Peter Norton's®
Upgrading and Repairing PCs

Peter Norton
Michael Desmond

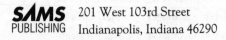 201 West 103rd Street
Indianapolis, Indiana 46290

To my wife, who helped me believe.
—Michael Desmond

Copyright © 1997 by Peter Norton

FIRST EDITION

International Standard Book Number: 0-672-31140-2

Library of Congress Catalog Card Number: 97-67495

2000   99   98   4   3

Interpretation of the printing code: the rightmost double-digit number is the year of the book's printing; the rightmost single-digit, the number of the book's printing. For example, a printing code of 97-1 shows that the first printing of the book occurred in 1997.

Composed in Goudy and MCPdigital by Macmillan Computer Publishing

Printed in the United States of America

Trademarks

Publisher	John Pierce
Executive Editor	Lisa Wagner
Managing Editor	Thomas Hayes
Director of Marketing	Kelli S. Spencer
Product Marketing Manager	Wendy Gilbride
Marketing Coordinator	Linda Beckwith

Acquisitions Editor
Grace M. Buechlein

Development Editor
Sunthar Visuvalingam

Production Editor
Gayle L. Johnson

Indexer
Chris Wilcox

Technical Reviewers
Dave Bixler
Brian Zucker
Joe Curley
Jeff Sloan

Editorial Coordinators
Mandie Rowell
Katie Wise

Technical Edit Coordinator
Lynette Quinn

Editorial Assistants
Carol Ackerman
Andi Richter
Rhonda Tinch-Mize

Cover Designer
Karen Ruggles

Book Designer
Gary Adair

Copy Writer
David Reichwein

Production Team Supervisor
Beth Lewis

Production
Bryan Flores
Julie Geeting
Kay Hoskin
Christy M. Lemasters
Julie Searls
Sossity Smith

Overview

Contents

Acknowledgments

Believe me, books don't write themselves. They are the compilation of months of hard work by dozens of people, including editors, contributors, vendors, and industry experts. I'd like first to thank contributing authors Dean Andrews and Jim Desmond, who wrote several key chapters of this book. Thanks also to Jim Rue, who provided welcome and timely input on repair issues. Of course, the hard-working folks at Sams deserve a lot of credit. Development Editor Sunthar Visuvalingam is as sharp an editor as I've ever crossed pens with, and Acquisitions Editor Grace Buechlein kept the project on track despite ferocious deadlines. I'd also like to thank Production Editor Gayle Johnson and Technical Reviewers Dave Bixler and Brian Zucker. In addition, I want to thank David Fugate, my agent at Waterside Productions, for ruining my summer by landing me this project.

Many hard-working public relations, marketing, and technical professionals helped make this book possible by responding to my always-urgent calls for photos and information. I owe deep thanks to all the people who dropped everything to get me the materials I needed before deadline. Here are the companies who contributed to this book: 1394 Trade Association; 3Com Corp.; ACTiSYS Corp.; Adaptec, Inc.; Altec-Lansing; AMD; American Power Conversion; ATI Technologies; CH Products; Cirque Corporation; Cirrus Logic; CMD Technology, Inc.; Creative Labs; Cyrix; Data Translation; Dell Computer; Diamond Multimedia; Epson America, Inc.; Hewlett-Packard; Hitachi America; IBM PC Corp.; Intel Corp.; Iomega; Kingston Technology; Lexmark International, Inc.; Logitech, Inc.; Micron Electronics, Inc.; Micronics; Microsoft Corp.; NMB Technologies; Olympus America; PC Power and Cooling; Pinnacle Micro Corp.; Plextor Corp.; Quantum Corporation; Ricoh America; Seagate Corp.; UMAX Corp.; Viewsonic Corporation; Winnov, Inc.; and Wireless Computing.

Finally, I want to thank my wife, Anne, without whom I never could have finished this book. She put up with a lot of late nights and lost weekends, remaining incredibly supportive even as the months wore on and the deadlines grew desperate. Thank you.

—Michael Desmond

About the Authors

Computer software entrepreneur and writer **Peter Norton** established his technical expertise and accessible style from the earliest days of the PC. His Norton Utilities was the first product of its kind, giving early computer owners control over their hardware and protection against myriad problems. His flagship titles, *Peter Norton's DOS Guide* and *Peter Norton's Inside the PC* (both from Sams Publishing), have provided the same insight and education to computer users worldwide for nearly two decades. Norton's books, like his many software products, are among the best-selling and most respected in the history of personal computing.

Norton's former column in *PC Week* was among the most highly regarded in the magazine's history. His expanding series of computer books continues to bring superior education to users, always in Norton's trademark style, which is never condescending or pedantic. From their earliest days, changing the "black box" into a "glass box," Norton's books, like his software, have remained among the most powerful tools available to beginners and experienced users alike.

In 1990, Norton sold his software development business to Symantec Corporation, allowing him to devote more time to his family, civic affairs, philanthropy, and art collecting. He lives with his wife, Eileen, and their two children in Santa Monica, California.

Michael Desmond is a senior associate editor at *PC World* magazine, one of the world's largest computer publications with a circulation of more than 1.1 million readers. He is also president of the Computer Press Association, an organization dedicated to promoting the technology media and its writers and editors. In 1996, he won a Jesse H. Neal award from the American Business Press as runner-up in the best investigative article category. Previously an executive editor of *Multimedia World* magazine, Desmond has a bachelor's degree in Soviet studies from Middlebury College in Vermont and a master's degree in journalism from Northwestern University's Medill School of Journalism. His work has appeared in numerous publications, including *Spin*, *Working Woman*, *Video*, and *DV* magazines. He is a coauthor of *Platinum Edition Using Windows 95* and a contributor to *Special Edition Using PowerPoint 97*, both from Que. A native of Cleveland, Ohio, Desmond is an inveterate Indians fan, and he will never *ever* forgive Art Modell for moving the Cleveland Browns football team to Baltimore. Desmond lives in Burlington, Vermont with his wife Anne and son Kevin.

Tell Us What You Think

As a reader, you are the most important critic of and commentator on our books. We value your opinion, and we want to know what we're doing right, what we could do better, what areas you'd like to see us publish in, and any other words of wisdom you're willing to pass our way. You can help us create strong books that meet your needs and give you the computer guidance you require.

If you have access to the World Wide Web, check out our site at http://www.mcp.com.

> **Note:** If you have a technical question about this book, call the technical support line at (317) 581-3833 or send e-mail to support@mcp.com.

As the Executive Editor of the group that created this book, I welcome your comments. You can fax or write me directly to let me know what you did or didn't like about this book—as well as what we can do to make our books stronger. Here's the information:

Fax: (317) 581-4669

Mail: Lisa Wagner
        Comments Department
        Sams Publishing
        201 West 103rd Street
        Indianapolis, IN 46290

Introduction

The PC is an appliance—at least that's what computer manufacturers want you to think. You buy the box, plug it in, and suddenly life is good.

In reality, buying and installing PC hardware is a daunting task. The rapid-fire pace of hardware advancement—couched in confusing acronyms and dubious benchmarks—makes it difficult to make informed buying decisions. What's worse, installing new hardware can be downright dangerous. PCs might be nearly as common as TVs and toaster ovens, but most folks don't spend their weekends cracking these devices open to add new hardware. If you botch the job, you can lose a lot of expensive equipment, not to mention valuable data.

This book will help you understand the workings of PC hardware, ranging from CPUs to printers, so that you can choose the products that will best help extend and enhance the life of your PC. You'll also find step-by-step instructions for installing and maintaining these devices. Along the way, you'll find tips that will help you get the most out of your PC.

Who Should Read This Book?

This book's intended audience is intermediate-to-advanced Windows 95 users who want to get the most out of their investment in PC hardware. Step-by-step instructions help you negotiate tricky installations, and useful explanations of products and technology help you make informed buying decisions. Whether you have a PC at home or in the office (or both), this book provides the information you need to handle your PC jobs yourself.

This is not a book for rocket scientists or system engineers. It is intended for people who rely on PCs to do their jobs and get things done at home—even if it's roaming the halls of Quake.

I've focused on PCs running Windows 95 because this is the most pervasive operating system for individual desktop PCs. However, you will find that the insights provided here apply to systems running other operating systems as well.

What You'll Learn

Here are some of the topics covered in this book:

- Step-by-step instructions for installing a wide variety of PC devices
- Comprehensible explanations of PC hardware and technology
- Useful advice for buying new products
- Strategies and tips for resolving hardware conflicts and breakdowns

- Advice for making the most effective upgrades for a wide variety of systems and applications
- An introduction to emerging PC technologies, including DVD, Universal Serial Bus (USB), FireWire, MMX, and Accelerated Graphics Port (AGP)
- Repair and maintenance advice for PCs and peripherals

A typical chapter covers a single topic, such as modems or monitors, in depth. Each chapter begins with an overview of the hardware technology and products, allowing you to understand how things work before you move on. Each chapter also includes a buying section that focuses on cost-effective upgrades, as well as on making sure that you get a fair deal when you buy new hardware.

Each chapter also includes a section covering upgrades, providing step-by-step installation and setup instructions for devices. Finally, a troubleshooting and repair section helps you deal with adversity when it arrives, providing hands-on instructions and tips.

How This Book Is Organized

This book is broken into sections by broad product categories. For example, I've grouped together chapters covering data storage, making it easy to explore related PC hardware and technology. In addition, you'll find an introductory section that provides an overview of PC hardware, an introduction to the Windows 95 operating system, and strategies for troubleshooting and repairing PCs.

Part I: Introduction

Part I provides an overview of what is to come. Here you will gain useful insights into PC technology, as well as key strategies for managing PC hardware. Chapters covering general upgrade and repair strategies (later covered in depth in chapters concerning specific hardware devices) will help you understand the issues raised later. This part also includes a discussion of the Windows 95 and Windows NT operating systems, because the OS plays a critical role in the management and operation of any hardware device.

Part II: Core Components

Our tour of PC hardware starts at ground zero, the CPU. The most critical and expensive component of your system gets in-depth treatment. You'll learn why a 233MHz Pentium II is faster than a Pentium MMX running at the same clock speed, and you'll learn how to tell if a faster CPU might be the fix you need for your aging system.

From the processor, we'll move on to other critical performance building blocks. We'll cover system RAM and cache memory, both critical players in application performance and compatibility, helping determine what you need to run your software. Memory in particular is critical, because a boost in the amount of RAM can be the most profound performance upgrade you can perform.

Also included in Part II is a chapter on PC power supplies and peripherals. Bringing it all together is the chapter on motherboards, the component that serves as the platform upon which all other components are connected. You'll find out why chipsets, rarely popularized in advertising, are the most important ingredient of your PC.

Part III: Basic Data Storage

This part introduces you to the workhorse storage devices inside your PC—hard disks, floppy drives, and CD-ROM drives. Here you will learn the role of these ubiquitous drives and how they work. Step-by-step installation instructions guide you through sometimes-tricky hard disk installations and help you deal with the complexities of master-slave relationships for IDE drives.

Virtually all these media run under one of two buses—IDE or SCSI—so Part III begins with a chapter that discusses IDE and SCSI controllers. You need to understand the key performance and compatibility issues of these bus types before you commit to buying a certain type of hardware. With an eye toward the future, this part includes a chapter on DVD drives. Here you'll find critical updates on compatibility problems with DVD, as well as useful tips to help you avoid disaster during the installation of these newest drives.

Part IV: Advanced Data Storage

Storage coverage continues in Part IV, which covers a variety of removable and cartridged storage media solutions. From slow-but-affordable tape backup drives to high-performance Apex media that provide near-hard-disk performance and capacities of 4GB, this part provides information on specialized storage products. Also covered are the confusing selection of recordable and rewritable media in the CD and DVD families. You'll find out which media types work best for long-term archiving and which are best for keeping large data files close at hand for immediate access.

Part V: Multimedia

Part V covers a variety of popular upgrade candidates, including sound cards, graphics and video boards, and monitors. You'll learn why a new graphics card might once again be your best bet for improving the performance of the latest multimedia titles. You'll also be introduced to the new bus on the block, Intel's Accelerated Graphics Port (AGP), which promises to double or even quadruple the data rate of existing PCI graphics cards. Also covered are video capture boards and videoconferencing products, including monitor-top cameras that can be used to take digital snapshots.

When it comes to displays, you'll learn how the balance between the monitor and the graphics board is crucial. You'll also receive useful advice on ergonomics, showing you which monitors might cause eyestrain and headaches, and you'll get helpful buying advice on power-saving products. An introduction to the burgeoning market of flat-screen displays is also featured.

Sound cards are in the midst of a transformation as Microsoft lays down new standards for Windows 95. PCI-based audio cards offer multiple channels of audio to produce realistic, interactive 3-D sound for games and titles—but watch out for your DOS games. These new boards might not work with your favorite games.

Part VI: Connectivity

More than ever before, PCs are the center of communication. Part VI helps you outfit your PC for the coming millennium, when virtually every PC will be connected to multiple devices and networks. The chapter on modems shows you what you need to gain fast access to the Internet and to make the most out of emerging applications such as videoconferencing, application sharing, and telecommuting. You'll see how to protect yourself when buying a 56K modem, and you'll get a glimpse of the intriguing digital technologies that lie underneath.

The chapter about I/O add-ons introduces some newly minted bus standards that promise to revolutionize PC connections. You'll also see how you can add this new technology to your existing PCs using simple PCI card upgrades. The networking chapter shows you how to turn your single stand-alone PC into a fully functioning network, where you can share data, applications, and hardware devices such as printers. You'll learn when it makes sense to pay more for pricey 100Mbps network hardware and why RJ-45 connectors make more sense than coaxial cable.

Part VII: Input and Output

This part covers devices that let you move data in and out of your PC. Input devices such as mice, keyboards, and game controllers get a close look, with an in-depth discussion of ergonomic issues and tips for avoiding painful hand, wrist, and shoulder injuries. You'll also learn about exciting innovations in the game controller market—such as joysticks that shake—as well as 3-D mice and keyboards with built-in pointing devices.

If you want to turn your PC into a digital photo studio, look no further than the chapters on scanners and digital cameras. You'll get a realistic assessment of the quality of these devices, as well as an eye-opening discussion of the confusing specs that vendors often publish. You'll also find out why anyone looking for top quality will want to buy a good scanner.

The chapter on printers will help you make sense of the confusing variety of printers available for PCs. You'll learn why color ink jets are such a terrific value for home PC owners, and why office users might want to stick with a fast and reliable laser printer. You'll learn how to eke the best quality out of your existing printer, and you'll see why you need to look closely at the cost of paper and media when choosing a printer.

Appendix and Glossary

This book finishes with an appendix on what to do with a PC that you don't want anymore. One intriguing option is to donate your system to a charity for a nifty tax deduction. You'll also find a useful glossary that can help you understand the fog of acronyms and technical jargon that go with any discussion of PC hardware.

Conventions Used in This Book

This book uses the following conventions:

Menus and the selections on them are separated by a vertical bar. For example, "Select File | Open" means "Pull down the File menu and choose Open."

Words that you must type or words that you see on-screen appear in a monospace font.

New terms appear in *italic*.

MBps stands for "megabytes per second." Mbps stands for "megabits per second." KBps stands for "kilobytes per second." Kbps stands for "kilobits per second." GBps stands for "gigabytes per second." Gbps stands for "gigabits per second."

Icons

This book contains many icons that help you identify certain types of information. The following paragraphs describe the purpose of each icon.

Architecture: Whenever you see the Architecture icon, I'm talking about the internal workings of PC hardware. Knowing how devices perform their jobs can help you determine why things do or don't work as they should.

Buying Tip: This books tries to help you get the most hardware for your money. The Buying Tip icon offers a valuable piece of advice for buyers. Whether it's the best way to get a bargain, or how you can avoid being ripped off by unscrupulous vendors, these tips will help keep more money in your wallet.

Case Study: When you've worked with as many computers as I have, you have plenty of war stories to share. The Case Study icon indicates useful first-person tales of hardware challenges and how I dealt with them.

Compatibility: Hardware technology moves fast, inviting all sorts of compatibility problems as you conduct upgrades. The Compatibility icon clues you in to tips, techniques, and notes that will help you get over the compatibility hurdle.

Looking Ahead: It's always good to know what you'll find down the road. A Looking Ahead box provides a road sign that tells you what will be discussed in a future chapter. That way, you can follow the path of a particular subject as I provide more detailed information later in the book.

Note: Notes bring interesting facts to your attention. I use Note boxes to explore useful tangents and provide information that I've picked up while using PC hardware.

PC97: With PC97 and PC98, Microsoft, Intel, and other market leaders are trying to push the PC platforms to higher ground. This icon denotes useful discussions on the latest technologies being addressed in this spec, including new Plug and Play buses and consumer-oriented multimedia features.

Performance: The Performance icon designates a performance-related tip. These tips cover optimization techniques and provide insight into how devices can boost overall performance.

Peter's Principles convey vital insights about important hardware issues. Boxes that have this icon might discuss key buying issues or help unravel confusing technical standards, but the focus is always on critical information with immediate value to PC owners.

Standards: When it comes to PC hardware, industry standards make the world go 'round. When you see the Standards icon, you know that I'm talking about important standards issues that can directly affect the effectiveness of an upgrade.

Technical Note: Technical Notes can help you understand how PC hardware works and help you get a handle on mysterious problems. Technical Notes can lead you to resolve intractable conflicts and make the right buying decisions.

Tip: Tips show you new ways of doing things that you might not have thought about before. Tip boxes also provide an alternative way of doing something that you might like better than the first approach I provided.

Troubleshooting: Everyone encounters problems occasionally, and this book is here to help. You'll find the Troubleshooting icon wherever there are useful tips and instructions for fixing hardware that has gone awry. In addition, every device-specific chapter includes a troubleshooting and repair section, where you will find valuable advice for handling common hardware problems.

Upgrade Advice: Upgrade Advice boxes offer important hands-on insights into adding new hardware to your PC. Expect to see information that helps you avoid dangerous upgrade conflicts or that helps you avoid obsolescence by guiding you to an upgrade that will last.

Warning: Warnings almost always tell you about some kind of hardware or data damage that will occur if you perform a certain action (or fail to perform others). Make sure that you understand a Warning thoroughly before you follow any instructions that come after it.

I

Introduction

Peter Norton®

1

The PC:
An Overview

Peter Norton®

The past five years have been nothing short of remarkable. Not since the invention of the automobile has the introduction of a new device so changed our society. More incredibly, the PC has become virtually ubiquitous in just 15 years, since its invention in 1982. From Fortune 100 businesses to home offices to college dorm rooms, PCs are a fixture.

There's just one problem: Most people are intimidated by PCs. It's no wonder. Some pretty amazing engineering goes into those putty-beige boxes. The rocket scientists over at Intel, for example, make their living from submicron magic, crafting intricate data-handling engines out of semiconducting silicon. For a populace stymied by VCR clocks, it's small wonder that the enormously powerful and complex PC can be so intimidating.

It doesn't have to be that way. This chapter will help break the ice by providing an overview of how PCs work. You will learn

- How the PC got its start, from a modest beginning as an in-house project at IBM
- About the workings of modern PCs, including all the requirements to meet the new PC98 specification
- About notebook PCs and how they work
- What to expect from PC technology in the future

What Is a PC, Anyway?

Today, personal computers are more powerful and diverse than ever before. From handheld personal digital assistants to multiprocessing Web servers and workstations, you will find a wide variety of devices that can legitimately be called personal computers. The vast majority of these devices, however, fit the description of personal computer that people are accustomed to—affordable desktop-based computers that are designed for general-purpose tasks ranging from spreadsheets and word processing to games and communications.

First, a Bit of History

The PC got its real start in 1981, when IBM released a modest little box by the name of The IBM PC. At the time, no one knew that the IBM PC was destined to create a multibillion-dollar market that would help power one of the greatest economic upturns in American history. Rather, it was regarded as the latest in a series of hobby computers—devices catering to an audience of ardent programmers, tinkerers, and electronics nuts.

So what helped propel the IBM PC beyond that fate of the dead-end computers that preceded it, including the Tandy TRS-80 and MIPS Altair? Two things:

- An open hardware architecture
- A third-party operating system and application market

Hawking Hardware

The IBM PC group took a very un-IBM-like approach to their little creation. The company's then-successful mainframe business made its fortune by requiring buyers to get everything from IBM. Everything from the new computer to replacement parts to operating system software all came directly from IBM. There was no competitive market of products or developers. When you bought IBM, you were committed to its products for the life of the machine.

Working on a shoestring budget, the IBM PC people cut deals with hardware companies to provide components for their PC. That decision would have an enormous impact on the nascent PC market and on the larger American business landscape. Here's one example: IBM single-handedly launched the rise of semiconductor powerhouse Intel Corporation when it tapped the company's 8080 chip to serve as the central processing unit (CPU) of the IBM PC.

More important, IBM invited other companies to build and sell products for its computer. Add-in card slots let companies such as Hercules create high-resolution graphics cards for early PCs. The result was that a cottage industry of peripherals arose that made the IBM PC an attractive option for business users.

Microsoft Gets Its Start

Along the way to launching the PC, IBM managed to give a start to another small company, Microsoft Corporation. IBM needed software to control its new machine, so the computing giant turned to a small Seattle company owned by Paul Allen and Bill Gates.

At the time, Microsoft had been creating programming tools—specifically, the Basic programming language—for the IBM PC and other platforms. But when IBM came calling, Gates and company quickly changed directions and started working on the first operating system for the IBM PC, which they called Disk Operating System, or DOS.

DOS became the software brains of the IBM PC. Behind every keystroke, file transfer, and screen display was Microsoft's DOS software. Most important, Microsoft kept the rights to its new creation, allowing it to later sell DOS and succeeding products to makers of IBM-compatible PCs.

The upshot was that both the hardware and the operating system software that were needed to make IBM-compatible PCs were both in the open. IBM held precious little control over the PC market it had just launched.

In Between

Today, literally thousands of companies are hard at work creating systems, peripherals, software, and tools for IBM-compatible PCs. Whether you're buying a brand-new system or making the best of one that is several years old, you enjoy a wide choice of products and vendors.

Hardware: The One-Cent Tour

No doubt about it—PCs can be intimidating. And it only gets worse when you find that you must upgrade or troubleshoot your system. Inside the chassis, you'll find a lot of delicate—and expensive—electronics. It can seem awfully complex and dangerous, but it doesn't have to be.

It helps to think of your PC in terms of its component subsystems. This quick outline of the PC's components can help put things in perspective:

- Outside the PC: You'll see the display, keyboard, mouse, and the PC's case, as shown in Figure 1.1. The case holds all the PC's vital components, and it also provides access to CD-ROM and floppy drives on the front and various ports along the back. The case also shields you from electromagnetic radiation produced by internal components and allows for channeled airflow to reduce overheating problems.

Figure 1.1.
Minitower PCs like this Micron system provide easy access to components while minimizing footprint. (Photo courtesy of Micron Electronics, Inc.)

- CPU: The *central processing unit,* or *processor,* handles all the arithmetic that drives your PC. The speed of the CPU, combined with its internal design, determines how quickly and efficiently the CPU can process data and program code.

- System memory: Called *random access memory*, or *RAM*, system memory stores the code and data being used by your PC. The more memory you have, the better your performance.

- Hard disk: The PC's permanent storage device. Programs and data held on the hard disk are transferred to system RAM for use. Today's hard disks feature capacities of 5GB and higher.

- CD-ROM drives: The ubiquitous large-capacity removable-media drive. CD-ROM drives let PC users access multimedia content, install large applications, and work with enormous databases and other resources.

- Graphics adapter: Everything you see on the display goes through the graphics adapter. This hardware component speeds the display of 2-D graphics and video playback. Newer systems include tweaks for quickly displaying complex 3-D images.

- Audio adapter: Anything beyond the basic beeps from your PC speaker go through the audio subsystem. Sound cards let you play digital audio over your PC speakers, as well as record analog sounds to digital format.

- Modem: Lets your PC talk to the Internet, fax machines, and other PCs using a standard phone line. Can be either an internal add-in card or an external box.

- Network interface card: Also called NICs, these add-in cards are used to connect a PC to a local area network, which is common in offices. Many PCs don't have a network card.

- Display: The TV-like cathode ray tube (CRT) display found on almost all desktop PCs. Today, 15- and 17-inch displays are most common. The larger monitors provide much better viewing.

- Keyboard and mouse: The primary input devices for your PC. Almost all PCs require—and come with—a keyboard and a mouse.

The Software Side

This being a hardware book, it's easy to lose sight of the importance of software in the operation of the PC. But, in fact, you can't separate hardware from software when talking about PCs. Software literally gives life to inanimate hardware.

In fact, your interaction with much of the hardware inside the PC comes through software. Graphics and sound-card features, for example, are accessed through on-screen control panels.

There are three types of software:

- Applications
- Operating systems
- Drivers

Applications

These are the programs you use every day, whether Quicken accounting software or Duke Nukem 3D. Application code and files are stored permanently on your hard disk or CD-ROM drive until you launch them. At that point, the bits are moved into system memory, where the CPU can quickly access the data and code it needs to perform actions.

Applications, particularly multimedia titles and games, interact with virtually every part of your PC. The keyboard and mouse provide input for the application, and files and data are accessed from the hard disk, CD-ROM drive, floppy diskettes, or even from the Internet through a modem. Graphics are sent to the display to let you view and manipulate program controls and features, collectively known as the *interface*. This is where the cycle closes: The graphical display lets you view your input and access on-screen controls.

The Operating System

You might think your applications access your PC's hardware. After all, when you click the diskette icon, the program saves the current file to disk. In fact, the operating system sits between your applications and hardware, providing a common set of rules for applications. This layer of software below your applications defines how applications access memory and the CPU, which can have a huge impact on functionality and performance.

It's difficult to overstate the importance of the operating system, also called the OS. The OS breathes life into your hardware, providing a common set of services and software-access systems that make it possible for your programs to perform their magic. What's more, the OS determines exactly what your applications and hardware can and can't do.

Here's a case in point: Before Microsoft introduced its DirectDraw video-handling code to Windows 95, even graphics cards that featured video-enhancing hardware lacked a standard means of making use of their video acceleration capabilities. Likewise, you need Windows NT or another optimized OS to take advantage of multiprocessor systems. Windows 95 simply doesn't recognize more than one processor.

Drivers

Finally, there is the software you don't see. Device drivers are the diplomats of hardware, opening lines of communication between your peripherals and the operating system. They are also the most underappreciated component of hardware performance. If you want to get the most out of your hardware, you need to be aware of the driver software that makes it run.

Why do you need drivers? Although operating systems such as Windows 95 provide a standard set of rules for applications, each hardware device has its own particular talents and ways of doing things.

It would simply be too complicated to provide support for every single peripheral in the OS itself, so drivers bridge the gap. Driver software is usually written by the hardware company because the company knows its products intimately.

> **Tip:** Device drivers get updated frequently—to add features, improve performance, and fix bugs. For this reason, it's a good idea to occasionally check your peripheral vendors' Web sites for updates. In almost all cases, driver updates are available for free download— essentially a free upgrade.

PC98: The PC Today

You've seen a quick outline of what goes into a personal computer, but this is hardly the complete picture. The PC is constantly evolving, adding capabilities and getting faster every year. In fact, this evolution is part of what makes buying and upgrading computers so difficult.

Are you looking for some help? There's a bit forthcoming from Intel, Microsoft, and other companies who sponsor the PC98 specification. PC98 is the latest in a series of system guidelines designed to help system and peripheral manufacturers improve the functionality of PCs. At the same time, PC98 is an excellent indication of what to expect in the year or so to come.

Actually, there are three flavors of PC98:

- Consumer PC98
- Office PC98
- Entertainment PC98

A basic PC98 specification serves as the common ground for all three.

PC98 Explained

Regardless of the kind of desktop system you want to buy, PC98 provides a set of common guidelines that apply. The technologies that PC98 demands for new PCs include the following:

- Universal Serial Bus (USB): An external Plug and Play bus that will replace serial and parallel ports, as well as provide connections for keyboards and mice
- Digital Versatile Disk- (DVD) ready: Graphics hardware that will allow MPEG-2 video playback (see Figure 1.2)
- 3-D graphics support: Driver support for 3-D graphics, allowing use of 3-D games and titles

- MPEG-2 video capability: Hardware that allows the display of high-resolution video used on DVD-based titles and applications
- 33.6Kbps modem: A step off the cutting edge, but the 33.6Kbps data rate is still the fastest you'll find for both receiving and sending data over phone lines

Figure 1.2.
DVD-ROM drives are among the exciting consumer technologies endorsed by the PC98 specification. (Photo courtesy of Creative Labs)

In addition, the PC98 specification calls for the phasing out of the venerable ISA (industry standard architecture) bus. ISA dates back to the very beginnings of the PC. If you look inside your PC, you can see three or four ISA slots, which accept compatible cards.

Looking Ahead: You can learn more about the ISA, PCI, and other PC buses in Chapter 10, "Motherboards and Cases."

Although there are many ISA-compatible add-in cards, the bus is limited to a paltry 5Mbps of data throughput. That might be fine for modems and low-end audio, but it won't do for graphics, networking, or multichannel audio. What's more, the aging ISA spec lacks built-in support for Plug and Play, bus mastering, and other important capabilities found in newer bus architectures such as PCI and AGP.

Note: Notebooks also get a nod in the PC98 scheme, with the inclusion of the CardBus. The successor to the successful PC Card specification, CardBus provides a fast 32-bit expansion bus for notebook PCs. Best of all, the peripherals comply with a svelte, credit-card sized format, which makes them perfect for mobile computers.

Consumer PC98

The Consumer PC98 adds a few tweaks to this baseline. This version of the specification deals with PCs intended for the home and therefore stresses multimedia features common in educational and gaming titles.

One thing the Consumer PC98 spec adds to the basic menu is the requirement of a 6X CD-ROM drive. It's worth noting that a 6X CD-ROM drive is hardly cutting-edge—in fact, today's drives often run at top speeds of 24 times that of the original 1X CD-ROM spec. However, a 6X drive speed will ensure that the PC can play virtually all CD-ROM-based titles.

In addition, the Consumer PC98 spec recommends the following:

- IEEE 1394 FireWire: A high-speed external bus that offers Plug and Play and that is suitable for video capture, external storage devices, and simple networking
- Device Bay: A standard for the easy installation and removal of peripheral devices, using Plug and Play USB and FireWire buses
- Accelerated Graphics Port (AGP): A high-speed dedicated graphics bus that allows for faster, more realistic 3-D graphics
- TV capability: An analog TV tuner and TV-out capability to allow viewing directly from the PC's monitor
- DVD-ROM drive: A next-generation optical disk drive that improves upon the 650MB CD-ROM drive by offering 3.7GB to 17GB of storage, depending on the type of media being employed
- Accelerated 3-D hardware: The graphics subsystem includes hardware to speed up and enhance the performance of 3-D graphics

Office PC98

It's no surprise that the Office PC98 spec deals with business-oriented PCs. Here, networking, reliable operation, and cost of ownership are paramount. Although multimedia capabilities are nice to have, they aren't critical to the mission of most business PCs.

Office PC98 demands two specific features:

- Managability enhancements to the PC's BIOS and the motherboard that allow IS managers to control and configure PCs over the network, as well as install software
- A network interface card with NDIS 5 driver support that ensures full compatibility with Windows 95 and NT

In addition, the Office PC98 spec recommends many of the same features included in the Consumer PC98 version. Among them:

- IEEE 1394 FireWire
- Device Bay
- Accelerated Graphics Port (AGP)
- TV capability
- DVD-ROM drive
- Accelerated 3-D hardware

Entertainment PC98

Microsoft and Intel aren't content with the traditional PC market. They want a slice of the home electronics business too—stereo equipment, TVs and VCRs, game consoles. PC98 is an important step toward melding the PC to these traditional devices (see Figure 1.3).

Figure 1.3.
Gateway 2000's Destination line of PCs, which broke new ground in consumer convergence, looks more like a consumer video setup than a traditional PC. (Photo courtesy of Gateway 2000)

Entertainment PC98 demands the following capabilities not found on other PC98 PCs:

- Two USB and FireWire ports, including one each mounted on the front of the PC for easy access
- Bundled joystick and gamepad, which conform to the standard human interface device specification governing USB-based input devices

- MPEG-2 video playback capability and TV tuner
- DVD-ROM drive
- Compliance with the OnNow specification, which provides for low-power sleep mode so that PCs can be left on permanently

In addition, Entertainment PC98 recommends several features, including the following:

- Device Bay
- Accelerated Graphics Port (AGP)
- TV capability
- DVD-ROM drive
- Accelerated 3-D hardware

The PC Tomorrow

You now know what's on the menu for 1998, but what about a couple years from now? If you're like most buyers, you want your system purchases and upgrades to keep you a step ahead of the obsolescence freight train. The following sections describe a few key applications and technologies to look out for.

Voice Recognition

There are two categories of voice recognition:

- Voice command and control
- Voice dictation

Just as the mouse helped redefine the PC interface, expect voice command and control to add a new dimension to PC interfaces. Voice control of PCs has existed for years, but less-than-perfect recognition and hefty performance overhead made it a clumsy solution. As PCs get faster and audio capabilities become better integrated, voice command becomes a viable option.

Perhaps the biggest stumbling block has been the inability of PCs to understand anything other than the exact words or phrases required to recognize a command. Say "File New," and your word processor will open a new document, but say "Create a file," and you'll get an error message. This creates more problems than it solves.

Voice dictation, on the other hand, is the vocal equivalent of typing in a word processor or spreadsheet. Here, the task gets much tougher, because the PC must understand tens of thousands of words on-the-fly. What's more, it must deal with grammatical nuances and pesky homonyms—words that sound alike but mean different things.

If you want voice recognition today, you'll want the fastest Pentium MMX or Pentium II processor you can afford—the MMX instructions will boost things considerably. Another critical element is RAM. 64MB is a pretty good minimum for effective voice recognition. Also look for a good sound board with a headset microphone for optimal gain.

High Bandwidth Net Access

The modem of the future will be all-digital—no more screeching telephone signals. Cable modems are getting play in test markets, while the telephone companies are looking at asymmetrical digital subscriber line (ADSL) service to provide megabit-range access to the Internet. Unfortunately, both technologies are years from general deployment.

The good news is that today's PCs will be able to access these technologies with simple card-based upgrades. That said, you'll want a fast CPU and a big hard disk to manage the larger data pipes.

Bigger Monitors

Expect bigger displays for both CRT and flat-panel LCD- (liquid crystal display) type screens. New 19-inch CRTs should become a viable midrange buy for people who want the most display area for their money.

More significantly, flat-panel displays should become a real option for desktop PCs in the next two to five years. Today, 14-inch LCD displays can be found on top-end notebook PCs. As production volumes of these displays increase, their relative cost will drop markedly. That said, expect to pay about twice as much for a 14-inch LCD screen as you would for a 15-inch CRT that provides the same relative viewing area.

Better Buses

USB is here today, but look for FireWire to emerge on multimedia desktop PCs. Over the next few years, FireWire will improve from its current minimum of 200Mbps to over 1 gigabit per second (Gbps), making it a match for the most demanding operations.

Inside the PC, the new AGP will get better. Intel has laid out a road map for the so-called 4x AGP, which will boast gigabyte-per-second data rates for graphics operations. Also expect some savvy network hardware companies to tap into this supercharged internal bus.

Device Bay

It's part of the PC98 spec, but expect Device Bay to be something that happens over the next two years. This standard approach to peripheral installations hopes to make swapping in drives and peripheral modules as easy as inserting a VHS tape. Plug and Play and on-the-fly system configuration (called *hot swapping*) both figure prominently in this technology.

A Note on Notebooks

No discussion of PC technology is complete without covering portable PCs. Notebooks occupy a growing segment of the market and are becoming more affordable as manufacturers get better.

In general, the same technologies and somewhat-altered components are used in notebooks as in desktop PCs. The main issues that affect notebooks are

- Compact size and light weight
- Low power consumption
- Low heat dissipation

The Package Defined

Because notebooks need to be small, you won't find any ISA or PCI bus slots for adding peripheral cards—unless you purchase a separate docking station unit that serves as a desktop home base for your notebook PC. Nor will you see any $5\frac{1}{4}$-inch disk drives and bays. Although notebooks aren't complete dead ends when it comes to performance and upgrades, their compact size can limit your options (see Figure 1.4).

Figure 1.4.
The compact design of notebook PCs make them more expensive to build and more difficult to upgrade than their desktop counterparts.

A typical notebook weighs between 6 and 12 pounds, including all the accoutrements such as battery packs, power bricks, and other components. The chassis is about 10 inches by 12 inches, or a little larger than a typical sheet of paper, and the height can range between 1 and 2 inches. As a rule, the faster and more feature-rich your PC, the more weight and size you'll have to contend with. For this reason, if you travel a lot, you might want to compromise features to improve portability.

Otherwise, a notebook is a lot like a desktop. There's a CPU, hard disk, display, keyboard, and even a pointing device (although it's not a mouse). You'll also find serial and parallel ports, as well as USB ports on some newer models, and virtually all notebooks now include integrated sound and speakers. Many notebooks today also include a modem and CD-ROM drive, making them the functional equivalent of desktop PCs.

Components

Notebooks might feature the same component set as desktops, but there are differences. Table 1.1 lists them.

Table 1.1. What's the difference?

Component	Desktop	Notebook
CPU	3.3- or 2.9-volt operation	2.2-volt operation, compact design
Display	15- to 17-inch CRT	12- to 14-inch LCD
Hard disk	$3^1/_2$-inch width	$2^1/_2$-inch width
PCI bus	Three or four add-in slots	Integrated bus, no expansion capability
PC Card bus	Not present	Two or more slots of PC Card peripherals
Pointing device	Mouse	Integrated pointer, port for using optional mouse
Power supply	200+ watt power supply	Lithium ion or nickel metal hydride battery

Notebook PCs might have many of the same components as desktop systems, but that doesn't mean the two are on equal footing. The low-power and space requirements of notebook PCs means that the newest technologies take a while to get to notebooks. In general, expect notebooks to be slower than their desktop counterparts and to be more expensive to upgrade with additional RAM or larger hard disks.

Summary

PCs are complex beasts, but they are not this way without reason. If you want to make sense of what makes a PC tick, you need to understand the parts that comprise it. Once you do, it's much easier to know what you need for your particular applications and needs.

Of course, PC technology is hardly standing still. The PC98 specification advances the capabilities and ease of use of the PC platform. As these technologies mature and propagate, PCs will begin to look more like consumer electronic devices and less like complex electronics gear aimed at hobbyists and programmers. In the meantime, it pays to stay on top of the acronyms and cryptic standards that are at the heart of PC products.

2

Inside
Windows 95

Peter Norton®

I admit it—I'm a hardware freak. I love megahertz, gigabytes, and the subtle science of submicron physics. There's something really neat about the fact that processor power essentially doubles every 18 months. But there is one simple fact that even hard-core hardware junkies must come to terms with: Software makes the world go 'round.

More specifically, operating systems and applications make hardware worth buying. The real value of a PC isn't in the hot new Pentium II processor with MMX technology or in the huge 7GB hard disk. What matters is what the software lets you do. If you can create better documents more quickly or play better games and titles, the hardware means something.

Ultimately, the operating system determines what your programs can do, so it really pays to be aware of what you're running. In addition, the OS provides key facilities and talents for configuring and troubleshooting your hardware. The good news is that Under Windows 95, users have more resources available to them than ever before.

In this chapter, you will learn about

- The operating system's role in the operation of your PC and its applications
- The evolution of the Windows operating system and its key features
- Windows 98
- Features within Windows 95 that can help you manage and configure your hardware

Windows 95: Inside the Operating System

When Windows 95 arrived in August of 1995, it was a very big deal. The successor to the hugely successful Windows 3.x operating environment, Windows 95 brought a number of key features to the mainstream desktop PC. Among them were these:

- 32-bit addressing: The 32-bit address scheme vastly simplified program code and eliminated key weaknesses in 16-bit Windows that invited frequent system crashes.
- Plug and Play: Perhaps the most important innovation in the history of personal computing, Plug and Play eased the treacherous game of trial and error that usually accompanied a hardware upgrade.
- Multitasking and multithreading: These features let capable programs do more than one thing at once, speeding performance when running multiple applications as well as when doing several things within a single application (for example, printing and scrolling at the same time).
- Hardware Abstraction Layer (HAL): This software layer sits between applications and hardware, preventing conflicts and problems that can arise when many applications try to work directly with many hardware products. Hardware makers provide an interface

between their hardware and the OS, while applications use standard pathways to reach hardware.

- Hardware management: Windows 95 tracks and provides an interface for managing hardware settings—features that previously were available only in third-party utilities.

- Integrated operating system: For the first time, Windows worked without separate DOS underpinnings. Although the DOS core still existed, Windows 95 presented a cleaner and more reliable structure to both users and programmers.

- Dynamic device drivers: Windows 95 VxDs allow hardware drivers to load and unload without restarting the system, making it possible to hot-swap components or share resources. This talent is particularly useful in notebooks.

32-Bit Revolution

Intel processors have provided 32-bit addressing since the 386 was introduced in 1988. Yet almost all PC software written before August 1995 was based on 16-bit addressing schemes. The reason is that without a popular 32-bit operating system, applications couldn't reach the full feature set of Intel's 32-bit CPUs.

Applications Get Better

What's so important about the number of address bits available to programs? For one thing, 16-bit addresses are too small to easily access all the data and code that applications typically use. In order to find data in memory, programmers had to resort to segmented addressing, a time-consuming scheme that takes several steps to hone in on bits stored in memory. Segmented addressing not only took longer to write, but it also hurt application performance.

32-bit addressing freed programmers to worry about other things. Large data sets could be addressed in a single chunk, not parsed and recombined after the fact. The result was faster, more stable, and less complex code. For users, it simply meant better software and better performance.

The Secure Operating System

In addition, the 32-bit Windows 95 operating system provides a much more stable environment than previous DOS-based systems. With the large address space provided by the 32-bit address scheme, Windows 95 can build secure walls around its applications.

Properly-written Windows 95 programs can crash and conflict all they want, but they can do so only within their own piece of memory real estate. The program itself might crash, but the bits owned by Windows 95 or other running applications won't get touched. No more wholesale system lockups and nasty Windows 3.1-style general protection faults (GPFs). In theory, at least, Windows 95's memory space is secure from application blow-ups.

Windows 95 also provides far greater resources for applications than the 16-bit version did. Applications under Windows 3.1 had to register themselves within memory stacks, which the OS used to track program activity. Unfortunately, not enough capacity was left to run more than a few large applications, leading to confusing out-of-memory errors, even on systems with 16 or 32MB of RAM. Windows 95 greatly increased the capacity of these stacks, enhancing stability when multitasking (see Figure 2.1).

Figure 2.1.
You can't see the reworked application resource infrastructure in Windows 95, but its effect is evident when you're multitasking. Now, Windows 95 stays stable even when you're running several large applications.

The truth is not quite so pretty. For one thing, Microsoft had to provide almost complete compatibility with the thousands of 16-bit DOS and Windows 3.1 applications. To do this, Microsoft exposed some of the Windows 95 memory space to these older programs. The technical details aren't important. What is important is that Microsoft essentially built a soft underbelly to its Windows 95 OS. If a program crashes and mucks with this shared memory space, the entire OS and other running applications can be compromised.

Note: Windows 95 kicked off the 32-bit software revolution, but it was hardly the first to market. In fact, IBM beat Microsoft to the punch by, oh, about four years. The OS/2 operating system provided true 32-bit support and outstanding DOS compatibility long before Windows 95 arrived. Although OS/2 remains a factor in mission-critical applications such as banking, corporate database management, and government applications, it failed to catch fire in the mainstream. Hefty hardware requirements and some very shrewd maneuvering by Microsoft helped keep OS/2 in the corner of the market despite its early lead.

Microsoft's other operating system, Windows NT, actually does the 32-bit thing better than Windows 95. Like OS/2, NT is aimed at corporate heavyweights and workstations. Despite its name, it bears little structural resemblance to Windows 95. NT forgoes 16-bit compatibility to provide a nearly bulletproof environment. So although your games and many older programs won't run under NT, no program gets to jump into shared memory space and topple the operating system. This kind of security is critical for businesses, who need their networks running every minute of every day. The constant watchdogging also affects performance and demands more system memory and other resources.

Multitasking

In addition to stabler, more feature-rich programs, the 32-bit OS helps boost performance. Windows 95 provides multitasking and multithreading, allowing several applications and operations to run simultaneously. There are two kinds of multitasking:

- Cooperative
- Preemptive

Cooperative multitasking, provided in Windows 3.1, basically gives the processor's attention to each running application. If an application happens to grab the system for a long time, other applications or operations might fail as they become starved for attention. The result is a scheme that can result in crashes or system lock-ups.

Preemptive multitasking allows software to butt in and grab the CPU, thus preempting the running operation. This scheme ensures that Internet downloads, for example, won't fail because a big spreadsheet recalculation is taking up 100 percent of the CPU. Instead, Windows 95 will make sure that the OS will stop working on the recalculation task for a bit to ensure that the big download gets the attention it needs.

Finally, multithreading provides smooth handling of multiple tasks within an application. For programs designed to have multiple threads, the OS can let Excel conduct a monster recalculation even as it spools a print job and saves a separate file. As with preemptive multitasking, the threads are tracked to ensure that none is forsaken.

Hardware Handling

Here is where the rubber meets the road. Windows 95 changed the hardware rule book, and almost entirely for the better. Better device management, better compatibility, and Plug and Play all make Windows 95 a vastly superior platform for hardware.

Plug and Play

The single most important innovation was the introduction of Plug and Play, or PnP. Windows 95 is actually just one leg of the PnP standard, which was formulated by Microsoft, Intel, Compaq, and others to provide automated recognition and configuration of hardware in the PC. Here are the three components:

- Hardware: PnP boards and devices include ROM that stores unique identifiers that let the OS and BIOS know the type of device, its manufacturer, and other key elements. Additional hardware allows for software-based configuration and the storing of data.

- BIOS: Because hardware must be polled and preconfigured before Windows 95 even starts, the BIOS must be set up to handle PnP hardware. The BIOS enumerates PnP devices, eventually handing its work over to Windows 95.

- Windows 95: The operating system interacts with the BIOS to ensure proper device configuration and includes facilities for automatically detecting new PnP devices.

In general, PC owners running Windows 95 fall into three categories when it comes to Plug and Play:

- Out of luck: Those with older 486 and Pentium systems probably lack PnP BIOS support. Without the PnP BIOS, neither the PnP logic on peripherals nor the PnP capabilities of Windows 95 can come into play. If your BIOS is Plug and Play, you should see the words "Plug and Play" appear along with the BIOS version number during startup. You can also check the BIOS version number against your system documentation to see if it supports Plug and Play.

- Mixed bag: Most users with new systems running Windows 95 will have a PnP BIOS in place. But there will be a mixture of PnP and non-PnP devices, often called *legacy hardware*. Windows 95 deals with legacy devices by moving PnP settings around the immovable resources of the older peripherals.

- Pure PnP: The best possible scenario. All the hardware and software can interact to determine the best settings for each device. Problems are reduced because hard-wired resource settings don't force other devices into odd configurations.

Buying Tip: If you have a system with a mixture of PnP and legacy hardware, make a point of upgrading to devices that include PnP capability. By adding intelligent hardware over time, you will end up with a system that is more stable and easier to configure.

Device Management

As I mentioned earlier, Windows 95 puts a standard layer between applications and all the hardware. The main benefit is that your applications don't need to support every hardware device on the market. Instead, they just need to talk to the operating system.

The key to this scheme is the driver software that comes with peripherals. Hardware vendors write specific driver software for their products, allowing Windows 95 programs to access hardware features. In order to offer top performance and capabilities, hardware vendors frequently update their drivers.

Three types of drivers work under Windows 95:

- 16-bit Windows 3.1 drivers
- 32-bit virtual device drivers (VxDs) for Windows 95
- 32-bit Win32 Driver Model (WDM) device drivers for Windows 95 and NT

16-Bit Drivers

Also called *real-mode* or *DOS-compatible drivers*, 16-bit drivers are written to work with Windows 3.1. Microsoft designed Windows 95 to be compatible with existing hardware, allowing it to work with device drivers written for Windows 3.1. The benefit is obvious: If a peripheral lacks a native Windows 95 driver, it will still work on Windows 95 systems using the original software.

Although you can usually get by with the old drivers, you won't want to. 16-bit drivers provide slower performance than native 32-bit drivers, meaning that disk drives, graphics cards, and other peripherals will fail to operate at optimal levels. More important, 16-bit drivers often lack features available in their contemporary counterparts. Graphics boards, for instance, feature drivers for switching resolutions or managing the desktop area—but those probably won't be available on 16-bit drivers.

32-Bit Windows 95 Drivers

Today, most peripherals use drivers crafted specifically for Windows 95. Called *virtual device drivers*, or VxDs, this software provides direct support for hardware within Windows 95. It's no surprise that these drivers deliver optimized performance and include the full feature set.

One key talent of 32-bit drivers is their ability to load and unload without requiring the system to restart. This dynamic driver scheme allows Windows 95 PCs to effectively share resources and add capabilities when called upon. Notebook PCs, for instance, can recognize and initialize a PC Card modem the instant it is popped into the slot. Likewise, desktops can access a portable scanner when it is plugged in—memory-consuming drivers need not be loaded all the time in the expectation that the scanner might be activated.

Win32 Driver Model: The New 32-Bit Driver

Microsoft is hard at work on a new driver scheme called Win32 Driver Model (WDM). This emerging class of 32-bit drivers is intended to provide driver services for both Windows 95 and Windows NT. Why the change?

Right now, if hardware vendors want their products to be sold to users of both Windows 95 and NT, they must write separate drivers for the two operating systems. The problem is, writing drivers isn't easy—in fact, it can border on black magic. Rapid-fire advancements in PC technology mean that driver software is simply trying to keep pace with the latest versions of hardware and software. If you add a second OS, the workload for a hardware company doubles.

Predictably, the OS with less market share gets less attention. This means that Windows NT often gets saddled with aging, less-than-polished drivers for the hardware running under it. Microsoft hopes WDM will bring NT into parity with Windows 95, since a driver written for one OS will work equally well for another. Don't expect too much right off the bat, because vendors face a learning curve with the new driver scheme. Microsoft intends to release WDM drivers first for storage devices, USB devices, and other less-complex driver sets. Expect graphics and audio drivers to require distinct Windows 95 and NT versions for some time to come.

Peter's Principle: The Applications Make the OS

Often, deciding on an operating system can be a calculated risk. If you purchase a computer that has an OS on the wane—say, OS/2 or, to a lesser extent, a Macintosh—you might be unable to use the best hardware and software. In fact, the market for software and driver development behaves a lot like the stock market: When confidence among developers of a certain OS wanes, the relative value of the operating system often declines.

Take the Mac OS, for example. Today, many software vendors won't invest their resources in a marketplace that is a fraction of that of Windows 95. Even firms that made their fortune as Apple developers, such as Adobe and Macromedia, now release Windows 95 or NT versions of their products either before or at the same time as their Mac counterparts. The reasoning is simple: Companies can realize greater returns by honing their products for Windows 95 rather than shifting to the Mac OS.

Before you buy a Mac or a PC, you should consider the health of the operating system you want to use. If you want to play fast-action games, the Mac is a dead end. Likewise, NT is not a good option. If you want home-education software, Windows 95 is your best bet, with the Mac close behind. Once again, NT's corporate focus means that many CD-ROM games and home peripherals (such as programmable joysticks or keyboards for children) might not work on the OS.

Often the story is told on store shelves. Just as VHS beat out Betamax as the home-video recording standard, Windows 95 and other OSs constantly jockey for market position. As a general rule, the OS with the most software wins. And in this case, that OS is Windows 95—while compatibility makes Windows NT the next choice. Despite its woes, the Mac OS continues to offer excellent software for creative endeavors such as desktop publishing and image editing. Before you commit to an operating system, make sure you know what software vendors are supporting.

Windows 98: The New Wave

It took nearly three years, but Microsoft has finally upgraded its mainstream operating system. If you're expecting anything close to the hype and impact that Windows 95 delivered, you'll be disappointed. Windows 98 is, for the most part, a series of measured updates that provide incremental improvements to the earlier OS. It's no surprise that Internet connectivity is a big feature, and the most visible. Here are some of the new features in Windows 98:

- A Web-savvy interface, including a Web-like browser view and desktop "channels" that turn your display into a cross between a PC monitor and Web-savvy TV (see Figure 2.2).

Figure 2.2.
If you right-click the Windows 98 desktop and select Web, you can set your system to automatically access Web-based channels for the latest content.

- FAT32 hard disk support, which eliminates the need for multiple drive letters on disk drives greater than 2GB. It also reduces the amount of wasted space, called *slack*, that is accrued with small files (generally less than 16KB).

- Advanced bus support, including USB, AGP, IEEE 1394 (also known as FireWire), and fast IR.

- Enhanced multimedia capabilities, including MMX accelerated code built into key Windows 98 components, such as the video- and audio-handling subsystems. The new ActiveMovie interface delivers better control than the old Media Player, while DirectX drivers provide hooks for compelling game play and multimedia playback.

- Advanced power management, including sleep mode for desktop PCs. PC Card peripherals also gain better low-power operation.

Is Windows 98 a slam-dunk upgrade? Maybe not. For one thing, many features of the operating system have been available from Microsoft's Web site or on new PCs for months or even years. It's very likely that many of these features are already on your system. If you've already downloaded Internet Explorer 4.0 (IE4), the DirectX 5.0 driver set, and the PowerToys utilities, you're well on your way to having Windows 98 on your desktop.

That said, there is something to be said for a wholesale upgrade. Core components of the OS get retrofitted, and the all-in-one update can ensure that you have the best of everything. This is also the only realistic option for people who ply the Web with a 28.8Kbps modem. IE4 is over 22MB in size—a nearly impossible download for analog surfers.

Windows NT: Microsoft's Buttoned-Down Operating System

Where Windows 95 was targeted at mainstream users, Windows NT caters to a more discerning crowd. Microsoft's bulletproof OS is designed to run in heavy-duty systems that demand complete reliability. Among them are

- Network servers
- Web servers
- Graphics workstations
- Heavy-duty corporate desktops

Windows NT will certainly run on stand-alone home and office machines, but most such users won't be tempted to move from Windows 95. Why? For one thing, NT demands more resources than Windows 95—32MB of RAM is a good starting point, for example—meaning that many users would face a stiff hardware upgrade in order to run NT effectively.

There are actually two flavors of NT:

- Windows NT Workstation
- Windows NT Server

The two employ the same core code, but you'll find a greater range of networking features in the NT Server package. NT 4.0 Server can do duty as a full Web server platform, but Workstation is limited in the number of connected systems it can support. You'll also find greater symmetric multiprocessing (SMP) support in NT Server. Unlike Windows 95, which can recognize only a single processor, NT can recognize up to four processors at once.

Advantages of Windows NT

Like Windows 95, Windows NT is a multithreaded, multitasking operating system, meaning that it can smoothly juggle many tasks at once. And with version 4.0, Windows NT even looks like Windows 95—a significant improvement over the Windows 3.1 look of its predecessor. NT 4.0 uses familiar tools such as Control Panel, Device Manager, and the Start button.

Most important, NT is a true mission-critical operating system, unlike Windows 95, which incorporates 16-bit code and a fragile memory structure in order to ensure compatibility. Windows NT was designed from the ground up to be bulletproof. Applications running under NT have no access to memory used by other applications or the operating system. If Excel crashes, it won't take NT down with it.

In fact, the core function of the operating system (called the *kernel*) is protected by an abstraction layer that prevents programs from tweaking with the OS proper. Instead, commands are handed off by applications and then handled internally by the operating system. The result is a sort of relay race in which the baton is handed to the OS to handle a function and then handed back to the application as soon as the task is complete. The drawback is that NT takes a lot of time to switch between internal and external operation, resulting in slower performance than under Windows 95.

How important is the reliability of NT? Businesses such as banks require that their systems run without fail, often 24 hours a day, seven days a week. Occasional reboots and the odd system crash aren't annoyances—they are service disruptions that result in lost sales and clients. NT is the first operating system from Microsoft that delivers that kind of rock-solid performance.

Perhaps most important, NT uses a familiar code base. Developers can write their applications for both Windows 95 and NT using the same code, creating an immediate and enormous market of NT-compatible software. Called Win32, this application programming interface (API) attracts more developer effort than any other in the market.

Drawbacks of Windows NT

NT isn't perfect. Mainstream users are still put off by NT's stiff hardware requirements and slower performance than Windows 95. What's more, although NT features the Windows 95 interface, it lacks Plug and Play capability. Hardware installations and resource settings must be handled manually, resulting in much more trial and error.

NT also lacks compatibility with some hardware and software—a big reason why the OS hasn't moved into the mainstream desktop market. Hardware devices must use NT-specific device drivers in order to work with the OS, requiring additional effort that some companies are unwilling to undertake. Although the roster of NT-compatible devices is growing quickly, buyers with NT systems must still be careful to make sure that the hardware they purchase will work with the operating system.

Software compatibility is a problem for games. Windows NT's strict security slows performance and rules out the kind of direct access that most games require. Microsoft is addressing part of this problem by bringing its DirectX technologies over to NT, but the transition is not immediate. Windows 95 typically enjoys a long feature lead over NT in handling games and multimedia; in some cases, games might not run at all under NT. If you have a PC that needs to run both business apps and entertainment titles, you'll need to stick with Windows 95.

Coming Up

Like Windows 95, NT is evolving. Microsoft has added multimedia savvy to the operating system with the DirectX technology set. The addition of DirectX should also further software compatibility. In addition, the Win32 Driver Model (WDM) promises to ease the driver development burden. WDM allows a single driver to work on both Windows 95 and NT, so a vendor needs to write a driver just once in order to reach both operating systems. In 1998, Windows NT 5.0 will finally add Plug and Play to the mix.

Is NT for you? If you run server applications or do heavy-duty graphical work such as 3-D computer-aided design (CAD) or video editing, it might be. And if you want to run Windows applications on a multiprocessor PC, NT is the only real choice. These advantages, plus the fact that NT uses the familiar Windows 95 interface, make NT an attractive option for businesses and professionals.

Living with Windows 95

Unless you're an affirmed UNIX junkie, you probably welcomed the move to Windows 95. The 32-bit OS mostly did away with the inscrutable command-line interface and the teetering Windows-on-DOS structure that was so prone to crashing. In many ways, Windows 95 actually surpasses the vaunted Mac OS, with features such as Plug and Play.

That said, Windows 95 has its share of problems. The interface might be vastly improved from Windows 3.1, but accessing hardware settings can be a trial. The Control Panel facility—the central repository for hardware configuration—is a veritable dumping ground of icons. Likewise, Plug and Play can fail spectacularly, creating greater problems than it solves. The following sections will help guide you toward the features in Windows 95 that can help you.

Control Panel

If you're dealing with hardware, you'll encounter the Windows 95 Control Panel. Control Panel provides one-stop shopping for finding and adjusting hardware settings, adding and removing peripherals, and changing drivers. Whether you plan on upgrading your hardware or keeping abreast of the latest driver software, you should be familiar with the Windows 95 Control Panel.

To access Control Panel, simply select Start | Settings | Control Panel. You will see a window with many icons, representing hardware devices and Windows 95 facilities (see Figure 2.3). When you double-click an icon, you are taken to the appropriate properties sheet. Here you will find crucial information for the device, such as driver versions, system resource settings (IRQ, DMA, and so on), and device settings.

Figure 2.3.
From Control Panel, you can gain access to virtually every peripheral attached to your PC.

Over time, you might notice that additional icons appear under Control Panel. Graphics card drivers, for example, might install a new icon in Control Panel. These new icons often provide enhanced features for installed hardware or address a peripheral type not supplied in the default Control Panel setup.

Control Panel also contains key upgrade facilities under the Add New Hardware and the Add/Remove Programs icons. We will step through some of these resources.

Accessing Device Properties Using Control Panel

Let's walk through this quickly. To access the properties of a device—say, a modem—do the following:

1. Select Start | Settings | Control Panel.
2. Double-click the Modems icon.

3. In the Modems properties sheet, click the modem you want to inspect. (You can have multiple modems set up.)

4. Click the Properties button to view the specific settings for this device.

5. In this case, the screen that appears provides information on COM port settings, device speeds, and speaker volume. You can also follow the Connections tab to inspect dialing settings for the device.

Once you get to the properties sheet, you'll see different interfaces for each device. After all, a graphics card doesn't use the same resources as a modem or a printer. A little digging should make you familiar with where the information is stored.

Adding New Hardware

This being an upgrade book and all, it seems logical to step through the procedure for adding devices to your PC. Windows 95's Add New Hardware icon is your upgrade gateway. This icon launches the Add New Hardware Wizard, a step-by-step interactive installation guide that prompts you to tell Windows what you're installing and how you want it done. This useful resource also fires up Windows 95's Plug and Play, so you can let the operating system do the installation automatically.

Actually, there are three ways to install new hardware, and it can get confusing. Here are the options you might face:

• New hardware detected at boot-up: The Add New Hardware Wizard launches when you start Windows 95.

• Use the Add New Hardware icon: You tell Windows 95 to fire up the Add New Hardware Wizard by using the generic hardware install facility.

• Use the specific device icon: You tell Windows 95 to install a specific device by clicking the Add button found on the properties sheet of the device type you want to install.

The most common upgrade is for Windows 95 to sense new hardware when it is started. After all, any internal device upgrade will require you to reboot the system. In this example, we will install a new sound card. Note that internal components such as modems usually don't require you to click the Add New Hardware button. That's because Windows 95's Plug and Play will detect the new device and launch the Add New Hardware Wizard at startup.

1. First, install the new card into your PC. Of course, you must shut down the system, remove the power cord, and open the case to do this.

2. Once the sound card is in, start up Windows 95. The operating system will detect the new hardware at boot-up and launch the Add New Hardware Wizard.

3. Click the Next button to kick things off.

4. Windows 95 asks to detect the hardware. Click the Yes radio button and then click Next to let Windows 95's Plug and Play go to work.

Upgrade Advice: You can speed up the upgrade process by telling Windows not to detect new hardware. If you do this, make sure you know exactly which device you're working with, the manufacturer name, and the model name. Also make sure that you have the driver disk handy so that you can load the device drivers and other utilities when prompted. Skipping the detection step can save 10 minutes or more of waiting around. Be careful, though. If you've just removed an older card and replaced it with a newer model, you should let PnP do its work so that Windows 95 knows about the change to the old hardware.

5. Get a cup of coffee or something. The detection process can take a while, particularly on slower machines.

6. Windows 95 will prompt you with the name of the manufacturer and model of the device it detected. If this information is correct, click Next.

7. When prompted to install device drivers, use the Browse button to select the drivers from the floppy disk. This usually means pointing the installation to the A:\ drive.

8. Wait while the drivers load. You might need to restart your system in order for the new device to work. Keep a close watch during this process.

9. Always try to test newly installed hardware immediately after setup. For the sound card, try playing some system sounds or MIDI files. You can also access the properties sheet from Control Panel to check the resources that Windows 95 has assigned.

The Add/Remove Programs Facility

Control Panel also contains the Add/Remove Programs icon. This useful resource guides you through software installation and, more important, provides a way to remove programs from your PC. These are your upgrade gateways, providing a structured approach to updating your system.

Double-click the Add/Remove Programs icon. You will see a dialog box that has three tabs, as shown in Figure 2.4:

- Install/Uninstall: Adds and removes applications
- Windows Setup: Adds and removes Windows 95 utilities and features
- Startup Disk: Creates an emergency boot disk for troubleshooting problems

As with the Add New Hardware process, a wizard interface guides you through the installation step by step. This useful approach can help keep novices out of trouble. But as with adding hardware, you don't have to use this facility to install new software. It's just one option.

Figure 2.4.

The Add/Remove Programs Properties dialog box is a powerful resource for updating Windows 95 with new software.

Here are the common methods that an application installation routine may start:

- CD-ROM setup file detected: Windows 95's AutoPlay feature detects a new CD-ROM disc and automatically fires up the installation wizard after you insert the disc.
- Use the Add/Remove Programs icon: You tell Windows 95 to fire up the installation wizard by double-clicking the Add/Remove Programs icon and clicking the Install button on the Install/Uninstall tab.
- Double-click the SETUP.EXE file directly: You bypass the wizard and launch the appropriate SETUP.EXE file by double-clicking it.

All these approaches yield the same result. And provided that the application conforms to Windows 95's guidelines for installation, you'll be able to uninstall the program using the Add/Remove Programs resource.

The System Tray

Another place to access hardware settings is from the system tray, which is found on the Windows 95 Taskbar (see Figure 2.5). Small icons on the far right of the Taskbar denote hardware with a system tray interface. Graphics card settings, sound card volume and settings, and the PC's system clock can generally be accessed from here. In addition, custom graphics and joystick drivers might place an icon in the system tray. Active print and fax jobs are displayed in the tray as well.

Figure 2.5.

The small icons at the far-right of the Taskbar provide instant access to volume controls, desktop icons, display settings, and modem status, among other things.

> **Tip:** You can enhance the Taskbar using Microsoft's PowerToys software. This free utility adds a Taskbar-based monitor icon for switching colors and resolutions on-the-fly, as well an icon for accessing desktop elements without having to close application windows. You can download the PowerToys utilities at the Microsoft Web site at
>
> `http://www.microsoft.com/windows/windows95/info/powertoys.htm`

Device Manager

Perhaps the single most important element when it comes to managing hardware under Windows 95 is Device Manager. Considering its importance in keeping track of resource settings and installed devices, Device Manager is surprisingly difficult to access. You will find it buried within the System Properties dialog box. There are two ways to get to Device Manager—from Control Panel and from the Windows 95 desktop.

To access Device Manager from Control Panel, do the following:

1. Open Control Panel and double-click the Systems icon.

2. In the System Properties dialog box, choose the Device Manager tab.

To access Device Manager from the Windows 95 desktop, do the following:

1. Right-click the My Computer icon on the desktop and choose Properties from the context menu that appears.

2. The System Properties dialog box appears. Choose the Device Manager tab.

> **Tip:** If you're too impatient to wait for context menus, you can fire up the System Properties dialog box by selecting the My Computer icon on the desktop and pressing Alt-Enter. The System Properties dialog box will come up right away.

Device Manager Explained

Device Manager provides a list of all the various hardware devices stored on your PC. Everything from CD-ROM drives to network adapters has an icon in this list. By clicking the + symbol next to the desired device type, you can see what hardware is installed on your system. Double-click the revealed devices, and you'll be transported to a useful configuration sheet that includes resource settings and driver information for the device. You can even change settings directly from this facility, making it easy to hunt down and resolve conflicts.

Most important, Device Manager lets you ferret out conflicts and problems. If a device is in conflict with another device, a yellow circle with a question mark appears next to the affected devices, as shown in Figure 2.6. This is an effective visual cue that immediately guides the user to hardware problems.

Figure 2.6.
Helpful icons draw your attention to devices that need troubleshooting—a big help when you're trying to get to the bottom of a mystery.

You'll also find an icon called System at the bottom of the list. Here you will find nitty-gritty details on resources for things such as the PCI bus, the ISA Plug and Play enumerator, and the system clock. In general, you won't need to—and won't want to—mess with these low-level settings. Still, you can browse these devices.

Print Settings

One of the most useful features is the ability to print your current system configuration directly from Device Manager. To do so, follow these steps:

1. Double-click the Systems icon in Control Panel. In the System Properties dialog box, choose the Device Manager tab.

2. Click the Print button. The Print dialog box, shown in Figure 2.7, appears.

3. If you want a complete report, click the All devices and system summary radio button. Otherwise, click the System summary radio button.

Figure 2.7.
*Make a point to
periodically record
your system con-
figuration using
Device Manager's
excellent system
summary tool.*

Windows 95 Utilities

In addition to the hardware-specific talents found in Control Panel and Device Manager, Windows 95 provides utilities to monitor and optimize your PC. These helpful applets are the result of years of agglomeration as Microsoft has incorporated more and more tools inside its DOS and then Windows operating systems. Today, Windows 95 comes with enough tools that you can do without third-party utilities—although these products still provide added value over Windows 95's tools.

Most of the useful programs can be found on the Start menu. Select Start | Programs | Accessories | System Tools. The fly-out menu will display up to a dozen or so icons, which represent built-in utilities.

Adding and Removing Utilities

Windows 95 doesn't install all the monitoring and management software by default. You need to tell it to add many of these programs. If you have the available hard disk space for them, you can add these applets in one of two ways:

- During the Windows 95 installation routine, select the Full Install option. All the utilities will be installed and available to you.
- After Windows 95 is installed, use the Add/Remove Programs Properties dialog box to selectively add some or all of the utilities.

To add utilities using the Add/Remove Programs Properties dialog box, do the following:

1. Select Start | Settings | Control Panel. In the Control Panel window, double-click the Add/Remove Programs icon.
2. In the Add/Remove Programs Properties dialog box, choose the Windows Setup tab.

3. You'll find utilities under the Accessories and Disk Tools items. To view the options, choose one of these items and click Details. A list of available applets will be displayed. Any item without a check in the box is not installed and is unavailable.

4. To install applets, go to the item you want to add, either within the individual component's Details view or from the main Components view. Check the boxes of items you want to add.

5. Click OK, and then click OK or Apply. Windows 95 will install the item you want. The OS will tell you if you need to reboot your system.

6. To remove an item (say, to save disk space), simply go to the specific utility or component and click the appropriate box so that no check appears. Again, click OK and then click OK or Apply. Windows 95 will remove the utility.

Windows 95's Inner Talents

Before you spend $50 on a third-party utility suite, it pays to know what Windows 95 can do itself. Many of its features are more than adequate for the majority of users. Of course, advanced users and inveterate tinkerers will want the extended features and optimizations offered by products such as Symantec's Norton Utilities.

Accessories

In the Add/Remove Programs Properties dialog box, in the Windows Setup tab, you will find an Accessories facility that has nearly 20 individual items. Among those, the following will help you manage your hardware:

- Backup: Lets you archive hard disk data to floppy disks or tape drive. Includes facilities for scheduling and customizing backup routines.

- Disk Defragmenter: Moves hard disk data together into contiguous sections, which reduces disk head travel and improves performance. You should defragment periodically to keep your hard disk running smoothly.

- ScanDisk: Evaluates floppy and hard disk media for bad sectors and other flaws. Useful in diagnosing disk-related problems and working around flaws in the media.

Tip: You should run both Defragmenter and ScanDisk periodically. Defragmenter will optimize performance by grouping related data on the disk. ScanDisk can catch flaws in media before they become critical and result in data loss.

- DriveSpace: On-the-fly hard disk compression helps make room for more data on smaller hard disks. Compression ratios can reach about 2 to 1, although ratios of 1.5 to 1 or 1.7 to 1 are more common. Be aware that the OSR2 version of Windows 95 is incompatible with DriveSpace, so compressed drives won't work on this later version of the OS.

Peter's Principle: Disk Compression Hurts Performance But Offers Real Benefits

Avoid using on-the-fly disk compression if you can. Any hard disk compression scheme will hurt performance, because the CPU must encode and decode all the data that comes to and from the hard disk. The added workload really hurts older 486 and Pentium PCs, but even the newest systems will suffer when running demanding games and multimedia software titles. Hard disk compression also adds complexity to your data management, because the disk must be partitioned to allow compression to occur. These changes can confuse older utilities and might cause problems with DOS-based software.

If you find yourself unable or unwilling to move to a larger hard disk, compression can help. DriveSpace lets you define the level and type of compression, allowing you to balance smaller file sizes against better performance. You can even identify levels of compression for particular file types.

- Inbox Repair Tool: Tries to repair corrupted inbox files (.PST) used by Microsoft's Exchange mail facility.
- Netwatcher: Lets you monitor the identity of connected systems on a network.
- Resource Meter: Lets you track available resources, which can run out as you run multiple applications. Can be helpful in avoiding system crashes.
- System Monitor: Lets you selectively observe the activity level of system components. Tracks CPU usage, memory transactions, and data flow to and from the hard disk, modem, and network interfaces, among other things. Useful for sniffing out bottlenecks.

All these tools are well worth installing; most take up very little space on your hard disk. The System Monitor and Resource Meter applets, for example, take up about 300KB combined. Although ScanDisk and Defragmenter are larger, they are well worth installing, because they play a key role in preserving your critical data, and they help your disk subsystem achieve peak performance.

Summary

Windows 95 is a quantum improvement over the sorry state of affairs under DOS and Windows 3.1. Intelligent device management, Plug and Play, and the performance and reliability of the 32-bit code base all combine to make Windows 95 a critical improvement.

Most important, Windows 95 has effectively transitioned the PC industry to 32-bit computing. The savvy combination of 16-bit compatibility and 32-bit native operation have helped thousands of hardware and software companies make the transition to 32-bit computing.

Consider this: When IBM touted its OS/2 operating system as an advanced 32-bit environment, developers stayed away in droves. The problem was that their OS/2-optimized applications wouldn't work under Windows 3.1, and Windows 3.1 applications wouldn't work optimally under OS/2. This combination stunted OS/2 application development and killed the market for OS/2-equipped PCs. Microsoft got its 32-bit operating systems onto PCs by ensuring that they could run 16-bit code, and system vendors and users were not faced with making the large universe of 16-bit code obsolete. Once Windows 95 was on enough PCs, software makers—led by Microsoft, not surprisingly— began cranking out 32-bit applications of their own.

If you're using Windows 95, it's worth the effort to make the 32-bit transition. If you're considering a hardware upgrade, replace your older non-PnP devices first. Also make sure that all your device drivers are up to date, because older 16-bit drivers can slow performance, hamper features, and invite conflicts. By the same token, you'll see vastly improved performance—particularly in multitasking—if you use only 32-bit applications.

3

Upgrade
Strategies

Peter Norton.®

If you own a PC, an upgrade is probably in your future. After all, you're likely to spend more time and money upgrading your PC than you will repairing or maintaining it. The reason is simple. When something goes wrong with a PC component, it's simply less expensive to replace it than to try to repair it.

But upgrading isn't easy. It often involves fishing around in the guts of your PC, removing cards and adding new ones. You also need to install drivers and update the operating system. These aren't trivial tasks; they all include some level of risk. For this reason, it's a good idea to think before you upgrade. This chapter will help you master the upgrade landscape. You will learn

- When an upgrade is called for and when it's better to buy a new system
- About the different types of upgrades
- How to best approach a hardware upgrade, including general strategies and tips

When Are Upgrades Worth It?

For most PC owners, upgrades are a fact of life. Old parts might need to be replaced, or new software might require additional resources. Whatever the case, any PC owner who expects to keep his or her machine for three or more years will probably end up investing in updated hardware.

In general, there are three reasons to upgrade a PC:

- To improve performance
- To add new functionality
- To replace a failing part

Performance Upgrades

Probably the most-talked-about upgrades are those that target performance. After all, when you boost the speed of your PC, the results are evident immediately. Windows 95 boots faster, programs snap to life, and complex graphics update without delay. No doubt about it—a certain satisfaction comes from improving your system's performance.

Certainly, there is always a need to consider performance upgrades. Every year, the software your PC runs gets bigger and more complex. Today's word processors—with their built-in grammar checkers, on-the-fly corrections, and whizbang graphics and layout tools—are a long way from modest DOS programs such as WordStar. And I have no doubt that word processors will get more complex still.

Peter's Principle: Don't Expect Too Much from Upgrades

It's important not to expect too much from your performance upgrades. Remember, replacing a CPU doesn't eliminate other performance bottlenecks, such as slower RAM, lack of secondary cache, or slow hard disk response. Don't expect an upgrade to make your PC as fast as new systems. Instead, a hardware upgrade can help extend the useful life of your PC for another year or two—long enough to let you gain access to some hot new technologies that might have yet to reach the market.

Keep in mind that you can spend a lot of money on upgrades that deliver only marginal or temporary performance gains. When planning an upgrade, you should always try to get the most bang for your buck. For example, with RAM prices at a historic low, adding memory to your PC might be the best option. Also be careful not to buy into technology that is soon to be replaced. For example, a graphics card upgrade that lacks 3-D features will leave your system without the ability to play some of the most popular games.

When I talk about performance upgrades, I am talking about speed, pure and simple. These are upgrades that shorten boot times, accelerate graphics displays, and smooth out jerky video playback. The following components are prime performance candidates:

- CPU and L2 cache
- System RAM
- Graphics card
- Hard disk
- CD-ROM drive
- Modem

Table 3.1 guides you to the proper upgrade for your needs.

Table 3.1. Performance upgrades at a glance.

Component	What It's Best For	Drawbacks
CPU	Overall performance, games, graphics, and spreadsheets	Expensive, risky upgrade
L2 cache	Overall performance	Cache sockets are sometimes unavailable
RAM	Overall performance, multitasking	Older PCs can't accept fast RAM

continues

Table 3.1. continued

Component	What It's Best For	Drawbacks
Graphics card	Graphics, video, and 3-D display	Limited impact on many applications
Hard disk	Database and multimedia operations	Older systems will require a separate add-in card for best results
CD-ROM drive rates	Multimedia applications	Many titles won't benefit beyond 8X spin
Modem	Internet access	Newest modems lack standards

CPU and L2 Cache

CPU and secondary cache upgrades have the main advantage of affecting performance across the board. From word processing to game play, a faster CPU and larger L2 cache will benefit your computing experience. But a new CPU can be quite pricey. Intel's Pentium MMX OverDrive upgrade, for example, can cost $500—enough money to buy more than 40MB of RAM.

A CPU upgrade can boost performance in several ways. Older Pentium systems can gain access to the latest MMX software by adding a new CPU, and the faster internal clock helps speed virtually all PC transactions. The newest CPUs also feature larger internal L1 caches, which help cut down bottlenecks in memory.

Any CPU upgrade is serious business. Depending on the type of CPU, you might encounter BIOS conflicts and other "gotchas." You should check the CPU vendor's documentation carefully to make sure your PC will work with the new processor.

System RAM

This is perhaps the best upgrade for machines that are on the downside of their careers. RAM is affordable—about $10 per megabyte—and it's particularly crucial for fat, multitasking operating systems such as Windows 95 and NT. With many people running Internet browsers alongside their other applications, the additional RAM can help relieve chronic disk swapping.

RAM is easy to install and well-standardized, but not all systems can access the latest, greatest stuff. Older systems use 30-pin sockets that won't work with today's fast EDO DRAM technology (see Figure 3.1). Likewise, Pentium Classic PCs won't be able to take advantage of the newest sync DRAM (SDRAM) memory. Still, adding RAM can be the most effective performance boost you can buy. Although Windows 95 can run in 8MB of RAM, 16MB is a good minimum, while 32MB of RAM provides the best combination of performance and affordability. Windows NT, meanwhile, requires 32MB of RAM but runs better in 64MB. Of course, more RAM is always better.

Figure 3.1.
Often the most effective upgrade, adding RAM to a PC can really speed up multitasking operations. But these 168-pin DIMMs won't fit into older Pentium PCs designed for 70-pin SIMMs. (Photo courtesy of Kingston Technology)

Graphics Card

All cards sold over the last three years provide more-than-adequate 2-D graphics handling. But the emergence of 3-D games and titles is making graphics card upgrades a hot item again. 3-D cards can add impressive rendering capabilities to your PC, allowing realistic and smooth game-play for software using a compatible 3-D display scheme.

Adding a card is easy, but 3-D technology is moving so fast that today's hot card is tomorrow's mangy dog. Try to put off your upgrade as long as you can in order to get the most features and value for your money. Also look for a card that has at least 4MB or more of graphics memory. If you're trying to get a card for an ISA or VL-bus machine, you might want to consider moving to a new motherboard or a whole new machine.

Hard Disk

A new hard disk will probably affect your ability to access files and programs more than it will affect performance. That said, today's disks spin faster, respond quicker, and move data more smoothly than ever before. The key spec is access time, measured in milliseconds (ms). Today's drives run at 9ms to 12ms, up to twice the speed provided by older drives.

A good enhanced IDE drive (see Figure 3.2) will suffice for virtually all mainstream applications, but if you want to capture video or do other professional-level work, consider a SCSI drive. These drives enjoy higher top data rates than their IDE cousins, and they can also move data without tying up the CPU. Of course, bigger is always better for hard disks, and you should look in the range of 4GB and above when buying a new drive.

Figure 3.2.
The newest IDE hard disks, such as the Quantum Bigfoot shown here, use the new ATA-33 specification to more than double maximum data transfer rates. (Photo courtesy of Quantum Corp.)

CD-ROM Drives

Speeds keep going up—from 8X just a couple years ago to 32X now. Don't be fooled. The higher spin rates aren't really accessed by most software, and in any case, access times are really the key to responsive performance. Look for access times below 200ms, and preferably below 150ms. Again, SCSI drives will improve multitasking performance but won't make much difference otherwise.

Down the road, look for DVD-ROM to replace this market. But be careful. Many DVD-ROM drives lack compatibility with CD-Recordable media, which means that some CD-ROM discs might not work in some DVD-ROM drives. In addition, many DVD-ROM drives run at the equivalent of 8X speeds when reading CD-ROM media—slower than most CD-ROM drives, which typically provide 24X spin rates. Look for second-generation DVD drives that provide 20X CD-ROM spin rate performance.

Modems

56Kbps is the end of the line for modem makers. Even then, the higher data rate applies only to downloads through an ISP or another connection that provides a digital connection to the phone network. Anything going upstream runs at 33.6Kbps. Still, when it comes to Web browsing and file transfers, every bit can help cut your connect time and expenses. If you have anything below a 28.8Kbps modem, you shouldn't hesitate to upgrade.

The biggest concern is with modem standards—or the lack thereof. Universal standards for 56Kbps modems should be laid down within the next six months. In the meantime, you'll have to make sure that any 56Kbps modem you buy matches the communications scheme used by your ISP or other PCs you're calling. Some vendors are also offering upgrades to the finalized standard, which can help ensure compatibility down the road.

Feature Upgrades

Feature upgrades can add new dimensions to your PC, letting you do things you couldn't do before. In fact, many performance upgrades provide a feature benefit. For example, an OverDrive MMX upgrade will let your older Pentium system play MMX-enhanced games and titles—a feature it didn't support before. Likewise, 3-D graphics cards might add support for previously inaccessible software.

In general, expect to get more value out of feature upgrades than performance upgrades—to an extent. An aging 33MHz 486 will gain only moderate benefit from that capacious 7GB hard disk or 24X CD-ROM drive. The main thing is to make sure that your upgrades fit your needs and that they will work within your system.

The following are typical feature upgrade alternatives:

- Displays
- Video peripherals
- Input devices
- Data storage

Table 3.2 guides you to the proper upgrade for your needs.

Table 3.2. Feature upgrades at a glance.

Component	What It's Best For	Drawbacks
Display	Increased display area, higher resolutions	Expensive; large size
Video peripherals	Videoconferencing, editing videotapes	Video files are large; complex installations
Input devices	Ergonomic design, better control	None
Data storage	Greater capacity, multimedia features	Expensive; soon to be replaced with more-advanced products

Displays

One of the most compelling overall feature upgrades you can make is to the display. A larger monitor can make a world of difference, whether you're working on spreadsheets or playing fast-action games. It's not like getting a larger television screen. You can pack much more information onto a larger monitor—more tasks and more columns of data. Anyone who runs multiple programs or works with complex applications will want the space afforded by a 17-inch monitor. Just be sure that the graphics board can handle the load. You'll need at least 2MB of graphics memory and fast refresh rates in order to enjoy the full benefit of the larger screen.

Video Peripherals

Fast entering the mainstream are video cameras that let you make video calls to other similarly equipped PCs. Kits such as Boca's BigPicture and Creative Labs' ShareVision provide a monitor-top video camera and capture card. These packages can also be used to capture video or stills to your hard disk, but you're limited by the length of the camera cord.

If you're creative, you might want to add a video capture card, which lets you record broadcast or taped analog video to your hard disk. The digital video may be sent to tape or digitally edited and enhanced with special effects and transitions. For acceptable results, you'll have to shell out about $800—quite a bit for anyone not doing professional video editing.

Inputs

If you use your PC for game play, a joystick or other game upgrade can really improve your level of play. You'll find everything from Nintendo-like gamepads to force feedback joysticks that actually buffet and resist to emulate the feeling of high-G turns and other effects. Likewise, 3-D input devices such as Diamond's GyroMouse are terrific for games such as Descent, in which you need to be able to quickly move up and down, side to side, and forward and back without cramping your fingers on obscure keyboard codes.

For more mundane tasks, ergonomic keyboards can help prevent painful repetitive strain injuries (RSI). Split models such as the Microsoft Natural Keyboard are the most common. Also look for enhanced mice, trackballs, and touchpads that help simplify scrolling and provide automated operation through programmable keys.

Data Storage

The big news here is DVD, shown in Figure 3.3. Over the next year, expect this enhanced CD-ROM-like media to provide data capacities of 4.7GB and beyond. If you're looking for convenient archiving and distribution, emerging CD-Rewritable (CD-RW) and DVD-RAM drives both let you write to standard optical media.

Figure 3.3.
PC software makers and Hollywood studios are both excited about DVD, which can hold over two hours of terrific-quality video and store from 4.7 to 17GB of data. (Photo courtesy of Diamond Multimedia)

Other storage options include magnetic-based Zip and Jaz drives, which provide fast access and capacities of 100MB and 1GB, respectively. Iomega has also begun shipping a 2GB version of its Jaz drive, further pushing the capacity of its removable media.

Repair Upgrades

The last type of upgrade is really a repair. Do you try to fix a three-year-old graphics board when it goes down? Of course not. It would cost more to have a tech noodle with the thing than the hardware itself is worth. By replacing the dead or dying component, you not only address the functional problem, but you also end up enhancing the PC itself.

In fact, when it comes to PCs, *repair* often means *replace*. Solid-state circuitry can't easily be fixed once it's fried, and disk drives and other sealed components are expensive to service. Given that PC components quickly fall behind the feature and performance curve, it makes sense to replace these failed components.

But before you decide to replace an ailing component, you should make sure that a less-drastic solution isn't available. What looks like a dead hard disk or CD-ROM drive, for instance, might simply be a loose cable or an improperly set IDE jumper. Here are a few things to consider before you run to the computer store:

- Check that all cables are snug and properly connected. Loose cables are a common cause of mysterious failures.
- Ensure that fans are operating and that proper ventilation is available to the PC. Overheating can cause intermittent and chronic failures in a variety of components.

- For drive problems, check the on-board jumper settings and the system BIOS to make sure that the drive is properly configured.
- Also try shutting down the PC and reseating boards and wires. Repeated heating and cooling of components over time can cause small movements that interrupt connections.
- Try installing updated drivers for appropriate peripherals. Driver conflicts can render devices inoperable.

General Upgrade Tips

Upgrading a PC can be a harrowing task, particularly when it involves internal components and messy driver installations. You can ease the pain by keeping a few general rules in mind both before and during the process. The following sections contain a few tips.

Preparation

Preparation is the key to any upgrade. From compiling the right tools to making sure that you have an up-to-date backup, a little preparation can save both time and data.

Weekend Warriors: Give Yourself Time

Complicated upgrades don't happen quickly. You need to give yourself enough time to remove the old components, install the new ones, and conduct all the troubleshooting and testing to make sure you've got things right. For anything more than an external printer or modem upgrade, try to give yourself the weekend to get the job done.

Also, it's worth checking to see if the manufacturer of the component you're installing provides weekend support hours. Depending on the company, telephone tech support can range from 24-hour toll-free support seven days a week to weekday-only support available just eight or nine hours a day via a toll call. If you think you'll need help with a weekend upgrade, it's best to go with a company that provides phone support when you need it.

Save the Data

Don't be fooled by slick documentation and colorful packaging. Upgrades can go seriously wrong. You can prepare yourself for the worst by saving your important files and applications. There are two things you need to do to protect yourself:

- Make a startup disk
- Make a full data backup

Make a Startup Disk

Windows 95 provides a facility for making a startup disk, which contains files needed to start Windows 95 from a floppy disk. In addition to startup and configuration files, this disk contains utilities for managing the hard disk and resolving problems that might be preventing normal operation.

To create a startup disk, do the following:

1. Go to Control Panel by selecting Start | Settings | Control Panel.
2. Double-click the Add/Remove Software icon, and then choose the Startup Disk tab.
3. Click the Create Disk button.
4. Insert a floppy diskette into your system's A:\ drive.
5. Once the files are done copying, mark the diskette as a startup disk and note the date on the disk. Store it in a safe location.

Tip: Remarkably, Windows 95 fails to include drivers for the installed CD-ROM drives on the startup disk. The result is that if you need to use the startup disk to recover your system, you won't be able to access the Windows 95 CD-ROM disk—making a reinstallation impossible! After you're done creating a startup disk, make a point to copy the file MSCDEX.EXE from your hard disk to a separate floppy.

Back Up Your Data

You don't need to have a dedicated backup software system in order to protect your data. Windows 95 includes a utility—cleverly named Backup—that lets you archive your data to tape or floppy disks. Since most people don't own tape backup drives, the floppy disk feature can be very attractive.

There's one hitch. Your Windows setup might not have installed the Backup utility. If you want to use this utility to back up your data, you can install it as follows:

1. Insert the Windows 95 CD-ROM disc into the CD-ROM drive (or, for floppy installations, have your diskettes handy).
2. Go to Control Panel (select Start | Settings | Control Panel) and double-click the Add/Remove Software icon.
3. Choose the Windows Setup tab.
4. In the Components scroll-down list, select the disk tools item and click the Details button.
5. In the sheet that appears, click the Backup entry. A check should appear in the box to the left of the description.
6. Click OK, and then click Apply. Windows 95 will search the CD-ROM for the drivers. You might have to prompt the program to find the right drive and directory.

Once Backup is installed, you can archive your data. Here's an example of how to do so:

1. Select Start | Programs | Accessories | System Tools. Select Backup to launch the program.

2. If you intend to use floppy disks for your backup, the program will notify you that it doesn't detect a tape backup drive. Simply click OK and disregard the message.

3. In the Explorer-like interface, click the empty check boxes next to the folders and drives you want to back up, as shown in Figure 3.4. If you want to back up an entire drive, simply click the check box next to the drive icon.

Figure 3.4.
Microsoft Backup's familiar Explorer-like interface makes it easy to set up intelligent backup routines that can save time and preserve data.

4. Windows 95 Backup will go through the files and begin the backup process.

5. When you're done, store the disks or tape media in a safe, cool place. Make sure that you mark the media with the date and a description of the backup.

Looking Ahead: For more information on backing up your data, see Chapter 18, "Tape Backup."

If you have your original system disks and a startup disk, you don't have to copy over the entire hard disk. You can simply copy relevant data files and keep them in a safe place. You can reinstall your applications from their respective CD-ROM discs if disaster strikes. This can help cut down the time involved in backing up your data, particularly if you're relying on floppy diskettes for this task.

Get Your Tools

Before you start working, think about what you'll need. Most internal upgrades require at least a Phillips-head or Torx screwdriver for removing the case and expansion backplanes. You'll also want to use a static mat with a wristband if you expect to go fishing around inside your PC. The static mat serves as a grounding device, eliminating the chance of a damaging static discharge. If you don't have a static mat, you can discharge any static electricity by simply touching the metal case before you work with any of the internal parts.

A good way to get yourself properly equipped is to pick up a simple PC toolkit. Ranging from less than $20 to $100 or more, a toolkit will often include the following useful items in a small carrying case:

- Bit driver
- $^1/_8$-inch and $^3/_{16}$-inch Phillips-head bits
- $^1/_8$-inch and $^3/_{16}$-inch flathead bits
- Torx T10 and T15 bits
- Chip extractor
- Chip inserter
- Tweezers
- Spare-parts tube
- Parts extractor

More expensive kits will include items such as a flashlight, wire cutters and crimper, exacto knife, and an extended set of bits. Soldering tools, including a soldering iron, solder sucker, and solder material, might also be included.

It's also a good idea to have all your documentation handy. Before you start opening the PC and making a mess of things, go through the new upgrade product first. Make sure that all the required parts are there, and review the documentation for the upgrade procedure. You might find some very useful tips that can save you time and trouble. Also be sure to keep your system documentation handy in case you need to set motherboard jumpers or make changes to resource settings of installed components. Without these documents, you will be flying blind.

Split Decisions: What to Upgrade

Upgrading a PC can pose some difficult choices. Do you bump to a faster CPU or buy more RAM? Does a faster CD-ROM drive make sense, or will a bigger *and* faster hard disk do the trick? Unfortunately, there are no easy answers.

Essentially, any upgrade can help your PC perform faster and provide more features and capabilities. But some upgrades are better than others. Some of them—depending on your specific situation—can be a waste of time and money, so you need to think before you purchase.

First, you need to ask yourself some questions:

- Can your PC really be upgraded enough to do the job effectively? Remember, older 486 systems might lack performance for some tasks.

- Do you need to upgrade for performance or to add functionality?

- Will a single component upgrade provide the enhancement you need, or will it take two or more component upgrades?

- How much do you plan to spend on the upgrade? If it's more than $1,000, think hard about what you're doing.

You Know You Need an Upgrade When...

How do you know what kind of upgrade you need? That's easy. Just observe. Table 3.3 describes common PC behaviors and the upgrades that can help resolve them.

Table 3.3. Symptoms and solutions.

Symptom	Possible Upgrade Solution
Incessant hard disk activity when you switch applications or open menus	Add more RAM (32MB is best for moderate Windows 95 use; 64MB is best for heavy multitasking and graphics)
Freezing of on-screen windows when you scroll through or switch windows	Consider a faster graphics card or CPU; add RAM
Digital video is jerky and grainy	Get a video-capable graphics card
Painfully slow Internet downloads	Install a 56Kbps-capable modem
Eye discomfort and headaches	Use a 17-inch monitor with high refresh rates for stable display (no flicker)
Slow loading of multimedia titles	Buy a fast CD-ROM drive (16X to 32X)
You can't hear sound on DOS-only applications	Switch to a Sound Blaster-compatible sound card
Out of disk space	Install a second hard disk
You can't play 3-D or MMX-enhanced games	Upgrade to a 3D-capable graphics card and/or install an OverDrive MMX or other MMX-enhanced CPU

Just following the advice in Table 3.3 won't cut it, however. The effectiveness of any upgrade depends on the PC being upgraded. Adding 32MB of RAM to a 25MHz 486 system won't resolve issues with the underpowered processor or the tiny 250MB hard disk. By the same token, upgrading a 90MHz Pentium to 150MHz will be a wasted effort if all you have installed is 8MB of RAM.

For this reason, you should try to prioritize your performance upgrades carefully. Assuming that you're running Windows 95, here is a list of suggested upgrades, in order of diminishing returns:

- Upgrade 8MB of RAM to 16MB
- Replace a 486 CPU with a Pentium-class CPU
- Upgrade 16MB of RAM to 32MB
- Replace an old graphics card with one that has 4MB and 3-D capability
- Replace a Pentium-class CPU with Pentium MMX-class CPU
- Boost an L2 cache to 256KB if possible
- Replace an old CD-ROM drive with one running at 24X or higher
- Add a new multigigabyte hard disk that has access times below 10ms

It's About RAM, Stupid

Many people get excited about CPU upgrades, but the slogan of every upgrader should be "It's about RAM, stupid." Anything less than 16MB of RAM will condemn you to long waits while the hard disk swaps out memory needed by applications.

The culprit is Windows 95's virtual memory scheme. Windows 95 lets you make use of more bits than you have RAM to handle by using your hard disk as a kind of RAM pool. Code that Windows doesn't think is needed gets sent to the hard disk to make room for active stuff. The drawback is that when that code is needed again—say, when you switch over to a background application—it can take long seconds of furious disk activity to restore those bits to fast main memory.

This slowdown isn't hard to understand. Even the fastest hard disk is much slower than solid-state system RAM. Transfers that took nanoseconds now take milliseconds as the disk head hunts and pecks for the necessary bits on the disk. By eliminating virtual-memory transactions, you can see an immediate benefit greater than any CPU upgrade. In fact, CPU upgrades will do little to improve things on a system that has too little RAM.

So how much RAM do you need? Windows 95 itself consumes 12MB of memory, leaving a meager 4MB for applications. So 8MB machines are already in the hole and must store hunks of active Windows 95 code on the hard disk just to allow the machine to operate at all. 16MB is OK for single-tasking, but anyone running multiple applications will want to go with 32MB.

When Not to Upgrade

Perhaps the hardest decision is the upgrade you don't make. At some point, the cumulative wear and tear and mounting bottlenecks on an aging PC make upgrades unworkable. A fast new CPU will only strangle on the narrow and slow motherboard bus, while the dwindling selection of VL bus peripherals makes it difficult to find decent graphics cards.

Right now, millions of 486 owners face tough decisions. Although products exist to help 486s stay afloat, the aging infrastructure results in diminishing returns. At this point, anyone running new Windows 95 applications on a 486 needs to think in terms of months, not years. For example, an upgrade can help stretch your system until the next financial quarter or can let you wait until the arrival of neat technologies that you want built into your next PC. But don't expect any upgrade to turn your aging warhorse into a modern workstation. Short of a new motherboard, no upgrade can overcome the ravages of time.

Why aren't 486 systems prime upgrade candidates now? Table 3.4 shows the bottlenecks on 486s that can't be resolved short of a motherboard upgrade.

Table 3.4. Bottlenecks that require a motherboard upgrade to eliminate.

Aging System	Today's PCs
80 to 100ns fast-page-mode RAM	50ns SDRAM
L2 cache is lacking or slow	512KB pipeline burst cache
ISA and VL-bus slots	PCI and AGP bus slots
33MHz motherboard speed	66MHz motherboard speed
32-bit system bus	64-bit system bus

The cumulative effect of these bottlenecks will limit the impact of any upgrade. Even the fastest MMX-enhanced CPU will be forced to wait for slow system memory to move data across the slow and thin system bus. The lack of fast L2 cache (or any L2 cache in some cases) means that faster CPUs will simply sit idle, waiting for the rest of the system to catch up.

If your needs are modest, a 486 can serve well, provided that it has enough RAM and hard disk space to do the job. But if you want to multitask Office 97 applications and work with big files, you will need to reconsider your platform. Multimedia titles and most games will be out of the question as well.

Summary

Upgrading a PC requires thought and planning. Play devil's advocate and ask yourself the hard questions. Often, people trying to avoid a $2,000 purchase end up wasting $500 on an upgrade that doesn't work. The result is that they end up spending $2,500.

Remember to consider the cost of the upgrade when planning. Does a $500 expenditure make sense for a component that will add six or 12 months to the life of your PC? And be sure to consider the fact that the extended life might not be perfect. You might have to forgo the newest applications and titles on that aging system, despite the upgrade, although your bread-and-butter programs might work fine.

If you keep that perspective, you should be able to make proper decisions. Try to think strategically. Do you expect to buy a new PC a year or three down the road? If you plan your upgrades, you should make the most of your money. Be careful out there.

4

Trouble-shooting and Repair Strategies

Peter Norton ®

Many users will never have to face the prospect of repairing their PCs. Properly maintained, the solid-state components inside the case can run for five or 10 years or more—certainly longer than the useful life of the system itself. At the same time, moving parts such as hard disks and CD-ROM drives have grown more reliable and durable. The net result is fewer repairs and less downtime.

That said, PCs still fall victim to a wide variety of maladies. Poor maintenance can result in overheating, which over time can destroy sensitive electronics. The working environment can be a major factor: Dirty work areas can gum up power supplies, floppy drives, and other moving parts and restrict the airflow and thermal conduction needed for silicon chips.

This chapter helps you deal with hardware maladies and shows you how to address them without replacing the components. Just be aware that very often, the age of affected hardware means that it would be less expensive to simply replace the item than to try to get it serviced or repaired. Not only will the new component be as good as new, but it will also offer performance and features that are superior to the original part, upgrading overall system behavior.

This chapter covers the following topics:

- Common causes of hardware breakdowns and how to avoid them
- Do-it-yourself repair opportunities for PC components
- A symptom guide for repair jobs

Looking for Trouble: What Causes Breakdowns

As the old saw says, an ounce of prevention is worth a pound of cure. When it comes to protecting your data, you'll want all the prevention you can lift. After all, when you're trying to repair a component, you're probably in a position where your data has been put at risk—not a pleasant feeling.

You can save yourself much anxiety by making frequent backups and taking proper care of your PC. If you know what can cause problems, you can take steps to ensure that problems don't crop up. Yes, occasional failures happen—hard disks will crash, power supplies will get tired, and RAM modules will punk out—but you can help avoid nasty surprises.

The Law of Averages

The key is to spare your PC any unnecessary stress. Although daily wear and tear will take their toll—and aging components sometimes fail without apparent cause—a properly maintained PC will tip the law of averages to work substantially in your favor. After all, a typical CD-ROM or hard drive sold today boasts a projected working life—called *mean time between failure*, or MTBF—of hundreds of thousands of hours.

Do the math. A device with an MTBF of 100,000 hours is rated to run 4,167 days. This is nearly 11$\frac{1}{2}$ years of constant, nonstop operation—no downtime, no vacation, and no weekends off. Consider the fact that most corporations depreciate PC hardware over five or even three years, and you find that much of the hardware inside a PC is rated for twice the useful life of the system itself.

Note: Don't be misled: MTBF is not a realistic projection of the life of your hardware. After all, a manufacturer can't know that a product that has existed for only six months will last for 10 years or more. What mean time between failure defines is the amount of time at which exactly half of the units might be expected to fail. In other words, for a hard disk line rated at 100,000 hours, half of the drives are statistically expected to die before 100,000 hours of operation, and half are expected to die after 100,000 hours of operation. A drive could fail after 300,000 hours or after just three hours (but, statistically, that possibility is very remote).

Another predictor of usable product life is the warranty. After all, when a company warrants a product against failure, it's putting its money where its marketing is. Until about three years ago, three-year warranties on PCs were all but unheard of. The hardware was just too unreliable for vendors to cover repairs beyond the first year. Today, most larger PC vendors offer three-year parts-and-labor warranties, and some extend that coverage to five or six years on solid-state components such as RAM and CPUs. They know that, once a device is installed and working properly, it will probably continue to work fine for the remaining life of the system or beyond.

When you purchase a new hardware device, look for products that have longer parts-and-labor warranties. Three years is a good minimum for most components.

Clean Up the Environment

Generally, things happen for a reason. Perhaps the most common cause of component breakdown with PCs is exposure to a hostile environment. A number of factors—alone or in combination—can place undue stress on your hardware. Key among these are

- Heat
- Airborne hazards (dust, dirt, smoke, and pet hair)
- Electrical stress

By reducing your hardware's level of exposure to these factors, you can significantly reduce the likelihood of having to repair or replace components.

Heat

Heat is the most consistent enemy of your solid-state hardware. Without moving parts, components such as the CPU, RAM, L2 cache, and graphics and sound boards are free of the debilitating effects of friction and kinetic stress. But semiconductors such as silicon chips operate best when they are cool. As these chips heat up, their conductive properties can break down, eventually leading to complete failure. The threat of thermal damage is the reason why you see massive heat sinks and extra fans mounted on Pentium and faster CPUs, and why so many new PCs feature one or more fans to provide internal airflow.

The components most affected by heat are

- CPU
- L2 cache and RAM
- Motherboard chipsets and traces
- Adapter cards

It's not just heat that is at issue. As PCs are turned on and off, the components inside must endure a repeated cycle of warming and cooling. It's no surprise that materials expand and contract with each cycle. Over thousands of on/off cycles, motherboard traces can crack, silicon chips can be damaged, and connector pins can creep out of alignment.

Peter's Principle: Leave It On or Turn It Off?

As long as there have been PCs, there's been a debate about whether it's better to keep a PC turned on all the time or to shut it down when it's not in use. The arguments cut both ways. PCs that are turned on and off are subject to some stress as power surges through circuitry and components are heated and cooled. Over time, this on-and-off cycle can stress sensitive PC hardware such as silicon chips.

Leaving a PC on reduces cumulative stress but invites other problems. For one, you'll face steeper electric bills as a result of constant operation—although newer PCs with energy-saving monitors and low-power sleep modes can ease the pain. A PC left on all the time is also exposed to variations in the power coming into your office or home, so a good surge protector or (preferably) a backup power supply would be a good idea. Finally, constantly running PCs is more likely to create problems in dirty environments, where the additional hours of operation draw more dust and particulates into the case.

There is no right or wrong answer. If your applications demand that the PC be ready at all hours to handle incoming faxes or voice mail, your best bet is to leave the system on. Otherwise, you might as well turn the system off to save a few cents on your electric bill. By most accounts, it's a toss-up between the stress created when the power goes on and off and continuous day-in, day-out service. Suffice it to say that a machine left on is subject to less stress as long as environmental hazards remain low.

To avoid thermal damage, the inside of the PC must be kept cool, preferably under 110 degrees. The best bet is to work in a cool environment. A PC in an air-conditioned office, for example, is less likely to suffer failure from overheating than one serving in a hot warehouse during the summer.

This is not to say that, for example, you must cool your warehouse if you have PCs in service there. After all, PCs are in regular use on shop floors, in steel mills, on ships and boats, and even on the battlefield. Don't let the possibility of system failure stop you from turning the machine on. Just realize that as environmental stresses increase, the threat of failure rises too. Remember that the precious part of your computer is your hard-won data. Keep good backups.

Follow these tips to avoid overheating:

- Work in an air-conditioned area where the room temperature doesn't go over 80 degrees.
- Ensure proper ventilation. Make sure that all fans are working and that the case is properly sealed to optimize airflow. If you've taken a peripheral out of a drive bay, replace it with a face plate so that air will circulate as it is meant to. If you pull out an internal modem or other adapter card, replace the backplane shield before putting the cover back on.
- Ensure that dust and debris don't block air vents and that the PC isn't placed such that air intake and outflow are restricted. Also, don't stack books or other objects in front of fan or ventilation outlets, and be aware that PCs set on the floor will gather more dust than those mounted on desktops.

Tip: Pets can be a major source of particulate build-up in a PC. If you own cats or dogs or other shedding animals, you should try to keep them out of the room where the PC is set up. Failing that, mount the PC on a desk so that it is not on the floor, where it will attract the most hair and fur.

- In hot environments, use a temperature sensor and alarm to notify you when the internal temperature gets too high (see Figure 4.1). Some models will automatically shut down the PC.

Symptoms of overheating include

- Intermittent system crashes and failures, including memory parity errors, system lock-ups, and random reboots
- System failures that consistently occur after several hours or minutes of operation
- Failure of a system to reboot after several hours or minutes of operation

Tip: One way that heat can become a problem is when the power supply's fan fails. If your system box seems hot, makes an unfamiliar noise (or doesn't make the noises you associate

continues

with normal operation), or is otherwise behaving oddly, and if you haven't made any changes to it lately, put your hand over the air vent on the back of the machine. If you can see the back of the system unit without moving the machine, you should see a fan there. You should feel a gentle air flow out of that vent. If you don't, even if your office temperature is normal, system failure is imminent. If the fan mechanism has failed, you need to replace the power supply immediately in order to avoid thermal damage to the PC during operation. In addition, if the power supply itself overheats, your system might be exposed to severe electrical stress.

Figure 4.1.
Internal temperature alarms like this one can help avoid hundreds or thousands of dollars in damage. (Photo courtesy of PC Power and Cooling)

Peter's Principle: Identifying Hot and Cold Breakdowns

Whenever I encounter mysterious behavior with my PC, I stick to the "hot and cold rule" of troubleshooting. You see, heat causes problems with silicon (CPU, RAM, cache), and cold causes problems with hardware (hard disk, CD-ROM drive). As a rule, heat-related problems occur after hours of use, while cold problems usually happen at first boot-up.

Keeping hot and cold in mind can help you figure out what seems to be unfathomable behaviors from your PC. For example, if a PC consistently fails to find the hard disk on the first boot attempt but boots normally thereafter, it's a safe bet that the drive isn't powering up quickly enough to be on call when the system BIOS reaches for it. The extra seconds afforded by the second boot give the sluggish component enough time to recover and respond. Behavior like this might be your system's way of telling you that the disk drive is wearing out or that the power supply is overtaxed. Likewise, system lock-ups or memory parity errors that occur consistently late in the day might be the result of cumulative thermal stress to the RAM chips or L2 cache.

By noticing *when* things happen, and not just what happens, you stand a good chance of narrowing down the potential culprit. And often you might find that the problem isn't with the pricey hard disk or RAM modules but with an inexpensive power supply or a $20 fan.

Problems that occur after several hours of use can often be tracked to silicon, and those that occur immediately after start-up can usually be tracked to hardware devices such as disk drives.

Dust and Dirt Devils

Another common cause of failure is dirty operating environments. PCs are designed to move air through the chassis in order to keep components cool. But if that air is dusty or dirty, particulates in the air stream will blanket internal components, impeding electrical connections and helping trap heat. Over time, dirt can gum up components such as the power supply fan or CPU fan, inviting potentially catastrophic failure. Static electricity built up within the case can also cause dust to adhere to components.

The components most susceptible to dirt-related problems are

- Power supply
- CPU and other fans
- Floppy disk drive
- CD-ROM drive
- Add-in card connections
- Cable and ribbon connectors
- Mouse and keyboard

Unfortunately, there might not be a lot you can do to clean up your environment. Dust or pollen might be a part of your everyday life. But there are some helpful tips that can really cut down on the PC's exposure to airborne dirt and grime:

- Make sure that all add-in card backplane slots are sealed tight. Open backplane slots allow unwanted material to gather in empty and occupied card slots, as shown in Figure 4.2.

- Place the PC on a desk or other raised platform. Dirt settles on the floor, so a PC set low will pull in unwanted material through its air vents.

- Always operate the PC with the case on. An open PC chassis will allow dirt to settle on top of all components. The open case also negates airflow, inviting thermal damage.

- Periodically clear dust from components. Use a soft, dry paint brush to loosen dirt lodged on the surfaces of cards and circuit boards, in card slots, and in CD-ROM and diskette drive mechanisms, and then either blow it away with a compressed air canister or use a service vacuum or other hosed vacuum to draw the dust out. Also blow dust out of the power supply, but don't intentionally spin the fan blade, because doing so works dust into the spindle of the fan motor, increasing friction and the possibility of failure.

- Periodically clean out the socket where the mouse ball sits. Cumulative grime will shorten the life of the mouse. Also avoid eating or drinking on the desktop. Food spills are among the most common causes of input device failure.

Figure 4.2.
Missing backplanes like the one shown here can allow dust to gather on the mother-board, clogging sockets and trapping heat.

How do you know when dirt is attacking your PC? Often you can tell by the looks of it. If the keyboard, mouse, and monitor all bear a nasty brownish film, your PC probably needs a good cleaning. After all, what has settled on the outside of the system has probably worked its way inside as well.

Troubleshooting: Dirt problems often present themselves as heat-related problems, because dirt insulates components and causes them to trap heat. If you discover that your PC is overheating, make sure that you take time to clean all internal components. Use compressed air to blow debris and dust out of the motherboard.

Here are some symptoms of a dirty PC:

- Failure to boot because the electrical contact to the graphics card or other key peripheral has been blocked. Dust bunnies were created for exactly this purpose.
- Failure of sound card or some other nonbooting device due to blocked contacts
- Heat-related symptoms
- Excess fan noise or lack of fan noise
- A sticking mouse or sticking keyboard keys

A Shock to the System

Although almost everyone knows that a severe electrical spike can fry system components, fewer people are aware of the cumulative effects that long-term exposure to uneven power can have. Over time, the stress of slight under- and over-voltages can strain power supplies, chipsets, and disk drives. The result is a shortened operating life that occurs with virtually no visible symptoms.

Cumulative Power Problems

In fact, this insidious power problem might be the most dangerous to your PC. If you work in an older home or office or in a neighborhood where the electrical grid is obsolete or overtaxed, you might run into problems. Also, if you work in an area that has a lot of heavy-use electrical appliances (air conditioners, laser printers, and so on), your PC might be subject to ongoing stress that can lead to eventual failure.

To prevent cumulative damage, you need a surge protector or, even better, an uninterruptible power supply (UPS). These devices act as a firewall for your PC, stopping damaging power surges, spikes, and other over-voltages in their tracks. UPSs take an extra step and actually provide power in the case of a sudden blackout or brownout. The best UPSs constantly condition incoming power, ensuring that your PC gets a steady diet that eliminates unneeded stress. These line-conditioning UPSs are the best choice for any PC owner and are a must for anyone working in a "dirty" electrical environment.

Static Electricity

Another form of electrical mayhem comes from static electricity. A single static discharge can fuse the submicron circuitry of a CPU or wipe clean the boot sector of a hard disk. Although the amperage from a "shuffleshock" is quite low, the voltage produced is actually very high—enough to fry a chip in an instant. Static electricity is a factor in all PC repair and upgrade jobs, so you must take precautions to avoid destroying vital components.

There are a number of ways to avoid static discharge:

- Use an antistatic mat and wristband to ground yourself during any inside-the-case procedure.

- Touch the metal edge of the PC's chassis or another metal object to discharge static electricity before handling components.

- Outfit your office with static-reducing flooring. Sprays are available for carpeted floors, which present the most static danger. These need to be applied periodically to control static buildup.

- If you have a home office, it's probably carpeted. Make a habit of safety in regards to static danger. Ensure that your PC and printer are well-grounded, and ground yourself by touching metal that runs to the ground before touching your PC—every time.

- Avoid extremely low humidity levels, which greatly increase the danger of static shock. Use a humidifier if necessary to keep adequate moisture in the work area. Winter months in northern climates are notoriously dry.

The Electrical Landscape

Virtually all components are susceptible to damage from electric shock, be it static or otherwise. Disk drive electronics, system chipsets, adapter board chips, and every other area of your PC can suffer catastrophic damage. Most important, the damage can come in a single burst, or over months or years of silent abuse.

How do you avoid electrical damage? Here are a few guidelines:

- Always use at least a surge protector to stop sudden power spikes. Also consider a line-conditioning UPS, shown in Figure 4.3, which will smooth out the sometimes unnoticed bumps and valleys in your power stream.

- Avoid placing too many heavy-draw devices on a single circuit. PCs and laser printers can both draw tens of watts of electricity, while air-conditioners, refrigerators, and other heavy appliances require much more power.

- When working inside the PC, always unplug the system from the wall.

- Also be sure to discharge static electricity during internal work. An antistatic mat is best, but you can also touch any piece of metal prior to handling components to discharge yourself.

- Don't turn off the PC from the power strip or wall outlet. Shut down the operating system completely, and then use the power switch to turn the PC off.

- Make sure that your power supply is rated to handle all the peripherals that it powers. If your supply is rated under 200 watts, you might need to replace the supply with a more powerful model.

Figure 4.3.
An uninterruptible power supply (UPS) with line-conditioning capability can help eliminate the cumulative effects of poor power input. (Photo courtesy of American Power Conversion)

Unfortunately, chronic power stream problems might not be visible. Over time, under- or over-voltages can quietly stress your power supply, chipsets, drives, and adapters. Eventually, the situation can lead to intermittent problems or even wholesale motherboard failure. Here are symptoms of possible electrical problems:

- Intermittent failures, including memory parity errors, random keyboard lock-ups, system freezes, and reboots

- Unusual power supply fan noises, or evidence of an overly hot power supply

- Unusual behavior that occurs when another electrical appliance on the circuit is switched on. Laser printers and air-conditioners are common culprits.

- Lights flicker or dim when the PC or other appliance on the circuit is turned on.

- Sudden failure of the PC from a power spike, particularly during a lightning storm or when the lights come on after a blackout. However, power spikes can happen without visible warning.

Do It Yourself: Things You Can Repair

When it comes to PCs, *repair* usually means *replace*. Quite simply, it's less expensive to replace a damaged CD-ROM drive than it is to try to have it serviced. In the PC industry, hardware costs drop so quickly every month that, within a year, the original component might not be worth salvaging.

What's more, the nature of PC hardware doesn't lend itself to simple repair. Obviously, damaged CPUs, chipsets, and other silicon components are simply beyond recovering. Meanwhile, the sealed and calibrated drive mechanisms of hard disks and CD-ROM drives makes servicing these components complex and expensive. Finally, power supplies, floppy drives, and mice are so inexpensive that it doesn't make sense to spend money to repair them.

Easy Fixes

This doesn't mean that you can't fix problems. In fact, routine PC maintenance might demand that you occasionally play Mr. or Ms. Fixit. Many problems that look to be pocketbook nightmares actually end up requiring no more than a little attention and perhaps a $10 part. Sometimes no parts are required at all.

Case Study: On the other hand, simple glitches can sometimes redouble into major problems. Here are two classic examples of unexpected dangers that can strike:

Attaching a tape drive to the side of a drive bay seemed simple enough, even though it required pulling the diskette drive out—a simple task. So far, so good. But when I reinstalled the diskette drive, a nonstandard power supply input connector was revealed, which could be attached to the diskette drive in two different ways (most power connectors attach in only one way). Failing to properly check the documentation, I took a guess, plugged in the power cord, and pressed the power button. I got quick results—a crackle and a wisp of foul-smelling smoke. The diskette drive was ruined and had to be replaced.

Another example is an intermittent hard disk problem, a serious problem that could require replacing the drive. Running Windows 95 Scan Disk failed to fix the drive, and an examination of the cabling revealed clean, securely attached connectors free of crimps or folds. But when I turned the system box on its side, I heard the distinctive sound of a metal part sliding across a surface inside the box. It turned out to be a screw that had fallen out of a backplane connector for an internal modem. The screw had been lying on the motherboard, shorting out two silver traces (the electronic leads printed onto the board). Removing the screw solved the problem, but I was lucky. The shorted-out circuit could have easily cooked the motherboard.

Getting Cable

One of the most common, and most easily addressed, breakdowns occurs with the cabling inside your PC. Wires and cables carry data and power to internal and external components. Often, these vital wires can get stretched, crimped, or twisted, leading to frayed contacts and shorted circuits. If a component ever goes down, whether a hard disk, CD-ROM drive, monitor, or printer, always be sure to check the cables first.

Another possible problem is hard disk failure. When the hard disk is down, your system is down—you can't boot, you can't run a disk scan utility, and you can't even tell for certain if your disk is the problem. Because getting a new hard disk can cost $300 and all of your data, it makes sense to exhaust other possibilities first. In fact, the problem might be limited to the hard disk cable.

This gray multiwire ribbon stretches from the IDE controller on the motherboard to the back of the PC. First, check to make sure that the connectors are firmly seated on both sides by pressing them firmly into their sockets. Also inspect the cable itself for any marks or tears. A hard fold in the cable—perhaps where it had been folded in the past—might indicate a broken wire inside. Just be sure to triple-check the cable alignment.

If reseating the cable doesn't help, try connecting the drive to the motherboard using an IDE cable that you know is working. Be sure to closely follow the drive's instructions for properly seating the cable in the sockets. If the cable was the problem, your system should boot normally.

> **Tip:** Use your senses. If you have doubts about a connection or about the sturdiness of a recently added component, be watchful during startup. Turn your radio off and make a final check to see that all components are where you want them to be. When you turn on the power, listen for any sound that is out of the ordinary for a PC. If the system speaker begins to yelp, with a steady beep or a continuous beepbeepbeep, turn the PC off. Likewise, if you hear a crackle, smell smoke, or see a spark inside the chassis, shut the system down right away.

Apply these same techniques to cables connecting the following peripherals:

- Hard disk
- Floppy drive
- CD-ROM drive
- Monitor
- Printer
- Mouse and keyboard

You can find replacement cables for internal devices at any computer store for just a few dollars. Unfortunately, mouse and keyboard wires are built directly into the housing themselves. If straightening and tweaking the damaged cord doesn't help, you can take it to a service center for repair. Just keep a close eye on cost. Anything more than $20 will probably prompt you to simply replace the ailing part. The same is true of power supplies. Connectors are built in. But PC power supplies have a number of physical configurations, so be careful. Translation: Make sure that the screw holes on your replacement match up with the holes in your chassis.

For printers, you can purchase an extra parallel cable at a computer store. These cables are pretty tough, but they can be damaged if they get squashed under a desk or other heavy object. Also check to see if the connector or the device's port have been damaged by excess stress—often a result of a hard yanking or chronic stretching of the cable.

For monitors, the data cable might or might not be able to be replaced. Some displays feature a 15-pin connector that plugs into one side of the cable, making it easy to simply replace the worn cable with a new one. However, some displays integrate the cable into the monitor housing, making such a replacement impossible.

Warning: Never attempt to work inside a monitor casing. The components inside the display can hold thousands of volts of electricity, even after the display has been shut off. The same goes for power supplies, which can also store a lot of energy even when turned off.

Buying Tip: When buying a new monitor, look for models that feature a generic 15-pin connector on the monitor housing. These models let you easily replace a damaged cable without having to service or replace the entire display.

Viral Threats

The next time your hard disk crashes, don't be so sure it's your hard disk that is the problem. Many viruses attach to the master boot record (MBR) of hard disks, resulting in symptoms identical to a hard disk crash. Unexpected or intermittent crashes and data loss of any kind should prompt you to check for viruses. You might find that your big repair job consists of hunting and killing viruses resident on your network or hard disk.

The best way to avoid viral infections is to run an antivirus program in the background at all times. These utilities keep a constant watch on your system, looking for telltale signs of viral attack, such as .EXE files that change size. These programs take inventory at every boot-up, ensuring that a virus hasn't entered the system, before allowing you to continue. Just expect to pay a price in longer boot routines.

Compatibility: Antivirus programs are, by definition, invasive. They must interact with the guts of your PC and operating system in order to protect against infection. Unfortunately, routines such as application installations can run afoul of antivirus trip wires. This is no surprise, since an installation might overwrite .EXE and .DLL file types, which the utility is designed to protect. When installing applications, you should always disable your antivirus program first to avoid problems.

Some games and other software might also disagree with the antivirus utility. Generally it's a simple matter to turn off the program while running such software. Just be sure that it's set up to start automatically during boot time so that you don't leave yourself unprotected.

How can you tell if a virus has trashed your hard disk? It might not be so easy. After all, if you end up reformatting your hard disk from floppy and reinstalling your operating system and applications, all trace of the virus will have been removed. One clue is if a hard disk scan fails to turn up any flaws on the disk surface.

Cleaning House

As I mentioned, accumulated dirt and grime can wreak havoc on finely tuned PC components. Dirt and dust can gum up fans and air flow, causing heat problems. They can even act as thermal insulators, leading to fried CPUs and other components. Particulates can also get between electrical contacts, rendering add-in cards and memory sockets inoperable. Dirt on exposed drive mechanisms can cloud the optics of CD-ROM drives and hinder floppy drive heads.

A Breath of Compressed Air

Before replacing a recalcitrant CD-ROM or floppy drive, try clearing the housing of dirt and dust. All you need is an inexpensive can of compressed air. A thin straw attaches to the nozzle end, allowing you to gain access to internal components and tight spaces. Fire a few bursts of air into the drive mechanisms, looking for evidence of heavy dirt build-up as you do so. Often this simple operation can clear up the problem.

Warning: Compressed air comes out of the can very cold, and the longer you press the trigger, the colder it gets. The sudden temperature change can crack IC chips and break the traces on circuit boards. Don't spray compressed air on hot components; let your PC cool for 30 minutes before using air on the motherboard. Also, spray in short bursts and wait a few minutes after spraying to start the PC. If the frost from a spurt of compressed air hasn't completely dissipated before you turn the power on, you can short out your motherboard.

Forced air can also help alleviate heat-related problems with the CPU, power supply, and on-board chips. Again, make sure that you reach all the vital components. The power supply in particular needs periodic attention, since the internal fan naturally draws a lot of dirt into the housing. When the power supply vents and fan get clogged up, the unit will overheat, eventually threatening the supply of clean power to the PC. A dying power supply can have a ripple effect on your system that can lead to serious component failures, including the CPU, hard disk, and motherboard.

Making Contacts

If you seem to be suffering from problems with system memory, the L2 cache, or add-in card peripherals, you might be having problems with electrical contacts. Cards and modules hook up to motherboard electronics by way of gold or tin-plated contacts that physically touch each other to pass electrical signals. Reliable operation demands clean conductivity.

Over time, a number of things can impede the smooth flow of electrons. The most pervasive is slow corrosion of the leads, which can be a particular problem in hot and humid climates, where moisture can help oxidize tin plating, resulting in rust. Dirt can also work its way between card leads and contacts in the slots. Finally, subtle expansion and contraction of components as the PC warms and cools can cause *chip creep*, a process by which contacts actually work themselves out of alignment over time.

Fortunately, all these maladies are easily addressed. If you notice problems with memory, for instance, don't be too quick to throw out the old SIMMs. Make a point to inspect the leads on the module and the pins inside the socket. The metallic surfaces should be clean and clear of debris. If you notice dust or dirt on either, use a compressed air canister to blow out the material.

If the leads are corroded, however, compressed air won't do the trick. You'll need to remove the obstructing layer of oxidized material. You can do this with a soft cloth moistened with linseed oil. Simply rub the cloth on the conductive material, brushing away from the card or module until the original tin or gold material is clearly visible.

Troubleshooting: Corrosion of leads is a problem in hot, humid climates, where moisture and heat serve to accelerate oxidation. Another catalyst is when gold and tin leads are mixed together. This can happen when tin-plated memory modules, for example, are installed into gold-plated memory sockets. The different properties of the gold and tin material cause more rapid oxidation. When possible, be sure that the contacts of all cards and modules match the material of that used in the corresponding sockets.

Note: If you live near the ocean, salt can be even more destructive. Over time, any piece of electronic equipment exposed to salty air will begin to exhibit the characteristics of a boat anchor. Tiny crystals of oxidation will grow all over the chassis, screws will corrode and stick, and connectors will short out and fail to make contact.

Hard Choices

Sometimes, what seems like a disaster might actually be a minor problem. However, there will be times when you must bite the bullet and either repair or replace an expensive component. What you do depends on several factors, including the relative age and value of the damaged component, and the prospect of actually repairing it.

Most of the components inside your PC simply can't be repaired if they're damaged. All solid-state silicon components, including RAM, CPU, cache, and various controllers, are simply irreparable if damaged. Likewise, most drives are too expensive to fix. It's cheaper and more effective to replace them.

If you do need repair help, you have several choices:

- If the component came with a system that is under warranty, contact the vendor for service. Often you will be able to avoid the cost of repair, and will simply receive a new replacement part directly from the system manufacturer.

- If you bought the component separately, check its warranty. If it's still covered, contact the manufacturer.

- If you purchased a new peripheral or system and it failed to work (often called "dead on arrival," or DOA), you should be able to return it for a new part or a full refund under the money-back guarantee provided by most retailers.

- Out-of-warranty repairs can be conducted by technicians at your local computer store. These can range from single-store garage shops to regional and national chains. Best Buy, for example, provides upgrade and repair service for PCs.

Warning: Before you take your PC to a technician for repair, always make sure you know as much as possible about the problem. Provide the repair tech with a complete history of the problem, including the symptoms leading up to it and your attempts to resolve it. By being knowledgeable about the problem, you might be able to save time and expense by focusing the repair effort.

If you do end up having your PC repaired by a technician, keep these tips in mind:

- Know as much about the malady as you can, and communicate what you know to the technician. Don't assume that the technician will be able to figure out the problem.

- If at all possible, make a complete backup before taking your PC in for repair. Too often, service departments of large chains assure the client that everything will be OK, and then return a system with a freshly formatted hard drive—even when the customer asked for nothing more than the installation of a modem. These are the things that get people started in home PC repair ("I can do a better job than that!").

- Don't authorize expensive part replacements until you've been given a quote on the job. You might decide to scrap the old PC altogether if the repair is too costly.

- Ask around for advice on where to go for repairs. Your local computer users group can be an excellent resource. Information about user experiences with national chain repair operations might be available via online forums.

- For big-ticket repairs, pay by credit card, not check or cash. That way, if the repair goes bad, you can dispute the payment with the credit card company and have some chance of getting your money back.

Summary

The good news is that PCs today are much more reliable than they were just five or 10 years ago. Hard disks and CD-ROM drives enjoy longer lives, and displays no longer suffer from annoying problems such as screen burn-in. Still, the complex electronics are sensitive. Stresses such as heat, power surges, and even dirt can all shorten the life of your PC and its components.

The best thing you can do is prevent problems before they start. Set up a PC-friendly environment. Make sure that adequate and clean power is coming to the system, even if this means spending a couple hundred dollars on a good UPS. Try to avoid computing in hot, humid environments, which invite both thermal failure and corrosion to metal leads. If you live near the ocean, don't keep your system box or printer near a window that is always open. And keep your workplace and the PC itself clean and clear of dirt. Take time to occasionally clear out vents and sockets using compressed air, and blow out the motherboard surface to avoid overheating.

If problems do arise, rule out the easy stuff first. Check the cables and make sure a virus or software glitch isn't the cause. If your hardware has headed south, try to get it repaired under warranty. New hardware can be replaced under the purchase guarantee. Finally, if you must seek out a technician, get references, and be as knowledgeable as possible when you go in.

5

Think Before
You Shop

Peter Norton®

Buying computer hardware is a dangerous business. Obsolescence lurks around every purchase, threatening to turn shiny new systems into worthless junk within a matter of months. As if that weren't bad enough, you have to run the gauntlet of compatibility worries, driver updates, and installation hassles. And let's not forget the usual price comparisons that need to happen.

This chapter will help you get the most hardware for your dollar. It offers the following:

- A guide to effective system configurations for various users
- Key strategies when you're deciding what peripherals and systems to buy
- What to look for in a hardware vendor

Building the Proper PC

The challenge of buying a new PC or peripheral lies in getting a handle on all the various components involved in such a decision. You can't just buy a new monitor. You must first factor in the amount of memory and other features found on the graphics board. Likewise, a new CPU upgrade needs to be undertaken with the amount of system RAM in mind.

Most important, you need to keep a steady eye on your computing priorities. Yes, faster is always better. But when it comes to spending computing dollars, faster is not always smarter. You can manage your budget by first deciding what you need in order to get your particular job done. By prioritizing your hardware needs, you can shift the money you budget to the proper area.

The following sections discuss a variety of buying profiles, providing a good system profile for each. Here are the buying profiles we'll discuss:

- A first system for a home user
- A home and office system
- A corporate desktop system
- A powerhouse multimedia PC

First-Time Buyer

First-time buyers don't want to spend $3,000 on a PC, but they also don't want to be facing another PC purchase two years down the road. In many ways, first-time buyers face the stiffest challenge. They want a low-cost PC that will enjoy a reasonable life span.

Service and support are a key concern for first-time PC buyers. A helpful illustrated manual can ease setup, but there is no substitute for toll-free technical support that has weekend hours. Longer warranties—three years for desktop PCs—can help reassure buyers that the company is willing to back up its products.

First-timers should look hard at software, too. A strong bundle of applications and multimedia titles can add immediate value to your new PC. Easy-to-use application suites such as Microsoft Works and Claris Works let you write letters, crunch numbers, and do the other workaday things that a PC is so useful for. Families should look for multimedia titles. From kids' education software to useful references and mapping programs, these titles can vastly enhance the value of your new PC.

What about the hardware? Table 5.1 summarizes a good novice PC configuration. Our target price is $1,500.

Table 5.1. A first-time PC profile for the novice.

Component	Description
Case	Minitower
CPU	Pentium MMX-166
	K6-200
	6x96mx-PR-200
RAM	16 SDRAM
Cache	512KB
Hard disk	2GB enhanced IDE
CD-ROM drive	12X enhanced IDE
Monitor	15-inch
Graphics card	3D-capable with 2MB of graphics RAM
Sound card	Software or hardware wavetable MIDI
Modem	56Kbps
Network adapter	None
Inputs	Keyboard, mouse
Other	None

The most important thing is convenience. The minitower case will fit nicely into tight home spaces, conveniently hidden under the desk or against the wall, while the monitor, keyboard, and mouse sit on top. The minitower design is spacious enough to allow easy upgrades, which might occur if you want to add a DVD-ROM drive or a Zip drive down the line.

For the most processor value, you can't beat AMD's K6 and Cyrix's 6x86Mx, shown in Figure 5.1. These CPUs are nearly as fast as Intel's top-of-the-line Pentium II, yet they're inexpensive enough to appear in systems costing less than most Pentium MMX-based PCs. If you feel uncomfortable going outside of Intel, don't despair. Intel has cut the price of its Pentium MMX line to defend against the renewed competition.

Figure 5.1.
The Micro Express MicroFlex-MX/200 uses a Cyrix 6x86Mx-PR-200 processor to offer excellent performance for less than $1,500. (Photo courtesy of Micro Express)

I strongly suggest 32MB of RAM for any Windows 95 machine, but if you don't plan on running multiple applications simultaneously, you can make do with 16MB. Just keep in mind that a RAM upgrade might be in your near future, as your computing becomes more sophisticated.

Otherwise, stick to the basics. A 56Kbps modem is a real must, since much of the value of today's PCs come from their Internet capability. You can go easy on the sound card—there's no need for whizbang 3-D sound and realistic wavetable MIDI unless your kids want to play games or get the most realism out of their titles. You will want a 3-D graphics chip, but this feature is rapidly becoming standard fare on PCs.

Home and Office System

Perhaps the most common home PC is the mixed-use workhorse that must act as a kids' machine by day and a second office by night. This system needs to run the latest multimedia games and titles while standing ready to handle large spreadsheets and complex documents. The multiuse PC will need to have many programs installed, so hard disk space will be at a premium.

This system can have a wide variety of options, but you can expect to pay $2,000 to $2,500 for a well-appointed model. Keep in mind that multimedia titles—and, in particular, games—push PC hardware to the limit. You can't afford to scrimp too much and still expect to get reasonable performance.

Service and support are crucial. High-traffic systems stand a greater chance of suffering from fatal software conflicts or simple wear-and-tear problems. Babies will bang on the keyboard, while gamers will hammer at the system and possibly spill drinks in the work area. If the work you keep on your home PC is crucial—be it work documents, tax information, or your bank files—be sure to make frequent backups. Also consider keeping occasional backups in a safe place outside the home, in case you need to protect vital tax data from fire. Table 5.2 provides insight into affordable, do-everything systems that cost under $2,500.

Table 5.2. A midrange PC for home and office must be a jack of all trades.

Component	Description
Case	Minitower
CPU	Pentium MMX-233, Pentium II-233 or faster
	AMD K6-233
	Cyrix 6x86Mx-PR-233
RAM	32MB of SDRAM
Cache	512KB
Hard disk	4 to 6GB enhanced IDE
CD-ROM drive	16X to 24X
Monitor	15- or 17-inch
Graphics card	Midrange 3-D-capable with 4MB RAM
Sound card	Wavetable MIDI and 3-D audio support
Modem	56Kbps
Network adapter	None
Inputs	Keyboard, mouse, joystick
Other	Consider tape backup

The most critical components are the CPU and hard disk. The processor must provide MMX instruction support to handle the latest games and titles. You'll want plenty of speed as well. A 6GB enhanced IDE hard disk will add $150 or so to your PC's cost, but this price is well worth it when you see how much space all those programs will consume.

You also need to beef up the audio and graphics subsystems for effective multimedia playback. A 17-inch monitor will make for thrilling play and will also benefit your evening work sessions, although you'll pay $300 to $400 over the price of a 15-inch model. If you get a Pentium II PC, consider one that has the new AGP Accelerated Graphics Port, which promises much higher levels of 3-D scene realism than earlier systems, once software gets tailored for it. The kids will love it. A good joystick, preferably digital, will provide great response and resist damage.

Finally, a tape backup or perhaps a Zip drive might be worth considering. Frequent software installations can lead to unexpected problems and lost data. If you put critical data on your PC, make sure you save it to disk periodically.

Corporate Desktop

PCs bound for office duty have some different priorities. For one, multimedia support and flexibility aren't a big concern. Instead, compact design and easy network management are important, whether for five PCs for a small office or department or 500 PCs for a Fortune 500 company. Table 5.3 shows some of the unique aspects of business-bound PCs, which typically cost about $2,000.

Table 5.3. A first-time PC profile for the corporate desktop.

Component	Description
Case	Slimline desktop
CPU	Pentium MMX-233
RAM	32MB
Cache	512KB
Hard disk	2GB enhanced IDE
CD-ROM drive	12X
Monitor	15-inch
Graphics card	2MB 2-D graphics
Sound card	Optional
Modem	None
Network adapter	10/100Mbps ethernet
Inputs	Keyboard, mouse
Other	Remote management features

In addition to compact design, corporate desktops need to be easy to maintain. Many new systems provide the ability to do system management remotes, allowing network administrators to update software and drivers from a central location during off hours. Network monitoring software helps maintain optimal network performance, while internal monitoring devices that check for heat and case removal can help reduce damage and theft of internal components.

Unfortunately, these features require dedicated motherboard hardware and up-to-date BIOSs. For this reason, older systems might not be able to take full advantage of these useful talents.

The Powerhouse PC

The powerhouse PC is more than a geek's fantasy. This is the kind of PC needed for top-notch game play, Web site and software development, and desktop publishing and image editing. These are different missions, certainly, but they all share requirements: lots of processing power and RAM, large storage capacities, high-resolution graphics, and fast performance.

The price tag can be steep. Expect to pay $3,500 or more for a top system. The good news is that this price will keep your initial hardware investment relevant for a longer time than a less-expensive model would. Table 5.4 provides a profile of a high-end PC suitable for demanding applications.

Table 5.4. A first-time PC profile for a multimedia powerhouse.

Component	Description
Case	Minitower or tower
CPU	Pentium II-300
RAM	64MB of SDRAM
Cache	512 to 1024KB
Hard disk	7GB EIDE or SCSI
CD-ROM drive	32X CD-ROM or DVD-ROM drive
Monitor	17-inch to 21-inch
Graphics card	AGP bus-based, 3-D-capable 4MB or 8MB card
Sound card	Multichannel PCI audio card with wavetable MIDI and 3-D sound
Modem	56Kbps or ISDN for remote networking
Network adapter	100Mbps (if in an office network)
Inputs	Keyboard, mouse, joystick
Other	Zip drive or other 100MB or greater removable storage drive

The 300MHz Pentium II CPU, shown in Figure 5.2, provides the best performance you can find in an IBM-compatible PC. It will be up to the task of handling software for years to come. It provides outstanding floating-point processing for computer-aided design (CAD) and image editing, as well as fast MMX support for the latest games and multimedia playback. 64MB of system memory allows large programs and data files to load without getting bogged down in virtual memory.

Consider going with a SCSI bus for storage. Although IDE peripherals offer nearly equivalent performance, you'll see differences when you multitask. SCSI can make a big difference during video capture and other very intense hard disk operations. Also consider a DVD-ROM drive, which will provide access to all the latest digital movies and upcoming multimedia titles. Its 4.7GB minimum storage capacity will attract many software and title developers.

Figure 5.2.
The Dell Dimension XPS D300 is the real deal: A 300MHz Pentium II PC with the new AGP graphics bus, ultra-DMA hard disk, and 64MB of fast SDRAM. (Photo courtesy of Dell Corp.)

You might have noticed the AGP graphics card. AGP stands for Accelerated Graphics Port, a dedicated graphics bus intended to enhance the realism of 3-D graphics. AGP allows your graphics card to use the large amount of main system memory for storing 3-D textures, adding realism to 3-D objects. As more and more games and software take advantage of AGP, expect this new bus to become an important feature on high-end PCs.

Upgrade Buying Strategies

When upgrading an existing PC, you have to keep a level head. No upgrade short of replacing the motherboard will transform the performance of an aging PC (see Figure 5.3). CPU upgrades will be hindered by the aging system bus and slow RAM. Graphics card upgrades will be limited by the lack of bus compatibility and the slower CPU.

So first things first. What do you want the upgrade to accomplish? Consider specifically the applications you want to speed up, as well as any new applications you want to gain access to through the upgrade. Often, you will find that a one-two punch (say, upgrading RAM *and* CPU) will provide a much better result than a single-component upgrade.

Turning Dollars into Hardware

There are so many upgrade options available that it can be difficult to focus on the most effective solution. One way to narrow your thinking is to set a budget. How much are you willing to pay to extend or incrementally enhance the performance and features of your existing PC? If you're willing to pour over $500 into your existing investment, you can choose from among some powerful upgrade options, such as a new motherboard or CPU replacement. If $200 is more your speed, a new 3-D-capable graphics board or 16MB of RAM can add appreciable zip, depending on your existing configuration.

Figure 5.3.
A motherboard upgrade can command a stiff price and entail a lot of work, but it's the only way to break through performance choke points in older systems. (Photo courtesy of Micronics Corp.)

The following breakdowns show how general upgrade options fall with regard to price. Perhaps they can help you decide where your upgrade dollars should go.

$500 to $1,000+

Motherboard upgrade

High-end CPU upgrade

17-inch monitor

DVD-ROM upgrade kit

$300 to $500

Low-end CPU upgrade

32MB of RAM

4 to 7GB hard disk

Jaz drive or other removable media drive

High-end 8MB 3-D graphics card

$200 to $300

16MB of RAM

3 to 4GB hard disk

Fast CD-ROM drive (24X to 32X)

4MB 3-D graphics card

Tape backup drive

High-end sound board

$100 to $200

8MB of RAM

1GB hard disk

16X CD-ROM drive

56Kbps modem

Zip drive or other 100MB removable drive

2MB 3-D graphics card

Software Alternatives

There is also a big market for performance-enhancing software. Disk caches, memory managers, and other utilities provide tweaks and tucks that can help maximize performance. But be careful. In some cases, these packages can provide modest improvements, but in many cases they will fail to provide any noticeable benefit. Almost certainly, these packages won't live up to the best-case claims that are printed on the box.

Whether you should consider a performance-enhancing utility depends on your situation. Although older Windows 3.1 systems benefited from these utilities, the more-robust 32-bit code found in Windows 95 doesn't need as much help. Still, there might be times when an aging system can benefit from software utilities.

There are several types of software acceleration:

- Memory managers (so-called RAM doublers)
- Hard disk caches
- CD-ROM caches
- Web browser accelerators

Memory Managers

A few years ago, memory managers made a whole lot of sense. After all, the DOS/Windows memory scheme was a mess. Large applications had to fit under the 640KB DOS memory ceiling, and memory managers helped them do that by lifting the ceiling a bit. These products also used intricate compression schemes to make 8MB of RAM seem like more than it was. The result was that more programs could run at one time, and the system spent less time in sluggish virtual memory. With RAM costing up to $50 per megabyte, these utilities were a boon to users who couldn't afford an expensive upgrade.

The market has changed drastically over the last three years. Windows 95 fixed most of the problems that memory managers were solving. Even with additional tweaks tailored for the new operating system, the need for a fix is vastly reduced. Perhaps more important, RAM prices dropped through the floor. Today, a megabyte of system RAM costs about $10, making it inexpensive to add memory.

So why consider a memory manager at all? Well, these programs can provide useful diagnostic features, allowing you to see what your system is using its resources on. Some market tools help alleviate system crashes and other problems. Several packages also try to accelerate specific operations, such as application launches.

But the upshot remains: Memory managers today aren't a great performance buy. Although you might get some nifty widgets and controls, don't expect much in the way of an overall performance boost.

CD-ROM and Hard Disk Caches

Like memory managers, there have long been third-party disk-caching utilities. Hard disk caches use system memory to hold small amounts of data that can be accessed much more quickly than data on the hard disk. CD-ROM caches, in contrast, actually use the hard disk to store cached data, since the disk is much faster than the CD-ROM drive.

You'll get the best results from a CD-ROM drive cache. If you have an older CD-ROM drive and sufficient hard disk space to serve as a cache (say, 10 to 50MB), you might consider this option. If your hard disk space is limited, however, the caching software might fall short of your expectations.

The picture on hard disk caches is not so clear. For one thing, Windows 95 already provides an excellent disk cache, limiting the performance improvement these utilities can deliver. Some disk-caching programs also optimize application launches, shaving up to 50 percent off the launch time. (Just keep in mind that a 10-second program launch means that you save five seconds.) But if you want effective overall acceleration, you might want to look elsewhere.

Web Accelerators

These programs don't actually accelerate your PC. Instead, they preload Web pages so that they come up faster when you access them. They work on the theory that modems often sit idle while users read Web pages or scroll among selections. Web accelerators look at the open page and begin downloading all the linked pages right away instead of waiting around for a mouse click to the next link.

The software usually works. A preloaded page sits locally on your hard disk, so when you click its link, the page snaps right up on-screen. If the page hasn't been accessed, it is loaded normally over the Web.

The downside is that these caching programs pollute the Internet with lots of unnecessary traffic. You might visit a Web home page and click through just one, or even none, of the many links provided there. Yet your Web accelerator will request all the linked pages from the server. The result is a sudden and intense surge in server traffic as users employ Web-accelerating software.

Note: Some Web sites have banned the use of accelerator caches because of the undue burden they put on the Web servers.

Buying Resources

If you want to buy hardware, you have a number of options, all of which have their own advantages and disadvantages:

- Retail
- Direct mail/catalogs
- Web-based services

Buying Retail

The most common option is to go to the local computer or electronics store and buy the hardware. Retail shopping has a number of key advantages. For one, you know exactly who you're buying from. If the store offers a return policy—and you should buy only from stores that do—you can simply return defective products for an immediate repair, refund, or credit. Many computer stores also offer on-site repair services, which makes it easy to address malfunctioning parts. Of course, the local store provides the distinct advantage of immediate gratification: You can buy the hardware and bring it home.

Retail stores also have a lot of drawbacks. Prices are often higher than that of bargain mail-order firms, because of the inevitable cost of inventory and maintaining retail outlets. Likewise, the presence of retail staff can make customers think that they can get questions answered at the store. Think again. Retail staffers can be woefully unknowledgeable about the products they sell, so plan to do your research well ahead of time.

Buying Tip: You should keep a couple of things in mind when visiting the local store. Know what you want before you go in. The sales staff won't be able to help you with in-depth questions, and the potentially large selection of products will only increase your confusion. Also be sure to inspect any product you purchase to make sure that it isn't defective or used. Make sure that boxes are shrink-wrapped and that the packaging hasn't been tampered with. If you find that products inside the box are improperly packaged, return the product immediately.

Catalog Shopping

Anyone who's ordered from an LL Bean catalog knows the drill. You browse through the pictures, check the descriptions, and dial the 800 number. Catalog shopping is convenient, fast, and often inexpensive. You can even avoid state taxes on your purchase if the company operates outside of your state.

Of course, you have to pay for shipping and then wait for the product to arrive, which can take weeks. Catalogs don't provide much in the way of product information—only the most basic specs and descriptions—so you need to do your homework before making any decisions. This is particularly important, because some catalogs are jammed with dozens of products in the same category.

Buying Online

The fastest-growing method of commerce is over the Internet. And no industry is more poised to market to its customers using the Web than the computer industry. In fact, online buying is rapidly becoming a service offered by all retailers, whether store-front chains, mail-order catalogs, or Web-only outfits.

The Web has helped revolutionize the mail-order PC business. Today, direct-order companies such as Dell, Gateway, and Micron provide Web "configurator" services that let you customize preset systems using easy-to-navigate drop-down lists. Want to bump up the 32MB of standard RAM on that Pentium MMX-233 PC? Just click the RAM drop-down list and select the 64MB option. Usually, a price for the upgrade from the initial configuration is displayed, allowing you to make informed decisions. Once you've tweaked the configuration, the Web site usually provides an amended price.

Buying Tip: Even if you aren't comfortable buying hardware from the Web, you should consider making use of vendor Web sites. You can take your time browsing different configurations and prices, and even visit a variety of vendors, to get all the information you need. Once you're ready, you can call the 800 order line and place your order without having to face a lot of complex decisions over the phone.

The advantages of online buying largely parallel those of catalog operations. Prices can be quite low because of the lack of expensive local operations. And in some cases you might be spared the expense of state sales taxes, provided that the vendor operates outside of the state you're ordering from. Certainly Web-based buying is convenient. You simply point and click your way to the product you want, often employing useful search facilities, and place the order. If you don't want to provide a credit card number over the Internet, you can usually complete the order via a toll-free call to the sales line.

Of course, you have to wait for your purchase. Depending on inventory and shipping policies, it can take weeks for hardware to get to your door. And you'll have to foot the bill for shipping. Be aware that any idiot can put up a Web page, so you need to be careful when doing business on the Web. If you don't know the company you plan to buy from, try to get more information before you order. The local Better Business Bureau is a good place to start.

What to Look for in a Company

When you buy hardware, you're taking a risk, pure and simple. The history of the computer industry is littered with the corpses of companies that didn't make it, and they left a lot of unsupported hardware in their wake. Once-prominent names such as Media Vision, Reveal Computer Products, and Leading Edge (later revived) all failed and left the owners of their products holding the bag.

The point is, you need to thoroughly research the company you plan to buy from. Why? Because once you buy the hardware, you need to keep it up-to-date. Driver software must be updated to take advantage of the latest OS tweaks and tricks, new features are always being added, and bugs need to be squashed. If your hardware vendor bites the dust, those updates and upgrades die too.

Here are a couple of ways you can protect yourself:

- Read reviews of vendor quality and support in industry-leading publications such as *PC World*, which uses a wide survey of reader experience to assess the quality and reliability of vendor support.

- Post inquiries at relevant forums on CompuServe, AOL, or other information services. You can get a lot of valuable feedback this way.

- Check the company's Web page or online forum. Check for recent software updates and signs of active support presence.

- Search online news archives or check at the library for financial details of the company.

- Call the Better Business Bureau in the company's area and inquire about any complaints outstanding with the vendor. Often companies in deep financial trouble will build a history of customer complaints.

In addition, make sure that the company provides adequate support policies. A one-year parts-and-labor warranty should be a minimum, and you shouldn't buy a product without a money-back guarantee that allows you to return defective products. You'll also want toll-free technical support—with weekend hours if available—to ensure a smooth installation.

Summary

The best way to avoid buyer's remorse is to do your homework. Take the time to research the product or system you're considering. Compare prices and features, talk to current users if you can, and be sure to look for strong warranties and effective support.

Most important, don't expect too much from your upgrade purchases. Updating hardware is a lot like piling sandbags along a flooding river. You can delay the flood, but eventually the river will break through anything you build. Upgrades are good for adding a year or so to the life of your PC, but eventually you'll need to buy a new system or upgrade the motherboard if you intend to access the latest software and features.

II

Core
Components

6

Heart and Soul: The CPU

Peter Norton®

Your PC might be made up of many different parts, but none is as important as the central processing unit. Also known as the CPU or processor, this unassuming square of silicon is the heart and soul of any PC. In fact, the CPU is so important to the performance and pricing of systems that computer makers routinely market PCs by the processor's type and speed. Whether you're buying a new PC or upgrading an aging system, you must understand the workings of the processor in order to make good decisions.

The good news is that there are plenty of choices available if you're buying or upgrading a system. The bad news is that the sheer number of CPUs can confound the most studious buyer. Intel alone sells more than 20 different types and speeds of CPUs, and AMD and Cyrix market more still. Add to that number the many upgrade-oriented processor products for 486- and Pentium-class systems.

Processor technology advances so quickly that even a system based on a high-end CPU will enjoy a useful life of, at most, five years. This might sound like a long time to your dog, but when you're talking about $3,000 for a new PC, it's not long. Behind the obsolescence freight train is something called Moore's Law, coined by Intel cofounder Gordon Moore. This law states that processor power— expressed in the number of circuits that can be packed into a given space—doubles every year.

You can stay ahead of the curve. This chapter will help you understand the workings of the so-called x86-compatible CPUs. In addition to the universe of Intel processors (including the 486, Pentium, Pentium Pro, Pentium MMX, and Pentium II), which account for nearly 90 percent of the desktop market, I will discuss x86-compatible processors from vendors such as AMD, Cyrix, and IBM. I'll also discuss CPU upgrade products—such as Intel's OverDrive product line as well as upgrades from Evergreen, Kingston, and others. Although these products vary in their operation and clock speed, all share the ability to run the DOS, Windows 3.x, Windows 95, and Windows NT operating systems and compatible applications.

This chapter covers the following topics:

- The basics of processor operation
- An overview of current CPUs and their features and advantages
- An overview of CPU upgrade products
- Step-by-step CPU upgrade instructions

Making Sense of Processors

CPUs perform their magic by doing very simple tasks very quickly. However, the many different CPU designs prove that there is more than one way to skin a cat. The PowerPC processors found inside PowerMacs, for instance, use a set of small, fast, and relatively simple instructions to achieve performance. Intel's P5 and P6 CPUs, in contrast, use a complex instruction set to muscle through calculations, which requires many more transistors.

Regardless of these differences, all CPUs employ innovative tricks to streamline operations and do more than one thing at a time. In addition, the same elements that affect CPU performance affect the performance of upgrade chips such as Intel's OverDrive processors.

Technical Note: The most-recognized aspect of CPU operation is clock speed, which indicates how many millions of times per second a CPU performs its most basic tasks. For years, the general rule of thumb said that a faster clock speed meant a faster CPU. Well, life is a bit more complicated nowadays.

First, the clock speed you see almost invariably refers to the internal operation of the CPU. Outside, most processors talk to the rest of the system at one-half or one-third the rate of the CPU core. The 100, 133, 166, and 200MHz Pentium CPUs all run at 66MHz on the outside, which means that the speed of L2 cache and memory access is unchanged despite the much higher clock rating on the 200MHz unit.

More important, some CPUs get more done in one clock tick than others. That's why a 150MHz Cyrix 6x86 can match the performance of a 200MHz Pentium. More confusing, a 200MHz Pentium Pro might outpace a 200MHz Pentium MMX under Windows NT but will actually lag behind under Windows 95. (The Pentium Pro is heavily optimized for 32-bit code, yielding more efficient operation under NT.) In other words, it's as much about what a processor does as how fast it does it.

With this conundrum in mind, Intel competitors now market their CPUs using a metric called a *P-rating* (Performance Rating). This rating system uses publicly available benchmarks to draw a comparison to the equivalent Pentium-based processor. The intention is to let buyers quickly compare Intel and non-Intel x86 processors. Cyrix, for example, calls its 150MHz 6x86 the 6x86 P200+, because P-rating benchmarks show that it roughly meets or exceeds the performance of a Pentium-200. Likewise, AMD's K5-PR166 runs at just 117MHz but tests close to Pentium-166 performance.

P-ratings attempt to clear the performance issue, but they can conceal the processor's true clock speed. This can become an issue when judging the performance of CPUs enhanced with MMX technology, which adds instructions to speed multimedia performance. Because the benchmark fails to address MMX operation at this time, you won't be able to tell that the slower core speeds of the Cyrix 6x86Mx make MMX operation much slower than that of Intel's Pentium MMX line.

For more information on the Performance Rating system, go to `http://www.datadepo.com/ prating.htm`.

What Makes a CPU Tick?

A typical CPU consists of millions of tiny transistors packed into a square or rectangular die less than 2 inches long on a side. What you see is the ceramic casing that protects the delicate submicron transistors and provides a ready means of pulling heat away from the CPU core (see Figure 6.1). The ceramic cover might feature silk screening to identify the CPU model and manufacturer. Recently, Intel began etching serial numbers into the casing in an effort to foil chip thieves.

Figure 6.1.
What you see is not what you get: Underneath the processor's ceramic packaging are millions of transistors. (Photo courtesy of Cyrix Corp.)

Modern processors are marvelously complex constructs that feature a number of key systems working together to drive the PC. Key among these systems are

- Data bus
- Address bus
- Primary or L1 cache
- Registers
- Instruction pipelines
- Floating-point unit
- MMX instruction

The Data Bus

The data bus is the collection of wires and circuits dedicated to moving information in and out of the CPU. Just like a highway, the wider the data bus, the more traffic that can move over it. Today's

Pentium and Pentium Pro CPUs employ 64-bit external data buses that can handle 8 bytes of data at a time, while older 486 processors use a thinner 32-bit (4-byte) data bus.

Bus width becomes particularly critical as clock rates increase and processors gain the ability to perform several operations simultaneously. With most system motherboards running at 60 or 66MHz, a wide data bus ensures that large scoops of data move into the CPU from slower main memory, keeping the processor well-engaged with data and instructions despite its much faster internal clock. In addition, Pentium and Pentium Pro CPUs employ a technique called *bursting* to rapidly move chunks of data into the processor cache in a single clock tick.

Generally, the data bus width is the same both inside and outside the chip. However, some older CPUs—such as the Intel 386SX and Cyrix's 486SLX—used a narrower external data bus in order to reduce cost, running 32 bits wide inside and 16 bits wide outside. The result is similar to what happens when you close lanes on a busy highway—a slowdown in traffic. In contrast, the Pentium CPU features a pair of 32-bit pipelines internally, making them a good match for the wide 64-bit external bus, since the 64-bit bus can fill both in one operation.

If data buses are so important, why not just make them 128 or even 256 bits wide? In a word, cost. Chip designers need to dedicate CPU pins for the data bus, which enlarges the CPU die and socket and requires more connector traces on the motherboard. Case in point: The 386DX CPU had 132 pins, and the 386SX with a 16-bit external bus used only 100 pins. The 64-bit Pentium processor uses a whopping 296 pins to connect to the motherboard. Not all those pins are for data, of course, but the widening bus accounts for its share.

Bus speed also comes into play. Just as a highway might have different speed limits, the data bus in newer processors usually runs faster inside the processor than out. The compact circuitry of CPUs allows for operation at 200MHz and beyond, but the longer trace wires on motherboards can't run nearly as fast. Today, most motherboards run at 60 and 66MHz, although a few run as fast as 75MHz and as slow as 50MHz. The result is that CPUs move data two to three times faster on the inside than they do on the outside, posing a challenge for CPU and system designers trying to ensure that a steady flow of data keeps the processor from waiting around. Engineers reach into their bag of tricks to keep things moving. The bursting just mentioned helps things, as does the use of fast cache memory to avoid transactions over the slower motherboard bus.

The Address Bus

As the name suggests, the address bus is the set of wires that carries bits describing the location of information in system memory. The larger the number (measured in bits), the more physical memory the CPU can access. How much more? To figure this out, you simply take the number 2 and apply the number of bits as an exponent. So a 32-bit wide address bus can access 2^{32} bits of memory, or 4,294,967,296 bytes.

From the 386 CPU through to the Pentium, Intel chips have employed a 32-bit address bus, allowing them to access up to 4GB of system memory. The Pentium Pro and Pentium II, which often power higher-end workstations and servers, feature a 36-bit address bus to access 64GB of system memory. The forthcoming P7 CPU—code-named Merced—expected in 1999, is expected to employ a 64-bit address bus capable of accessing millions of *terabytes* of data.

Level 1 (L1) Cache

Cache design has gotten much attention from CPU designers over the last five years, and for good reason. These small, incredibly swift pools of memory can significantly boost performance by keeping frequently used data and instructions close at hand.

There are two types of caches: the internal level 1 cache found inside processors, and the larger, external level 2 cache. Caches aren't simple. L1 caches can eat up a lot of valuable on-chip space and require complex algorithms to guess what the CPU needs next, but the performance payoff is undeniable.

The concept behind caching is simple enough. A processor can grab bits internally much more quickly than it can fish them out of main system memory. Not surprisingly, the larger the cache, the greater the performance payoff. The downside is that if the necessary code or data isn't found in the cache, the processor loses time searching the cache. That's where those complex algorithms come in—helping predict what the CPU will need so that the proper data can be made available.

The first Intel CPU to use an internal cache (or L1 cache) was the 486, with an 8KB reservoir shared for both instructions and data. The Pentium doubles this with separate 8KB instruction and data caches, the same amount found in the Pentium Pro. Even bigger caches figure in the latest chips from AMD and Cyrix: Both the K6 and 6x86Mx CPUs feature 64KB of L1 cache memory.

Floating-Point Unit

The floating-point unit (FPU) in a processor is dedicated to handling complex noninteger numbers such as 3.000001. Most PC applications don't use floating-point arithmetic, so the FPU often sits idle. However, applications that do require floating-point operations—such as photo editing, 3-D design, and CAD software—rely on the FPU heavily. In addition, some 3-D games rely on the FPU, causing it to have growing importance for a mainstream audience.

The FPU might be rarely used, but some software requires its presence in order to run. Since the Pentium processor, all Intel CPUs include an integrated FPU. And although the 486DX line of CPUs were the first Intel chips to provide built-in floating-point capability, the less-expensive 486SX left it out. Competing designs from Cyrix, AMD, and IBM also provide floating-point capability.

MMX Instructions

An extension to the x86 instruction set, the 57 MMX instructions built into the Pentium MMX, Pentium II, AMD K6, and Cyrix 6x86Mx processors boost graphics, video, and other multimedia functions. The performance boost can be big—up to 400 percent in some operations, according to Intel—but software must first be written specifically for MMX (see Figure 6.2). Many companies are developing MMX-aware applications, including UbiSoft's Pod racing game. Microsoft has already released MMX versions of its ActiveMovie playback module and DirectX game-development APIs.

Figure 6.2.
If you try to run an MMX title without the proper CPU, you could get stopped in your tracks.

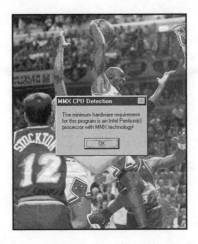

In addition to new instructions, MMX provides a one-instruction, multiple-data scheme that allows a single operation to be conducted on a large set of data. This technique boosts performance with functions such as image filtering, because the CPU doesn't have to reissue the same instruction for every piece of data.

Intelligence Inside: A Day in the Life of a CPU

In many ways, the CPU acts like a tiny bit factory, taking raw material in the form of data and instructions from system memory and turning them into usable bits on the other end. Like any factory, the CPU employs a production line to work raw bits into finished material, as well as a loading dock—called a *bus*—to move bits on and off the factory floor. The CPU even produces pollution, in the form of electromagnetic radiation and heat.

Although each operation a CPU performs is very small, the assembly line in a 200MHz CPU completes operations at a pace of 200 *million* times per second. The newest CPUs employ more than one assembly line—a concept called *superscalar pipelining*—which allows modern PCs to keep pace with video playback and application multitasking.

Note: The Pentium processor, introduced in 1993, was the first Intel CPU to employ a superscalar design. This feature was one reason that 60MHz Pentium systems often performed better than 486DX4 PCs that had faster-clocking 100MHz processors.

Buying a CPU

Make no mistake—there are a lot of CPUs out there. In fact, there are so many different models and speeds that many buyers are simply overwhelmed. Imagine a scenario in which you have about $2,500 budgeted for a new PC. Here are your possible CPU choices:

- Pentium II (266, 233, 200MHz)
- Pentium MMX (233, 200, 166MHz)
- Pentium Pro (200, 180MHz)
- AMD K6 (233, 200, 166MHz)
- Cyrix 6x86Mx (200, 166, 150MHz)

These CPUs cover a very wide price range. Intel sells its Pentium II-266 CPU for about $740, while Cyrix sells its 150MHz Cyrix 6x86MX PR-233 for just $175. Yet you can easily buy a PC that has either CPU for $2,300 to $2,800. To meet our budget, the Pentium II system will require a stripped-down configuration, while the 6x86Mx PC can be loaded with RAM, large hard disk and monitor, and fast CD-ROM and graphics card. The point is that users shouldn't assume that they can't afford the fastest processors. If they want the speed—and are willing to sacrifice for it—they can have it.

So how do you go about choosing a CPU for a new system? I'll try to answer that question in this section by providing a rundown of the various processors available. In addition to the usual specs, you'll find information about how each behaves.

You might notice that no 486-class CPUs are discussed in this section. The reason is simple: I cannot recommend 486-level processors for new systems. They simply lack the performance to address the computing needs of the coming five years.

Table 6.1 helps you focus your attention on the CPU that best fits your needs. Keep in mind that Intel competitors AMD and Cyrix have both introduced processors that can match the performance of Intel's Pentium MMX and Pentium II lines. These CPUs cost considerably less than Intel products, helping stretch your performance dollars considerably. But be on the lookout for "gotchas" with software such as games, which can sometimes fail to recognize non-Intel CPUs during startup.

Table 6.1. Choosing a CPU.

CPU	What It's Best For	Notes
Pentium Classic	Entry-level	166 and 200MHz Pentiums can cost as little as $1,000, but the lack of MMX support makes them unsuitable for cutting-edge games and multimedia.
Pentium MMX	Midrange	200 and 233MHz Pentium MMXs can be had for under $2,000. Great for mixed-use home and office PCs.
Pentium Pro	Servers/workstations	NT-savvy CPUs were upstaged by the Pentium II, but multiprocessor support makes them appropriate for networks and workstations.
Pentium II	High-end/workstations	This has a Pentium Pro core, but with a faster clock, larger cache, and MMX. Windows 95 and NT performance is unrivaled. Prices start as low as $2,800 and go up fast.
AMD K6	Entry-level/midrange	This MMX-aware CPU is a terrific value for mixed home-office use. Performance is just shy of the Pentium II, but systems sell for well below $2,500.
Cyrix 6x86Mx	Entry-level/midrange	Another MMX clone that matches K6 performance but costs less. It's good for people who need real performance at prices below $2,000.

Performance: Measuring processor performance is a tricky business. After all, no benchmark works exactly the way you do, and benchmark designers must make a lot of assumptions to address all the usage patterns in the real world. What's more, the CPU is only one ingredient in overall system performance.

Intel expresses its processors using the iCOMP index, shown in Figure 6.3. This amalgam of various benchmarks helps Intel explain where CPUs fall on the performance ladder. By Intel's reckoning, a Pentium II-266 CPU is four times faster than a Pentium Classic-120.

continues

Cyrix and AMD, on the other hand, employ the WinStone 97 benchmark from Ziff-Davis, shown in Figure 6.4. Because buyers are familiar with Intel CPUs, these clone makers use the benchmark to peg their products against existing Intel clock speeds. The 150MHz Cyrix 6x86Mx CPU, for example, gets a Performance Rating of 200, allowing Cyrix to market the CPU against Pentium MMX-200 competition.

Figure 6.3.
Intel's new iCOMP 2.0 benchmark uses a variety of tests to provide insight into CPU performance. But remember that your mileage may vary. (Figure courtesy of Intel Corp.)

Figure 6.4.
Cyrix and AMD use Ziff-Davis's Winstone 97 to come up with Performance Rating number that compare their products against Intel's Pentium line. (Figure courtesy of Cyrix Corp.)

Intel Pentium Classic: The Real Thing

When Intel shipped the first Pentium CPUs to vendors in March of 1993, it was a big deal. After all, the Pentium, shown in Figure 6.5, was the first x86 CPU to provide superscalar pipelining, using two instruction pipes to work on more than one instruction at a time. It also broke ranks with the naming conventions of earlier 486, 386, and 286 CPUs. Intel adopted the Pentium moniker after a court ruled that it could not trademark-protect a number.

Figure 6.5.
Intel's Pentium CPU introduced multiple instruction pipelines for enhanced performance and established Intel's unassailable position in the market. (Photo courtesy of Intel Corp.)

The first Pentiums got off to a rocky start. The 60 and 66MHz Pentiums ran extremely hot, dissipating an incredible 16 watts during normal operation. In 1994, Intel improved things by shrinking the CPU to allow cooler operation and to push clock speeds to 75, 90, and 100MHz. These newer chips used the same clock multiplication technique found in Intel's 486 DX2 and DX4 processors, running at one-and-a-half or two times the speed of the motherboard bus. The result was significantly improved performance without the need to redesign motherboard components for higher clock speeds. Table 6.2 provides an overview of Pentium CPUs.

Table 6.2. Intel Pentium specs.

Specification	First Generation	Second Generation	Third Generation
Internal clock speed	60, 66MHz	75, 90, 100MHz	120, 133, 166MHz
L1 cache size	8KB/8KB	8KB/8KB	8KB/8KB

continues

Table 6.2. continued

Specification	First Generation	Second Generation	Third Generation
L2 cache clock speed	60, 66MHz	60, 66MHz	60, 66MHz
MMX support?	No	No	No
Number of pipelines	Two	Two	Two
Data bus (internal/external)	32-bit/64-bit	32-bit/64-bit	32-bit/64-bit
Number of transistors	3.1 million	3.3 million	3.3 million
Manufacturing process	.8 micron BiCMOS	.6 micron BiCMOS	.35 micron CMOS
Pin count	273	296	296

Intel launched speedier Pentium versions in pairs, based on the clock multiplier factor over the system bus speed. In 1995, for example, the 120 and 133MHz Pentiums ran at two times the speed of their respective 60 and 66MHz motherboards. The Pentium-150 and Pentium-166 boosted this factor to 2.5, while the 200MHz Pentium runs at three times the speed of the motherboard.

Note: Intel introduces CPUs in pairs because the clocks match up with the 60 and 66MHz motherboards in the market. In some cases, the faster CPU of the pair might be in short supply while Intel works the kinks out of its processors. The company tests CPUs after manufacturing and rates them for a certain clock speed based on the results. This is why, for example, 90MHz Pentium systems were so prevalent about two years ago and 100MHz PCs were not: Not enough CPUs were achieving the quality needed for 100MHz operation.

Inside the Pentium CPU

The Pentium delivered more than just faster clock speeds than the 486. These CPUs feature a 64-bit external data bus and 16KB of L1 cache (with 8KB each dedicated to instructions and data), both double that of the 486. Furthermore, the cache improves on the 486's *write-through* scheme, which stores only incoming data. The Pentium's *write-back* scheme stores outgoing data, freeing the CPU from the time-consuming process of writing data back to main system memory. (Note that the 8KB L1 instruction cache doesn't provide write-back operation, because instructions are read-only.)

The big win came from the twin pipelines, which allow the Pentium to work on two sets of instructions at once, as shown in Figure 6.6. The five-stage pipelines (pre-fetching, instruction decoding, address generation, execution, and write-back) mean that the CPU can be executing operations even as the pre-fetch stage is gathering bits for upcoming operations.

Figure 6.6.

The Pentium's advanced plumbing streamlines the flow of bits through the processor. (Figure courtesy of Intel Corp.)

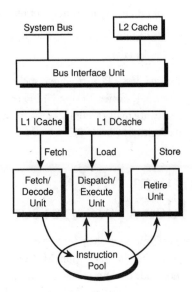

The Pentium employs a scheme called *branch prediction* to attempt to get the right bits into the right pipeline. The *branch target buffer* helps this process by looking at program code over time and making decisions based on past branches in the code.

Intel also paid attention to the Pentium's floating-point unit (FPU), beefing it up considerably from the FPU inside the 486 processor. The faster FPU makes the Pentium platform appropriate for the complex mathematics found in programs for image editing and computer-aided design (CAD).

Finally, Intel groomed its Pentium franchise for life on the road. The Mobile Pentium line, which started at 75MHz, uses *Tape Carrier Packaging* instead of the familiar ceramic packaging in its desktop CPUs to reduce weight to less than 1 gram and thickness to less than 1 millimeter. The 3.3-volt CPU is soldered directly onto notebook motherboards so that heat can be dissipated through the bottom without fans. Today, 133MHz Pentium notebooks sell for less than $2,000.

The Buying Line

The Pentium might have catapulted Intel's fortunes in the PC market, but that won't spare this CPU from becoming a part of history. Intel has moved its attentions to the Pentium MMX CPU, launched in January of 1997. By the time you read this, Intel will have transitioned most of its production and marketing entirely away from the Pentium Classic design.

So where do Pentium CPUs make sense? The focus is squarely on bargain hunters at this point. The following are typical examples of Pentium-based PCs:

- Affordable home or office systems that don't require strong multimedia performance
- Bargain PCs for buyers unwilling to consider x86 clones from Cyrix or AMD
- Inexpensive notebooks PCs

When it comes to Pentium Classic PCs, trouble is spelled "MMX." As optimized software and games emerge for the instruction set, owners of standard Pentium systems will find themselves frozen out of a big portion of the software market. For this reason alone, buyers should think twice before going for a cut-rate deal on a Pentium Classic PC.

Intel Pentium MMX: A Good Idea Gets Better

If Pentium represented an important leap for x86 computing, Pentium MMX (shown in Figure 6.7) is the pretty flourish at the end. With Pentium MMX, code-named P55C, Intel hopes to address the growing multimedia demands of software ranging from games to Web browsers. Still, the internal workings of the CPU—the dual pipelines, FPU, and data buses—remain largely unchanged, although Intel doubled the L1 cache to 32KB.

Figure 6.7.
The multimedia-savvy Pentium MMX features new instructions and a bulked-up cache for superior all-around performance. (Photo courtesy of Intel Corp.)

The first Pentium MMX desktop CPUs were introduced at 166 and 200MHz—at the top end of the Pentium clock speed range—running three times faster than the 66MHz system bus. A 233MHz version—reported to be the last Pentium MMX CPU—was introduced in June of 1997. This fastest processor runs at three-and-a-half times the speed of the 66MHz motherboard.

A Look Under the MMX Hood

What Intel did change was the instruction set, extending the original set of x86 instruction that has existed since the 386 CPU. MMX adds 57 new instructions, specifically targeting graphics, video compression/decompression, 3-D display, audio, and signal processing. The new instructions allow the Pentium MMX to do in one step what the Pentium Classic would need dozens of steps to accomplish.

Another important revision was support for so-called Single Instruction, Multiple Data (SIMD) operation. This technique allows the CPU to issue one command and to apply it to a range of data—eliminating the need to reissue the command for every piece of data that comes along. SIMD can make quick work of image-editing operations such as filtering, where wide swaths of visual data get updated with a single type of operation.

MMX doesn't come for free. Software makers must write their software with the new instructions in mind, or the chip's MMX capabilities won't be accessed. Microsoft has already moved components of its Windows 95 operating system to MMX and has released MMX-enhanced tool sets for game developers and application programmers. Numerous CD-ROM title makers have also begun work on MMX-enhanced applications.

Table 6.3 provides an overview of Pentium MMX processors.

Table 6.3. Intel Pentium MMX specs.

Spec	First Generation
Internal clock speed	166, 200, 233MHz
L1 cache size	16KB/16KB
L2 cache clock speed	66MHz
MMX support?	Yes
Number of pipelines	Two
Data bus (internal/external)	32-bit/64-bit
Number of transistors	4.4 million
Manufacturing process	.35 micron CMOS
Pin count	296

Even with non-MMX software, Pentium-MMX provides a significant boost over Pentium Classic. The new CPU doubles the L1 cache to 16KB each for data and instructions, immediately improving overall performance. Intel also tweaked its pipelining schemes, improving branch prediction to reduce costly pipeline stalls.

Technical Note: In order to fit the new MMX instructions without expanding the transistor count, Intel overlays the eight 64-bit MMX registers over the existing FPU registers. The approach has its drawbacks: It's a little bit like setting up shop in a living/working loft. You save the expense of renting a dedicated office, but you must deal with the hassle of additional furniture, housecleaning, and the like.

The performance hit comes when applications switch between floating-point and MMX operation. The CPU needs about 100 clock ticks to reset the registers from FPU to MMX or vice versa—a long time by a processor's reckoning. However, most PC applications fail to use the FPU at all, and those that do will rarely—if ever—jump repeatedly between floating-point and MMX operation. Multitasking MMX- and FPU-intensive applications isn't a problem either, because the operating system takes much longer to switch among programs than the CPU does to reassign its registers.

The shared register scheme has been employed by Intel, AMD, and Cyrix. However, Intel's CPUs are the only ones that employ multiple MMX pipelines. That should give Intel CPUs the performance edge in handling MMX operations.

Pentium MMX CPUs use a lower 2.8-volt internal operation to reduce heat dissipation while still running 3.3 volts externally to the motherboard. The split voltage requires motherboards to be outfitted with voltage regulation—something that manufacturers started adding several months before the January 1997 launch of the CPU line.

Pentium MMX quickly proved to be the swiftest Windows 95 CPU you could buy, outstripping the performance of 32-bit optimized Pentium Pro-200 CPUs in most benchmarks. However, Pentium Pro continued to enjoy the performance advantage in the true 32-bit Windows NT environment.

MMX-optimized operation shows even more impressive gains. Intel's boast of 400 percent improvements in some areas might be based on isolated program code (see Figure 6.8), but real-world applications such as Adobe PhotoShop and Macromedia Director still enjoy big gains on the order of 50 to 70 percent. Clearly, Pentium MMX delivers the goods.

Intel also launched a mobile version of Pentium MMX; 150 and 166MHz CPUs were available at launch time. 133 and 200MHz versions shipped later to fill out the notebook-ready line. Mobile CPUs are functionally identical to their desktop mates, but they use the slim and trim tape carrier packaging to reduce weight and thickness (see Figure 6.9). They also run at an even lower 2.45 volts internally.

Figure 6.8.
How fast is fast? Intel's MMX benchmarks show big performance gains over Pentium Classic when running MMX-optimized software. (Figure courtesy of Intel Corp.)

Figure 6.9.
The Pentium MMX for notebooks loses the bulky ceramic coating. The CPU weighs less than 1 gram and is less than 1 millimeter thick. (Photo courtesy of Intel Corp.)

Buying Tip: If you buy a Pentium notebook, especially for multimedia use, make sure that it's MMX-capable. Because of their compact design, notebooks typically lack sophisticated coprocessors for graphics, audio, and other functions. The enlarged cache, faster clock speed, and tweaked pipelining on Pentium MMX processors make a big impact on notebook performance. With MMX support being woven into Windows operating systems (MMX is a key component of Windows 98), notebooks will come closer than ever to matching desktop performance.

The biggest challenge with the mobile Pentium MMX chips is heat. Most notebook makers can use passive heat dissipation techniques with the Pentium MMX-150, but the 166MHz CPU runs hot enough that fans are often needed to move cool air over the processor. The heat issue delayed many Pentium MMX-166 notebook systems, forcing higher prices and affecting battery life.

Warning: In their zeal to be first with the fastest notebooks, small vendors sometimes sell systems using desktop CPUs. These notebooks are fast, no doubt about it. But short battery life combined with the risk of chronic overheating—to the point of damaging the CPU and system board—make such notebooks a risky buy. If you find a vendor selling a notebook PC at unheard-of CPU speeds, check the CPU make closely. If it isn't a notebook-specific version, walk away.

The Buying Line

Pentium MMX is fresh out of the blocks, but don't expect it to be around as long as the Pentium Classic. Intel faces stiff competition from AMD and Cyrix, but history shows that Intel will walk away from a crowded market by pushing the Next Big Thing (that is, Pentium II).

Still, Pentium MMX will remain the mainstream processor of choice at least through 1998. Performance is good, prices are right, and the CPU should enjoy an MMX performance advantage over its competitors. Expect prices anywhere from $1,600 to $2,500. If you're in the market for a PC (or a CPU upgrade), consider Pentium MMX for the following:

- Mixed-use home and office systems that need to run everything from e-mail and spreadsheets to presentations and multimedia titles
- Bargain PCs for buyers unwilling to consider x86 clones from Cyrix or AMD. The Pentium MMX-166 CPU works here.
- Almost all mainstream notebooks PCs

Who shouldn't consider Pentium MMX? Power users, graphics professionals, and even avid game players should all take a hard look at Pentium II. Advanced chipset support for AGP and fast SDRAM memory now make Pentium II more attractive than ever.

Intel Pentium Pro: The Future of Mainstream Computing

January 1996 was an interesting and somewhat worrisome time for Intel. Word on the street was that the venerable x86 instruction set, with its variable instruction lengths and rigid in-order execution requirements, was too unmanageable to move forward. Simple designs such as Motorola, IBM, and Apple's PowerPC drew praise for their fresh, streamlined, and forward-looking architectures.

> **Technical Note:** There are two philosophical camps of CPU design. Reduced Instruction Set Computing (RISC) looks to gain performance by quickly executing a stream of simple instructions, while Complex Instruction Set Computing (CISC) employs a wider set of instructions to get more done in each step. Today, most CPUs—including Intel's newest CPU—incorporate RISC technology, because it provides the best path to higher clock rates.

Pentium Pro proved a lot of folks wrong. Intel pushed the superscalar design found in the Pentium CPU, employing techniques with names such as dynamic execution and speculative branch prediction to work around the CISC bottlenecks. In essence, what Intel did was build a rapid-fire RISC core inside a fully-compatible CISC interface.

The Pentium Pro

On the outside, Pentium Pro, shown in Figure 6.10, is an absolute monster. The processor core alone packs 5.5 million transistors. What's more, Intel moved the L2 cache—usually placed externally on the motherboard—inside a second cavity in the ceramic PGA packaging. The 256KB L2 cache uses 15.5 million transistors, and the 512KB L2 cache uses 31 million transistors. The result is a 387-pin CPU with as many as 36.5 million transistors—10 times that of the Pentium CPU! Table 6.4 provides an overview of the Pentium Pro.

Figure 6.10.
The massive dual-cavity design delivers swift performance but is too unwieldy to manufacture cheaply. (Photo courtesy of Intel Corp.)

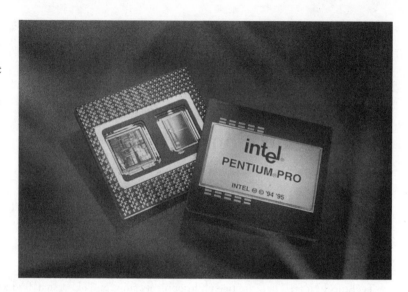

Table 6.4. Intel Pentium Pro specs.

Specification	First Generation	Second Generation
Internal clock speed	133MHz	150, 180, 200MHz
L1 cache size	8KB/8KB	8KB/8KB
L2 cache clock speed	133 MHz	150, 180, 200MHz
MMX support?	No	No
Number of integer pipelines	Three	Three
Data bus (internal/external)	32-bit/64-bit	32-bit/64-bit
Number of transistors	5.5 million	5.5 million
Manufacturing process	.6 micron BiCMOS	.35 micron CMOS
Pin count	387	387

The first versions of the mammoth CPU threw off tons of heat (14 watts) and cost well over $1,000, but the integrated L2 cache with its dedicated backplane bus provided an immediate performance jump. The L2 cache on other x86 CPUs runs at motherboard bus speed (60 or 66MHz), but the L2 cache inside the Pentium Pro runs at CPU speed. The 180 and 200MHz Pentium Pros, therefore, enjoy a 3x performance advantage in this critical pool of local memory. Furthermore, the Pentium Pro's L2 cache enjoys a dedicated cache bus rather than sharing time with the general frontside CPU bus as traditional caches do.

Inside the CPU core, Intel applied some nifty tricks to break out of the CISC closet. First, engineers extended the five-stage P5 pipeline to 12 stages, breaking tasks down into smaller, if more numerous, sections. The extended pipeline opened the door for still higher clock rates (now being seen in the 300MHz Pentium II, for example). More important, the CPU includes a decode unit at the front of the pipeline that breaks unwieldy x86 instructions into a series of RISC-like micro-operations. These micro-ops can move through the pipeline much more quickly and smoothly than traditional x86 code.

Technical Note: Intel went to great lengths to create a fast RISC core inside the CISC interface. Why not just go with the streamlined RISC instruction set entirely? One very important word: compatibility. Intel's entire market success is built on the simple fact that millions of programs have been written for its processors using the x86 instruction set. Abandon that legacy, and Intel loses the key competitive advantage over competitors ranging from the Motorola-IBM-Apple PowerPC processor to CPUs from Digital, MIPS, and Sun Microelectronics. By wrapping CISC compatibility around a RISC core, however, P6-class CPUs can achieve the performance of optimized RISC designs while still being able to run 10-year-old DOS applications.

AMD, Cyrix, and now IDT (with its new Centaur CPU) leverage the huge market for Intel-compatible CPUs by designing their chips with x86 instructions in mind. Like Intel, all three employ streamlined RISC cores to handle translated x86 instructions.

The RISC techniques help, but out-of-order execution is the key to the P6 design. When a CPU reaches an instruction that requires data still to come, the processor must wait. The Pentium Pro can move on to code that it can operate on by storing results in a holding area called the *instruction pool*. This buffer allows the CPU to speculatively execute instructions, holding the results until the proper data can be moved into registers in the proper order.

The addition of *symmetric multiprocessor* (SMP) support makes Pentium Pro well-suited for work inside network servers, Web servers, and high-end workstations. One challenge is keeping the data that is stored in each Pentium Pro L1 cache in sync with the others. Intel uses a protocol called MESI, which defines the four states of cache data (modified, exclusive, shared, and invalid). This scheme ensures that one processor doesn't overwrite a valid piece of data with older data stored in its cache. Up to four Pentium Pro CPUs can be set up in an SMP configuration using the built-in design.

The Buying Line

For all its technical merits, Pentium Pro carries a lot of baggage. The architecture is heavily optimized for 32-bit code. (Rumor has it that Intel expected Microsoft to transition the market to

Windows NT by 1996.) The P6 can't process the 16-bit code inside Windows 95 using out-of-order execution. As a result, Pentium Pro fails to deliver superior performance under DOS and Windows 95.

What's more, the Pentium Pro's integrated L2 cache is difficult to manufacture, with low yields keeping supply constrained. The big cache also makes it impossible to drive CPU clock speeds much above 200MHz. For all the performance of a dedicated internal L2 cache, the architecture doesn't work for a mainstream CPU that needs to be manufactured in the tens of millions of units.

Pentium Pro might not be a mainstream hit, but the CPU has a real future in niche networking and workstation markets. Pentium Pro's four-way SMP capability in particular makes it a good buy in the following cases:

- Web servers
- Network servers
- High-end graphics and engineering workstations
- Windows NT-based desktops for departments that require CPUs that have a proven compatibility history

Those footsteps you hear are from Pentium II, the Pentium Pro's brother. If you are considering a Pentium Pro system, make sure you look into this latest-generation CPU.

Intel Pentium II: Revenge of the P6

Intel quieted a lot of talk about AMD and Cyrix with this blockbuster processor. Introduced in May of 1997, Pentium II ups the ante with peerless x86 and MMX performance and a new system connector design that strategically alters the way Intel CPUs work with motherboards. What's more, Intel clearly plans to ride this P6 architecture into the next century. Table 6.5 provides an overview of the Pentium II.

Table 6.5. Pentium II specs.

Specification	First Generation	Second Generation
Internal clock speed	233, 266, 300MHz	333+MHz
L1 cache size	16KB/16KB	16KB/16KB
L2 cache clock speed	112, 133, 150MHz	166+MHz
MMX support?	Yes	Yes
Number of pipelines	Three	Three
Data bus (internal/external)	32-bit/64-bit	32-bit/64-bit

Specification	First Generation	Second Generation
Number of transistors	7.5 million	7.5 million
Manufacturing process	.35 micron CMOS	.25 micron CMOS
Package type	Socket 1 SEC	Socket 1 SEC

Pentium II Builds on P6 Success

Essentially, Pentium II takes the existing Pentium Pro core, with its RISC-like, out-of-order execution, and adds the same MMX support found in the Pentium MMX CPUs. This means that MMX-optimized software will enjoy a significant speed increase with Pentium II systems. Intel also doubled the L1 data and instruction caches over those in the Pentium Pro, boosting each to 16KB.

Like the latest Pentium Pro CPUs, Pentium II is built on a .35 micron CMOS process. It also features built-in SMP support, although the first Pentium IIs are limited to two-way SMP versus Pentium Pro's four-way SMP capability (see Figure 6.11). Forthcoming Pentium IIs should offer four- and eight-way SMP capability.

Figure 6.11.
Micronics' Dual Fortress motherboard features two massive Pentium II SEC cartridges for symmetric multiprocessing capability. (Photo courtesy of Micronics Corp.)

Bigger changes occur outside the core. Intel has adopted a cartridge carrier scheme for Pentium II that puts the CPU and L2 cache inside a cigarette pack-sized module. This package, called a Single Edge Connector (SEC) cartridge, mounts vertically into the new Socket 1 slot on Pentium II motherboards.

Inside the SEC, the L2 cache now sits separately from the CPU, connected via a dedicated backside bus that runs at half the speed of the CPU proper (see Figure 6.12). Intel calls the separated CPU system and CPU cache bus design the Dual Independent Bus (DIB) Architecture.

Figure 6.12.
Inside the cartridge, Pentium II uses an external L2 cache running at half processor speed to balance speed and affordability. Oh, and there are MMX instructions too. (Figure courtesy of Intel Corp.)

The new SEC design achieves three things:

- It separates the L2 cache from the CPU, improving production yields, lowering cost, and allowing core CPU speeds of 300MHz and higher.
- Like the Pentium Pro, it enables fast L2 cache performance by using a dedicated backside cache bus that runs faster than motherboard-mounted designs.
- It prevents competitors such as AMD and Cyrix from selling compatible CPUs, because they can't plug into the Intel-patented P6 bus and Socket 1 connector.

Intel introduced Pentium II at internal clock speeds of 233, 266, and 300MHz. Clock speeds will go higher still in 1998, once Intel shrinks the CPU to a .25 micron CMOS process. The so-called Deschutes processor will allow clock speeds to increase to 400MHz or higher. The .25-micron variant will also be the first Pentium II appropriate for notebook application, probably in the second half of 1998.

The Buying Line

No doubt about it: Pentium II is the future of Intel-based computing. In an effort to stay ahead of the competition, Intel will gladly kill its own. It publicly iced the 286 processor to move customers to faster 386 designs. And now the company is pushing the SEC cartridge and Socket 1 motherboard connector on system makers. If you want a system with maximum life span, Pentium II is your best bet.

Pentium II has its limits. Expect Pentium II's limited two-way SMP support to move up to four-way SMP, making the CPU more appropriate for server applications. Finally, Pentium II notebooks are several months off. With key advancements on the way, Pentium II appeals to a wide market. Expect prices to start at over $2,500 and move to $5,000 and above for multiprocessor configurations:

- Graphics and engineering workstations
- Powerful home systems for multimedia titles and game play
- Mixed-use home or office PCs for multimedia playback and presentations
- Future four-way SMP Pentium II versions for network and Web server applications

AMD K6: A Challenger Returns

AMD launched its latest processor, the K6 (see Figure 6.13), in April of 1997. For the first time, a non-Intel CPU stood atop the x86 performance heap, as K6 proved faster than both Pentium MMX and Pentium Pro. AMD's latest could even keep pace with Pentium II CPUs running at the same clock speeds under Windows 95.

Figure 6.13.
AMD's latest CPU brings close-to-Pentium II performance, yet plugs into affordable Socket 7 motherboards. (Photo courtesy of AMD Corp.)

K6 enjoys one big advantage in the marketplace over Pentium II: AMD's processor plugs into the same Socket 7 motherboards used for Pentium and Pentium MMX CPUs. Although system vendors will have to adopt expensive new motherboards for Pentium II, K6 systems can cut costs by using the same motherboards and componentry found in millions of Pentium PCs.

Buying Tip: Because K6 plugs into Socket 7 motherboards, the CPU can serve as the core of a processor upgrade for Pentium MMX and some newer Pentium Classic PCs. Evergreen Technologies intends to offer K6 upgrade products.

A Look at K6

Socket 7 compatibility makes for good economics, but it hands the performance advantage to Pentium II and its faster L2 cache. K6 makes up some of the difference with an oversized L1 cache that, at 64KB (32KB for instruction and 32KB for data), is twice the size of that in Pentium MMX and Pentium II. Expect the performance difference to widen as Intel pushes the Pentium II clock beyond 300MHz. Still, the L2 cache will be limited to the 66MHz clock speed of the motherboard bus.

In many ways, K6 resembles the Pentium Pro and Pentium II CPUs it targets. Like these processors, K6 wraps a CISC interface around a superscalar pipelined RISC architecture. x86 instructions are decoded into fixed-length RISC86 instructions (AMD's version of Intel's micro-operations) for efficient processing in the K6's two six-stage integer pipelines. Table 6.6 provides an overview of the K6 processor.

Table 6.6. AMD K6 specs.

Specification	First Generation	Second Generation
Internal clock speed	166, 200, 233MHz	266, 300MHz+
L1 cache size	32KB/32KB	32KB/32KB
L2 cache clock speed	60, 66MHz	60, 66MHz
MMX support?	Yes	Yes
Number of pipelines	Two	Two
Data bus (internal/external)	32-bit/32-bit	32-bit/32-bit
Number of transistors	8 million	8 million
Manufacturing process	.35 micron CMOS	.25 micron CMOS
Package type	Socket 7 PGA	Socket 7 PGA

You'll find other familiar tricks inside the K6. The processor supports out-of-order execution and uses branch prediction to avoid stalls in its two integer and one floating-point pipelines. The K6 also supports MMX instructions, using eight 64-bit MMX registers to process MMX instructions broken down into RISC86 operations.

The current K6 is built on a .35 micron CMOS process and runs as fast as 233MHz. AMD expects to move to a smaller .25 micron process before 1998, which should allow clock speeds of 266 and 300MHz.

The Buying Line

AMD K6 changed everything. Finally, buyers can consider a viable competitor to Intel's top-of-the-line CPUs. The result has been healthy price competition that allows you to buy that much more PC for your dollar.

But is K6 for you? Many individuals and companies will stick with Intel for the assurance of x86 compatibility—although AMD's compatibility record is very strong. Perhaps more important, you simply might not be able to find K6 CPUs from major vendors. Big names such as Dell, Compaq, IBM, and Gateway have all stayed on the sidelines. As a result, buying a K6 system often means taking your chances with smaller vendors who might not offer the full range of service and support provided by major firms.

On the performance side, expect K6 systems to fall a bit short in MMX performance. Otherwise, the K6 tucks neatly above the fastest Pentium MMX PCs, matching the speed of the low-end Pentium II-233 CPU. Look for prices ranging from $1,500 to $2,500.

K6 works best for

- Affordable mixed-use home and office PCs that need to handle moderate multimedia, presentations, and game play
- Affordable general-purpose home PCs

Cyrix 6x86Mx: The Competition Heats Up

Introduced in June 1997, Cyrix's 6x86Mx has a lot in common with AMD's K6. Performance is a close match for K6 in both standard x86 and MMX instructions. And like K6, the 6x86Mx uses a 64-bit external bus that plugs into existing Socket 7 motherboards. But Cyrix has priced its new CPU very aggressively, making 6x86Mx PCs possibly the best bargains around.

In fact, Cyrix and AMD share many of the same prospects and problems. Both have good manufacturing capacity, strong processor designs, and sustained histories as x86-compatible CPU makers. Unfortunately, few first-tier PC makers will carry their products, making it difficult for them to break into larger markets.

6x86Mx Details

Like K6 and Pentium MMX, the Cyrix 6x86Mx is built on a .35-micron CMOS process and uses a pipelined, superscalar design to achieve more than one operation per clock tick. The 6x86Mx, shown in Figure 6.14, also provides full MMX instruction support—with MMX registers laid on top of the floating-point registers. Key to 6x86Mx performance is the big 64KB L1 cache, which is unified so that instructions and data share space in the cache.

Figure 6.14.
A little late to market, 6x86Mx runs head-to-head against K6 in both price and performance. (Photo courtesy of Cyrix Corp.)

6x86Mx runs initially at 166, 200, and 225MHz, using system bus speeds of 60, 66, and 75MHz, respectively. Faster speeds are expected in 1998, once Cyrix shrinks the chip to a .25-micron process.

6x86Mx gets the most out of each clock tick, using an aggressive superscalar design and large cache to help power performance. However, MMX performance doesn't enjoy this advantage. Expect 6x86Mx to trail Pentium MMX and Pentium II considerably in MMX-optimized tasks. Table 6.7 provides an overview of the 6x86Mx processor.

Table 6.7. Cyrix 6x86Mx specs.

Specification	First Generation
Internal clock speed	150, 166, 188MHz
L1 cache size	64KB unified
L2 cache clock speed	60, 66, 75MHz
MMX support?	Yes
Number of pipelines	Two
Data bus (internal/external)	32-bit/64-bit
Number of transistors	8 million
Manufacturing process	.35 micron CMOS
Package type	Socket 7 PGA

Socket 7 compatibility allows for lower system prices and the possibility of 6x86Mx-based upgrade CPUs. Also, Cyrix has pushed a faster 75MHz motherboard speed, so some 6x86Mx systems might employ the faster design.

> **Buying Tip:** All things being equal, you're better off looking for a 75MHz motherboard in an M2-based PC. The faster clock will speed accesses to both the L2 cache and system memory, making the CPU more effective.

The Buying Line

Cyrix markets its CPUs using the Performance Rating scheme. In fact, you might have a hard time finding the actual core speed of the processor you're buying—an annoying bit of marketeering that makes assessing performance potential difficult. Table 6.8 shows the actual clock and bus speeds of each P-rated 6x86Mx processor.

Table 6.8. Clock speeds of P-rated 6x86Mx CPUs.

6x86Mx P-Rating	Internal Clock	Motherboard Clock
PR166	150MHz	60MHz
PR200	166MHz	66MHz
PR233	188MHz	75MHz

The buying outlook for the 6x86Mx is nearly identical to that of K6. Again, expect system prices ranging from $1,500 to $2,500. The following are good applications for the 6x86Mx:

- Affordable mixed-use home and office PCs that need to handle moderate multimedia, presentations, and game play
- Affordable general-purpose home PCs

Cyrix 6x86 and AMD K5: Better Than Pentium

Although they are now out of production, the Cyrix 6x86 and AMD K5 both helped set up the competitive processor market. Both were able to provide performance slightly ahead of Pentium CPUs running at the same clock rate, and both were significantly less expensive.

Unfortunately, neither broke out in the market. Large system makers declined to pick up the new CPUs for fear of drawing the ire of Intel, the critical supplier in the market. More important, problems plagued both lines. AMD suffered a series of delays that kept K5 a step behind the competition, while the 6x86 suffered from a series of minor glitches that helped impede sales. In addition, Cyrix lacked relationships with major system vendors, a critical ingredient for marketing a CPU.

Inside the Cyrix 6x86

For all its problems, the 6x86 is a good entry-level CPU. The slimmed-down .5-micron process has allowed faster clock speeds in a smaller, cooler die. Like the Pentium, the 6x86 features 16KB of L1 cache and a superscalar core that can process multiple operations at once. To tweak performance further, Cyrix has tried to get system makers to adopt 75MHz motherboards—20 percent faster than standard 66MHz models—for its fastest 6x86 CPU.

Table 6.9 provides an overview of the 6x86 processor.

Table 6.9. Cyrix 6x86 specs.

Specification	First Generation	Second Generation
Internal clock speed	100, 100MHz	120, 133, 150MHz
L1 cache size (data/instruction)	16KB unified	16KB unified
L2 cache clock speed	50, 55MHz	60, 66, 75MHz
MMX support?	No	No
Number of pipelines	Two	Two
Data bus (internal/external)	32-bit/64-bit	32-bit/32-bit
Manufacturing process	.6 micron CMOS	.5 micron CMOS
Package type	Socket 7 PGA	Socket 7 PGA

Inside the AMD K5

Table 6.10 provides an overview of the K5 processor.

Table 6.10. AMD K5 specs.

Specification	First Generation
Internal clock speed	100, 117MHz
L1 cache size (data/instruction)	16KB/8KB
L2 cache clock speed	60, 66MHz

Specification	First Generation
MMX support?	No
Number of pipelines	Two
Data bus (internal/external)	32-bit/32-bit
Number of transistors	4.3 million
Manufacturing process	.35 micron CMOS
Package type	Socket 7 PGA

Behind the Pentium-beating performance is a superpipelined, superscalar core that runs more efficiently than the Pentium CPU. Like Cyrix's 6x86, the K5 can simply do more per clock tick than the Pentium CPU. However, like the 6x86, K5 lacks MMX support.

Upgrading a CPU

So you've decided that your aging system needs a faster processor to keep pace with the latest applications. This section will show you the options you have when it comes to upgrading your processor. It will also guide you through an upgrade and give you strategies and tips for avoiding problems.

Buying Tip: A new processor can boost performance, but it won't resolve bottlenecks that exist with memory, graphics, and other areas. Before opting for a processor upgrade, make sure that you aren't overlooking other possible upgrades that might do a better job of improving performance.

How CPU Upgrades Work

No doubt about it, a processor upgrade is serious business—the PC version of a brain transplant. Although most CPU upgrades entail replacing the existing processor with a faster chip, the real payoff comes from the more-sophisticated processing features of the upgrade CPU (see Figure 6.15).

How does a CPU upgrade work? In most cases, the upgrade chip plugs into the same socket occupied by the existing CPU. The new chip communicates with the PC using the same pins employed by the original processor but adds all the talents of its more-sophisticated core. Depending on the upgrade, the new CPU might add new functions to the PC—such as floating-point math or MMX instructions—or it might simply augment existing performance with a faster internal clock, larger L1 cache, or optimized internal operation.

Figure 6.15.
Upgrade products such as Intel's OverDrive MMX can significantly boost clock rates and add new features such as MMX support. (Photo courtesy of Intel Corp.)

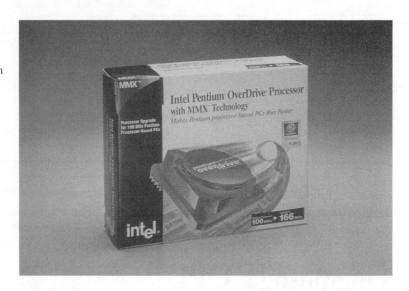

In general, CPU upgrades will enhance performance by doing the following:

- Boost internal CPU clock speed.

- Add or improve floating-point capability for some 3-D and imaging applications.

- Add MMX instruction support for multimedia applications.

- Provide a superscalar pipelined architecture to increase the number of operations performed per clock tick.

- Add or enlarge the L1 cache to reduce wait states in the processor.

- Work with motherboard settings to allow faster external bus speeds.

The level of benefit to your system depends on several things. The important thing is not to overestimate what a CPU upgrade can do, particularly for older 486 systems. The following bottlenecks all share one aspect: They will force a fast processor to halt operation while it waits for data to come from the system.

- Slow motherboard speed: Many 486 motherboards are limited to 33MHz operation, half the speed of current motherboards.

- Narrow external bus: Older systems with 32-bit memory buses will starve a fast CPU.

- Slow system RAM: Today's PCs feature enhanced RAM running at 60ns or faster, versus the 80ns RAM that you might find in a 486. The 30 percent speed difference and inefficient design can force your new CPU to wait.

- Lack of L2 cache: Because they didn't need to keep up with super-fast CPUs, older PCs might lack the ability to use a fast L2 cache. Again, your new CPU might end up waiting for data.

- Slow graphics bus: If your 486 lacks PCI or VL-bus slots, a processor upgrade can't help solve problems with graphical programs. At the very least, you'll need to consider a motherboard upgrade.

- Slow hard disk: Today's hard disks feature access times of 11 milliseconds. Four years ago, 25ms was common. This means that programs take longer to load, data crawls into RAM, and virtual memory is a swamp.

> **Peter's Principle:** A CPU Upgrade Extends—Rather Than Renews—the Life of Your PC
>
> If you think of a CPU upgrade as a way to extend—rather than renew—the life of your PC, you will avoid inevitable disappointment. A processor upgrade is a terrific way to wait out the arrival of The Next Big Thing while keeping your PC in useful shape in the meantime.

How to Upgrade Your CPU

A processor upgrade might be PC brain surgery, but that doesn't mean it has to be difficult. In fact, compared to installing a hard disk or CD-ROM drive, upgrading the CPU can be a breeze—usually. This section will help you understand how an upgrade happens, complete with step-by-step instructions.

First, be warned. The complexity and diversity of the PC marketplace makes CPU upgrades a fairly uncertain proposition. There are hundreds, if not thousands, of system vendors, most of which have produced hundreds, if not thousands, of individual models. No CPU upgrade vendor can anticipate and design for this wide universe of platforms.

The leading culprit in this compatibility soup is the system BIOS (Basic Input/Output System), the code that underlies all the workings of the PC. BIOS programming can be half science and half black magic. Bugs and twitches turn up all the time in even the most up-to-date BIOS code working inside of unaltered systems. Plug in a processor purchased four or six years after your system BIOS code was written, and there's no telling how the two will interact. That's why I'll mention this piece of sage advice now (which will be repeated mercilessly throughout this book): Back up your hard disk first.

Back up to tape, to cartridge media, to floppies, or to your network. One way or another, put those valued bits someplace where they can be retrieved after disaster strikes. Also faithfully record your current BIOS settings—hard disk sectors, bus I/O, the works. If you have a flash BIOS—a BIOS that can be software-updated—store the current BIOS code onto a floppy disk and keep it handy. Also make a startup/rescue disk with the usual data.

For more on backing up before an upgrade, see Chapter 3, "Upgrade Strategies."

Physically Installing a CPU Upgrade

Surprisingly, the physical installation of a new CPU can be quite easy. This is particularly true for Pentium-based systems sold over the last four years. All these PCs include so-called Zero Insertion Force (ZIF) sockets, which use an easily accessed lever to socket and desocket the CPU. ZIF sockets eliminate the need to tenderly pull chips out of their sockets—harrowing work that can result in snapped pins and broken hearts.

A typical ZIF socket installation works like this:

1. Shut off the PC, remove the power cable, and remove the system chassis. Allow the system to sit for about 10 minutes so that the CPU is cool enough to handle.

2. Ground yourself to avoid electrostatic shock. The best method is to use a static mat with the cord attached to your wrist. Lacking that, be sure to touch the metal of the PC chassis before touching any componentry.

3. Place the system so that the motherboard is facing the ceiling. (For tower and minitower systems, this means placing the unit on its side.)

4. Remove the upgrade CPU from its packaging, and place it pins-up on the mat.

5. Locate the system CPU. If the processor has a fan or heat sink with a wire attached, you need to detach it first. Also clear any cables or wires that block access. If necessary, unplug cables or remove drives from their bays.

6. Find the ZIF lever (the metal lever with a plastic tip that lies next to the socket) and gently pull it up. The CPU should lift a little from the socket.

7. Making sure that you're well-grounded, grasp the CPU with your thumb and forefinger and pull straight upward. Avoid raising one edge or the other, because this can result in bent or broken pins. Place the original CPU in the packaging supplied with the upgrade processor.

8. Take the upgrade CPU and orient it so that pin 1 aligns with pin 1 in the CPU socket. Usually, the pin 1 corner will have a beveled edge or will have a dot silk screened on top of the CPU in the corner, as shown in Figure 6.16. (Refer to the vendor's documentation to make sure you have properly identified pin 1.)

9. Slowly place the processor into the socket, taking your time to make sure that the edges are aligned and that the pins seat smoothly into the socket holes. Don't force it!

10. Once you're satisfied that the CPU is properly aligned and seated, press gently on the top of the CPU to make sure that all pins are in contact.

11. Lower the ZIF lever slowly. You should be able to feel some resistance as the lever brings the socket into contact with the CPU pins.

12. Make sure that you haven't disturbed any wires or boards inside the chassis, check to make sure that the CPU fan is properly connected. Also check to make sure that no tools or other objects are inside the case.

Figure 6.16.

Lining up the pin 1 position is critical to avoid damaging the CPU. You'll need to spot the subtle pin 1 clues that chip makers provide, including a beveled edge, silk-screened dot, and the absence of a corner pin. (Figure courtesy of Intel Corp.)

13. Before putting the case back on, plug in your PC and boot it up. You'll be in violation of FCC emissions compliance for a few minutes, but it's a good idea to see if things work before going to the trouble of screwing on the case.

14. If the machine boots up normally, congratulations! Your PC has a new brain. Go ahead and put on the case. If the machine doesn't boot normally, refer to the section "Trouble-shooting: Fixing CPU Problems."

Most older 486 systems don't have a ZIF socket, so you need to pull the chip out of the socket using a tool called a chip puller, which looks a little bit like salad tongs. The chip puller lets you put even upward force on two sides of the CPU so that you don't end up bending pins.

Here's how to handle the physical installation of a non-ZIF-socketed CPU:

1. Shut off the PC, remove the power cable, and remove the system chassis. Let the CPU cool off by leaving the system alone for about half an hour.

2. Ground yourself to avoid electrostatic shock. Use a static mat, or at least touch the metal of the PC frame before going inside.

3. Place the system with the motherboard facing up toward you. (Tower and minitower systems go on their sides.)

4. Remove the upgrade CPU from its packaging, and place it on the static mat pins-up.

5. Locate the system CPU. If the processor has a fan or heat sink with a wire attached, you need to detach it first. Also clear any cables or wires that block access. If necessary, unplug cables or remove drives from their bays.

6. Grasp the chip puller with your thumb and forefinger, and lower the tool so that the tongs are level with the bottom of the processor. Squeeze the tongs between the CPU and socket, working them so that the tong teeth fit between the CPU pins.

7. Once you're confident that the tongs have a good grip, pull evenly and gently toward your body. To help unseat the pins, you can pull one side up slightly and then even up the opposite side. Be very careful, because tipping the CPU too far to one side will bend or break the pins!

8. If necessary, remove the chip puller and reseat the tongs on the other two sides of the CPU. Repeat step 7. Repeat this as necessary until the CPU comes up. Take your time, and work slowly.

9. Once the CPU is lifted, use your hand to slowly pull it straight up and out of the socket. Place the CPU in the packaging used by the upgrade processor.

10. Take the upgrade CPU from the mat, and lower it slowly onto the socket. Align pin 1 of the upgrade chip with pin 1 of the socket. Usually, the pin 1 corner will have a beveled edge or will have a dot silk screened on top of the CPU in the corner. (Refer to the vendor's documentation to make sure that you've properly identified pin 1.)

11. Slowly lower the processor into the socket, taking your time to ensure that the edges are aligned and that the pins fit neatly into the socket holes.

12. Once the CPU is aligned and seated, press gently on the top of the CPU, slowly adding force to lower the chip. The CPU should press flush against the socket. Don't force it!

13. Reattach any wires or drives you cleared earlier, and check to make sure that the CPU fan is properly connected. Also make sure that you haven't disturbed any boards or the inside of the chassis, and check that no tools or other objects are inside the case.

14. Plug in the PC and boot it up before sealing the case. This will let you see if the installation worked before you seal the case.

15. If the PC boots up normally, put on the case. If it doesn't, refer to the section "Troubleshooting: Fixing CPU Problems."

Software Needed for an Upgrade

Like almost any hardware upgrade, there's a software side to installing a CPU. Specifically, you need to determine whether the upgrade processor will work with your system. Upgrades such as Intel's

OverDrive processors come with a disk to diagnose the system BIOS and to determine whether it will work with the chip. If not, you need to install a new BIOS.

If your system has a flashable BIOS—that is, if it can be upgraded from software—you can update it easily. The first step is to determine the exact model of both your PC and its motherboard. Also look for the maker and version of the current BIOS. You can find this information by watching the display during boot-up. With that information, you can visit the Web site or BBS of the system manufacturer or motherboard maker to get the latest compatible BIOS version. To upgrade a BIOS, do the following:

1. Download the BIOS code from your vendor's Web site and copy the update file to a floppy disk.

2. Turn off the system and insert the diskette into the floppy drive.

3. Turn on the PC, boot from the floppy, and follow the instructions to update the flash BIOS.

4. Wait for the BIOS flashing sequence to complete. The computer should automatically restart itself with the new BIOS installed.

For more information on the system BIOS, see Chapter 10, "Motherboards and Cases."

Older systems might be equipped with an EPROM (Electrically Programmable Read-Only Memory), which can't be readily reprogrammed. In this case, you can try to order an updated EPROM chip from your system or motherboard vendor. However, the cost and difficulty of installing the new chip can be prohibitive. In addition, the system vendor might not offer an EPROM update for older motherboards. In this case, your upgrade options might be limited.

Performance: Even if your CPU upgrade doesn't require a BIOS update, you should look into one anyway. Quite often, motherboard manufacturers and third-party BIOS vendors release performance-optimized updates that can deliver a big boost to existing systems. Key updates include the addition of write-back cache support or streamlined memory access, as well as the occasional bug fix.

CPU Upgrade Options

So you have an older system that you hope to keep around a while longer. You have plenty of options. A number of companies sell CPU upgrade kits based on Intel, AMD, and Cyrix processors.

Peter's Principle: When a CPU Upgrade Turns into a Motherboard Upgrade

Before you go too deep into exploring CPU upgrade alternatives, make sure you don't really want a motherboard upgrade instead. In addition to providing a fast new CPU, motherboard upgrades feature quicker system RAM, faster graphics capability, and attractive features such as Plug and Play, enhanced IDE, and USB.

The following are key points in deciding whether a CPU upgrade can really work. If any of these points describes your current PC, you might consider upgrading the motherboard instead:

- Lack of PCI bus slots for fast graphics
- Lack of Plug and Play BIOS and chipsets for easing peripheral installations under Windows 95
- Lack of support for quick (60ns or faster) and enhanced system RAM such as EDO DRAM and SDRAM

Also, anyone upgrading a 486 PC should at least look into a new motherboard. The slow and narrow 486 motherboard bus alone makes any CPU upgrade problematic at best. Combine that with the lack of VL bus and ISA graphics boards for these systems, and a new motherboard makes sense.

For more on motherboard upgrades, see Chapter 10.

These upgrade kits include everything you need to replace your old CPU with a faster chip. Inside the box you will usually find a CPU, a heat sink or fan, a chip puller tool, step-by-step documentation, and sometimes diagnostics for testing the compatibility of your PC's BIOS.

Table 6.11 lists vendors who sell CPU upgrades.

Table 6.11. Vendors who sell 486-to-Pentium upgrades.

Company	Phone Number	Web Site
Evergreen Technologies	(800) 733-0934	http://www.evertech.com
Gainbery Computer Products	(800) 825-7331	http://www.gainbery.com
Intel Corp.	(800) 538-3373 (408) 765-8080	http://www.intel.com
Kingston Technology Corp.	(800) 337-8410	http://www.kingston.com

486 Upgrade Options

If you own a 486DX system, the easiest and most certain upgrade is a clock-multiplied 486-class CPU. The Intel DX4-100, for example, triples the internal clock of the 486DX-33. The downside is that a 486-grade CPU lacks the architectural features of a Pentium-class CPU.

Another, potentially better, option is to use a Pentium-class upgrade that uses the 486 pin-out. Intel's 486-to-Pentium OverDrive chip—since discontinued—was the first such product. Although the 486-to-Pentium OverDrive (also known as P24T) boasts the same superscalar core found in the Pentium CPU, the results failed to impress in benchmark tests. What's worse, the complexity of the 486-to-Pentium upgrade caused all sorts of compatibility problems. DX4-based upgrades generally matched the performance of the 486-to-Pentium OverDrive in most applications.

Behind the poor showing was the 32-bit data bus employed by 486 motherboards, which is half the width of that of true Pentium CPUs. The narrow bus prevents the superscalar architecture from running at full tilt. Still, some applications—in particular, those employing floating-point operations—can see significant jumps.

You can find 486 upgrade products from Kingston and Evergreen that use Cyrix's 586 and AMD's K5 processors. Like P24T, these chips provide Pentium-like characteristics. And like P24T, their ability to improve the performance of an old 486 motherboard is limited.

Pentium Upgrade Options

The outlook for owners of Pentium systems is better. Pentium PCs feature a wider 64-bit motherboard bus running at 60 and 66MHz, providing four times the bandwidth of 486 systems. What's more, most Pentium PCs are outfitted with PCI add-on cards, providing superior graphics performance for both ISA and VL bus-based systems.

Although Intel has sold its Pentium OverDrive processors for years, you should look for the more recent MMX versions. The addition of Pentium MMX features—the enlarged L1 cache and MMX instruction set support—make OverDrive MMX one of the most compelling CPU upgrades yet.

OverDrive MMX supports Pentium PCs running from 75 to 166MHz. Clock speeds vary by model but range from 120 to 200MHz. The OverDrive upgrade includes an attached heat sink and fan, as well as a voltage regulator for allowing the 2.8-volt CPU to run on existing 3.3-volt motherboards.

Table 6.12 shows the clock-speed improvement provided by OverDrive MMX products for existing Pentium CPUs.

Table 6.12. OverDrive MMX products.

Pentium PC Clock Speed	OverDrive Clock Speed
75	150
90, 120, 150	180
100, 133	166 or 200*
166	200

*200MHz operation is available for Socket 7 motherboards. Older Socket 5 motherboards run at 166MHz.

A more recent Pentium upgrade entry is Evergreen Technologies' MxPro. Based on AMD's K6 CPU, MxPro upgrades any compatible Socket 7 PC to speeds of 166, 200, and 233MHz and adds MMX support. Significantly, slower Pentium-75 systems can be upgraded all the way to 233MHz. Intel's OverDrive scheme, in contrast, only allows an upgrade to 125MHz for a Pentium-75. The K6 has also proved faster than Pentium MMX CPUs in benchmark testing, making the MxPro an attractive upgrade option.

Peter's Principle: Overclocking: Live Fast, Die Young

There is a way to wring more performance out of an aging system without throwing money at it: Run it faster than its rated speed. Although this is relatively simple to do, overclocking a CPU will, at best, shorten the processor's life. At worst, it can cook the chip in its socket, instantly killing the PC.

I'm going to do the proper thing and say that you shouldn't consider overclocking as an option for boosting performance. The cost of failure is simply too great to justify what is really only an incremental boost in performance. And if you push the clock aggressively to get a sizable boost, you will almost certainly fry the CPU. Either way, the risks outweigh the benefits.

Risky or not, overclocking a CPU is very easy to do. You simply find the jumper switches on your PC's motherboard that control CPU speed and adjust the settings to higher settings. Doing this fools the motherboard into thinking that a faster CPU is installed in the socket.

To make a 90MHz Pentium system into a 100MHz model, set the jumpers to the documented settings for a Pentium-100 CPU. The quartz crystal on the motherboard will now resonate at a higher rate, driving the CPU to the higher clock speed. This is possible because system makers use the same motherboard in a wide variety of CPU models and speeds.

Note that driving the clock will cause the CPU to run hotter. If you're planning to overclock your CPU, make sure that you get a CPU fan from a company such as PC Power and Cooling. If your overclocked system starts acting erratically after being on for a while, the reason might be overheating. Aggressively cooling the CPU might allow normal operation.

CPU Buying Strategies

I've said it before, and I'm going to say it again: When you buy computer hardware, you must consider what you will do with it. A lot of books urge you to pay for all sorts of wild-eyed technology, unmindful of the fact that all you need is something to send e-mail and update a recipe list.

When you're buying a new PC, think about the following concerns when it comes to the CPU:

- Look for the best value
- Think two years ahead
- Consider upgradability
- Know your needs

Look for the Best Value

If you want to get the most processor for your money, buy a step or two off the cutting edge. Intel's 300MHz Pentium II processors cost $700 or more at the time this chapter was written, while the very-capable Pentium MMX-233, K6-233, and Cyrix 6x86MX-PR233 CPUs cost less than $300. You won't get the fastest system on the block, but you'll save $500 or more and have the opportunity to spend money on vital components such as RAM. The downside is that you'll end up having to replace such a system sooner than you would have to replace one based on cutting-edge technology.

Generally you can get a better deal with an Intel-compatible processor. AMD and Cyrix price their chips very aggressively, making them a better price-performance value for most applications. AMD K6-based systems, for example, can sell for $1,000 less than similarly configured Pentium II PCs. On the downside, these processors are generally sold by smaller, little-known vendors, which can be a concern for some buyers.

Note: Both AMD and Cyrix enjoy good compatibility records with x86 software, but problems can arise with non-Intel CPUs. Some games mistook Cyrix's 6x86 processor as a

continues

486-class CPU, failing to load because they required Pentium-level processing. The problem was that there was no ID number for the 6x86 in Windows 95's CPU database. The programs simply defaulted to the Cyrix CPU they could find—an old 486SLC.

Think Two Years Ahead

You should also try to predict your needs a few years down the road. Will your basic e-mail expand into heavy Web browsing and HTML editing six months or a year from now? Will your recipe lists evolve into HTML documents that incorporate photos and interactive animation? If you go with a rock-bottom processor based on your current needs, you will have no room to advance into more sophisticated work.

The key is to balance the raw power in the processor with the other components in your system. You might be able to buy a Pentium II-266 system for $2,300 if you get it with just 8MB of RAM, a 500MB hard drive, and a 14-inch monitor—but you'll be sorely disappointed with the performance and features of such a lopsided configuration. A better choice is to step back a bit on the CPU—maybe a Pentium MMX-233 will suit you—and boost the RAM, hard drive, and monitor to provide a better overall balance.

Consider Upgradability

Moore's Law basically says that any processor you put in your new system will be obsolete within a few years. That leaves you with two options: Buy big up front and hope to stretch the useful life of your original hardware, or spend less now and pay a premium to upgrade down the road.

The concept of a processor upgrade sounds good, but don't overvalue it in your decision. Bottlenecks in main memory, graphics, and other areas reduce the effectiveness of a faster CPU. Still, a system with an upgrade path ahead of it is better than one without.

As it looks now, the faster Pentium MMX CPUs don't offer much opportunity for upgrading. Intel doesn't plan to go beyond 233MHz with Pentium MMX, and the company has begun transitioning to its newest P6 CPU, Pentium II. Unlike previous Intel processors, Pentium II sits inside a cartridge housing equipped with a slotted connector—an approach called Single Edge Connector (SEC), as shown in Figure 6.17. This approach allows for better performance (thanks to faster L2 caching and a more sophisticated CPU bus), but the real story is that Intel competitors AMD and Cyrix lack rights to the P6 bus. That is a big incentive for Intel to push new PC buyers to the new platform.

Figure 6.17.
Intel lauds the performance of the SEC cartridge and its Dual Independent Bus (DIB) for optimizing the externalized L2 cache, but the real target is AMD and Cyrix. Intel hopes to shake the competition by moving the market to its patent-protected P6 bus motherboards. (Photo courtesy of Intel Corp.)

Those who bought Pentium Classic processors do have something to look forward to. Intel's MMX-enabled OverDrive upgrade chips provide a better performance boost than we've historically seen from CPUs. What's more, firms such as Evergreen sell AMD K6-based upgrade chips for Pentium systems. Tests have shown that K6 provides significantly better performance than even the fastest Pentium-MMX CPU.

Know Your Needs

If you work with 3-D graphics or computer-aided design (CAD), don't skimp. Make sure you get top-flight floating-point capability and aggressive pipelining in your CPU. This means that Pentium II or perhaps Pentium Pro in a four-way multiprocessing system. The same goes for hardcore image editing and mathematical applications.

Home PCs for Web browsing, e-mail, and the occasional multimedia game will do well with Pentium MMX, AMD K6, or Cyrix M2. Bargain hunters should look at the same CPUs but consider the lower range of clock speeds.

Repair a CPU? Think Again

CPUs provide remarkable power, flexibility, and reliability, but they aren't bulletproof. The heroes of the Information Revolution can suffer any number of maladies that will render a $3,000 PC lifeless.

Here's just a short list of the bad things that can happen to good processors:

- Bent or broken pins
- Overheating
- Static discharge
- Over-voltage from a blown fuse or power spike

Fortunately, these things don't happen without cause. Pins usually get broken or bent during the installation or removal of the CPU, a tricky process that requires a steady hand, a good eye, and lots of patience.

Should you accidentally break or crush a CPU (say, by stepping on it) or inherit a microprocessor that has been damaged, you're probably out of luck. Any damage to the ceramic body will almost certainly disrupt the microscopic traces on the chip. Likewise, a snapped pin is almost certainly irreparable. But if a pin (or pins) is simply bent, you might be able to straighten it using a pair of jeweler's pliers.

Warning: Even if you manage to straighten a bent pin, you aren't out of the woods. The deformation of the metal will weaken the pin considerably, making it especially susceptible to bending or breaking in the future. If you try to install a pin that has been bent and straightened, you might run the risk of having a pin snap off inside the CPU socket itself. If this happens, you will lose both the CPU and the motherboard. So be careful!

Overheating is a common problem, particularly because some CPUs run awfully hot and leave little room for error. Many processors now rely on chip-mounted fans and a constant flow of air inside the PC chassis to stay cool. If that fan dies—and you don't notice it right away—the CPU will sit there and cook itself dead, sometimes within minutes.

A constant concern for those who tinker with their PCs is static discharge. The electronics inside a PC are very delicate, and a simple static shock can be enough to fuse submicron circuitry and wipe out bits in solid-state memory, such as the BIOS.

In the case of the processor, the stakes can be very high. A brief moment of contact can lay waste to a brand-new CPU that cost hundreds or even thousands of dollars. For this reason, it's always advisable to use a static mat or other device that grounds both you and the PC when you're working inside the chassis.

Warning: Older buildings might lack grounded three-prong outlets. Be aware that your system must be properly grounded (via the round socket in the three-prong outlet) in order to avoid potentially catastrophic damage. If you do have a two-prong outlet, consult an electrician who can properly ground the wiring.

A similar situation can occur when too much voltage gets sent into the CPU. Unlike static discharge, this can occur due to user error or a power spike. Misaligning the cables to the power supply is one quick way to fry a system, as is plugging into an outlet of the wrong voltage. And even nonupgrades need to be concerned about power spikes. Lightning strikes are a common source of crippling power surges, although the power level can fluctuate for no apparent reason as well. Also make sure that the power leads to and from the power supply don't get reversed.

Tip: When electricity comes on after a blackout, it often spikes, posing a threat to your PC. If you have a power outage, it's a good idea to unplug your PC until the power is back up.

Troubleshooting: Fixing CPU Problems

When a CPU dies, it is dead. Still, you might be able to fix some scary problems. The following are classic symptoms of a dead or dying CPU:

- The system fails to boot
- The system boots, but the OS fails to load
- Erratic behavior and unexplained system crashes during startup or operation
- Error messages indicating parity errors and other problems
- The system locks up or dies after several minutes of operation

If you encounter these symptoms, you should consider the possibility that the CPU is the culprit. To check the problem, do the following:

1. Perform a visual inspection of the CPU. First, turn off the PC and open the case. Let the system sit for about 10 minutes or until the CPU is cool enough to touch.

2. Clear away any obstructing wires, cables, or bays. Check to see if any material was in direct contact with the CPU or its pins.

3. Check the heat sink and fan. Are the fan wires attached (if present)? Are the heat sink and fan properly secured to the CPU?

4. Boot up the PC with the case off. Watch the CPU fan for activity. If it doesn't rotate, the probable culprit is overheating due to a malfunctioning fan.

5. With the PC still running, place your hand near the CPU fan, and check for proper airflow. Do the same near the power supply to see if that fan is working. Check the chassis to see if any cables or other objects are blocking the air vents.

6. Turn off the PC. With your fingers, gently and evenly press along the edges of the chip. Notice if any movement occurs that might indicate that the CPU had come unseated.

Tip: If you think your PC is prone to overheating, check out a CPU temperature monitor. PC Power and Cooling's 110 Alert, shown in Figure 6.18, costs $22 and plugs into any spare drive connector, emitting an alarm when the temperature inside the chassis climbs above 110 degrees.

Figure 6.18.

For about $20, you can protect that $500 CPU. (Photo courtesy of PC Power and Cooling)

If everything seems in order, the problem might be with your system setup. Do the following:

1. Check your system documentation to ensure that the CPU clock jumpers are set properly for the speed and model of your processor.

2. Examine the CPU if possible. Check the silk screening on the top of the unit or the etched markings on the bottom. Does the indicated CPU speed match what you're supposed to have?

3. If possible, boot up your PC and enter the BIOS program. Look for any discrepancies in the CPU and system settings. Compare the settings against the factory defaults in your documentation.

You should also call technical support. Your system vendor might know about an issue with its PCs that could lead to apparent CPU failure.

Remember, these steps just cover CPU diagnostics. Several other problems can cause the same symptoms. Other areas to suspect are

- BIOS settings
- System RAM
- Power supply
- Graphics board and drivers
- Hard disk
- Operating system and drivers
- Virus infection

Peter's Principle: If the CPU is the Culprit, Consider
Where the Problem Came From

If you find that the CPU is the culprit, consider where the problem came from. For example, an unreliable power supply can nuke a CPU. Replace the processor without fixing the power supply, and your bad luck is likely to recur. Likewise, an overheating problem won't go away until you resolve problems such as dead CPU fans or blocked airflow.

In general, your best defense against CPU failure is prevention. Avoid overcrowding your PC's case or blocking air vents with books or papers. Also try not to jar the PC, because this can unseat the CPU or break the CPU fan.

Periodically clean out the inside of your system box with a soft brush or compressed air. Take special care to ensure that the air vents on the power supply aren't blocked by debris. That simple problem will eventually lead to overheating, followed by failure of the power supply, fan, or CPU.

Troubleshooting: You should be especially conscientious about cleaning your PC's insides if the system sits in an area with pets or where people smoke. Both tend to leave extra blocking matter in the PC's chassis. Also, if you system box sits on the floor, those vents tend to clog over time.

Also, be sure to act on problems swiftly. If you notice a lack of fan noise from your power supply or auxiliary CPU fan, make sure you replace the unit promptly to avoid overheating. If you notice problems cropping up soon after a power outage, a power spike might have damaged the CPU.

Summary

The past year has been a hectic one in the CPU market. Not long ago, Intel called all the shots, making routine price changes and rolling out new products at a measured pace. AMD and K6 are pushing the chip-making giant, leading to lower prices and faster product cycles.

Power users can look forward to a new level of performance from Intel's Pentium II CPU, which should continue to advance in speed and feature support over the next three years. As a case in point, Intel demonstrated in 1997 a Pentium II running at 450MHz—a clear indication that big things are ahead for this chip.

In the mainstream market, systems under $2,500 get multimedia-savvy MMX support and x86 performance that is significantly faster than that of 200MHz Pentium Classic PCs. AMD and Cyrix will both continue to push the envelope in the existing Socket 7 motherboard scheme. And even $1,500 bargain boxes can include advanced features such as MMX support and Pentium MMX-class performance.

Of course, the glut of CPUs makes choosing a system difficult to do. The processor introductions are starting to muddy the upgrade waters too, as first OverDrive MMX and soon K6- and M2-based upgrade products emerge.

Ultimately, the CPU is just one piece of the performance puzzle—albeit an important one. The motherboard bus, system RAM, and L2 cache all determine how quickly data can get to and from the CPU. If any of these poses a bottleneck, a fast CPU will simply sit idle while it waits for data to arrive from your system.

7

RAM

Peter Norton®

If the CPU is the heart of your PC, system RAM is its lifeblood. Adding RAM to an aging PC can infuse new life into demanding applications and provide a greater boost than either a CPU or graphics card upgrade. Without enough memory, your PC ends up spending too much time reading data from the hard disk and starving the CPU in the process.

This chapter introduces you to the silicon memory that is at the core of your PC's operation. It also shows you how to manage upgrades. You will learn the following:

- What system RAM is and how it works
- How to shop for RAM and make sure your new memory is compatible with your system
- How to recognize RAM-related problems and deal with them
- How to upgrade your system RAM

Overview

Simply put, the memory in your system makes all the compelling stuff possible. Rapid-fire CPU advancement and all the wonders of the Internet would mean little without the recent affordability of system memory. Cheap, plentiful RAM allows complex multimedia applications and robust, 32-bit operating systems such as Windows 95 and Windows NT to exist.

Just three years ago, a megabyte of RAM cost $40 to $60, limiting most systems to 8MB at the most. The tight supply put a noose around the PC industry and choked the life out of innovative software such as IBM's OS/2. Today, a megabyte of RAM costs less than $10, and most new PCs come with 32MB or even 64MB of RAM. The result is that many old systems are begging for an upgrade, and tough decisions need to be made on new PCs.

What Is RAM?

System memory is your PC's "scratch pad." Often called *dynamic random access memory*, or DRAM, system memory is the place where data and code that the PC is working on get stored.

Consider the analogy of an office desk. When you do your taxes, you probably clear the desk of other material, pull out your files, and spread tax forms, receipts, and other documents across the desktop. To make space for this mess, you put last week's vacation planning in the file cabinet.

Your PC uses RAM much like you use your desk. Things that are being worked on are placed in system memory, where the processor can reach them quickly. Your system assigns addresses to data, specifying exactly where in system RAM the specific bits can be found. Data that isn't being worked on gets sent back to the hard disk—the PC's version of your file cabinet—or deleted, making room for the work at hand.

Let's Get Physical

System memory is easy to spot, as shown in Figure 7.1. With your PC chassis removed, look at the motherboard and look for one or more low, thin cards sitting in rows (you will probably see some empty sockets as well). Measuring just over 4 inches long by ³/₄-inch high, the RAM modules include a number of small black chips mounted on the cards. These chips are the physical memory itself.

Figure 7.1.
RAM modules are easy to spot, laid out as they are in rows on the motherboard.
(Photo courtesy of Micronics Computers)

Inside these little black chips are thousands or millions of tiny transistors, which your PC uses to store information in the form of 0s and 1s. If a transistor has no voltage applied to it, your PC sees it as a 0. In contrast, if a transistor is charged, it is a 1. By stringing thousands of these voltage-induced 0s and 1s together, your PC—and, by extension, your operating system and software—can manipulate complex data and code.

Unlike a hard disk or CD-ROM, system memory is volatile—that is, the contents of RAM are lost when the system powers down. The reason is that system RAM must constantly be refreshed with electrical signals to prevent the charge in the transistors from bleeding away (and setting everything to 0s). That's why even a brief disruption in power can result in the loss of all your working data.

The Speed Thing

If you've looked into getting a memory upgrade, you've probably seen cryptic references to the "speed" of the memory—often expressed as something like 70ns or 60ns. Actually, speed is the wrong word. What these numbers show is how quickly RAM can turn itself around (measured in nanoseconds, or billionths of a second). The faster the RAM, the more frequently it can be refreshed by your system—and the more frequently it can be updated or accessed.

Older systems frequently employ 70ns, 80ns, or even 100ns RAM, while newer Pentium-class PCs use RAM running at 60ns. Two things determine what speed of RAM your system can use—the speed of the current RAM installed, and the speed supported by your system chipset. You could buy fast 60ns RAM for that 486SX-25 machine in your office, but the chipset that plays traffic cop will strictly enforce a 100ns speed limit. You'll be wasting your money on that fast memory.

Tip: Have you lost your system manuals? You can usually glean the rated speed of your RAM by reading the silk screen on the top of the chips. (Figure 7.2 shows silk-screened codes on memory chips.) Look for a dash followed by a number. –7 indicates 70ns RAM, –6 is 60ns, and so on. If you see a –10 or –12, you have a relic—that's dog-slow 100ns or 120ns RAM.

As a general rule, installing faster memory than what is expected by the system won't improve performance. If your PC is designed to handle 60ns memory modules, installing 50ns modules won't improve things. More important, installing slower memory can actually hang your PC, because the memory won't be able to return data at the expected rate.

Plug In and Turn On

Life isn't simple, and neither is RAM. There are several variations of system RAM, all of which are important to know about if you want to perform an upgrade. First, RAM usually comes in a standard format, allowing you to plug new memory into sockets on the motherboard. There are two types of memory modules you need to worry about:

- Single inline memory modules
- Dual inline memory modules

Most upgraders will probably encounter SIMMs, which have been widely used in PCs for years and which remain popular today. These modules feature either 30 or 72 connector pins with individual RAM chips mounted on either side of the card. You'll find the shorter 30-pin SIMMs in 386 and old 486 PCs, while newer 486 and later machines employ the 72-pin variety.

Technical Note: SIMMs plug into motherboard sockets, which are organized in banks. A *bank* is the number of sockets needed to correspond to the CPU's bus width. So the 32-bit RAM SIMMs on a 64-bit Pentium motherboard are organized in banks consisting of two sockets each. By the same token, each 64-bit DIMM socket constitutes a bank, because its data width matches that of the 64-bit external Pentium bus. On 486 or 386 systems that have 32-bit buses, a single 32-bit SIMM does the job.

Figure 7.2.
Memory speed can often be gleaned from the silk screening on the top of RAM chips. (Figure courtesy of Kingston Memory)

MANUFACTURER	SAMPLE DRAM PART NUMBER
Fujitsu	MB 814400-80L $\overline{F}$ 9445 T14
Hitachi	KOREA A107 9516 FFF HM5116100AS7
Micron	9512 C USA MT4C4007JDJ -6
Mitsubishi	M5M44100AJ 222SB29-7
Motorola	MCMSL4800AJ70 TQQKX9236
NEC	NEC JAPAN D4216160G5 -70-7JF 943LV200
Samsung	SEC KOREA 522V KM44C4100AK-6
Toshiba	TOSHIBA TCS514100AFTL-70 JAPAN 9409HCK

30-pin SIMMs fell out of favor because they lack capacity and performance: The fewer pins on the module limit the number of bits that the system can move in and out of the SIMM at any one time. Most 30-pin SIMMs feature capacities of 4MB and less. 72-pin SIMMs offer capacities as high as 32MB per module.

For example, to install 40MB of RAM into a Pentium system, you would need to pair two 16MB modules (called 2×16MB) and two 4MB modules (2×4MB) to total 40MB. No matter what the memory size, all RAM must be installed into banks in pairs.

Tip: You can tell if your system uses 30-pin or 72-pin SIMMs by measuring the length of the modules. 72-pin SIMMs are $4^1/4$ inches long across the top, while 30-pin versions are shorter, measuring just over $3^1/2$ inches. Some SIMMs also put an indicator number (either 30 or 72) next to the pins themselves.

New to the scene are DIMMs, which feature a wider 168-pin connection for improved performance and higher capacities. Most DIMMs also run at 3.3 volts, versus 5 volts for many SIMMs, to match the lower-voltage operation of Pentium II motherboards. You can find DIMMs that put 64MB of memory on a single module. Unlike 72-pin SIMMs, they can be installed singly. The reason is that DIMMs provide a 64-bit data path that equals the bit width of a single memory bank—a perfect fit for Pentium and faster CPUs. DIMMs began showing up in PCs in 1996, when PC makers introduced a new memory variant called *synchronous DRAM (SDRAM)* in Pentium-class PCs. Expect the entire PC market to move toward DIMM designs as new memory types are adopted.

You can recognize DIMM sockets from their greater length and more numerous electrical leads, as shown in Figure 7.3. DIMMs themselves are also longer than SIMMs and usually pack RAM on both sides of the module board. Many Pentium MMX motherboards provide both DIMM and SIMM sockets as manufacturers transition to the new SDRAM technology.

Figure 7.3.
Many Pentium MMX and Pentium II motherboards, such as the Micronics Stingray motherboard shown here, provide sockets for both SIMMs and DIMMs. (Photo courtesy of Micronics Computers)

Not all standard DIMMs and SIMMs are identical. Some use gold-plated connectors, and others use tin-plated connectors. The main difference is cost. Tin connectors save precious pennies of manufacturing cost, which add up when you talk about tens of millions of units annually. But they lack the higher conductivity and reliability of gold.

As a rule of thumb for upgrades, you should try to match the lead material with that in your PC. Check your documentation and also the original memory that shipped in the system. If the leads are silver in color, make sure you buy RAM with tin connectors; if they are gold, get gold connectors. This will avoid possible corrosion, which can lead to system crashes.

Parity and Other Religious Wars

But wait—there's more. Even if you match the speed, module format, and connector material, you have to worry about something called *parity*. When it comes to RAM, there are two schools of thought: Data security nuts want system RAM to constantly check itself for errors, and cheapskates don't want to pay for extra diagnostic chips. Don't laugh—people get upset over this stuff.

Parity RAM is PC memory that checks on itself to detect errors, using extra chips to keep count of bits. In this scheme, a ninth bit is added to every set of 8 bits (1 byte) with the sole purpose of checking up on the others. The ninth bit would perform an operation called a *checksum* to make sure that its addition matched up with the contents of the 8 bits. If the checksum failed, the system would know right away that something was amiss, before bad data got written back to the hard disk.

Parity has two disadvantages: One, it costs money, and two, it rarely gets used. To make a 16MB RAM SIMM with parity, a manufacturer must produce 18MB of capacity. This means that users must pay for an extra 2MB of memory—equal to almost 15 percent of the 16MB capacity. Today, 16MB of RAM SIMM with parity costs about $130, compared to $100 for the same RAM without parity.

The main reason why many PCs lack parity is because RAM errors rarely occur. Most PCs will never experience a noticeable problem with system memory, and if they do, the error is often perceived as a software glitch. Given that most users don't see RAM errors—or misdiagnose them when they do happen— it's not surprising that folks don't want to pay for a parity-checking feature.

Intel played a key role in making nonparity memory prevalent when its chipsets for mainstream PCs dropped parity support. On such a system, parity memory behaves exactly like nonparity RAM: The system simply ignores the ninth bit and the extra $20 you spent for it. Memory makers, anxious to trim costs and boost their manufacturing capacities, quickly moved to nonparity designs. Of course, parity remains a necessity for servers and other critical applications.

New Pentium and Pentium Pro motherboards now boast enhanced data protection, using error-correcting code (ECC) memory. This memory can actually fix corrupt data, allowing operation to continue when a parity SIMM would simply return the location of the error. ECC memory costs more than parity memory and runs more slowly, but the enhanced protection is excellent for critical applications such as network servers. Support for the new memory is enabled by Intel's latest Pentium II chipset—the 440LX.

Warning: Be careful! Parity memory will work in a nonparity system, but the reverse is not true. A system that requires parity memory will not recognize nonparity memory. If your system chipset employs parity checking, be sure to buy memory with parity.

Keeping Up with the New RAM

Not long ago, there was only one flavor of system RAM—basic fast page mode (FPM) DRAM. Those days are gone. With processor speeds pushing 300 MHz, more efficient memory types are needed to keep pace. The result is an explosion of exotic memory designs. Of course, older systems won't recognize the new memory schemes, so you should purchase the type of memory documented in your PC's manuals.

If you're purchasing a new system, take note. The type of system RAM can significantly affect performance. Upgraders, meanwhile, need to gauge whether these new memory schemes make buying a new PC a better option than upgrading the existing system.

The following system memory technologies exist:

- Fast paging mode DRAM (standard DRAM)
- Extended data out DRAM (EDO DRAM)
- Synchronous DRAM (SDRAM)

Fast Paging Mode (FPM) DRAM

FPM DRAM has been around for years, but it has largely been replaced by faster EDO DRAM. Like EDO, FPM DRAM comes mounted on SIMMs. FPM DRAM gets its name from the paging scheme it employs. The memory gets broken down into a series of pages up to several kilobytes in size. Once the system accesses data within a page, subsequent accesses inside that page happen without delay.

The scheme works by first addressing the row of memory to be accessed and taking the first column address to pinpoint the address. Data in sequential columns along the selected row is accessed without wait states. If the next access occurs in a different row, a significant delay occurs while the new row is accessed and set up for multiple column reads.

Extended Data Out (EDO) DRAM

EDO DRAM became prevalent in 1994 as clock-multiplied 486 and fast Pentium CPUs started to outpace memory speeds. EDO DRAM adds circuitry to speed subsequent reads by optimizing the timing of accesses. The memory can be set up for a new access even as a read is already in progress.

EDO DRAM takes just two clock ticks to perform subsequent read operations, versus three ticks for FPM DRAM.

Overall, EDO DRAM performance generally enjoys about a 5 to 10 percent advantage over FPM DRAM of the same rating. However, your system's chipset and BIOS must be EDO-aware in order to work with it.

Performance: If you upgrade a system that has an EDO-aware chipset but that contains FPM DRAM, consider dumping the old memory in favor of EDO DRAM. Not only will you get the benefit of additional memory, but you'll see improved performance as well. And although Intel chipsets can recognize different memory types, system vendors don't generally test their designs using mixed memory, which might invite unanticipated problems.

There is a variation on EDO DRAM called Burst EDO (BEDO) DRAM that further boosts performance. BEDO DRAM doesn't require an address for every address point. Instead, it requires only the first address point and the length of the read, and then it sends everything in between in a single data stream. This scheme allows sequential data to move out of memory at a rate of one operation per clock tick.

Both EDO DRAM and BEDO DRAM are limited by the speed of the system bus. Neither memory architecture works beyond 66 MHz. With Intel setting its sights on a 100 MHz system bus down the road, memory makers are moving toward other options.

Synchronous DRAM

Synchronous DRAM employs the same bursting technique found in BEDO DRAM, but it adds the ability to run in synch with a 100 MHz system bus and CPU. By synchronizing with the system clock, SDRAM enjoys faster and more efficient operation with the system bus and CPU. Expect SDRAM to provide a 5 to 10 percent performance boost over EDO DRAM, depending on the application involved and the size of the L2 cache.

Unlike earlier RAM types, SDRAM comes in DIMM format, which provides a 64-bit data width that matches Pentium and faster PCs. Today, SDRAM is found in most Pentium, Pentium MMX, and Pentium II systems. Some Pentium Pro PCs still use EDO DRAM, because their chipsets don't support SDRAM.

Buying Tip: If you're buying a new SDRAM system, watch out. Motherboards based on Intel's 430TX chipset can't provide L2 cache support for any more than 64MB of SDRAM, which makes upgrades beyond this point unadvisable.

Table 7.1 shows the enhanced efficiency of burst-mode memory designs used by SDRAM and BEDO DRAM in a 66MHz motherboard. As you can see, all these memory types take five clock ticks to find and return the first bit of data requested. However, the time to gather subsequent bits drops from three clock ticks per bit to just one clock tick per bit—a 300 percent improvement!

Table 7.1. Slow out of the block.

Memory Type	First Bit	Second Bit	Third Bit	Fourth Bit
FPM DRAM	7	3	3	3
EDO DRAM	6	2	2	2
BEDO DRAM	6	1	1	1
SDRAM	6	1	1	1

Shopping for SIMMs (and DIMMs)

Once you've tackled compatibility questions—such as what type of memory will work in the system—buying RAM is fairly straightforward. You can take your business to a local retail store, such as CompUSA or Office Depot, or a local computer repair shop. You can also purchase memory via mail order, whether from large firms such as Micron Technology or small memory brokers that often advertise in the classified sections of many computer magazines. Of course, many system vendors sell RAM module upgrades for their PCs as well.

One option you might be considering is buying secondhand or used RAM from a small computer dealer or even a friend. Although RAM, being solid-state, is immune to the kind of wear and tear associated with moving components, don't jump into this trap too quickly. Over the life of a computer, system RAM is exposed to the cumulative electrical and thermal stress of thousands of hours of operation. Over time, this can cause circuits to fail, resulting in intermittent errors that occur only after hours of operation. Given that memory costs less than $10 per megabyte, the risk is high for relatively small savings.

Warning: Because memory is small, valuable, and hard to trace, there exists a healthy black market for stolen memory products. Unscrupulous mail order vendors who deal in stolen goods often rip off consumers by shipping substandard DRAM or products that are rated slower than what you ordered. You should try to verify the legitimacy of an unfamiliar mail order broker before you buy.

More than any other PC component, RAM is a true commodity. As such, its price and availability can fluctuate like pork belly futures on the Chicago Board of Trade. In less than a year, the once-lucrative RAM market collapsed, as prices tumbled from over $50 per megabyte to as low as $5. Things stabilized in 1997, and RAM prices have settled down to about $10 to $15 per megabyte. However, moves to higher-capacity chips, lower-voltage operation, and new memory types will likely push prices up again.

If you want to get the best deal on RAM, keep your ear to the ground. If you hear of upcoming price hikes, it might be worth your while to move forward with a RAM upgrade sooner rather than later.

The Checklist

With so many variations of RAM available, it's important to know exactly what you need. The following checklist guides you through all the variables present in standard memory products. Use your PC's documentation and a little observation to ensure that you get RAM that is compatible with your system.

Characteristic
SIMMs or DIMMs
30-pin or 72-pin SIMMs
FPM, EDO, or SDRAM
Parity or nonparity
Rated speed
3.3-volt or 5-volt
Gold or tin connectors

Most of these items should be apparent from your system documentation. If you've lost your documentation, the following sections will help you identify the RAM you currently have installed.

SIMMs or DIMMs

As a general rule, systems with FPM or EDO DRAM use SIMMs, and those with SDRAM employ DIMMs. Your PC's documentation will specify which type of memory you have.

Although DIMMs and SIMMs look quite similar, you can distinguish DIMMs by their slightly greater length and more tightly spaced contacts. If you're still unsure of your memory type, remove one of the modules and bring it to your retailer for examination. That person will make sure that they match your existing memory.

30-Pin or 72-Pin SIMM

The visual clue is the length of the SIMM. 72-pin SIMMs are about 20 percent longer than 30-pin SIMMs and also feature more tightly spaced connector leads. If you own a Pentium PC, it's very unlikely that your memory is of the 30-pin variety.

FPM, EDO, or SDRAM

You'll need your system documentation to be sure, but you can also check your system BIOS to find out whether you have FPM, EDO, or SDRAM. During boot-up, press your PC's BIOS key combination and look for the entry memory type.

Parity or Nonparity

Look closely at the memory chips on the module. Telltale signs of a parity SIMM or DIMM include the following:

- An odd number of chips mounted on the SIMM or DIMM
- Larger memory chips accompanied by one or two smaller chips (these are the parity chips)

You can also check to see if your BIOS is set for parity operation.

Rated Speed

Most RAM chips display the nanosecond response time of memory on the top of the chip. Look for a dash followed by a number on the chip's silk screening. For example, –7 indicates 70ns RAM, and –6 indicates 60ns RAM. Remember, it's OK to match faster RAM with slower chips in your system, but not the other way around. Buy no slower than what you own now. The exception is newer SDRAM memory, which is typically rated in MHz on the chip. A marking of –10, for example, indicates an SDRAM chip running at 100 MHz.

3.3-Volt or 5-Volt

This is an important consideration, because using the wrong voltage will result in a fried memory module (and no, your warranty probably won't cover it). System makers began to employ 3.3-volt components with the introduction of second-generation Pentium PCs. If you own a 75 MHz Pentium or faster PC, look closely at your documentation to determine whether the memory operates at 3.3 volts.

Gold or Tin Connectors

It's not critical, but you should match the material used in your PC's SIMM or DIMM sockets. Look in an empty socket. If the leads are silver, you should buy memory with tin connectors. If the leads are gold, look for gold connectors for your modules. Matching materials can help extend the life of your memory.

Buyer Beware

System memory might be one of the most effective upgrades you can make, but it can also be among the most dangerous. And it's not because of compatibility concerns. The problem is that it's easy to get ripped off buying system RAM, particularly when you buy from mail-order companies offering cut-rate prices.

Buying Mail Order

Despite the potential dangers, there is good reason to buy mail order—cost savings. By ordering RAM from an out-of-state vendor, you can often avoid paying sales taxes, in some cases saving up to 8 or 9 percent of the total purchase. With SIMMs weighing just a few ounces, it is often much less expensive to pay for shipping than it is to pay sales tax.

Because memory brokers can operate with little or no inventory, unscrupulous dealers can shut down their operations and disappear before authorities can react. Dealers who lack inventories might also encounter lengthy delays in shipping products as they wait for affordable products matching your order to become available.

There are a few things you can do to protect yourself:

- Choose a mail-order company based on a personal recommendation from someone who has had a good experience in the past.
- Check with the local Better Business Bureau for complaints outstanding against the firm.
- Make sure the company offers a money-back guarantee so that you can return flawed memory with no questions asked. Also look for a warranty, if possible.
- When your memory arrives, inspect it closely. Do the chip markings look fresh and undoctored? Does the rated speed match that of your original order? If not, notify the vendor immediately.

Playing It Safe: Going Retail

If all this makes you too nervous, you can buy RAM from a local retailer. In addition to the security of being able to see the operation, you get a chance to inspect the memory before you take it home. If something does go wrong, you can always return to the store for a refund.

Another big plus is that you might be able to get the RAM tested at the store, using a device called a SIMM tester. This device will verify the memory type, speed, and parity support, as well as detect flaws in the chips and connectors.

Note: You probably won't be able to test brand-name memory sold in shrink-wrap packaging until after you've actually purchased the SIMMs. On the positive side, this memory might be easier to return under store and manufacturer policies.

Troubleshooting Memory

When it comes to problems with system memory, the news is both good and bad. The good news is that chronic memory failures are quite rare. What's more, these problems often occur in the first couple of days of use, which means that repairs can be made under warranty. The bad news is that when something goes wrong, it is very difficult to diagnose without outside intervention. More often than not, you'll end up replacing SIMMs that display flaws.

A number of things can cause RAM to fail:

- Corrosion or cracks in the connectors due to humidity and prolonged use
- Loss of contact between the SIMM and the socket due to repeated thermal expansion and contraction of components
- Failure of solid-state components due to overheating or normal thermal stress over time
- Damage caused by a power spike or a static discharge during installation
- Temporary errors due to external radiation or overheating

Your first and best defense against any RAM-related problem is to own a PC that employs parity-checked memory. As I explained earlier, parity memory employs an extra bit as a watchdog for each byte of memory. If the parity bit expects an odd value, but main memory returns an even value, the system BIOS knows that something is amiss.

Symptoms of Memory Trouble

How do you know something is wrong with RAM rather than the CPU, cache, or some other component? Quite often, you don't. But the nature of the failure can help you pinpoint the problem. The following symptoms might indicate a RAM failure:

- Text-only parity error messages that halt system operation (on parity-equipped PCs only)
- Error message or lock-up during POST (Power On Self Test)
- Seemingly random system lock-ups or reboots
- The system fails to boot successfully and can't be booted from a floppy disk
- Lost or corrupted data, including corrupted executable files or a corrupted operating system

In fact, because memory sits at the core of nearly every transaction made inside the PC, problems with system memory can crop up anywhere. They can also vary in their character, persistence, and consistency. For example, if a certain area high in the memory space is corrupt, you might not encounter symptoms until programs and files manage to occupy all the system memory. These kinds of variables make some memory problems difficult to diagnose.

Making Sense of Parity Error Messages

If your system has parity checking and a memory problem occurs, you will generally see a message that says something like

```
Memory parity interrupt at [address]
```

When a parity error occurs, a special BIOS interrupt is invoked that halts system operation. In some cases, the CPU might be halted, forcing the user to cold-boot the system. Other systems might allow the user to either reboot the system or resume operation with parity checking disabled.

Not only does parity checking provide an immediate warning of memory problems, it helps pinpoint the source of the flaw. Because the message provides address information in segment:offset format, you can take note of whether the problem occurs in a single place or happens in different places.

Tip: If you get a parity error message, write down any memory address information that appears. If the problem occurs again, you will be able to tell if a certain area of memory is having trouble. Once you know that, you might be able to isolate which SIMM is having a problem by selectively removing SIMMs and seeing when the error disappears.

Isolating Memory Problems Without Parity

If you don't have parity-checked memory, getting to the bottom of a persistent memory flaw might be more difficult. If you notice unexplained failures, start observing. Take note of what sequence of actions causes the problem, and try to recreate it. Once you isolate the actions that cause a memory error, do the following:

1. Shut down your system.
2. If you haven't already, try reseating the SIMMs and boot the computer. Retrace the steps that lead to the RAM failure.
3. If the failure persists, shut down the system again.
4. Remove two SIMMs and swap their positions. Restart the machine and retrace your steps.
5. If the problem recurs as before, shut down the machine.

6. If your machine has only one pair of SIMMs, the problem is probably with the SIMM socket, not with the RAM itself.

7. If there is a second pair of RAM SIMMs, remove one pair and restart the system. Retrace your steps as before.

8. If the error doesn't recur, the problem is probably with the module you removed. If the problem recurs, try repeating this process, but with one of the other modules. If the problem persists, one of the SIMM sockets might be flawed.

Note: If you suspect a memory problem is locking up the memory exam routine during boot-up, try swapping the memory as just described. Then see if the point of failure changes. If it does, you've isolated the problem to one of the two SIMMs. A little more swapping might help you narrow it down to a single module.

If you narrow down the behavior to one of your SIMMs, take the chip to a computer store for testing (actually, you should take all your SIMMs in for testing, regardless) and replace it with a SIMM of the same type and speed. If the problem seems to be with your SIMM sockets, you might be facing a motherboard replacement.

Upgrade Signs

As bad as a memory failure might be, eventually you might find yourself facing an even greater enemy—obsolescence. Applications and operating systems get larger each year. In 1995, when Windows 95 first came out, most people said you needed at least 8MB and preferably 16MB. Today, the bare minimum is 16MB, but 32MB is better for anyone who multitasks two or more applications.

One thing is for sure: When your system needs more memory, it will let you know. Here are a few telltale signs of a system needing a memory upgrade:

• Constant disk activity, particularly when you're running fewer than three applications

• Slow performance, particularly when you're switching between applications or opening large files

• Sluggish screen updates

There are tools that help you track how much memory your applications and files are using. These utilities—including some that are part of Windows 95 itself—can help you determine exactly how much memory you should invest.

Windows 95 Memory Utilities

Your system makes it easy to determine how much physical memory you have installed. Information about your system's memory can be found at the following:

- The Power On Self Test (POST) memory diagnostic
- The Windows 95 System Properties sheet
- The DOS-based MEM utility
- The Windows 95 System Monitor utility
- The Microsoft System Info applet, which comes with Microsoft Office and Microsoft Windows 98

Any of these facilities can tell you how much memory is installed in your system, but they won't tell you what kind of memory it is or how fast it runs. For that kind of information, you'll need your documentation or the ability to decipher the cryptic numbering found on RAM SIMMs and DIMMs.

- POST: The most reliable way to determine the amount of memory is to simply watch your display during boot-up. As part of the POST routine, the BIOS checks system memory, counting the number of kilobytes in your system. If you have 16MB of RAM, for example, the POST will report that you have 16,384KB of memory. A 32MB system will report 32,768KB. On some machines, you might see the memory split into conventional memory (640KB) and extended memory (the remaining amount).

- System Properties sheet: If you have Windows 95 running, you can find the installed RAM amount displayed in the System Properties sheet, as shown in Figure 7.4. To view it, right-click the My Computer icon and select Properties. You will see the RAM amount displayed under both the General and Performance tabs.

Figure 7.4.
The Windows 95 System Properties sheet states the memory amount up front.

- Microsoft System Info: If you're running Microsoft Office 95 or 97, you can find the RAM amount displayed in the application's Microsoft System Info dialog box. To access it, select Help | About *Application Name*, and click the System Info button.

- MEM.EXE program: This one is familiar to DOS users. In Windows 95, click the Start button, select Run, and type mem in the Open text box in the Run dialog box. A DOS box will appear, displaying the standard text-based MEM utility output. In addition to displaying the total memory found in the system, MEM reports how much memory is available below 640KB—the once-critical area known as conventional memory.

  Despite its 16-bit history, MEM remains very useful for people who run resource-intensive DOS-based software on Windows 95 machines. Game players in particular need to scrounge up conventional memory for high-performance flight simulations and other DOS games, although any DOS-based application will need access to conventional memory.

- Windows 95 System Monitor: This little applet can be found under the Start menu. Select Programs | Accessories | System Tools | System Monitor. Actually, System Monitor does a lot more than snoop memory. It tracks everything from processor usage to network data packets to file accesses (see Figure 7.5).

Figure 7.5.
Don't be fooled by the lack of free memory reported by System Monitor. Even if you have just one application open, Windows 95 will horde all the RAM space it can to provide disk caching and other performance-boosting services.

If System Monitor doesn't appear on your Start menu, you can install it by running Add/Remove Programs from the Windows 95 Control Panel. First, make sure your original Windows 95 CD-ROM is in the drive. In the Add/Remove Programs Properties dialog box, choose the Windows Setup tab and select Accessories from the list in the Components box. Click the Details button, and in the Accessories dialog box, scroll through the Components list box until you reach the entry for System Monitor. Make sure that the check box on the left is checked, and click OK. Click OK again, and Windows 95 will begin installing the utility.

Third-Party Memory Utilities

A number of utilities address system memory. The most popular programs are called *RAM doublers* or *RAM enhancers*. Although these utilities played an important role under the memory limitations of DOS and Windows 3.1, the 32-bit memory scheme of Windows 95 removes much of the reason for these utilities.

What's more, the precipitous drop in RAM prices makes it more economical to buy new RAM than to purchase a software package that tries to extend your current memory. These utilities use compression techniques and other tricks to make your existing RAM look larger than it is. However, the processing and resource overhead involved can actually slow system performance. Compatibility problems aren't unheard of, either.

Although I don't recommend memory-enhancing utilities, diagnostic packages can offer valuable services for users trying to determine how much memory their applications need. Programs such as Symantec's Norton Utilities and Connectix's Agent 97 give you detailed information about memory usage, virtual memory, and all other aspects of system performance.

You can also find useful third-party utilities on the World Wide Web. For instance, Tessler's Nifty Tools' SuperMonitor program snoops your system to provide snapshots of memory consumption while you work. Much like Windows 95's System Monitor, it lets you see various aspects of memory usage. You can find this program at `http://ourworld.compuserve.com/homepages/nifty_tools/tnt.htm`.

Upgrading

So the plaintive thrashing of your hard disk has finally convinced you that it's time for a RAM upgrade. How do you go about it? The following sections show you.

How Much RAM Is Enough?

Before you buy new memory, you should look at your needs and your system's setup. RAM is cheap these days, but some combinations of SIMMs might force you to throw out your system's existing memory. For this reason, you should tailor your upgrade to both your applications and your motherboard.

Weighing Applications

First, you should determine what your needs are. If you have a Windows 95 system with 8MB of RAM, it's likely that almost any upgrade will feel like a huge improvement. Likewise, someone using large databases or multimedia applications will notice immediate improvements going from 16MB to 32MB.

So how much memory do you need? As much as possible, really. The reason is that your computing usage will probably adjust to the upgraded configuration. After an upgrade, you will feel comfortable multitasking more programs or keeping a Web browser or other application fired up all day, whereas in the past you would have shut the application down.

Software developers from Redmond to Boston are scheming to make even a hearty RAM upgrade obsolete. Microsoft talked everyone's ear off about how Windows 95 could run comfortably in 8MB of RAM (not true, by the way), yet today the company's Internet Explorer Web browser (bundled with Windows 95) needs 12MB just to load. Lotus Notes, meanwhile, chokes on anything less than 16MB.

The fact is, low RAM prices and the flat 32-bit memory model of Windows 95 and Windows NT have unleashed the memory hogs. There is a stampede of fat code (redolent with complex features), interactive help, and animated widgets that make conservative upgrade estimates look foolish.

So how much do you really need? Table 7.2 provides low and high RAM estimates for specific application profiles.

Table 7.2. RAM requirements by usage.

Usage Type	Low End	High End	Examples
Light office use	8MB	16MB	Minimal multitasking: word processing, e-mail, some Web browsing
Light home use	16MB	32MB	Minimal multitasking: e-mail, home finance software, some Web browsing, some CD-ROM titles
Heavy office use	16MB	64MB	Multitasking four to six applications: word processing, spreadsheets, presentation software, e-mail, Web browsing, some database work
Heavy home use	32MB	64MB	Multitasking three or four applications: games, multimedia titles, heavy Web browsing, word processing, graphics design software
Design professional	64MB	256MB	Multitasking four to six applications: 3-D design and CAD software, database applications, imaging
Software developer	64MB	256MB	Multitasking four to six applications: software development tools, database applications

These figures are merely estimates. You should keep a close eye on your personal usage and your system's behavior to make decisions. Still, this table can at least help guide you in your purchase.

How Much Can Your Motherboard Handle?

The tricky part is making sure the additional RAM you buy will fit in your system configuration. Motherboards are designed to recognize specific combinations of memory in the SIMM sockets. So if you want to add 64MB of RAM to your system, for example, you need to think about what combination of RAM SIMMs adding up to 64MB will work in your motherboard. It's not hard to figure out. First,here are a few ground rules:

- SIMMs should be installed into a bank in pairs. (DIMMs, however, can be installed singly.)
- SIMM pairs often must be of the same capacity and preferably come from the same manufacturer. Sometimes, particularly with 30-pin SIMMs, a bank of four must be of the same capacity and come from the same supplier.
- Many motherboards require that the first two sockets (also known as bank 0) be occupied before you install SIMMs into the next two sockets (bank 1).

For example, the documentation for the Micronics M54Hi-Plus Pentium motherboard says that it can accept RAM SIMMs of 4MB, 8MB, 16MB, and 32MB capacities. Table 7.3 shows a chart from the M54Hi-Plus motherboard manual, which describes common memory configurations.

Table 7.3. Memory configurations for the Micronics M54Hi-Plus motherboard.

Memory	Bank 0	Bank 1
8MB	(2) 1MBx36	
16MB	(2) 1MBx36	(2) 1MBx36
16MB	(2) 2MBx36	
24MB	(2) 2MBx36	(2) 1MBx36
32MB	(2) 4MBx36	
32MB	(2) 2MBx36	(2) 2MBx36
40MB	(2) 4MBx36	(2) 1MBx36
48MB	(2) 4MBx36	(2) 2MBx36
64MB	(2) 8MBx36	
64MB	(2) 4MBx36	(2) 4MBx36
72MB	(2) 8MBx36	(2) 1MBx36
80MB	(2) 8MBx36	(2) 2MBx36

continues

Table 7.3. continued

Memory	Bank 0	Bank 1
96MB	(2) 8MBx36	(2) 4MBx36
128MB	(2) 8MBx36	(2) 8MBx36

As you can see, this motherboard—like that inside many Pentium-class systems—can accept up to 128MB of RAM. However, you might not be able to get there without first removing the installed SIMMs. To handle 128MB of RAM, most motherboards employ four 32MB SIMMs, or 64MB per bank.

The problem is that this configuration demands all four sockets. So if you currently have 32MB installed in your PC (16MB apiece in the two SIMM sockets that make up bank 0), you need to yank those two 16MB SIMMs and replace them with 32MB SIMMs.

This case is a bit extreme. After all, 128MB RAM configurations are the stuff of graphics workstations and network servers—but the same problem plays itself out at more reasonable levels. For example, a 486 with 8MB of RAM might have 1MB SIMMs in each of its eight sockets (4MB per bank). To move up to 16MB or 32MB, you will have to remove at least half, and possibly all, of the existing RAM to make room for higher-density SIMMs.

What You See Is What You Get

The easiest way to assess your personal upgrade situation is to pop the top and look inside. Look for parallel SIMM modules and possibly a few empty SIMM sockets as well. If all those sockets are filled, you will have to remove some memory to effect an upgrade.

Figuring out the capacity of the individual SIMMs can be tricky. You can try dividing the total amount of memory by the number of SIMMs, but this assumes that all the SIMMs are of the same capacity. You might also try inspecting the SIMMs themselves. Depending on where the modules are on the motherboard, you might need a flashlight or other light source to read the silk screening on the SIMM chips. You might even need to remove the SIMMs to view them. Ultimately, the best way to be sure is to remove a pair of SIMMs and see how much memory is reported when you boot up the machine.

Tip: A dental mirror can help you read component markings without having to pull them out of the motherboard. You can pick one up cheaply at most drug stores.

You can also check your system's documentation, which might specify the SIMM configuration. Also keep in mind that some motherboards include memory laid down on the board itself, in the form of DIPs or dual inline package.

Plugging In

This section gives you step-by-step instructions for installing new RAM SIMMs and DIMMs in your PC:

1. Attach yourself to a grounding mat or touch the PC's metal chassis. Turn off the PC and unplug it. Remove the case.

2. If necessary, remove the existing SIMMs. Press the tabs on the edges of the sockets away from the SIMM so that the SIMM falls forward.

3. If the SIMM doesn't fall forward, simply press the back of the module while continuing to press the tabs away from the module. Pull the SIMM vertically out of the socket and place it in an antistatic bag.

Tip: If the tabs give you trouble, you can use a pair of flathead screwdrivers to loosen their grip. Slide the heads between the tabs and the card, and gently press the tabs outward.

4. Repeat as necessary.

5. Install the first SIMM. Line up the notched bottom edge of the module with the notch in the SIMM socket, as shown in Figure 7.6.

Figure 7.6.
The pin notch is easy to spot on a SIMM. (Figure courtesy of Micronics Computers)

6. For SIMMs, insert the module into the sockets at a 45-degree angle. DIMMs are inserted straight into the slot.

7. Rotate the SIMM to an upright position until the card squeezes past the tabs and locks into place.

Warning: Take a moment to inspect the inserted SIMM, and make sure the connector is seated uniformly. A SIMM often might appear seated when it actually isn't. Make sure that the bottom edge of the SIMM module runs parallel to the socket. If you see any angle or deviation, you must reseat the SIMM.

8. Repeat until all the SIMMs are installed.

9. Remove all tools from the inside of the PC. Plug in the PC and boot the system. Watch the display closely to see how much RAM is recognized at boot-up.

10. If you hear two beeps during boot-up, try entering your CMOS setup utility and then exiting, saving the settings. Doing so will allow the CMOS to update itself to the new memory amount.

11. If everything seems in order, shut down the system and replace the case.

Summary

It would seem as though RAM should be an easy upgrade. But the wide variety of RAM speeds, technologies, and module combinations can make for a daunting purchase. Many new systems use SDRAM DIMMs, and older Pentium and 486 PCs use FPM or EDO DRAM in SIMM format. Before you decide what to buy, you need to check your system requirements closely.

The work is worth it. Without a doubt, system RAM is one of the most important ingredients for efficient performance. Regardless of the speed of the CPU, it takes adequate system RAM to keep bits flowing freely. And as operating systems and applications get bigger, expect the demand for system RAM to increase.

8

Secondary Cache: A Vital Helper

Peter Norton®

Today's microprocessors literally run too fast for the rest of your system. Since the introduction of the Pentium CPU in 1994, the clock rate of new chips has jumped from about 60 to 300MHz, a 500 percent increase. During that time, motherboard bus speed—which determines the rate of system RAM access—has been stuck at 66MHz. The quickness of system RAM, meanwhile, has improved marginally, from 70 or 80 nanoseconds to 50 or 60 nanoseconds.

The result is predictable: diminishing performance returns as CPU clock speeds increase. The problem is a recent one. Until the introduction of the 486DX2 CPU, all Intel processors ran at the same speed as the motherboard—in other words, they talked both to the system and to themselves at the same rate. But clock-doubled CPUs such as the 486DX2 delivered significant speed-ups by running internally at twice the speed of the external motherboard.

Today, processors run two to almost four times faster than the motherboard. To help the rest of the system catch up, motherboard makers such as Intel and Micronics began putting a small store of very fast memory between the CPU and RAM. Called *Level 2 (L2)* or *secondary cache*, this fast memory holds the most recently accessed data so that the CPU can make subsequent accesses from the fast cache rather than from slower memory. Today, L2 cache is present in virtually all Pentium-class PCs.

Note: A smaller and even faster cache is found inside most CPUs. It's called the *primary*, or *Level 1 (L1)*, cache.

This chapter will

- Help you understand what L2 cache is and how it affects system performance
- Show you how to buy and add L2 cache memory to an existing system
- Help you deal with possible cache-related problems

The Workings of Cache

The L2 cache in most Pentium and faster systems is made up of extremely fast silicon memory, called *static RAM* or *SRAM*. Running at blistering speeds of about 10 to 15 nanoseconds, SRAM is about six to eight times faster than main system memory. And unlike system memory, which must constantly receive electrical signals to keep data present, SRAM requires no refresh signal from the system, just power. This static design cuts down access times, resulting in much faster performance.

The memory chips themselves are broken into two sections: the main data cache chips and a single tag RAM cache chip. The tag RAM stores address information for bits residing in cache. These tag bits are used by the system to determine if and where needed data resides in the L2 cache.

Not surprisingly, SRAM is expensive—about 10 times more expensive, in fact, than common EDO DRAM SIMMs. Cost is one reason why L2 caches are generally quite small. Most Pentium Classic PCs feature 256KB cache memory, while Pentium MMX and Pentium II systems use somewhat larger 512KB cache pools. But older Pentiums, sold when RAM and cache memory were exceedingly expensive, might have used cache as small as 64KB or even no cache at all.

Note: Thinking about upgrading the cache on your Pentium Pro or Pentium II system? Think again. The two CPUs take different approaches to handling L2 cache, but both integrate SRAM memory into the chip packaging itself. The design optimizes performance but makes cache upgrades impossible. The only way to boost the cache is to replace the CPU or CPU module (in the case of Pentium II) with a version that has a larger cache.

What a Cache Can Do

How much does L2 cache help system performance? A lot, actually. Tests consistently show that a 256KB L2 cache can boost system performance by about 20 to 25 percent over that of a cacheless PC. And a smaller 128KB cache still delivers performance just a few percentage points shy of the larger 256KB pool.

The law of diminishing returns really goes to work after the 256KB level. Under Windows 95, doubling cache size to 512KB provides only an incremental performance boost, while moving up to an extra-large 1024KB cache fails to nudge performance higher at all.

At issue is the critical hit rate that these caches achieve. Sophisticated predictive algorithms and smart access schemes let your cache wait with the proper bits fully 95 percent of the time. That 95 percent hit rate means that your processor needs to reach into slow main memory only once every 20 transactions.

Caches can provide this efficiency because data access isn't random. Operations or data that have been accessed once will probably be called on again soon. Likewise, data located close to currently accessed bits has a good chance of being accessed in the near future. This predictable behavior makes it possible for cache to preload bits into fast SRAM memory before they're actually needed.

However, although a 256KB cache can achieve a 95 percent hit rate, doubling the cache yields a meager 1 percent or so improvement in efficiency. At this point, the cache has already covered most of the predictable accesses—the easy yardage has been gained.

Technical Note: If system performance doesn't benefit that much from adding L2 cache past 256KB, why do many new Pentium MMX and Pentium II PCs ship with 512KB standard? There are a couple of reasons. First, the larger cache helps keep hit rates high even as applications get bigger and more demanding. Second, some motherboards require 512KB of installed L2 cache in order to cache main memory in excess of 64MB.

Peter's Principle: Cache Is Critical

A system without L2 cache is not an option if you want reasonable performance. Some vendors sell bargain systems without L2 cache, reasoning that enhanced memories, such as EDO DRAM, provide enough performance for entry-level users. But even low-end PCs use 100 to 150MHz CPUs that run 2 to $2\frac{1}{2}$ times faster than the motherboard bus, making fast access to memory critical.

Clearly, any Pentium or faster system needs L2 cache in order to keep the processor from waiting around while data makes its way out of main memory. Look for at least 256KB of L2 cache in most Pentium models and 512KB in newer Pentium MMX- and Pentium II-based PCs. If a system you're considering lacks L2 cache, find out if it can be configured with at least a 256KB cache. Also, if you intend to use more than 64MB of RAM in your PC, you should consider going with a Pentium II PC using the Intel 440LX chipset, which can generally cache up to 512MB of RAM. Otherwise, any memory over 64MB will be uncached and therefore very slow.

The Hard Science Behind Cache Magic

Staying a step ahead of a processor that ticks 200 or 300 million times a second is no easy task. However, as I mentioned, the predictable nature of program code makes the concept of caching possible. Two rules come into play:

- If a bit has been accessed, it is likely to get accessed again soon.
- If a bit has been accessed, bits close to it are likely to be accessed.

Knowing this, cache designers can keep recently-accessed information in the L2 cache pool and access memory addresses around the specific address being called. This is simple enough, but more sophistication is needed to wring performance out of systems. That's because the cost of a *cache miss*, when data being called on is not found inside the cache, is very high. Not only must the CPU first check the L2 cache, but it must then get data from slow main memory, resulting in wait states.

There are two major caching schemes: write-through and write-back. Write-through caches can provide better performance by allowing new or changed data to be written to both the cache and to main memory simultaneously—the CPU doesn't have to take the extra step of writing to each separately. However, if there is much write traffic, the write-through scheme can actually tell the CPU to wait for the cache to empty before it can make further writes to main memory. Still, write-through keeps cache and memory in sync, eliminating the need for consistency checking. In most applications, it can boost performance 5 to 10 percent over that of write-back caches.

Technical Note: There are two types of cache schemes: direct-mapped and set-associative. The L2 cache is direct-mapped, which means that the system sees it as a single pool of memory. Set-associative designs, used for internal L1 caches, split the cache into segments. Each segment is called a *way*, so a four-way set-associative cache—a common L1 configuration—features four independent sections of memory.

Splitting up the cache allows a piece of data to exist in more than one location. Most L1 caches use a four-way design that breaks the cache memory pool into four segments. This speeds up access to frequently needed data, since it is less likely that data will be written over when new data is written into one of the cache segments.

You'll find two-way and four-way set-associative caches. The designation defines how finely the cache pool is broken down. The smaller the segments, the faster data can be found within them—but the more time that must be spent locating the proper segment. Today, most caches use a four-way set-associative design.

The Three Faces of L2 Cache

There are three kinds of L2 cache. Older asynchronous SRAM has been largely replaced by faster synchronous burst (sync-burst) and pipeline burst SRAM designs. Table 8.1 lists the cache types and their data output cycles, expressed in number of clock ticks.

Table 8.1. Both sync-burst and pipeline burst caches achieve optimal performance, completing one transaction per clock tick after the initial setup work is complete.

Cache Memory Type	Cycle Profile
Asynchronous SRAM	4-2-2-2
Synchronous SRAM	2-1-1-1
Pipeline burst SRAM	3-1-1-1

If you're considering an upgrade, you must determine whether your motherboard supports the cache type you want to use. See the section "Upgrading" for specific instructions.

Asynchronous SRAM

This cache generally operates at speeds of 20, 15, or 12 nanoseconds. The memory is called *asynchronous* because the processor must provide an address for each cache access and then wait while the cache delivers the requested data. This asynchronous operation can cause a faster processor (more than 33MHz externally) to sit idle while the information is retrieved.

The oldest and slowest cache type, asynchronous SRAM can be found in 386 and 486 systems.

Synchronous Burst SRAM

As its name implies, *synchronous burst SRAM* works in lock-step with the system clock to provide data to and accept data from the processor. By synchronizing with the clock, the SRAM eliminates the need for the processor to wait an undetermined amount of time for incoming bits.

Sync-burst SRAM uses an input buffer to store address requests, which allows the cache to receive orders even as it retrieves another piece of data for the processor—in effect, the cache does two things at once. Once the first bit in a set is retrieved, the cache can burst bits across the bus very quickly.

Although synchronous burst SRAM is the fastest cache scheme on buses operating at 66MHz and below, it's also the most expensive. For this reason, most mainstream systems don't use this scheme any longer. In addition, faster 75 and 100MHz bus speeds will outpace the ability of this cache type to deliver subsequent bits in a single clock tick.

Pipeline Burst SRAM

Affordable pipeline burst SRAM can be found in the L2 caches of most Pentium-level systems. Like synchronous burst SRAM, pipeline burst SRAM bursts data across the bus. This allows for single-clock tick access for subsequent data bits. However, pipeline burst cache adds an output buffer to hold outgoing data at the ready for the CPU. This scheme can speed data access of sequential bits, letting the cache provide one-cycle burst mode transfers on bus speeds higher than 66MHz.

Although the pipeline scheme allows for single-clock burst operation at up to 133MHz (twice the speed of sync-burst SRAM), filling the output buffer takes an extra clock tick. In other words, pipeline burst SRAM is generally slightly slower than sync-burst SRAM on current 66MHz motherboards.

Finding Cache on the Motherboard

Your system motherboard determines the cache type, form factor, and capacity. In fact, some motherboards might not allow an L2 cache upgrade at all. Older PCs have SRAM modules that are soldered directly onto the motherboard (as shown in Figure 8.1), while high-end Pentium Pro and Pentium II systems integrate the cache with the CPU. Even if your motherboard does feature socketed cache memory, the motherboard might not be able to accept any more than is already installed.

Figure 8.1.
The soldered cache chips on this motherboard make an L2 cache upgrade impossible.

Generally, cache comes in two forms:

- DIP modules, which are soldered directly to the motherboard
- Socketed edge-connected modules, which are plugged into a standard SIMM-like socket

If you have socketed cache memory, it probably conforms to a standard known as COAST, which stands for "cache on a stick" (cute, huh?). The COAST format defines cache SIMMs to a length of 4.35 inches wide by 1.14 inches high. This L2 cache mini-SIMM looks very much like your RAM SIMMs. You can distinguish it from RAM SIMMs because the module is usually shorter and contains fewer chips and is not laid next to other sockets or modules.

> **Troubleshooting:** Even if your system has an empty COAST socket, you might be out of luck. If L2 cache is soldered to the motherboard, you might not be able to add additional cache memory. Always check your motherboard documentation for specifics before attempting an upgrade.

Also like RAM SIMMs, a little observation can go a long way. If you see a COAST module in your PC, Table 8.2 will tell you what you probably have.

Table 8.2. When is more not better? If you see nine small chips on your cache SIMM, you probably have older (and slower) asynchronous cache memory.

What You See	What You've Got
Nine or more large chips	Asynchronous SRAM
Two big chips and one small chip on one side	256KB of sync-burst or pipeline burst SRAM
Two big chips on both sides plus a single small chip	512KB of sync-burst or pipeline burst SRAM
Two big chips and one small chip on one side with the number 64 silk screened on the chip	512KB of sync-burst or pipeline burst SRAM

Whether the SRAM chips are mounted on a COAST module or on the motherboard, you can glean important information by inspecting the chips. You should see the name of the SRAM manufacturer, such as Toshiba, Micron, or NEC, silk-screened on the top of the chips. You'll also see the usual jumble of part numbers.

More importantly, though, the memory speed might be displayed on the chips. As with DRAM chips, the speed (in nanoseconds) is often displayed with a dash followed by a one- or two-digit number. –20 and –2 both indicate a 20ns SRAM chip, while –1 and –10 indicate a faster 10ns SRAM.

Purchase Decisions

Buying an L2 cache upgrade is pretty simple. You can purchase COAST-format L2 cache upgrades from retail stores or from many memory brokers. You can also purchase cache memory from your system vendor. In fact, doing so might help ensure that your upgrade is successful, since the vendor can match the new SRAM with that required by your system.

Before you buy cache, you need to know the following:

- The amount of cache you can install
- The type of cache supported by the motherboard
- The speed of the SRAM (in nanoseconds)
- The speed of the tag RAM (in nanoseconds)

The amount is easy to find. Your motherboard documentation should tell you clearly. In general, most new motherboards for mainstream systems can accept up to 512KB of secondary cache, although some go as high as 1024KB. Older systems, on the other hand, might top out at 256KB or even less.

The type of cache refers to asynchronous, pipeline burst, or sync-burst. Again, you need to check your documentation for the exact type that your motherboard supports.

Buying Tip: You can do more than merely boost the amount of cache during an upgrade—you might be able to improve cache performance as well. If the original cache in the system is the asynchronous type, don't assume that you must buy asynchronous cache. Check your motherboard or system documentation. If it can accept a pipeline-burst cache, you can realize a nifty performance boost.

The last two points regarding speed are important. Most motherboards run at speeds of 60 or 66MHz. In order to work with these systems, the L2 cache SRAM must run at a minimum speed. Intel's 430TX chipset, for example, requires 10ns SRAM for 60MHz operation and 8.5ns SRAM for 66MHz operation. In both cases, the tag RAM must be 15ns. Don't buy L2 cache that runs any slower than the rate required by your motherboard.

Otherwise, when buying cache, you should follow the same guidelines you do when you buy RAM SIMMs and DIMMs. Like RAM, cache modules are small, valuable, and virtually untraceable. That makes these components good candidates for theft and resale by unscrupulous vendors. If you buy through a mail-order memory broker, you should make sure that the company has a good track record, whether by getting a personal reference or by calling the local Better Business Bureau.

For more on buying advice, see Chapter 7, "RAM."

Diagnosing/Troubleshooting

In most respects, you should regard L2 cache the same way you do system RAM. Together, L2 cache and RAM make up your PC's memory system, working in tandem to move data and code in and out of the CPU. They are also functionally very similar, which means that RAM and cache might suffer from some of the same problems.

Diagnosing L2 Cache Problems

If your L2 cache fails, you're probably suffering system-locking conflicts—much the way a memory error will stop a system cold. The following are possible indications of cache problems:

- Unexplained system crashes or lockups
- The system fails to boot, or it stalls during a POST routine
- Seemingly random data errors
- Unusually slow performance

Unfortunately, not many utilities can help you when it comes to L2 cache. The cache interacts with your PCs processor and main memory at the lowest level, well below the notice of the operating system or its applications. On Pentium systems, the chipset knows if a cache is present and how large it is. It then sets internal bits that the BIOS can read. On older 486 systems, jumpers are used to set cache information independent of the BIOS.

If during the POST test you see the message `System Cache Error - Cache Disabled`, the cache SIMM is probably bad. Although the PC will continue to run, it will do so without the benefit of L2 cache, affecting performance significantly. Although you can try the usual tricks, you might be looking at cache purchase.

You can use a low-level diagnostic program, such as AMIDiag 5.0, to check on your cache. AMIDiag 5.0 can be downloaded from the American Megatrends, Inc. Web site at `http://www.ami.com`.

If you're experiencing system lock-ups that don't seem related to RAM or other components, you can easily isolate the problem if it resides in COAST-format L2 cache. After you've encountered the symptom, do the following:

1. Shut down the machine, unplug the power supply, and remove the cover.
2. Making sure you're properly grounded, lift the L2 cache module from its socket. If the module won't budge, try getting it started by pulling up one edge slightly and then evening the second edge.
3. With the cache removed and placed in a safe location, plug your computer in and reboot.
4. If your PC uses manual settings for cache configuration, enter your computer's BIOS setup routine. Go to the section that controls cache settings and change the setting to `0` or `No Cache`.
5. Exit the BIOS setup environment, making sure to save changes.
6. Complete boot-up and use the computer normally.

If the problem fails to recur, you're probably experiencing trouble with the cache SIMM, or perhaps with the way it was seated. You should note whether you experience any noticeable degradation in performance after removing the L2 cache. If not, your cache might not have been working properly in the first place. If this is the case, replacing the module should result in a welcome 20 to 25 percent performance boost.

Troubleshooting Cache Problems

So you think your cache might be the culprit? Like RAM, the news is good and bad. If the cache memory modules themselves are bad, they're gone. There is simply no repairing 15ns static RAM chips.

The good news is that the problem could just require a software tweak or minor adjustment. Here are a couple of things your should try before heading out to buy a new cache module:

- Reseat the cache module: Press the module firmly into the COAST socket to make sure there is adequate contact between the pins.

- Check your BIOS: Go into the BIOS setting and try changing the cache settings. One possible culprit is that your BIOS is trying to conduct write-through cache operations when only write-back caching is supported.

- Check for overheating problems: If problems occur only after sustained use, make sure you have proper ventilation in the chassis and that no wires are impeding airflow around the cache SIMMs.

Upgrading

Although some of the dealings with L2 cache can be arcane, the actual process of upgrading is relatively straightforward. The main thing is to be patient. Cache SIMMs aren't rugged devices. You can snap a socket pin or card connector by trying to force a SIMM where it doesn't belong. If things don't seem to fit, back away, take a breath, and try again. Of course, you need to exercise the usual precautions against static discharge.

Follow these steps to upgrade your cache:

1. Make sure you are properly grounded. Shut off and unplug the PC. Remove the case.

2. Identify the L2 cache SIMM. It should be standing alone, close to the CPU.

3. With the thumb and forefinger of each hand, grasp the cache SIMM at the top at each end. Pull it straight up and out of the socket.

4. If the SIMM doesn't budge, try pulling one edge up a little first, followed by the other. Then try pulling straight out again.

5. Pull the cache SIMM clear of the socket, and put it in a safe place.

6. Grab the new cache SIMM and lower it into the case. Align the notched corner of the SIMM with the notched corner of the socket.

7. Fit the gold edge connectors into the socket and apply gentle pressure straight down. Ease the module into the socket until it's firmly seated.

8. Make sure you remove any tools or objects from the inside of the chassis. Plug in the computer and start the system.

9. Watch the boot process closely. Make note of any odd beeps or error messages.

Most newer systems automatically detect the new cache at boot-up. However, if you notice that performance doesn't improve, or if you don't trust that little black box of code to make the adjustment, dive into the BIOS setup application to make sure the change gets recorded.

You should be able to find the cache settings in the Advanced section of the BIOS utility. Make sure that cache operation is set to Enabled. If there is a choice to select between cache memory types—such as asynchronous and pipeline burst—select the one that matches your new cache module.

Summary

Cache in many ways acts as an extension of your system RAM, and it's part of the memory pool in your PC. For this reason, the problems and solutions for cache are similar to those applied to RAM.

The fact of the matter is that L2 cache might be an overlooked upgrade. In particular, entry-level PCs sold following the introduction of faster EDO DRAM suffer from a cache shortage. System vendors, seeking to shave $100 off their sales price, sold these machines with the claim that the enhanced performance of the EDO memory provided speed comparable to cached systems. Not true.

With CPUs getting faster, and system RAM failing to keep pace, the importance of L2 cache will continue to grow. Larger applications and more aggressive multitasking will drive the cache sweet spot from 256KB to 512KB. If your system is falling behind the performance curve, it might be time to give that L2 cache a long, hard look.

9

Power
Supplies
and UPSs

Peter Norton®

Personal computing is a funny thing. People get so tied up in clock speeds and standards wars that they lose sight of what makes it all possible—reliable power. After all, without juice, your Pentium II powerhouse is one very expensive doorstop.

The problem is that people pay too little attention to the electrical diet that their systems need to run effectively. Overtaxed circuits, old wiring, and even power-hogging neighbors can all pose problems that can lead to the early—and sometimes sudden—demise of your PC.

This chapter covers the issues related to PC power, including internal power supplies, uninterruptible power supplies (UPSs), and surge protectors. Here are some topics this chapter covers:

- The workings of electrical systems in PCs and what is needed to make sure a system stays healthy
- Coverage of external UPSs and surge protectors, as well as mobile computing issues such as battery technologies
- Buying a new power supply or peripheral
- Buying considerations with notebook systems
- Installing a power supply and power peripherals
- Troubleshooting power-related problems

Overview

Like a car's engine, your PC relies on a steady and reliable flow of fuel in order to operate. Everything from the CPU and hard disk to motherboard chipsets and RAM SIMMs requires a steady source of electricity. Unfortunately, reliable power can be elusive, particularly in older buildings. Everything from lightning strikes to air conditioners can disrupt the normal flow of power and pose a threat to both your data and your hardware.

Of course, PC makers know all this, and systems include basic protection against the power sags and surges that are common in day-to-day operation. Unfortunately, more severe electrical disruptions can and will overwhelm circuitry built into the PC's power supply and motherboard.

Trouble doesn't always come from the outside. Sometimes it's right under your nose. For example, consider your PC's power supply. The heart of your PC, the power supply is responsible for taking incoming current and turning it into the 5 volt or 3.3 volt stream that your PC's components are designed to handle. It must also be able to keep up with the power demands of peripherals, which can get pretty severe on decked-out machines.

Whether your PC's power supply is on the blink or has simply become outmatched by upgrades, you might need to consider a new unit.

When it comes to PCs, there are two general categories of power components:

- Power supplies
- External power maintenance and interdiction

A Peek at Power Supplies

PC power supplies aren't marvels of submicron engineering like CPUs, RAM SIMMs, and cache modules. Nor do they improve at an astronomical rate the way hard disk capacities and CD-ROM speeds have. No, power supplies are pretty boring.

There's just one thing: Without them, nothing else works.

Your PC's power supply is easy enough to spot after you remove the case. On most systems, the power supply is a large silver box fitted into one corner of the chassis (see Figure 9.1). A number of wires, bundled in groups of four, run to various cards and peripherals or, in some cases, just hang loose in the chassis. On the outside of the case, you'll notice a fan outlet and a three-prong plug that accepts a matching female adapter.

Figure 9.1.
Start at the CPU, take a right at the bus slots, and look for the big silver box—you can't miss it. Even specialty dual-power supplies like this one from PC Power and Cooling look alike. (Photo courtesy of PC Power and Cooling)

> **Note:** If you own a compact desktop system from a vendor such as Hewlett-Packard, Compaq, or IBM, it might use a custom-designed power supply. These supplies are designed to maximize usable space and, often, accessibility—but at the cost of standard design. Before you buy a new supply for any system, you need to look inside the case and verify its dimensions. Obviously, custom units need to be purchased directly from the vendor or its authorized dealers.

Power supplies might look alike, but they aren't (see Table 9.1). The biggest difference is output wattage. Most desktop PCs feature a power supply that can produce 200 to 250 watts of electricity.

Compact or slimline systems, however, typically use lower-rated supplies. Older systems also frequently use less-robust power plants.

Table 9.1. Typical power supplies for different PCs.

PC Type	Power Output
Slimline	100 to 150 watts
Standard desktop	150 to 200 watts
Minitower	150 to 250 watts
Full tower	250 to 300 watts

The main concern with any healthy power supply is that it be rated to handle the load being put on it. Add-in cards, additional disk drives, and other hardware upgrades all draw power from the system, placing a greater electrical load on the supply. On older PCs, or on compact models with slimline cases, this can mean that the supply lacks the horsepower to push additional devices along. At some point, your hardware upgrades will demand a power supply upgrade to make them work.

Warning: When buying a new PC, be sure to check the rated wattage of the power supplies. It isn't unheard of for vendors to put underpowered supplies in their systems in order to save money. Also, if you use SCSI devices, be prepared to beef up your supply. SCSI peripherals are among a system's biggest power hogs.

Probably the most noticeable feature of any power supply is its fan. On some less-expensive models, the fan is noticeable indeed. Fan noise—that constant hum coming from the back of your PC—can be quite distracting. Many power supply models are marketed specifically on their quiet operation.

PC97: Quiet operation is a target of the PC98 and Microsoft Simply Interactive PC (SIPC) specifications. The goal is to eliminate fan noise in order to make PCs a viable entertainment fixture—along with TVs and stereos. Obviously, the distracting whir of a PC fan doesn't cut it when you're trying to enjoy your favorite CD.

Fortunately, power supplies are inexpensive and easy to upgrade. If something goes wrong, you can effect a repair within a few minutes. Still, monkeying around with your PC's power source is serious business. If you run the wrong wires, you'll fry the motherboard, CPU, and other expensive components.

Surge Protection: The First Line of Defense

Power supplies might be simple devices, but they act as the interface between your PC and the electric company. That's no small task—running point when a lightning storm is raging outside, for example. Surge protectors act as armor, providing an enhanced level of protection against power surges and spikes.

These devices do their thing when an over-voltage hits the line. Most suppressors use a metal-oxide varistor (MOV), which clamps on the line and draws away excess energy. The over-voltage is sent to a ground wire to be dissipated, ensuring that your PC doesn't take the hit. More expensive units have additional circuitry to finesse their way through less-intense surges, as well as physical circuit breakers or fuses to cut the circuit entirely should a catastrophic surge hit.

If too much power hits a suppressor, your PC is at risk. Surge suppressors are rated as to the amount of energy—measured in joules—that they can withstand. Generally, you should look for a rating of at least 240 joules.

> **Warning:** Those cheap power strips you see advertised as surge protectors often lack even rudimentary protection. Their voltage ceilings might be very low, allowing even moderate surges to get past them and into your PC. What's more, they can be so slow to react that the damage is done to your hardware before the circuit is broken.

Some surge protectors also feature phone line inputs. These protect your modem and telephone from power surges that can occur over phone lines when a catastrophic event, such as a lightning strike, occurs. You can also find power panels that let you turn equipment on and off from a central location, as shown in Figure 9.2. Just be aware that these panels will disable useful features in newer PCs, such as wake-on-ring and wake-on-LAN.

Uninterruptible Power Supplies (UPSs)

The next step up the electrical food chain is the uninterruptible power supply (UPS). This device provides all the amenities of a good surge suppressor and adds features such as battery backup, power conditioning, and even monitoring and management software.

The biggest advantage of a UPS is that it lets you recover from even a complete blackout. Depending on the size and cost of a UPS unit, you can get about five to 10 minutes of battery-powered operation after a complete power failure—enough time to save your documents and shut down your system. In fact, some models even include software that automatically closes your applications and shuts down the system when the power goes out. A serial cable connection allows the UPS to tell the system to shut down.

Figure 9.2.
Monitor-base surge
protectors let you turn
devices on and off
from a central
location. (Photo
courtesy of American
Power Conversion)

In addition, many UPSs condition incoming power, letting you work unimpeded through summer brownouts, power sags, and other conditions that can result in mystery lock-ups and reboots. Although many of these problems wouldn't cause a system shutdown, the conditioning of line power reduces strain on the power supply and components, thereby extending the life of the PC.

The Juice

The most important feature of any UPS is its power rating. A UPS must be built to handle the load presented by your hardware. A $100 UPS box just can't meet the demands of a dual-processor Pentium II tower with a RAID disk array, CD-ROM jukebox, and 21-inch monitor.

The thing to look for is the UPS's voltage-ampere rating, or VA. Before you can buy a UPS, you need to determine the load your equipment will put on the unit. Although in theory you can try to add up all the power requirements of your PC's components, you are unlikely to get an accurate figure. Consider 250 VA a good low-end target (see Figure 9.3). Fully stocked multimedia Pentium MMX PCs will need a UPS with a VA rating of 350 or above.

Types of UPSs

There are three types of UPS products to choose from:

- Standby UPS
- Online UPS
- Line-interactive UPS

Figure 9.3.

With its compact design, modem jacks, and replaceable batteries, the APC Back-UPS Office is great for small offices. But its 250 VA rating won't do for big network servers. (Photo courtesy of American Power Conversion)

Standby UPS

The least-expensive UPS type, standby models provide battery backup and little else. The UPS is plugged into the outlet, and power flows straight through the UPS. If a blackout or major voltage sag occurs, the standby UPS's battery kicks in, providing power to the PC. During normal operation, a small amount of power is fed to the battery to keep it charged.

The drawback is that there is a slight delay while battery power comes on after a blackout. Although most new systems can handle the transition, older models might reboot. More of a concern is the fact that these models don't actively condition power. Power sags and surges might put wear and tear on your PC's power supply.

Online UPS

Online UPSs improve on things by actively managing the incoming power stream. Voltages are monitored and adjusted to meet the PC's parameter, a process called *line conditioning.* If voltages sag, the battery makes up the difference. Power runs directly into the battery and back out through an inverter, which converts DC power to AC format. This means that if power ever cuts off, the battery is already actively in the power stream. The result is a virtual elimination of transition time to battery power.

Online UPSs have their drawbacks, too. For one thing, active management and battery interdiction mean that these models produce a bit of heat and fan noise. You can also expect the UPS battery to have a shorter operating life than that of standby models. In addition, cheaper online UPSs lack a way to provide a pass-through; if the battery dies, the UPS will no longer run power to the PC. You're better off getting a more expensive model that includes a pass-through feature.

Despite these drawbacks, online UPSs are the best way to go. Although the advantage over standby models during an actual blackout is minor, their workaday line-conditioning service can help avoid cumulative trauma to your PC's power supply and components. If your power is particularly unreliable, an online UPS is a must.

Line-Interactive UPS

A recent hybrid innovation, line-interactive UPSs provide line-conditioning services without relying on battery power (see Figure 9.4). When voltages sag—a common occurrence—these products actually work to pull more energy out of the outlet. A small amount of juice is used to keep the battery charged.

Figure 9.4.
APC's Back-UPS Pro line uses line-interactive technology to maximize battery life while providing active line conditioning. (Photo courtesy of American Power Conversion)

Line-interactive UPSs are less expensive than their online siblings, yet they provide line conditioning without shortening battery life. However, you'll get more robust line conditioning from an online UPS—particularly in highly variable environments.

Other Features

Some UPSs have many bells and whistles—which is important for network administrators and other pros who need to make sure their mission-critical servers are working smoothly. Among the features you'll see are these:

- Line monitoring: Provides real-time data on incoming voltages, sine wave character, and other aspects. Also provides a power-flow history, which can be useful for tracking down intermittent problems.

- Battery power status: Lets the user know how long the estimated battery charge will last if there is a shutdown.

- Automatic shutdown: In the event of a blackout, the UPS closes all open applications and shuts down the PC. The device sends a signal to a software utility over a serial cable.

- Remote management: Allows network administrators to track and manage UPS activity over a network or modem, using standard SNMP (Simple Network Management Protocol) facilities.

- Pager and fax: Lets the UPS send a message to an administrator's beeper, fax, and e-mail.

Although these features are nice, most small-office or home users can probably do without them. However, for larger offices, these features represent an important set of tools in the administrator's troubleshooting arsenal.

Warning: In most cases, it is inadvisable to run your laser printer off a UPS. The extreme electrical load limits the ability of an affordable UPS to provide even five minutes of battery run time. What's more, laser printer data isn't irreplaceable. If a print job is killed because of a blackout, you can simply reprint the document later.

Also, if you have an ink jet printer connected to a UPS, be aware that these devices often have long shut-down routines in which the ink nozzles are cleaned. If you shut down your devices from the UPS switch, you'll kill this self-maintenance step.

A Word About Portables

When it comes to power, no one has more to worry about than the notebook PC owner. The batteries in these units can be capricious, losing life as they age. Depending on the notebook PC, batteries might last six hours or less than two.

There are two popular battery technologies on the market:

- Nickel metal-hydride (NiMH)
- Lithium ion (Li)

Of the two, lithium ion is much preferred. These batteries can provide 30 percent more charge (or greater) than NiMH batteries of the same size. Although supply constraints and engineering problems (remember Apple's burning PowerBook batteries?) slowed down the acceptance of lithium batteries, today you shouldn't buy a notebook without one. You will get longer battery life and much more reliable operation.

Tip: One of the biggest problems with nickel metal-hydride batteries is the so-called memory effect. If you have a battery that runs four hours at a charge, and you use it repeatedly for two hours and then charge it up again, the battery remembers the shorter cycle. Before long, it will run only two hours at a time. Your best protection is to run the battery all the way down before recharging it. Better yet, get a notebook with a lithium ion battery; these products don't suffer from memory problems.

For those who use their notebooks in hotels and want to protect them from power problems, there are even portable-oriented power-managing devices (see Figure 9.5).

Figure 9.5.
APC's SurgeArrest Notebook is a compact module that plugs directly into the outlet. It provides both power and modem surge protection. (Photo courtesy of American Power Conversion)

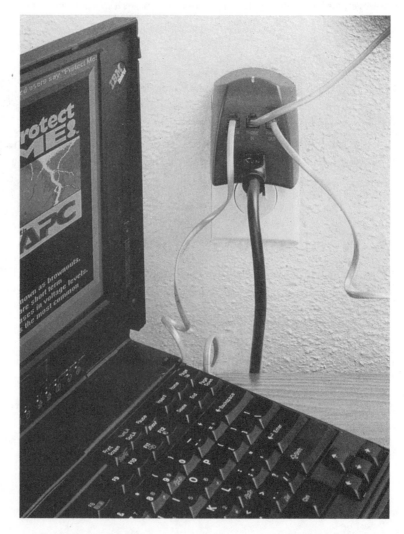

Buying a Juice Machine

Two purchases are covered here: Internal power supplies and external power protection devices. Both are equally critical, because they affect the performance of the rest of your PC. We'll deal with power supplies first.

Power to the PCs: Power Supplies

Power supply upgrades are a fairly frequent occurrence, so don't be surprised if you find yourself in the market for a new supply. Old supplies get dirty and gummed up or simply wear out after years of use and abuse. Overheating and chronic voltage sags can also bring the early demise of a power supply. And, of course, upgrades can leave your system with greater power needs than the original supply can handle.

How Much Is Enough?

Fortunately, supplies are cheap. Fifty bucks or so should get you a basic slimline power supply that can dish out about 230 watts of power—enough for a midrange desktop. That said, you're better off buying more power supply than you need. A supply that is running at or beyond capacity will produce excess heat and wear out quickly.

> **Warning:** Make sure you have enough power supply for your system. Overworked supplies produce excess heat and place unneeded thermal stress on every component inside your system. That puts expensive hard disks, CPUs, RAM, and CD-ROM drives at risk for failure or shortened operating life. It can also lead to lots of mysterious quirks such as frozen keyboards, data loss, and random reboots.

So how much power supply do you really need? As a general rule, you can estimate based on the case type of the PC. Compact systems draw a lot less power than big, rangy towers, simply because there aren't as many drives and add-in cards inside the system. Remember, external devices such as monitors, scanners, and printers can get their own power, so these usually won't factor into the supply purchase.

If the Shoe Fits

The other critical buying issue is size. Any power supply you purchase must fit into the existing space inside your PC. Before you order anything, take a close look at the power supply. Note its dimensions, measure it if you have to, and check to make sure a matching product is offered. Fortunately, the vast majority of supplies comply with a handful of size formats. Here are some of the standard sizes:

- Baby AT format: 8.35"×5.9"×5.9"
- Desktop format: 8.35"×5.5"×3.4"
- ATX or slimline format: 5.9"×5.5"×3.4"
- Tower format: 8.35"×5.9"×5.9"
- Custom format: Varies

If your machine uses a nonstandard power supply, you should contact the system vendor directly about a possible replacement. You must either purchase the supply from the vendor or get it from a third party. In either case, you will probably pay extra for the custom design.

Okay, so you've got enough juice, and the space is just right—but your work still isn't done. People often buy new power supplies in order to get away from distracting fan noise. Many companies market quiet power supplies, which might add $20 or more to the cost of a standard power supply. Often, these products cut rated noise from about 45 or 50 decibels (dB) to about 35dB.

For mission-critical systems such as network servers, you can buy redundant power supplies. These two-in-one models actually integrate a pair of power supplies into a single enlarged casing. If one supply fails, the second takes over the entire load without missing a beat. These products also feature warning lights and beeps so that you know a power supply has failed. Some high-end servers, such as IBM's 704 line, come with dual power supplies.

You can buy power supplies from any computer store or via mail order. In general, make sure you look for a money-back guarantee (you want to be able to return any DOA product, after all) as well as a three-year or longer warranty. The warranty, in particular, says a lot about a company's confidence in the product.

Buying Protection: UPSs and Surge Protectors

Buying a surge protector or a UPS is a two-step process. One, you need to decide if you want simple surge protection or more-robust power maintenance. Two, you need to find a surge protector or UPS that meets the specific power draw and protection needs of your equipment. Features and outlet layout are considerations too.

If you have set money aside for a good surge protector, you should probably stretch for a UPS. These devices don't cost much more, and they offer the ability to ride out even a complete power failure—something a surge protector can't do.

The Urge to Surge

For surge protectors, expect to pay anywhere from $20 to $100, depending on the level of protection (again, measured in joules) and the presence of circuit breakers and other devices. Here are things to look for:

- Adequate surge protection: At least 240 joules
- Some guarantee against equipment damage
- Enough power receptacles
- RJ-11 data line surge protection

The most important issue is the level of protection. Cheap surge protectors will do little to stop a big surge or spike, leaving your power supply and components open to assault. Also, look for some form of guarantee from the surge-protection company, insuring against power-related damage to equipment hooked to the product.

Another concern is to make sure there are enough receptacles for your needs. Most protectors provide six spaces for plugs; however, you won't be able to use them all if you have many devices that use power bricks. In these cases, you might find a model that spaces out some of the receptacles to prevent lost capacity. Also, consider a model that includes an RJ-11 telephone jack for modem hookups.

Buying Power Protection

When it comes to UPS, size matters. The bigger your PC and the more plentiful your peripherals, the more UPS you need to buy. The VA (voltage-ampere) rating is key.

If you can afford the extra $50 to $100, you should go for an online UPS rather than a standby model. The active line conditioning will help extend the life of both the power supply and motherboard components. Of course, all UPSs give you a few precious minutes to shut down during a power outage. Although more capacity—say, up to 15 minutes of battery run time—is always welcome, in reality, all you need is enough battery to shut your PC down.

Diagnosing/Troubleshooting

When it comes to power problems, the symptoms can be tough to read. In fact, most users fail to recognize power-related failures, attributing them to software glitches, sun spots, acts of God, and the like. There are two aspects to consider here: problems from the electrical source (that is, the line) and problems within the hardware (power supply, UPS, surge protector).

Check Your Power Line

The nature of the power your PC receives can vary widely, depending on where you live, the time of year, and the power usage habits of your neighbors. In summer, for example, the sudden load change as air conditioners click on and off is guaranteed to send surges and sags running through your electrical lines. Laser printers, refrigerators, and other power-hungry devices do the same thing. Older wiring is also a problem.

The following are common symptoms of unreliable power:

- Flickering or dimming lights
- Mysterious keyboard or system lock-ups
- Random reboots or shutdowns

If you experience any of these problems, you probably need a UPS more than a surge suppressor. Suppressors, after all, only handle over-voltages. But under-voltages from excess power draw or sudden load increases need the active management that online UPSs can provide.

Also be aware that in some cases a UPS won't help you. Older buildings might lack the ability to support a full office setup. Laser printers and large monitors in particular will add to the problem. You should consult with an electrician to make sure that the local circuit provides enough amperage to service your PC.

A Failing Power Supply

With the exception of flickering lights, any of the symptoms just noted can also indicate a failing power supply. However, there are a few other telltale signs to look for:

- Fan noise sounds rough or louder than usual
- Fan noise is absent altogether
- The power supply chassis is unusually hot to the touch

If you note any of these symptoms, shut down the PC immediately—it's time to buy a new power supply. Although power supplies can be repaired, their low cost, coupled with the presence of dangerously high voltages inside, makes this a matter for professionals. You can also use the failure as an excuse to upgrade to a beefier model or to get one designed specifically for quiet or cool operation.

Here's one thing to keep in mind before you replace a dying unit: Make sure that you know the cause of its demise. If the supply went south soon after you loaded up on a bunch of new peripherals, you should double-check to make sure your new supply will be up to the more demanding task.

Putting in Power

Installing surge protectors and UPSs is as easy as it gets. If you can figure out which way is up on a grounded three-prong plug, you've pretty much got it licked. Installing a new power supply, however, is a bit more complex. After all, you need to fish around inside the case, unplug about a dozen cables, and unscrew a lot of screws. Still, it's hardly brain surgery. Here's how you install a power supply:

1. Shut down the PC, unplug the power supply, and open the case.

2. Disconnect the four-cable connectors attached to the motherboard and drives.

3. Disconnect the front panel switch if it's connected to the power supply. If the switch has terminals, disconnect the power supply from the switch. If the switch is soldered on, you must unfasten the switch from the computer chassis.

4. Use a Phillips-head screwdriver to remove the screws holding the power supply chassis to the case. Slide or lift the power supply clear. Be careful not to snag the power switch wire or assembly.

5. Get the new power supply. On some units, you need to check that the voltage selection switch (115/230 volts) is set properly.

6. Move the power supply into place, and use the provided screws to secure it to the chassis.

7. Attach the large 20-pin connector to the matching connector on the motherboard, as shown in Figure 9.6. Attach the drive connectors, making sure to align the tapered edges of both the plug and the connector.

8. Connect the remote switch wires, matching the colored wires as shown in Figure 9.7.

Figure 9.6.
Make sure you align the pins carefully.

Figure 9.7.
*Make sure you get the
wire colors right.
Otherwise, your
switch won't work!*

REMOTE SWITCH WIRING DIAGRAM

Tip: Most power supplies provide four sets of cables. If you're running out of power connections, you can avoid upgrading the entire supply by purchasing a Y-splitter cable from just about any electronics store. The splitter plugs into a disk drive power connector and provides two connectors for internal devices. Just be sure your power supply provides enough output to handle the additional load.

Summary

Power is an overlooked area when it comes to troubleshooting. CPU overheating, memory parity errors, hard disk data loss, and random lock-ups and shutdowns can all be attributed to irregular power flow. Whether it's the fault of a failing power supply or of an unreliable utility, the end result is a lot of headaches.

It's important to keep power problems in mind whenever you're sleuthing out a hardware problem. Overheating problems could be from a broken CPU fan or a dying hard disk, or they could be from a laboring power supply that's pushing too many peripherals. Likewise, old wiring or your air conditioning might cause sags and surges that create problems with your motherboard chipsets.

Ultimately, the best protection is an online UPS that provides constant line conditioning and the insurance of a 10-minute shutdown window. If you have data that you absolutely can't afford to lose, you should make room in your budget for such a device.

10

Mother-boards and Cases

If you look inside the case of your PC, you will see that almost everything inside is mounted on a single large circuit board, called the *motherboard*. This circuit board is the backbone of your PC. Everything from graphics cards and hard disks to CPUs and RAM plugs into the motherboard and communicates with the other components using the motherboard's connections.

In fact, the motherboard defines exactly what your PC can and can't do. You can make better upgrade and maintenance decisions when you understand how the motherboard works. This chapter will help you

- Learn what goes into a motherboard and how it works
- Understand how to buy a new motherboard and the role the motherboard plays in a new system purchase
- Diagnose and resolve motherboard problems

Overview

The motherboard is the foundation of your PC. Without it, CPUs, disk drives, and add-in cards are nothing but a bunch of disparate parts. The motherboard provides more than a place to plug these devices in; it determines how quickly and efficiently they can communicate and work.

The Grand Tour

Motherboards are complex beasts, but they're easy to understand if you break them down into individual components. In fact, a company's motherboard models are often distinguished by incremental differences among integrated parts. This chapter will help you understand what those differences are.

Want to see for yourself? Pop the top off your PC (after shutting down and unplugging the unit, of course) and have a peek inside. If you look closely, you'll find that the components of a motherboard are easy to identify. Looking straight down into a PC, you will see the following (as shown in Figure 10.1):

1. CPU socket or sockets
2. Add-in card bus slots for ISA, PCI, and perhaps EISA or MCA
3. Memory and (usually) secondary cache sockets or chips
4. System chipsets and BIOS CMOS
5. Motherboard clock crystal and battery
6. Backplane I/O ports for serial, parallel, PS/2 mouse, keyboard, and USB
7. Pin-outs for disk drives, power, and (possibly) SCSI connectors

Figure 10.1.
Micronics' Stingray motherboard includes all the components needed to make a PC run. (Photo courtesy of Micronics Corp.)

The RED square specifies pin 1 of the component (Jumper, Connectors, and Sockets).

CPU Socket

It all starts here. Motherboards must be closely tailored to the CPUs they serve, providing the correct number and types of data and address lines to the CPU. A Pentium MMX processor, for example, uses very different connections than the dual-cavity Pentium Pro or single-edge connected Pentium II. The type of CPU socket in any motherboard directly affects its performance and upgradability.

That said, motherboards can generally host a number of different CPUs designed for their connectors. Jumpers let you set the motherboard to run at different speeds, allowing the same board to support both a 90MHz Pentium CPU and a 233MHz Pentium MMX CPU. Intel-compatible processors from AMD and Cyrix can likewise plug into the processor socket.

In Pentium and later motherboards, the CPU socket is one of the most prominent features on the circuit board landscape. Pentium and Pentium Pro motherboards feature a large square or rectangle of pin holes. Often, a silver lever is positioned next to the socket. This is the zero insertion force (ZIF) lever, which allows easy insertion and removal of CPUs.

New Pentium II motherboards depart from this familiar scheme: You'll see a long slot for the CPU instead of a large square, as shown Figure 10.2. The slot accepts so-called single-edge connector (SEC) cartridges, which Intel uses to house its Pentium II CPUs. Although the effect is the same—

conductive gold-plated leads make contact and allow electrical signals to pass to and from the CPU—the change means that Pentium II motherboards won't accept other Intel or non-Intel processors.

Figure 10.2.

Notice a difference? This Pentium II motherboard doesn't feature the familiar square CPU module of past generations. The CPU goes into the dark slot near the bottom-right. (Photo courtesy of Tyan)

Technical Note: Intel will give you all sorts of good reasons why they moved to a slotted CPU package with Pentium II. But the rub isn't what it does for Intel's CPUs—it's what it does to Intel's competitors.

The so-called Slot 1 design is a well-protected piece of property. Patents and trademarks surround both the P6 CPU bus (used with Pentium Pro and Pentium II motherboards) and the Slot 1 design. Unlike earlier 486 and Pentium CPUs, AMD, Cyrix, and other processor makers lack access to the technology through licensing agreements. The upshot is that you won't see CPUs from competing vendors that will fit into those Slot 1 motherboards.

If you have an existing motherboard you want to upgrade, you can usually do so with the same class of processor. Table 10.1 lists your direct upgrade options.

Table 10.1. Motherboard upgrade options.

Original CPU	Socket Type	Upgrade Options
Pentium	Socket 5	Pentium MMX OverDrive, K5, 6x86, faster Pentium
Pentium or Pentium MMX	Socket 7	Pentium MMX, K6, 6x86Mx, faster Pentium or Pentium MMX

Original CPU	Socket Type	Upgrade Options
Pentium Pro	Socket 8	Faster Pentium Pro
Pentium II	Slot 1	Faster Pentium II

As you can see, your upgrade options get slim once you move to a P6-bus motherboard (that is, Pentium Pro and Pentium II). The best upgrade picture exists for Socket 7 motherboards, where Pentium MMX, AMD K6, and Cyrix 6x86Mx CPUs all vie for a piece of the mainstream computing market.

Technical Note: Some motherboards can accept two or more CPUs, providing enhanced performance for computationally intense operations. Called *symmetric multiprocessing*, or SMP for short, these advanced PCs require a specialized operating system that can recognize and take advantage of the additional CPUs. Microsoft Windows NT Server, for example, can use up to four CPUs right out of the box, while enhanced versions can recognize even more processors. OS/2 and various UNIX operating systems also provide SMP support, but you won't find SMP inside Windows 95.

How much does SMP help, really? Not as much as you might think, although it depends mostly on the application. Often, the second CPU will yield an impressive performance boost, in the range of 70 percent. However, successive CPUs tend to deliver less and less return, diminishing to the point where additional CPUs fail to appreciably affect performance. The reason is that the CPUs are waiting for the system bus, memory, hard disk, and other components to deliver data to them. Making them faster simply increases the percentage of time that they sit idle.

SMP sounds good, but it isn't for everybody. Web servers, network servers, and professional workstations are the types of PCs that can make SMP pay off—particularly since SMP systems are significantly more expensive than single-processor PCs. SMP motherboards and chipsets must contain additional logic to keep the various CPU caches (L1 and L2) in sync, so that data altered by one CPU doesn't accidentally get overwritten by older data in the cache of a second CPU. The processors also need a fast connecting bus to allow them to achieve top performance.

Intel has made SMP more accessible by crafting a standard that eliminates the need for every PC maker to cook its own SMP design. Intel's newest CPU, Pentium II, provides SMP capability, but only in limited two-way configurations. The Pentium Pro CPU is actually Intel's premier SMP processor, able to be set up in four-way and higher configurations. For this reason, Pentium Pro remains the primary CPU of large servers, despite the fact that its top clock speed is 100MHz slower than the top speed of Pentium II processors (see Figure 10.3).

Figure 10.3.
Tea for two: This dual-processor Pentium Pro motherboard is well-suited to server and workstation tasks. But it needs a special operating system to put both CPUs to work. (Photo courtesy of Intel Corp.)

Get on the Bus, Gus

Another important consideration is add-in card support, which you can discern by looking at the motherboard. In most Pentium systems, you will see parallel slots lined up perpendicular to the backplane. You'll usually see two separate types of slots, corresponding to the type of bus being used by the system.

These slots are important because they determine what kind of cards you can add to your system down the road. Graphics cards, sound cards, network adapters, and other internal peripherals all plug into the add-in card buses. The number and type of slots are both key considerations.

There are six major PC buses:

- ISA: The workhorse low-speed system bus present on virtually all PCs.
- PCI: The reigning standard found on all new Pentium-class PCs sold in the last two years.
- AGP: The Accelerated Graphics Port is the new graphics-only connection for Pentium II PCs that runs at two or four times the speed of PCI and provides intriguing features for 3-D graphics.
- VL bus: The first high-speed add-on card bus, it was tailored to 486 systems but never caught on with Pentium PCs.
- MCA: IBM's enhanced Plug and Play add-in bus never took off in the mainstream market.
- EISA: The industry's answer to MCA, it too enjoyed only limited market share and today is found only in servers.

Of these six, the vast majority of PCs today incorporate just two—the ISA and PCI buses. You should make sure that any new system or motherboard you buy comes equipped with both. You can recognize PCI slots by their light color, shorter lengths, and closely-spaced pins. ISA buses often come with brown or black plastic slot housings.

In fact, the bus type of a motherboard might make or break an upgrade decision. Older VL bus-based motherboards, for example, have reached the end of their useful life, as graphics board vendors have abandoned VL bus almost entirely in favor of the nearly-ubiquitous PCI standard. The upshot is that if you want a hot 3-D graphics accelerator, you'll need a PCI motherboard to plug it into. Most 486 owners need not apply.

What's so special about PCI? Well, for one thing, it's fast. With a 132MBps burst transfer rate, PCI can push bits about 25 times faster than ISA. It also boasts built-in Plug and Play capability, bus mastering, and a compact slot design that shaves precious pennies off manufacturing costs.

Many new Pentium II systems feature a new bus called Accelerated Graphics Port (AGP). AGP is a "PCI bus on steroids" that is dedicated to graphics, allowing 3-D-savvy graphics adapters to use the large pool of system memory to create visuals in 3-D textured scenes.

What's more, AGP can help undo bottlenecks for all graphics operations, whether 2-D, 3-D, or video. Early AGP peripherals will be able to push 528MBps (versus PCI's 132MBps), but Intel plans to push that number up to as high as 1GBps over the next year. Because only one device sits on this bus, graphics performance should benefit (see Figure 10.4).

Figure 10.4.
This schematic shows how AGP-based graphics boards sit above the PCI bus and gain direct access to main system memory. The result is better performance potential and more-realistic 3-D texturing. But you need an AGP motherboard to get AGP. (Figure courtesy of Intel Corp.)

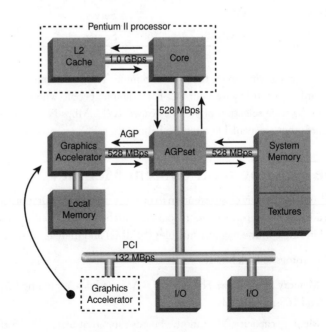

What's the catch? AGP is available only on Pentium II motherboards until chipset-maker Via Technology releases its AGP-capable VP3 chipset for Socket 7 systems. Expect AGP-equipped systems featuring AMD and Cyrix processors in the second half of 1998.

Table 10.2 helps you understand how PCI and other buses compare with each other.

Table 10.2. Buses compared.

Bus Type	Data Rate	What It's Best For	Notes
ISA	5MBps	Desktop PCs, sound cards, modems, low-bandwidth peripherals	On its way out
PCI	132MBps	Desktops and servers, graphics, network adapters, sound cards	Great hardware selection, and it's fast
AGP	264MBps/528MBps	High-end desktops, gaming PCs, and 3-D workstations	Future of PC 3-D games and titles
VL bus	120MBps	486 desktop PCs, graphics cards	Going, going, gone
EISA	33MBps	Servers	Replaced by PCI
MCA	33MBps	Servers	Never took off

Why all the worrying about those slots? Simple. The bus installed in the motherboard determines what cards you can buy for your PC. For example, people who have older VL bus systems simply can't find a wide selection of graphics cards, 10/100Mbps NICs, or other high-speed peripherals. The cards that are available often lag behind their PCI counterparts by several months.

The Lowdown on System Memory

You'll also want to pay close attention to memory support in your motherboard. As with add-in cards, there are different types of memory sockets, which can affect performance and capabilities. Memory is sold in single inline memory modules (SIMMs) and in dual inline memory modules (DIMMs).

The key things to look for are

- Memory form factor: The types of RAM modules, including 30-pin SIMMs, 72-pin SIMMs, and 168-pin DIMMs.
- Memory capacity: Most motherboards support at least 128MB, although some might require a cache upgrade in order to provide caching services to all the installed RAM.

- Memory type: The most common types, in order of increasing performance, are Fast Page Mode (FPM DRAM), Extended Data Out (EDO DRAM), and Synchronous (SDRAM).

Technical Note: Why can't Pentium Pro and some Pentium II systems accept the fastest memory? It's not as if Intel or others can't build DIMM sockets into the motherboards. For a variety of reasons, chipsets for Pentium II and Pentium Pro are about a half-step behind Pentium MMX chipsets—and recognition of SDRAM memory is one of the features that was lacking in these motherboards. The introduction of the Intel 440LX chipset has added SDRAM and more to its P6 lines.

Memory vendors use a cryptic scheme to market their products. You'll see a megabyte amount (1MB, 2MB, and so on), and then an x, and then a number that denotes the bit width of the module. If the second number is divisible by 8 (32, 64), the module is a nonparity-checking SIMM. If the second number is divisible by 9 (36, 72), the SIMM provides error checking. To figure out how much memory sits on a single module, divide the bit width number by either 8 or 9, and multiply the result by the number of megabytes.

For example, a SIMM marked as 1MBx32 has a capacity of 4MB. A SIMM marked as 1MBx36 also has a capacity of 4MB, but it includes error correcting. Table 10.3 shows a typical RAM configuration on a motherboard, using the number scheme just explained.

Technical Note: The markings on RAM modules can be cryptic, but they tell a story. The first number indicates the rows in the memory array, and the second shows the bits in each row. To figure out the size of the array, measured in bits, multiply the row figure by the columns. (Remember that 1MB equals 2^{20}.) Then divide the product by 8 or 9 to get bytes.

Table 10.3. Common memory configurations.

Memory	Bank 0	Bank 1
8MB	(2) 1MBx36	
16MB	(2) 1MBx36	(2) 1MBx36
16MB	(2) 2MBx36	
24MB	(2) 2MBx36	(2) 1MBx36
32MB	(2) 4MBx36	
32MB	(2) 2MBx36	(2) 2MBx36
40MB	(2) 4MBx36	(2) 1MBx36

continues

Table 10.3. continued

Memory	Bank 0	Bank 1
48MB	(2) 4MBx36	(2) 2MBx36
64MB	(2) 8MBx36	
64MB	(2) 4MBx36	(2) 4MBx36
72MB	(2) 8MBx36	(2) 1MBx36
80MB	(2) 8MBx36	(2) 2MBx36
96MB	(2) 8MBx36	(2) 4MBx36
128MB	(2) 8MBx36	(2) 8MBx36

As this table shows, motherboards can be particular about how memory is installed in the SIMM or DIMM sockets. Again, only the documentation can guide you here, but a good rule of thumb for SIMMs is to occupy the first two sockets with equal-capacity modules that should be larger or equal in capacity to any SIMMs in adjacent sockets. DIMMs, on the other hand, may be installed singly.

System Chipset

There are many very important components on the motherboard, but the system chipset is arguably among the most critical (see Figure 10.5). The chipset consists of a number of silicon chips soldered directly to the motherboard. These chips handle the flow of data between all the various components and buses on the motherboard.

Figure 10.5.
Intel's new 440LX chipset is an important advance for Pentium II systems, providing access to faster SDRAM memory, the AGP bus, and intelligent power management. (Photo courtesy of Intel Corp.)

Peter's Principle: Don't Underestimate the Chipset in Evaluating Motherboard Performance

Looking for performance? Check out the chipset first. The supporting silicon can make a big difference in performance, by streamlining data transfers and providing access to the fastest memory and bus types.

The most prevalent example was when Intel released the 82430FX chipset, also known as Triton, to replace the older 82430, or Neptune, set for Pentium motherboards. The result was that Triton-based systems running at the same clock speeds gained a 5 to 15 percent performance edge in application benchmarks, thanks to its support for EDO DRAM and faster L2 caches. The 440LX chipset for Pentium II and Pentium Pro motherboards does much the same thing. It adds support for SDRAM memory, the new AGP bus, and enhanced data transfers targeting MMX-enhanced multimedia operations.

One important thing to remember about chipsets is that they can't be upgraded. The only way to gain new features not supported in your existing system's chipset is to either replace the motherboard or purchase a new system. Before you upgrade a motherboard or buy a PC, it pays to research the chipset market first. Early buyers of Pentium II PCs, for example, missed out on the key AGP bus and enhanced SDRAM memory. The lack of these features doesn't spell doom for these buyers, but it could shorten the useful life of the PC—particularly for those wanting top 3-D game play.

The chipset determines exactly what your PC can and can't do in terms of technological support and performance. Make sure you know what chipset is in a system before you buy it.

The chipset is part and parcel of the motherboard—it can't be upgraded. So when you make a motherboard or system purchase, you should consider the chipset carefully. The biggest danger is that a new chipset introduces support for enhanced buses or memory types, cutting into the long-term availability and support for components designed for the older technology.

Over the last five years, Intel has become the leading maker of both chipsets and motherboards. (This is hardly a surprise. Intel uses these businesses to ensure healthy support for its CPUs.) Table 10.4 provides information about Intel chipsets.

Table 10.4. Intel chipsets.

Chipset	CPU	Key Features
430HX	Pentium	EDO DRAM
430TX	Pentium, Pentium MMX	SDRAM, power management
440FX	Pentium Pro, Pentium II	EDO DRAM
440LX	Pentium II	SDRAM, AGP bus

BIOS

BIOS stands for Basic Input/Output System, and it's the lowest level of software operating on your PC. The BIOS is responsible for all the behind-the-scenes work, configuring hard disks and parallel ports, managing bus transfers, and providing support for various memory schemes and other technologies.

But if the BIOS is the great facilitator, it can also be the source of many mysterious problems. An out-of-date or flaky BIOS can cause all sorts of crashes and incompatibilities. Worst of all, most users fail to consider the BIOS as a potential trouble source, so they waste days going through hardware and drivers and applications before they even consider the invisible code that runs their PC.

The BIOS can also determine whether your PC can accept certain upgrades, such as CPUs, video-handling hardware, and other devices. For example, an older BIOS might not be able to recognize enhanced IDE hard disks that use Large Block Addressing (LBA), limiting your ability to upgrade to a hard disk that has capacities as high as 8GB.

There are two types of BIOS: flash and nonflash. Most systems sold over the past two or three years use a flash BIOS, which can be easily updated using software. In contrast, older nonflash BIOSs can be updated only if you physically replace the BIOS chip itself.

> **Tip:** If you have a flash BIOS, it's a good idea to periodically update it. BIOS makers and motherboard vendors frequently update BIOS code to add support for new device types and technologies and to squash bugs and performance problems in existing code. You can easily download BIOS update modules from a vendor's Web site and then follow the installation routine's instructions to update the system. Be sure to keep a backup of the original BIOS code handy and to back up all your data. Also consider a BIOS upgrade if you are unable to successfully install a new peripheral on your PC—the BIOS might be the culprit.

How do you know what BIOS make and version you have? When your machine first boots up, the BIOS information will be displayed briefly at the top of the screen. But unless you have a photographic memory, you won't have time to write down the information before it disappears. It's better to enter the BIOS utility. On most machines, you do this during the initial boot—before the Windows 95 splash screen appears—by pressing the Delete key or some other key or key combination. Your system documentation will specify how to launch the BIOS utility.

Once inside, the text-based utility provides choices for managing settings and capabilities. You'll be able to navigate using the keyboard's cursor and the Esc and Enter keys. You'll also see the specific BIOS make and version. Remember that system makers often tailor BIOS code for their PCs, so the AMI BIOS in a Dell system might be different from that found in another PC.

Inside the utility, you should see controls for the following:

- Basic device settings for keyboards, mice, and display adapters

- Boot device order, which can be set to start with a floppy drive or ignore floppy drives altogether

- On some systems, cache algorithm settings for both L1 and L2 CPU caches let you choose from among write-through, write-back, and disabled settings

- External port configuration, including parallel port settings for enhanced parallel port (EPP), extended capabilities port (ECP), or basic bidirectional (PS/2) port operation

- Hard disk configuration, including auto-detection of the hard disk layout, and settings for optimized IDE data transfers

- On some systems, PCI bus management is provided, including bus mastering settings and burst mode support

- Plug and Play management, including confirmation of a PnP-aware operating system, DMA (direct memory access) resources for ISA peripherals, and reserved memory spaces for legacy cards

- Power management settings, including CPU clock slowdown, and time-out settings for devices such as displays and hard disks

- Security features, including the ability to set a BIOS-stored password

- Time and date settings

Warning: As most people know, Windows 95's password facility is a farce. Anyone can get around it by simply rebooting the machine in safe mode. For true password security, use the BIOS's facility. Just don't forget your password! Although some motherboards include a jumper to defeat the password, the only way to get into a password-protected system without the password is to remove the motherboard battery—wiping clean the BIOS settings—and then rebuilding the BIOS configuration from scratch.

If there is one technology you need in your BIOS, it is Plug and Play (PnP). In order to enjoy the automated installation and configuration talents of Windows 95 and PnP hardware, the system BIOS must be compliant with the PnP specification. A PnP BIOS plays a critical role during system startup, identifying and enumerating resources for boot devices. In effect, the BIOS sets the stage for Windows 95's ability to recognize hardware devices.

Motherboard Clock

You can thank the PC industry for turning the word *megahertz* into a household term. A PC's MHz rating comes from the system clock, which provides the cadence for activity in both the CPU and system bus. The clock is actually a chip of quartz crystal that resonates in response to an electric charge. By adjusting the electrical input, the frequency of the resonance can be controlled.

The motherboard clock is usually visible as a black rectangle of silicon mounted near the edge of the motherboard. Most older motherboards feature a clock from Dallas Semiconductor.

Most motherboards today run at 60 or 66MHz, with the CPU running internally at some multiple of that rate. Why not run the motherboard at the same 200MHz or higher rate found inside the CPU? Simple physics. The submicron transistors inside can be run at much higher speeds than the long trace wires and disparate components and connectors found on motherboards. Table 10.5 shows you how the speed of different CPUs relates to the motherboard clock.

Table 10.5. Motherboard speeds and processors.

Motherboard Speed	Clock Multiplier	Speeds in MHz
60MHz	1.5, 2, 2.5, 3*	90, 120, 150, 180*
66MHz	1.5, 2, 2.5, 3, 3.5	100, 133, 166, 200, 233
75MHz (Cyrix 6x86 only)	2, 2.5	150, 185

*Very few 180MHz Pentium and Pentium Pro CPUs have been sold.

Technical Note: Boosting bus speeds is tough, but it can be done. Cyrix already runs its CPUs off 75MHz motherboards. Intel, meanwhile, plans to push its motherboards to 100MHz in the future.

If you own a Pentium or newer machine, your motherboard is probably moving as fast as any CPU can handle. The actual speed of the motherboard and the CPU can be set using jumpers found along the edge of the circuit board. These jumpers are often marked with silk screening, but you are well advised to check the documentation to confirm which jumpers control speed.

Backplane I/O

Turn your attention to the back of the system chassis, and you'll notice a series of connectors sticking out the back. Here you will find the serial and parallel ports, as well as connectors for keyboards and mice. Pentium systems sold over the last year also often include a pair of USB ports. All these connectors run directly from the motherboard and out the back.

Serial Ports

Most PCs have two compact 9-pin serial port connectors, while older systems feature one 9-pin connector and a larger 25-pin connector. These ports are frequently used by external peripherals, including modems, personal scanners, PDA communications, and low-end tape backup.

The serial ports use the logical COM ports to talk to the system. COM1 and COM3 service one serial port connector, and COM2 and COM4 service the second connector. Because the higher COM port addresses can change, COM1 and COM2 are the best to use, effectively limiting the number of permanent serial-based peripherals to two—one on each port. The serial port can move 115Kbps or up to 300Kbps of data.

Parallel Port

On most desktops, the parallel port is used to connect to printers. Able to move up to 2Mbps of data, the parallel port is fast enough for most medium-strength data transfers, including print jobs and direct-connect networking provided by Traveling Software's LapLink Pro and Windows 95's Direct Cable Connect facility. Scanners, tape backup, portable CD-ROM drives, and external near-disk storage such as Jaz and Zip drives are also designed to use the parallel port.

Not all parallel ports are created equal. Newer systems feature an enhanced capabilities port (ECP) that can provide duplex operation and higher data rates. ECP-equipped PCs can cut down print times, but not all peripherals recognize the optimized signaling. In addition, they require a DMA channel.

Troubleshooting: Parallel port pass-through adapters and some peripherals won't work with ECP-enabled ports. If your parallel port devices aren't working, try setting the port back to standard bidirectional Centronics (also called PS/2) operation. You'll lose some performance, but the more standard signaling may well fix the problem. To switch parallel port modes, access your system's BIOS at boot-up and look for the parallel port entry. You should be able to toggle among EPP, ECP, and Centronics modes. Set the BIOS to Centronics, save the results, and continue with the boot process. If the problem resolves itself, a signal mismatch was probably the culprit.

Universal Serial Bus

A newcomer to the PC backplane, USB will probably take over many of the duties served by serial and parallel port buses over the coming years. Most desktop PCs include two USB connectors placed at the level of the motherboard. These compact snap-in connectors serve as the physical starting point of a network of external peripherals. Up to 127 USB peripherals can be linked.

What will run off USB? Mice, keyboards, scanners, joysticks, digital cameras, and even audio speakers can function off the Plug and Play bus. USB provides 12Mbps data rate, about six times that of the parallel port and sufficient for a wide variety of peripherals.

Compatibility: If you have a USB-equipped system and you plan to add USB peripherals, consider upgrading to Microsoft's Windows 98 operating system when it comes out around mid-1998. Although individual vendors will provide add-on software to enable USB on existing systems, your best bet is to get your operating system patches from Microsoft itself. Windows 98 integrates USB functionality and provides a single target for all hardware vendors to shoot for. The use of these source OS drivers and updates can help reduce incompatibilities down the road.

Mouse and Keyboard Ports

Finally, nearly every desktop PC will include PS/2 mouse and keyboard ports. These circular connectors provide compact, dedicated plug-ins for the vast majority of mice and keyboards. The biggest advantage is that these connectors don't require the use of scarce COM port resources to operate these peripherals.

There are two types of circular connectors: DIN5 and MiniDIN6. The MiniDIN6 connectors are the most common today and are preferable because they are also found on notebook PCs. Mice and keyboards designed for the smaller MiniDIN6 connector can be used by notebooks without modification.

Down the road, expect these ports to get replaced by USB. Mice and keyboards can both benefit from the emerging bus standard.

On-Board Connectors

A variety of connectors located on the motherboard handle everything from power and disk drives to the lights on the front of the computer chassis.

Power Connectors

You'll find connectors inside the case, too. Most prominent among these are the power connectors, which accept the main leads coming from the power supply. You can easily spot the connector by the raised white plastic edging that surrounds the pins.

IDE Bus Connectors

Another prominent feature is the IDE connectors. On most motherboards, two of these connectors are present: one for the primary IDE bus and another for the secondary IDE bus. The boot drive must be plugged into the primary adapter and set as the master device on that primary bus. For this reason, most users will have their hard disk plugged into the primary connector, while CD-ROM drives or other internal IDE devices occupy the secondary bus slot. The two IDE channels can handle up to four devices.

SCSI Connectors

Less common are integrated SCSI bus connectors. These sockets allow the installation of internal SCSI hard disks, CD-ROM drives, and other peripherals without requiring a separate add-in card. Because of the added expense of SCSI circuitry, these connectors are more likely to be found on specialized systems aimed at higher-end applications.

Floppy Drive

Near the IDE sockets, you'll find the single connector for the floppy disk drive. A standard cable plugs into the motherboard socket and usually includes a pair of connectors for driving two devices.

Assorted Lights and Things

Along the front edge of the motherboard, you might see a number of small connectors. These serve the PC's speaker, the hard disk and power indicator lights, and the front-panel power and reset buttons. Wires from the connectors run directly to these devices. However, you'll need to check your system's documentation to be sure which connectors go where.

Battery

This unassuming device plays a critical role in the smooth operation of your PC. The battery supplies the constant electrical charge needed to maintain CMOS settings and the PC's clock. There are several types of batteries, including nickel metal hydride, lithium ion, and alkaline cells. Newer PCs use lithium batteries, which generally last five to 10 years before needing replacement.

Buying a Motherboard

As you can tell from what's been covered so far in this chapter, there is much to think about when you're looking at a new system or motherboard. What's more, everything from the CPU to your hard disk and graphics card is affected by the motherboard that they're plugged into. The same Pentium MMX-200 CPU will run faster on some motherboards than others.

Regardless of whether you're buying a new system or upgrading an existing one, the same buying issues apply. There are four key areas to consider:

- Compatibility/reliability
- Upgradability
- Performance
- Price

Compatibility and Reliability

Any motherboard you purchase has got to work. It must be able to make use of the processor and peripherals you own or want to buy, and it must be compatible with your software. If you are upgrading, that motherboard must also fit in the case you own.

Physical Compatibility

Your motherboard must work with your existing hardware. A variety of system cases are available, ranging from slimline and standard desktops to vertically standing minitower and midtower models to large, full-tower PCs. You'll find a number of different motherboard configurations inside each of these.

The following are common motherboard sizes:

- AT: Fits older 486 and Pentium desktops and minitowers.
- Baby AT: Fits older 486 and Pentium desktops and minitowers.
- ATX: Works with Pentium and faster PCs sold in the last year and a half. Basically a Baby AT board rotated 90 degrees.
- NLX: A new compact motherboard specification for slimline desktops.

ATX: The Best Board for New Systems

Most newer Pentium and faster PCs conform to the recently adopted ATX form factors. The standard motherboard specification, minted by Intel, places the processor back and to the right, in proximity with the cooling airflow produced by the power supply fan. Meanwhile, RAM sockets and cache are presented in the clear, not wedged beneath drive bays as they often are on older systems.

If you're buying a new system, you should consider one that has an ATX motherboard. These boards are space-efficient and well laid out. You'll find that the tasks of installing memory, cache, and CPUs are made easier by the logical placement of components. Most ATX motherboards also feature built-in USB connectors that go alongside the familiar ports for serial, parallel, mouse, and keyboard devices. ATX motherboards usually sport seven add-in card slots—three ISA, three PCI, and a single shared space that can accept either an ISA or a PCI card.

AT and Baby AT: Old Standards Begin to Wane

If you're upgrading an older system, you probably have a baby AT or an AT-style motherboard. Like ATX motherboards, these models feature as many as seven or eight add-in card slots mounted directly in the motherboard. However, the CPU is often located front and center on the board, which blocks access for full-length add-in cards. If you plan on installing peripherals for videoconferencing or other applications that demand such space-hungry boards, an AT or Baby AT motherboard might not be suited to the task.

Slimline and Custom Motherboards: Big Trouble in Small Packages

Here's where things get ugly. Many manufacturers roll their own motherboard designs for their slimline systems. The reason is simple: The tightly tailored design lets them build a full-featured PC in a small amount of space—but your upgrade prospects will suffer for it.

One distinguishing feature of slimline motherboards is a vertical riser card in the center of the motherboard. PCI or VL bus slots are mounted on one side of the vertical riser, and ISA slots are located on the other side. The total number of slots is usually limited to about five, but that number can be deceptive. CPUs, RAM SIMMs, and drive bays can all block some of the slots. In fact, the lowest slot facing the CPU is often unusable because the CPU fan and heatsink assembly block access.

These custom motherboards can pose a number of other problems. For one, power supplies are often custom-made, which means that you probably won't be able to buy an inexpensive model from a power supply vendor. Your only choice might be to purchase a tailor-made unit from the original vendor—at a premium, of course. You'll also find that the graphics and video subsystems are soldered directly to the motherboard. Although these can almost always be disabled and upgraded using add-in card products, the ability to add memory or wavetable capability to the installed subsystem itself is generally limited.

NLX: Small Made Smart

Slimline motherboards are troublesome, but Intel and others are seeking to fix matters with the newly minted NLX specification (see Figure 10.6). This motherboard spec puts the expansion riser on the right edge of the motherboard, while the RAM and processor sit on the far-left edge. This layout eliminates card blockage while allowing the motherboard to fit into the low-profile PCs favored by businesses.

Figure 10.6.
The new NLX form factor provides a standard motherboard layout for compact PCs. (Photo courtesy of Intel Corp.)

Other Compatibility Concerns

Even if the shoe fits, it might not be right for your kind of use. For example, any motherboard built before 1995 will lack Plug and Play capability. And if your BIOS lacks flash capability—that is, if it must be physically replaced in order to be updated—you might find yourself with a PC that is falling behind the curve. Here are some of the "gotchas":

- The system chipset lacks Plug and Play capability
- The system BIOS isn't flashable
- The motherboard uses 30-pin RAM sockets
- The system lacks PCI expansion slots, or the PCI slots lack bus-mastering facilities

If your existing PC matches any of these descriptions, you should beware of pouring too much money into upgrades. Before long, you might be forced to move to a new platform if you want access to the latest applications and hardware.

Motherboard Upgrades: Anyone for a Heart-Lung Transplant?

Of all the upgrades, replacing the motherboard is the most extreme. It is also the most expensive and most effective upgrade you can conduct. But you're talking hundreds of dollars, not to mention a lot of risky messing around with components and wires. So before you decide to embark on a motherboard upgrade, you should answer a few questions:

- Have you ruled out that a less-extreme procedure, such as a CPU, RAM, or graphics card upgrade, might deliver the capabilities you need?

- Have you considered purchasing a new system while keeping the monitor, keyboard, and mouse to cut down the purchase cost?

- Are you confident of your ability to successfully remove and replace the system's main board?

Buying a New System Versus a Motherboard

If the motherboard defines the character of a PC, what is the difference between buying a new motherboard and getting a new system? There are several key things to be aware of.

When you buy a motherboard, you're keeping a lot of the components around it. The result can be a nifty cost savings over a new system. Among the things you can keep are

- External devices: Keyboard, mouse, monitor, and modem
- Internal disk drives: Hard disk, floppy drive, and CD-ROM drive
- Add-in cards: Graphics, sound, and network cards, among others
- System RAM
- Power supply

If most of these components still meet your needs, a motherboard upgrade might be a very good idea. You can move up to a new level of CPU performance and take advantage of the latest chipset innovations. Depending on whether you're willing to replace an older VL bus graphics card, you will also be able to enjoy the benefits of the PCI bus.

When does buying a new system make sense? Usually, the break point is decided by the peripherals. If the new motherboard requires that you replace several drives or cards in order to get reasonable features and performance, you should consider a new system instead. Of course, you'll need to do something with your old PC, whether pressing it into limited service elsewhere in your home or office, or donating it to a charity, school, or church. (See Appendix A, "What to Do with a PC That's Beyond Recovery," for ideas.)

When does buying a new system make sense? Table 10.6 helps you decide.

Table 10.6. When a new system makes sense.

Old Motherboard	New Motherboard	The Problem
VL bus slots	PCI bus slots	You must replace all VL bus add-in cards.
30-pin SIMMs	72-pin SIMMs or 168-pin DIMMs	You must replace all system memory.
Basic IDE	Enhanced IDE	Your current drive might work, but it won't match the capacities of EIDE units.

Making the Upgrade

So you've decided you want to take the plunge. Where do you start? Well, first of all, make sure all your data is safely backed up onto a medium that you know you can access elsewhere. If things go bad with a motherboard upgrade, the situation can be dire. Remember the golden rule of upgrades: Plan for the worst and hope for the best.

Once you have your motherboard and all the tools you'll need to make the transfer, it's time to get started. The following steps will help you through the process, but nothing can take the place of good documentation. Make sure you review the new motherboard's documentation before you start, and keep it handy throughout the process. You'll need to refer to it in order to properly hook up power and data cables and jumper settings.

Out with the Old

First you need to remove the existing motherboard. This is nearly as complicated as putting the new one in, so plan ahead. Use masking tape to label wires as you unplug them. That way, you can tell the difference between two identical wires leading to the hard disk activity and power-on lights. You'll thank yourself later, when you're trying to connect the new board.

1. Turn off the PC, unplug the power cord from the power supply, and remove the case.

2. Remove all external connectors, including those for the monitor, modem, keyboard, mouse, and any other external devices.

3. Unscrew the Phillips-head screws holding the cards in place. Then pull out the cards one by one, applying firm but gentle upward force while grasping the card by the top at each end. Put all the add-in card screws in a single place—you'll need them later.

4. If you plan on using the existing RAM in your new motherboard, you can pull out the SIMMs now. To do this, apply pressure with your fingertips on the silver or plastic tabs holding the SIMMs at each end. Use your thumb to nudge the module forward, where it

will fall out of the SIMM. Repeat for each module. Make sure to place the SIMMs in a static-free place.

Warning: If those SIMMs aren't all the same capacity and type, be sure to label them so that you remember the original layout. Many motherboards require you to mate SIMM pairs of the same size and speed. If you had a mix of SIMMs in your old machine, you should try to install them in the new machine in the same order.

5. Find the floppy and IDE connectors on the motherboard, and find the corner of each that has the socket 1 indicator. The cables should have a red line on the socket 1 edge. If they do not, mark the appropriate edge with a felt tip marker. This will let you correctly plug the cables in later.

6. Now unplug the IDE and floppy disk cables from the motherboard sockets, but leave them connected to the drives. Again, use firm but gentle force to ease the connectors out.

7. Find the serial and parallel connectors. Unplug their cables from their motherboard sockets, again labeling the cables as appropriate. Then unscrew the connectors themselves from the chassis's backplane (unless the connectors are attached directly to the motherboard).

8. Follow the wires from the power supply to the white connector near the edge of the board. Usually, you'll see a pair of six-wire connectors inserted edge to edge. The inside two wires of each set are black. Be sure when you insert these later that the inside two wires are black.

9. Finally, you'll need to disconnect the wires for your power and disk activity lights, on/off and reset switches, and other sundry front bezel stuff. The function of each wire might be noted on the motherboard. If it isn't, check the documentation. You should make a point of identifying each wire with a masking-tape label before removing it from its motherboard socket.

10. If you're lucky, you can start unfastening the motherboard. Unfortunately, most systems have a drive bay or two that must be cleared out first. Look the system over carefully and determine which drive bay or bays might need to be removed to allow egress. Use a Phillips-head screwdriver to remove the bays from the chassis.

11. Most motherboards are attached to the case bottom by a combination of screws and plastic fasteners. Remove all the screws and work the fasteners through the holes in the motherboard. Be very careful to avoid any bending or stretching of the motherboard, because this can break leads and contacts, rendering the board worthless. When the motherboard is clear, set it to the side.

In with the New

You're halfway there. If you've managed to extricate the original motherboard, much of the hard work is done. That said, a few perils lie ahead. Among them: Making sure that the motherboard has sufficient support, and avoiding a botched power cable installation that can fry the new motherboard. You need to be observant as you install. Check and double-check to make sure you're lining up the pin 1s of connectors, modules, and wires. When in doubt, check the documentation and look it over again.

1. What was it that the scarecrow used to sing? "If I only had a brain?" Well, it's time to give your new purchase one. For all non-Pentium II motherboards, locate the large CPU socket assembly and find the pin 1 corner (there should be a silk-screened dot on the assembly, and the corner hole will be missing). Lift the plastic ZIF lever located next to the socket. Now line up the beveled edge of the CPU with pin 1 of the socket, and lower it gently into the holes. Don't force the pins. When the CPU is seated, gently lower the ZIF lever to secure the CPU and make positive contact (see Figure 10.7).

Figure 10.7.
Easy does it: You need to properly align the CPU to make it fit in the socket. (Figure courtesy of Intel Corp.)

2. Next, attach the fan to the CPU as indicated by the fan's documentation. In some cases, you will need to apply a layer of thermal adhesive to ensure good contact. Plug the power wire into one of the free wires coming from the power supply.

3. Find those SIMMs you set aside (assuming that you want to use them) and plug them into the open SIMMs on the motherboard. If you've purchased new RAM, install that too. Align pin 1 of the RAM SIMM (the side with the bottom corner cut out) with pin 1 of the socket (see Figure 10.8). Lower the edge into the socket at a 45-degree angle, and rotate it back until the tabs click into place.

Figure 10.8.
Both RAM and cache modules plug easily into standard tabbed sockets on the motherboard. (Figure courtesy of Micronics Corp.)

4. You might have to tape those pesky cables and wires to the edge of the case to keep them out of the way. Place the motherboard carefully into the waiting chassis, being careful to align the keyboard port with the matching hole in the case. You should find that several holes in the motherboard align with those on the bottom of the case. Insert the plastic fasteners and screw the case down. You might need to provide paper or felt "washers" to be placed around the screw so that the metal screw head doesn't come into contact with any circuitry.

5. The most dangerous part is reconnecting the main power cables to the main board. Botch this, and you'll be serving up motherboard flambé. Make sure that the twin power cables are aligned so that the black wires are matched together in the middle. Plug the cables into their respective connectors.

6. Attach the serial and parallel port assemblies to the appropriate spaces on the back of the case. Before you plug the serial ports in, you'll need to check the system documentation to determine which uses COM1 and which uses COM2. You'll want to make sure that the logical connections comply with any labeling present on the back of the PC. Once the assemblies are screwed in, plug in the connectors, being careful to identify pin 1 on the cables with pin 1 on the ports. Usually, the red wire orients with the connector's pin 1.

7. You'll need to check the motherboard documentation to make sure that you get all the lights and buttons on the front of the case properly connected to the sockets along the front edge of the motherboard.

8. Plug the hard disk cable into the primary IDE interface, aligning the red wire with pin 1. Do the same with the CD-ROM drive, but plug it into the secondary IDE interface. Don't mix these up, or the system will fail to recognize the hard disk as a boot device. Finally, plug the floppy cable into the dedicated floppy drive connector, being sure to align to pin 1. Attach power leads to each of these devices.

9. Reacquaint your PC with those add-in cards. If you've gone from a VL bus motherboard to PCI, you no doubt will have one or two new cards to install into the case. Secure the cards with a Phillips-head screwdriver.

10. Reattach the monitor, modem, keyboard, and mouse. Plug the power cord into the power supply. Make a final preflight check. Cards should be firmly seated and secure, and cables and wires should fit snugly and be properly aligned. Turn on the monitor now so that it is partially warmed up prior to boot-up.

11. Take a deep breath, look sharp, and flip the switch. Note whether the CPU fan is running. If it isn't, you need to shut down and check the connection. Assuming that the fan is OK, watch the monitor like a hawk. Observe the initial BIOS readings, POST results, and RAM count. You should also hear the single beep from a normal boot—provided that the internal speaker was properly set up. Multiple beeps mean trouble. You should also hear the floppy drive being accessed.

12. Assuming that all goes well, you might spend two or three reboots getting Windows 95 to sort out the new hardware and altered settings. This is normal. But keep a close eye out for intractable problems. They might indicate a problem with your installation.

Upgrade Troubles

So what happens if things don't go smoothly? First, don't panic. There's probably a simple fix that can bring the newly upgraded system back to life.

Check the Hard Disk

If the machine fails to start, the hard disk might be the problem. Try the following:

1. Make sure that the drive cables are firmly set and that power is getting to the drive. Look for any evidence of drive activity during the boot process.

2. Check that the hard drive is plugged into the primary IDE connector. Also check that jumpers on the drive are correctly set to master, not slave.

3. If neither of these fixes works, enter the BIOS setup program during boot-up. Check the IDE hard disk settings and select automatic hard disk recognition.

4. If this doesn't work, the BIOS might be confused. You should manually enter the cylinder configuration data for your hard disk.

Card Troubles

Another possible problem comes from the add-in cards, which might conflict with the operating system or the state of the new motherboard's resources. If you suspect that peripherals are the issue, it's time to strip down the PC to isolate the problem. Do the following:

1. Shut down the PC and unplug the power.

2. Unplug any unnecessary external devices, including modems, scanners, joysticks, and printers.

3. Remove any unnecessary internal cards and devices. Sound boards, LAN cards, I/O cards, even CD-ROM drives should all be unplugged.

4. Start Windows 95 and follow the start-up process. The operating system should recognize the lack of devices and adjust to match.

5. Reboot the system as soon as it's done changing settings, observing behavior carefully. If the problem is resolved, you can now start adding components one by one.

6. Install each device singly, allowing the operating system to configure it and run successfully. Repeat until all devices are successfully installed or the problem recurs.

7. If the problem happens again after a specific piece of hardware has been installed, you can focus on it as the likely culprit. For many devices, new driver software might do the trick. Likewise, a quick BIOS update for flash-type BIOSs is a good idea as well.

Diagnosing/Troubleshooting

What if your current motherboard is in trouble? Unfortunately, motherboards aren't terribly easy to repair. Age and handling can cause cracks in the motherboard itself, disrupting trace wires and rendering the board worthless. Among the biggest problems are

- Overheating
- Power surges
- A dead CMOS battery

Overheating

Overheating is a cumulative problem. The stress of motherboard components heating and cooling can create a great deal of wear as the material expands and contracts. Eventually, cracks can result in trace wires and the motherboard material. So-called "chip creep" can also result, in which slight movements in the motherboard gradually push electrical leads out of contact.

More than other problems, overheating can seem like a mystery. A system might boot normally in the morning, only to suffer mysterious crashes, memory failures, and other maladies later in the day. Or a system that boots fine in the morning might have trouble rebooting after several hours of operation.

Generally, heat problems will come from the power supply, from the CPU, or from problems with airflow through the chassis. The upshot is that if you replace a damaged motherboard but fail to address the ongoing thermal problem, your new investment might be at risk. (See Chapter 4, "Trouble-shooting and Repair Strategies," for more information.)

Power Surges

Funny thing about power surges: You often know when they occur. In this respect, they are among the easiest motherboard problems to identify. But that's small comfort when you consider that even a mild over-voltage can destroy sensitive electronics. Here are some common sources of power surges:

- Catastrophic power surges from lightning strikes or similar events
- Power over-voltages from external peripherals or phone lines
- Intermittent problems from power sags or mild over-voltages

In most cases, a UPS or surge protector can help avoid damage to the motherboard.

Battery Problems

A common—and thankfully repairable—problem is with the motherboard's built-in battery. The CMOS battery ensures that critical configuration data is available to the BIOS at all times. Even if a system is shut down for months or years, the tiny motherboard-based battery ensures that the PC will boot properly.

But batteries die eventually, and often within five years you might find troubling symptoms cropping up. For example, if the PC can no longer keep the proper date after being shut down, a dead battery is probably the culprit.

You can buy PC batteries from any computer store. Your first task is to determine exactly the type of battery you have and to find one to replace it. There are generally three types of motherboard batteries:

- Alkaline
- Nickel metal hydride
- Lithium

Of these, lithium lasts the longest and is common on PCs sold within the last two years. If you buy a new motherboard, a lithium CMOS battery is a good idea.

Summary

The motherboard is where it all starts and ends. Most people worry about processor speeds, RAM, and hard disks when buying a new PC, but they should pay more attention to the motherboard. These components are the *terra firma* of PCs—the foundation that makes performance possible.

Of all the components on motherboards, the most important is the system chipset, or PCIset, to use Intel parlance. This set of one to four chips orchestrates every data transaction that occurs inside the PC. Critical features such as direct memory access (DMA), PCI bus concurrency, power management, and enhanced memory support all come from the chipset.

The upgrade picture is improving as well. Standard motherboard form factors are easing the travesty of blocked add-in card slots and buried RAM SIMMs. Still, you'll need to be very, very careful when choosing a motherboard. Keep the old carpenter's axiom in mind: Measure twice; cut once.

III

Basic Data Storage

11

Control Freaks: IDE and SCSI Controllers

Peter Norton®

Controllers work like traffic cops, managing the interface between peripheral devices (hard disks, CD-ROM drives, and more) and the PC system itself. When your CPU requests data from a disk, for example, the disk controller handles the transfer of the request to the drive and the passing back of the retrieved information over the PC's bus.

As with all PC technology, controllers have undergone significant enhancements over the years. The original PC controllers were all hardware boards inserted into slots on the motherboard and connected to disk drives via a ribbon cable. Over time, disk drive manufacturers advanced the electronics aboard the drives, allowing the drives to do more of the data management themselves, turning the controller into a fairly simple mechanism (a traffic cop with an easy job). New controllers no longer always require a large hardware board to hold the circuitry.

Motherboard manufacturers have begun integrating these simple controllers directly into the motherboard, and you'll find connectors for disk drives on the motherboards of almost all new PCs. Controller cards still exist on older machines, though, and they remain useful for adding new drives and adding other devices to new ones, so I'll discuss them in a moment.

Controllers come in several different standards and use different protocols for managing the disk drive data. The original controllers had interfaces called ST-506 and ESDI, but today these are found only on archaic PC systems. Faster, more efficient standards have stormed onto the scene. Now the two main controller types for PCs are called IDE and SCSI. I'll limit this discussion to these two.

SCSI Versus IDE

SCSI stands for Small Computer System Interface, and IDE stands for Integrated Drive Electronics. Understanding them is becoming more confusing as the two standards evolve.

SCSI's second iteration was called Fast SCSI (or SCSI-2). It provided support for several device types beyond hard disks and increased the data transfer potential. Recently, a newer version called Ultra SCSI (SCSI-3) was released, improving data transfer speeds even more. A variation on both Fast SCSI and Ultra SCSI increases the data path (and data transfer rates) from 8 to 16 bits. You'll see these referred to as FastWide SCSI and UltraWide SCSI. Table 11.1 gives a breakdown of controller specifications.

Table 11.1. Controller specs.

Controller Type	Number of Devices Supported	Types of Devices Supported	Data Transfer Speeds
IDE	Two	Only hard disks	Less than 10 MBps
EIDE	Four with primary and secondary channels	Hard disks, CD-ROM drives, tape drives, optical drives	11.1 to 33.3MBps

Controller Type	Number of Devices Supported	Types of Devices Supported	Data Transfer Speeds
SCSI-1	Eight (one of which is the host adapter card)	Hard disks, CD-ROM drives, scanners	5MBps
SCSI-2	Eight to 16 (one of which is the host adapter card)	Hard disks, CD-ROM drives, scanners, removable drives, optical drives	10MBps (Fast SCSI); 20MBps (FastWide SCSI)
SCSI-3	16 (one of which is the host adapter card)	Hard disks, CD-ROM drives, scanners, removable drives, optical drives	20MBps (Ultra SCSI); 40MBps (UltraWide SCSI); 80MBps (UltraWide Low Voltage Differential SCSI)

The original IDE evolved from the hard drives aboard IBM's PC AT, the first 16-bit personal computer. The name Integrated Drive Electronics is as literal as they come. These drives put most of the controller electronics in the drive housing itself rather than on a separate card. The resulting design cut costs, helping make it an enduring standard on the PC.

Like SCSI, the IDE standard improved over time. The newest and most popular version found on most motherboards is called EIDE (Enhanced Integrated Drive Electronics). EIDE allows for primary and secondary controllers, connecting up to four devices to one controller set. It also adds support for devices other than hard disks.

Buying Tip: Never consider a controller purchase or upgrade on its own. Always lump disk drives (or other peripherals) in the equation with controllers before deciding what you need. First, read Chapter 12, "Hard Disks," and determine whether you want to purchase an IDE or SCSI hard drive. Then check which type of controller you currently have in your system. Depending on your circumstances, you might not even need to upgrade your controller.

Note: Most people think of SCSI and particularly EIDE as disk drive controllers, but both standards now support control of other device types. SCSI hosts many devices and is popular for scanners and CD-ROM drives as well as disk drives. EIDE also now supports several types of devices, including CD-ROM, CD-Recordable, and tape drives in addition to hard disks.

There are some general differences you should think about when making upgrade decisions. The following is a brief look at the pros and cons of both types of controllers.

IDE: Pros and Cons

IDE grew out of the original PC architecture. It was closely matched to the BIOS specifications of most PCs, and as a result, it was reasonably easy to install. In fact, the vast majority of new systems come with IDE or EIDE controllers already in place on the motherboard, requiring no installation at all. They are also cheaper than SCSI controller installations.

It sounds great, but you pay a price in performance. The method by which IDE transfers data can't match that of the faster SCSI technology. New SCSI-3 hard drives, for example, boast stunning 40 to 80 megabytes per second (MBps) transfer rates, while most EIDE drives remain in the 10 to 16MBps range. A brand-new EIDE variation called UltraDMA, developed by Quantum in cooperation with Intel, extends the data transfer rate up to 33.2MBps. The first of these drives are just beginning to appear on the market. EIDE doesn't handle multitasking with the same grace as SCSI drives. IDE can make your CPU wait while it retrieves disk drive data, while SCSI allows the CPU to perform other jobs while it fetches data. Both EIDE and SCSI support bus mastering, which relieves the CPU from handling data transfer, but EIDE's approach isn't as robust as the SCSI method.

Recognition of large-capacity drives has also been a problem. Until a couple of years ago, IDE drives were limited in capacity to 528MB. If you owned a larger IDE drive, you had to partition the drive in order to trick the controller and the operating system into thinking it was two or more drives. Even the improved EIDE struggles with very large (several gigabyte) hard drives. Today, most manufacturers continue to produce their largest drive sizes only in SCSI format.

SCSI: Pros and Cons

SCSI got its start in the Macintosh world, where it flourished. SCSI host adapters let you chain several different types of devices together (hard disks, scanners, printers, and so on), running them all off a single adapter card. A SCSI-2 host adapter, for example, supplies eight different device addresses, one of which the adapter itself must use. That means up to seven independent devices may share one controller.

> **Technical Note:** Sophisticated bridge controllers can actually connect seven devices per device address. This means that you can link up to 49 devices from a single SCSI adapter! Compare that to the four-device limit of EIDE controllers.

SCSI's problem is that it is, well, difficult. SCSI controllers usually require additional setup for assigning SCSI ID numbers to devices and to get the PC to recognize the entire chain of devices. More importantly, vendors typically charge $100 to $200 more for SCSI controllers and devices than their IDE counterparts. When an EIDE 3GB hard disk sells for just $299, that premium becomes more than the mainstream market will accept.

Purchase Decisions

In terms of buying advice, a good start is determining whether you're interested only in upgrading your hard disk drive or adding several new devices to your PC. Despite SCSI's superior technical specifications, real-world hard drive speed tests generally don't show SCSI performance to be so much better that it makes up for the added cost and hassle of SCSI format. If you don't need the biggest or fastest hard drive, go for EIDE. But if you plan to add several new devices, such as scanners and CD-ROM drives, or if you need a very large, fast drive, consider SCSI.

When should you buy SCSI? If you perform the kind of operations described in the following list, you might consider going with a SCSI controller for your hard disks and other peripherals:

- Do you anticipate adding more than one new hard disk, CD-ROM drive, CD-Recordable, or scanner to your existing system in the next three years?
- Do you aggressively multitask disk-intensive applications, such as database software or multimedia titles and tools?
- Do you need very large disk capacities of 7GB or higher?
- Do you plan to use your PC to capture full-motion video or audio?
- Will you incorporate one or more external hard drive, CD-ROM, scanner, or other device(s)?

Who should buy EIDE? Again, if the following items describe your approach to computing, an EIDE controller might be your best bet. Keep in mind that EIDE serves the majority of desktop users very well.

- Are you unwilling to pay a premium for hard disks, CD-ROM drives, and other peripherals?
- Do you generally run classic productivity applications (word processing, spreadsheets, light desktop publishing) and titles?

- Do you plan to add two or fewer storage devices in the next two to three years?

- Does your existing system provide USB (Universal Serial Bus) connectors for upcoming peripherals?

Of course, the decision isn't entirely cut and dried. Ultimately, if you place a lot of value on maximum flexibility, performance, and upgradability, a SCSI controller is your best bet. For the majority of users, however, one of the new generation of EIDE controllers should do just fine—and save you a few bucks in the process.

PC97: Purists have argued the benefits of SCSI over IDE and EIDE for years, but they might have a new target to contend with. The new Universal Serial Bus (USB) standard promoted by Microsoft, Intel, Compaq, and similar industry heavyweights is poised to become an important peripheral bus architecture for the PC. Although it will largely augment and replace tasks currently performed by serial and parallel port buses, it also serves some SCSI applications, such as scanners.

USB capability is required for systems that adhere to the PC97 specification, and most PCs sold during the last year include two USB ports on the backplane. Although USB peripherals have been slow to emerge, the pace should pick up in 1998 as device makers enjoy assured operating system support and a large installed based of USB-capable PCs.

If you already own or are planning to purchase a USB-ready PC, consider going with the USB interface for external devices such as scanners, monitors, keyboards, and joysticks. Components such as hard disks and CD-ROMs, however, require faster data transfer than the 12MBps USB ports can provide. So you'll still need to contemplate IDE or SCSI interfaces for those devices.

Controllers On-Board: Finding Out What You Have

Most PCs have installed IDE or EIDE controllers, but how can you tell what you have? Fortunately, it's pretty easy once you pop the top off your system.

SCSI controllers generally inhabit hardware boards, which you will find in the PC's ISA or PCI slots (see Figure 11.1). Typically, these boards contain a number of chips, as well as a ribbon cable connector along the top edge or interior vertical edge of the board. Look at the port that sticks out the back of your PC. The dead giveaway for a SCSI adapter will be the single long, thin port (a Centronics latch style or a shielded D style connector or the 50-pin connector). This indicates that this is a SCSI controller, because EIDE controllers don't have external connectors.

Figure 11.1.
Most SCSI-equipped systems use a separate add-in card, such as the PCI-based Adaptec 3940 shown here. The fast PCI bus provides key data-handling features that enhance SCSI's multitasking capabilities. (Photo courtesy of Adaptec, Inc.)

Some older computers did supply on-board SCSI controllers, but most if not all PC manufacturers have stopped offering this feature because the SCSI interface has changed (and improved) more frequently than IDE.

Most newer PCs feature an on-board IDE or EIDE controller. These controllers are pretty easy to distinguish from one another. Examine the motherboard, looking for connectors laid down on the motherboard itself (you might have to push some cabling aside and use a flashlight to get a good look). You should be able to find and read labels next to the connectors that indicate IDE or Enhanced IDE. Otherwise, look for a 40-pin connector sticking up from the board (20x2) with a "1" indicating pin 1 in one corner. An older Pentium-based or 486-based machine might have the EIDE or IDE interface on a circuit card occupying one of the expansion slots.

If you find only one 40-pin connector on the motherboard, you have an older IDE controller that is unable to support CD-ROM drives; new, larger hard disks; or EIDE-compliant media such as Iomega Zip and Jaz drives. You'll probably also notice a separate port labeled "floppy," which controls the floppy disk drive.

If you see two ports labeled "primary" and "secondary," the system is equipped with a modern EIDE controller. Unless you need to connect more than four EIDE-compliant peripherals, you should be able to avoid a controller upgrade.

Technical Note: SCSI enjoys one key advantage over EIDE: It allows for external peripherals. EIDE lacks the more robust grounding and electrical specifications required for

continues

external device operation—that's one of the reasons these devices are less expensive than their SCSI counterparts. If you want an external CD-ROM or other drive, or if your current PC is running out of drive bay space, SCSI might be your only choice—this by virtue of the fact that the IDE (and EIDE) standards allow for a maximum of only 18 inches of cabling. SCSI allows a much more flexible six feet.

Managing IDE Resources

Older IDE controllers are very limited in their capabilities. They can drive only two devices, both of which must be hard disk drives. You can't run a CD-ROM or other drive from a standard IDE connection. What's more, IDE throughput—the speed at which data passes through the bus—is limited to 10 megabytes per second. That was plenty for disk drives three or four years ago, but it's woefully inadequate today.

EIDE controllers are much improved over the older IDE type. For one thing, they now allow operation of a variety of internal devices, including hard disks, CD-ROM drives, CD-Recordables, removable media drives, and even new DVD-ROM drives. Performance has improved as well. New ultra-DMA-compliant drives can push up to 33MBps through the EIDE bus, as much as all but the swiftest—and most expensive—SCSI drives.

Multiple-device support is added as well. On the typical PC with two EIDE ports, each port (one primary and one secondary) supports up to two devices. EIDE maintains a rigid pecking order, designating one device on each port as the *master* and the other as the *slave*. That means that a system with a total of four EIDE devices will have two master drives (one on the primary port, the other on the secondary port) and two slave drives.

Each device will have jumper settings (referenced in the documentation) that configure the device to operation as either a master or a slave. When you're using more than one EIDE device, the primary port's master device will be the boot drive of your PC.

Troubleshooting: If you set the device jumpers incorrectly, you will have difficulty booting or accessing the drives. Be sure that the drive you want to boot from—that is, the one containing your operating system and start-up files—is correctly set as the primary port's master device.

Tip: Always keep the plastic jumper connector on your device, even if the master or slave setting you're using doesn't require the plastic jumper. Just hang the plastic nub off one pin, leaving the other end unattached to a pin. That way, you won't lose it. You might need it if you change the configuration of your PC in the future.

Multiple IDE Drives

For both IDE and EIDE controllers, setting devices as master or slave is done on the devices themselves through jumper settings. The cabling on IDE controllers is fairly simple. One end of the ribbon cable connects to the 40-pin controller interface, and the two drives plug into the two other 40-pin connectors that split off further up the cable. Unlike SCSI, no terminators need be set on these IDE devices, because a termination circuit is built into the drives themselves.

Unfortunately, variations in the IDE standard over the years mean that there is no guarantee that any two IDE drives will run successfully off the same IDE controller. This is particularly true if the drives come from different manufacturers. For this reason, you should try to match any hard drives intended to run off the same IDE port.

Troubleshooting: If a drive isn't recognized by your PC, first check the jumper settings to make sure that one drive is set to master and the other to slave (see Figure 11.2). Then double-check for snug fit and proper placement for all the cabling (ribbon cable and power adapter cable). If you still have difficulty, consult with the drive manufacturer's technical support.

To install the cable, you need to match the red line that runs along the side of the cable with the pin 1 location on the device. All ports, whether on the motherboard or an IDE interface card, include a label identifying pin 1. Make sure that these match up when connecting, or your devices won't work correctly.

If your system has an on-board EIDE controller (with primary and secondary interfaces), you can add an extra EIDE drive to the secondary port if it is unused. But keep two things in mind. First, the primary controller's drive will be the boot drive of your PC. Second, even though you have two drives in this configuration, both drives' jumper settings will be set to master, because the primary and secondary ports are seen by the system as two separate controllers.

Figure 11.2.
You need to properly set jumpers on EIDE hard disks to enable them as boot devices. Otherwise, your system won't see the drive at startup. (Photo courtesy of Seagate)

Technical Note: Most users won't notice any performance difference between attaching two hard drives to one controller (as master and slave) versus installing one hard drive on the primary controller (as master) and a second on the secondary controller (as master). Theoretically, drives located on the primary controller can enjoy a performance edge. Moreover, older systems don't have independent timing control for master and slave. Thus, putting a slow drive and a fast drive on the same controller channel forces the timing to the slower drive's settings.

Multiple Controllers

One thing's for certain: IDE and EIDE sure don't like company. Do not try to add a second IDE or EIDE controller to your system if you plan to keep the on-board controller active. You'll probably encounter system conflicts and have difficulty accessing all the IDE devices you're trying to install.

What you can do, as mentioned earlier, is upgrade your on-board IDE controller to a newer EIDE board. This will increase the number of possible disk drives from two to four or allow you to run devices other than disk drives from the new controller. Performance should get a boost, too.

After you've installed the new controller, you'll have to disable the on-board controller via the system BIOS. Boot your PC and hold down the key sequence that launches the system BIOS setup screen (usually the Delete key, but see your PC's documentation for the correct key sequence). Then look for the item that disables the on-board controller. Once you have disabled the original controller, save the new settings and exit the BIOS setup.

One way to take advantage of new technology controllers without throwing out your IDE hard drive is to add a SCSI controller to your system but keep the on-board IDE (or EIDE) controller active. Remember, even if you add other SCSI hard drives, your boot disk will still reside on your on-board IDE controller. Attempting to set a SCSI drive as the boot drive while your on-board IDE controller remains enabled will create headaches and won't work on most systems.

Managing SCSI Resources

In the majority of cases, a SCSI host adapter card can be made to control any SCSI devices you add to you system. See the section "Adding an Internal Controller Card to Your PC" for instructions on installing a controller card.

SCSI-2 adapters are most prevalent in today's PCs, so they are the focus of this discussion. A SCSI-2 host adapter can drive seven different devices (while SCSI-3 can chain up to 16). As I mentioned earlier, using expensive and sophisticated bridge controllers, you can actually run several chains off one adapter. But you won't find that scenario in a typical home or office PC, so I won't go into those details.

Although SCSI controllers are more flexible and powerful than their EIDE counterparts, they tend to be more difficult to work with. For example, the daisy-chaining capability that makes SCSI so useful also requires users to juggle device IDs and set electrical termination. These are not huge hurdles for experienced users, but novices might find themselves stopped cold by the stubborn behavior (or refusal to behave) of SCSI-based peripherals.

SCSI Software

Windows 95 users have an edge in SCSI adapter installations, because this operating system already includes drivers to run most adapters without the need for additional software. If the operating system fails to recognize your particular adapter, it will prompt you to provide the supplied drivers from a floppy or CD-ROM disk from the vendor.

Most SCSI adapter kits and devices ship with their own drivers, but some companies have tried to ease your installation burden by creating general SCSI management software packages that include drivers for many peripherals. Two of the most popular are EZ-SCSI from Adaptec, Inc., and CorelSCSI Network Manager from Corel Corp.

EZ-SCSI's SCSI Explorer lets you install, interrogate, and manage SCSI devices including hard disk spin-up, start times, power management, and other controls with a graphical representation of your SCSI chain. SCSI Tutor gives you an online tutorial of SCSI software, host adapters, and peripheral devices. SCSI Bench helps measure the data-transfer performance of your SCSI devices. You'll also find a host of utilities, including an audio CD player, a PhotoCD viewer, and a backup program. EZ-SCSI runs on Windows 95, Windows NT, and Windows 3.1.

Corel provides both server and workstation modules for its Network Manager, allowing you to track SCSI networked devices across a Novell Network. This package includes utilities for troubleshooting peripherals as well as CD-ROM jukeboxes, WORM, and rewritable drives.

If you have several SCSI devices on a chain and are concerned about correcting problems quickly, consider one of these packages.

SCSI IDs: Get Your Ducks in a Row

IDE has a master-slave setup, and SCSI uses unique device IDs to keep track of connected peripherals. There are eight ID numbers in all, with the SCSI controller itself usually assigned the ID number 8. Each device on the chain must be assigned a number from 0 to 7.

ID numbers are usually set using hardware control on the SCSI device itself—often a jumper device, dip switch, or pushbutton counter. External devices place this mechanism on the back of the box, and internal devices usually supply jumpers at the back of the metal casing.

When it comes to SCSI IDs, you're on your own. You may set whatever value you please (within the 0 to 7 range). But read your adapter's documentation carefully, because devices such as a bootable hard disk require a specific ID number. What's more, this requirement can differ from adapter to adapter.

Without the supporting documentation, there is no way to prevent a boot drive installation from becoming an ugly exercise in trial and error. Most SCSI adapter cards come from the factory set for SCSI ID 7, which is the highest priority SCSI ID.

Map out which ID numbers you give to each device. If you're planning to add devices in the future, keep the list around. This will save you time and hassle checking the switch settings on the devices at a later date.

Generally, SCSI adapters come with installation and configuration software that lists the devices that the card recognizes at each ID. You'll also find it handy for printing and keeping a record. Simply ensure that each device's ID remains unique.

> **Tip:** Better yet, write or print the SCSI IDs and their corresponding devices on a label and stick it to the back of your PC. That way, you will always know what the IDs are.

The Terminator

Another difference between IDE and SCSI is terminating devices. With multiple devices (or even one device) running off a SCSI controller, the controller needs to know exactly where the chain ends. Under IDE, each device carries a self-terminating circuit, so users don't need to worry about telling the controller where the end of the device chain resides. SCSI devices generally don't carry these circuits, and your SCSI chain (or SCSI bus) requires manual termination at both ends.

Like SCSI ID settings, SCSI terminators come in different forms. For external devices, you'll probably find terminating resistors—plugs that fit into the SCSI interface socket on the back of a device. You may also have a device with terminators built in. In this case, jumper settings are used to specify whether the device marks the end of the chain.

External devices generally have two SCSI ports on the back—one for an incoming cable and one for an outgoing cable. This makes setting up a daisy chain simple. You just connect the outgoing cable of the previous device on the chain (or from the SCSI host adapter) to the incoming port of your new device. Then you either insert a cable on the outgoing port and attach it to the next device in the chain, or terminate the outgoing port with a terminating plug if it's the last device in the chain.

Although you supposedly can set up devices in any order along the chain, some devices need to be further up the pecking order than others. Bootable hard disks, for example, must occupy the 0 ID in order to be recognized as a boot device and should be at the front of the chain.

Some external SCSI devices feature only one port on the back. In this case, a pass-through terminating plug fits between the incoming cable and the port itself. Finally, other SCSI devices, such as NEC's external CD-ROM drives, offer a self-termination feature that can be set by a dip switch. Check the product's documentation to see which method applies to your SCSI device.

> **Troubleshooting:** Keep in mind that both ends of the SCSI chain need to be terminated. Normally the SCSI host adapter sits at one end of the chain and comes with an auto-terminating mechanism from the factory. If for some reason you decide to have the adapter reside inside the chain (if you've added one internal and one external SCSI device, for example), you'll need to terminate both the internal and external devices, because the host adapter now sits in the middle of the chain.

Internal SCSI devices will either have jumper settings or use a pass-through plug for setting termination. Check the documentation for any internal SCSI devices to determine which you'll need to use. Most SCSI devices, whether internal or external, come with terminators in the box (or use jumpers), but if yours doesn't, you can purchase one from any computer electronics store for a minimal cost.

While we're discussing terminators, I'd like to briefly mention SCSI cabling. Unlike IDE, you'll find a variety of SCSI cables. Regular SCSI uses 50-pin connectors, while Wide SCSI employs a 68-pin connector.

You'll also see variations between external SCSI connectors. If your kit, device, or SCSI card doesn't come with the cabling you need, you can pick up adapter plugs that match any of these different connections at your local computer store.

Avoiding Trouble

SCSI may be powerful, but it can be maddening as well. To avoid system crashes, conflicts, and other headaches, follow the advice in the next three sections.

Delayed Start

If you have several drives on one SCSI chain, you might want to specify that they use a *delayed start* via jumper settings on each drive. Spinning up multiple drives simultaneously upon booting your computer can drain power resources and cause mechanical failure or system crashes. If you set each device as *delayed start,* the host adapter sends a *start* command to one device at a time along the chain upon boot-up.

Add One Device at a Time

Don't attempt to save time by simply daisy-chaining several SCSI devices all at once. Instead, install each device, one at a time, reboot your PC, and make sure that the device is recognized and accessible by the operating system. Then proceed with the next installation. You'll save time in the long run by avoiding troubleshooting problems. This precautionary step requires you to move the terminator as you add each new device, but the time saved in troubleshooting will be worth it.

Secure the Cables

With the number of cables involved in a large SCSI daisy chain, it's easy for connections to come loose. Make sure all the cable screws are tightened down and all the fittings secure. You'll save yourself the trouble of tracking down this problem later, when you can't access devices.

Adding an Internal Controller Card to Your PC

In most respects, controller cards are very similar to any other hardware card you might plug into your PC. Controller cards come with a variety of PC bus interfaces, like ISA and PCI. Keep in mind that whether a card is ISA or PCI is completely independent of the standard the controller uses (EIDE or SCSI). You need to make sure that the controller card you buy corresponds to the bus slots inside your PC.

SCSI controller cards differ from some other hardware cards in that they usually feature internal and external connectors. The internal connectors are on the card itself and are accessible only while your PC's cover is off. They provide controller interfaces for devices that will be installed inside the PC, such as an internal hard drive or an internal CD-ROM drive.

External connectors reside on the end of the card and can be found on the backplane of the PC when the card is installed. These connectors are available for plugging in cables for external devices such as scanners, external CD-ROM drives, and so forth.

Multifunction cards often include everything but the kitchen sink. Modem/sound cards are becoming common, and even an inexpensive interface card might include an EIDE and a floppy-disk interface, several serial ports, a parallel port, and a game port. When you're attempting to solve a problem with a PC, it might be tempting to opt for one of these comprehensive solutions. But be careful. If the documentation is anything less than complete, clear, and accompanied by a working technical support number, don't choose this "everything card." The reason is that any option on the card that duplicates preexisting, working functions in the PC will have to be disabled by the judicious setting of interface card jumpers. Most interface cards now include a table of switch settings silk-screened on the card itself. This is an encouraging sign, but it won't replace thorough documentation, whether printed or on a disk.

Troubleshooting: When you're upgrading a PC, whether you're working in a Plug and Play environment, Windows 3.1, Windows NT, or even plain DOS, most of your problems will be caused by resource conflicts—SCSI ID conflicts, IRQ (interrupt) conflicts, or com port or I/O addressing conflicts. It's a good idea to print or write out a record of the PC's system settings before you begin upgrading. Especially when an automated procedure promises to do everything for you, it's important to ensure that you can back out of the procedure if it fails.

An example is when your PC encounters an error in reading a critical file right in the middle of an installation. You're far better off if you know in advance what you will do next if this happens. Calling the company is sometimes a less-than-optimal solution, especially when the system in question needs to be up and running.

As you troubleshoot a problem installation, document each change to jumpers and system configuration in sequential order. Don't wait until the changes begin to accumulate—or worse, something else unexpected occurs—before you begin to lay your trail of bread crumbs that will lead you back to the system you had when you began.

Controller Upgrades: Rules of the Road

With any card installation, always remember the following:

- Never remove or insert any card, tighten or loosen any screw, or remove any cables while the PC's power is on. With any installation, be sure to turn off the PC and remove the power cable from the back of the system. Some PCI cards are now *hot-pluggable*, or meant to be swapped with the power on. But these are few, expensive, and intended for very specific purposes. In the absence of clear instructions to the contrary, assume that removal from or insertion of a card to a live motherboard will result in fried circuits.

- Avoid static electricity shocks to your equipment. Wear an antistatic (grounded) wristband while installing cards, or at least touch the PC's grounded internal metal frame before you touch any cards.

- Systems in dusty or dirty environments often pick up grime and/or corrosion on electrical contacts. Systems operating where there are smokers, pets, or salty air are especially prone to problems with making solid connections. A fine jeweler's file can restore dubious expansion slots, but this isn't a procedure to use too often, lest the metal plating inside the slot be worn completely away. Similarly, dirty or oxidized edge connectors (tin connectors tend to oxidize, while gold ones get dirty) can be cleaned up using an old-fashioned ink eraser—the technician's friend. The best kind of ink eraser (although it's hard to find now) is shaped like a pencil and can be sharpened like a pencil. At the other end (where a pencil eraser would be) is a small plastic brush. Any residue should be vacuumed up with a technician's hand-held vacuum (keeping it well away from any magnetic media) or blown away using canned compressed air.

- Determine whether your PC, operating system, and controller card are Plug and Play- (PnP) compatible. If all these devices comply with PnP, you won't need to concern yourself much with your cards' IRQ and DMA settings. If they aren't PnP-compatible, read the cards' documentation to determine the jumper settings required to set the cards' IRQ and DMA to avoid conflicts with devices that are already installed on your PC. If necessary, set these jumpers before installation.

Warning: Even in you have soup-to-nuts PnP support, don't wander in unprepared. Take inventory of your system's IRQ and DMA settings so that you know what's free and what's not. If something goes wrong with the automated installation—and this has been known to happen—you won't be left in the dark.

- Connect any internal cables before you insert the card into the PC's slot. Once cards have been installed in the slots, the distance between cards is so small that it's impossible to connect internal ribbon cables and so forth after insertion. Connect cables to the cards as required, and then insert the card into the slot.

- Tighten bracket screws. Unsecured cards can come loose when a PC is moved or bumped. Be sure to finish installing any card by fastening the bracket screws.

- Cards often seat very firmly. If a card is mis-seated or must be removed for any reason, take great care in the removal. If the card balks, use a small, flat-bladed screwdriver to carefully pry between the card backplate and the chassis. Don't force the card in or out. Don't use pliers, a vise grip, or a monkey wrench to try to wrench the circuit card from its socket. As with children, be firm but attentive and gentle.

Controller Card Installation

After preparing, and after having read through your controller card's documentation for any specific instructions relating to installation, you can begin.

1. Turn off your PC and unplug the power cable.

2. Remove the PC system case using either just your hands (for thumbscrew cases) or a screwdriver (for older designs).

3. Unscrew the metal flap that protects the open slot where you'll be installing the card. Normally, this will be secured with a small Phillips-head screw.

4. Connect internal cabling if necessary. For example, if you're connecting the controller to an internal drive, attach the ribbon cable (red line on cable to pin 1 on card) to the controller that will later connect to the drive.

5. Align the card with the open bus slot. Be careful to avoid catching the card's back port on the metal bracket at the back of the PC. Try easing the card's port below the top of the bracket so that, once the card is inserted, the connector will be positioned properly out the back of the PC's case (see Figure 11.3).

Figure 11.3.
Ports on the card's backplate provide cable access to external devices. Some also include internal connectors, such as those found on the Adaptec AHA-2940AU. (Photo courtesy of Adaptec, Inc.)

6. When you're sure that the card is properly aligned and that the edge connector won't bind against the plastic sides of the expansion slot, gently push the card into the slot. Using two hands, push the card down evenly at each end simultaneously until the card is fully in position in the slot. A card that isn't fully inserted won't be accessible through the operating system, and a misaligned insertion can cause smoke and a trip to the computer store when the power is turned on. Press firmly down on the card once it's in the slot to seat it correctly.

7. Ensure that the top edge of the interface card backplate is flush against the chassis, and then replace the bracket screw to secure the card.

8. Attach any external device cable and any external devices that are required.

9. Reattach the PC's power cable, and turn on the PC.

10. Test the system to ensure that the operating system at least knows that something new has been added.

11. Put the PC case cover back on, and secure the case.

Summary

This chapter focused on the controller interfaces: IDE and SCSI. I discussed the pros and cons of both technologies and guided you through the purchase decisions and management of each interface. You read complete descriptions of accessing on-board IDE controllers and adding a SCSI board to your computer.

12 Hard Disks

Along with memory and graphics cards, hard disks are probably the most often upgraded component inside the PC. The reason is obvious. Every year, programs get bulkier, file formats get more
complex, and operating systems encompass more tasks. Microsoft Windows and Microsoft Office—
the most popular operating system and office suite on the planet—keep disk drive companies such
as Western Digital, Seagate, Maxtor, IBM, and Quantum very busy indeed. Add the explosive growth
of disk-consuming files from the Internet, and it's no wonder that disk capacities double every year.

Most people are probably well-acquainted with the hard disk. The central mass storage element of
the PC system, it is where all your files and programs reside. Using a quick magnetic-based recording
format, the disk retains information even if the power supply is shut off.

This chapter covers the hard disk and related issues. You will learn

- About the workings of hard disks and the various types of disks available for PCs
- How to troubleshoot disk-related problems and how to recover from disk crashes
- What to look for in a new hard disk purchase
- How to install a new hard disk, whether you're adding a second disk to the existing unit or
  replacing the original disk altogether

Overview

If you recall the office desk analogy from Chapter 7, "RAM," the hard disk acts a lot like a file cabinet. When the operating system or any application is launched, its data is read from hard disk storage and loaded into RAM for processing by the CPU. The RAM acts a lot like the top of the office
desk: Papers that are being worked on sit conveniently on the desktop, and other files are stored.

When you launch a word processor application, for example, its executable program is read from the
hard disk and loaded into RAM. Then, when you open a saved document, that file is also read from
the hard disk and loaded into RAM. Any subsequent changes you make to that document are written back out to the hard disk as the file is saved.

Windows 95 and other operating systems also make the hard disk serve double duty, using it as an
overflow reservoir for system RAM. When too many applications and files are loaded, those least
recently used get stored back on the hard disk. Programs are tricked into thinking that the bits are
still in RAM, but when the data is called up, the operating system goes off to the hard disk to fetch
the information. Called *virtual memory*, this scheme extends the functionality of all PCs but exacts
a hefty price in performance: Hard disks are 100 times slower than system RAM.

Inside, the hard drive unit resembles a vinyl record turntable, as shown in Figure 12.1. A *platter*,
circular and flat like a record, is covered in a magnetic coating called *thin film*, where the data is
written to and read from. One round platter (or several platters stacked on top of each other) spins
around a center *spindle*, which is driven by a *spindle motor*. Each platter is lined with concentric circular *tracks*. These are divided into sectors that can be read from or written to in blocks of data. (For

the sake of precision, realize that a vinyl record has one continuous "track," or spiraling groove, per side, while a hard disk platter has separate concentric tracks that are not connected.)

Figure 12.1.
Inside the sealed chamber, a hard disk drive resembles a series of vinyl records read by high-performance needles.

When you have several platters stacked together, the tracks that line up with each other across several platters are called a *cylinder*. The *head actuator* (like the phonograph's tone-arm) guides the read-write heads (record needle and stylus) to the tracks of the disk from the data transfer. When heads move to a particular track in a stacked-platter drive, all the tracks in one cylinder are accessible at the same time.

Note: Hard disk *crashes* are aptly named. The read/write heads of a Head Disk Assembly (HDA) float about three micro-inches above the platters on a cushion of air, never coming in direct contact with the disk during normal operation. A malfunction in the drive unit can cause the head to literally crash into the disk surface and gouge out a piece of the recording material. In a bad crash, the drive usually ceases working, and your only option is to replace the drive. Fortunately, with improved manufacturing clean-room techniques, hard drives don't crash as often as they used to.

A surefire way to kill a perfectly good hard drive is to slide the system box of an up-and-running system across a desktop so that the chassis shudders against the surface. It takes only a few inches of that sort of motion to generate a resonant vibration that generates substantial G-forces on the heads, causing them to come into contact with the spinning recording surface of the drive. When that happens, you're finished.

continues

Hard disks are constructed more securely today than in the past, but the data is much denser than ever before (see Figure 12.2). As capacities have gotten larger, the margin of error has gotten much smaller. Larger drives also make recovering data from a dead drive more expensive than ever if the data isn't backed up.

Figure 12.2.
Modern hard disks are complex, finely tuned mechanisms.

You won't find upgrading hard drives to be the easiest task you can perform inside your PC. (For example, upgrading RAM is much easier.) But if you follow the steps listed in the section "Installing a Hard Disk Step by Step," you can get through the process with a minimum of hassle. Hard disk vendors offer drives in different controller types (as discussed in Chapter 11, "Control Freaks: IDE and SCSI Controllers") and in an amazing range of sizes. I'll walk you through the options.

Hard drive problems come in two main categories: setup/format troubles and hardware failures/disk crashes. Setup/format problems can be dealt with using disk utilities or by modifying your CMOS. Hardware failure/disk crash, on the other hand, generally means that you need to replace the unit, because the sealed Head Disk Assemblies (HDAs) of hard drives make them impossible to fix using standard home or office tools. Additionally, opening the sealed unit almost always invalidates your warranty. Fortunately, it isn't too difficult to find companies that specialize in performing data recovery on failed drives, often allowing you to recoup some of your lost data—albeit at a substantial fee.

Tip: Just as it's easier to find a job when you already have one, it's easier to replace a hard drive that hasn't yet completely quit.

Technical Note: Hard disk engineers focus much of their energy on improving the density of information on a disk, called the *areal density*. Higher density means more data storage in a smaller space. Areal density is measured by multiplying the number of bits per inch (BPI) on a particular track by the number of tracks per inch (TPI) (calculated from the edge of the disc inward toward the center). High-end drives now feature areal densities of over 700 megabits per square inch, resulting in drives with 1 gigabyte (GB) on a single platter. Recently, areal densities of more than 1 gigabit per square inch of thin film recording media have been achieved. That top limit rises by 60 percent per year, compounded, according to IBM researchers.

Packing these bits on the disk requires the precise integration of different component technologies. The BPI potential depends on disk rotational speed, the read/write head technology, and the disk media type. The TPI potential depends on the read/write head technology, the disk media, and the positioning of the head actuator arm:

> **Rotational speed:** This is the number of revolutions per minute (RPM) that a platter spins. As disks have diminished in overall size from $5^1/_4$ inches to $3^1/_2$ inches (even $2^1/_2$ to 1.7 inches for notebooks), the linear speed of the disk has decreased. To understand this concept in real-world terms, think of an amusement park carousel. Suppose you're standing on the moving carousel and you want to stay even with a tree that's next to the ride. You would need to run (in the opposite direction that the carousel is spinning) in order to stay in one place at the outer rim. But at the innermost point, you would only need to walk in order to stay even with the tree, due to the decrease in linear speed of the carousel surface. Unfortunately, for inductive read/write heads, the signal strength from bits decreases as the linear disk speed slows. So drive manufacturers have been increasing rotational speeds to

continues

compensate. Typical drives now run from 3600 to 7200—even 10000—RPM. Speed tests generally show that the faster the rotational speed, the better the overall performance of the drive.

Read/write head technology: State-of-the-art manufacturing allows read/write heads to float about 3 micro-inches from the surface of the platter. Unfortunately, as bits get packed closer and closer together on the disk surface with improved technology, even that tiny head height distance reduces the ability of the read/write heads to pick up the diminished magnetic signal strength of the individual bits. Engineers are plotting how to reduce this head height distance even more and possibly even have the heads ride on the surface of the platter itself (but this causes wear and tear on the disk and heads).

In addition, improvements in head technology continue. Inductive read/write heads, the most popular technology, simply pick up and amplify the bit's magnetic field as they pass over it. Newer Magneto-Resistive (MR) heads use a sense current that constantly runs through the head. When the head passes over a bit, the resistance changes and the amperage of the sense current fluctuates, passing on the needed data. MR heads increase areal density, because they're more precise in distinguishing between tightly packed bits.

Disk media: Disk platters now come in aluminum alloy, ceramic, glass, and glass-ceramic combinations. The goal is to develop a platter that is strong and lightweight and that doesn't expand or contract with temperature changes. The recording media, which covers the platter and holds the magnetic data, is generally a 1 to 3 micro-inch layer of cobalt alloy. Engineers keep working to make the recording media thin, defect-free, and capable of withstanding head crashes without damage.

New Technologies

Keep your eyes open for changes in the hard disk landscape. This segment of the computer industry evolves as rapidly as any other. Four years ago, an average PC shipped with a 500MB hard drive. Now the average drive size for a new PC is about 3GB, and many mainstream systems feature 4GB drives.

The standard controller interfaces for hard drives are still SCSI and EIDE (see Figure 12.3), but you'll start to see high-tech modifications to these protocols that will increase performance and overall drive capacities. On the EIDE side, vendors are working on ultra Direct Memory Access (DMA) EIDE drives, which increase throughput by bypassing the CPU during data requests. Similarly, in SCSI drives, the recently announced UltraWide Low Voltage Differential (LVD) SCSI drives push data transfer rates up to 80MBps.

Figure 12.3.
SCSI hard disks offer higher data rates and better multitasking performance. But many PCs need a separate SCSI add-in card, such as the Adaptec AHA 3940UW, shown here. (Photo courtesy of Adaptec)

Western Digital Corporation will release SDX (Storage Data Acceleration) technology hard disk drives in late 1997. SDX technology drives connect directly to CD-ROM drives (via a 10-pin cable), foregoing the need to transfer CD-ROM data over the EIDE bus. Theoretically, SDX gives you a significant performance boost by using the hard drive as a cache for CD-ROM data. (Western Digital claims that an 8X drive performs like a 20X drive.) Western Digital hopes to later apply the SDX interface to CD-Recordable and DVD-ROM drives. Whether SDX will have a significant impact on the hard drive market remains to be seen.

Additionally, other drive manufacturers continue to come up with improved disk drive components. New PRML (Partial Response Maximum Likelihood) disks, for example, use data-detection techniques in conjunction with MR heads to improve data throughput and increase areal density. You should read the latest technology "white papers" that major drive manufacturers post on their Web sites. For example, Quantum Corporation (www.quantum.com) and Seagate Technology (www.seagate.com) frequently provide technology papers online.

Drives that have these technological enhancements should all be available before the end of 1997. How much these drives will cost and their overall impact on the hard drive market have yet to be determined.

Drive Replacement or Add-On

You should decide whether you're simply adding a drive to your PC or replacing your current hard drive. If you've run out of room on your hard drive but you're happy with its performance, consider just adding an extra hard drive. You'll save yourself the time-consuming hassle of backing up and transferring all your data to the new drive. This also gives you the opportunity to go for the cheaper, smaller drives, and you won't have to dispose of a perfectly good drive just because it doesn't hold enough bytes. If you can use the old drive, you probably won't need 8GB of extra space.

If you do decide to add a larger, faster drive to your system, but you intend to keep the old hard drive, some people think you should go through the data backup and transfer hassle so that the new, more efficient drive will be your PC's boot drive. You'll gain overall performance advantages by having the disk that contains the operating system and its virtual memory file be the better drive. Some hard drives come with a disk mirroring utility to make the data transfer process easier.

When you're adding a drive, be aware that not all drives are compatible under EIDE's master/slave relationship (see Chapter 11). Older IDE drives that don't support PIO (programmed I/O) modes 3 and 4 (the faster data transfer protocols) sometimes have difficulty working with another drive running on the same EIDE controller. Unfortunately, experimentation is often your only option. Generally, your boot drive should be the master drive, to take advantage of the theoretical, if not practical, performance gains.

On the other hand, if your drive is slow, deteriorating, showing an increasing number of bad sectors or intermittent errors, or altogether dead, it's time for a replacement drive. You should choose the biggest drive you can afford. After all, you'll be using it for a long time, and you'll want as much storage as your budget will allow.

What size hard drive should you buy? If you answer yes to at least two of the following questions, you should consider a 3GB drive or larger:

- Do you often use image, video, sound, or animation production tools on your PC?
- Do you store large video, image, or sound files on your hard disk?
- Do you store or work with large database files on your hard disk?
- Do you install five or more new applications (or application upgrades) within a six-month time frame?
- Do you regularly download new files from the Internet?

Generally, the bigger the drive, that better your ratio of dollars per megabyte. Even if the preceding questions don't necessarily apply to you, but you can afford a few more dollars for a hard drive, you can divide the disk into several logical partitions for various uses.

If you purchased your PC before 1994, your system's BIOS might not be able to handle the larger than 528MB drive capacity of new EIDE drives, due to changes in IDE's method of interpreting hard disk geometry and the newer EIDE's LBA (Logical Block Addressing) approach. If your BIOS isn't enhanced, you might be able to upgrade just your BIOS through your system vendor. In the worst case, you could upgrade your motherboard itself in order to take advantage of these high-capacity EIDE drives.

Tip: Don't dwell on hard drive performance when making your purchase decisions. Comparative hard drive review test results show that performance differences between drives usually hover around 5 percent or less. Just make sure that any drive you're considering falls within these standard ranges of performance specifications.

Key Specs

The following hard drive specifications flow in order from most important to least important in terms of understanding and evaluating hard drive decisions:

- Average seek time: The average amount of time required to move the heads to a track, measured in milliseconds. Fast drives now offer 7.5ms average seek times. Almost all new drives are 10ms or faster. This is three times faster than the hard drives of a decade ago. The lower the number, the better.

- Transfer rate: The rate at which the drive and controller pass data back to the PC system, measured in megabytes per second. A higher number is better. This rate varies greatly, depending on the controller type. EIDE controllers and drives range from 11.1 to 16.6MBps, due to PIO (programmed I/O) modes 3 and 4, which were part of the specifications. Newer UltraDMA EIDE controllers have the potential to transfer up to 33.6MBps. SCSI controllers and drives now normally run from 10 to 40MBps. Don't let the differences scare you. The CPU clock speed, the amount of RAM, and even your video graphics accelerator card more clearly define your PC's overall speed.

- Disk cache: Hard drive disk caches are extra memory buffers that are included with many new drives. To reduce the total number of times the hard drive spends time seeking data on disk, read request information gets stored in the cache temporarily. Many times, the following read request's data can be supplied directly from the cache without accessing the hard disk again. A typical new drive can come with a 512KB drive cache. Here, a larger number is better.

- Disk rotational speed: The number of revolutions per minute (RPM) that a platter makes after spinning up to speed. Ranges normally run from 3600 to 7200RPM. Generally, in hard disk drive comparisons, the faster the drive's RPM, the better the overall performance of the drive during real-world operating system and software application testing.

Planning Your Purchase

With the multitude of options you have when shopping for a new hard drive, you might be confused if you don't have a plan. This section gives you a structured way to decide on which disk you need.

Tip: Before you shop for a drive, take measurements of the available drive bay. At the same time you buy your drive, make sure you will have all necessary cables, connectors, screws, and brackets to install it both physically and electronically. Save yourself a trip back to the store.

- Size (capacity): Before anything else, determine the size of hard disk you need. This might determine for you which controller type you'll be using, because SCSI drives dominate the high-end capacities (8GB or bigger). If you're planning to run many large applications (database, image processing, multimedia production tools), or if you store and manipulate huge files (database, image, video, sound), get the largest hard disk you can afford. The applications and data files you use in the next three years will only get larger, so plan for big storage demands. Once you've picked a drive size, calculate the cost per megabyte of different drives from different vendors, and make a short list of the cheapest.

Technical Note: When it comes to hard disk capacities, your mileage will vary. First, vendors overstate capacities by marketing hard disks with the assumption that there are one million bytes in a megabyte and one billion bytes in a gigabyte. In fact, the true numbers of bytes are 1,048,576 and 1,073,741,824, respectively. So when a drive is advertised as 4.3GB, for example, the vendor often means that the drive has 4.3 billion bytes. A true 4.3GB drive would contain a little over 4.617 billion bytes. You're being cheated out of over 300MB!

What's more, formatted drives won't match the exact capacity stated on the box. And you will get different capacity readings from different utilities. All this makes accounting for disk space a fuzzy area. Don't sweat it too much. Although these phantom bits might be vexing, your drive actually loses much more data to slack in the Windows 95 filing system than to any amount of accounting weirdness.

- Controller type: If the size you choose hasn't decided the controller type for you, you must decide between an EIDE and a SCSI controller. SCSI drives theoretically supply faster data transfer and definitely provide more flexibility in adding devices, so go that way if you can afford the extra cost. Otherwise, choose EIDE for the convenience and cost savings of leveraging off your on-board controller.

- Warranty and service policies: Evaluate your short list of drives by the manufacturer's service and warranty polices. Typically, drives have warranties of about five years. Check computer publications for service records and reader complaints about vendor service.

- Performance: Finally, double-check that your potential new drive falls within the performance specs just listed. Again, in real-world tests, the performance differences between drives isn't that significant.

Tip: Chapter 11 has a breakdown of these different controller technologies. Keep in mind that SCSI generally offers the largest drives available and more flexibility in adding devices in the future, but you'll pay $100 to $200 more for a SCSI drive than an EIDE drive. Additionally, a SCSI controller card costs about $150. If you don't have an on-board EIDE controller (which is free), you can pick an EIDE controller hardware card for about $50.

Some newer motherboards allow you to switch from an EIDE boot drive to a SCSI boot drive. (This is useful when you want to run Windows 95 sometimes and Windows NT other times.) If you own such a motherboard, adding a SCSI drive will enable this feature.

Diagnosing/Troubleshooting

Hard disks are much more reliable than they used to be, but that's small comfort when 3GB of your favorite data goes down with your hard disk. It can be a heartbreaker. Disks always seem to drop out at the exact moment when you've saved a substantial quantity of essential and irreplaceable data.

Fortunately, most troubleshooting consists of routine maintenance to keep the drive running smoothly or to fix minor problems. The next sections will help you identify and fix problems and give you insights into the tools available to do so.

Disk Utilities and Facilities

If you notice problems with your hard disk, you'll find two tools close at hand inside Windows 95 (see Figure 12.4). Disk Defragmenter and ScanDisk both provide handy tools for assessing and fixing routine disk problems. You access these utilities from the Start button by choosing Programs | Accessories | System Tools.

Disk Defragmenter

Windows 95 can be a real space-waster. When data is constantly read from and written to a hard drive, the operating system often leaves small blocks (fragments) of hard disk space wasted between current (and usable) data blocks. Over time, these useless fragments can build into quite a collection and ultimately lead to vast wasted hard disk space and potential disk errors. They can also degrade performance, because the disk head must jump among thousands of scattered blocks.

The Disk Defragmenter utility shuffles the bits around your hard disk, reuniting all those separated blocks by copying the useful data together into contiguous blocks. Wasted space and leftover bits are removed. Defragmenting the hard disk can often resolve vexing problems with lost files or slowed performance.

Figure 12.4.
You'll find useful hard disk management tools in Windows 95. Simply right-click the drive and select Properties.

ScanDisk

Another, more disturbing, problem relates to physical defects on the surface of the hard disk. These flaws make it impossible for the read/write head to read from or write to the disk. Any data located where flaws occur is lost.

ScanDisk examines the entire disk surface, finding and marking bad sectors so that they won't be used in normal operation. If your disk is crying for help, run ScanDisk in "thorough" mode and set it to correct any disk errors it can.

Additionally, Norton Utilities supplies several disk diagnostic and recovery tools. You can even handily recover erased files using the manual "unerase" utility.

If you've got a full disk on your hands, you might have some wasted space remaining from installing and uninstalling applications. Downloadable shareware utilities such as CacheCompactor (available at CNET's www.download.com) find and delete unnecessary files hogging space on your disk.

Finally, Windows 98 will deliver Disk Defragmenter Wizard, Automatic ScanDisk, and other new disk utility features.

Going Out with a Bang: Symptoms of a Dying Disk

A hard drive on its last legs makes itself known. The key symptoms include loud noises, excessive heat, and constant data errors when you're booting or running applications. If you're concerned about the health of your hard drive, first back up the entire disk. Data is almost always the most important part of any disk drive.

Table 12.1 is a checklist of symptoms and solutions to try before deciding whether to replace the drive. You'll have to remove your PC's cover to check some of these items.

Table 12.1. Troubleshooting hard disks.

Symptom	Solution
Constant disk errors	Run disk utilities ScanDisk and Disk Defragmenter (DOS 6.0 and higher and Windows 95) or third-party applications such as Norton Utilities to find and correct bad sectors on your disk. Also check your PC's CMOS settings to see if the disk drive is set up properly.
Loud disk noises (whining or clicking sounds while the hard disk is booting or running)	With the PC cover off, make sure the disk is secured in the drive bay and is situated either flat or standing on end (not slanted) for proper operation. Also check that both the power supply cable and the data cable are firmly connected at both ends.
Excessive heat from the drive	Your disk drive will be warm to the touch (but not really hot) during normal operation. Make sure your PC's internal fan is working properly. Some fans have a switch that disables them while the PC cover is removed, so check for normal fan sound and air flow with the cover on. If the fan appears disabled, check its connections inside the PC.

Warning: When blowing out the inside of your PC, try not to blow air and dirt through the blades of the fan, causing the blade to turn. This forces dirt in between the axle and bearing, causing squeaking and eventual failure.

If none of these solutions corrects your problem, consider upgrading your hard drive. Back up your data first, because these problems foreshadow a hardware failure.

Upgrading

The hard disk is a component you'll probably upgrade over the life of your PC. The two main reasons to upgrade are that you need more room for applications and/or data, or that your disk has crashed and you need to replace it. A third reason to upgrade, popular with people who like to improve their overall computer performance component by component, is simply to gain a faster and more responsive drive from which to run the operating system and applications. Sizes go up and prices go down continually, so this would be an affordable and effective upgrade.

When Do You Need to Upgrade?

The following is a short list of questions that will help you decide if it's time to upgrade. If you answer yes to two or more of these questions, it's time to consider a hard disk upgrade:

- Have you been unable to install a new application due to an insufficient disk space warning?
- Have you noticed unusual application slowdowns due to a reduction in temporary storage space on your hard drive?
- Have you had to search your hard drive to delete files due to insufficient disk space warnings while running applications?
- Do you continue to encounter disk errors even after performing troubleshooting operations such as checking connections and CMOS settings and running disk utilities?

Installing a Hard Disk Step by Step

If you've never installed a hard drive, try to buy a hard disk upgrade kit that includes all the necessary cables, brackets, and screws (and possibly controllers) you'll need to complete the task. It's no fun having to stop in the middle of a hard drive installation in order to make another run to the store. Once you've decided on the type of drive to install and you've made your purchase, follow the steps listed in the next sections.

Back Up Your Data

If you're replacing your drive, a full backup is critical. After you remove your old hard drive, your operating system, applications, and data files must be copied over to the new hard drive. Strongly consider a backup medium such as tape, CD-Recordable, zip, or jazz drives. As soon as you get over 5MB, you'll find floppies woefully inadequate as a backup medium. Let's do the math. A 1GB drive would require one billion divided by 1.4 million bytes, or about 700 diskettes.

Backup devices will ease your burden and allow you to easily back up your data on a regular basis. Even if you're simply adding a drive, a backup is a good idea for avoiding problems.

> **Tip:** Whatever backup medium you use (floppies, tape, zip, and so on), you should check the data integrity of the backup once it's complete. File copy methods aren't always 100 percent accurate, and all backup devices include ways to reread the backed-up information to verify a successful copy. There is no more woebegone feeling than beginning to restore a lot of data, only to discover that it is all unexpectedly gone.

Choose Your Drive Bay

If you're installing an external drive, you don't need to concern yourself with drive bays (just desk space). For an internal drive, open the PC case and check for available drive bays. Check your system's documentation, because some PC designs include bay spaces that aren't obvious just by peering inside. Hard drives come in either $3^1/_2$-inch or $5^1/_4$-inch (across the front of the drive) sizes. You can install a $3^1/_2$-inch drive into a $5^1/_4$-inch bay with the help of mounting brackets.

Check Cabling

When replacing a drive without changing to a new controller, simply use the old power supply connection and controller connection for the new drive. If you're adding a drive, check for free power supply and controller connections that can reach to the drive bay you've chosen for the new drive. Power supply connections are four wide-pin sockets usually encased in white plastic, as shown in Figure 12.5.

Figure 12.5.
Make sure you properly connect the power supply cable to avoid potential damage to your components. (Figure courtesy of Quantum Corp.)

Set Up the Drive

As discussed in Chapter 11, an IDE device can be either a master or a slave. Set the jumpers on an IDE device before installation. Hard drives generally come from the manufacturer set as the master drive for a one-drive only setup, so if that's your scenario, you won't have to modify the jumpers. If you're adding a drive, you might have to set the jumpers on both your original hard drive and the new hard drive. Ultimately, you'll want your boot drive set as master and the new drive as slave. You might have to set a jumper on the original drive to tell it that a slave is present, as shown in Figure 12.6.

Figure 12.6.
You'll need to set jumpers to make sure your hard disk assumes its proper place in the IDE pecking order.

SCSI Devices Require Proper SCSI ID and Termination Settings

Set the jumpers on your hard drive to a unique SCSI ID. For the hard drive, due to faster startup and even general operating performance advantages, choose a low SCSI ID, either 0, 1, or 2 (the lower the better). Then set the termination jumpers if the drive is at the end of a SCSI chain of devices. You might need to remove termination from the SCSI controller host adapter card if you have both internal and external SCSI devices, because now the host adapter is in the middle of the chain, not at the end.

Replacing Your Hard Drive

If it's time to take out an old drive and put in a new one, follow these steps:

1. Turn off your PC and disconnect the power cable.
2. Open the PC case.

3. Remove the data cable and the power cable from the old drive. IDE data cables often include a white strap at each connector so that you don't need to grasp the ribbon cable or the connector itself. If not, you can pull on the ribbon cable, but get your fingers as close to the connector as possible. Use both hands, and pull gently but firmly until the connector detaches. The power supply cable usually requires a little extra effort. Grasp the white plastic connector on both sides (use just one hand, because it's too small for both hands to fit around it) and pull firmly.

Warning: There is a reason to be careful here. The connectors used in the manufacture of ribbon cables are often cheaply made, so they pull apart easily.

4. Unscrew the mounting screws that hold the old drive in place. PC case designs vary tremendously. Traditionally, drive bays are rack-like slots where you slide the drive in or out and secure it with bracket screws into the sides of the drive. But sometimes hard drives are mounted on swing-out metal brackets. If so, remove the screws that hold the swing arm in place, rotate the bay so that the mounting screws are exposed, and remove them. Other times, PC designers trap the drive in the drive bay and protect it from escaping by brackets and screws on the front of the system box. If your drive is in a traditional slot-type drive bay, remove the mounting brackets on both sides of the drive. Newer systems sometimes let you attach the drive to a metal bracket (with two screws) before you slide it into a bay where the bracket just clicks into place.

5. Slide out the old drive. Drives should slide easily as soon as all the mounting screws have been removed. If you feel resistance as you try to remove the drive, you might have missed a mounting screw.

6. Insert the new drive. If your new drive is smaller than your original drive (for example, if the new one is $3^1/_2$ and the old one is $5^1/_4$), you first need to attach the mounting brackets that make the smaller box fit properly into the larger bracket frame. Then slide in your new drive.

7. Screw in the mounting screws for the new drive. Don't over-tighten the screws. (See Figure 12.7.)

8. Reattach power and data cables. Note: Both of these attach correctly in only one way. The ribbon data cable has a red line running along the edge for pin 1 out of the cable. Your hard drive should have a small "1" marking pin 1 on the data cable connector at the back of the drive. If not, read the device's documentation to determine which device is pin 1. Make sure the red line edge of the cable and pin 1 match up, or you won't be able to access this drive.

   Your cable length (particularly in the shorter IDE cables) might determine which drive bays you need to use. Master and slave IDE drives often need to be adjacent to one another.

The power supply cable should have a rounded edge on the top two corners of the connector. The power supply port on the back of the drive will also have these rounded edges designating the top edge of the port. Make sure that the power cable is firmly secured in the correct position.

Figure 12.7.
Check the disk's documentation to make sure you're correctly fitting the new drive. Make sure that you don't accidentally turn the screws into the hard disk's sealed case.

9. Close the PC cover and connect the power cable.

10. Go to the section "Setting the PC's CMOS."

Adding a Second Drive

1. Turn off your PC and disconnect the power cable.

2. Open the PC case.

3. Locate the free drive bay that will hold your new drive. If your new drive is a $3^1/_2$-inch unit and your bay is a $5^1/_4$-inch bay, insert and screw in the mounting brackets.

4. Mount your new drive in the bay. Slide in the new drive so that its back end ports are closest to the data and power supply cable connections. Screw in all the mounting screws, but don't over-tighten them.

5. Connect the data and power supply cables. Internal cables have several connectors running along the length of one cable. Use one of the open connectors for both the data cable (coming from your controller) and the power supply cable (coming from the power supply). Check step 8 of the preceding section to ensure that you are connecting the cables correctly.

> **Technical Note:** If you've already added several internal devices to your PC, it's possible that your power supply might not handle an additional drive. Check your PC's documentation regarding your power supply. The effects of an insufficient power supply would cause data errors or difficulty in accessing your new drive. Anything under 200 watts of power might be a little suspect if you plan to add several devices—particularly SCSI devices.

6. Close the PC case and reconnect the power cable.

7. Now follow the instructions in the next section on setting your PC's CMOS and preparing your new drive for data.

Setting the PC's CMOS

Now that you've finished the physical installation part of the hard drive upgrade process, you have to ready the system to recognize the new drive.

IDE Drives

Your PC needs to know what types of drives and ports are attached (among other things) before it boots and turns control over to the operating system. Check your PC's documentation on how to adjust its CMOS settings (also called *entering setup*). Normally this involves pressing a particular key on your keyboard (such as F1 or Delete) while the PC boots.

Most modern PCs have an Auto Detection setting for IDE drives that tells the PC the drive details it needs to know, such as the number of cylinders on your disk, the number of heads, and the number of sectors per track. Once you've entered your PC's setup program, simply set your IDE drive setting to Auto. Then press the key or key combination that will reboot your PC.

If your PC doesn't have Auto Detection, you need to get the cylinder, head, and sector/track information from your drive manufacturer and enter it manually into your BIOS setup. Most drive vendors now supply this information on their Web site. You also might find it on the case of the drive unit or in the documentation that comes with the drive.

SCSI Drives

Your SCSI host adapter has its own BIOS that handles the SCSI devices that are attached to it. Read the part of your host adapter documentation that covers installing a hard drive. Sometimes SCSI host adapters require a boot drive to be a particular SCSI ID, so check that as well.

Low-Level Hard Drive Formatting

Generally, modern hard drives come with a low-level format already performed by the hard drive manufacturer. It's best not to try to override this low-level format by performing another on your own. If you're having problems with a new drive *and* you've already attempted the troubleshooting procedures covered in this chapter, try a low-level format with the DOS (and Windows 95) FORMAT command.

Partitioning Your Hard Drive

You can *partition* (divide) your new physical hard drive into several logical drives, each designated by a letter (C, D, E, and so on). The key thing to understand about drive partitions is that large ones (from 1024MB to 2048MB) waste an incredible amount of space due to large cluster sizes, the minimum size the operating system takes to store data on the disk. In a 2048MB partition, for example, a small 1KB file actually takes up 32KB of disk space.

Table 12.2 lists partition sizes and their corresponding cluster sizes.

Table 12.2. Bigger drives waste data.

Partition	Cluster Size
From 16 to 128MB	2KB
Between 128 and 256MB	4KB
Between 256 and 512MB	8KB
Between 512 and 1024MB	16KB
Between 1024 and 2048MB	32KB

The latest release of Windows 95 (OSR2) includes a file system called FAT32, which handles this problem and doesn't waste space in large partitions. If you have Windows 95, go to Control Panel, click the System icon, and check the General tab. If the System: entry reads anything other than Windows 95 4.00.950 B, you don't have the OSR2 release. If you don't have this release, or if you're using Windows 3.x, you should choose a partition size of 512MB or less, dividing your disk into multiple logical drives and saving precious disk space.

PC experts sometimes use these logical drives to separate applications from the operating system or to simply categorize their disk like a file drawer (drive C contains business software, drive D has home software, drive E has kids' software, and so forth). Choose the number and size of partitions that make the most sense for you.

Use the FDISK command (DOS and Windows 95) to partition your drive. If you've added a second hard drive, make sure you specify the correct drive to partition, because you'll destroy any data that resides on the drive you partition.

High-Level Hard Drive Formatting

Congratulations! All your hard drive installation difficulties are behind you. Simply format the partitions as you would a floppy disk (use Format.com under DOS or My Computer under Windows 95), but make sure you're formatting the new drive, not your old one, if you've just added a drive! If this is your boot drive, be sure to install the system files on it. Then copy your applications and data from your backup to your newly installed drive.

Repair

As I mentioned, you will deal with hard disk repairs through software utilities, correcting CMOS setup, or fixing cabling mistakes. Don't attempt to fix your hardware by opening the sealed drive box! That requires special tools that you won't find at home.

If you encounter hard disk errors, follow these steps:

- Check the power supply and data cable connections. Make sure everything is secure and properly connected regarding pin numbers. For SCSI, double-check all jumper settings and termination.

- Double-check CMOS setup. Locate the BIOS information regarding your drive and determine whether the auto-detection features have correctly recognized your drive. For SCSI, use the host adapter's BIOS settings.

- Run through the gamut of disk utilities, especially Disk Defragmenter and ScanDisk. Many a disk problem can be resolved by cleaning up and marking off bad sectors.

- Finally, if you've had a disk crash and your drive is inaccessible, consider shipping the disk to a service bureau, which can perform intensive data recovery procedures using specialized equipment. You can find these bureaus by looking in the yellow pages or searching the Web under "Computer Service and Repair." These services will likely cost several hundred dollars, so make sure you really need the missing data. Also, make regular backups so that you won't need this type of expensive service.

Summary

This chapter discussed both the current and the upcoming technologies of hard disk drives, choosing from among IDE and SCSI drives, and whether you need to add to or replace your PC's hard drive. You also saw step-by-step instructions on hard drive installation.

As performance upgrades go, a hard disk won't usually have that great an impact. However, if your hard drive is nearly filled with data, a new hard drive that increases your storage space will have a noticeable effect on your ability to get work done. A new hard disk can let you install and run the latest applications and operating systems, which are often twice the size of versions that came out just a few years before. A new hard disk can also save you a lot of time searching for files to delete.

13

CD-ROM Drives

Peter Norton®

CD-ROM (compact disc read-only memory) drives ushered in the multimedia boom in personal computing. Compact discs allowed for 650 megabytes (MB) of portable storage on a single easy-to-transport platter, which allowed software and multimedia developers to include large sound and video data in their applications and games. Consumers quickly embraced these low-cost, durable (compared to floppies), high-capacity discs. As a result, CD-ROM drives have become the most successful removable mass storage element that the PC has known to date.

Today, virtually all home PCs and over 50 percent of business PCs ship with CD-ROM drives, according to the research firm Dataquest. With CD-ROM discs virtually ubiquitous, everyone from application vendors to game companies has chosen CD-ROM discs as their delivery medium of choice. But CD-ROM technology moves fast, with drive speeds increasing by a factor of five or six in just two or three years.

This chapter will help you stay ahead of this fast-moving area. You will learn how to

- Understand the workings of various types of CD-ROMs
- Examine CD-ROM drive buying issues that may affect your upgrade decisions
- Properly install and optimize your CD-ROM drive for your system
- Identify and resolve conflicts and problems that may arise with the drive

Overview

The first major use of CD-ROM drive technology came in the stereo component consumer market, where CDs ultimately led to the death (or at least an endangered species classification) of the vinyl LP (long-playing) record format. Their 74-minute audio capacity and ability to last for years with no quality degradation made them a hit with music consumers.

CD-ROM technology then stormed the computer market with the ability to store 650MB of data, including sound and video segments, on its shiny 4.72-inch discs. CD-ROM discs now rank as the most-used format for distributing computer software, games, and new music. Almost every new PC on the market comes with a CD-ROM drive.

Unlike magnetic-based recording formats such as hard disks or floppies, CD-ROMs use a laser light method for reading (and writing in the case of CD-Recordable drives) digital data from their discs. A laser (normally yellow) scans the rotating disc surface, and the light reflected back from the disc is interpreted as bit data. A pit (only microns deep) etched into an aluminum alloy coating indicates a binary one, and no pit indicates a binary zero. The laser light reflection only changes in the transition from no pit (called land) to pit or from pit to land.

Note: The issues of keeping CDs clean has often been overstated by computer guide books and magazines, leading to the sale of cleaning kits and paranoia among users. The truth is, if you use them properly, you won't need to clean your CDs for many years. First and foremost, avoid touching your CD's shiny recorded surface, because this tends to leave oil deposits from your skin on the surface of the CD. When you pick up a disc, touch only the edges. Adults can easily grasp a disc in one hand. Children should use two hands if they can't grasp the disc with one. When you're done using your CDs, store them in their jewel cases so that they won't collect dust or become scratched while resting on a rough surface.

The most dramatic change in CD-ROM drive technology (other than recordable media and drives, which are covered in Chapter 16, "Optical Storage") relates to speed. The initial drives had transfer rates of 150 kilobytes per second (KBps), called 1X speed. Manufacturers quickly began improving drive mechanics, and it became standard to refer to drive speed in multiples of this original transfer rate. Therefore, a 2X drive transfers at 300KBps, a 4X drive at 600KBps, and so on. In the beginning, these faster drives had premium prices.

You might have paid $800 for a 10X drive a few years ago. Over time, as more vendors jumped into this popular market and flooded stores with drives, prices dropped tremendously. Today, you can purchase an IDE 16X drive for as little as $150. Currently, CD-ROM drive transfer rates top out at about 24X speed.

As for the future, in addition to even faster drives from various vendors, Western Digital Corporation plans to add what might be an interesting wrinkle to CD-ROM technology. Their new hard drives, shipping in late 1997, use SDX (Storage Data Acceleration) technology. SDX hard drives feature a 10-pin cable connection that can hook directly into CD-ROM (bypassing the EIDE controller bus) for improved performance. Western Digital claims that SDX makes 8X speed drives perform like 20X drives.

Technical Note: Manufacturers use two distinct methods to spin a CD-ROM disc: CAV (constant angular velocity) and CLV (constant linear velocity).

Hard disk drives traditionally use CAV technology, which means that the speed of the platter is kept constant, no matter where the head is over the platter. As the head moves in from the outer rim of the disc toward the center, the speed of the disc moving underneath it is slower (see the nifty carousel analogy in Chapter 12, "Hard Disks"). With the magnetic-based disk/head technology of hard disk drives, this method works well.

When CD-ROMs first came out, engineers believed that a more workable method for the optical heads of CD-ROM drives was CLV, where a set speed under the head is maintained no matter where the head is. In this method, the disc itself must speed up or slow down as the head moves in and out to keep the linear velocity constant.

continues

The CLV approach worked fine until CD-ROM drives started spinning above 12X speeds and the disc RPM (revolutions per minute) began reaching 6,300. At these speeds, speeding up and slowing down the disc would cause a slight shudder, and the optical heads needed time to settle down after a move. As the data transfer rates of CD-ROM drives have reached 20X and 24X, almost all vendors are now using CAV technology for their high-end CD-ROM drives.

Most of these CAV drives come qualified as *variable-speed* CAV technology (such as the Plextor 12/20PleX, shown in Figure 13.1), meaning that two different constant angular velocities are used when reading: one for the outer rim data, and one for the center of the disc. As data is written to the CD starting with the inner track and moving toward the outer track, if a disc isn't full, you won't be able to take advantage of the faster outer rim data transfer speed of variable-speed drives.

Figure 13.1.
Plextor's 12/20PleX variable-speed drive reads data at 12X speeds near the center of the disc, and at 20X speeds at the outer edge. (Photo courtesy of Plextor Corp.)

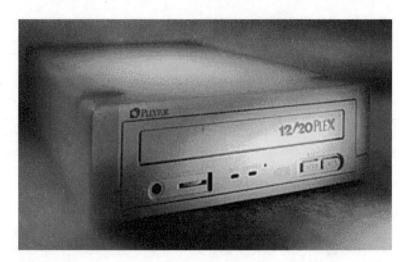

Upgrading a CD-ROM drive is a fairly straightforward process. It's easier than replacing a hard disk, but slightly more involved than adding RAM. The most difficult part of the process is deciding which drive to buy. The options (speed, controller type, caddy or tray, internal or external) can make a drive purchase confusing, but the following section walks you through the decision.

However, repairing a CD-ROM drive, other than a simple cleaning or reconnecting of cables, is a job best left to professionals. Like hard disk drives, the technology inside the sealed unit requires special tools and environments that you won't find around your home or office. Fortunately, drives are so cheap now that replacing a drive would probably be less expensive than attempting to fix a broken one.

Peter's Principle: Buy a CD-ROM Drive Now or Wait for Cheaper, Faster, More Flexible DVD-ROMs

The hype surrounding the new DVD (Digital Versatile Disc) technology suggests that DVD-ROM drives will replace CD-ROM drives in computers. DVD drives allow for 4.7 gigabytes per disc (as opposed to 650MB for CD-ROMs) and include MPEG-2 video and Dolby AC-3 Surround Sound audio data. Unfortunately, the first generation of DVD-ROM drives, which are shipping now, leave something to be desired.

First, although DVD-ROM drives do read and play CD-ROM discs, they do so at relatively slow 6X to 8X transfer speeds. Moreover, because they use a different color laser (red as opposed yellow for CD-ROMs), most of the first-generation DVD-ROM drives can't read the greenish-tinted CD-Recordable discs, which are popular in the desktop publishing business and other markets. The next generation of DVD-ROM drives promises to fix these problems. You will read more about DVD in Chapter 15, "DVD: More Than Hype." For now, understand that at this time, CD-ROM drives remain an affordable and useful upgrade to consider.

Purchase Decisions

Just like hard disk drives, CD-ROM drives come in both SCSI and IDE controller types. But, unlike hard disks, the limited access speeds of the CD-ROM drives (generally 150ms for CD-ROM drives versus a typical 10ms for hard drives) don't stress the transfer rate capabilities of either standard. Both IDE and SCSI controllers can easily handle the "slower-than-hard-disk" transfer rates of even the fastest CD-ROM drives, so don't look at the IDE or SCSI decision in terms of performance. In fact, currently the fastest drives available are 24X EIDE drives (with fast 90ms average access times) from both Hitachi and Toshiba.

If convenience is key, go with an IDE CD-ROM, which should be the easiest to install and your cheapest option, particularly if you can leverage off of your on-board IDE controller. Because all IDE drives are internal, make sure you have an available drive bay that is accessible via a removable space holder through the front of the machine.

If you already have a SCSI controller (saving some of the cost) and/or your IDE controllers are full, consider a SCSI CD-ROM, where you have the option of internal or external drives. Be sure to read Chapter 11, "Control Freaks: IDE and SCSI Controllers," which covers the termination of SCSI devices.

How fast a CD-ROM drive do you need? It depends on what you plan to use it for. Multimedia producers plan their CD-ROM games and titles for play on lower-end CD-ROM drives so that they can capture a large market share. Currently, this lowest-common-denominator approach has most CD titles optimized for 4X speed drives. If you have an older CD-ROM (1X or 2X speed), you might notice that some titles won't even install or play on your drive. With a 4X speed drive, you should have no trouble running any of the latest games or titles, although a year or two down the road, this threshold could conceivably move up to 8X- or 10X-speed drives. Overall, you should get the fastest drive you can afford in order for it to be useful for the foreseeable future.

Who needs the fastest drives? If you answer yes to two or more of the following questions, you should consider a 16X or faster drive:

- Do you regularly transfer CD data (database, image, sound, or video) from discs to your PC?
- Do you install more than 10 new titles (applications, games, or reference) in a month's time?
- Do you use PhotoCDs on a regular basis?
- Do you regularly receive and install update discs from CD-ROM publishing services (legal, clip art, reference, or others)?

Keep in mind that multimedia games and titles are currently optimized for 4X speed playback, so a faster drive will offer no significant advantage in playing back these discs. But installing applications and transferring data from your CD-ROM drive to your hard disk will run the CD-ROM drive as fast as it can go, so a faster drive will save you more time in these situations.

Technical Note: The following is a list of performance specifications for CD-ROM drives. Unlike with hard disk drives, performance really matters when you're shopping for CD-ROMs.

Data transfer rate: How fast the CD-ROM drive transfers data back to the PC. This is usually measured in kilobytes per second and is also referred to as an X-speed (meaning a multiple of the original CD-ROM drive transfer rate of 150KBps). A 4X drive transfers at 600KBps, a 10X drive at 1,500KBps, and a 24X drive at 3,600KBps. A larger number is better.

Average access time: The average amount of time from a CD-ROM drive's receipt of a data request until it reads the first byte of data. This is measured in milliseconds (ms). A smaller number is better. 4X drives usually have 150ms average access times. The fast 24X drives now have 90ms times.

Buffer size: The amount of cache memory on board the CD-ROM drive, usually measured in kilobytes (KB). A larger number is better. These buffers help keep the transfer of data between the PC and the CD-ROM drive continuous so that video and audio playback flow smoothly. Drives normally have 256KB or larger buffers. In read-only CD-ROMs, buffer size specs are less important than data transfer rate and average access time. This cache memory becomes more important in CD-Recordable drives when the buffer can make the difference between a successful recording and a disc recording error (see Chapter 16).

To access this cache setting, do the following:

1. Select Start | Settings | Control Panel.
2. Double-click the System icon.
3. Choose the Performance tab of the System Properties dialog box.
4. Click the File System button.
5. In the subsequent dialog box, choose the CD-ROM tab, as shown in Figure 13.2. In the Settings section, you'll see a slider control called "Supplemental cache size" for adjusting the cache size, as well as a drop-down box called "Optimize access pattern for," which lets you choose a speed setting for your drive. Generally, you should set the supplemental cache size to Large (with the slider all the way to the right) and the access pattern to the speed of your CD-ROM. (The list doesn't go beyond Quad-speed or 4X, so choose Quad-speed for any drives that are faster than 4X.) However, if you're running on very limited hard disk space—say, 10MB or less of free hard disk—you might disable this cache altogether. Do so by selecting "No read-ahead" from the "Optimize access pattern for" drop-down list.

Figure 13.2.
You can try to squeeze a little extra performance out of the drive by tweaking Windows 95's cache settings from the Performance tab of the File System Properties sheet.

Buying Tip: As a rule, it's more difficult to deliver faster access times than it is to improve raw data rates. What's more, access time will have a more profound effect on your day-to-day computing, since this spec determines how quickly the drive can find the first piece of data.

The Tray-Versus-Caddy Controversy

There are two different methods for loading and unloading discs into CD-ROM drives. A caddy mechanism encloses the disc in a removable plastic case (about the size of a jewel case). When you eject a disc, the entire caddy pops out, allowing you to switch discs without ever touching the CDs themselves (provided that you have several plastic caddies). When you're loading a disc into a tray-style CD-ROM drive, on the other hand, a plastic tray slides out from the drive but remains attached to it. You drop the disc directly onto the tray and press the close button.

In general, caddy drives aren't as fragile during loading and unloading discs as tray-style drives. Experts often suggest that caddy drives more accurately read CD-ROMs, but this might be overstated. On the downside, purchasing additional caddies adds cost, and most people never purchase more than a dozen, thereby losing the advantage of never having to touch the discs for large CD collections.

Tray drives (see Figure 13.3) are somewhat faster in loading and unloading discs and are usually cheaper to purchase. But again, trays are slightly more fragile than caddies.

Figure 13.3.
Tray-fed CD-ROM drives, like this remote-controllable model from Creative Labs, are generally more convenient to use than caddy-fed models. (Photo courtesy of Creative Labs)

Additionally, some work environments force people to stand their desktop PC cases on end to make room for other equipment. In these scenarios, the CD-ROM player would sit vertically, not horizontally, in relation to the ground. Unfortunately, not all tray-style CD-ROMs can play discs in this way. Those that can have plastic tabs that secure the CD in the tray even when it's situated vertically.

Unless you're particularly paranoid about banging the sliding tray, go for the tray-style drive. The extra expense and hassle of caddy drives are generally not worth it.

CD-ROM Jukeboxes:
A Small Circle of Friends

The technology of CD-ROM jukeboxes (also called CD-ROM changers) has vastly improved over the years. Now jukeboxes store up to six discs at a time, run up to 10X speed, and swap discs in less than 10 seconds. If you have a small group of discs (from four to six) that you use constantly, a jukebox can save you valuable time by allowing you to keep your discs loaded and available all the time inside one drive.

Companies such as Panasonic, Pioneer, Smart and Friendly, and Nakamichi offer a variety of jukeboxes that come with the same type of options as regular single-disc drives (controller interface, internal and external, speed, buffer size, and so on), but they are differentiated by classifications such as "four-by-eight," "five-by-ten," and so forth, which describe the number of discs that the unit holds by the speed that the drive spins. "Four-by-eight," for example, means that the drive holds four discs at one time and runs at 8X speed.

Normally jukeboxes feature only one actual CD-ROM reader but contain slots where the other discs reside when not in use. Each disc is usually represented by a separate drive letter on your desktop. A game might be at drive E:, a reference title at drive F:, and so on. When you click a different drive letter, the jukebox quickly swaps the old disc out of the drive, inserts the new one, and spins the disc up to speed.

One feature that differs between single disc drives and their jukebox brethren is the loading mechanism. Instead of the tray-versus-caddy issue, jukeboxes have one of the following:

> A slot: This is similar to car stereo CD players, where you just slip the disc through a rectangular hole in the front of the unit.

> A tray: You drop the discs, usually one at a time, into a tray.

> A cartridge (my favorite): You insert all the discs into a sandwiched-sized cartridge and then plug the whole cartridge into the front of the jukebox.

The beauty of cartridges is that, if you have more than one cartridge, you can keep libraries of related discs preloaded and ready to insert into the jukebox. Imagine one cartridge full of games, another full of reference CDs, and so forth.

Unfortunately, although they are ideal in concept, jukeboxes aren't for everyone. Jukebox prices currently range from about $250 to $900—far more than for a typical CD-ROM drive. Moreover, top-end jukeboxes still spin at only about 10X speed, while regular CD-ROMs go up to 24X. The extra money and slower speeds of jukebox drives are only worth it if you have a set of discs that you use frequently. Otherwise, stick with single-disc drives.

Taking It on the Road: Portable CD-ROM Drives

Due to the space restrictions and the difficulty of manufacturing, notebook CD-ROM drives can be quite expensive and can add $500 or more to a notebook purchase. If you can't afford an internal CD-ROM drive in your notebook, but you miss the convenience of playing discs while traveling, check out portable drives such as those from Sony and Panasonic.

These external drives usually connect to notebooks via a Type II PC Card (also known as PCMCIA) slot (see Figure 13.4). Available in 6X to 8X speeds, they often use AA-size batteries, which can keep them running for about three hours without being plugged in. Expect slower access times (from 180ms to 280ms) and smaller buffers (128KB) from these lightweight, portable units.

Figure 13.4.
If a CD-ROM isn't built into your notebook, you might need to use a SCSI PC Card to provide the interface. (Photo courtesy of Adaptec)

If you plan to buy one of these portable drives, in addition to the standard price and performance features, you should look for the following features:

- Rechargeable battery options
- Rugged case designs
- Sturdy PC Card interfaces

Also, realize that many newer notebook manufacturers incorporate specially designed internal CD-ROM units that can be swapped out by extra battery packs or internal floppy drives. Unfortunately, you might be stuck with whatever speed drive the manufacturer offers and therefore won't be able to upgrade when you feel the need. You'll have no alternative company from which to choose a drive.

Troubleshooting

CD-ROM drives usually are reliable. If you're having problems, first check the Windows 95 Device Manager to see if the OS recognizes the CD-ROM as working properly. To access Device Manager, select Start | Settings | Control Panel, double-click the System icon, and choose the Device Manager tab, shown in Figure 13.5. Table 13.1 lists potential problems and their corresponding solutions.

Figure 13.5.
Check Windows 95's Device Manager to make sure your CD-ROM drive is working properly.

Table 13.1. Troubleshooting CD-ROM drives.

Symptom	Solutions
The CD-ROM drive is not accessible through the operating system.	The installation hasn't been successfully completed. Run through the steps in the section "Installing a CD-ROM Drive." When you've successfully completed the installation, you should see the drive referenced in the operating system. In Windows 3.1, you'll notice an icon with a drive letter for the CD-ROM (usually D or E) next to the hard and floppy disk icons in File Manager. Under Windows 95, you'll see an icon for the CD-ROM drive when you click My Computer.

continues

Table 13.1. continued

Symptom	Solutions
The CD-ROM drive immediately ejects the disc every time you insert it.	The disc probably is mis-seated in the tray or caddy. Make sure that the disc sits firm and flat in the tray or caddy. Also, read the following Tip if you're using your drive vertically.
The CD-ROM drive makes whirring sounds while spinning a disc, and error messages pop up about difficulty accessing the CD-ROM drive.	The disc might be scratched or dirty. Clean the disc using a cleaning kit or water and a nonabrasive, lint-free cloth. Inspect the disc for scratches. You might ultimately need to replace the disc if the problem continues. You can also try cleaning the drive itself with a compressed air canister (traditionally used to clean camera equipment).
You receive constant error messages about accessing the CD-ROM, even when you use different discs.	Check all the cable connections, and make sure the drive itself is clean. If the problem continues, you might need to replace the drive.
Excessive heat emanates from the CD-ROM drive.	Check the power cable connection and the power supply specifications for your CD-ROM and the power supply output specs for your power supply. If they check out, it's likely that the CD-ROM drive needs replacing.

Tip: Not all CD-ROM drives were designed to work on their sides. Read the documentation to see if your drive supports this feature. A tray-style drive that allows vertical play will have plastic tabs embedded in the tray that snap out to secure the disc in place for proper seating of the CD disc while it's vertical.

Upgrading

Fortunately, upgrading a CD-ROM drive is a relatively cheap option. If you answer yes to two or more of the following questions, you should consider a CD-ROM upgrade:

- Is your current CD-ROM drive a 1X or 2X speed drive?
- Does your current drive have difficulty reading CD-Recordable discs?
- Does your CD-ROM still generate constant read errors, even after troubleshooting?
- Does your CD-ROM consistently make loud noises, even after troubleshooting?
- Do you often transfer data from CDs to your hard disk?
- Is your current drive incompatible with popular CD-ROM formats such as Photo-CD, multisession discs, Video CD, and so on?

Before the Installation

If you've never installed a CD-ROM drive before, consider purchasing a CD-ROM upgrade kit, because it will include all the necessary cabling, screws, and rails. If your PC doesn't already include a sound card and speakers, check into getting a full multimedia upgrade kit, which will add both to the mix. However, be warned that computer press product reviews have often found these kits to be overly expensive and of poor quality. Carefully check each component of a kit to ensure you're getting a good deal.

Once you've made your purchase, follow these preparatory steps:

1. Choose a drive bay. For internal CD-ROM drives, you need a bay that opens from the front of your PC. If your system is bulging with components, you might need to move your hard drive to a bay that doesn't abut the front of the PC. External CD-ROM drives, of course, require only desk space.

2. Check cabling. Make sure you have the necessary power cable socket (usually a white plastic molding with four large pin openings) and controller cable (IDE or SCSI). Make sure they both reach the drive bay in which you intend to install the CD-ROM drive.

3. Set up the drive. As discussed in Chapter 11, an IDE device can be either a master or a slave. Set the jumpers on an IDE device before installing it. CD-ROM drives generally come from the manufacturer set as the master drive, so if that's your scenario, you won't have to modify the jumpers. In fact, to avoid potential compatibility or performance issues, it's a good idea to put the CD-ROM on the secondary controller (assuming, of course, that your boot drive is on the primary controller). If you're adding a CD-ROM to an IDE controller that already has a drive attached (a hard disk, for example), you might have to set the jumpers on both your CD-ROM and the hard drive.

SCSI devices require proper SCSI ID and termination settings. Set the jumpers on your CD-ROM drive to a unique SCSI ID. Then set the termination jumpers if the drive is at the end of a SCSI chain of devices. You might need to unterminate the SCSI controller host adapter card if you have both internal and external SCSI devices, because now the host adapter is in the middle of the chain, not at the end.

Installing a CD-ROM Drive

Once you've finished the drive preparation, you can start the installation process. If at all possible, try to keep the cabling inside the PC neat and organized during your work and after you've finished the job. You'll thank yourself the next time you delve inside the PC case.

1. Turn off your PC and disconnect the power cable.

2. Open the PC case and remove the front placeholder panel, which will be taken up by the front of the CD-ROM drive unit.

3. If your drive bay requires slide rails, attach them.

4. Attach the controller cable and the power cable. (With all the cabling and cramped spaces, attaching the cables after the drive is secured in the bay can be difficult.)

5. Both the controller cable and the power cable attach correctly in only one position. The ribbon data cable has a red line running along the edge for pin 1 out of the cable. Your CD-ROM drive should have a small "1" that marks pin 1 on the data cable connector at the back of the drive. If not, read the device's documentation to determine which pin is pin 1. Make sure that the red line edge of the cable and pin 1 match up, or you won't be able to access this drive.

6. The power supply cable should have a rounded edge on the top two corners of the connector. The power supply port on the back of the drive will also have these rounded edges, which designate the top edge of the port. Make sure that the power cable is firmly secured in the correct position.

7. Attach the audio cable from the CD-ROM drive to your sound card. The audio cable transfers the audio signal (converted to analog from the digital source) from audio CDs. The audio port of the CD-ROM drive is usually adjacent to the power cable port. Read your sound card's documentation to find where the connector goes on the sound card.

8. Slide the CD-ROM drive into the drive bay, as shown in Figure 13.6. Make sure that the front edge fits flush with the front of the PC case. Also make sure that the drive sits level in the bay.

9. Close the PC case and reattach the power cable.

Repairing

Checking cabling and operating system settings will fix most CD-ROM drive problems. If the drive itself isn't working properly, it must either be replaced or sent to a professional, because the internal components can't be manipulated in a home or office environment.

If you encounter problems with your drive, follow these steps:

- Double-check cabling. Mis-seated or reversed controller connectors will make your CD-ROM drive inaccessible.

- Check that your operating system correctly identifies the drive. Under Windows 95, right-click the CD-ROM drive icon under My Computer and select Properties. The resulting dialog box should correctly identify your drive. Contact the drive's technical support if this is not the case.

  In DOS (and therefore Windows 3.x) you need to check your settings in CONFIG.SYS and AUTOEXEC.BAT. The AUTOEXEC.BAT line that refers to your CD-ROM should look something like this:

  ```
  C:\WINDOWS\MSCDEX.EXE /d:mscd001
  ```

This is the reference for the Microsoft CD Extensions for DOS.

Your CONFIG.SYS will have a corresponding line that specifies a device driver to match the AUTOEXEC.BAT file's mscd001 CD-ROM device name. Your drive's installation instructions will spell out the details of the CONFIG.SYS line, but it will look something like this:

```
DEVICE=C:\CDDRVER\CDDRV.SYS /D:MSCD001
```

If you generally use Windows 95 but occasionally boot or shut down to DOS (perhaps to play DOS games), you'll also need these AUTOEXEC.BAT and CONFIG.SYS entries in your PC's configuration files.

Figure 13.6.
For internal drives, you'll need to make sure there's a free drive bay to slip the unit into.

- Inspect the medium: It might be that the problem lies with your disc, not your drive. Make sure your discs are clean and free of scratches. If you're using CD-Recordable discs, it's possible that your drive has compatibility problems with that type of CD-ROM. Check with the drive manufacturer.

- Clean the drive: Used compressed air to clean the tray/caddy of the drive.

Summary

CD-ROM drives are a critical piece of the PC puzzle. Not only do faster drives provide quicker response and file transfers, but they also can ease the load on your CPU. Most users opt for enhanced IDE drive models, which are affordable, quick, and easy to find. But if you do a lot of multitasking or you want a CD-ROM drive that sits externally on your desktop, you'll need to consider a SCSI device.

Of course, DVD looms on the horizon. Although this high-capacity medium comes with a lot of hype and more than a few attractive features, the technology is clearly in its infancy. Early drives lack compatibility with common media such as CD-Recordable, PhotoCD, and audio CD discs. They are also limited to slow 6X or 8X data rates when playing CD-ROM discs.

The ubiquity of CD-ROM discs, rapid increases in drive performance, and questions about DVD all make CD-ROM drives a viable upgrade. Combine these traits with incredibly low prices, and a CD-ROM drive upgrade might be a good way to extend the life of your PC.

14

Beyond Floppies: Removable Storage for PCs

Peter Norton®

Much is changing with the PC platform, and nowhere is it more overdue than with the venerable floppy drive. The $3\frac{1}{2}$-inch floppy diskette is the universal medium for sharing data among systems, but it has been around for well over 10 years.

Change is in the air. New removable storage technologies are vying for a shot at becoming the standard, thus inviting all sorts of difficult upgrade decisions. Meanwhile, floppy drives are often prone to problems since their mechanisms aren't sealed and drives read diskettes in all sorts of states of disarray.

This chapter will help you

- Understand existing and developing removable media technologies
- Master buying issues associated with a changing market
- Troubleshoot and resolve problems with removable media and their drives
- Install new removable-media drives

Overview

The floppy disk drive was the first removable storage device for the PC. The term "floppy" came from the original $5\frac{1}{4}$-inch diskettes, which could actually bend because they had only a thin coated paper (or flexible plastic) covering, not a hard plastic shell. These original floppies could hold only 360KB of data and recorded on both sides. These diskettes were soon followed by "high-density" versions, which increased the number of available tracks per side and could store 1.2MB of data.

The $3\frac{1}{2}$-inch diskettes, covered in a hard plastic case, quickly converged on the PC after enjoying success on the Apple Macintosh. The first $3\frac{1}{2}$-inch diskette held 720KB of data, but improvements in track density led to 1.44MB and then 2.88MB-capable drives and diskettes. Unfortunately, the 2.88MB format was never widely accepted, and now it's difficult to find drives that accept this format, which can be a problem when you're sharing diskettes.

Floppy Drives

The innards of a floppy drive somewhat resemble the magnetic-based recording internals of the hard disk drive unit. Included are the following:

- Magnetic read/write heads: These read and write the data to and from the diskette surface.
- A head actuator: This moves the heads in and out across the diskette to position them over specific tracks.
- A spindle motor: This spins the diskette in a circle so that the track/sector data passes underneath the heads.

Floppy drives have two spring-loaded read/write heads that actually grip the diskette surface on both sides (unlike hard disk drives, which don't touch the disk surface). The direct connection between the heads and the diskette surface causes wear over time, which is why it's a good idea to replace diskettes that you use frequently.

Floppy drive capacities now seem sorely lacking when you consider the large sound, video, image, and database files that are common today. A single large TIFF image file might exceed the storage capacity of a floppy diskette. Distributing applications and other software on diskette has mostly vanished as the number of floppies per title needed grew past 30. Now vendors mainly use the popular CD-ROM medium for distributing software.

Manufacturers no longer attempt to increase the performance or even the potential density of these original floppy drives. What manufacturers *have* done is delve into research and development of new removable storage technologies such as LS-120 and Zip-style drives, which offer much larger capacities. The goal is to replace floppy drives with these new technologies. But which medium will dominate is still up in the air.

Keep in mind that faster access and larger-capacity removable drives such as Iomega's 1 GB Jaz drive do exist, although high prices will probably keep them out of the running as floppy replacements.

Troubleshooting: If you're unexpectedly having trouble accessing a $3\frac{1}{2}$-inch diskette, eject the diskette and try sliding the metal shutter plate back and forth with your fingers. Occasionally, the plate can become stuck, keeping the floppy drive from sliding it back to access the data.

Sometimes you can fix the snag by gently but firmly sliding the plate back and forth before reinserting it into the drive. Be careful not to touch the disk surface itself with your fingers or anything else when you pull the shutter back. It's easy to damage the surface of the recording material.

LS-120 Drives

LS-120 stands for Laser Servo-120MB. Compaq and other PC vendors have begun to include LS-120 drives in their new desktop products, and you can now purchase these drives separately (see Figure 14.1). O.R. Technology's a:drive and Imation's SuperDisk 120MB (both LS-120 drives) are being sold as upgrades.

LS-120 drives, first developed by 3M, use the same size diskettes and the same basic concentric track concept as standard floppy drives. However, the LS-120 medium is specially formatted during manufacturing with a laser to contain a high-density track guide called a "servo" pattern. This pattern, which is never disturbed or removed during reads or writes, is used as an index by an optical laser head inside the drive.

Figure 14.1.
LS-120 drives stand a good chance of being the next floppy. (Photo courtesy of O.R. Technology)

The optical head precisely guides a cooperative magnetic read/write head to track locations with densities of up to 2490 data tracks per inch (compared to just 135 tracks per inch for conventional high-density floppy diskettes). Higher disk rotational speed allows LS-120 drives to transfer data about five times faster than traditional floppy drives.

Moreover, LS-120 drives sport dual-gap read/write heads, which can read and write 1.44MB and 720KB 3½-inch floppy diskettes. (And no, their capacity doesn't increase just because they're used in the LS-120 drives.) Still, the faster disk rotation means that old floppies transfer data about three times faster in LS-120 drives than when used in floppy drives.

LS-120 media come with a dual-layer coating and metal particle pigment, different from the ferrite material of floppy media, which allows for the higher density. All LS-120 disks come preformatted, although you can delete and rewrite information on the diskettes as you normally would with a floppy diskette. Unlike Zip drive disks, LS-120 diskettes can be used as boot diskettes for your PC. Internal models use the standard IDE interface, and external models use the parallel port connection.

Zip Drives

Iomega Corporation introduced a $149 removable storage drive, called the Zip drive, and it has gained tremendous popularity over the last few years. These drives use proprietary 3½-inch disks that are twice as thick as standard 3½-inch floppies and that store 100MB of data per disk. Zip drives can't read traditional floppy diskettes.

Zip drives win hands down in terms of interface options. Among the various types of Zip drives are these:

- SCSI internal
- SCSI external
- Parallel port external
- Enhanced IDE (internal)

SCSI connections (see Figure 14.2) and IDE connections offer the fastest performance for Zip drives with 29 millisecond access times, although this speed still remains significantly slower than hard disks.

Figure 14.2.
SCSI-based drives will give you the best performance, but you might have to pony up for a separate adapter card, such as the Adaptec 2940 Ultra shown here. (Photo courtesy of Adaptec Inc.)

The parallel port option increases the unit's flexibility, because you can quickly connect to different computers, and it's perfect for use with notebook computers. But the parallel port becomes a performance bottleneck for data transfer and can noticeably slow drive access.

Zip drives can't be used as boot drives for the PC, and you'll find it difficult, even impossible, to launch applications directly from Zip disks. These drives are better used for data storage, backup, and archiving files.

One key issue remains with floppy drives and their potential replacements—sharing data. The beauty of the floppy medium was that it was widely accepted and became a standard feature on all PCs. As the floppy's domination erodes, it might get harder to swap data to other computers using a less common medium.

Currently, Zip drives have a popularity edge over LS-120-style drives—Iomega Corporation has sold over 7 million units. This lead might dissolve as the larger and higher-performing LS-120 drives and diskettes arrive on more desktop computers from the factory. Overall, it's difficult to determine which way the trend will go. Stay abreast of the media used by the people you share data with. If you all work with the same medium, you'll encounter fewer hassles down the road.

Purchase Decisions

Never consider upgrading a floppy drive because you need a "better" one. Your floppy drive either works or it doesn't. If it doesn't, you can consider a cheap replacement. In terms of upgrades, you might think about moving up to the new drives, which feature 100MB or more on a single removable disk. LS-120 and Zip drives are relatively cheap, are easy to install, and might suit your needs. In this chapter, we'll discuss how to install both.

One way to go is to purchase a combination drive, which comes with different devices and includes a floppy drive. One style combines a CD-ROM drive and a floppy unit in the same drive. Another style offers both floppy and PC Card (also know as PCMCIA cards).

Your best bet with a combination drive would most likely be the floppy/PC Card combo. The CD-ROM drive that is included in such a combo might be of inferior performance, while the PC Card interface will likely be standard-issue. Keep in mind that LS-120 drives read 1.44MB standard floppies, so you might consider that route as well.

If you already have a high-capacity portable storage device (CD-Recordable drive, tape, and so forth), you might decide on a straightforward floppy drive replacement. If you do plan to simply replace your current floppy drive with another plain-vanilla floppy, here's a quick checklist to help guide your purchase:

- Don't concern yourself with performance. Floppy drives all perform alike.
- Don't concern yourself with brand names. You'll probably just pay more for the name.
- Shop around. You shouldn't have to spend more than $50 for a new floppy drive.

Thinking about higher-capacity drives? If you answer yes to three or more of the following questions, you should consider buying a Zip drive:

- Do you plan to use your new drive mostly for data backup, archive, and temporary storage?
- Is it unlikely that you'll need to use the drive as a boot drive?
- Is fast access unimportant to you?
- Do the people you share data with use Zip drives?
- Is it unnecessary for the new drive to be able to read floppy diskettes?

On the other hand, if you can answer yes to two or more of the following questions, you should consider spending a little more money for an LS-120-style drive:

- Do you need to boot from the drive?
- Do you need to launch applications from the drive?
- Do others you share data with use the LS-120 medium?
- Does the new drive need to be able to read floppy diskettes?

Table 14.1 compares floppy, Zip, and LS-120 drives.

Table 14.1. A comparison of removable media.

	3½-Inch Floppy Drive	Zip Drive	LS-120 Drive
Single-disk capacity	1.44MB or 2.88MB	100MB	120MB
Boot drive potential	Yes	No	Yes
Interface options	IDE	IDE, internal SCSI, external SCSI, parallel port	IDE for internal, parallel port for external
Ability to launch applications from disk	Yes	No	Yes
Price	About $50	About $149	About $199

Diagnosing/Troubleshooting

Floppy drives are notoriously flaky. Heat and cold and variations among drives and diskettes can cause errors. Table 14.2 is a guide to help you fix your problems.

Table 14.2. Floppy fixes.

Symptom	Solution
Disk errors while accessing a particular diskette	Make sure that the diskette is formatted correctly for your drive. Macintosh-formatted diskettes can't be read by PCs without special utilities. Additionally, 2.88MB formatted diskettes can't be read by all floppy drives. If the data isn't vital, try reformatting the diskette, or simply replace it.
You're unable to access the floppy drive at all	Check data cable and power cable connections inside the PC. Make sure that the cables are aligned properly and that the fittings are snug. Try replacing the data cable. Make sure that your computer's BIOS settings have an entry for the floppy drive.
Diskettes frequently become stuck in the drive	The ejector arm of the drive might be broken. For $50, replacing the drive might be your best option. If you feel like tinkering, you can take the drive apart to see if you can fix the problem.

continues

Table 14.2. continued

Symptom	Solution
Frequent disk errors while accessing diskettes	Try cleaning the read/write heads with a cleaning kit, available from any computer store. Usually these kits come in wet or dry options. The wet kits cause less wear on the head. If the problem continues, consider replacing the drive.

Troubleshooting: Unlike hard disk drives and CD-ROM drives, floppy drives can be taken apart for repair. The most common reason to do this is that a floppy diskette is stuck in the drive unit. Be sure to completely remove the drive from the computer before attempting to disassemble it. Getting the floppy diskette out is simply a matter of unscrewing the case screws, removing the metal casing that surrounds the drive internals, and pulling the diskette free. Before completely closing your PC case again, attach the reassembled drive to the computer with the PC case off, and determine if it works.

To extend the life of diskettes, follow these simple rules:

- Never expose them to extreme temperatures, hot or cold.
- Never expose them to strong magnetic fields, including resting them on audio speakers or your monitor.
- Never touch the recording surface with anything.
- Avoid spilling anything on the diskette case.
- Store diskettes in a dust-free area or inside a case with a cover.

Upgrading

Because floppy drives reside alone on their own controller ports, you don't need to worry about the jumper settings that most internal device installations require. Just follow the next steps.

Upgrading a Floppy Drive

To replace a floppy drive, do the following:

1. Turn off the PC and disconnect the power cable.
2. Remove the PC case.

3. Remove the data and power cable from the back of the floppy disk drive, and then remove the drive itself.

4. Unscrew the mounting brackets that hold the drive in place.

5. Slide the floppy drive out on its drive bay.

6. If your new drive is a $3\frac{1}{2}$-inch drive and your old drive was $5\frac{1}{4}$-inch, you mighufiDeed to attach mounting brackets that will hold the smaller drive in the larger bay. If so, screw in the mounting brackets now.

7. Attach the data and power cables to the back of the new floppy drive unit before inserting it into the drive bay. It might be difficult to access the ports after the drive is installed in the bay, so avoid this hassle by attaching them now. You can use the same ribbon data cable that was attached to your old floppy drive, but if you want to replace it, you can do so now.

Note: To replace the ribbon data cable, locate the floppy drive controller port on the motherboard of your PC. It should have the word "floppy" etched into the board directly underneath. It generally resides right next to the primary and secondary on-board IDE controllers.

Remove the old ribbon cable and attach the new one. Make sure the red line along the new ribbon cable aligns with pin 1 of the controller. You should also see a "1" etched into the motherboard, pointing out the proper side of the on-board floppy controller.

Now attach the ribbon data cable and the power cable to the new floppy drive. Both of these cables attach correctly in only one way. The ribbon data cable has a red line running along the edge for pin 1 out of the cable. Your floppy drive should have a small "1" marking pin 1 on the data cable connector at the back of the drive. If it doesn't, read the device's documentation to determine which pin is pin 1. Make sure the red-line edge of the cable and pin 1 match up, or you won't be able to access this drive.

The power supply cable should have a rounded edge on the top two corners of the connector. The power supply port on the back of the drive will also have these rounded edges, designating the top edge of the port. Make sure that the power cable is firmly secured in the correct position.

Note: Both ribbon cables and the power cables inside PCs usually have connectors along the length of the cables, as well as connectors at both ends of the cable. These simply let multiple devices share the same cable. There is no order to these connectors, so attach your floppy drive to whichever connectors along the floppy controller ribbon cable (and the power cable) are closest to the drive itself.

8. Slide the floppy drive into the drive bay. Make sure the front of the drive is flush with the front of the PC unit. Make sure there are no gaps between the edges of the drive and the metal frame that surrounds it.

9. Attach the screws that secure the drive in place. Do not over-tighten them.

10. Close the PC case and secure the case screws.

11. Reinsert the PC power cable.

12. If you just replaced the floppy drive with an identical unit, no BIOS adjustments should be necessary. However, if you've moved from a $5\frac{1}{4}$-inch drive to a $3\frac{1}{2}$-inch drive or made some other configuration change, you should check your computer's BIOS settings to ensure that it has correctly identified the drive through auto-configuration.

Installing a Zip Drive

Currently, Iomega Corporation (www.iomega.com) offers Zip drives in parallel port and internal and external SCSI versions. At the time this chapter was written, an internal IDE version had been announced but was not yet available. Installing the parallel port version is a breeze, and you have the flexibility to quickly move the drive to another computer. But, as I mentioned, you sacrifice some performance for what you gain in flexibility.

Installing the Zip Drive on a Parallel Port

The Zip drive comes with a *pass-through* parallel port connection, which lets you keep both the Zip drive and your printer attached to the parallel port at the same time.

1. Attach the Zip's pass-through connector to the parallel port. If you have a printer attached to the parallel port, remove your printer cable from the parallel port of your PC, and then attach the Zip drive connector to the parallel port.

2. Connect your printer cable to the back of the Zip's pass-through port.

3. Install the Zip drive software, which will recognize your drive as the next available drive letter.

Installing an External SCSI Zip Drive

If you don't have a SCSI controller, you'll need to purchase one and install it. See Chapter 11, "Control Freaks: IDE and SCSI Controllers," for details. The Zip drive uses a SCSI-2 thin 50-pin female, but it can attach to any SCSI controller card with the right cable adapter. If you already own a SCSI card, check which type you have. You must purchase an adapter cable if you don't have the SCSI-2 connector.

1. Connect the SCSI cable to your SCSI controller and to the back of the Zip drive.

2. Set the SCSI ID settings. If you have other SCSI devices, check them to determine if either SCSI ID 5 or 6 is free. These are the two IDs that the Zip drive can use. You might need to set the switch (or jumpers) of another SCSI device to a different ID if both are currently being used. Choose either 5 or 6 for the Zip drive, and then set the switch.

3. Set the termination of the Zip drive. The default setting is terminated for the end of the SCSI chain. If you have other SCSI devices, you might need to adjust this switch. (You can read about terminating devices in Chapter 11.) First, simply try to access the drive after you finish the installation. It's likely you won't need to adjust this switch.

4. Turn on the power for the Zip drive before turning on your PC. In order for the PC to recognize the drive, you must turn on the Zip drive first.

Installing an LS-120 Drive

LS-120 drives from Imation (www.imation.com) and O.R. Technology (www.ortechnology.com) come in external parallel port versions and internal IDE versions. As with Zip drives, you'll sacrifice performance for the flexibility of the parallel port versions.

Installing the Parallel Port LS-120 Drive

Just like with the Zip drive, you can still operate your printer through the pass-through capabilities of the LS-120 connector. Unlike Zip drives, LS-120 drives are made by more than one manufacturer, so their installation procedures might vary. Make sure you read and follow the directions included with your drive. In general, the instructions should be similar to these steps:

1. Attach the LS-120's pass-through connector to the parallel port.

2. Connect your printer cable to the back of the Zip's pass-through port.

3. Install the LS-120 drive software, which will recognize your drive as the next available drive letter.

Installing the Internal IDE LS-120 Drive

Follow the manufacturer's instructions to install the internal IDE LS-120 drive. In general, the steps will be as follows:

1. Turn off your PC's power, and remove the power cable.

2. Remove the PC's case.

3. Choose your drive bay. If you're replacing your floppy drive (because the LS-120 drive reads floppy diskettes in addition to LS-120 media), remove your floppy drive and use that drive bay for your LS-120 drive.

4. Attach the ribbon data cable and power cable. Make sure that the cables connect in the proper way. You can use any connector of your IDE controller cable.

5. Insert the drive into the bay. Make sure that the front of the drive is flush with the front of the machine.

6. Secure the LS-120 drive in its bay with screws.

7. Close the PC's case and reattach the power cable.

8. Read the manufacturer's instructions regarding your BIOS. You might need to upgrade your BIOS to recognize the LS-120 drive as a boot drive.

Repair

Unlike hard disk drives and CD-ROM drives, you can actually disassemble a floppy disk drive with standard tools. Unlike fast-access drives, floppy drives are not sealed against the contaminants in the air (dust, dirt, and so on).

The problem is that you'll probably find it easier (and less expensive) to just replace the drive than to either fix it yourself or have someone else do it. Floppies currently cost $50 or less. First, though, follow these steps to determine if you can fix your drive:

1. Check cabling and power connections. Make sure that pin 1 is aligned with the red edge of your ribbon data cable and that the power cable is inserted properly.

2. Make sure that your system BIOS correctly identifies your drive.

3. Try cleaning the drive heads with a store-bought wet cleaning kit.

4. Check your diskettes to make sure they aren't the problem. Format new diskettes, copy files to them, and read and write to them. Throw out any old, beat-up diskettes.

Summary

Floppy drives should be given a lifetime achievement award by the computer industry. Due to their relatively simple technology, sufficient speed, and cheap but durable medium, floppy drives have been an integral component aboard almost every PC ever manufactured. For many years, floppy disks were the main distribution medium for software and data.

Times have changed. With the large-scale files now involved in multimedia applications, a single file can be larger than the 1.44MB capacity of the standard high-density floppy format.

You can easily replace your broken floppy drive with an inexpensive replacement, but for a little more money, you can extend the capacity of a single disk drive to 100MB with a Zip drive or even to 120MB with an LS-120 drive. These new-wave removable storage drives come in a wide array of interfaces, including parallel port, external SCSI, and internal SCSI. Although no one yet knows whether any of these new formats will ever be as popular as floppy drives, you can take advantage of their large capacity in the meantime.

15

DVD:
More Than
Hype

Peter Norton®

Your PC has a problem. There's a burgeoning universe of cool theater-quality video, audio, and animation out there, and no way to get it into your PC. Internet connections aren't fast enough, and CD-ROM discs aren't large enough to handle sharp MPEG-2 compressed video and immersive AC-3 audio. What do you do? Why, upgrade, of course.

The new Digital Versatile Disk (DVD) technology is classic convergence stuff. DVD-ROM drives and DVD players promise to change the face of both computing and home theater. If you have a fast Pentium-class PC and you want access to the best and brightest content, you'll need to upgrade to a DVD-ROM drive.

This chapter covers the following:

- The workings of DVD media and drives
- Buying advice for those considering a DVD-ROM drive in a new or existing PC
- Upgrading and installation insights for a new DVD-ROM drive
- Troubleshooting and maintenance tips for DVD-ROM drives

The CD-ROM Revolution, Part II

They say necessity is the mother of invention. Well, Mom was hard at work when the DVD specification was being cooked up during the last two years. It all began in the early 1990s, when it became apparent that the existing capacity of CD-ROM discs was running out of steam. The culprit was high-quality, high-bandwidth video compression schemes featured on direct satellite systems (DSS) such as DirecTV and PrimeStar.

Birth of a Spec

Several companies began investigating ways to increase the storage capacity of existing CD-ROM discs and drives. New manufacturing techniques and improved laser technology had begun to pave the way for storage potential far beyond the CD-ROM limits of 650MB per disc. Two competing organizations and design specifications quickly emerged: Super Density, from a group of companies led by Toshiba, and Multimedia CD, from Philips and Sony.

It was becoming a classic standards standoff, and one that could imperil the success of the new standard. Considering the costly '80s battle between competing videocassette standards (VHS and Betamax), the two groups decided to work together in 1996 to complete one unified standard. The result was called Digital Versatile Disc.

Input from the movie industry added much complexity to the initial designs. This group saw DVD as a terrific medium for the distribution of higher-quality home movies. To make it happen, they wanted the following:

- MPEG-2 video support
- Dolby AC-3 surround sound audio support
- Subtitling capability
- The capability to handle multiaspect ratios (full screen, letterbox, and wide screen)
- Encryption

Not surprisingly, hammering out these aspects took time. Hollywood studios were particularly concerned about encryption, since the digital nature of DVD invites the potential for large-scale piracy that could prove financially ruinous to these businesses. In fact, encryption remained a sticking point until the first DVD drives and media were released in mid-1997.

DVD readers come in two forms:

- DVD players
- DVD-ROM drives

Intended for the family room, DVD players are set-top boxes that plug directly into your television. Essentially, they are the successor to today's VCRs and Laserdisc players.

For PCs, DVD-ROM drives look and act like existing CD-ROM drives, as shown in Figure 15.1. However, they come with additional hardware—usually an add-in board—that handles the demanding tasks of video and audio processing, as well as the decryption of the disc data.

Figure 15.1.
DVD-ROM drives such as Creative Labs' Encore-DVD drive look like CD-ROM drives but offer up to 30 times the storage capacity. (Photo courtesy of Creative Labs)

The Four Faces of DVD

Actually, DVD is four specs in one, with separate schemes for storing anywhere from 4.7 to 17GB of data on a single disc. By taking advantage of media layering and using both sides of the disc platter, four capacity levels are supported:

- Single-sided, single-layer: 4.7GB
- Single-sided, dual-layer: 8.5GB

- Double-sided, single-layer: 9.4GB
- Double-sided, dual-layer: 17GB

All DVD discs, regardless of capacity, have the same diameter and thickness as traditional CD-ROM discs (a 12cm diameter and a 1.2mm thickness). Only the first and smallest DVD disc type—4.7GB—is currently available. Subsequent media are expected to roll out over the next year. Fortunately, all DVD players and DVD-ROM drives sold today will be able to read all the various formats.

One bit of good news is that manufacturing improvements have allowed existing CD-ROM production facilities to be refitted to generate DVD-ROMs. The major change comes in the bonding process, where two 0.6mm-thick discs (called *substrates*) must be bonded to create a single 1.2mm-thick disc. This second substrate, which is not present on CD-ROM discs, provides the "dual-layer" feature, where another level of data storage is contained. In essence, DVD discs are two discs in one.

Other DVD Details

But wait—there's more. Lots more. Other DVD advances include

- Laser wavelength
- MPEG-2 video
- Dolby AC-3 surround sound audio

Laser Light

DVD-ROM drives use a red laser, as opposed to the yellow laser used in CD-ROM drives. The red laser light has a shorter wavelength than yellow lasers, which allows the drive to focus on smaller data bits than CD-ROM drive lasers. By cramming data bits closer together on the disc, much greater capacities (4.7GB versus 650MB) can be stored on a single layer of disc material.

The new color also plays an important role in the layout of the dual-layered DVD disc. The disc's underlayer is silver-colored and reflective, and the overlayer is semitransparent and gold in color. By setting the red laser to low power, the drive reads the outer gold layer. Increase the laser power, and the drive punches through to read data on the silver underlayer.

MPEG-2: Theater-Quality Video

By now, most PC users are familiar with MPEG-1 video, often found on existing CD-ROM titles. This VHS-quality video compression scheme was designed to put lots of video onto 650MB CD-ROM discs and to allow it to play back even on the slowest CD-ROM drives. There's just one problem: The highly-compressed video lacks visual fidelity and gets downright chunky during the fast-action sequences routinely encountered in movies and sports broadcasts.

Enter MPEG-2. Designed by the Motion Pictures Experts Group (MPEG), MPEG-2 dramatically improves on the MPEG-1 standard while using the same basic compression principle of storing only changes that occur between specific frames, called *key frames*. Thus, in a talking-head sequence (such as a newscaster talking), only the movements of the announcer's head, mouth, and eyes get stored, not the unchanging background.

That's where the similarities end: MPEG-2 delivers video quality that is superior to both Laserdisc and Super VHS. MPEG-2 provides more than four times the resolution of MPEG-1, making it appropriate for full-screen video and television broadcasts. It also shoots out video at 60 fields per second—essentially 60 frames interlaced—versus MPEG-1's 30 frame-per-second limit. Most important, it allows for high data rate transfers so that enough data is available to store even action-packed sequences. Table 15.1 compares MPEG-1 and MPEG-2.

Table 15.1. MPEGs compared.

Characteristic	MPEG-1	MPEG-2
Resolution	352×240	720×240
Frame rate	30 frames per second	60 fields per second
Data rate	150 Kbps	1.5MBps compressed, 20MBps uncompressed

The Ears Have It: Dolby AC-3 Sound

Also called 5.1 Surround Sound, AC-3 uses five separate channels of digital audio, plus a dedicated subwoofer channel, to produce true surround sound. The five channels designate left, right, and center in front of the listener, and left and right behind the listener. The subwoofer, which produces deep bass sounds, sits front and low.

More important for PC users, AC-3 can be used in traditional two-speaker setups. Algorithms are applied to produce the illusion of surround sound from two speakers, although you'll get much more realistic results with all five speakers in place. In order to decode AC-3 data, most DVD kits use a special chipset on the DVD add-in boards (see Figure 15.2). Some kits, like the Sony DDU100E, decode AC-3 data in software, but this method makes greater demands on your PC's CPU.

Peter's Principle: DVD-ROM Software Might Be
Recycled CD-ROM Software

Currently, only a few DVD titles are available in stores. By the beginning of 1998, you should see about 150 movies and live music concert discs from companies such as Warner

continues

and Columbia, but computer-related games, reference, and entertainment titles might take a bit longer before they arrive en masse.

Some vendors have begun porting CD-ROM titles that came in multidisc sets into single-disc DVD packages. Unfortunately, there are two key issues involved in porting CD-ROM to DVD-ROMs that consumers should be aware of.

First, games that were created for CD-ROM might not include the superior MPEG-2 video or Dolby AC-3 sound that DVD offers without having undergone significant and expensive rework. The main advantage of a ported game would be that you would no longer need to swap discs in and out of your ROM drive as you progress through the game. Don't expect stunning sound and video on a CD-ROM ported game unless the improvement is specifically mentioned on the box or in a computer press review.

Second, reference titles that were originally designed to reside on a series of CD-ROM discs will have a different indexing system (used for searches) than titles that were specifically designed to reside on one large DVD disc. Thus, don't except fast searches on a DVD reference title that was ported from CD-ROM without an indexing overhaul. Again, computer publications would be your best source for information about particular titles.

Overall, before you buy, make sure you carefully check any DVD title that you suspect might have been ported from CD-ROM multidisc sets. It might not include the stellar attributes that original DVD titles offer.

Figure 15.2.
Most DVD-ROM kits use a separate AC-3 board to handle the demands of surround sound audio.

The Future Looks Bright: Buying into DVD

Will DVD-ROM drives ultimately replace CD-ROM drives? Probably. However, the first-generation drives that are currently available (such as Toshiba's SD-M1002 DVD-ROM) won't be the DVD drives to achieve this. Although the first-generation drives do read most CD-ROM formats, they can't read CD-Recordable discs. (The greenish tint of CD-R media conflicts with the red laser of DVD.) Moreover, the performance of first-generation DVD-ROM drives playing CD-ROM media leaves something to be desired (currently, only 8X speed or 1200Kbps is supported).

Look for second-generation drives, which solve both of these problems. Fortunately, they are in the last stages of development and should start to become available by the time you read this. These drives use a second laser to read CD-ROMs, which doesn't conflict with CD-R. Additionally, the spindle motors will run CD-ROMs at 24X speed.

Just like the dramatic drop in CD-ROM drive prices as newer CD-ROM drives arrived, DVD-ROM drives should dip well below their $400 to $800 original price points as second-generation drives emerge.

Down the Road: Improvements to Wait for in DVD-ROM Drives

Muddying the buying waters is the changing face of the DVD market. Over the next year, several variations on the base DVD-ROM drive will emerge that might make a purchase worth putting off. Here are some of the coming products and when you should see them:

- Second-generation DVD-ROM: Fall-winter 1997
- High-density DVD-ROM discs: First half of 1998
- Recordable DVD (DVD-R): Mid-1998
- Rewritable DVD (DVD-RAM): Second half of 1998

Second-Generation DVD-ROM

Second-generation drives were just emerging when this book was published. They are the minimum you should purchase. These newer DVD products will push CD-ROM speeds to 24X and read all CD formats, including CD-R discs. Also expect faster, more responsive DVD disc playback from these products.

In addition, DVD kits are getting needed improvements in video quality and compatibility. Some first-generation kits lacked full compatibility with Windows 95's Media Control Interface, resulting in crashes and scrambled video. In addition, more-sophisticated MPEG-2 decode chips on second-generation products deliver sharper MPEG-2 video playback.

Getting Dense: Higher-Capacity DVD-ROM

To steal a line from the Rolling Stones, DVD capacities are going up, up, up, up, up. Those first 4.7GB DVD discs will be peanuts compared to the 17GB capacity medium that uses a dual-layer, double-sided design. Fortunately, you don't face a huge decision here. All DVD drives now come with multipowered lasers, so they can read both the translucent outer data layer and the reflective inner data layer. However, expect some pricier drives and players to be able to automatically read both sides of a double-sided disc. Otherwise, you would have to manually flip the medium over in order to read data found on the other side.

For the Record: DVD-R and DVD-RAM

Over the next year, expect to see recordable DVD drives (DVD-R) emerge on the market. Basically, these are CD-Recordable discs on steroids. They're excellent for data archiving and document distribution.

However, many vendors plan to skip the write-once, read-many style drives altogether and move directly to a rewritable DVD spec called DVD-RAM. The first DVD-RAM drives will be able to write and rewrite on 2.6GB discs, which means that they won't offer the full capacity of professionally produced media. However, they will be readable on standard second-generation DVD-ROM drives.

Looking Ahead: For more on DVD-RAM, see Chapter 16, "Optical Storage." These high-density, high-speed recordable drives may well revolutionize the way people back up and archive data.

Purchase Decisions

Unfortunately, DVD ain't cheap. First-generation DVD-ROM upgrade kits initially cost from $500 to $1,000. These prices are very high when you consider that a 16X CD-ROM currently costs only about $130 and that almost no DVD-based content actually exists. Essentially, you'll be using a very expensive DVD drive to play CD-ROM discs.

What's It Good For?

With these stiff prices, who should consider buying a DVD-ROM drive? Mostly home entertainment enthusiasts. Almost all planned DVD software is arriving from either game vendors or movie production houses. At the time this chapter was written, only two DVD reference titles were available:

- Encyclopedia Electronica: A multimedia encyclopedia from Xiphias
- PhoneDisc PowerFinder USA One: A U.S. phone number database from PhoneDisc that was simply ported from a multidisc CD-ROM set

The message here is that DVD will take a while to make an impact on the business and reference market. Most publishers aren't willing to add the expense of a new media type until the installed base of DVD drives runs into the millions or even tens of millions.

The Game's the Thing

On the other hand, if you're looking for the latest and greatest in computer entertainment, you'll find it in DVD. Games and other titles that have been designed specifically for DVD's strengths feature stunning sound and video and hours of interaction without the need to switch discs. Here are some things to keep in mind when you shop:

- Planned use
- Drive technology
- Graphics card compatibility

Planned Use

If you're interested mainly in DVD's superior movie technology, consider a DVD player (which hooks directly to your television) instead of a DVD-ROM computer drive. Although most DVD-ROM kits provide TV out ports on the back of the DVD decoder boards, you still need to control the movie from your computer (pause, play, stop, rewind, fast-forward, show subtitles, and so on). If you're using a PC/TV system such as Gateway Destination, this won't be a problem. But if your TV and computer are separate, the hassle involved will be frustrating. Gamers have only one way to go—DVD-ROM drives.

Which Generation?

If you do decide on a DVD-ROM drive, go for a second-generation model. It will be able to read CD-R discs and run CD-ROMs at speeds of at least 20X. What's more, you'll probably pay only a little more for the more-advanced drive than for early first-generation products. If you plan to use the DVD-ROM drive as a CD-ROM drive replacement, you absolutely need this capability.

Graphics Card Compatibility

At the moment, DVD-ROM kits use video overlay techniques to incorporate the MPEG-2 video stream into your graphics card's output. The MPEG-2 video is literally laid on top of your desktop's graphics as a separate video element. However, not all kits do this the same way, and the result can be problems with video playback.

DynaTek's DVD471TII kit, for example, requires your PC to have a graphics chipset that supports *linear memory addressing* over the PCI bus. This means that the DVD decoder board writes in bursts directly to the graphics card's memory. It's a fast and efficient way of doing things, but compatibility is limited. At the time this was written, the DynaTek kit had been tested successfully with only eight different graphics chipsets.

> **Buying Tip:** Before you purchase a DVD drive, check your existing hardware. Make note of your graphics card's chip. Also make sure your PC's PCI bus slots support bus mastering—you'll need it to move the gobs of video information that DVD titles employ. Also take a look at your BIOS version and sound card model. Once that's done, check with the kit maker to ensure that your hardware will work with the product you want to buy.

At the time this was written, DVD-ROM drives weren't available individually—only in the kits, because the included DVD decoder boards are required to work in conjunction with the ROM drives.

The other approach is a simple pass-through method, which is used by kits such as Diamond Multimedia's Maximum DVD Kit. In this setup, after the installation procedure, you attach a cable (known as a VGA loopback cable) from the back of your graphics card's VGA port to the back of the DVD decoder board. The analog video signal from your graphics card is then passed through the cable to the DVD board, which handles the overlay process and outputs the result to your monitor. With this style of kit, your monitor is attached to the DVD board instead of your graphics card.

Which overlay method is better? It's hard to say. Theoretically, the linear memory addressing approach has a performance edge over the pass-through approach. In my testing of DVD kits, though, the difference (to my eyes) seems negligible. Additionally, the pass-through method can work with almost any video card, whereas the linear addressing method can be a compatibility issue for many PC systems. As a general recommendation, the pass-through method seems more trouble-free.

Minimum System Requirements

Make sure you check the system requirements of these kits carefully. Most require at least a 133MHz Pentium or equivalent processor with 16MB of RAM. There might also be video graphics card and sound card requirements. All the kits available thus far require a free PCI-bus slot for the DVD decoder board and must be run on a Windows 95 system. You won't be upgrading a low-end PC with a DVD-ROM drive.

> **Buying Tip:** Some kits don't include mounting rails with the DVD drive. If your PC's drive bays lack mounting rails, you'll need to make a second trip to the computer store to get all the hardware you need to install these railless kits. Therefore, before you buy, check

to see if your PC has drive rails in place. If it doesn't, either make sure the kit provides them, or pick up a pair from the computer store at the time of purchase.

Price

Don't rush to buy the least-expensive DVD-ROM drive. As is sometimes the case with other computer equipment, with DVD-ROM drives, a higher price might mean a better product. Check computer publication reviews that feature roundups of several kits, and look carefully at the pros and cons. The good news is that with so many companies competing in this arena, the prices will likely drop quickly. Expect to spend at least $400 for a DVD-ROM drive until at least mid-1998.

Peter's Principle: DVD-ROM Versus CD-ROM

Are you trying to choose between DVD-ROM drives and CD-ROM drives? With first-generation DVD-ROM drives, there is no comparison. A fast 24X CD-ROM drive will cost only about $200 and will read all CD-ROM media, including CD-R discs, while first-generation DVD-ROM drives cost about $500 and have CD-ROM playback issues (as mentioned earlier). For home-office or business use, a fast CD-ROM upgrade is still well worth the money and will probably remain useful well into 1999 (this is much more than you can say for most computer components). Companies have announced no plans to stop producing CD-ROM discs as of yet.

With second- (or third-) generation DVD-ROM drives, the choice becomes more difficult. If you can afford the premium that DVD begs, you lose nothing regarding CD-ROMs, and you gain the ability to enjoy a major advancement in computer entertainment. Check your budget and make your own call.

Upgrading

If you've upgraded a CD-ROM or hard disk drive, you'll be well-prepared to handle the physical issues involved with a DVD installation. That said, DVD upgrades are among the most challenging you'll find. Why? Because a new DVD drive affects so many areas of your system, including

- Disk drive
- Graphics subsystem
- Audio subsystem

For this reason, you need to be aware of what is inside your system before you upgrade. Many graphics subsystems, for example, are incompatible with the linear addressing scheme used by the highest-performance DVD kits. Older Pentium PCs might also lack bus mastering PCI add-in slots necessary to stream video and audio from the drive to your display and sound system.

See You Later, CD-ROM?

Not if you can help it. If you have an extra drive bay and your PC is not otherwise loaded with components, I advise you not to replace your CD-ROM drive with a DVD-ROM drive. You will always find occasions when more than one ROM drive is beneficial.

You should consider a DVD drive as your lone optical media reader when at least one of the following is true:

- The new DVD drive plays CD-ROM discs significantly faster than your existing CD-ROM drive.
- The new DVD drive can read CD-R media, or you never use CD-R discs.
- Your PC lacks an open externally accessible drive bay for both CD-ROM and DVD drives.
- Your PC's power supply lacks the output to support two optical drives in addition to the existing power load.
- You already have four EIDE devices and you can't add another without replacing one.

Before You Go

Prior to installation, decide whether your DVD-ROM drive will operate as a master or a slave on the enhanced IDE bus. If another drive (hard disk or CD-ROM) resides on the same IDE controller cable, you must set the DVD-ROM drive to slave via a jumper on the back of the drive. If the DVD-ROM drive alone connects to the IDE controller, it must be set as master.

Warning: Unlike CD-ROM drives, which invariably come from the factory set as master, I've seen DVD-ROM drives come set both ways. Make sure you examine the drive before you begin the installation. Otherwise, you're asking for serious conflicts that could knock out your boot drive and add hours to your installation.

Note: Are you looking for a DVD drive for your SCSI setup? Bad news. Unlike CD-ROM drives, current DVD-ROM drives are available only for the EIDE interface. The significantly lower cost and higher market penetration of EIDE has convinced early manufacturers to play to the widest possible market. Still, there is no reason why DVD won't work on SCSI. In fact, it should enjoy the same multitasking advantages enjoyed by SCSI-based CD-ROM drives. You'll just have to wait a while for them.

Just so you understand the big picture, Windows 95 recognizes a DVD-ROM drive as a regular CD-ROM drive. Although the next release of Windows should fix this glitch, don't be alarmed if you run across the Properties of your DVD-ROM drive listed as "CD-ROM" under My Computer. When you place a regular CD-ROM in the drive, the DVD-ROM device plays it as a CD-ROM drive would normally play a disc. When you insert a DVD-ROM disc, your kit's included DVD player software (the last step of the installation) will kick in to play the disc.

Installing the DVD-ROM Drive

Okay, enough talk. Let's install the kit:

1. Turn off your PC, disconnect the power cable, and remove the PC's case.

2. On the front of the PC, locate an available $5^1/_4$-inch drive bay (one of the wide ones). Remove the plastic placeholder from the front of the bay.

3. If your computer requires mounting rails, check to see whether they are present in the bay. Some DVD kits don't include the rails, so you might have to purchase them separately at a computer store. If you do need them, install them now.

4. Slide the DVD drive in from the front of the PC. Make sure that the front of the drive is flush with the front of your PC case and that there are no gaps between the edges of the drive and the borders of the front PC panel.

5. Connect the IDE controller cable and the power cable.

Warning: Both of these cables attach correctly in only one way. The ribbon data cable has a red line running along the edge for pin 1 out of the cable. Your DVD-ROM drive should have a small "1" marking pin 1 on the data cable connector at the back of the drive. If it doesn't, read the device's documentation to determine which pin is pin 1. Make sure the red-line edge of the cable and pin 1 match up, or you won't be able to access this drive.

The power supply cable should have a rounded edge on the top two corners of the connector. The power supply port on the back of the drive will also have these rounded edges, designating the top edge of the port. Make sure that the power cable is firmly secured in the correct position.

6. Here's the step that many DVD-ROM kit installation guides leave out: Before you insert the DVD decoder card, you should boot up your system and verify that your PC recognizes this drive properly. This step will save you troubleshooting headaches (or tech support calls) later if you've made a mistake or there is a problem with your DVD-ROM drive unit.

7. Don't close the PC's case just yet. Make sure that you've removed all the tools you've used and that cables are firmly connected, and then reattach your PC's power cable and power up the system.

8. After Windows 95 comes up, double-click the My Computer icon and look for a new drive letter that corresponds to the DVD-ROM drive. (You can also highlight the drive, right-click, and select Properties to find the "CD-ROM" entry mentioned a moment ago.)

9. Insert your favorite CD-ROM disc and make sure it plays properly.

> **Note:** Don't insert one of the DVD-ROM discs that came with the kit! You haven't yet finished the DVD installation, so these discs won't play.

If there's a problem, step back through the instructions and make sure you haven't missed any. Contact the kit vendor's tech support if a problem remains. Your DVD-ROM drive should be acting like a CD-ROM drive at the moment.

Once you've resolved any problems (or if you haven't had any), shut down Windows 95, power off your PC, and disconnect the power cable before continuing to the DVD board installation.

Installing the DVD Decoder Board

Installing a DVD board is much like any card installation, except, perhaps, for the final stage, in which you attach cables to your video graphics card. Even if you've never attempted a card installation, the following steps will walk you through the process:

1. Locate an available PCI-bus slot, preferably one with clearance for a full-length board.

> **Upgrade Advice:** Sometimes CPUs, RAM SIMMs, and other components stick up from the motherboard and prevent a full-length card from being pushed all the way down and secured in the slot. If this is a case, you must find another PCI slot to install the board into.
>
> A full-length card insertion can be tricky due to the fact that you have several things to watch at the same time: The card connector fitting into the slot on the motherboard, the ports fitting through the opening out the back of the PC, and the opposite end of the card fitting into the plastic guide.

2. Unscrew the screw that keeps the slot's metal placeholder bracket in place, and slide the bracket out of its slot.

3. Insert the DVD decoder board into the slot. If the DVD card is full-length, the card edge that doesn't contain the output ports must slide into a plastic guide slot, which you'll find inside your PC case, opposite the bracket you just removed. Using two hands, position the card carefully, and then press down gently yet firmly until the card is seated in the slot.

4. Screw in the mounting screw that holds the card in place.

5. You might need to attach a cable from the DVD board to your sound card. This differs from kit to kit, depending on whether this cable is internal or external. Read your kit's documentation and connect the internal sound cable if required.

6. Next, check the graphics card setup. If your DVD board uses linear memory addressing (explained in the earlier section "Graphics Card Compatibility"), you won't need to make a connection between your DVD board and your graphics card, because the PCI bus handles the data, so you can skip to step 9. If your kit uses a pass-through approach, disconnect the monitor cable from the graphics card.

7. Now connect the provided pass-through cable to the "VGA in" port on the back of the DVD board, and plug it into the graphics card's VGA port.

8. Connect the monitor cable to the back of the DVD board's "VGA out" port. Check your kit's documentation, and make the connections your kit requires.

9. Now attach your two-speaker cables, TV-out cables, or surround sound speakers to the back of the DVD board as needed.

10. Replace the PC case.

11. Reattach the power cable.

Installing the DVD Player Software

You'll need to install software. In addition to the usual device drivers, these kits need a DVD player module installed because Windows 95 doesn't yet recognize DVD drives. You'll also need software for handling MPEG-2 video and AC-3 audio.

1. Power up the PC. After Windows 95 starts, you'll see the New Hardware Found dialog box, which asks you to insert the manufacturer's diskette.

2. Insert the kit's DVD driver diskette into the A: drive, and click OK. Windows should find the drivers and install them. Now check your kit's documentation on loading the DVD player software. You might need to take another step in which you run SETUP.EXE for the player software.

3. Congratulations! You're now ready to enjoy DVD.

Repair

Here's the good news about DVD-ROM repair: Unless you found this book sitting in a used-book store, your DVD-ROM drive probably is still under warranty. Therefore, you should contact your kit vendor's tech support with any problems.

As with CD-ROM drives, DVD-ROM drives are sealed devices that aren't intended for home repair. Working inside the unit requires special "clean room" environments to maintain the precision of the mechanics.

That said, gremlins can plague your DVD device, causing it to seem to fail when nothing serious is wrong. Before calling the vendor, run through this list of fixes:

- Make sure all cables are properly connected and secure.

- Make sure your DVD-ROM drive is recognized under My Computer as a CD-ROM drive under Windows 95. If it isn't, there was a mistake in the installation, or the unit has a hardware problem.

- If you own an older PC, make sure you installed the PCI board into a bus-mastering PCI slot. Also ensure that the PCI slot you're using is active. You can check both in the PC's BIOS.

- Ensure that the CD-ROM and DVD-ROM discs you use in the drive are clean. You should clean DVD-ROM discs just as you would CD-ROM discs—usually with a cleaning kit or just water and a scratch-free, lint-free cloth.

- Double-check that the drive itself is clean. Use canned compressed air products to blow dust and debris off the disc tray and inside compartment.

Summary

As upgrades go, DVD is a big deal. These new drives provide access to a whole new level of content and software, including theater-quality video and audio. And with storage capacities of up to 17GB, you'll eventually see comprehensive encyclopedia titles packed with hours of broadcast-quality video.

Just be cautious, particularly if you own an older system. DVD applications will be written for cutting-edge PCs, which means that adding DVD to slower PCs might make for problematic performance. In addition, there are pesky graphics compatibility issues to contend with. You'll need to do a little sleuthing to ensure that you buy what you need.

Of course, the biggest concern with DVD is that it is still a market in its formative stages. Drives for DVD-R and DVD-RAM have yet to arrive, which means that compatibility for these upcoming media types can't be ensured with existing DVD-ROM drives. Even if compatibility works out, the performance, capabilities, and prices of these drives will improve. So be careful.

IV

Advanced
Data Storage

16

Optical Storage

Peter Norton®

Optical recorders let PC users create (or *master*) their own optical discs, such as CD-ROMs and DVDs (Digital Versatile Disks) without needing to send data to a service bureau for processing. Although they're not the easiest products to use, optical recorders do allow for relatively cheap and fast mass storage that can easily be distributed to others.

This area is becoming increasingly important. The universal installed base of CD-ROM drives, for instance, makes CD recordable and rewritable drives a terrific tool for archiving and distributing large amounts of data for playback on any machine. The emergence of DVD promises to make similar drives for high-density media important as well. This chapter will help you

- Learn about the four major types of optical recorded media and how they work
- Understand key buying issues associated with optical recording devices in general and with certain types in specific
- Recognize and resolve problems associated with optical recording drives and media

Overview

Optical recorders serve a growing number of applications, ranging from casual home use to publishing and data management. Table 16.1 lists some of the most important applications.

Table 16.1. Applications served by optical recording media.

Task	Examples
Home entertainment	Creating custom audio discs, PhotoCDs, multimedia productions
Publishing	Mastering copies of critical data, software publishing
Data backup and archiving	Saving important files, such as e-mail archives, to permanent media in case of system failure; saving data and storing off-site in case of flood, fire, or other catastrophe
Data distribution	Forwarding database updates to colleagues and businesses; software distribution within companies

Not all recording drives are best suited for each of these uses, so I'll break down which drive does what as we go along. Additionally, not all disc formats can be read by all drives—a critical point when you're making a purchase. We will cover all these points in this chapter.

There are several flavors of recordable optical media spanning the CD and DVD media spectra. We will cover the four most important and widespread optical formats and drives:

- CD-Recordable (CD-R)
- CD-Rewritable (CD-RW)

- DVD-Recordable (DVD-R)
- DVD-Rewritable (DVD-RAM: DVD Random Access Memory)

CD-R: First Out

The first mainstream recordable laser-based medium now enjoys the greatest market share. You will find CD-R drives under a number of different names, including

- CD-WO: CD-Write Once
- CD-WORM: CD-Write Once Read Many
- CD-R: CD-Recordable

These labels call attention to a key element of CD-R technology: Any given portion of the medium can be recorded to only once. Although the data can be read back from the disc as long as the disc remains intact, you can never again record over a track after it has been "burned" by a CD-R drive.

The biggest advantage of CD-R discs and drives is that this medium can be read by almost any CD-ROM drive—an important point given that CD-ROM drives are ubiquitous on today's PCs. The installed base of CD-ROM drives makes CD-R particularly useful for distributing data to others.

Compatibility: Unfortunately, first-generation DVD-ROM drives can't read CD-R discs. The green tint of the CD-R medium's coating conflicts with the frequency of DVD drives' red lasers, making the medium unreadable. Second-generation DVD-ROM drives resolve this problem by using a second, yellow laser head to read CD-R media.

Burn, Baby, Burn

How does CD-R work? Basically, these drives replicate the professional CD-ROM creation process through the use of chemicals. With a professionally recorded CD-ROM disc, data is stored on the medium by using a laser to create pits and rises along the concentric spiral track. At playback, the reading laser of the CD-ROM drive detects changes in the reflection between a pit and a nonpit (called a *land*). A microprocessor in the drive makes sense of the varying returns and converts this into bits, which can be sent to the PC and interpreted as data.

CD-R recording differs somewhat, mainly because the equipment on your desktop can't easily burn pits into waiting media. Rather, CD-R drives employ a special medium that provides a chemical interaction to create the illusion of burned pits and lands. It is this medium that accounts for the greenish tint of CD-R discs (regular CD-ROM discs are silver-colored).

The green color is produced by a green dye that reacts with the gold layer below when exposed to a laser of specific frequency and strength. When the recording laser heats a point on the disc, the gold layer below the dye and the dye itself interact to change the reflective property of that point on the disc. Although no physical pit is formed, the resulting chemical change mimics the reflective property of a real pit.

CD-R and CD-ROM

Back in 1994, CD-R units could cost as much as $6,000—limiting them to corporations that had a real need to quickly produce limited runs of CD-ROM discs. But as with all computer technology, competition has lead to steady and significant drops in price. At the time this was written, you could purchase a CD-R unit for as little as $400.

That said, you can expect to always pay a premium for optical recorders over CD-ROM player or reader drives because of the extra hardware involved in the mastering technology. Although CD-R drives can read CD-ROM media like a standard drive, they might not be appropriate as the primary reading drive. That's because CD-R read speeds lag considerably behind that of standard CD-ROM drives. Whereas CD-ROM drives today read at up to 24X speeds, most CD-Rs are limited to 8X operation.

Also, CD-R drives record at a different rate than they play back. Typically, a drive capable of 8X read performance will be able to record at a maximum speed of 4X. And many drives are still limited to recording at 2X speeds. The main advantage of faster recording spin rates is the time it takes to burn a disc. Depending on your CD-R software, your PC system, and the method of recording, a typical CD-R drive with a 2X record speed can burn one 650MB disc in about 40 minutes. 4X drives won't halve that number (the drive won't always reach peak spin rates since it must wait for data and verify operation), but it can shave 10 minutes off that time.

Note: The usability of your CD-R software makes a big difference when you prepare to burn (or premaster) a CD. In fact, many people believe that a CD-R drive is only as good as the software that drives it.

The best premastering software features automated wizards that walk you through the format of the disc you'll be creating (audio CD, PhotoCD, data CD, and so on) and let you drag and drop files you want to record. This software also determines whether your PC is powerful enough to successfully make it through the planned recording session. Finally, an effective help system can get you through jobs without too much pain.

One of the better packages is Adaptec's Easy CD Creator, shown in Figure 16.1, but you should check reviews in computer publications for the latest information on CD-R software products. Almost every CD-R drive includes CD-R software in the box, but if you find yours to be ineffective, you can purchase off-the-shelf CD-R software for about $100.

Figure 16.1.
Adaptec's Easy CD Creator software provides packet-writing capability for drives that support it, but you'll still want a powerful PC to avoid problems during recording. (Photo courtesy of Adaptec, Inc.)

Performance Matters in Recording

The process of mastering CDs can be fraught with frustration and errors. First-time users of CD-R drives often fail at their first few attempts at recording discs and have to throw out the partially recorded blank discs that were ruined in the process. At about $5 per blank CD-R disc, learning the proper recording technique can get expensive quickly.

Recording to CD is done in "sessions." You can record an entire CD in one session or add to a partially recorded disk with additional sessions on CD-R drives that support this multisession technique. In traditional CD-R drives, a successful recording session requires your entire PC system to keep a continuous stream of data flowing from your hard disk to your CD-R drive. The CD-R drive must record an entire track of the disc without stopping. If your CD-R drive ends up waiting on data when it's in the middle of recording a track, it fails to correctly record that track, and the resulting disc becomes unreadable and worthless. This is called a *buffer underrun* error.

Fairly recently, a technique called *variable-packet writing* emerged. It eliminates the need to record an entire track at once. The software and drive can record a single file at a time and leave the disk ready for additional recording in later sessions. Unfortunately, many manufacturers include this technology only in their CD-RW (CD-Rewritable) products (which we'll discuss later), so many current CD-R drives still suffer from troubling buffer underrun problems.

How do you avoid underruns? Here's a list of hardware factors that can help ensure a successful burn:

- CPU: When it comes to CD-R recording, the more powerful the processor, the better. Experts recommend at least a Pentium 133MHz processor or the equivalent for trouble-free recording.
- RAM: Have at least 16MB of RAM for recording. 32MB or higher will greatly decrease your chances of buffer underruns.

- CD-R buffer size: The bigger the buffer of your CD-R drive, the better. If your PC can feed data to a large CD-R drive buffer, the chances of buffer underrun will be minimal. Many CD-R devices come with only 512KB buffers, but this seems adequate. If you can afford one with a 1MB or larger buffer, you'll be increasing your chances of error-free recording.

- Large hard disk: CD-R software usually gives you the option of creating a physical or virtual image of your data to set up a recording (we'll discuss this in a moment). A physical image is the most effective for a successful burn, but this requires large amounts of spare hard disk space, because the software will literally create a 650MB premaster copy of your data on your hard drive before writing the data to the CD-R disc. Only you know how much hard disk space you need on a regular basis, but having a spare 650MB for recording will probably demand a 2.5GB or larger disk.

- Fast hard disk: A fast SCSI hard drive will lessen the chances of buffer underrun. Also, be sure to defragment the drive (see Chapter 12, "Hard Disks") and uninstall any hard disk compression you're using before recording.

- SCSI versus IDE: Just like CD-ROM drives, CD-R drives come in SCSI and IDE interface drives. The superior performance of SCSI drives (11.1 to 16.6MBps for typical IDE versus 10 to 40MBps for typical SCSI) becomes a factor in recording. If you can afford the extra cost, go for a SCSI drive. But keep in mind that real-world testing of these two types of CD-R drives indicates that the performance differences aren't all that significant. You can successfully record CDs with an IDE CD-R drive.

- Internal versus external: Some columnists in computer publications claim that the electromagnetic fields generated by your other computer equipment (monitors, PCs, and so on) can negatively affect an external CD-R drive during recording, causing an unsuccessful write session. This might be overstated, because many people (including me) have recorded using external CD-R drives without difficulty. The shielded casings on most drives are quite adequate for blocking out any EMF interference. Still, if your environment is rife with electronic equipment, consider going with an internal drive, which will have extra EMF protection from your PC case.

Note: Most CD-R software lets you set up either a physical or virtual image of the data you want to record to disc. The physical image approach builds a complete disc image on your hard drive (complete with indexes required by your chosen CD-ROM format) before the recording begins. During recording, the physical image is simply copied bit by bit to the CD-R disc. A virtual image approach, on the other hand, performs an on-the-fly recording. You build a template of all the data you want to record in the session, but no full disc image is constructed on your hard drive. The software copies the data file by file during the recording session and builds the indexes on-the-fly.

The physical image approach greatly increases the chances of a successful recording session, because the only processing left to do is copying files. The downside is that it can require up to 650MB of free hard disk space. The virtual image method doesn't require massive free hard disk space, but it can lead to buffer underrun problems during the on-the-fly recording due to processing overhead.

Fortunately, your decision here is actually a simple one. If you have the free disk space, always go with the physical image method. It's much safer, and the CD-R software usually cleans up the physical image from your hard disk once the burn completes. If you're pressed for space, go with the virtual approach, but first run the premaster test (almost all CD-R software provides one), which performs a "dry run" with your data to see if the whole PC system can maintain the necessary data transfer rate. The test will return either a high-confidence result or a low-confidence result on your chances of success before writing any data to the CD-R disc.

CD-RW

New CD-RW (CD-Rewritable) drives have begun arriving from Ricoh, Yamaha, and other manufacturers. These drives use a combination of the variable-packet writing scheme and a phase-change disc medium (first developed by Panasonic-Matsushita) to allow writing and rewriting on CD-RW discs. In fact, a CD-RW disc can be rewritten up to 1,000 times. CD-RW drives might bridge the gap between CD-R drives (which can't be rewritten) and DVD-RAM drives (which are not yet available).

As discussed earlier, variable-packet writing negates the problems of buffer underrun, because the CD-RW drive doesn't need to write an entire track at once. In fact, even if the CD-RW buffer does underrun, the laser can mark off that section of the CD-RW disc as unusable and continue writing, much like a hard disk drive would.

The phase-change medium, on the other hand, departs from the usual CD-ROM approach. Here, a tiny dot of the crystalline medium is subjected to a laser pulse to write bits. The energy alters the crystal structure of the medium, causing the substance to toggle from absorbing light to reflecting light. A drive can then determine the value of a bit based on whether the read laser light bounces back to the detector or is absorbed by the medium. Each portion of the medium can be toggled up to 1,000 times.

Unfortunately, CD-RW discs can't be read by older CD-ROM or CD-R drives. Newer models, such as Plextor's $269 12/20PleX CD-ROM drive, feature modifications that let it read CD-RW discs in addition to CD-R and CD-ROM media.

These newly released CD-RW drives have the added feature of being able to record on write-once CD-R discs. Expect drives to be somewhat more expensive than existing CD-R models. Ricoh's

MP6200S CD-RW drive, for example, costs about $600 (see Figure 16.2). The CD-RW medium is also pricier than its CD-R sibling, costing about $20 per disc.

Figure 16.2.
Ricoh's CD-RW drive looks like any CD-ROM or CD-R drive but uses a pulse laser to change the properties of crystalline media. (Photo courtesy of Ricoh Corporation)

DVD-R and DVD-RAM

With DVD-ROM set to all but replace CD-ROM in the PC marketplace, it's no surprise to see similar recordable devices planned for the DVD format. After all, the prospect of multigigabyte storage, accessible from millions of mainstream desktop PCs, is appealing. Just don't get ahead of yourself. Neither DVD-R (DVD-Recordable) nor DVD-RAM (DVD-Random Access Memory) drives were available when this book was published.

In the DVD specifications, the first DVD-R drives will be able to record once on 3.8GB discs (single-layer, single-side)—almost 1GB less than the capacity of DVD-ROM discs, which hold 4.7GB single-layer, single-side. The first DVD-RAM drives will handle even less data—2.6GB on a single-layer, single-side disc—but will allow multiple rewrites. Why the lower capacities for these recordable media? The phase-change medium used in these discs is difficult to manage at very high densities.

In fact, expect many manufacturers to go right past DVD-R and offer DVD-RAM drives as their only recordable solution. DVD-RAM is much more flexible than DVD-R and will appeal to a larger mainstream market that will use DVD-RAM as a super-duper floppy drive. Both Matsushita and Hitachi expect to ship DVD-RAM drives near the beginning of 1998, much more quickly than first predicted. In fact, Hitachi has already announced the GF-1000 DVD-RAM drive, which will feature 1.38MBps data transfer rates. (Pricing and shipping information is not yet available.)

Manufacturers say that DVD-R and DVD-RAM drives will be compatible with all the earlier optical media, including CD-ROM, CD-R, CD-RW, and DVD-ROM discs. The drawback? News reports say that the DVD-RAM medium might cost as much as $80 per disc—prohibitively expensive for many users.

In very recent developments, Sony, Philips, and Hewlett-Packard have announced their plans to produce optical storage drives that compete with DVD-RAM technology, offering more capacity per disk than DVD-RAM drives. None of these companies has yet released the capacity specs or even the name of these new drives.

In other optical storage news, NEC states that it will ship Multimedia Video File (MMVF) recording drives around the middle of 1998. MMVF drives will be able to write 5.2GB per side.

Waiting to purchase these as-yet-unreleased drives might be a risky maneuver, however. New products often go through a bug shakeout stage, even as consumers are buying the first releases.

Purchase Decisions

With all the choices in optical recorders, how do you decide which one to buy? First, you should determine your needs. What's more, patience might be the key. If you can afford to wait six months, affordable DVD-RAM and CD-RW are probably attractive options. But if you must buy now, you might be limited to write-once technologies—unless you have the money to spend for early technology.

In all cases, you should consider optical recording media over magnetic media for the following applications:

- Permanent or long-term data archiving and backup
- Software or data distribution and publishing (CD-R only)
- Multimedia production and distribution

Peter's Principle: Speed: Optical Storage Versus Magnetic Storage

When do optical technologies not make sense? Most often when very fast, responsive performance is needed. Magnetic technologies, such as the Iomega Zip and Jaz drives, operate on the same principles as hard disk drives. Here, focused magnetic fields are used to switch bits on and off on a magnetic medium. This process is much quicker than laser-based drives. The magnetic polarity can be switched instantly, whereas optical media must be heated before the bit switch can occur.

continues

Generally, access times for hard disks can be as low as 7ms, while Iomega's Jaz drive provides 12ms access times. Optical CD and DVD media, on the other hand, feature access times of about 150ms and above. The faster access times make magnetic media great for running applications from a removable platform. For example, you could run Word or Excel off a Jaz drive.

The price you pay for the speed is reduced durability. Magnetic media can be easily corrupted. In other words, on bits can easily be switched to off bits. When that happens, files get lost. For example, any household magnet can corrupt magnetic media.

To help you make sense of the media, I've provided a list of pros and cons for each type.

CD-R: Mainstream Media

CD-R is the most prevalent recordable optical medium, and it's also the most affordable. If you want to produce finished content for distribution or you want permanent data archives, CD-R is the most economical choice.

Pros

- Records all the popular CD formats (audio discs, video discs, PhotoCD, data CDs) except CD-RW.
- Fairly inexpensive—about $400.
- Great for home use, data distribution, creating masters of software titles, and archiving data.
- Blank CD-R discs are the cheapest of the lot at about $5 per disc.

Cons

- Can't read DVD or CD-RW media.
- Slow playback speeds make CD-R drives ineffective as your sole CD-ROM drive.
- Writes only once on a track.
- Ineffective for data backup due to the write-once restriction.
- Few CD-R drives support variable-packet writing; therefore, they can suffer buffer underrun errors.

CD-RW: Floppy of the Future?

CD-RW is a good option for people who want more flexibility than the write-once character CD-R provides. CD-RW discs can act as super-floppy discs, for example, provided that the CD-ROM drives in your organization can recognize the phase-change medium. And despite their write-many character, the optical medium is quite robust—a stray magnetic field won't corrupt the data. These drives are also faster and can read more formats than their CD-R cousins.

Pros

- Records all the popular CD-ROM formats, including CD-R and CD-RW.
- Can rewrite on CD-RW media.
- Fast CD-ROM playback (up to 20X on some CD-RW drives).
- Inexpensive. The cheapest CD-RW drives cost about $600.
- Variable-packet writing and phase-change media solve buffer underrun recording problems.
- Great for home use, data distribution, creating master CDs, backup, and archiving.

Cons

- CD-RW media isn't cheap; it costs about $20 per disc.
- Can't read DVD discs.

DVD-R: The Next Generation

DVD-R has real promise. In an age of 7GB hard disks, the viability of 650MB CD-ROM media for mass storage backup is in question. DVD-R lets you burn to 3.8GB discs and enjoy the enhanced bandwidth of DVD-ROM playback. In addition to reading DVD-ROM and DVD-R discs, these drives can handle all the CD varieties.

Pros

- Can read all CD-ROM and DVD-ROM media, including CD-RW and CD-R.
- Likely to feature fast CD-ROM playback.
- Useful for home use, data distribution, mastering DVD titles, and archiving.

Cons

- Currently, no drives are available. Initial pricing might be high.
- Not effective as an incremental backup device due to its write-once restriction.

- Might become obsolete if DVD-RAM drives succeed.

- Expensive media at almost $80 per disc.

- Writes only 3.8GB single-layer, single-side, as opposed to DVD-ROM's 4.7GB single-layer, single-side.

DVD-RAM: Now This Is Cool

Unless your needs are immediate, it might make sense to hold out for this still-developing technology. Although DVD-RAM isn't perfect—its 2.6GB capacity is less than that of DVD-R, for example—DVD-RAM drives will let you read virtually every CD and DVD format there is. In addition, DVD-RAM approaches the appeal of near-disk magnetic storage devices such as Iomega Jaz and magneto-optical devices such as SyQuest. If CD-RW is a super-floppy, DVD-RAM is a super-duper floppy.

Pros

- Reading-compatible with all ROM formats, including CD-ROM, CD-R, CD-RW, and DVD.

- Can write and rewrite at 2.6GB single-layer, single-side.

- Great for home use, data distribution, master DVD titles, backup, and archiving.

- Likely to support high-speed CD-ROM playback (24X).

Cons

- Currently unavailable. Initial pricing might be high.

- Can't write full DVD-ROM capacity (only 2.6GB single-layer, single-side, as opposed to DVD-ROM 4.7GB single-layer, single-side).

- Expensive media at almost $80 per disc.

Optical Media Buyer's Wrap-Up

The best deal going in optical recorders is the CD-RW drive. At about $600, these drives are affordable for recorders and worth the extra $100 to $200 over a CD-R drive because of their added backup and temporary storage capabilities. The CD-RW medium costs more than CD-R but significantly less than the initial DVD-RAM discs. Even if the CD-RW format becomes obsolete after DVD-RAM emerges, it will still cut CD-R discs, which will be useful for some time to come.

If you need to start recording right away, go with a CD-RW drive. The initial DVD-RAM drives will be expensive and are likely have a few bugs. If you can wait for DVD-RAM price drops due to competition—possibly around the middle of 1998—DVD-RAM drives might be a universal solution to all your recording needs.

Upgrading

If you use your PC for multimedia production work, an optical upgrade might be in your future. You might also want to opt for one of these technologies for your backup needs instead of using a less-flexible tape drive or lower-capacity Zip or LS-120 drive.

Should I Stay or Should I Go?

One question is whether you should keep the existing CD-ROM drive in your system when you upgrade. That depends. IDE CD-ROM drives could be forced out of the mix if you already have a pair of IDE hard disks and an IDE Zip drive, for example. Remember that you're limited to four IDE devices. Regardless of the system mix, slower CD-ROM drives are probably best retired in favor of faster-moving recorders.

If you're going with a CD-R drive, it's unlikely that it will outperform your CD-ROM drive for playback (unless your CD-ROM drive is 4X speed or slower). For this reason, it makes sense to add a CD-R drive to the CD-ROM drive in your system rather than swapping it out. CD-RW, on the other hand, might spin CD-ROMs faster than your existing CD-ROM drive, in which case replacing the CD-ROM drive with the CD-RW drive is a reasonable option. However, if you have the space and power, leave your CD-ROM drive in so that you won't have to swap titles as much.

For DVD media, performance goes up a notch. DVD-RAM drives will reportedly run CD-ROMs at high speeds. This, combined with the drive's ability to read all existing CD-based formats, makes it attractive to replace the older CD-ROM drive with a DVD-RAM drive.

The following section steps you through adding a CD-R drive to your PC. Except for the final software installation, the process is identical to adding a CD-ROM drive to your system, so you'll notice a similarity between the following instructions and those in Chapter 12.

Tip: For SCSI CD-R drives, it's a good idea to consider installing the CD-R drive on its own SCSI controller card instead of adding the CD-R to a SCSI controller with other devices already attached. Multiple devices riding on the same SCSI controller can slow data transfer speeds. In recording, the required data rate to avoid buffer underruns demands all the performance advantages you can muster. Another, less expensive solution is to simply not power on your other SCSI devices when you're entering into a recording session. If you're using a SCSI hard drive, however, this won't be an option.

Preparing a CD-R Drive Installation

If you've never installed a CD-ROM or CD-R drive before, consider purchasing a CD-R upgrade kit, because it will include all the necessary cabling, screws, and rails. Once you've made your purchase, follow these preparatory steps:

1. Choose a drive bay: For internal CD-R drives, you need a bay that opens onto the front of your PC. If your system is bulging with components, it's conceivable that you might need to move your hard drive to a bay that doesn't abut the front of the PC. External CD-R drives require only desk space.

2. Check the cabling: Make sure you have the necessary power cable socket (usually a white plastic molding with four large pin openings) and controller cable (IDE or SCSI). Make sure they both reach the drive bay in which you intend to install the CD-R drive.

3. Set up the drive: As discussed in Chapter 11, "Control Freaks: IDE and SCSI Controllers," IDE devices can be either a master or a slave. Set the jumpers on an IDE device before installation. CD-R drives generally come from the manufacturer set as the master drive, so if that's your scenario, you won't have to modify the jumpers. If you're adding a CD-R to an IDE controller that already has a drive attached (such as a hard disk), you might have to set the jumpers on both your CD-R and the hard drive. Before you add the CD-R to the primary channel where the hard drive is located, check for free space on the secondary IDE connector. You can avoid potential compatibility and performance issues this way.

SCSI devices require proper SCSI ID and termination settings. Set the jumpers on your CD-R drive to a unique SCSI ID. Then set the termination jumpers if the drive is at the end of a SCSI chain of devices. You might need to unterminate the SCSI controller host adapter card if you have both internal and external SCSI devices, because now the host adapter is in the middle of the chain, not at the end.

Installing the CD-R Drive

To install a CD-R drive, do the following:

1. Turn off your PC and disconnect the power cable.

2. Open the PC case and remove the front placeholder panel, which will be taken up by the front of the CD-R drive unit.

3. If your drive bay requires slide rails, attach them now.

4. Attach the controller cable and the power cable. With all the cabling and cramped spaces, attaching the cables after the drive is secured in the bay can be difficult.

> **Tip:** Both of these cables attach correctly in only one way. The ribbon data cable has a red line running along the edge for pin 1 out of the cable. Your CD-R drive should have a small "1" marking pin 1 on the data cable connector at the back of the drive. If it doesn't, read the device's documentation to determine which pin is pin 1. Make sure that pin 1 and the red-line edge of the cable match up, or you won't be able to access this drive.
>
> The power supply cable should have a rounded edge on the top two corners of the connector. The power supply port on the back of the drive will also have these rounded edges, designating the top edge of the port. Make sure that the power cable is firmly secured in the correct position.

5. Attach the audio cable from the CD-R drive to your sound card. The audio port of the CD-R drive is usually adjacent to the power cable port. Read your sound card's documentation to find out where the connector goes on the sound card.

6. Slide the CD-R drive into the drive bay. Make sure that the front edge fits flush with the front of the PC case. Also make sure that the drive sits level in the bay.

7. Close the PC case and reattach the power cable.

8. Congratulations! The only step remaining is to install the CD-R software that came with the drive. Follow the instructions included with the software. The first time you launch the software, it will scan your PC system for your CD-R drive. From there, you're ready to begin recording.

Repair

Checking cabling and operating system settings will fix most CD-R drive problems. If the drive itself isn't working properly, it must either be replaced or sent to a professional, because the internal components can't be manipulated in a home or office environment.

Troubleshooting

If you're encountering problems with your drive, step through these procedures:

- Double-check cabling. Mis-seated or reversed controller connectors will make your CD-R drive inaccessible.

- Check that your operating system correctly identifies the drive. Under Windows 95, right-click the CD-R drive icon under My Computer and select Properties from the list of choices. The resulting dialog box should correctly identify your drive. Contact the drive's technical support if this is not the case.

Note: In DOS (and therefore Windows 3.x), you need to check your settings in CONFIG.SYS and AUTOEXEC.BAT. The AUTOEXEC.BAT line that refers to your CD-ROM should look something like this:

```
C:\WINDOWS\MSCDEX.EXE /d:mscd001
```

This is the reference for the Microsoft CD Extensions for DOS.

Your drive's installation instructions should include information about the matching CONFIG.SYS line, but it should look like this:

```
DEVICE=C:\MYDRIVER\MYDRVR.SYS /d:mscd001
```

Additionally, if you ever boot or shut down to DOS from Windows 95, you'll also need these entries in your AUTOEXEC.BAT and CONFIG.SYS configuration files.

- Inspect the medium. It might be that the problem lies with your disc and not your drive. Make sure that your discs are clean and scratch-free.

- Clean the drive. Used compressed air to clean the drive's tray or caddy.

Recording Tips

In addition to the tips mentioned throughout this chapter, keep the following in mind when you're setting up a recording session:

- Always start with clean discs. Make sure that there are no scratches or marks on your blank CDs.

- Have your CD-R software perform a test before the recording to check the system throughput. This can alert you to a problem before you end up ruining a blank disc.

- Try not to perform any other PC tasks during your recording. For CD-R recording, this is vital to keep up the necessary transfer rate. It's a good idea for CD-RW or DVD-RAM recording as well.

- Verify the integrity of the session after recording. All CD-R software includes an error message window that lists any problems encountered during a session. Be sure to check this window before distributing the disc.

Summary

The PC platform is changing rapidly, and the area of recordable optical media is one of the fastest-moving technologies. In just over a year, the recordable storage volumes available to mainstream users have increased five times over. And with DVD-RAM and CD-RW, optical media is poised to take over many applications heretofore limited to fast, magnetic technologies.

With all the change in the air, my current advice is to wait—if you can. Buying big into CD-ROM-based recordable technologies might end up being a big mistake two years down the road, when you want to move all your home movies from camcorder tapes to DVD. Even worse, you might end up having to buy a DVD drive just 12 months or so after getting a recordable CD unit, since many titles will be moving to the high-density format.

Of course, the choice depends on your needs. CD-ROM will continue to be the universal medium for at least a couple of years, and the price of these discs is attractive if you're on a budget. The good news is that all these choices represent opportunities that simply didn't exist a couple of years ago.

17

Near-Disk Storage: Large Removable Disk Drives

Peter Norton®

Even if they have hard disk drives of several gigabytes, many people still find use for large removable storage drives. Constant archival backup, large-scale multimedia production use, storing inventory records, and network storage needs are just a few of the reasons to incorporate one of these work-horse mass-storage devices into your computer environment.

You can think of "near-disk storage" as removable drives that approach hard drives in terms of both size and performance. This chapter introduces you to the many flavors of near-disk storage, ranging from removable magnetic cartridges to magneto-optical disk drives. The common thread is that these devices provide gigabytes of storage on removable disks and can be read from and written to like any hard disk.

In this chapter, you will learn

- What near hard disk storage is and what types of drives fall in this category
- How to choose from among the different near-disk options
- How to install and use near-disk storage devices
- How to troubleshoot problems with near-disk devices

Overview

Microsoft watchers predict that the next version of the Windows operating system, Windows 98, might consume more than 200MB of your hard disk with a full installation. If this is any indication of where storage requirements are headed, we might all need removable storage with near hard disk capacities to back up your least-used data. These devices let you offload data that is not used daily from your main hard disk, yet still keep it handy for quick access. Moreover, for confidential or critical data, these large removable drives allow you to easily transfer data off-site or secure it in fireproof storage.

The Two Faces of Near-Disk Storage

Chapter 14, "Beyond Floppies: Removable Storage for PCs," discussed floppy-drive alternatives such as LS-120 and Zip drives. Although these drives work similarly to the drives we'll walk through here, the key difference is capacity. The disks used as floppy alternative drives store only 120MB or less per disk. The drives we'll talk about in this chapter—such as the SyQuest SyJet, Iomega's Jaz, and magneto-optical drives from a number of vendors such as Fujitsu—work with disks that start at 230MB and run up to several gigabytes.

Prices are higher too, ranging from about $200 to about $2,000. Right now, the floppy-alternative market is essentially a popularity contest with few real contenders. In contrast, the near-disk market segment includes several viable companies and a broad range of performance, capacity, price, and interfaces.

The two basic recording technologies of these large removable disk drives are

- Magnetic
- Magneto-optical (MO)

How Magnetic Media Work

Magnetic-based drives, such as the Iomega Jaz and SyQuest SyJet, employ recording techniques very similar to those used in hard disk drives. The main difference is that the disk itself resides inside a removable cartridge, while the drive head and mechanism are stationed permanently inside the drive housing. A drive head, similar to a record player's spindle, floats above the spinning medium. Think of it as a souped-up floppy diskette and drive.

Like any hard disk, each point on the medium contains a magnetic charge that is either positive or negative. When reading data, the drive head senses the magnetic charges of the points spinning below it. These charges are interpreted as binary 1s and 0s. To write data, the drive head applies a magnetic charge to the medium, toggling bits on or off as appropriate.

Because these devices work like hard disk drives, they can approach the quick performance provided by these devices. Average access times of 10ms (milliseconds) are possible. These speeds are equal to that of average nonremovable hard disk drives. For this reason, magnetic-based near-disk products are best if you want to use them for very quick data access and backup.

Hey, MO!: The Story of Hybrid Drives

MO drives, on the other hand, use a combination of laser and magnetic heads to read and write data on cartridge media. When reading data from disks, the drive head reads the magnetic charge of points on the medium, just like a hard disk or other magnetic drive.

Writing data is more complex. Before the charge on MO media can be altered, the medium must be heated. To do this, MO drives pass a laser over the medium to be written, preparing the section of the disk through an increase in temperature. The magnetic drive head follows close behind, switching the polarity of the heated medium. As the medium cools, the magnetic value of that point is locked in.

The main advantage of MO is extended shelf life. Data stored on MO drives is not as susceptible to loss or corruption as that stored on magnetic disks. Everything from stray magnetic fields to simple aging can cause magnetic media to degrade within as little as three to five years. MO media, on the other hand, can be expected to last 10 years or longer.

Buying Tip: Most of these large removable disk drives use either $3^1/_2$-inch or $5^1/_4$-inch cartridges (although you'll see some variations, such as the Avatar Shark 250's $2^1/_2$-inch disks). The capacities of these disks vary tremendously, from 230MB (the SyQuest EZ-Flyer) to 4.6GB (the Pinnacle Micro Apex, shown in Figure 17.1). So, when choosing from among the options for large removable drives, be aware of how much the medium costs. You might be ecstatic over a new, inexpensive drive, only to find out that media expense will put you in the poorhouse.

Just like with hard disk drives, you should calculate the cost per megabyte of storage. For these drives, the range will typically run 20 cents or less per megabyte. Consider it a bargain when the medium costs 5 cents or less per megabyte. Think twice when the medium costs 15 cents or more per megabyte. Other factors, such as drive performance and interfaces, are certainly important, but when calculating the price, don't forget the disks!

Figure 17.1.

No near-disk storage option comes close to matching the quick response and enormous capacity of Pinnacle Micro's 4.6GB Apex drive. (Photo courtesy of Pinnacle Micro, Inc.)

As you would expect during performance tests, generally hard disk-like magnetic drives outrun MO drives for backing up, restoring files, and retrieving individual files from disk. Next come the high-capacity MO drives (such as the Pinnacle Apex), which now spin about 3,600 revolutions per minute.

These drives perform better at reading than writing due to the two-head (laser and magnetic) recording process. Finally, the low-capacity MO drives (such as the Fujitsu DynaMO 230) typically fall to the bottom of the pack for speed.

Most important, understand that the removable nature of all these drives makes their maximum performance slower than that of hard drives. Don't expect to be able to launch applications directly from their media or even to continually load data files from these disks. Even with state-of-the-art design, large removable drives are best suited for data backup and archiving.

Purchase Decisions

For many, backing up and archiving data is an unpleasant prospect. If the only time you plan to access your backup medium is when your hard disk drive fails, you should look to a less-expensive technology, such as tape drives, to meet your needs. In this case, speed is not an issue, and the slow, sequential tape access won't drive you crazy. You'll save money with both the drive and the medium over removable disk drives.

On the other hand, if you regularly go back to your backups or data archives, retrieving and reinstalling files, these removable drives can be a cost-effective solution. In this product category, what you're really paying for is reasonable-speed random access of your stored data.

The following sections list the different factors involved in choosing from among the wide range of options. The items run from most-important to least-important for purchase decisions.

Size Matters

These products can be divided into three tiers of storage: 230 to 750MB drives, 1 to 1.5GB drives, and drives over 2GB.

- 230 to 750MB: Choose this when floppy-alternative drives are just a little too small for your needs but you're still mainly concerned with selective backup and transporting files between systems. These drives cost about $250 to $700, depending on the technology used. Drives in this category include the SyQuest EZ-Flyer 230, the Nomai 540 and 750.c, the Pinnacle Micro Tahoe 640MB, and others.

- 1 to 1.5GB: Choose this when you need to store large multimedia files for periodic access or perform regular archiving and retrieval of data. These drives can be especially useful in desktop and Web-publishing applications. Drives in this tier include the SyQuest SyJet and Iomega Jaz Drive, both of which cost about $500.

- Over 2GB: Choose this when you require regular PC or network hard drive backups. If you need an ever-expandable second hard drive, if you work in digital video production, or if you use multiple operating systems on a single PC, these drives will provide the storage you need. Drives in this tier include the Hewlett-Packard SureStore Optical 2600fx Multifunction Disk Drive, the Pinnacle Micro Apex 4.6GB and Vertex 2.6GB (see Figure 17.2), and others. Generally, drives at this storage capacity cost about $2,000.

Figure 17.2.
At under $1,000, the internal Pinnacle Micro Vertex drive provides quick performance and 2.6GB disk capacities. (Photo courtesy of Pinnacle Micro, Inc.)

Getting Connected

Removable disk drives now offer the whole range of SCSI, IDE, and parallel port connections. Computer publication reviews will make head-to-head comparisons for you, but in terms of reading and writing performance, SCSI is generally fastest. IDE is slightly slower, and parallel port connections run at a snail's pace.

Of course, parallel port connections might be the only option for mobile computer users, although some manufacturers now offer internal drives for notebooks. Some drives, such as the Avatar Shark 250, are targeted directly at mobile users and feature rugged case designs and tiny (2^1/$_2$-inch) portable disks.

One important note about SCSI drives: Many of these drives don't include a SCSI host adapter card in the box, requiring you to obtain your own. This can add to the price and hassle involved in installing the drive.

Recording Technology

Although we're discussing magnetic and MO technologies together, there are key differences. If you want quick performance, magnetic is the way to go. These drives can provide average access times as fast as 10ms, making it possible to launch applications from the removable medium if necessary. The access times for MO, on the other hand, can be as slow as 30ms.

Speed isn't everything. If you plan to use a drive for permanent backup or archiving, faster magnetic drives might not be suitable. The problem is that the integrity of magnetic media might degrade over time, resulting in lost data. Because MO media must be heated before the magnetic charge can be changed, data stored on the disks is less prone to corruption.

Versatility

Some drives read and write more than one media format. If you're sharing disks with others, determine the most common disk type and then look for a drive that can handle it. If the drive has flexibility in its formats, you might not be sacrificing anything for the ability to share files.

Price Per Megabyte

As I mentioned, always double-check the cost per megabyte of the medium. Factor in how many disks you think you might need in a year when figuring out prices. This can be an illuminating part of your purchase decision.

Backing Up Data

Most large removable disk drives come with backup software in the box. If for some reason your drive doesn't include backup software, or the software doesn't meet your backup needs, several options await you.

Windows 95 Backup

Windows 95 features a utility called Backup, shown in Figure 17.3. You can access it by selecting Start | Accessories | System Tools. If you don't see it listed, it wasn't installed during the original operating system installation. To install it, select Start | Settings | Control Panel and double-click Add/Remove Programs. Choose the Windows Setup tab. Highlight Disk Tools and then click the Details button. Put a check next to Backup, and then click Apply. You will be asked to insert your Windows 95 installation CD-ROM.

Windows 95 Backup offers only limited backup features and does not support scheduling. If you need more powerful tools, check into other options.

Figure 17.3.
*Windows 95's
integrated Backup
facility won't schedule
your backups, but it's
free with the operating
system.*

Free Backup Software

Backup software is a popular topic on shareware bulletin boards and Web sites. Partial-function (or limited-timed use) demos are available for free at many sites. One example is Search on Reflex Backup (from Genius Technologies) at www.download.com (CNET's shareware page). Reflex Backup supposedly works with any removable disk drive. Demos usually include information on where and how to purchase the full package.

Additionally, you can often find free applets that extend the features of your existing backup package. For example, for Iomega Jaz drives, you can add scheduling capability through a free utility called 1-Step Backup System Agent Extension (also available through www.download.com). You must have Iomega Tools and the Microsoft Plus packages in order for this applet to work.

Off-the-Shelf Backup

One of the higher-rated packages is the $80 Cheyenne Backup for Windows 95 (www.cheyenne.com). It features diskette-based disaster recovery and antivirus protection. Check computer press reviews for more on the latest software.

Upgrading

With the wide variety of drive types and models, it is simply not possible to detail every large removable disk drive installation. Instead, we'll discuss installing the highly regarded SyQuest SyJet (www.syquest.com).

The $3^1/_2$-inch SyJet uses magnetic-based recording on 1.5GB removable disks. It offers fast 12ms access times and therefore is suitable for loading files (and occasionally launching applications) from its medium. The SyJet comes in internal SCSI ($400), external SCSI ($500), and external parallel port models ($530). SyQuest has announced that an internal IDE version is under development. You can purchase individual 1.5GB disks at $125 or a three-pack for $300.

What follows are the instructions for the internal SCSI model. You'll need your own SCSI host adapter card (see Chapter 11, "Control Freaks: IDE and SCSI Controllers"), because SyQuest doesn't supply one in the box.

Before you begin, do the following:

1. Choose a drive bay: You need a bay that opens onto the front of your PC. If your system is bulging with components, it's conceivable that you might need to move your hard drive to a bay that doesn't abut the front of the PC. External drives, of course, require only desk space.

2. Check the cabling: Make sure that you have the necessary power cable socket (usually a white plastic molding with four large pin openings) and controller cable (SCSI). Double-check that they both reach the drive bay in which you intend to install the SyJet.

3. SCSI devices require proper SCSI ID and termination settings (again, see Chapter 11). Check the ID of your SCSI host adapter and any devices that connect to it (using your SCSI management software) before beginning this installation. You'll need to choose an unused SCSI ID for the SyJet.

4. The SyJet comes with a default SCSI ID of 4. If another device holds this ID, you must either change that device's ID or change the SyJet's ID. To alter the SyJet's ID, follow these remaining steps:

5. Remove the four screws that hold the SyJet drive into its $5^1/4$-inch mounting boot.

6. Pull the drive out from its $5^1/4$-inch mounting boot.

7. Turn the drive upside down.

8. Locate the JP2000 jumper on the bottom of the drive. Pin 1 is toward the center of the drive, and pin 8 is on the outer edge of the drive. Page 13 of the SyJet Installation Guide shows the jumper settings map. Using this map, move the jumpers to a new setting.

9. Before putting the drive back into the mounting boot, check the termination jumper (pin 8). If the jumper covers both pins, the drive is unterminated. If it covers only one of the two pins, it is terminated. If your SyJet is to be the last device on a SCSI chain (see Chapter 11), it must be terminated. Otherwise, leave it unterminated. Remember, if the SyJet is to be at the end of your SCSI chain, the device that was previously at the end must now be unterminated.

10. Reinsert the drive into the mounting boot, and screw in the mounting screws.

Installing the Internal SCSI SyJet

Follow these steps to install the internal SCSI SyJet:

1. Shut down the PC, turn off the power, and remove the PC power cable from the back of the PC unit. Open the PC case.

2. Remove the plastic cover from the front of the chosen drive bay.

3. Connect the 50-pin SCSI cable and the power adapter cable to the back of the SyJet drive.

Upgrade Advice: Both of these attach correctly in only one way. The ribbon data cable has a red line running along the edge for pin 1 out of the cable. Your SyJet has a small "1" marking pin 1 on the data cable connector at the back of the drive. Make sure that the red-line edge of the cable and pin 1 match up, or you won't be able to access this drive.

The power supply cable should have a rounded edge on the top two corners of the connector. The power supply port on the back of the drive also has these rounded edges, designating the top edge of the port. Make sure that the power cable is firmly secured in the correct position.

4. Insert the SyJet into the drive bay. If it is a $3^1/_2$-inch bay, first remove the SyJet mounting boot. You won't need it in this case.

5. Make sure that the front of the SyJet drive is flush with the front of your PC case and that no gaps exist between the edges of the drive and the PC.

6. Screw in the four screws that hold the SyJet into the bay. Don't over-tighten them.

7. Double-check that the cabling is correctly attached.

8. Put the PC case back on.

9. Reattach the PC power cable.

10. Insert a SyJet cartridge into the SyJet drive. This cartridge is preformatted. Make sure that the cartridge snaps into place after you push it all the way in.

11. Turn on your PC.

12. Use your SCSI diagnostics to determine whether the drive is recognized correctly. Do not reformat the cartridge.

Installing the SyJet Software in Windows 95

Follow these steps to install the SyJet software in Windows 95:

1. Under Windows 95, select Start | Settings | Control Panel.

2. Insert the SyJet Installation diskette and click Install.

3. Follow the on-screen directions.

Troubleshooting

Although large removable disk drives vary in type, many of the problems that users encounter with them are very similar. Table 17.1 lists the most common difficulties and their solutions.

Table 17.1. Fixing problems.

Symptom	Solution
You receive constant disk errors when accessing the removable drive.	If the drive is SCSI, there's a good chance that you haven't terminated the drive correctly. Read the manual to find out how to terminate the drive properly.
The new preformatted disk is unreadable/unwritable.	This is a very common mistake. It's likely that your diskette is preformatted for Macintosh computers, not PCs (most drive vendors offer both types). You should be able to reformat it with your SCSI host adapter software, but first check your drive's documentation and follow the instructions.
You receive `Drive not ready` error messages.	It's likely that the disk isn't completely inserted. You should hear a click when the removable drive is secured into place.

Summary

Near hard disk storage devices are an attractive solution for a wide number of users, particularly as program and data files get larger. Fast magnetic media such as the Jaz and Shark drives can put gigabytes of removable storage on your desktop. Best of all, these drives are quick enough that you can use them as a primary data store for your applications.

Magneto-optical drives, on the other hand, are excellent for backup and archiving. This medium is slow enough that you won't want to use it as the primary data store for your applications, but MO provides excellent durability. Data recorded to an MO drive will last 10 years or more, whereas magnetic media can suffer data loss in less than five years.

If you need to move very large files among systems, either of these media will work. The biggest concern is that you need drives that will recognize the medium wherever you plan to use it.

18

Tape
Backup

Peter Norton®

When it comes to computing, nothing is more important than your data. Quite simply, data is the currency of personal computing, whether it is in the form of word processing and spreadsheet documents, e-mail archives, or complex page and Web layouts. And with the expanding role of PCs in everyone's lives, there is more data to protect than ever before.

Unfortunately, most users don't adequately protect this valuable resource. This chapter discusses tape backup drives, the most common device used to archive large amounts of data. With hard disks pushing 7GB in size, it's no longer possible to archive data on 1.44MB floppy diskettes, yet a high-capacity floppy standard—such as the Iomega Zip or the LS-120 drives—is still years off.

This chapter introduces you to tape drives. It covers the following topics:

- How tape backup drives work and what they're useful for
- How to install a tape drive
- Troubleshooting tape drives

The Tale of Tape

If you've browsed through this book, you've already read about affordable 7GB hard disks, 17GB DVD-ROM drives, and fast magneto-optical drives that can hold nearly 5GB. So why would anyone want to use cassette tapes, a technology used on desktop PCs back in the early '80s? Three words: cost per megabyte. Cassette tape drives remain the preferred means of backing up large amounts of data because data cassettes are much less expensive than removable disks such as Syquest, Jaz, and Apex. How much less? Table 18.1 shows the relative prices of various types of media.

Table 18.1. Cost per megabyte.

Medium	Capacity	Cost	Cost Per Megabyte
Tape (Travan TR2)	3276.8MB	$35	1 cent
CD-ROM	640MB	$12	1.5 cents
Apex	4710.4MB	$99	2.1 cents
Vertex	2662.4MB	$79	3 cents
Jaz	1024MB	$79	7.7 cents
Hard disk	7168MB	$700	9.8 cents

In addition to its low cost, tape can be rewritten freely, a feature that CD-ROM drives can't offer. But tape isn't appropriate for general data handling because of the linear nature of the medium. In other words, the drive can't simply jump to the desired place on the medium to access data the way hard disks and CD-ROM drives do. Instead, it must scroll to a spot on the tape, which can take tens of seconds. That kind of delay—hundreds of times slower than CD-ROM drives or hard disks—means that tape drives are too slow to act as general data storage.

How Tape Backup Works

If you're familiar with how an old eight-track tape works, you already have a good idea of how tape drives store data. To write data to tape, a drive head changes the magnetic charge on the tape medium as it passes beneath it. To read data, the head simply senses the charge of the medium, which the drive interprets as a binary 1 or 0.

Like eight-track tapes, tape backup media are divided into tracks, each of which runs the length of the tape. The tracks run one into another, forming a long chain of tracks. When the drive reaches the end of one track, it simply reverses the direction of tape motion and picks up the next track. On a 740-foot-long tape, 72 tracks yields a total of 53,000 feet of recording surface.

Note: The side-by-side tracks used in data cassettes help shorten the length of the tape. After all, a 72-track tape measuring 750 feet in length would be over 53,000 feet long if the tracks were all laid end-to-end. These tracks allow the drive to access data on the tape more quickly.

But how does the drive know where one bit starts and the next ends? Like other media, the tape is segmented into defined spaces called *bit cells* within which the drive knows to look for a magnetic charge. If the drive detects a change in charge between two bit cells, it interprets a digital 1. If the bit cells are of the same charge, a 0 is identified. These bit cells are contained within larger sectors, which may be called *sectors* or *frames*. They contain both data and error-correction bits to ensure precision.

These sectors or frames also include *slack space*, which provides enough travel for the drive head to start and stop the medium without overrunning data on the tape. This is important, because sometimes the PC can't maintain a continuous data stream to the tape, requiring the drive to pause while the processor catches up. Without gaps in the sectors, any pause in the data stream could result in lost data, much like CD-R recording sessions can be ruined by a buffer underrun.

Compression is an important part of tape drive operation, but it can be a source of confusion as well. Tape drive vendors often quote capacities based on compressed data, usually assuming a 2-to-1 compression ratio. But the effectiveness of compression can vary widely, depending on the type of data being compressed. If you need to back up JPEG images and MPEG movies—both already heavily compressed—the vendor's 2-to-1 compression assumption won't pan out. Always look at the uncompressed capacity when you're considering storage.

Types of Backup Media

A few years ago, the tape backup market was a mess. Tapes for one manufacturer's drive wouldn't work in another, leading to incompatibilities and limiting data-recovery options. If you switched to a different tape drive, you had to purchase all-new media to go with it.

Today, there are several types of tape backup media, including

- DAT: Digital Audio Tape
- DLT: Digital Linear Tape
- 8mm cartridge
- QIC-format Travan

Of these, only the QIC-format tape is designed for use on single desktops. The others are priced for larger network duty and can handle capacities of 25 to 35GB or more (see Figure 18.1).

Figure 18.1.
With its autoloading cassette mechanism, fast performance, and large capacities, this DAT backup drive is ready-made for network servers and other demanding backup environments. (Photo courtesy of Seagate Corp.)

Established in 1987, the QIC standard gets its name from its quarter-inch cassette, which defines the width of the tape. The QIC standard started at 400MB with the QIC-40 specification and has moved up as hard disk capacities have increased. Today, new QIC media provide 2GB and greater capacities of uncompressed data.

Behind the higher capacities is a technology called Travan, which was established by 3M and several hardware makers in 1992. Key to the new standard is the relative density of magnetic charge changes that can occur on each inch of tape, called *flux transitions*. The more flux transitions per inch (ftpi), the more data the tape can store.

Table 18.2 lists four variations of the Travan specification.

Table 18.2. Travan flavors defined.

Travan Type	Capacity	Flux Transitions Per Inch
TR-1	400MB	14,700
TR-2	800MB	22,125
TR-3	1.6GB	44,250
TR-4	4GB	50,800

In fact, ftpi determines the capacity of a Travan tape, because all Travan media employ the same amount of physical surface area. All tapes are a quarter-inch wide and measure 750 feet in length. Greater ftpi densities mean that more bits are stored per inch and also allow for more tracks to be packed into the medium. The TR-1 spec, for example, provides 14,700 flux transitions per inch, resulting in 400MB of data stored in 36 tracks. In comparison, the 4GB TR-4 spec employs 50,800 flux transitions per inch on 72 tracks.

Making Backups

Advancements in tape drives have vastly improved performance—a good thing considering the amount of time it would take to move gigabytes of data otherwise. Today, fast tape drives can move data at up to 500Kbps, enough for video playback directly from tape media. The problem is that accessing data in a random fashion will always take an unacceptably long time with tape drives. For this reason, tape backup can't compete with spinning-disk media, which provide access times in milliseconds.

One of the most critical elements of any backup drive is the software that makes it work (see Figure 18.2). Backup software varies widely, so it makes sense to look for software that provides the features you need. Virtually all these packages let you select the files to be backed up.

Better software provides powerful options to tailor backup routines. Scheduling features let you back up data every day, every week, or at any other specified interval. In addition, backups can be tailored to save all the selected data on the disk, or only data that has been changed since the last backup. There are three categories of backups:

- Full backup: Writes everything on the disk to tape.

- Incremental backup: Writes to tape anything that has changed since the last incremental backup.

- Differential backup: Writes to tape anything that has changed since the last full backup.

Figure 18.2.
Microsoft Backup provides the ability to selectively back up files and filter them by date. But you'll want a more sophisticated program for automated scheduling of backups.

Full backups take the longest time and chew up the most media, but they also provide the most sure-fire security. With a full backup, you know everything you need is on the tape. Incremental backups are the most problematic, because only altered data appears on the tape. You need to make sure that you have both the original full backup and all subsequent incremental backups on hand in order to restore all the data. However, incremental backups are the most economical in terms of media space and time.

In between are differential backups. These backups save all the changed data since the last full backup. Although you repeat the work of earlier incremental or differential backups, you need to keep only two tapes handy at any time—the first full backup and the latest differential backup.

Table 18.3 helps untangle backup strategies.

Table 18.3. Examples of backups.

Backup Type	Tapes Needed to Restore
Full	One
Differential	Two
Incremental	Up to five for a weekly rotation

Warning: Backups can go bad. Media can fail, or the drive might simply fail to write to the medium properly. You can reduce data loss by setting the backup software to conduct a full verification after the backup is complete. This feature causes the drive to review the entire tape. Although this process significantly increases the time it takes to complete a backup, it can catch flaws before they become a problem. Also be sure to do test restores of your data on a regular basis. This will let you verify the integrity of your data backups before you find yourself in a do-or-die situation.

Buying Backups

When it comes to buying a tape backup, you need to make sure that the drive you purchase can meet your needs. A computer that has a stuffed 8.4GB hard disk simply can't be backed up with an 800MB Iomega Ditto drive. You'll also need to think about the interface type and compatibility with other tape formats if you have older media around that you need to access.

Capacity Concerns

The biggest challenge in buying a tape drive is figuring out the maximum data capacity it supports. Often, manufacturers market their drives based on compressed data capacities, usually based on a 2-to-1 compression ratio. The result is that you might think the drive can handle more data than it really can.

In fact, 2-to-1 is an optimistic estimate. In general, you can expect data compression ratios to fall around 1.7-to-1 overall, with document files enjoying higher capacities. If you're compressing a lot of previously compressed data—Internet images, video, or program files—scale your expectations downward.

Today, the highest-capacity tape drives can store 4GB of data before compression. If you have a large hard disk over 4GB in size, you'll need to consider a higher-end tape drive.

Upgrade Advice: If you already own a tape drive and are upgrading to a larger hard disk, consider your new backup needs. Odds are you might have to update the tape drive as well in order to handle the expanded data capacity of the new hard disk.

Interface Options

Another critical concern is the device interface. You'll also want to consider whether you want an internal or external model, because this might determine which interface you use. Tape drives are sold with interfaces for the following bus types:

- SCSI
- Parallel port
- Enhanced IDE
- Floppy drive
- USB (soon)

For the fastest and most trouble-free backups, SCSI drives are the way to go (see Figure 18.3). You'll spend more money for the fast SCSI bus and interface, but you won't have to share ports the way you must with parallel port drives. In addition, higher-speed tape drives can move data at their full 500Kbps data rate. SCSI also provides superior multitasking, allowing the system to perform other activities more efficiently during backup routines.

Buying Tip: If you already have external SCSI peripherals installed, go with a SCSI tape drive. After all, you already have the SCSI host controller in place, so you can simply add the tape drive to the daisy chain. Otherwise, the SCSI decision will rest on your usage. If you make frequent and large backups, you'll enjoy quicker backups on a SCSI bus. This is particularly true if you tend to conduct backups while working with the PC.

Parallel port tape drives are an option if you need light-duty backup facilities. Home and home-office PCs might do well with parallel port drives. In addition to being very simple to install, parallel port models are much less expensive than their SCSI counterparts. They can also be shared easily among several PCs, making them a great option for people who have a desktop and notebook PC, for example.

Figure 18.3.
The fast SCSI connection employed by the internal Seagate TapeStor 8000 helps speed backup jobs to the 4GB TR-4 medium. (Photo courtesy of Seagate Corp.)

That said, these drives must often share the parallel port with the printer, which can invite conflicts and prompt a lot of annoying port swapping. Drive throughput can also be limited by the parallel port.

Another common option is for floppy or IDE controller-based drives. Often, if you have two floppy drives already installed, you might need to install a separate controller card. Of course, both floppy-based and IDE drives need to be internal models, but the interfaces provide faster performance than low-cost parallel port models.

Finally, look for a new generation of tape backup devices, based on the Universal Serial Bus (USB). USB provides 12Mbps throughput that is much faster than parallel port connections while avoiding the expense and complexity of SCSI. To a large extent, device makers are waiting for the arrival of Windows 98—the first USB-aware operating system—before introducing products. Of course, USB is an option only for newer systems outfitted with the bus connectors—or for those upgraded with a USB card.

And what about the choice of external versus internal? Generally internal drives are less expensive and more convenient than external models. Not only do internal models conserve desktop space, but they also avoid adding yet another power cord (and sometimes an enormous adapter module) to the tangle behind the PC. Of course, if you want to use an IDE interface, you must go with an internal drive. Of course, external models (see Figure 18.4) are excellent for PCs that don't have drive bays, as well as for offices in which a tape drive is shared among more than one system.

Figure 18.4.
*Form and function:
The Seagate TapeStor
3200 uses 1.6GB
TR-3 media and
sports a stylish,
vertically mounted
design. (Photo
courtesy of Seagate
Corp.)*

On the downside, internal drives consume drive bay space and require internal connections for power. If you own a slimline system or a PC with a paucity of bays, you might want to pay a little more for an external device.

Compatibility

Another critical concern is compatibility. In general, tape drives with larger capacities can at least read tapes made for smaller capacities. In many cases, these drives can both read from and write to smaller media.

Of course, if you have one drive that you use on your system, compatibility might not be a huge concern. But if you need to read tapes from a previous drive or share tapes from other systems, this ability to read and write different media is a valuable one.

Installing a Tape Backup Drive

Installing a tape backup device is very similar to installing a CD-ROM or other drive. Windows 95's Plug and Play facility will guide you through the routine, automatically detecting the new device. Or you can decide to identify the device to the OS yourself. The biggest difference among drives is between external and internal devices.

Physical Installation

It's far more complicated to install an internal backup drive. To install the unit, do the following:

1. Shut down the PC, remove the power cord, and remove the case.

2. Make sure you're well-grounded (an antistatic wrist strap is a good idea) before reaching into the case. Find an open externally accessible drive bay, and pry off the front cover.

3. Connect the drive cable to the drive, being sure to match pin 1 of the cable to pin 1 of the connector.

4. Slide the drive into the bay, and align the screw holes with those in the mount.

5. Use the screws provided with the drive to affix the drive to the bay. Be sure to follow the instructions that came with the drive to make sure that it is properly mounted.

6. Attach the data cable to the appropriate SCSI, EIDE, or floppy connector, as determined by your drive's interface (see Figure 18.5).

Figure 18.5.
For floppy-based drives, the presence of two floppy drives will require a third cable to split off of the existing leads. Often, this cable will be provided. (Figure courtesy of Seagate Corp.)

7. Attach one of the free power leads from the supply to the power connector on the drive. Make sure you properly align the connector.

8. In some cases, you might need to set jumpers found near the back of the drive to match the settings on your motherboard. Consult your documentation for specific information.

If you have an external drive, you simply need to plug the drive into the appropriate cables. If it's a SCSI drive, you'll need to make sure you have the proper cable connectors to mate with your SCSI card or the connector on other daisy-chained SCSI devices. Also check the device's documentation on how to terminate and enumerate SCSI devices.

Parallel port drives might include a printer pass-through port. If so, you might need to check your system BIOS and set it to standard Centronics (or PS/2) operation. ECP- and EPP-enabled parallel port configurations might get confused by the pass-through port.

To install the drivers, do the following:

1. Plug in the PC and power it up.
2. Windows 95 will detect the new hardware during boot-up and prompt you to install the new device.
3. Click through the Add New Hardware Wizard. When Windows 95 prompts you to detect the new device, click No.
4. Select the Other Device item and click Next. Insert the tape drive's driver disk into the floppy drive.
5. In the next dialog box, click Have Disk and select the .INF file from the appropriate drive and directory.
6. Windows 95 will update the new driver information. When you're prompted to restart the system, click Yes.
7. Your tape drive should now be installed.

You'll also need to install the backup program that comes with the device (or a third-party program of your choosing). Once this is done, you can test the drive and make sure it works.

Tape Management: Handling with Care

Dealing with backup drives can get tricky. The cassettes themselves are sensitive to environmental stress, and the physical logistics of juggling backup media can get complicated. In both cases, it makes sense to have a strategy to avoid trouble down the road.

Establishing a Smart Backup Scheme

Before you get started backing up data, establish a routine. Decide how often you need to back up your data and how thorough you want to be. Usually, you can avoid burning too much time (and money on tapes) by establishing a set of incremental backups between full backups.

Imation Corp., the 3M spinoff that invented the Travan tape medium, provides the following guidelines for scenarios using three or six cartridges a week.

Three-Cartridge Weekly Backup

This backup principle requires daily backups and a single weekly off-site backup copy to provide a data history of up to two weeks. Friday backups are full backups. Monday-through-Thursday backups are incremental (all on the same tape). Note that restoring incremental changes might be more difficult using the three-cartridge principle.

- Start the cycle on a Friday, and back up your entire hard disk to a cartridge labeled Friday 1. This is a full backup of your system. Store this data cartridge off-site.

- On Monday, back up only the files that have been created or updated since the last backup (Friday 1); use a cartridge labeled Daily for this. Store this cartridge on-site.

- On Tuesday, Wednesday, and Thursday, use the same Daily cartridge to back up files that have been created or updated since the preceding day. Store this cartridge on-site.

- On Friday, do a full backup using a cartridge labeled Friday 2. Store this cartridge off-site.

- Continue the weekly routine of incremental backups for Monday through Thursday using the same Daily data cartridge. On Fridays, alternate the Friday 1 and Friday 2 cartridges.

Six-Cartridge Weekly Backup

This backup principle requires daily backups and a single weekly off-site backup copy to provide a data history of up to two weeks. Friday backups are full backups. Monday through Thursday backups are incremental.

- Start the cycle on a Friday, and back up your entire hard disk to a cartridge labeled Friday 1. This is a full backup of your system. Store this data cartridge off-site.

- On Monday, back up only the files that have been created or updated since the last backup (Friday 1); use a cartridge labeled Monday for this. (Or, for easier restoring, do a full backup.) Store this cartridge on-site.

- On the appropriate days, use cartridges labeled Tuesday, Wednesday, and Thursday to back up files that have been created or updated since the previous day. (Or, for easier restoring, do a full backup.) Store these on-site.

- On Friday, do a full backup using a cartridge labeled Friday 2. Store this cartridge off-site.

- Once you get this far, you continue the weekly incremental backups for Monday through Thursday using the same Monday-through-Thursday data cartridges. On Fridays, alternate the Friday 1 and Friday 2 cartridges.

Caring for Cassettes

Cassette tape media can be tricky. The flexible tape can suffer from exposure to dirt, humidity, and temperature. Over time, tape can stretch as it is pulled time and again through the drive mechanism. For this reason, it's a good idea to stay on top of potential problems.

Watch the Environment

Give your new tape cartridges time to acclimate. The media material expands and contracts in relation to room temperature. So when you bring new tapes in from outside—say a delivery truck—you should give them at least eight hours or so to adjust to the temperature of the room you will use them in. In fact, for this reason, it's a good idea to keep your tapes close to where they will be used.

Of course, it's a good idea to avoid constant temperature and humidity fluctuations, because this can stress the medium and shorten its useful life.

Cleaning Up

Tape drives aren't sealed like hard disks, so dirt can be a problem. Dust that gathers on tape heads can end up on the medium, impairing the drive's ability to read and write. The problem is that the head must be in contact with the medium in order to function. If dust or other particulates block this contact, the device can't operate properly.

The best approach to this problem is to keep your work space reasonably clean to avoid exposure. In addition, you should periodically clean the drive heads and motor assembly using a cleaning media tape. This cassette fits into the drive like any other data cassette, but it's designed to clear the internal components of dirt.

Get Tense

Over time, environmental stress and normal operation can loosen the medium in its spools. The result is lost precision as the tape slips with each drive movement. You can avoid this problem by periodically running the tape from beginning to end in a single run. Some backup software includes a retension command that performs this operation automatically. If a tape is subject to extreme temperature changes, the tape should be run from beginning to end. In fact, it's a good idea to do this every time a tape is loaded.

Take Care of Media

You'll get longer life out of your media—and, consequently, better data protection—if you take care of cassettes. Keep in mind the following points when handling cassettes:

- Remove cassettes from the tape drive when they're not in use.
- When you're finished using a tape, reset it to the very beginning or the very end.
- Store cassettes in the same room where they will be used, and keep them in their protective covers.
- Keep tapes away from destructive exposures such as magnetic fields and sunlight.

Summary

Surprisingly, tape backup drives are more important than ever. These slow devices provide affordable, flexible data storage for everything from home PCs to network servers. Although cassette technology has been around almost forever, the buying landscape can get tricky. Tape capacity, compatibility, and interface choices are all part of any buying decision.

Don't overlook the importance of software, either. Yes, Windows 95 does include a backup utility that can get the job done. But if you want to make consistent and effective backups, you'll want the automated scheduling capability provided by third-party products. When buying a backup drive, look for the quality of the software.

Tape backup drives aren't sexy, but they can really be a lifesaver. After all, with more and more of our personal and working data on PCs, the effects of loss or damage to the system can be disastrous. Tape backup drives are the best way to avoid losing your investment.

V

Multimedia

19

New Dimensions: Graphics Accelerators

Peter Norton®

When it comes to performance upgrades intended to make their systems faster, people think of two things: CPUs and graphics boards. To a large extent, the arrival of Windows 3.0 in 1990 helped develop this belief that graphics boards are important to performance. The upgrade picture these days is a bit more complex—RAM and cache upgrades are now just as important to consider as CPU and graphics—but the basic truth still holds.

In fact, graphics board upgrades have renewed importance these days. The emergence of 3-D graphics standards has created a new class of software, written to display realistic and smooth 3-D images (see Figure 19.1). Every kind of software, from arcade-style games to business presentation packages, can make use of complex 3-D graphics to boost visual impact.

Figure 19.1.
Diamond Multimedia's Stealth 3D Pro 2000 is typical of today's graphics accelerators. It packs 2-D, 3-D, and video acceleration into a low-cost PCI add-in card. (Photo courtesy of Diamond Multimedia)

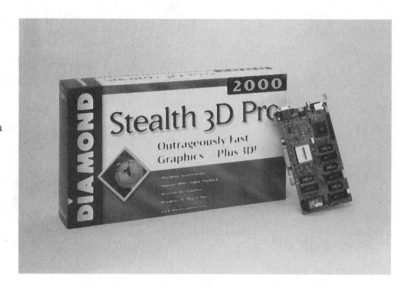

If you have a 486 system, you might have to consider a new motherboard or system if you want to enjoy the exciting 3-D and video features of the latest graphics boards. Board makers have largely abandoned the older ISA and VL-bus slots in favor of the PCI scheme that is ubiquitous on Pentium and faster PCs. And the landscape is starting to change again, as new Pentium II systems feature the AGP bus that is dedicated to graphics.

There's just one problem: If you don't have a 3-D-capable graphics card, you might not be able to play. And even if you can, you might lack the performance to avoid distracting (and sometimes fatal) delays in screen updates. This chapter shows you how to move into the third dimension. You will learn

- How graphics cards speed up and enhance 2-D and 3-D graphics and video
- What to look for when buying a new graphics card for games, business, and other applications

- How to diagnose and troubleshoot common graphics problems
- How to upgrade your system with a new graphics card, including complete installation instructions

Packin' Pixels: How Graphics Boards Speed Performance

Graphics boards speed up system performance in two ways: They free the system CPU from the mundane chores of displaying and updating graphics information, and they accomplish these chores many times faster than a general CPU ever could. The result is rapid-fire screen updates that make possible wonderful things such as Deathmatch Quake, super-scrolling spreadsheets, and really smooth animated text in PowerPoint presentations.

In order to understand how graphics boards do their tricks, you need to know how Windows works. In fact, Windows made the graphics accelerator board market possible by providing a standard way to draw text, graphics, and other elements on-screen. Under DOS, most applications wrote to the display in a custom way that confounded graphics board makers and demanded a different driver for each application.

Getting Under the Graphics Hood

Windows provides a standard interface for display interaction. Under DOS, programs each displayed information to the screen in their own way, working directly with hardware to display graphics, fonts, and other information.

Windows put several layers of software between your applications and graphics hardware, establishing a standard set of rules for doing graphics work. This new scheme, shown in Figure 19.2, allowed graphics boards to use hardware to speed up common graphics operations that used to be the responsibility of the host CPU. The result was improved overall performance.

2-D Graphics Acceleration

The rule book for 2-D graphics, established firmly with the release of Windows 3.0, is called the *Graphics Device Interface* (GDI). Applications send GDI calls to Windows to do everything from moving blocks of graphics to scrolling text to displaying color.

Software on the other side—the graphics board driver—is queried by the GDI to determine what capabilities are available, allowing the driver to direct the flow of work to the dedicated graphics chip on the board or to the host CPU. If no acceleration hardware is in place, all the GDI calls are handled by the processor.

Figure 19.2.
Microsoft employs a series of function-specific software layers to address graphics capabilities such as 2-D, 3-D, and video. (Figure courtesy of Microsoft Corp.)

Compatibility: Watch out for cards that use a scheme called *GDI bypass* to boost performance. These boards have drivers that intercept inbound GDI graphics calls and replace them with custom code that is designed to perform the same operation more quickly. Although performance might get a boost—GDI is a very slow component of Windows 95—the prospect of incompatibilities in the vital graphics-handling area of the OS is a real concern. In particular, the multimonitor support being built into Windows 98 can run into trouble if the GDI is bypassed. Microsoft has stated that GDI bypass isn't an acceptable solution and that systems employing it will have their PC97 standing revoked.

Graphics boards handle several key 2-D operations:

- Bit block transfer: Perhaps the most important function of a graphics board is the *bit block transfer*, also called a *bit blit*. A bit blit moves chunks of graphics data from one place in graphics memory (and on-screen) to another. Scrolling text and dragging a graphic across the screen are both examples of bit blits.

- Line drawing: Speeds the drawing of lines by defining the beginning and end point and filling in the pixels in between. This approach is faster than operating on each pixel individually. Similar approaches are used for drawing arcs and polygons.

- Color and pattern fill: The process of applying color and patterns to an area of the screen, usually a polygon, circle, or other geometric shape. Instead of updating each pixel individually, the card can identify a range on the screen to update in one step. Gradients are supported as well.

- Clipping: Allows the quick display of items that obscure other items, such as a drop-down menu that covers part of a spreadsheet.

- Off-screen memory caching: Employs unused graphics memory to store frequently-needed graphical information such as fonts and application menus. Caching eliminates the need to go to main system memory for updates.

In the past, some graphics boards provided a greater range of acceleration features than others. Today, almost all graphics boards deliver similar capabilities, with performance differences coming from the type of memory. The result is that demanding multimedia titles, such as DeLorme's Mag'n'Go, shown in Figure 19.3, enjoy much-improved performance.

Figure 19.3.
DeLorme's Map'n'Go street map software is an excellent example of graphics-heavy software that benefits from 2-D acceleration.

Video Acceleration

Around 1994, software such as Apple's QuickTime and Microsoft's Video for Windows helped introduce digital video playback to PCs. The new software allowed Windows-based PCs to recognize compressed video files and play them back on-screen.

But even today's fastest Pentium MMX and Pentium II PCs struggle to display video of a quality approaching that of a standard VHS tape. Like the reels in a movie, digital video consists of a series of individual images, or frames, played in swift succession to create the illusion of motion.

The amount of data involved is tremendous: In order to display 30 frames of uncompressed digital video, a PC would have to move nearly 200MBps of data. To make digital video possible, that number needs to be cut down to as little as 150 kilobits per second. To do this, video is stored in compressed format so that it can be moved more quickly and efficiently until it reaches the processor.

The problem with compression is that it takes a lot of work from the processor to decode the video stream. There is so much processing to do that video frame rates can drop from a smooth 30 frames per second (fps) to a jerky 5fps or less. Not surprisingly, the responsiveness of other applications suffers as well.

Video-capable graphics boards help improve things by easing the burden on the CPU and by improving the quality of stretched video windows. Although compression schemes such as MPEG-1, MPEG-2, Indeo, and Cinepak might do things in different ways, they all share characteristics that allow standard video accelerating hardware to boost performance.

DirectDraw: Crucial Shortcuts

Before any hardware could help video playback, Microsoft had to provide an efficient path for video data under Windows. GDI might be a useful standard for static images and simple animations, but it's slow-moving death for consumer applications such as video playback and game play.

To this end, three years ago Microsoft began working on a set of standards called *DirectX*, which provides programming tools and pathways for efficiently moving multimedia data and handling complex controls. On the graphics side, the DirectDraw application programming interface (API) allows hardware and software makers to move multimedia graphics more quickly and efficiently. The version of DirectDraw found in DirectX 2 provides the crucial programming hooks that allow video clips to access video-accelerating hardware.

As with any peripherals, you need the proper drivers in order to gain access to all the features in the operating system and the peripheral's hardware. You might have a video-capable graphics card, but unless you install DirectDraw drivers, those features will go unnoticed by your applications.

For more on installing drivers, see the section "Installing a Graphics Board."

Tip: The best place to get drivers is online, from the vendor's Web site or from a forum on CompuServe, AOL, or another online service. Make a point to visit these sites every few months to see if a significant upgrade or feature release is available. You might be able to extend and enhance the life of your graphics card with these occasional downloads.

The DirectDraw API provides the following key features (among others):

- Direct frame buffer access
- Double frame buffering
- Color space conversion
- Pixel interpolation

Direct Frame Buffer Access

The essential shortcut that makes video and game play possible under Windows 95, direct frame buffer access lets programs cut through layers of GDI code to get bits on-screen quickly. Under GDI, software sends commands to Windows 95, which interprets them and turns them into specific graphics commands. The extra layer ensures compatibility but exacts a penalty in performance.

Direct frame buffer access cuts through the thick levels of code, replacing them with a thin layer that allows direct access to memory without inviting all sorts of incompatibility shenanigans. Even on a card that doesn't have video acceleration features, direct frame buffer access can speed video frame rates and the display of 2-D and 3-D graphics.

Double Buffering

Like direct frame buffer access, double buffering has applications outside of video. This scheme lets the graphics controller store two pictures in its memory—the current image and the image that is next to come up. By staying ahead of the game by constantly displaying an image of what's to come, graphics boards can avoid distracting flaws such as frame dropping, slow screen updates, and image shearing (in which the image on-screen splits in half as part of it fails to update quickly).

Double buffering is particularly important in video and 3-D graphics, in which a frame rate of about 30 frames per second maintains the illusion of smooth motion. By splitting graphics memory with this efficient scheme, the graphics card can stay ahead of the game.

Color Space Conversion

In order to save space, the color information in video clips is stored in a format called YUV. This format, which is the same as the one used by your TV, breaks video data into separate color and brightness components. Y represents the luminance, or brightness, value of each pixel, U defines the color, and V represents the saturation value of each pixel. A YUV value of 4:2:2, which yields 16 bits of data per pixel, equals 24 bits per pixel using standard graphics format. The result is smaller files.

In contrast, your PC's monitor uses a red-green-blue (RGB) color scheme in which colors are created by mixing varying levels of the three colors within each pixel. Because of this, the YUV color information in a video clip needs to be converted to the standard RGB format recognized by the display.

The problem with color space conversion is that it takes a lot of processor power. In fact, about 30 percent of the video playback workload using the popular Indeo codec consists of changing YUV into RGB. Video accelerating hardware immediately boosts the performance of all video playback by freeing the CPU from this task.

Pixel Interpolation

Pixel interpolation improves the visual quality of video clips that are stored at lower resolutions than they are played back. This feature is needed because many clips are stored at resolutions of 320×240 pixels but are played back full-screen on systems running at 640×480 or 800×600 pixels. Although you can have the host CPU double up pixels to fill the extra space, the results can be very unattractive.

Pixel interpolation makes expanded video look more realistic by averaging color information when pixels are added. That way, smooth curves don't break into jagged boundaries; instead, the color averaging keeps the illusion of smoothness.

Note: One downside of pixel interpolation is that sharply contrasting areas—such as what is found on a checkerboard kitchen floor—sometimes get averaged into softer grays. This can make the original image look hazy or undefined. Better interpolation hardware will detect edges and keep them intact.

The color interpolation feature on graphics boards can vary. Some less-sophisticated graphics chips only average information between pixels running horizontally—what is called an *x filter*. Most chips today provide both x and y filters. In other words, they average going up and down and side to side.

In addition, some chips take more pixels into account when doing their work. Older or less-sophisticated chips compute averages using two pixels—the pixel in question and the one adjacent to it (called a *2-tap filter*). Today, most graphics chips average color values among 4 pixels (a *4-tap filter*), allowing the hardware to make a better approximation of reality when it expands the video image. Often, the higher pixel count can smooth out the distracting stair-stepping of colors, known as *banding*.

Peter's Principle: How to Discern Video Quality

If you look closely, you can tell the difference in the way video accelerators affect playback. Although all video compression schemes introduce some degradation, often the lack of proper video accelerating hardware will make a bad situation worse.

Look for telltale signs such as banded or blotchy colors. Skin tones in particular are a challenge for video chips. Also check for stair-stepped or jagged effects on diagonal lines (see Figure 19.4). Bicycle spokes are a classic example of an interpolation challenge, although nearly any angled surface will do. In addition, look for high-contrast points, where very different colors meet head-on. You might be able to see some hazing as the hardware unintentionally wipes out detail.

Figure 19.4.
Look closely at the wing and tail edges of this dogfighting F/A-18 Falcon, and you'll note stair-stepped edges. There are also banded colors on the fuselage.

Hardware-based interpolation does more than enhance image quality—it boosts performance as well. Think about it. During video playback, your CPU is busy enough just pushing out the video stream. Double the size of the video window, and you're asking it to take time out to calculate additional pixels in up to 30 frames every second. What's more, the considerably larger video stream must be ushered across the bus and to the graphics card.

With hardware interpolation, the driver software can tell the system CPU to just handle the decompression tasks and to route the native resolution (and still YUV-encoded) video stream to the graphics board. Once there, the video-savvy chip handles interpolation in hardware, and the CPU gets busy with succeeding frames. Because video isn't expanded until after it has reached the card, the system bus carries less data. Be aware that different codecs, such as Indeo and MPEG-1, use different types of YUV formatting—some of which might not be supported by older graphics hardware.

Motion Estimation

More recently, some graphics cards have begun adding a feature called *motion estimation*. Targeted for the high-quality MPEG-2 video found in DVD titles, motion estimation allows high-end PCs to play back MPEG-2 video without requiring a dedicated decompression card. Performance won't match that provided by dedicated MPEG-2 hardware, but this feature opens up the next level of video playback at a very affordable price.

Motion estimation allows the graphics card to ease the processing burden of determining what information is redundant in a video frame. In clips where little action is taking place—say, a video of someone giving a speech—these cards can simply keep all the unchanged visual information already in graphics memory and send it to the screen. Only changed pixels need to be processed.

Performance: When it comes to general-purpose video acceleration hardware, don't expect too much. The most demanding component of video playback—decompression—still falls entirely on the CPU, which is also busy with other system tasks. Video acceleration can ease the load and extend the quality of video, but it won't fix it outright.

Nowhere is this more true than with the coming generation of MPEG-2 clips used in DVD-based titles. The MPEG-2 compression scheme is extremely complex and data-heavy. Even the most effective general-purpose video hardware can't do enough to make MPEG-2 playback entirely effective.

PCs that use MMX-enhanced processors enjoy a big advantage when it comes to video playback. MMX extends processors' instruction sets to allow them to handle multimedia tasks such as video playback and decompression. Although a video-savvy graphics card already handles many of the tasks that MMX is tailored for, these enhanced CPUs still provide added performance for video playback. If you expect to play a lot of digital video, consider getting a system that has an MMX processor.

By the same token, this hardware won't make poorly captured or compressed video look better than it is. A Cinepak-compressed clip captured at low 160×120 resolution in 8-bit color and at 10 frames per second will look awful and jerky on the most sophisticated hardware (see Figures 19.5 and 19.6). Likewise, video encoded without a sufficient number of reference frames, called *key frames*, will lack clarity.

Figure 19.5.
Video hardware won't help low-resolution video, such as that found on many Web sites.

Figure 19.6.
Lots of motion forces compression schemes to throw out more visual data to keep the data rate low. The result is degraded image quality. Compare this image to Figure 19.5.

3-D Acceleration

If the introduction of video playback to PCs was important, it pales in comparison to the impact that 3-D graphics will have on personal computing. From rapid-fire gaming to immersive Web browsing, the emergence of 3-D standards and acceleration hardware promises to redefine the visual experience.

It's no surprise that popular 3-D programming standards form the basis of accelerated 3-D applications. It's less surprising that Microsoft put the standard in place. The Direct3D API, like DirectDraw before it, gives hardware and software vendors a single interface to hook into 3-D-accelerated features. Most important, everyone who creates a 3-D game or graphics card knows that Direct3D will be part and parcel of the Windows 95 operating system, helping create a large audience for compatible products.

Peter's Principle: 3-D Standards Are in Transition

Microsoft enjoys the upper hand, but the 3-D market is very much in transition. In addition to Direct3D, many 3-D APIs are available to programmers and hardware vendors. Boards from Diamond Multimedia and STB that use S3's Virge graphics chips, for example, offer support for the S3D API. Creative Labs' GameBlaster, meanwhile, comes packaged with CGL (Creative Graphics Library) support. Of course, these boards also provide compatibility with the Direct3D API from Microsoft.

In fact, virtually every 3-D-capable graphics board has its own native 3-D API. The reason is that neither hardware nor software companies can afford to wait while Microsoft perfects its Direct3D scheme. To get a leg up on the marketplace, graphics chip companies use their own custom 3-D APIs tailored for their chipsets. They then motivate game vendors to customize their existing titles for their own API and graphics chip. Although this activity helps get 3-D on the market a bit sooner, it also results in incompatible 3-D games that won't run on graphics chips other than the one they are written for. In other words, it's a lot like DOS.

What should you do? If possible, wait it out. PC-based 3-D graphics, being a young industry, has a steep development curve. A couple months can yield huge differences in performance and features as next-generation chips arrive that run rings around their predecessors. No matter what, make sure that Direct3D support is provided and that the vendor plans to stay on top of the latest developments. Over the next year or two, you can expect most software vendors to flock to the Direct3D standard, leaving those individual APIs to gather dust as vendors fail to update aging titles.

So you're not convinced that Microsoft is on its way to wrapping up the 3-D standards battle? This list from Microsoft shows some of the software companies that are supporting its 3-D work:

3D/EYE Inc.
47-Tek Inc.
Acclaim Entertainment Inc.
Accolade Inc.
Activision Inc.
Caligari Corp.
Chaco Communications
Computer Artworks Ltd. London
Dimension X
DreamWorks Interactive
Gemini Technology
Hash
id Software
INFOGRAMES Multimedia
Interactive Magic
Intervista Software Inc.
Katrix Inc.
Looking Glass Technologies
Macromedia Inc.
Maxis
Mechandeus
mFactory Inc.
Microsoft Softimage
NAMCO
OnLive!
Origin
Radical Entertainment
Reality Bytes
Sense8
SingleTrac Entertainment Technologies Inc.
Template Graphics Software
Trimark Interactive
Virgin Interactive Entertainment
Virtus VREAM Inc.

Understanding 3-D Graphics

Part of the reason that 3-D graphics are so compelling is that they consist of virtual models of reality called *scenes*. In general, your PC uses thousands of small triangles to build objects such as buildings, people, clouds, or whatever else populates the space. For example, with the frame of a house, the PC first creates a wireframe model, on top of which materials, colors, and textures can be applied.

A lot of complex math is involved. Every face of every object in a 3-D scene must be computed, positioned, and visually described. Variables such as lighting, atmospheric effects (fog), and camera angles all add to the workload. Finally, the PC even has to contend with objects in the scene that can't be seen from the current camera angle—a challenging process that can chew up processing time, memory, or both.

Let's say you're displaying a 3-D scene in a flight simulator program—one of the most common 3-D applications. Here is a typical chain of events:

- Geometry: The PC computes the position of triangle vertices and assigns effects such as textures, z-buffering, lighting, atmospherics, and other attributes. Generally, this work occurs on your host CPU.

- Setup: The PC determines where line edges of triangles need to be in order to form desired objects—in this case, airplanes and clouds. All of this work occurs on your host CPU.

- Texture mapping: To provide realistic appearance, bitmap patterns are draped over the wireframe objects. An enemy plane gets matte black treatment with a few embellishments, such as tail and wing markings. For maximum effect, the interior cockpit is rendered, showing the pilot and controls. Clouds are draped in white. Accelerated graphics cards can boost these operations.

- Bilinear or trilinear filtering: Further realism can be attained by smoothing out blockiness in texture-mapped graphics. Filtering averages pixel color information to smooth out bitmaps. Trilinear filtering provides better results because it averages over a wider range of pixels than bilinear filtering does. Filtering can be applied to virtually any 3-D scene to provide the effect of greater realism.

- Flat or gouraud shading: Gouraud shading blends color values of triangles to further the illusion of smoothness. Less-sophisticated flat shading, often seen in unaccelerated games such as Falcon Gold and Hornet, yields a cartoonish look. Both games and 3-D design applications employ gouraud shaded scenes.

- Atmospheric effects: If your dogfight occurs on a hot, muggy day, your PC might wrap the scene in a slight haze. A translucent effect can also be used on the enemy plane's canopy to provide a glassy effect. The same process creates a semitransparent missile contrail. Newer accelerated graphics cards can boost these operations.

- Lighting: Your PC computes a primary light source—in this case, the noonday sun—revising surface appearance based on the type, angle, and brightness of the light. Secondary sources—say, the flame from a missile's firing—might also affect the appearance of a nearby craft as the reflection of the light source is computed. Most graphics cards accelerate light effects, though to different extents.

- Z-buffering: Much happens on a busy battlefield. Planes can be hidden behind clouds or mountains, or even behind other planes. Your graphics card can avoid drawing these obscured objects and pixels using a scheme called *z-buffering*, which keeps positional data in memory to decide whether or not a particular object is visible. The payoff is improved performance, although many graphics cards require an additional 2MB or more of memory to handle the z-axis data. Newer graphics cards offer z-buffering capability. Additional benefit comes from z-sorting, in which the card can eliminate handling of occluded bits altogether.

Technical Note: I know the preceding list reads like a vocabulary test, but it's important to at least become familiar with the terms of 3-D acceleration. Graphics card vendors are slapping these and other terms onto their boxes and making claims about how their product is better than the next because it supports certain features. However, be aware that although a graphics card might support some high-falutin' features, much of the software you now own might fail to take advantage of them. Still, a more feature-rich 3-D graphics card stands a better chance of keeping pace with upcoming software.

What's in a Graphics Board

In a sense, graphics boards are like a miniature PC inside your PC. Like your system, graphics boards have a single CPU that calls the shots and determines performance. And like your PC, graphics boards contain memory and an internal bus for moving bits from memory to the processor and back. As with systems, there has been an improvement in price and performance with graphics boards.

What goes into a graphics board? The following systems help determine a board's features, performance, and cost:

- Graphics chip
- Memory
- RAMDAC (the card's digital-to-analog converter and color palette)
- VGA-compatible BIOS
- Software drivers

Together, these components help determine the relative performance of your PC's graphics. The amount of memory will determine the maximum resolution and color depth that your PC can support. The more memory you have, the more colors and pixels you can potentially display on your monitor. The type of memory can also make a big difference in graphics performance.

The speed of the RAMDAC, as shown in Figure 19.7, helps determine the maximum refresh rate, which is the number of times per second that the graphics hardware sends an update to the monitor. Finally, driver software lets the operating system and programs talk to your graphics hardware, allowing everything to work together.

Figure 19.7.
The Diamond Fire GL 1000 provides 2-D and 3-D graphics for high-end workstations. Note the chip in the upper-right corner. This is an external RAMDAC that most lower-cost boards usually integrate into the main chip. (Photo courtesy of Diamond Multimedia)

The following sections will run through these various systems so that you can understand how graphics boards accomplish their magic.

Inside the Graphics Coprocessor

This chip is the heart of any graphics board and, as such, determines exactly what the board can and can't do. Key features for accelerating 2-D and 3-D graphics and video playback are all designed into the square of silicon sitting in the center of the board.

Today, most new graphics chips provide video and 3-D graphics capabilities, as just described. One key factor in predicting chip and card performance is the data width of the graphics chip, measured in bits. Most coprocessors feature 64-bit data paths. This is the minimum that you should consider for any graphics upgrade. Anything narrower will invite performance-sapping data bottlenecks.

A few graphics cards use chips that are 128 bits wide. Tseng Labs' ET-6000 and Number Nine's Imagine 128 chips employ wide 128-bit data paths. Expect to pay more for these boards because of the extra cost that the larger chip and numerous data lines exact. However, these chips can move much more data smoothly, providing a difference during the most demanding tasks.

Often, chipset cores are designed for one or more memory types. For example, you'll find S3 chipsets using both EDO DRAM and Synchronous DRAM.

Inside Graphics Memory

Two considerations are important with memory—how much you have and what type it is. The more graphics memory, the more pixels and colors you can display on the monitor. 3-D graphics and image and photo editing are examples of applications that require 4MB or more of graphics memory.

Most boards today come with 2 or 4MB of memory, although some come with as much as 8MB. Some boards also allow memory upgrades, making it possible to boost the maximum colors and resolution without actually installing a new graphics card.

To determine how much memory is needed to display an 800×600 image at 24-bit color, you need to do a little math. Multiply 800 by 600 to determine how many pixels (in this case, 480,000) the graphics memory must track. Then multiply that number by the color depth (24 bits), which is the number of bits used to store color data for each pixel. Divide the result by 8 to get the number of bytes required. In this case, you need 1,440,000 bytes, or just under 1.4MB, of memory to display true-color graphics at 800×600 resolution.

The type of memory is also an important consideration. Your graphics card uses memory very similar to that in your system. In fact, some cards use the same type of memory as that found in many PCs. The following memory types are common:

- EDO DRAM (Extended Data Out Dynamic RAM)
- VRAM (Video RAM)
- SDRAM (Synchronous DRAM)
- SGRAM (Synchronous Graphics RAM)
- WRAM (Windows RAM)
- RDRAM (Rambus DRAM)
- MDRAM

In general, memory can be broken into two categories: single-ported and dual-ported. Like standard system memory, EDO DRAM, SDRAM, and SGRAM are single-ported memory architectures. These memories use a single door to move data in and out of the frame buffer. These memories enjoy an advantage in that they are cheap to manufacture (and allow cards to carry more memory affordably), but the single data port limits bandwidth at the high end.

New memories get around the single-port limitation by doing things more efficiently. EDO DRAM and SDRAM, both discussed in Chapter 7, "RAM," cut down the amount of time it takes for each bit to be accessed. SGRAM adds graphics-specific tweaks to the optimized SDRAM interface, boosting common graphics operations such as bit blits.

One problem is refresh rates. Because the same port must be used to both accept incoming data from the controller and send data to the monitor, a bottleneck exists. At higher resolutions, color depths, and refresh rates, this bottleneck can restrict performance and cause slowdowns. Faster single-ported memory now on the market can eliminate this problem, because the higher bandwidth leaves enough room to handle both refresh and graphics output. For more on refresh rates, see the next section.

Dual-ported memory, although more expensive, allows boards to break through the refresh-rate bottleneck. VRAM and WRAM architectures use two doors—one going in, the other going out—to improve the flow of data through the frame buffer. The difference is that WRAM adds some graphics-specific enhancements to the memory design that can help squeeze additional performance out of some 2-D graphics operations. However, dual-ported RAM pushes up the price of the card and requires the use of an external DAC, further adding to the cost.

Performance: Despite its extra cost, dual-ported memory doesn't always provide a performance advantage in day-to-day use. People running applications at 800×600 resolution and below 24-bit color will find that single-ported memories can keep pace with their graphics demands. Graphics professionals and anyone running at 1024×768 and 24-bit color might consider VRAM or WRAM memory for their next card purchase. At these higher settings, the second data port can make a difference—particularly if you run your monitor at high refresh rates of 85Hz or more.

An important newcomer to the graphics memory fray, Rambus DRAM, or RDRAM, is also worth mentioning. New boards based on Cirrus Logic's Laguna chip employ this memory type. RDRAM does its thing by moving bits very, very quickly along a narrow path. In fact, the RDRAM bus runs at an astounding 500MHz (versus 80 to 100MHz for other memory types) but is only 8 bits wide (versus 32 bits for other memories).

Recent drops in Rambus DRAM pricing and expected enhancements that will improve responsiveness have made RDRAM an attractive option. However, the memory still suffers from slowdowns during highly random accesses.

RAMDACs and Refresh Rates

RAMDAC determines how frequently the graphics card can refresh the image on the monitor. The faster the RAMDAC, the more quickly the board can update things, and the more stable the images that appear on-screen.

Most affordable graphics boards don't have separate RAMDACs at all. Instead, this componentry is built directly into the graphics chip, allowing board vendors to cut costs.

RAMDACs generally run at speeds of 135MHz, 170MHz, 185MHz, or 220MHz. What is the difference between these speeds? On larger monitors, it can be a lot.

At 1024×768 resolution and 16-bit color, a 135MHz RAMDAC can manage a refresh rate of only 60Hz. The same graphics card with a 220MHz RAMDAC can refresh the screen at twice that rate—120Hz—at the same setting.

Driver Software: The Secret Ingredient

Drivers aren't actually part of the board per se, but in many ways this software plays the most critical role of all. In general, drivers are the sophisticated chunks of code that allow peripherals (such as graphics cards) to talk to and take orders from the operating system and its applications. Without driver software, your 1-2-3 for Windows spreadsheet wouldn't be able to put its numbers and interface on the display, since Windows 95 would have no idea that the card is there.

Although the board vendor itself is the main source of driver code, the following parties might write drivers for products:

- The board vendor
- Microsoft (as the operating system vendor)
- The graphics chip vendor
- The third-party driver vendor

Generally, hardware vendors write drivers for their products, and this is where you should look first for updates. The board maker has the greatest vested interest in adding value and performance to its products and is usually responsible for providing service and support for the card.

Microsoft gets involved in driver development mainly to ensure support for its operating systems. When Windows 95 came out, few hardware makers had adequate programming experience in the new driver scheme to have drivers ready for the August 1995 launch, so Microsoft helped them write drivers for the most popular existing peripherals and included these drivers on the CD-ROM disc.

One overlooked source is the graphics chip vendor. Board makers, because they often carry a wide variety of graphics chips on their various lines, don't build drivers from scratch. Instead, they enhance the base-level chip code provided from the maker of the graphics coprocessors, such as S3 or Cirrus Logic. In fact, the basic drivers provided on the Windows 95 disc might be directly from the graphics chip company.

Tip: Although it's always best to get your drivers from the board maker, it might sometimes be advisable to check with the chip vendor for a driver update when something in the operating architecture changes. Often, the maker of the graphics chip is on the front lines of driver development, building in the baseline features required to access new capabilities. In these situations, a visit to the maker's Web site might be in order.

All drivers are the same in that they access the standard graphics interfaces (GDI, DirectX) of Windows 95. This allows support for virtually every Windows 95-compatible application. However, the quality of driver software does vary. Often, larger vendors have the resources to keep a software development staff on hand to fine-tune drivers, while the smallest no-name vendors will use the base-level drivers provided by Microsoft or the builder of the graphics chip. Be warned: Company size is not a real predictor of driver quality, and no one can predict how much a vendor will stress driver development in the future.

Peter's Principle: Keep Your Drivers Up to Date

Graphics performance is critical to overall system operation, and driver software plays a big role. Whether you want the best performance or enhanced features and reliability, your best bet is to periodically check for updated driver software.

The best way to get new graphics drivers is from your board vendor's Web site. Typically, vendor Web sites will provide several drivers for each board, serving different operating systems, such as Windows 3.1, Windows 95, Windows NT, and OS/2. The key thing to look for is the driver version number and the driver date. Always look for version numbers that are higher and dates that are newer than those of your current driver.

Purchase Decisions

When you buy a graphics card, the decisions you make depend on both your existing system and your application needs. Sometimes these two things might be at odds. Before you decide to spend money on a graphics board upgrade, consider whether the system you're upgrading can accomplish the tasks you want to accomplish.

Suppose that you have a 486DX-33 PC and you want to buy a VL bus graphics card to let you play the latest 3-D games. Although that graphics board might support some 3-D features, chances are that old warhorse PC isn't up to the task. The lack of L2 cache and effective floating-point capability in the processor, as well as a slower system board bus, combine to hinder performance. Even the fastest graphics board can't overcome these long odds. What's more, you'll find a very limited selection of VL-bus-compatible 3-D graphics cards, possibly making a move to a PCI-equipped motherboard a necessity.

That same 486 might be eligible for an upgrade for different purposes. The original graphics board might have only 1MB or even just 512KB of RAM, but you need to be able to view spreadsheets on a large 17-inch monitor. An affordable $150 card can get you 2MB or even 4MB of graphics RAM, as well as additional video and 3-D acceleration functions.

Accelerated Graphics Port: The New Graphics Bus

For over four years, PCI has been the bus of choice for graphics on Pentium-based PCs. Now Intel has introduced a faster, graphics-only bus for Pentium II motherboards called Accelerated Graphics Port (AGP). AGP is basically a super-PCI bus that runs at 66MHz (twice the speed of most PCI cards, although the PCI 2.1 spec allows for 66MHz operation) and provides 264MBps data rates. An enhanced AGP version, called AGP 2X, uses a clock-doubling technique to allow graphics boards to talk to the system at an effective rate of 133MHz, for data rates of 528MBps. Down the road, expect Intel to introduce AGP 4X, which will boost AGP to 1GBps.

Unlike PCI, which is a general-purpose system bus, AGP does one thing and one thing only—graphics. With its higher speed, AGP is already an improvement over PCI, and AGP graphics cards won't have to share time with other peripherals as they do under PCI, providing another performance edge.

Most important, AGP allows AGP-tailored software to reach directly into system RAM to access large amounts of texture data used to create realistic 3-D scenes—a feature called *AGP texturing*. The payoff is in 3-D applications, in which access to more RAM to build 3-D scenes can result in greatly enhanced realism. Right now, mainstream graphics boards (read: affordable) ship with 4MB of memory, which allows a meager 2MB of RAM for 3-D data. Cards that support AGP texturing can access tens of megabytes of unused system memory and apply them directly to 3-D scenes.

Why should you care? For one thing, Intel has clearly positioned AGP as the future of PC graphics. This means that graphics board vendors will start delivering innovative and powerful boards for the new bus, particularly when it comes to 3-D. If you're buying a Pentium II PC, make sure that it includes AGP slots. If you plan a Pentium II motherboard upgrade for an existing system, be sure that the motherboard you purchase includes AGP. In all cases, AGP-capable systems and motherboards use Intel's 440LX chipset.

> **Buying Tip:** Be careful when buying an AGP graphics board! Intel doesn't require boards
> to offer key features such as AGP texturing and 2X mode operation. As a result, many first-
> generation AGP boards basically act like fast PCI graphics cards and lack 3-D features that
> are likely to show up in future games and software. Check to make sure such a board offers
> AGP texturing (also called *direct memory execution* or *execute mode*) if you intend to use the
> board for 3-D graphics.

System Considerations

The easy (but very critical) part is buying a board that will work in your existing system. By far, the
most important issue is the system bus. The vast majority of Pentium-based PCs employ the Peripheral Component Interconnect bus, better known as PCI. Most 486 systems, on the other hand, use
the VL bus add-in card standard—although older PCs might lack a high-speed bus.

Why all the talk about buses? The bus inside your PC determines what type of card you can buy and
the extent of your selection. It also affects performance.

Also consider the size of your PC's monitor when you're buying a new graphics board. It doesn't
make much sense to spend extra money on a card that has 8MB of RAM and can display 1600×1200
pixels when all you have is a 14-inch monitor. That said, memory not used for the display is put to
use for caching fonts and bitmaps, rendering 3-D objects, and playing back MPEG video. Still, a
4MB graphics card is a good minimum for mainstream users.

Finally, your board needs to work with your operating system. Virtually all boards now come with
drivers for Windows 95, and most provide Windows NT support as well. However, the existence of
drivers doesn't mean that a board is appropriate for your environment. For example, 3-D gaming
cards such as Creative Labs' GameBlaster might offer 2-D graphics acceleration under NT, but their
advanced 3-D and video features might be tailored specifically for Windows 95. Be sure to ask the
vendor which operating system the graphics card is tuned for. In particular, make sure that the card
supports the latest version of DirectX, which was version 5 at the time this chapter was written.

Usage Considerations

It's no surprise that what you buy depends on what you expect to do with it. A graphics card intended for basic office use—word processing and spreadsheets, for example—differs greatly from a
board for 3-D games and multimedia.

What should you buy? Table 19.1 gives you some ideas.

Table 19.1. A graphics board buying guide.

Applications	Memory	Features	Price
Office applications	2MB SDRAM/SGRAM	2-D graphics	$120
Office applications and presentations	2MB SDRAM/SGRAM	2-D graphics/ video	$120
Mixed home/office use	2 to 4MB SDRAM/SGRAM	2-D and 3-D graphics/video	$120 to $150
Gaming and multimedia	4 to 8MB SGRAM, RDRAM, WRAM	2-D and 3-D graphics/video	$160 to $400
Photo editing	8MB WRAM or VRAM	2-D graphics	$400
Professional 3-D design	8 to 16MB SGRAM or VRAM	2-D and 3-D graphics	$999 to $1,500

For many home gamers, 3-D graphics capability is a must. Emerging games and titles make heavy use of 3-D graphics, and these titles will become more prevalent as Microsoft's Direct3D scheme takes hold of the market. Unfortunately, the current state of the market isn't friendly to consumers. 3-D features are advancing so quickly that today's hot new board can be old news within 12 months.

Although the standards and features for video and 2-D graphics are well set, the 3-D landscape continues to change. Your best bet is to make sure that the board you buy provides up-to-date support for the latest version of Direct3D. One good benchmark is to buy a board that has a graphics chip from an established vendor, such as Diamond Multimedia (see Figure 19.8).

Figure 19.8.
Diamond Multimedia's Monster 3D card is tailored for 3-D game play under Windows 95. (Photo courtesy of Diamond Multimedia)

If you're buying a 3-D card, consider one that has at least 4MB of RAM—perhaps even 8MB. The extra memory gets used by 3-D applications for z-buffering, speeding the display of 3-D scenes by telling the coprocessor not to draw obscured objects. Matrox's Millennium II and Number Nine's Revolution 3D come standard with 8MB.

Where to Buy

Graphics boards can be purchased almost anywhere computer hardware is sold, from the local consumer electronics chain or superstore to mail-order catalogs and even vendor Web sites. The wide availability makes price comparisons easy, allowing you to get the best deal.

> **Buying Tip:** Vendors cycle through graphics board products quickly, and cut-rate pricing of aging boards is common. Be careful if you find a certain board or chip being widely sold at discount prices. This might be a signal that the board is on its way out, which means that driver support will wane, and its features and performance will lag behind more current products.

Certainly, price is an important consideration, and you can often find lower prices from mail-order companies than you will at CompUSA and other retail outlets. But more important than a $10 or $20 savings in the short term is the quality of a board vendor's software drivers and commitment to supporting its products.

> **Buying Tip:** Some companies, such as Diamond Multimedia and Number Nine, offer trade-ins on older boards when you buy a new model. Before you simply replace a graphics card, it makes sense to check with the manufacturer of your existing card to see if you might be able to get credit toward a new purchase.

You will probably own the graphics board you buy for two, three, or even five years. During that time, the vendor will likely refresh its drivers a dozen times or more, introducing new features, fixing bugs, and playing catch-up with operating system modifications. These driver updates can also squeeze more performance out of your existing hardware.

Tracking driver quality and support is a tricky thing, and the quality of a certain vendor's work can wax and wane, depending on existing management, the number of products in its lines, and other variables. Your best bet is to visit online forums at CompuServe and AOL, or Internet newsgroups, and find out what others recommend. Look for a history of behavior from the company, and ask people what their experiences are. If possible, try to find people who are using the product you're looking to buy. Also look for real-time online support, which can be found on some vendors' CompuServe or AOL forums. On the Internet, IRC-based (Internet Relay Chat) services can help you get immediate replies to your questions.

Also visit the vendor's Web site before you buy. See if there is any late information about the product, and check for evidence of recent driver updates. Driver updates can be a two-edged sword. On the one hand, frequent updates indicate a commitment by the vendor to improve the product. On the other hand, too-frequent updates can indicate a "driver *du jour*" policy in which half-cooked bug or feature fixes get rushed to the market and then fixed incrementally after the fact. That kind of approach can invite a lot of vexing compatibility problems for users.

Buying Tip: The first thing you should do after bringing home a new graphics board is download the latest drivers from the vendor's Web site or other forum. Chances are the drivers in the box are up to six months old, which means that they might be one or more versions old. Depending on how the board's installation routine works, you can avoid installing the older drivers altogether and simply install the downloaded software during the standard Windows 95 installation routine.

Diagnosing/Troubleshooting

Under Windows 3.1, graphics-related problems were nearly an epidemic. Buggy driver software caused inexplicable crashes and problems and could even cause problems that seemed unrelated to the graphics card altogether. Fortunately, Windows 95 has improved this situation. Vendors have much less leeway in how they write their code, and the operating system's 32-bit architecture resolves most of the memory space conflicts that caused so many problems. In addition, graphical utilities, such as Number Nine's HawkEye suite, shown in Figure 19.9, help you avoid inadvertent driver setting mismatches that can lead to trouble with your monitor and applications.

That said, graphics remain a lightning rod for problems, particularly on the driver side. When incompatibilities crop up with a new software program, it's always a good idea to suspect your driver software.

Other problems can present themselves. For instance, a mismatch in the refresh rate or graphic settings between your board and monitor can cause the display to distort or even fail to appear. Older driver software might lack the ability to support certain titles (specifically, DirectX-optimized games), causing them to fail when they are launched.

Figure 19.9.
Graphics board utilities, such as Number Nine's HawkEye suite, provide useful troubleshooting information and controls, including color and resolution settings.

Problems Caused by Graphics Settings

One of the most common problems is a mismatch between the signals going out of your graphics board and the signals your monitor can recognize. This is particularly true during a graphics board upgrade, because the enhanced board might dangle advanced capabilities beyond the reach of your aging monitor. Typically, your board sends signals at a higher frequency than your monitor can handle.

Warning: A mismatch in signal frequency represents one of the gravest dangers to your PC's hardware. When your graphics board sends more than your monitor can handle—known as *overdriving* the monitor—this can cook the internal components and damage or even ruin the display. Overdriving can even pose a fire hazard.

Three settings can cause your card to overdrive the monitor:

- Refresh rates
- The resolution setting
- The color-depth setting

Symptoms of Overdriving

How can you tell when your graphics board is too much for your display to handle? The symptoms can vary, but typically you will observe the following on the monitor:

- A scrambled or distorted image
- Shrunken or multiple instances of an image

- A blank screen or other unusual display activity
- A high-pitched whine from the display

If you encounter any of these symptoms, the graphics board might be talking too fast for your monitor to understand. Unfortunately, the display isn't equipped to just ignore out-of-match incoming signals, so it will try to handle the signal and display what it can.

The important thing is not to panic. Actual monitor damage is unlikely, except in the most extreme cases. However, you do need to stop the overdriving as quickly as possible, because the longer you stress the monitor circuitry, the greater the chance of permanent damage.

Fixing an Overdriven Display

When does overdriving happen? Typically, this problem occurs after you have changed the resolution, color, or refresh rate settings of your graphics board.

This problem often occurs when Windows is misinformed about the monitor it's working with. To make sure you have installed the proper monitor, do the following:

1. Right-click the Windows 95 desktop and select Properties from the context menu that appears.
2. Choose the Settings tab, and click the Change Display Type button.
3. If the item displayed in the Monitor Type text box doesn't match your hardware, click the Change button.
4. Click the Show all devices radio button.
5. In the Manufacturers scrolling list box, select the name of your monitor's vendor.
6. Select the name of the monitor in the Models scrolling box. (If your monitor doesn't appear here, you will have to insert a driver diskette and use the Have Disk button to install the monitor profile.)
7. Once the proper monitor is selected, click OK and Close. Then click OK or Apply.

If your monitor is installed correctly, Windows 95 provides a facility for backing out of a signal mismatch. The following steps detail how to change your resolution and color depth and back out of the problem.

Note: When Windows 95 first came out, it lacked the ability to change color depths on-the-fly—that is, to change the settings without rebooting the computer. Although later versions of Windows 95 and a software patch called PowerToys added on-the-fly color changes, your configuration might require you to restart. Windows 98 will build this useful feature into the OS. It is already included in the version of Windows 95 (called OSR2) that can be found on PCs sold during the last six months.

1. Right-click the Windows 95 desktop and select Properties from the context menu that appears.

2. Choose the Settings tab. You will see a drop-down list on the left called Color palette and a slider bar on the right called Desktop area.

3. Adjust the slider bar to the desired resolution and then select the desired color depth from the Color palette list. Click OK or Apply to make the settings take effect.

4. Windows 95 will display a box that tells you that it will test the display for 15 seconds. Click OK.

5. If the display looks normal after the screen updates, click Yes. If you notice any problems with the display but can still make out the control buttons, click No to return to the previous settings. If you do nothing, the display will return to its previous settings after 15 seconds (good for when a blank or very garbled screen makes clicking No impossible).

Not all settings get changed on-the-fly from the Properties dialog box. Many Windows 95 systems lack the ability to change colors without a restart. And refresh rates are generally controlled by vendor-specific utilities that also might require you to restart. In these situations, you won't get a friendly notice that offers you a chance to back out.

In these situations, you will go through the steps required to change color depths or refresh rates. Windows 95 will prompt you to restart the computer before new settings can take effect. Before you restart, make sure that all open documents are saved and that your applications are closed.

When the system reboots, look for any signs of trouble. If the screen looks badly garbled or distorted, you should try to return to your old settings. If the distortion is too severe to navigate, do the following:

1. Press Ctrl-Esc.

2. Press the U key to select Start | Shut Down.

3. Press the R key to tell Windows 95 to restart.

4. Watch the display closely. When you see the message Starting Windows 95, press the F8 key.

5. In response to the text list of choices, select 3, Restart in Safe Mode.

6. From the safe mode of Windows 95, restore your graphics settings and restart the PC normally. You should now have your display back.

Better yet, try to avoid these situations by first checking the specifications on your graphics board and monitor before changing the settings. Your monitor documentation should state the maximum resolutions and refresh rates it can handle.

Dealing with Driver Problems

More problematic are driver-related problems. In fact, graphics driver-related problems can cause problems that seem unrelated to video performance. Symptoms of driver conflicts include the following:

- Windows 95 fails to start
- Application and system crashes or lock-ups
- On-screen distortion
- Certain applications (such as games) fail to launch
- Slow performance or poor video display

How do you know if a driver conflict is at issue? Usually it's a matter of timing. If the problem occurs immediately after you installed a driver update, you might have an older driver that is unable to handle the latest software demands. Look into restoring the old driver or finding an updated version that might resolve the problem.

Unfortunately, troubleshooting driver problems can involve a lot of trial and error. You might need to go through a couple different driver versions, installing and uninstalling them, before you find the one that works properly.

The DirectX Dilemma

On a related note, the introduction of DirectX gaming APIs has introduced a new facet of Windows 95 graphic driver development. Windows 95 games and multimedia titles often require DirectX software components to be installed in the operating system before they will run. Often, this means getting a driver update.

How do you know if the lack of DirectX capability is holding you back? Usually, games will fail to launch, displaying a dialog box saying that DirectX version 2.0 or some other version is needed to run the game. What's more, upon installation, the title should offer to add the necessary code and to update your drivers.

Warning: By default, Microsoft's DirectX installation routine found in games will check your driver software to see if it is certified. Ironically, this process can actually downgrade your drivers from the latest version to an earlier "certified" version of the drivers. During the DirectX installation, if the routine finds uncertified drivers, it will tell you that the driver software is not certified and recommend that you replace the existing driver set with the generic one provided in the DirectX routine.

If you know your drivers are a recent version with proper DirectX support (for example, if you downloaded them from the vendor's Web site just weeks ago), click No at the dialog box. The routine will install all the proper DirectX components into the operating system while leaving your graphics board alone. If you experience problems with the game that seem related to the DirectX functionality, you can always reinstall the generic code later—or, better yet, seek a tailored fix directly from the board vendor.

Note that not only will knocking out your drivers for Microsoft's affect performance, but it could also nuke all the enhanced features in your current board. Custom graphics controls, such as Number Nine's HawkEye utilities and Diamond's InControl Tools, will be lost, as will enhanced refresh-rate settings for specific boards. What's worse, boards that provide TV broadcasts or video capture will lose all these enhanced features. In other words, Microsoft's "fix" will kill your hardware until you reinstall the original drivers.

You can tell if DirectX is installed on your system by searching for a few key files in your Windows /System directory. If you find the file ddraw.dll, your card has some level of DirectX support in place.

Upgrading the Graphics Board

One of the most frequent upgrades, the task of installing a new graphics board got considerably simpler with the advent of the PCI bus and Windows 95 Plug and Play support. Under DOS, ISA-based cards required DIP switch changes to set memory exclusion areas and other settings. Today, all this is handled automatically with new cards.

When Does Upgrading Make Sense?

First of all, when does an upgrade make sense? The following scenarios make an upgrade worthwhile:

- The new hardware can significantly improve system performance, particularly with video playback and 3-D graphics display.
- You want access to higher resolutions and color depth settings—crucial for getting the most out of 17-inch and larger monitors. If you're upgrading to a larger monitor, you might want to consider a new graphics board at the same time.
- You want to access hybrid features such as video capture or TV broadcast reception on the PC. Some boards build these features in.

- Chronic hardware conflicts or lack of driver support make your aging board a liability. A new model will fix this situation.

- You need more graphics memory for high-resolution operation, but the current board doesn't accept memory module upgrades.

In all these cases, a less-drastic software driver upgrade won't solve the problem. What's more, a proper upgrade can add new applications and functions to your PC, ranging from video capture and TV reception to cutting-edge support for 3-D graphics.

However, there are times when a graphics board update doesn't make sense. Any systems limited to ISA or EISA add-in card slots won't be able to take advantage of current-generation hardware. For one thing, graphics board companies have stopped supporting these bus types entirely (can you say PCI?), and, for another, the slower buses will completely bottleneck even the most advanced graphics chip architecture.

Unfortunately, owners of VL bus systems are falling into the same trap. Despite the bus performance, board makers have largely moved away from the VL bus architecture in favor of PCI. And with the next-generation AGP specification now appearing in systems, you can bet that what meager resources were going to old VL bus machines will be shifted to other tasks.

Installing a Graphics Board

Windows 95 makes upgrading add-in cards easier than ever. Although Plug and Play is hardly perfect, the scheme does a good job of sniffing out new components and guiding you through the installation. To install a new PCI-based graphics adapter, simply do the following:

1. Shut down the PC, remove the power cord, and open the case.

2. Making sure you are well-grounded, use a Phillips-head screwdriver to free the existing graphics adapter from the backplane.

3. Grasp the card at the top at each end, and apply even upward force. If the card doesn't budge, try rocking out the back end a bit first, and then raise the front end.

4. Set the existing card aside and fit the new card in the slot. When placing it, make sure there is adequate clearance for the entire card. (Some multifunction graphics cards can be full-length, limiting the slots they can fit into.)

5. Inspect the expansion slot for debris, dust, or obstacles that might prevent the card from seating properly. Once the card is seated in the slot, press down firmly to make sure you have good contact.

6. Plug in the power cord and start the PC. Keep a close eye on the monitor. (You might see a new video BIOS text message appear at the very beginning of boot-up.)

7. Wait while Windows 95 starts. The New Hardware Detected dialog box should appear. Click Yes to detect the new hardware.

8. Place the floppy or CD-ROM disc from the packaging into the drive. When Windows 95 asks where to look for drivers, click Get drivers from disk and select the proper drive location.

Tip: If you downloaded the latest drivers from the Internet prior to installation (always a good idea), you can simply tell Windows 95 to install this driver from its existing location. The best thing to do is to download the driver code and expand the compressed files into a temporary directory dedicated to the new driver. When Windows 95 asks where to install the drivers from, simply use the Browse tool to select the proper directory.

9. A dialog box will tell you when the driver installation is complete. At this point, you can restart Windows and access the new functions.

10. If all is working properly, turn off the PC and screw the backplane down to avoid possible problems with the connector. Seal the case and restart.

11. If your board has custom utilities or software controls, you can install them now. Place the board's setup disk into the drive and double-click Setup.exe from Windows Explorer.

Adding Memory to an Existing Graphics Board

Some graphics boards use socketed memory, memory modules, or even standard SIMMs (in rare cases) to allow upgrades down the line. If you have a graphics board that meets your acceleration needs but lacks the ability to display the highest color and resolution settings, a memory upgrade might save you money over buying a new board outright. In addition, some feature upgrade modules, such as for MPEG playback for video capture, might include additional memory as part of the package.

Your best bet when buying new memory is to go directly to your board vendor, because the company will know the proper memory type, capacity, and form factor for your board. Otherwise, peruse the documentation carefully. If you have a board with two 1MB EDO DRAM modules, for instance, you must be sure to purchase a second pair of 1MB EDO DRAM modules for your upgrade. Like systems, upgrades generally have to happen in paired increments, because the graphics controller might not recognize odd memory configurations such as 3 or 6MB.

If the board uses SIMM-style memory, you might be able to buy the new RAM the way you would system memory. Again, you need to match memory type, speeds, form factors, and capacities. Review the documentation carefully and check the SIMMs themselves for clues as to their specifications.

Installing new memory is easy. Follow these steps:

1. Shut down the PC, remove the power cord, and open the case.

2. Making sure you are well-grounded, use a Phillips-head screwdriver to free the existing graphics adapter from the backplane.

3. Remove the board. Grasp the card at the top at each end, and apply even upward pressure. Don't force it. If the card doesn't budge, try rocking out the back end a bit first, and then raise the front end.

4. Fit the new memory modules into the open sockets, being sure to orient them properly, as shown in your documentation. With the board lying face-up on a flat, hard surface, place the modules so that they sit even in the sockets.

5. Once the module is fitted to the socket, put even downward pressure on each end using your thumb and forefinger. The module should press into the socket and lock into place. Don't force the module. If it fails to seat, try lifting the module and reseating it.

6. Repeat this step for the other module or modules, and then put the card back in its original slot.

7. Restart the PC. If everything is working properly, turn off the PC and screw the backplane down to avoid possible problems with the connector. Seal the case and restart.

Upgrade Advice: Now you can check your new configuration. Just right-click the desktop, select Properties, and choose the Settings tab. Check the Color palette and Desktop Area controls. You should notice additional resolution and color depth options that were not available before the upgrade.

Summary

For the last several years, graphics boards have waned as a prime performance-boosting upgrade. Most boards provide closely matched 2-D graphics capabilities, while video playback features affect only a minority of graphics operations. In addition, the advent of the PCI bus in 1993 widened the data pipes to the graphics card enough to ease much of the bottleneck.

Now it's time for users to pay attention again. 3-D graphics standards and software are driving a new generation of graphics hardware. The impact that 3-D-capable boards can have is remarkable. Everything from Quake to AutoCAD can enjoy a sizable performance boost. What's more, these cards also enhance visual impact, providing more realistic 3-D environments that turn ho-hum blocks and triangles into stunning virtual worlds.

Before long, even common Web browsing might benefit from 3-D acceleration. The VRML (virtual reality modeling language) standard promises to bring fully navigable 3-D worlds to your desktop. And 3-D graphics can do wonders for everything from business presentations to school reports. If you have a Pentium-class PC, a 3-D graphics board should be on your short list of upgrades.

20

Audio

Peter Norton®

For a long time, personal computers were to be seen and not heard. Despite the runaway appeal of the built-in audio found on Macintosh computers, most early IBM-compatible PCs demonstrated few audio talents beyond the occasional monotone beep from the built-in speaker to begin with, and later the obnoxious repetition of oversimplified Bach fugues.

We've come a long way. A little company called Creative Labs helped give PCs a voice with its Sound Blaster audio card. Since then, progressive generations of Sound Blaster and competing boards have helped bring the entire range of digital audio recording, editing, and playback functions to the PC. In the process, they've helped transform the buttoned-down old business box into a creative medium and an entertaining center for the home.

This chapter covers PC-based sound. You will learn about the following:

- The workings of PC-based audio under Windows 95, including the emergence of new PCI-based sound boards

- Shopping for a sound board for Windows 95 and DOS-based applications

- Diagnosing and resolving audio problems

- Upgrading your system with a new sound board

- How to choose PC-based speaker systems and microphones

The Ins and Outs of PC Audio

In the last few years, sound has become as important to many PC applications as graphics. Games need engaging sound effects and music scores, multimedia titles employ audio and video clips, and business presentations and even Web sites gain impact from music and sound. More recently, 3-D audio has become big in both titles and games—a feature you'll find in newer sound cards.

Today, any multimedia PC worth its salt needs a sound card that can process CD-quality digital audio files, as well as the ability to play back realistic-sounding scores from so-called MIDI (Musical Instrument Digital Interface) files. For best results, though, you'll want multichannel audio (to play several independent sounds simultaneously) and polyphonic MIDI (to play MIDI scores that incorporate dozens of instrument sounds). Don't let the dizzying array of specs and terms overshadow the most important issue: compatibility. Whether you want to record music under Windows 95 or hear realistic sounds in your DOS-based flight sim game, you need to make sure that your audio hardware will handle the task.

Sound on Board

Sound boards didn't introduce the ability to handle digital audio to PCs. After all, the first IBM PC could play musical tones, after a fashion, over its crude speaker by sending electrical impulses corresponding to the frequency and amplitude of the desired sound. What sound boards did was introduce the first tools needed in the evolution toward handling sophisticated sound transactions. Digital-to-analog converters transform digital signals into analog waves for waiting speakers. In the other direction, analog-to-digital converters (ADCs) take incoming sounds from a microphone or line input and convert them into 1s and 0s for storage on disk.

Most sound boards consist of the following components:

- Digital-to-analog converter
- Analog-to-digital converter
- Audio processing chip or digital signal processor (DSP)
- On some boards, an amplifier chip for boosting outbound signals for unpowered speakers
- Analog input ports for microphone, line-level signals, CD audio, and MIDI devices
- Analog output ports for speakers, line-level signals, and joysticks

Some boards also add a MIDI controller chip and dedicated memory (either RAM or ROM) for storing wavetable MIDI sounds.

Sound boards handle several types of sound. The most common is wave audio, or the Windows .WAV files that your system plays back. Another audio file type, MIDI audio (.MID), has seen much activity in the past few years as an effective way to play back musical scores. More recently, though, there have been big advances (and even bigger hype) in 3-D audio technologies, as well as the emergence of full-duplex boards for telephony and videoconferencing. The following sections explain these file types and how sound boards work with them.

The least-common denominator for PC audio is frequency-modulated (FM) synthesized sound. Popularized by the original Sound Blaster cards, FM was used by many DOS games to produce simple music and sound effects. FM synthesis sound is produced by mixing two or more modulated sine waves to produce a desired sound. The quality is poor, but this technique was the first baby step of PC-based audio.

Wave Audio

The most common sound type is wave audio—essentially, a digital reproduction of real-world sounds. The frequency and amplitude of analog sound—which is essentially vibrations in the air or some other medium—is represented as a series of 1s and 0s. The *digital to analog converter* (DAC) recognizes and converts these bits into familiar sounds such as musical instruments and people's voices.

Note: The waveform character of audio is where the Windows audio format, called a *wave file* (.WAV), gets its name. Wavetable MIDI, discussed a little later in this chapter, refers specifically to the use of waveform representations of sounds from musical instruments.

The problem with wave audio is that the files get big—really big. In order to represent an analog wave form, your PC slices up the analog curve into lots of small portions—as many as 44,100 separate slices for each second of audio. Each slice is then given a digital value corresponding to its audio character, up to 16 bits per slice.

If you do the math, you'll see that 44,100 slices, each needing 16 bits of data, consume over 700,000 bits per second. Stereo audio uses two independent channels, doubling this total to 1,400,000 bits per second. To store a single minute of audio, your PC might need more than 10MB of storage space. A 10-minute uncompressed .WAV file will fill a 100MB Zip disk.

44.1kHz 16-bit audio is the highest range of audio fidelity, corresponding to the fidelity of audio CDs and the limits of human hearing. Doubling the size of already-large files by pushing them to 88.2kHz, for example, adds nothing to the experience. Although older boards were limited to 8-bit audio (the original Sound Blaster and Sound Blaster Pro, for example), today virtually all sound boards can record and play back 44.1kHz 16-bit wave audio.

Sampling at lower rates can save a lot of disk space, though at the expense of audio quality, as shown in Table 20.1.

Table 20.1. Wave audio settings and capacities.

Quality Level	Audio Setting	Size of One Minute of Uncompressed Audio
CD quality	16-bit 44.1kHz stereo	10MB
Radio quality	8-bit 22.05kHz mono	1.25MB
Telephone quality	8-bit 11.025kHz mono	.6MB

Sound boards sample the incoming analog wave form, taking thousands of snapshots each second (up to 44,100 snapshots, to be precise) and using up to 16 bits of data to store the snapshot or sample in memory (see Figure 20.1). The resulting wave audio file can be played back on any compatible PC.

MIDI Audio

Another audio file type got an early start in the world of professional music. The Musical Instrument Digital Interface (MIDI) is a standard for letting electronic instruments and synthesizers work together. Jazz keyboardist Herbie Hancock was one pioneer willing to experiment with the new medium, hooking it up to his Apple II. Rock musician Todd Rundgren was so impressed by the potential of the new technology that he essentially changed careers. The MIDI standard defined an index of instrument types, as well as instructions corresponding to musical notes and other parameters. The standard also defined communications and control, so a user could send instructions to a MIDI device and always get the same results, as well as protocols for interpreting the output of old-fashioned acoustic instruments.

Figure 20.1.
Using a lower sampling rate loses much of the analog "data" that is contained within the curve of the audio waveform. (Figure courtesy of Microsoft Corp.)

Higher sampling rate
Lower sampling rate

Standards: The standard instrument library, known as General MIDI, provides 128 standard instruments. General MIDI-compliant sound cards work with any MIDI file, producing the score using the proper instruments. Virtually all PC sound cards conform to the General MIDI standard, although some might offer extended sounds and capabilities.

MIDI is a perfect fit for the PC. Not only does the established specification spare everyone the usual standards battle, but it also solves many of the thorniest problems with PC-based wave audio. Most notably, MIDI files are very small. A minute of MIDI music often requires just 10KB of disk space. What's more, MIDI files are easy to edit, so users can change instruments or invent new ones, alter the composition, and change the relative amplitude and pitch of instruments using software tools.

Note: MIDI is good only for playing and creating musical scores. To reproduce voices, animal sounds, or most other sounds, you need to digitize the sound into a wave audio file.

There are two types of MIDI:

- FM MIDI synthesis
- Wavetable MIDI synthesis

FM MIDI

Until about two years ago, most affordable sound boards provided so-called FM MIDI synthesis. This scheme emulates the sound of instruments by mixing sine wave signals. This approach is inexpensive, but acoustically, the results are horrendous. Rich orchestral scores sound cheap and thin on an FM MIDI card. The subtle nuances created by 10 or more simultaneously playing instruments get cut down to a synthetic-sounding baseline. You can recognize the tune, but the richness of the original score is lost. Still, FM synthesis MIDI cards can play any general MIDI score—they just won't do it well.

Wavetable MIDI

Wavetable MIDI synthesis provides realistic music playback by using actual recorded instrument sounds during playback. During MIDI playback, sound samples of French horns, oboes, violins, and other instruments are accessed from memory and played. Not every variation of every note is stored, so the card does a little math on the digital sample to create the desired instrument note and aspect from the original sample. Although the results aren't perfect, they're much, much better than those produced by FM synthesis.

Wavetable MIDI became prevalent when the cost of silicon memory dropped. Most boards use anywhere from 512KB to 8MB of on-board ROM or RAM to store instrument sounds, with more memory allowing a greater selection of instrument notes and samples. Creative Labs' Sound Blaster AWE 32, for example, comes with 2MB of MIDI sounds in ROM and even lets you add up to 32MB of RAM SIMMs for storing custom MIDI sounds.

To get the most realism, a wavetable MIDI card must be able to play multiple instrument sounds at one time—critical for orchestral sound. Called *polyphony*, this multi-instrument capability is described in terms of the number of simultaneous instruments (or voices) that can be played. The new Sound Blaster AWE 64, for example, can output 64 separate instrument sounds at once—more than enough for even the most demanding scores. 20- or 24-note polyphony is a good baseline for most boards.

Note: Many cards today provide *software-based wavetable MIDI*. With this approach, no on-board storage is needed for instrument sounds. Instead, sound samples held permanently on the hard disk are moved to system RAM and then played as needed. New PCI-based sound boards such as the Ensoniq Audio PCI and Diamond Monster Sound employ this scheme, as do Creative Labs' Sound Blaster 64 cards.

Software-based MIDI reduces hardware costs on the board and allows a much greater variety of potential sounds, including custom sounds—such as weapons and sound effects—that might be loaded by games and titles. The drawback is that software wavetable MIDI takes CPU power, which can degrade performance on older Pentium PCs. In addition, these cards can't provide MIDI playback for DOS-only games, because they rely on Windows 95's resources to move MIDI sounds from system memory to the sound card.

Creative Labs' Sound Blaster AWE 64 actually does both hardware and software wavetable MIDI. This board includes 512KB of on-board MIDI samples and the ability to play 32 instrument sounds simultaneously (32-voice polyphony). This card can also juggle an additional 32 voices in software, providing 64-voice polyphony for software running under Windows 95 or a Windows 95 DOS window.

Upgrade Advice: Because of its compact file size, MIDI makes an excellent audio format for the Web. Many Web pages include background MIDI scores that play when a page is loaded.

Technical Note: Another MIDI variant is *wave guide MIDI*, which actually produces sounds based on mathematical models of the instrument produced by the host CPU. Although the computation involved is quite complex, wave guide allows MIDI scores to go beyond the stilted stitching together of individual notes. What you end up with are scores that have the individual flavor and dynamics of a real composition.

Don't expect wave guide MIDI to push wave table MIDI aside. Many instruments, such as pianos, present so many variables that current PCs can't effectively render them in real time. Some sound boards, such as Creative Labs' Sound Blaster AWE 64 Gold, use a mixture of wave table and wave guide, depending on the instrument being played.

3-D Audio

3-D audio began coming on strong about two years ago, when competing technologies such as SRS (Sound Retrieval System) and Q Sound hit the market. What all 3-D audio schemes try to do is improve the immersive quality of PC-based sound, giving the illusion of depth and direction to sounds coming from a pair of stereo speakers.

Unfortunately, 3-D audio has been more about market confusion than innovation. The same term—3-D audio—describes the general sound enhancement scheme used by SRS and the specific positional audio features of DirectSound3D. AC3, with its roots in home theater systems, gets tagged as a 3-D audio technology as well.

> **Standards:** DirectSound is one component of Microsoft's multimedia initiative, called *DirectX*. DirectX is a collection of Windows 95 components, interfaces, and driver software that provide enhanced multimedia performance under Windows 95. This technology addresses everything from graphics and audio to network game play and input devices. For sound cards, DirectSound and DirectSound 3D provide a standard way for software titles to access your sound hardware. Most important, DirectSound guarantees that a sound will be played in sync with graphics and other elements, something that wasn't assured under Windows prior to DirectX. DirectX updates are often provided as part of CD-ROM-based games, but they can also be downloaded from Microsoft's Web site.

Stereo-Enhancing 3D (SRS)

The least-relevant of these is SRS, which adds depth to sound. SRS attempts to restore spatial information captured by stereo microphones during the recording of sound. This scheme uses algorithms to add this spatial information using two-channel stereo hardware.

Surprisingly, SRS can be effective. Depending on how audio was captured initially, instruments in a song can sound as though they are coming from places other than the speakers. However, SRS also uses a brute-force approach, boosting volume and adding distortion to the original signal—potentially making it more distracting than useful.

Programmatic Positional Audio (DirectSound3D)

More relevant to PC users is the emerging generation of games and titles that support positional 3-D audio. Technologies such as Microsoft's DirectSound3D let programmers pinpoint individual sounds in three-dimensional space.

The illusion can have a huge impact on gaming. With stereo speakers properly spaced on the desktop, players can hear the footsteps of approaching enemies. They can also hear chopper blades move from left to right as an enemy dashes across the screen. But positional 3-D audio won't happen overnight. Software makers must retool their games for DirectSound3D, and PCs must have the DirectSound3D components installed into the operating system. Finally, a hardware interface component—those pesky drivers again—is needed to allow compatible sound cards to accelerate the process of positioning sound on a two-speaker system.

Home Theater 3-D Audio (AC-3)

A third type of 3-D audio makes its debut courtesy of the DVD (Digital Versatile Disc) standard. Dolby's AC-3 digital audio specification is used in DVD-equipped home theater systems and with MPEG-2 broadcasts over digital satellite systems (DSS) such as DirecTV and PrimeStar. As a home theater-based technology, AC3 applies mostly to the playback of digitized linear content such as films and music.

AC3 brings a couple of important talents to the PC. For one, it's identical to the scheme implemented on high-end consumer electronics and upcoming HDTV systems—a key convergence point. In addition, PCs will be able to reproduce AC3 3-D audio in a two-speaker setup. A key point for reducing system cost, two-speaker capability mimics the rich surround sound accomplished using the 5.1 setup of home theater systems, in which four corner speakers, a center speaker, and a subwoofer combine to provide surround sound (see Figure 20.2).

Figure 20.2.
Home theater-oriented AC3 audio employs six speakers strategically placed to produce true surround sound. (Figure courtesy of Microsoft Corp.)

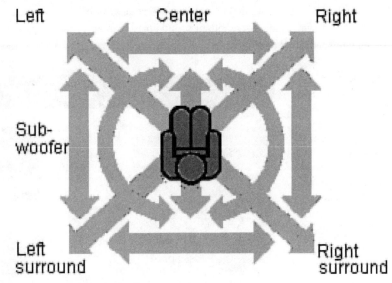

The New Face of Sound Boards

1998 will be an exciting year in the sound board business—and a hectic one for upgraders. For the first time since the late 1980s, Creative Labs' Sound Blaster standard will face a competitive challenge. In fact, by the end of 1998, Sound Blaster compatibility will be a fading issue. The new standard will be Microsoft's DirectSound.

DirectSound: The Emergent Standard

Under DOS, software needed direct access to hardware in order to access its features. Because of Sound Blaster's enormous market share, harried software developers—and in particular, game companies—focused their efforts first on the Sound Blaster architecture from Creative Labs. To this very day, titles that run exclusively in a dedicated DOS session (as opposed to a DOS box within Windows 95) require compatibility with a Sound Blaster or other supported sound card model.

Windows 95 changes all that. The operating system puts a level of software between hardware and applications—called a hardware abstraction layer, or HAL—in order to preserve stability and compatibility in the face of changing hardware. As long as sound cards and other peripherals comply with the standards put into place by Windows 95, any Windows 95-compatible application or game can make use of any sound device. Individual game makers no longer need to write separate interfaces for a dozen or more sound boards.

The real catalyst is DirectX—and, more specifically, the DirectSound API that addresses audio within DirectX. Under DirectSound, audio gets treated much like graphics do under DirectDraw and Direct3D (see Figure 20.3). Audio features ranging from MIDI playback and reverb effects to 3-D positional audio can be handled by either the host CPU or by logic on the sound board. And, like graphics cards, DirectSound-compliant sound boards can boost the performance of these functions by applying dedicated hardware.

Figure 20.3.
DirectSound abstracts audio functions from the hardware, allowing either the host CPU or customized audio hardware to handle audio functions. (Courtesy of Microsoft Corp.)

How do you get DirectSound? Like the rest of the DirectX components, DirectSound drivers and software are included with Windows 95 multimedia titles and games. You can also download the latest version of DirectSound from the Microsoft Web site.

Sound Blaster-Compatible: The Sound Board Today

For more than 10 years, Creative Labs' Sound Blaster standard has been the target of DOS and Windows software developers. Today, millions of compatible sound boards are installed in PCs. These boards run on the ISA bus and provide wave audio and MIDI sound capability.

Why hasn't Creative Labs moved to the PCI bus? For one thing, the company enjoys legal protection for its Sound Blaster chip architecture. In order to ensure full Sound Blaster compatibility for DOS applications, many companies license chipsets from Creative Labs, providing a healthy revenue source for the company. Despite Windows 95's move to Microsoft-driven standards, Sound Blaster compatibility will remain a concern for DOS software for years to come.

As shown in Figure 20.4, line and microphone inputs are available for recording analog sound to digital files. Speaker and line-out ports send analog sound to speakers or external recording devices. These boards also include a MIDI port for controlling external MIDI devices such as musical (and even acoustic) keyboards.

Figure 20.4.

The input and output ports for the Sound Blaster AWE 64 Gold are available on the PC's backplane. Note the gold-plated line-in and line-out ports, which Creative Labs says produce higher-quality audio. (Photo courtesy of Creative Labs)

Left RCA jack (white)

Microphone in

RAM board connectors   CD in   Line in

Joystick/MIDI

Right RCA jack (red)

Depending on the board, MIDI support might be simple FM synthesis or more-realistic wavetable synthesis. Refer to your sound board factory documentation. Often, the type of MIDI can be determined by the chipset found on the board. A Yamaha OPL-3 chip indicates a board with FM MIDI, while a Yamaha OPL-4 indicates wavetable MIDI capability.

Most wavetable MIDI cards come with 2 or 4MB of MIDI instrument sounds in RAM or ROM. The more memory dedicated to MIDI instruments, the better the potential range of instrument sounds. The quality of the algorithms used to create musical notes from the samples and the compression applied to the sample sounds themselves can also have an impact.

Many sound boards also include EIDE or SCSI interfaces for connecting to CD-ROM drives. Older sound boards might also include proprietary interfaces for CD-ROM drives from Panasonic, Mitsumi, and other vendors.

Sound Boards Go PCI

With the Sound Blaster standard no longer a mandate, vendors are moving sound cards off the trouble-some ISA bus and onto the same PCI bus used by graphics cards. This will not only ease often-painful installations, but it will open enhanced applications to these peripherals. For example, PCI's high bandwidth allows the use of 20 or more independent channels of audio to be hanlded simulta-neously (see Figure 20.5). The ability to play back many audio sources at once allows rich soundtracks to play even as dialog and 3-D positional sound effects are output. What's more, each channel can react differently to user input, so one sound can grow louder as a person moves through an environ-ment while another sound (on another channel) becomes fainter. ISA cards, with their limited band-width, can't support this sophisticated interaction.

Figure 20.5.
Diamond Multimedia's Monster Sound board is among the first of many PCI-based sound boards designed to the Microsoft DirectSound specification. (Photo courtesy of Diamond Multimedia)

PCI also allows sound cards to use system memory to store MIDI sound sample sets. On ISA boards, these sounds must be stored in board memory, which adds cost and limits the quality or quantity of MIDI samples. Finally, PCI sound boards don't require an IRQ, an important consideration for PCs that often ship with all 15 IRQs already taken.

Why the change now, years after PCI became an industry standard? Again, the answer is compatibility. The Sound Blaster standard requires that IRQ and DMA settings remain fixed. PCI, however, might change these settings as part of the Plug and Play specification. PCI-based sound boards forego compatibility with Sound Blaster cards to provide optimized performance under Windows 95 and DirectSound. New software is now emerging that demands PCI bandwidth, even as PCI-equipped systems become ubiquitous.

Buying a Sound Board in a Changing Market

Buying a sound board is very much like buying a graphics card or modem: You can safely purchase these products from mail order or retail vendors. You can usually find lower prices through mail order, but you'll lose the security of being able to return the product directly to the store if something goes wrong. Just be sure that the mail-order vendor honors returns with a 30-day money-back guarantee, and ask about restocking fees before you purchase. These fees can cost you up to 15 percent of the purchase price if you need to return the product.

Key Buying Considerations

Before you purchase a new sound board, you should decide what you hope to do with the upgrade. The following are good reasons to upgrade a sound board:

- Enhanced wave audio fidelity (16-bit 44.1kHz sound)
- Enhanced wavetable MIDI capability, to provide greater realism than FM synthesis as well as 32-voice or better polyphony for orchestral scores
- 3-D audio capabilities for games and multimedia titles
- Better compatibility with games and software
- Full-duplex audio for telephony and videoconferencing
- Digital studio functions, including multichannel recording and effects generation, such as reverb and chorus effects

In addition, you need to worry about a few things. Even if you find a sound board that meets your needs, there might be characteristics that make it unsuitable for your system. For example, many systems (in particular, compact desktop PCs), such as those that have been manufactured by Compaq and Packard Bell, lack the space for full-sized add-in cards. You need to check whether the card you want to buy will fit in the available space inside your PC.

Compatibility: You might find the best sound board in the world, but it's worthless if it can't fit inside your PC's chassis. Keep in mind that some sophisticated sound boards are full-length or three-quarters-length add-in cards. The circuitry required for wavetable effects processing, drive connectivity, and wavetable MIDI memory might be getting smaller, but these modern-day miracles often require the greater space found on a full-length card.

In general, expect to pay anywhere from $70 to $350 for a sound board. That's quite a range, I know, but it's easy to narrow down. Table 20.2 provides general price ranges for boards required for specific types of uses. Of course, peripheral prices are volatile, so it pays to shop around.

Table 20.2. Choosing a sound board.

Application	Type of Sound Board	Cost
Business audio	PCI audio	$120 to $200
Mixed-use home office	PCI or Sound Blaster audio	$120 to $300
Home and gaming	Sound Blaster audio	$120 to $300
Professional audio and production	PCI or Sound Blaster audio	$300 to $350

Compatibility First, Last, and Always

The PC audio market is in transition. Even as Windows 95 and DirectSound help redefine sound boards, popular titles such as Duke Nukem 3D and Quake are still being written for DOS. Sound Blaster compatibility remains important even as PCI audio cards promise to deliver improved performance and functionality.

Compatibility: PCI-based audio boards might have many advantages over Windows 95-based DirectSound-compliant games and titles, but be sure you're ready to make the leap. Older DOS games simply might not work with these PCI cards.

The changing market means that you have to plan an upgrade purchase carefully. If you run DOS-based games or software, your best bet is still a Sound Blaster-compatible card. The Creative Labs Sound Blaster 64 or the Sound Blaster AWE 64 Gold, shown in Figure 20.6, both offer better audio fidelity than earlier boards and provide support for up to 64 simultaneous MIDI voices (through mixed hardware and software).

Figure 20.6.

Creative Labs' Sound Blaster 64 improves on previous models with better audio fidelity and enhanced MIDI capability, yet it maintains compatibility with Sound Blaster-compatible software. (Photo courtesy of Creative Labs)

For DOS gamers in particular, a Sound Blaster board from Creative Labs offers an important level of comfort. Because DOS game makers must build drivers for individual sound cards into their titles, the number of supported products is often small. A vendor might include support for cards from companies such as Advanced Gravis and Ensoniq, but you can't count on this for every title. The Sound Blaster compatibility of these boards can also be suspect.

If you're buying a Sound Blaster-compatible card, make sure that it supports wavetable MIDI audio. For Sound Blaster and compatible boards, this usually means a wavetable MIDI controller chip or DSP will be on board, as well as dedicated memory. Without wavetable MIDI on board, MIDI playback will sound unrealistic.

Looking a year or so down the road, a Windows 95-based PCI audio card will enjoy the best compatibility and features. These cards are less expensive than Sound Blaster-compatible boards, yet they provide the same realistic wavetable MIDI playback that adds cost in traditional sound cards. The trick is the PCI cards' ability to use system memory to store MIDI sounds, eliminating the need for on-board ROM or RAM.

Note: PCI audio has its costs, particularly with wavetable MIDI. Because these boards use system memory to store wavetable MIDI sounds, MIDI playback can consume 2 to 4MB of system memory. On PCs with 16MB or less of main memory, that can cause unwanted disk swapping and degraded performance.

Tip: If you have a Sound Blaster-compatible board for your DOS games, you might consider upgrading to a PCI board while keeping the existing board in the system. The older board will provide support for DOS games while the new board provides advanced features under Windows 95. Of course, you'll need to switch your speaker input jack between the two boards—unless you don't mind the extra expense and clutter of a second pair of speakers. Remember, games that run in a DOS box under Windows will be able to use a PCI board. It is software that runs only in a dedicated DOS session that is a problem.

Sound Card Fidelity: Lower Your Expectations

As the PC begins to look and act like a consumer electronics device, many heretofore hidden weaknesses will be revealed. Chief among them is audio fidelity. Although virtually every major sound board maker claims that its products produce CD-quality audio, the actual quality of wave audio produced by sound boards is significantly below that of consumer audio equipment. The problem is that electromagnetic interference inside the PC's case introduces noise to the original signal. Creative Labs' Sound Blaster 64 Gold tries to reduce this problem by using digital output and gold connectors for speakers and other devices, which can boost response at the very low end (below 150Hz). Just make sure that you have a good subwoofer and audiophile cables to make this feature pay off. Ultimately, the digital-to-analog conversion step must be moved outside the PC case—something that the upcoming generation of USB speakers might provide.

How do sound board companies justify their claim? CD quality means that the boards can handle the same bit depth and sampling rate employed in audio CDs (16 bits, 44.1kHz); by this definition, nearly all sound cards are indeed of CD quality. However, actual tests of signal quality indicate that sounds boards consistently perform more poorly than audio equipment, producing lower signal-to-noise ratios, higher total harmonic distortion levels, and greater channel crosstalk.

Several characteristics go into audio fidelity. Some boards will include specifications on the side of the box defining performance, and others will provide no information at all. However, the lack of benchmark standards in the PC audio industry makes it difficult to know how printed specs were produced. Here are the primary specs to look out for:

- Signal-to-noise (S/N) ratio: The level of desired signal compared to the level of unwanted noise, expressed in decibels. The higher the number, the better. Consumer audio equipment produces S/N ratios of 80 to 90dB, while tape recorders produce about 60dB. S/N ratios below 70dB can be perceived as an audible hiss.

- Frequency response: The precision with which the board reproduces a signal across the 20Hz to 20kHz frequency range of human hearing. Most boards suffer at least moderate degradation at the highest and lowest ends of the range. This degradation can impair the quality of sound by reducing the impact of low bass and high treble sounds.

- Crosstalk: Leakage that occurs between the two stereo channels. Severe crosstalk can eliminate the effectiveness of stereo altogether.

- Total Harmonic Distortion (THD): Changes that occur to the original signal due to distortion produced by the amplifier. At peak volumes, THD levels increase considerably.

Tip: If you want to get the best fidelity out of your sound board, do not use the speaker-out port or make use of the internal amplifier. The amplifier on the sound board is of low quality. It introduces significant levels of noise and distortion to the original audio signal. For best results, use amplified speakers plugged into the line-out port.

Unfortunately, assessing audio quality isn't easy. To measure the electrical characteristics of a sound board, you need specialized audio testing equipment, such as the Audio Precision System Two, which costs $100,000 or more. Of course, your ears are the ultimate judge. Listen to your new board and test its range of performance on different audio clips that run the gamut of high and low frequencies. Listen for distortion.

Full-Duplex Audio

The Internet has helped transform PCs into a vital communications tool, but your sound board might not be up to the task. Applications such as Internet telephony and videoconferencing work best when both parties in a conversation can speak and hear each other at the same time. Known as *full-duplex audio*, this capability requires that a sound board be able to juggle inbound and outbound audio data simultaneously.

Many older sound boards lack duplex audio functionality. Although you can still run many telephony or conferencing applications, you will be unable to speak simultaneously. The abrupt cut-outs produced by these older boards make natural conversation difficult. In addition, some software requires full-duplex capability on the sound board.

Diagnosing/Troubleshooting

Under Windows 3.1, sound boards earned a deserved reputation for being a pain to install. The problems start with the heavy resource demands of Sound Blaster-compatible devices. These boards require dedicated IRQ, DMA, and port address settings in order to operate, which invites conflicts with other devices. In addition, many problems arise due to spotty Sound Blaster compatibility.

Troubleshooting: The inside of your PC is polluted with electromagnetic signals—the kind of stuff that can wreak havoc with analog audio signals. If you aren't satisfied with your sound quality, try moving the board away from electromagnetic field (EMF) sources such as disk and CD-ROM drives and the system CPU, as shown in Figure 20.7. Also make sure that speaker and microphone wires aren't draped over power cords or other EMF sources.

Figure 20.7.
Install your sound board as far away as possible from interference-producing components such as hard disks, CD-ROM drives, and processors. Also note how the hands grip only the top edge of the board, pressing evenly in a straight-down motion to avoid damaging any on-board components. (Photo courtesy of Creative Labs)

With all these problems to contend with, it's fortunate that hardware breakdowns with sound boards are rare. Still, little mistakes can cause vexation. Speaker and microphone cords attached incorrectly can seem like serious breakdowns. Likewise, a slipped audio cable to an internal CD-ROM drive can disable audio CD playback. And running from store to store trying to find connectors not included with the hardware can hold you up for days, especially if the performance of your sound card isn't the only important thing in your life right now.

Managing Resources

In order to function, Sound Blaster-compatible boards must have access to the following system resources:

- Interrupt Request (IRQ)
- Direct Memory Access (DMA)
- Memory address

IRQs, DMAs, and memory addresses provide the vital data pathways between your sound board and your PC. IRQs are the dedicated resources that allow sound boards and other peripherals to get the CPU's attention, while DMA provides a shortcut to your system's memory. Meanwhile, the memory address reserves a section of your PC's memory for the sound board, ensuring that no other peripheral or program attempts to grab it.

The Plug and Play Solution

The problem is that these resources are limited. Any PC loaded with multimedia peripherals will have, at most, one or two available IRQ addresses, which can lead to hardware conflicts and system crashes. DMA ports can also become scarce.

Windows 95 Plug and Play tries to resolve this problem by keeping tabs on each peripheral's resource needs. The operating system works with the motherboard BIOS to set the IRQs, DMAs, and other resources of peripherals, including sound boards. This scheme ensures that all peripherals get the resources they need.

There's just one problem: Older systems lack PnP capability, leaving you to figure out which resource settings are available when you upgrade your sound board. If you're replacing an old sound board, make a point to write down all the original settings so that you can simply point the new board at these freed resources when you install it.

Tip: If you have a Sound Blaster-compatible board that includes DOS-compatible drivers for games, you can find key information in your AUTOEXEC.BAT file. Use a text editor such as Windows' NOTEPAD.EXE and find the line that starts with the phrase Set Blaster =. The number following the letter I indicates IRQ, the number after the D indicates the DMA settings, and the number after the H indicates the High DMA setting. Windows 95 will have this information recorded under Device Manager, of course, but sometimes the operating system will change these on-the-fly as part of the PnP specification. To ensure operation under DOS, you'll want to know these numbers.

Using Windows 95 to Manage Sound Board Settings

Whether or not you have a Plug and Play system, the built-in facilities in Windows 95 make it easy to determine your sound board settings. You can adjust your sound board's IRQ, DMA, and address port settings from the Hardware Device Manager. If your sound board is experiencing problems, this is a good place to start. To access the Hardware Device Manager, do the following:

1. Select Start | Settings | Control Panel.

2. Double-click the System icon to launch the System Properties dialog box, and choose the Device Manager tab, as shown in Figure 20.8.

Figure 20.8.
Check your sound board's resource settings from the Windows 95 Hardware Device Manager.

3. Click the plus sign (+) next to the Sound, video and game controllers item.

4. Double-click the sound card item that appears. The sound adapter's properties sheet will appear.

5. Choose the Resources tab, shown in Figure 20.9, to view the settings in the Resource settings list box.

6. Select the resource you want to edit. To change settings, click the Use automatic settings check box, and then click the Change Setting button.

7. In the Edit Interrupt Request dialog box, shown in Figure 20.10, you can change the existing settings by using the spin control.

8. Click OK to save the new settings, and then click OK in the other two dialogs to return to Control Panel.

Figure 20.9.
Prior to setup,
Windows 95 gives
you an inventory of
your new card's
resource settings.
Take a moment to
print these.

Figure 20.10.
The Edit Interrupt
Request dialog box
lets you edit IRQ
settings for your
sound board.

Troubleshooting: Scratchy-sounding wave file playback can result from DMA conflicts. Use the Hardware Device Manager as just explained to reassign the existing DMA setting. If the original DMA is 1, your card might be conflicting with an enhanced-capabilities parallel port (provided that your system has one). If the original DMA setting is 5 or higher, your card might have problems working with a 16-bit DMA channel. Try reassigning it to a low DMA setting of 1, 2, or 3.

Upgrading a Sound Card

Despite all the horror stories, upgrading a sound card can be a painless experience. Plugging in a single add-in card, after all, is a lot less complicated than squeezing a new hard disk into an internal drive bay. Still, the possibility of a catastrophic conflict means that you should proceed carefully.

Who Needs to Upgrade?

First, you need to figure out if you need to upgrade. If your sound board lacks any of the following, you might consider an upgrade:

- Wavetable MIDI playback
- 3-D positional audio
- 16-bit 44.1kHz wave audio processing
- Sound Blaster compatibility

Although any of these situations can motivate a sound board upgrade, you might consider a more incremental approach. Some sound boards feature connectors for accepting wavetable MIDI add-on cards; they are called *daughtercards*. You can also purchase separate ISA boards that add functionality to your existing Sound Blaster-compatible card.

Here are some of your audio upgrade options:

- Sound board upgrade
- Install a wavetable MIDI daughtercard
- Install a wavetable MIDI ISA card
- Add RAM for wavetable MIDI instrument sounds

Installing a New Sound Board

The following steps describe how to install a new Sound Blaster-compatible sound board into a Windows 95 PC:

1. If you have an installed sound board, remove its software first. In the Windows 95 Control Panel, double-click the System icon and choose the Device Manager tab.

2. Select Sound, video and game ports and click Properties. Click the Remove button.

3. Once the removal process is finished, exit Control Panel, shut down your applications, and turn off the PC. Unplug the power cable and remove the system case.

4. Remove all plugs from the sound card backplate, such as those for speakers and a microphone. Also remove any joystick or MIDI device connectors from the MIDI/game port.

5. After grounding yourself, remove the backplate screw using a Phillips-head screwdriver.

6. Disconnect any cords or cables connected to the sound card, including the CD-audio cable that runs from the CD-ROM drive to the top edge of the sound card.

7. Grasp the card by the top edge at each end and pull directly upward. If the board doesn't budge, pull the inside end up a bit and then rock the backplate end upward.

8. Seat the new card into the add-in slot. Apply even downward pressure until the card fits firmly in the slot. If the card won't seat completely, try rocking it in by pushing the interior edge down first.

9. Reconnect the original wires. Read the port ID markings first and attach devices for the bottommost port. Then work your way up. This will allow you to read ID markings for subsequent ports.

10. Make sure that the speakers are plugged in and powered up.

11. Boot the system and watch for any changes. After Windows 95 boots, your PC should detect new hardware, and the Add New Hardware dialog box should prompt you to search for devices.

12. Click No to tell Windows not to initiate a search (this can take a very long time). Click Next.

13. In the Hardware types scrolling list box, select Sound, video and game controllers and click Next.

14. You will probably see a box called Building driver information database. Once this operation completes, the Add New Hardware Wizard box lets you select your board from a list of manufacturers and models.

15. Select the appropriate item from the Manufacturers scrolling list box. Then select the desired item from the Models scrolling list box. If the board you're installing isn't shown, click the Have Disk button.

16. In the Install From Disk dialog box, enter the drive and subdirectory containing the installation and driver files for your sound board. Usually these files will be located on a floppy disk included with the packaging.

17. Once the new hardware is selected, a dialog box will show you the new settings for your peripherals.

Note: You might need to change the configuration of your hardware to match that assigned by Windows 95. You should check your documentation for the factory defaults set by the vendor. You can try changing the settings used by Windows 95 to the board's default settings by going to Control Panel and using Device Manager to switch assigned IRQs, DMAs, and addresses. Or you might need to refer to your board's documentation to determine how to change its settings to match that of Windows 95. Of course, PnP-compliant cards and systems don't require this intervention.

18. Test the new sound board under Windows 95 by selecting Sounds from Control Panel. In the Sounds Properties dialog box, select one of the sound files shown in the Events scroll-down list box. Click the play button (the right-pointing arrow).

19. If you hear the sound, your wave audio configuration is correct. If you don't, make sure that your speakers are on and that all cables are properly set up. If the problem persists, you'll need to troubleshoot the installation.

Installing a Daughtercard Upgrade

The following steps describe how to install a Wave Blaster or similar daughtercard upgrade to sound boards that have the proper connectors. These daughtercards can add wavetable MIDI capability to older boards.

1. Shut down the PC, unplug the power cable, and remove the system case.

2. Remove all plugs from the sound card backplate, such as those for speakers and a microphone. Also remove any joystick or MIDI device connectors from the MIDI/game port.

3. After grounding yourself, remove the backplate screw using a Phillips-head screwdriver.

4. Disconnect any cords or cables connected to the sound card, including the CD audio cable that runs from the CD-ROM drive to the top edge of the sound card.

5. Grasp the card by the top edge at each end and pull directly upward. If the board doesn't budge, pull the inside end up a bit and then rock the backplate end upward.

6. Install the daughtercard. Place the sound board face-up in one palm, and align the daughtercard so that the rows of sockets on the daughtercard line up with the parallel rows of pins.

7. Seat the daughtercard on the pins and apply even downward pressure until you feel the card seat firmly.

8. Replace the upgraded sound card. Grasping the card by the top edge at each end, align the board with the original add-in card slot and apply even downward pressure to fit the card firmly in the slot. If the card won't seat completely, try rocking it in by pushing the interior edge down further.

9. Reconnect the original wires. Read the port ID markings first, and then attach devices for the bottommost port and work your way up. This will allow you to read ID markings for subsequent ports.

10. Make sure that speakers are plugged in and powered up.

11. Boot the system and watch for any changes. After Windows 95 boots, your PC should detect new hardware, and the Add New Hardware dialog box should prompt you to search for devices.

Installing Wavetable MIDI RAM SIMMs

Some wavetable MIDI-capable sound cards, such as the Sound Blaster AWE 32 and AWE 64 Gold, let you add more RAM beyond the ROM soldered to the board itself.

1. Shut down the PC, unplug the power cable, and remove the system case.

2. If there is sufficient room on the component face of the sound board to readily access the empty SIMM sockets, you can try to install the SIMMs with the board installed. If you can do this, proceed to step 6.

3. Remove all plugs from the sound card backplate, such as those for speakers and a microphone. Also remove any joystick or MIDI device connectors from the MIDI/game port.

4. After grounding yourself, remove the backplate screw using a Phillips-head screwdriver.

5. Disconnect any cords or cables connected to the sound card, including the CD audio cable that runs from the CD-ROM drive to the top edge of the sound card.

6. Grasp the card by the top edge at each end and pull directly upward. If the board doesn't budge, pull the inside end up a bit and then rock the backplate end upward.

7. Install the RAM SIMMs. Place the sound board face-up in one palm, and seat one SIMM into the lower socket at a 90-degree angle to the board face. Be sure to align pin 1 of the SIMM (the notched edge) with pin 1 of the socket.

8. Rotate the SIMM in the socket toward the top edge of the board. The SIMM socket clips should click into place on the small holes in the module.

9. Repeat steps 6 and 7 as necessary.

10. Replace the upgraded sound card. Grasping the card by the top edge at each end, align the board with the original add-in card slot and apply even downward pressure to fit the card firmly in the slot. If the card won't seat completely, try rocking it in by pushing the interior edge down further first.

11. Reconnect the original wires. Read the port ID markings first, and then attach devices for the bottommost port and work your way up. This will allow you to read ID markings for subsequent ports.

12. Make sure that speakers are plugged in and powered up.

The Ins and Outs of Microphones and Speakers

A sound board isn't much good without speakers. Although most new PCs that have a built-in sound board do sell with speakers, boards sold individually lack them. Many boards also include microphones for recording voice snippets, telephony, and voice recognition.

PC Speakers

Speakers might be the most important part of your new sound system. If you have an older system, upgrading the speakers might be a good idea (see Figure 20.11). Many older PCs came with cheap, low-end speakers that produce less than 5 watts of output and fare very poorly when reproducing deep bass sounds.

Figure 20.11.
Altec Lansing's ADA305 speakers can add oomph to tinny PC speakers. A pair of shielded satellite speakers and a central subwoofer provide effective audio across a wide range of frequencies. (Photo courtesy of Altec Lansing)

Note: Don't expect to use standard stereo speakers on your desktop. All speakers produce magnetic radiation that interferes with the operation of PC monitors and that can wipe floppy diskettes and other magnetic media clean of their data. For this reason, PC speakers incorporate shielding to limit magnetic emissions.

Warning: PC speakers might be shielded, but radiation still emits from the front of the speaker. In addition, some speakers leak more magnetic radiation than others (they have very strong magnets inside), so it's always a good idea to keep magnetic media a safe distance away.

Troubleshooting: If you notice waviness or distortion in your monitor's image, try moving your speakers away from the display. If magnetic leakage from the speakers is the culprit, the image will stabilize right away.

When you shop for speakers, you will face the same spec game common with sound boards. For example, speaker vendors tend to trumpet wattage figures based on maximum output (often called *peak power output* or PPO) as opposed to the *root-mean square output* (RMS) figures generally quoted by consumer audio companies.

RMS wattage figures are based on operation at low distortion levels—typically below 1 percent—and indicate wattage per channel. PPO figures, in contrast, provide inflated wattage outputs that are achieved only when the amplifier introduces significant distortion to the sound. Sometimes vendors also add the wattage of each channel together, calling a 40-watt speaker system 80 watts because there are two 40-watt speakers in the set.

Today, many PC speakers include a subwoofer to provide enhanced performance for low-end bass audio. Particularly effective for adding impact to the sound effects in combat-oriented games, a subwoofer also enhances music and other content.

Not everyone needs the same kind of speakers. After all, that thumping subwoofer might get a tad disruptive in the office. Business-oriented setups can get by with a standard two-speaker set with power output under 10 watts. Game players and people who put on presentations should consider a little more muscle—20 to 40 watts per channel, with a subwoofer if you need the punch for low-end audio. Stereo speaker companies such as Bose and Cambridge Soundworks produce high-quality PC speakers and subwoofers.

Microphones

Most sound boards come with a microphone for recording voices and sounds. Microphones generally plug into the microphone-in port on the back of your sound card, and they may stand on your desktop, mount onto your monitor, or even be packaged as a lapel microphone.

Many microphones feature unidirectional designs to avoid picking up extraneous noise common in work environments. However, microphone input quality on PC sound boards tends to be poor. Although a higher-end microphone might help, the real problem is often with the sound board's microphone input line. The line might lack the ability to handle the input signal strength, resulting in lost audio data.

Microphones also play a key role in voice recognition. Many boards include basic recognition tools for navigation and interface controls. In addition, third-party recognition programs from Dragon Systems, Kurzweil, and IBM let your computer recognize spoken dictation.

In addition, some monitors and even keyboards now come equipped with speakers and microphones. However, the microphones on these devices might lack the tight focus of some unidirectional models, and their placement might make them unsuitable for precise tasks such as voice recognition.

Summary

People often underappreciate the importance of audio quality in a multimedia PC. Everything from games to presentations to educational titles gets a big boost from a good sound board and speakers. Even the mundane beeps from Windows 95 get richer with a better sound system.

Expect the importance of audio to grow as the PC becomes more of an entertainment and education device. DVD will bring AC3-encoded surround sound to the desktop, and Windows 95 games will employ 3-D positional audio to make it sound like the bad guys are right behind you. Meanwhile, Web pages and presentations will leverage the realistic playback produced by wavetable MIDI-capable sounds cards. And with Windows 95 Plug and Play, sound boards can finally claim to provide easy listening.

21

Displays

Peter Norton®

How important is the PC's display? The monitor that comes with a new PC can represent up to 25 percent of the total cost of the computer. What's more, the display acts as the computer's primary output device—a device that you might look at for eight hours or more each day.

Recent price drops have made 15-, 17-, and even 19-inch monitors (measured diagonally) more affordable than ever. What's more, Windows 95's multitasking talents, combined with the visual demands of multimedia applications and Web browsing, make screen real estate extremely valuable.

This chapter will help you understand the workings of CRT displays and their role in your system's operation. You will learn

- How displays work
- How to buy a new display
- How to recognize and resolve display problems
- The best way to upgrade to a new monitor

Overview

If you're like most office workers, you probably spend hours reading text from a PC's monitor. That makes your monitor the most critical element of your system. A poor display can hurt productivity and potentially affect performance more than any CPU or memory upgrade. Small screens limit productivity, and low refresh rates and lack of tight focus can cause eyestrain and headaches.

Despite the importance of the display in any computing environment, many users tend to skimp when they buy a new system. Buyers often try to get the fastest processor or the largest hard disk they can, anticipating that upcoming software will outstrip their existing PC. Retail systems are at fault as well: In an effort to hit attractive price points, vendors use smaller, older displays that can shave $200 to $400 off the cost of a new PC.

Peter's Principle: Choosing the Right Monitor Size

Generally, monitor sizes match up with standard resolutions used by Windows 95. Older 14-inch monitors, for example, are useful mainly at 640×480 pixel-per-inch resolution. Any higher, and the text gets too small to read.

A 15-inch monitor will do well at 800×600 and 640×480 resolutions. A 17-inch model can push up to 1024×768 pixels comfortably, while a 19- or 21-inch display is needed to make 1280×1024 resolution readable (see Figure 21.1).

Keep in mind the resolution you might like to work in when buying a new monitor. If you want to see large swaths of financial spreadsheets or view several open programs, a 17-inch or larger display running at least 1024×768 is your best bet.

Figure 21.1.
*Larger 17-inch
models allow crisp
1024×768 resolu-
tions, great for
multitasking and
graphics work.
(Photo courtesy of
ViewSonic)*

More Than Television:
How Monitors Work

The monitor on your desktop has a lot in common with the TV in your family room. Both are cath-ode ray tube (CRT) displays that use a beam of focused electrons to excite phosphors on the surface of a large glass vacuum tube. But your PC's monitor might have a lot less in common with your TV than you think.

For one thing, PC monitors are much more sophisticated than TVs, which is why a 17-inch moni-tor can cost about the same as a 32-inch TV. Your monitor provides much crisper output than a TV, up to 1280×1024 or even 1600×1200 pixels. In contrast, TV resolutions in North America are limited to about 525×700 pixels, as defined by the NTSC (North American Television Standards Commission) standard.

Most important, PC monitors use a process called *progressive scanning* to paint images on-screen. Unlike televisions, which paint every other line of the screen and then fill in the unpainted lines during a second pass, PC monitors paint every line on every pass. The result is a much more stable display that makes it possible to read small text and view detail without eyestrain. This is why it's so hard to read text on TVs, which use less-sophisticated interlaced scanning.

A Picture Is Worth a Thousand Pixels

How do graphics, text, video, and animation get to your screen? The process starts with a device in the back of your monitor called an *electron gun*, which sprays a focused beam of electrons toward the surface of the glass vacuum tube. The inside of the glass screen you look at is layered with phosphorescent material, which, when excited by electrons, glows a specific color.

If you look closely enough at a monitor or hold a magnifying glass to one, you'll see lots of tiny red, green, and blue dots. These dots are the individual color elements that make up pixels (which stands for "picture elements"). Each pixel gets its color from the combination of the three color dots.

The electron gun firing away in the back of the monitor determines what those dots look like. If it lays a big electron charge on the red color dot and then sprays no electrons on the green and blue dots, that pixel will appear pure red. Often, all three dots will get varying strengths of electron charges to produce literally millions of colors. The dots are defined by the monitor's *shadow mask* or *aperture grill*, a thin layer of material with tiny spaces for allowing electrons through. This mask focuses electrons on precise points, ensuring sharp images and precise color positioning.

The electron gun is one busy worker. It paints every dot of every pixel at least 70 times per second. The reason is that the phosphors on your screen fade quickly and require a constant stream of electrons to remain lit. Keeping up with the demands of refreshing high-resolution displays is one of the things that distinguishes high-end monitors from less-expensive products.

Firing Line: Refresh Rates Explained

The process of updating the screen is called the *refresh rate*. It's a key ergonomic concern with any CRT display. A refresh rate of 75 updates per second (or 75Hz) is the minimum you should consider. Lower refresh rates can result in perceptible flicker in the display, causing eyestrain and headaches.

Upgrade Advice: Older monitors, even those capable of resolutions as high as 1280×1024, lack the advanced electronics to handle higher refresh rates. If you experience discomfort or eyestrain from frequent use of your monitor, you might need to upgrade to one that can support 75 hertz (Hz) or higher operation at the resolutions you use.

Here's how refresh works: The electron gun shoots its beam of electrons at the topmost pixel on the left side of the screen and then works its way across to the right side. The beam turns off and the gun moves to the leftmost pixel on the second row and begins painting the screen again from left to right. This operation is repeated for every row on the screen. On a 15-inch monitor running at 800×600 resolution, this means that 600 rows (each containing 800 pixels) are painted in each screen pass.

To keep the phosphors properly lit, this process must be repeated 70 or more times per second. When the gun reaches the bottom-rightmost pixel, the beam is again turned off, and the gun then shoots at the top-leftmost pixel to start the whole process again.

To update the screen 70, 80, or even 100 times per second, the electron beam must be targeted quickly. Rather than having a moving gun, which could never keep up with the task, magnetic fields are used to quickly and precisely target the beam to the desired location.

Tip: Your monitor's refresh rate capabilities are documented in your manual, but you can figure this out yourself. Look for the monitor's maximum vertical frequency, which is expressed in kilohertz (kHz). (Hint: It's often printed on the back of the monitor.)

To determine if your monitor can handle a certain refresh rate at a specific resolution, just multiply the number of rows (for example, there are 768 rows in a resolution of 1024×768) by the refresh rate (say, 75 Hz). Now, multiply that number by 1.04, which is a fudge factor that accounts for time lost reorienting the beam between rows.

In our example, 768 times 75 equals 57,600. Multiply that by the 1.04 fudge factor, and you get 59,904Hz (or 59.904kHz). So your monitor must be able to support a vertical frequency of 60kHz or higher in order to produce a 75Hz refresh rate at a 1024×768 resolution.

Upgrade Advice: Remember, your graphics boards must be able to produce the refresh rates and resolutions that end up on your monitor. A new 21-inch monitor that can display 1600×1200 resolution at a rock-solid 100Hz refresh rate will be wasted on an old 1MB graphics board with a 135MHz RAMDAC that limits refresh rates to about 75Hz.

Screen Types

The display quality of a monitor is directly affected by the type of shadow mask that is used. Most monitors use an Invar shadow mask, made of a special composite that resists expansion when heated. Shadow masks like these feature tiny holes for the electron beam to shoot through.

Some monitors use Sony's Trinitron shadow mask technology and have names such as Diamondtron and SonicTron. The Trinitron tube produces brighter and sharper images but typically costs $100 or more than similar shadow-mask monitors. Behind the enhanced display is a grill with thousands of tiny rectangular openings rather than the round openings in standard tubes. However, pixels are slightly malformed due to the rectangular holes in the mask. In addition to several of Sony's displays, Gateway's Vivitron line of monitors uses this scheme.

Buying Tip: You can identify a Trinitron-style screen by two faint horizontal bands that appear about one-third of the way from the top and bottom of the glass. These are wires that hold the Trinitron mask in place, helping provide exceptional precision. However, some users might find the band distracting, particularly on bright white backgrounds, where the contrast of the wire is most evident.

In either case, the potential image fidelity of a monitor can be measured in the *dot pitch* (or *aperture grill pitch*) of the shadow mask. The pitch defines how far apart the centers of contiguous pixels are from each other. The smaller the number, the better the precision of the tube and the sharper the images.

Most 15-inch monitors today feature .28 or .26 millimeter dot pitches. Older 14-inch displays often had wider .39 or .41mm dot pitch measurements, which translated into fuzzy text and lack of fine detail. The larger your monitor, the lower the dot pitch number needs to be, since pixels must be much more precise at higher resolutions (see Table 21.1). The distance you sit from a display also makes a difference. For example, the monitor on Gateway's Destination PC, which measures 31 inches diagonally, is intended to be viewed from across the room, much like a TV. For this reason, its dot pitch doesn't have to be in the .25mm range desired for most mainstream displays.

Table 21.1. Recommended dot pitches for monitors.

Tube Size	Maximum Recommended Dot Pitch
14 inches	.39mm
15 inches	.28mm
17 inches	.26mm
19 inches and larger	.21mm

Features to Look For

Beyond pixels and refresh rates, there are several other key issues to consider, including

- Electromagnetic shielding
- Power consumption
- Display controls
- Speakers

Most newer monitors feature shielding that blunts the leakage of electromagnetic radiation from the display. Most monitors comply with the MPR-II specification, and others comply with the more rigorous TCO standard. Both specifications originate from Swedish government standards that have since been adopted internationally.

Tip: If you suspect that your monitor is a health hazard, you can easily protect yourself. Just sit back further from the display. Electromagnetic energy dissipates at an exponential rate based on your distance from the source. By setting the monitor back by about two feet, you can drastically cut your exposure.

Power consumption is another critical area. Larger 17-inch displays, for example, can run at 700 watts of power. So-called *green monitors* can reduce your electric bill, minimize heat output, and extend the useful life of the monitor tube by shutting down display components. Look for an Energy Star-compliant display.

When it comes to power consumption, most displays support two levels of low-power operation: stand-by and sleep modes.

- Stand-by mode: The electron beam and the electron gun are shut down, blanking the screen. This mode reduces stress on the gun and relieves wear and tear on the phosphor material. Energy consumption can be cut by about 74 percent over normal operation. Return to operation is immediate.
- Sleep mode: Monitor components are shut down to the point that the gun and components will cool off. Power savings are significant. Power draw can drop to nearly 0 watts, but returning to operation can take several seconds or more.

Tip: Whether or not you have a shielded monitor, the display will leak electromagnetic radiation. If you're concerned about EMF exposure, avoid working with your face close to the display. The level of electromagnetic radiation decreases exponentially as the distance from the monitor increases.

Displays are persnickety things that can fall out of alignment over time. To help keep things in order, most monitors feature controls for straightening, resizing, and unbending images that have gotten out of whack. Among the controls, you will find the following:

- Vertical size and position: Moves and sizes the display area to fit the viewable area of the screen.

- Horizontal size and position: Moves and sizes the display area to fit the viewable area of the screen.

- Trapezoid: Adjusts the vertical aspect of the display so that the top and bottom are both the same width.

- Pincushion: Adjusts the corners of the display area to resolve bowing that can distort images.

- Rotate: Untilts the display area.

- Degauss: Refreshes the display and clears distortion by reasserting magnetic field controlling display.

Finally, you might consider a monitor with integrated speakers. The advantage here is space savings. If you have a crowded desktop, a multimedia monitor can help cut down on clutter. However, the magnetic output of the speakers puts display fidelity at risk, and monitor-bound speakers invariably provide poor audio quality. Unless your space situation is dire, I recommend that you stick with desktop speakers.

Flat-Screen Displays: A View of the Future

Larger displays are a good thing. They let you comfortably multitask several applications without losing sight of their interfaces. And they're a boon to anyone involved with graphics, whether designing Web pages and brochures or playing games and multimedia titles. Anyone buying a PC should consider a 17-inch display.

But large monitors have big problems. For one thing, 17-inch and larger CRTs are huge, hogging all sorts of valuable desk space and making it difficult to maintain an ergonomic layout. These jumbo displays also suck a lot of juice when running and produce enough heat to turn a room into a sauna on a warm summer day.

Enter flat panel displays. Anyone who has used a notebook computer is familiar with LCD screens. Ranging in size from 10.4 to 13.3 inches, today's notebook displays are now approaching the viewable area of 14- and 15-inch CRTs. In 1998, even larger 14.1-inch LCD screens will push that limit even further.

LCD displays seem to be a win-win situation. After all, even the largest LCD screen consumes a fraction of the space of its CRT cousins. Power consumption and heat dissipation are both radically reduced as well. The drawback is price. A 14.1-inch display costs $1,500 or more, nearly twice the price of most 17-inch CRTs. Still, manufacturing and design advancements are pushing prices down, and most experts expect LCD displays to grab a growing segment of the desktop display market.

How LCD Displays Work

Flat displays take an entirely different tack from CRTs when it comes to putting images on-screen. Instead of shooting a beam of electrons at phosphorescent material stuck to the glass, most flat displays use an electrical charge to excite liquid crystals suspended between two layers of glass.

There are two main types of LCD screens:

- Passive-matrix (Super Twist Numatic, or STN)
- Active-matrix (Thin Film Transistor, or TFT)

Passive-Matrix

Passive-matrix screens enjoy the advantage of being cheap to produce. However, display quality is unacceptable for many applications. Brightness and contrast are both limited, and passive-matrix screens can't be viewed from some angles.

Passive screens light individual liquid crystals by sending intersecting charges from the horizontal and vertical edges of the display. The level of the charge determines the relative color value of red, green, and blue emitting crystals found in each pixel element. However, because charges are sent across the screen to each pixel, individual pixels can't be refreshed quickly enough to produce exceptional brightness or contrast.

Dual-scan passive screens improve on the original idea by splitting the display into top and bottom halves. This way, two sets of intersecting charges come into play—one set lighting the top half of the screen, and the second set lighting the bottom half. The quicker response makes for a brighter display. It also reduces the sluggishness of STN displays.

> **Buying Tip:** You can spot a dual-scan passive-matrix screen easily. The split point between the two halves is usually easily visible, particularly with white backgrounds when the screen brightness is pushed up.

Active-Matrix

Active-matrix screens, also known as TFT displays, provide very bright, high-contrast images—nearly matching that of desktop CRTs. The secret is that each pixel in the display is activated by a charge provided from its own transistor. The one-for-one pixel-to-charging device ratio solves many problems, but the complexity of these screens makes them expensive.

Perhaps more of a concern is that when a transistor goes dead, a pixel on the screen goes out. With so many thousands of transistors on each display, manufacturers run into so-called *yield problems*, where a high percentage of screens coming off the production line are unacceptable. Wear and tear during ownership can also lead to dead pixels—a distracting flaw. The basic rule is this: The bigger the glass, the more likely a flaw.

That said, 12.1- and 13.3-inch TFT displays have become standard equipment on all high-end notebooks, while some less-expensive notebooks use 11.3-inch TFT displays. The cost of displays is dropping as manufacturers improve production techniques and yields. In general, LCD screens bound for desktop use will be active-matrix models.

Flat-Panel Applications

Flat-panel technology is intriguing stuff, to be sure. After all, large, bright flat-panel displays could dramatically cut the space and power requirements of desktop PCs. And advances in this area have already transformed portable computing. Also expect flat panels to become very popular among users who need to use multiple monitors.

Portable Computing

Of course, you won't be upgrading your display on an existing notebook. The fact that you can't change a notebook screen down the road makes the display decision all the more critical. If you choose the wrong display type, your entire investment might go south. For general-purpose computing, consider getting an active-matrix screen of at least 11.3 inches. 12.3-inch screens are even better.

Table 21.2 will help you determine your display needs when you buy a new notebook.

Table 21.2. Choosing a notebook display.

Application	Display Type
General-purpose/business portable	11.3- or 12.1-inch active-matrix
Desktop replacement (without separate CRT)	13.3-inch active-matrix
Multimedia sales presentations	13.3-inch active-matrix
Low-end general purpose/business portable	11.3-inch active-matrix or 11.3-inch dual-scan passive-matrix
Lightweight notebook	11.3-inch dual-scan passive-matrix

Peter's Principle: Wide 13.3-Inch Notebook Screens Are More Vulnerable Than Compact 11.3-Inch Screens

Do you travel a lot, or subject your notebook to abuse? If so, you should stay away from the new, larger displays. Wide 13.3-inch screens are subject to much more torque and twisting force than more-compact 11.3-inch models, which can result in screen damage. Similarly, an impact on larger screens is more likely to result in damage, because the reinforcing frame material is located further from the center. Even if you don't abuse your notebook, keep in mind that, historically, the largest displays generally produce more problems than more-established, easier-to-manufacture screens.

Desktop Computing

The story of desktop LCDs is not so clear. Although vendors such as IBM and NEC sell desktop-style LCD monitors, they are generally marketed to businesses seeking small-footprint peripherals. As a result, these monitors sell at a healthy price—as much as $5,000 or more.

LCD prices might come down soon. In July of 1997, a new specification was ratified to allow digital signals to be easily piped from graphics boards to LCD displays, overcoming a hurdle in performance and cost. As manufacturers perfect techniques for large 14.1-inch TFT displays, expect desktop vendors to begin offering these types of screens with their systems.

In the meantime, don't consider anything less than an active-matrix LCD for desktop use. Light from windows or other sources can wipe out a passive-matrix screen. In addition, these screens update more slowly than TFT models, making them unsuitable for animation or video playback—a particular concern for presentations and multimedia.

Other Visions: LCD Panels, Head-Mounted Displays, and More

Beyond desktop displays, you'll find all sorts of things to hook up to PCs. There are inexpensive LCD panels that sit atop projection machines, enabling multimedia presentations. For brighter output, a PC projector lets you pump your VGA output directly to the screen, as shown in Figure 21.2.

Gamers have welcomed head-mounted displays and eyeglasses. Although they are limited in resolution, these devices offer unmatched realism. Combined with a head-tracking device, the tiny LCD screens placed in front of the user's eyes actually display whatever the user looks at in his or her virtual environment.

Figure 21.2.
*ViewSonic's PJ800
projector lets you put
your PC's graphics up
on the big screen.*

Note: The immersive quality of head-mounted displays can be so effective that it can lead to nausea and neck strain. It pays to be careful.

Purchase Decisions

Buying a new monitor isn't as tough as it might seem from all the specs and technical jargon you've just read about. For one thing, compatibility is almost a nonissue with displays, unlike virtually every other component of your system. With a few exceptions, any new monitor you purchase will work with existing systems bought during the last five years. The only time problems really crop up is with older displays, which might lack the capacity for the high-resolution, high-refresh operation provided by today's graphics boards.

The key decisions you need to make boil down to the following:

- Price
- Tube size
- Refresh rate support
- Control and management features
- Plug and Play capability
- Image quality

Price

In general, price is a direct function of the size and quality of the monitor you want to buy. The larger tube and more-complex electronics inside a 17-inch display generally make it more expensive—by about $150 to $300—than a 15-inch CRT. However, there are enough variations that price can differ widely among products.

Buying Tip: If you're waiting out the market, hoping for 17-inch monitor prices to drop the way RAM did a couple of years ago, don't. Unlike most other PC components, the price of monitors is constrained by the cost of heavy glass vacuum tubes, plastics, and shielding. You won't see huge price drops as silicon-based manufacturing processes advance—although refresh rates and other features might improve—because electron tube technology dates back to the 1930s. The biggest price driver is economies of scale. When enough 17-inch tubes are being built, the cost of each tube will come down.

Tube Size

Tube size defines the distance from one corner of the tube to another, measured diagonally across the screen. A 17-inch monitor, therefore, measures 17 inches from corner to corner. The vast majority of monitors use a standard 3×4 aspect ratio (three units tall for every four units wide), so the shape of the screen is constant among products. There are even a few models that turn the monitor screen on its end, allowing for high-resolution display of documents in full screen (see Figure 21.3).

Peter's Principle: Specs Do Lie: Check the Viewable Screen Measurement, Not the Physical Dimensions of the Tube

In 1996, several major monitor vendors settled a suit brought against them by the California Attorney General's Office. The suit claimed that display makers falsely advertised the size of their monitor screens.

At issue was the common computer industry practice of using the CRT glass measurement to describe the size of the monitor. Since the bezel of the monitor (the plastic material around the edges) obscures part of the visible screen, the actual viewable area of a display is always less than the stated tube size. In fact, a so-called 17-inch monitor can have 16 inches or less of viewable area.

continues

Today, monitor makers are compelled to prominently display the actual viewable area of their products. This practice puts manufacturers in line with practices in the consumer electronics field, where television makers have long used viewable area exclusively. You should make a point of checking the viewable screen measurement, since the usable size of some monitors can be up to a half inch or more larger than others.

Figure 21.3.
The ViewSonic VP140 caters to document imaging with its vertically-oriented screen.

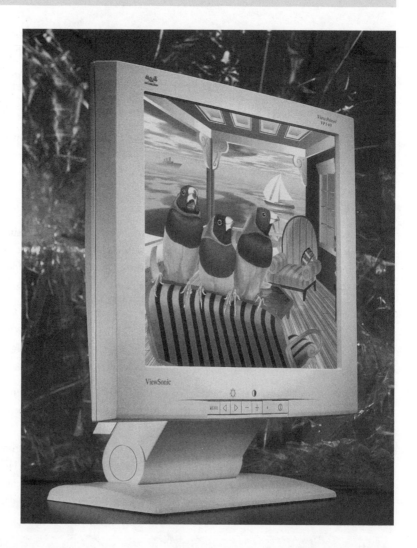

17-inch displays are becoming the sweet spot product for new PCs. Driving the larger models is Windows 95's graphical interface and the multitasking it promotes. Compared to 15-inch monitors, a 17-inch monitor adds about 30 percent more viewable area, making it possible to multitask a spreadsheet on one side of the screen while a Web browser updates on the other.

The larger size doesn't come without cost. You need to consider your workspace when upgrading to a new monitor. 17-inch and larger monitors need a lot of desk space, and they can weigh 40 pounds or more. Make sure that you have enough room and a strong-enough desk to handle the load of a larger monitor. Another consideration is power consumption. Operating wattage for 17-inch models runs about 70 watts, up from 40 watts for a typical 14-inch display. Larger tubes, of course, will consume even more power.

In general, expect to pay about $250 to $300 for a 15-inch monitor. Because high-resolution operation (1024×768 and higher) is unnecessary on these smaller screens, 15-inch monitors can get by with less-sophisticated electronics and a coarser shadow mask dot pitch.

Warning: Be careful not to run your display at higher color and resolution settings than it was designed for. Your graphics board can damage or destroy your display by sending frequencies outside its range. If you hear a whining noise, or the display looks all rattled or squished, you're probably overdriving the monitor. Try to shut down Windows 95 immediately by pressing Alt-F4. If that doesn't work, simply turn off the PC. When you reboot, press F5 when you see Starting Windows 95 appear on the screen, and then select Safe Mode to go into straight VGA operation. You can choose a safe graphics mode from there.

Which size of display is best for you? That depends on your needs. Unless your needs are particularly modest or demanding, a 17-inch display is your safest bet. It provides great viewing for nearly all applications and gives you room to grow. Table 21.3 can help guide your decision.

Table 21.3. Size matters: which monitor do you need?

Tube Size	Price Range	System Type	Applications
14-inch	$150 to $200		Not generally recommended. Only for the most basic text-based applications.
15-inch	$250 to $400	Budget-oriented home PCs	Low-demand office applications such as e-mail or word processing.
17-inch	$550 to $1,000	Mainstream PCs	Spreadsheets, light-to-heavy multitasking, general-purpose graphics, multimedia.

continues

Table 21.3. continued

Tube Size	Price Range	System Type	Applications
19-inch	$800 to $1,600	High-end mainstream PCs	Heavy multitasking, very large spreadsheets, moderate to heavy graphics use. Great for intensive game play and multimedia.
21-inch and larger	$1,200 to $3,000	Workstation-level PCs	Professional graphics, computer-aided design, application development.

Refresh Rate Support

As with dot pitch, refresh rate demands change with monitor size. The industry group VESA (Video Electronics Standards Association) recommends a 75Hz refresh rate for ergonomic operation. However, 17-inch and larger monitors running at high resolution will benefit from even higher refresh rates. The real breakpoint occurs at 1280×1024 resolution, where most bargain displays are unable to manage more than 75Hz at this setting.

Tip: Perceived flicker is much greater on a white background than on a darker, more subdued background. If you can't shell out $700 for a hot new monitor, you'll be glad to know that you can ease eyestrain and discomfort for free. Just adjust your application backgrounds to a neutral color like gray. To do this, right-click the Windows 95 desktop, choose Properties, and select the Appearance tab. Click the area labeled Window Text and choose the Color drop-down item. Choose the desired color (a light gray might work) and click OK. Now the white background on your word processor, spreadsheet, and other programs will appear in a subtler shade.

Keep in mind when purchasing that your graphics board must be up to the task. If you have an old graphics card with 1MB of graphics RAM, it simply won't be able to deliver the goods to a flashy 17-inch CRT. In these cases, you might need to consider a double upgrade of the graphics card and display.

Control and Management Features

Monitor control features such as degauss and pincushion (discussed in the earlier section "Features to Look For") can help ease the frustration caused by a display that just doesn't look right. But keep in mind that these settings can be tough to get exactly right, and monitor controls—even on-screen ones—tend to be hard to use.

Graphics professionals need exacting display controls, including color matching and calibration, to ensure utmost precision. These features can boost monitor price by as much as $500 to $1,000, so they're not for everybody. Most people can get by with a minimum of screen resize and position controls, manual degauss, and tilt, trapezoid, and pincushion controls.

Often, your best bet with a new monitor is to get one with DDC (Display Data Channel) compliance, a Plug and Play technology developed by the Video Electronics Standards Assocation (VESA) that lets your monitor talk to your graphics board. Under the DDC-2b specification, for example, the monitor can tell Windows 98 what display is installed so that it can employ optimal settings, boosting refresh rates to their best level for the selected resolution.

The expense associated with this scheme (because it requires separate wiring for an access.bus connection) keeps DDC-2a on the sidelines. But DDC-2b is widely supported and provides a method for the display to identify itself to the system over a single pin on the existing 15-pin VGA connector. Windows 98 can then load the appropriate monitor profile to match the installed monitor.

Many monitors feature a set of preset display modes, hard-wired frequency settings that provide optimal display at various resolutions and color depths. Provided that your graphics card can synch with these modes, this feature can help you avoid annoying problems such as display images that slide off to one side of the screen or get squished vertically or horizontally.

Better monitors also include memory for storing user-programmed display modes, allowing you to lock in an optimal profile, which you can select using the front panel buttons or on-screen controls when your graphics card is set to take advantage of this. All you need to do is tweak your settings to eliminate any visual problems and then press a save button or click an on-screen control.

Improper display information can cause mismatched signals. Squished or distorted screens are a common symptom of this failure. Most new monitors come with a driver disk for placing the display's exact preferences into the operating system. This way, your graphics card will know what to do.

Image Quality

Ultimately, you must decide what looks good to you. Keep in mind that not all displays are right for all people. NEC's mid- to high-end monitors, for instance, tend to be bright, sharp, and clear—perfect for most business applications and, in particular, multimedia presentations. MAG Innovision's displays, on the other hand, produce more subdued—but equally sharp—images.

Which do you need? Look for yourself. If possible, arrange to use a monitor for some time before purchasing it. Often, the quirks of a particular model won't make themselves known until you've used it for several hours. Also consider your environment. Bright lights overhead or behind could lead to a lot of glare, so consider a screen with an antiglare coating.

You can also use a monitor test program to ferret out hard-to-see flaws. Sonera Technologies' DisplayMate, for example, is almost universally accepted as a visual benchmark for monitors (see Figure 21.4).

Figure 21.4.

*The intricate patterns
of DisplayMate's
various test visuals let
you detect hidden
flaws that might
annoy you over time.*

In general, subdued monitors are best for long hours spent reading text or figures. However, these displays might not compete well with other light sources in a brightly-lit environment. Brighter displays are excellent for full-motion video, animation, and graphics. Much like your TV, the heightened brightness adds impact to moving images.

Discerning image quality doesn't take much—just a pair of good eyes and a little patience. Remember that a simple control tweak might fix what looks like a serious problem, so don't be afraid to twist a few knobs and push a few buttons during this process.

- Pay special attention to details in the far corners of the screen. Many monitors produce hazy images at these extremes, reducing the usable visual area of the display. Precise display is very difficult at the screen corners because of the sharp angle required for the electron gun to paint these regions. The result is that round pixels might distort to an oval shape and lose their sharp edges.

- Turn the monitor brightness up as far as it can go, and look closely for spreading pixel colors. Called *blooming*, this occurs when pixel edges bleed into each other, reducing contrast and sharpness.

- Look at the lit area of the display. Does it appear perfectly rectangular, or does it have a trapezoid look in which one horizontal edge is wider than the other? Also check to see if the display area looks slightly tilted or askew. If the monitor you're looking at lacks controls for these imperfections, walk away.

- Display an image with straight, thin vertical lines along the outer edges of the screen. (The scroll bars and application window frames of any word processor or spreadsheet will do.) Look for any curvature or bending along the line.

Diagnosing Display Ailments

Things can and do go wrong with monitors. Magnetic interference can warp displays, and a power surge can blow fuses or cook sensitive electronics. Even daily wear and tear adds up to perceptible loss of fidelity.

Fortunately, you won't find yourself worrying about monitor software going bad. In contrast to other PC components, monitor compatibility is very good. However, you might find yourself chasing what looks like a monitor problem, only to find that the culprit is your graphics board. Table 21.4 lists some common maladies.

Table 21.4. Common monitor maladies.

Problem	Symptoms
Frequency mismatch	Squished or distorted display, blank display, rolling display, high-pitched whine
Loose or overlong cable	Intermittent image loss, incorrect colors, poor focus and image fidelity
Blown monitor fuse	Black screen
Power supply problems	Intermittent clicking on and off, incorrect colors, brightness changes

Troubleshooting: As a rule, always keep the graphics board and its drivers on your short list of suspects when it comes to display problems. A squished or distorted display might result from a frequency mismatch, which can be best addressed by changing the refresh rate or resolution of the graphics board.

You might notice that your monitor clicks and snaps a lot when switching on or going into DOS mode to display. What you're seeing are the electronics of the monitor struggling to sync up with the new frequency being put out by the graphics board. Often this process—which was described by one product manager as a mating dance between the graphics board and the monitor—can take several seconds to complete.

Utilities and Facilities

For monitors, the best weapons in your troubleshooting arsenal are your eyes. Close attention to detail can help you discern simple vagaries in display quality, allowing you to avoid needless driver updates or graphics board installations.

Windows 95 provides a few useful tools for managing monitor quality. As with graphics boards, most of the action occurs in the Display Properties sheet under the Settings tab. To access your monitor's profile, do the following:

1. Right-click the Windows 95 desktop, and then choose Properties from the context menu.
2. In the Display Properties dialog box, choose the Settings tab.
3. Click the Change Display Type button to bring up the Change Display Type dialog box.
4. Under Monitor Type, you should see the brand and model of the monitor installed under Windows 95.
5. Click the Change button to access the Select Device dialog box for changing or updating the monitor profile.

There are several instances when this control can come in handy. For example, you might find that after moving up to a new resolution or color setting, your display looks wrong. A squished or distorted image is a common symptom of a frequency mismatch—basically, a breakdown in communication between the graphics board and the monitor. This can occur because Windows 95 doesn't know the exact model of monitor installed, so it prompts the graphics card to pump signals at a frequency that is slightly off spec. If you need to update the monitor profile from a floppy, simply click the Have Disk button and select the appropriate .INF file from the dialog box.

Dealing with Interference

More than drivers or other software, monitor problems arise because of outside interference or issues with the incoming signal. Many factors can lead to display problems, including

- Uneven electrical current
- Interference from speakers, fans, or telephones
- Poorly connected or overlong cabling

Power Problems

Monitors need a lot of juice, particularly larger 17-inch models. The hefty draw can outstrip older wiring found in aging buildings. Problems can also arise when several devices are running off the same circuit.

This problem is particularly acute in home offices. Laser printers, fax machines, and televisions can all draw significant amounts of power. Although a blown fuse or tripped circuit breaker is a common result of such a situation, other problems can arise short of a power shutdown.

If your monitor clicks on and off spontaneously, uneven power flow might be the culprit. This kind of oscillation can damage the monitor, causing blown fuses or fried circuitry. An air conditioner, laser printer, or other heavy-drawing device can cause this kind of problem.

There are two ways to resolve this problem: Make sure that the monitor is running off a circuit free of unwanted oscillation, or purchase an uninterruptible power supply (UPS). A UPS ensures that incoming electrical flow is consistent, and it employs a battery to supplement power should there be a loss of electricity. Even an inexpensive $25 surge-suppressing power strip can help alleviate the cumulative punishment that display electronics can take from variable power input.

Interference from Other Devices

As everyone knows, a home office can be a pretty crowded place. Phones, radios, printers, fax machines, and other devices all compete for space on your desktop. In addition to drawing power, all these devices produce electromagnetic fields that can interfere with your display's normal operation.

Magnetic interference usually appears as a visible discoloration or distortion of the screen. Often, the area of the display closest to the magnetic source will show greater change, making it easy to determine the source of the interference.

If you're having trouble, look around the vicinity of the monitor and identify electric devices. Try removing them one by one from the area of the monitor until you see the problem go away. This way, you can isolate the culprit, rearranging your setup.

Tip: Just because your PC speakers are shielded, don't ignore them as a possible source of interference. All speakers produce some amount of magnetic radiation, particularly toward the front of the speaker, where sound is produced. Imperfections in the speaker casing, due to poor manufacture or cracks from an impact, can nullify the benefits of shielding. If you encounter interference problems, make sure that your speakers aren't the culprit.

Cabling Problems

Another suspect when things go awry is your monitor's cable. Analog signals traveling along the 15-pin VGA cable are subject to interference from outside sources, as well as from degradation as signals are pushed over longer distances.

Most monitors use cables that are less than 5 feet long, ensuring that the length of the connection won't affect the signal quality. Cable extenders, additional cable lengths that let you place the monitor further away from the PC, add convenience but also increase the possibility of signal problems. If you use a cable extender and you experience trouble, you should consider removing the extra cabling to eliminate the problem.

Also be aware that a loose connection is one of the most common causes of a funky display. Make sure that the VGA connector is plugged in firmly and is screwed into the port to avoid problems.

Also make sure that the graphics card itself is screwed down, because pushing in the VGA cable can partially unseat the card, inviting potential damage to the card in addition to occasional display outages.

Troubleshooting: The analog signals that travel through your monitor's cable are especially susceptible to outside interference. Make sure that power cords and other potential sources of trouble aren't draped across the cable. If you notice problems, interference introduced at the cable might be the culprit.

Upgrading

Monitor upgrades are among the least-difficult of any PC upgrade. However, they don't come cheap. A new 17-inch monitor can cost anywhere from $600 to $1,000—more than virtually any other upgrade short of a full motherboard purchase. Still, the impact it can have on your computing experience makes a new upgrade well worth the price.

Who Needs to Upgrade?

Almost any PC can benefit immediately from a larger monitor. Although a new display won't make your PC any faster, the extra viewing area can significantly improve your productivity. Because a 17-inch monitor provides nearly 40 percent more viewing area than a 15-inch display, you can cut down on the time you spend scrolling through documents or switching among various applications.

A monitor upgrade makes particular sense if you often multitask several applications. A 17-inch or larger display lets you run two, three, or more applications and keep them visible on-screen. A wide view can also come in handy when you're browsing the Web, because you might have two or more browser windows open at a time.

A monitor upgrade might not make sense on older systems, particularly those with graphics boards that have 1MB of RAM or less. If you own a 486 PC with 8MB of RAM, for example, your system probably won't be able to effectively multitask applications, thus reducing the usefulness of the larger monitor.

Upgrading Your Monitor

Follow these steps to upgrade your existing monitor:

1. Set Windows 95 to VGA resolution by right-clicking the Windows 95 desktop and choosing Properties. Click the Settings tab.

2. Click the Color palette drop-down list and select 256 Color.

3. Click the slider bar in the Desktop area control, moving the control to the left until it reads 640 by 480 pixels. Click OK to make the new settings take effect.

4. When prompted to restart the PC, click No. Then shut down the PC.

5. Locate the monitor connector that plugs into the back of the graphics board. Unscrew the two securing screws, and pull the connector clear of the adapter board.

6. Remove the old monitor from the desktop, and place it out of the way.

7. Place the new monitor on the desktop and plug the cable into the back of the graphics adapter.

8. Secure the cable connector by twisting the two screws clockwise.

9. Boot up the PC and turn on the monitor.

10. Install the new monitor driver software. Place the floppy diskette from the monitor package into your PC's A:\ drive.

11. Right-click the Windows 95 desktop, choose Properties, and click the Settings tab. Click the Change Display Type button.

12. Click the Change button. In the dialog box that appears, click the Have Disk button.

13. Use the dialog box to locate the .INF file, and click OK.

Once installation is complete, you can change the graphics settings to suit your desired resolution and color depth.

Repair

Repairing a monitor is an unlikely scenario. In fact, attempting to open a monitor to repair it can result in fatal injury, because thousands of volts of electricity can be stored inside. Even after the display has been unplugged, a lethal charge can reside inside the monitor.

Warning: At the risk of sounding redundant, I'm going to say it again: Do not tinker with the inside of your CRT monitor. CRT displays produce thousands of volts of electricity in order to create the focused electron beam that lights up your monitor screen. This energy can remain in the electron gun assembly well after the monitor has been turned off and unplugged. You are risking fatal injury by prying open the case. And if that's not enough, you're also voiding the warranty.

Summary

Ultimately, the monitor is your window to the digital world inside your PC. If you spend long hours working at the computer, a large, high-resolution display can make all the difference. Additional screen real estate will cut down on time-consuming scrolling and hunting through windows, while high refresh rates and sharp images will reduce eyestrain and headaches.

As with so many other purchases, choosing a monitor is a subjective decision. Some people like the bright, TV-like output of NEC and Sony displays, and others opt for the subdued tone of monitors from MAG Innovision. Still, no matter what your preference, one rule holds firm: Bigger is better. You should buy as much monitor as you can afford.

22

From PC to TV: Video Capture Board

Peter Norton®

Three or four years ago, the marketing whizzes at Intel figured that the PC buying public needed a good reason to keep spending money for faster and faster processors. Word processors and spreadsheets, they figured, had all the horsepower they needed (this was before the release of Office 97). Intel's solution was to push PC-based digital video as a central productivity application.

This effort had an impact that can be seen throughout this book. PC-based videoconferencing got much early attention from Intel through its ISDN-based ProShare product, and Intel successfully positioned its Indeo compression scheme as a standard for delivering software-based video clips.

Today, several years after Intel's first efforts, video enjoys an expanding role in PC communications and interaction. The Internet provides a standard transport for low-cost videoconferencing, while the growing availability of digital ISDN phone lines and 33.6Kbps and faster modems allow home- and business-oriented videoconferencing applications. Sophisticated editing software, low-cost video capture hardware, and the emergence of cheap, multigigabyte hard disks have all contributed to the availability of video as a mainstream endeavor.

Add Intel's video-savvy MMX processor enhancements, and most mainstream PCs now possess the horsepower and storage capacity to handle video playback and editing. With digital USB or analog parallel port cameras, you don't even need a dedicated adapter card to get videoconferencing on your PC.

This chapter covers the following:

- The basics of video capture and key issues such as compression and file formats
- Videoconferencing hardware and applications
- Installing video hardware
- Troubleshooting and repair for video capture hardware

Video Capture Comes Home

If you read Chapter 19, "New Dimensions: Graphics Accelerators," you know that boards sold over the past two or three years have included enhancements to boost the quality of digital video playback. However, only a few boards include the ability to accept incoming analog video (from a VCR or TV, for example) and turn it into a digital video file.

In order for older PCs to capture reasonable-quality digital video, you'll need a dedicated video capture board that specializes in turning analog video into digital format. These boards include hardware to compress incoming signals into popular compressed video formats, easing the load on your system and enhancing the quality of the compressed video. Just as important, your PC needs to be up to the task of handling video capture. Newer USB-equipped PCs can produce 15 frames per second, provided that the USB camera precompresses the video data before sending it to the PC.

Inside a Video Capture Card

Video capture boards can range widely in price and features. For example, low-cost hybrid boards such as ATI's PC2TV provide inputs for a VCR or TVs in addition to functioning as a graphics and video accelerator. True video capture cards, on the other hand, limit themselves to capturing and compressing incoming analog video. Even these products can range widely in price and features, from $199 to $2,000 and above.

You'll generally find the following components and functions on a typical video capture board:

- Analog video inputs
- Analog video outputs (to a TV or VCR)
- Analog-to-digital converter (ADC) and filtering hardware
- Digital video compression hardware
- Effects acceleration hardware
- System bus connection

All these features typically reside on a single add-in card, as shown in Figure 22.1. When the board is installed in a PC, the backplate reveals a number of ports for moving data in and out of the PC. Video and audio inputs and outputs let you move video to and from TVs and VCRs.

Figure 22.1.
Full-featured video capture cards are busy animals, as evidenced by the amount of silicon mounted on Data Translation's Broadway 2.5 MPEG capture card. (Photo courtesy of Data Translation)

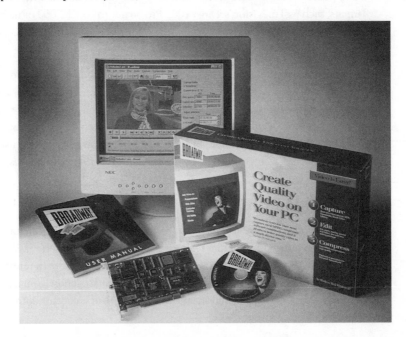

Analog Input

Needless to say, video capture boards are all about input. In order to capture video, you need to send an analog signal from a source such as a TV or VCR. The input ports on the board determine what quality the board can produce. There are three types of input: S-Video, Composite, and Component:

- Composite: The least expensive video connection, composite video mixes all the elements of the video signal into a single port. Although it's useful for saving space and reducing cost, bundling the video signal together results in lost fidelity and limits its usefulness for high-quality video clips.

- S-Video: These ports are found on almost all capture boards. They represent the best input choice for budget-minded home and business video capture. Most VCRs and camcorders, for example, use S-Video connections to move video out to other devices. S-Video splits the signal into two parts: One part has color information, and the other has brightness information. For this reason, S-Video cables usually feature two video leads (plus a third for audio).

- Component: Professionals will want to look for component video inputs for their capture boards. This scheme splits the video signal into three parts—brightness, color, and hue. Component video is more precise than S-Video. Expect boards with component video inputs, such as Truevision's Targa 1000 Pro board, to cost $2,000 or more. Of course, your analog device—whether a camera or VCR tape deck—must provide component video outputs.

In addition, better capture boards provide audio inputs. Although the audio capture components probably duplicate what is present on your sound board, the added cost yields better playback quality. The reason is that integrated audio capture allows for much more precise timing when stitching sounds and images into a video clip. When audio is handled on a separate board, several clocks get involved in determining which audio bits are matched with which image bits. When this process happens on one board, a single clock is used to synchronize audio and images.

Analog Video Output

Although many video capture boards might be intended for producing digital video to other PCs, the most common distribution format remains the familiar VHS cassette tape. Analog output ports let you move edited video clips to tape as well as review your work on a television monitor before saving. The output ports used by video boards (just described) generally match up with those provided for input. The PC97 specification encourages the use of broadcast output for large-screen display of entertainment content.

Analog-to-Digital Converter (ADC) and Filtering Hardware

Once analog video signals get onto the board, they must be converted to 1s and 0s. As just mentioned, some boards accept both audio and image streams, and others allow the existing sound card to do the work of digitizing audio for incorporation into the video stream later. In either case, a dedicated audio cable delivers the analog signal to an analog-to-digital converter (ADC) for conversion.

In either case, both audio and video signals are filtered to remove extraneous noise and interference that can impair quality. All boards provide this service, although the quality of filtering varies. Generally, expect to pay more for better filtering.

Audio sampling takes place as it does with any sound board. The incoming waveform is sampled up to 44,100 times per second, with as many as 16 bits of data dedicated to each sample. The resulting digital version of the audio stream is kept in lockstep with the video so that it can be stitched together with it later.

Like audio, inbound video is sampled from an analog signal. The board takes snapshots of the incoming series of images—called *frames* or *fields*—taking up to 60 snapshots each second. The video is then interleaved with the digital audio signal to create a digital video stream.

Digital Video Compression Hardware

Turning an analog video stream into digital bits is tough, but compressing these bits is the real challenge. Until just two years ago, only boards costing $2,000 or more featured on-board compression hardware that let you capture directly to a compressed video format. Most boards captured to an intermediate format featuring only modest compression, putting a lot of strain on the system CPU, bus, and hard disk. The result was that frame rates and fidelity suffered.

The professional compression standard for video capture is a scheme called Motion JPEG (Joint Photographic Experts Group). This codec compresses data within each frame—a process called *intraframe compression*—to squeeze video down by a factor of 5 to 100. By keeping each frame intact, authors can use editing software such as Adobe Premiere to conduct precise frame-by-frame edits of the digital video file. Some boards offer different on-the-fly compression schemes, such as MPEG and Indeo Video Interactive.

Peter's Principle: Which Video Compression Scheme Do You Need?

Capturing video is all about compression. Raw digital video files are simply too huge to be managed by desktop PCs. Thirty frames of true-color video at a modest 320×240 resolution adds up to over 6.5MB of data per second. That's over 395MB each minute before you add in sound.

All compression schemes, called codecs, cut video down to size by doing two things: coding blocks of redundant information in each frame into space-saving format, and selectively filtering visual data to reduce the amount of data in the video stream. In addition, many video codecs identify and discard redundant data between frames. Called *interframe compression*, this scheme demands much processing work on both the compression and playback side, since several frames must be assessed at one time.

If you want to be able to edit the video you capture, you should use an intraframe compression scheme, such as Motion JPEG. The file will be a little larger than it needs to be, but each frame contains all the data used to display the video image to enable frame-accurate editing.

On the other hand, if you want to simply convert analog video to digital format, an interframe codec such as MPEG or Indeo Video Interactive is your best bet. These produce more compact files than intraframe codecs and enjoy a wider installed base of playback drivers on mainstream PCs. Of course, interframe compression will limit your editing options down the road.

Technical Note: Compression schemes that throw out unneeded data are called *lossy*, meaning that they lose some of the original data. Those that strictly crunch existing bits (such as PK Zip) are called *lossless*. Obviously, lossy schemes won't work on data and executable files, which must remain intact in order to work. This is one reason why PK Zip and disk compression systems attain top compression ratios of about 2 to 1, while the lossy Motion JPEG codec reaches 100 to 1. The M-JPEG scheme can discard reams of visual data without incapacitating the video file—although the quality of the clip suffers as more data is discarded. Loss compression works because the eye and brain are lenient when it comes to images that whip by in a 30th or 60th of a second.

System Bus Connection

When it comes to video capture, there really is no question—the PCI bus is by far the best option. Even with on-board, on-the-fly compression to squish video streams down to size, the amount of data is enormous. Heavily compressed MPEG-1 video might require only 150Kbps of data, but higher-quality clips will go much higher. A good Motion JPEG-compressed video can run at 5Mbps or higher.

The PCI bus brings a couple of key talents to the capture game. For one, a capture board can take advantage of the 132Mbps peak sustained throughput of the PCI bus (versus just 5Mbps for ISA). Furthermore, PCI bus mastering capability means that the board can send digitized video directly to a SCSI hard disk without the intervention of the system processor. The PCI bus also provides much lower latency than ISA, reducing the time that devices are left to wait for control of the bus or to receive commands and data. Both characteristics enable high-quality digital video capture at high frame rates.

Video Capture Applications

Video capture might seem like a neat application, but who really needs it? After all, capturing video takes a fast Pentium system with a large and fast hard disk and plenty of RAM. In other words, you need a cutting-edge setup to do video capture right.

Recent market advances, however, make professional-quality video capture available to most new systems. A Pentium MMX-200 PC with 64MB of RAM and a large 4GB EIDE hard disk costs about $2,500. Throw in a $999 video capture card, and this mainstream desktop PC can support all but the most demanding video compression. Of course, people who have older systems might have to lower their expectations.

Still, not all video input is about producing professional-looking clips. Videoconferencing, for example, employs low-bandwidth (and low-quality) video along with audio and data communications. Other products, such as Play, Inc.'s Snappy, can produce brief clips and high-quality snapshots from an analog source.

Videoconferencing

Probably the fastest-growing video application, videoconferencing lets PC users make video calls over standard or digital ISDN phone lines. Unlike traditional video capture, videoconferencing melds modem-based communications, video capture, and real-time video playback into a single application. Although videoconferencing requires much less video fidelity than traditional capture applications, the need to juggle other sundry tasks makes it an extremely demanding application.

You need the following components in order to make videoconferencing happen on your PC:

- A monitor-top camera
- A video-enabled V.80 modem (33.6 or 56Kbps) or ISDN adapter
- A video input for the camera (a video input card, parallel port, or other device)
- Recommended: A video-accelerating graphics card and an MMX-enhanced processor

- Videoconferencing software
- Someone on the other end with a similar setup to receive your video call

Most of these components are provided in videoconferencing upgrade kits. Upgrade kits from companies such as Intel, Creative Labs, and Diamond Multimedia cost anywhere from $199 to $599 and give you everything you need to make video calls over standard analog phone lines (see Figure 22.2). ISDN-based videoconferencing systems, which generally cost $200 to $500 more than analog systems, provide higher-quality communications due to the 128-bit potential data rate provided by the digital connection. Other protocols also support conferencing over networks. If you purchase a new system, you can have it preconfigured for videoconferencing.

Figure 22.2.
Diamond's Video Phone Kit includes a video-capable modem and parallel port monitor-top camera to let Pentium-class PCs handle video calls over standard phone lines. (Photo courtesy of Diamond Multimedia)

For more on ISDN, see Chapter 23, "Modems."

Performance: Have you seen those AT&T commercials showing a doctor teleconferencing with a patient? If so, strike it from your memory—that ain't reality. The simple truth is that any video that happens over a phone line (even a digital ISDN line) will look terrible. Small video windows, blurry graphics, lost frames, and poor lip-synching all plague desktop videoconferencing. The problem is bandwidth.

Analog calls produce frame rates between one and 10 frames per second, depending on the quality of the hardware, noise in the connection, and the nature of the video. Motion in the camera's viewing area will drop frame rates drastically as the codec throws out visual bits in an effort to keep the video data stream within the requirements of a 33.6Kbps connection. Audio and video synching will also suffer under these conditions. Even

ISDN-based videoconferencing won't provide professional-quality results, although it can pass muster for one-on-one business conferences.

Low-End Video Capture

Another video capture application is the use of inexpensive cameras and devices to capture short clips or still images. Play's $99 Snappy adapter, for example, plugs into a parallel port and grabs high-resolution still images from an analog video source. The Connectix QuickCam camera also uses the parallel port. Available in both black-and-white and color versions, this small camera can capture video at 15 frames per second and at resolutions of 320×240 pixels.

Another affordable option is graphics cards that include video inputs. ATI's Expert@Play and Diamond Multimedia's DTV 2000 (see Figure 22.3) both let you capture video from an external camera, TV, or VCR.

Figure 22.3.
Diamond's DTV 2000 captures video from broadcast or cable TV and displays it on your monitor. (Photo courtesy of Diamond Multimedia)

These applications are appropriate for spot capture duty and low-resolution video production. The QuickCam even comes in a videoconferencing package, although the quality of the call falls below that of dedicated conferencing products. Still, for spot work, the QuickCam and similar products are a versatile option.

Purchase Decisions

If you're in the market for a video capture board, you need to consider what you expect to do. A video capture board that is appropriate for producing low-bandwidth MPEG video for playback on a CD-ROM drive won't fit the bill for producing high-resolution output bound for super-VHS tape.

Types of Capture Boards

There is a wide range of video capture boards. When you're looking, the following points should guide your buying decision:

- Video source: VHS, 8mm; super-VHS, super-8; Beta 1
- Video target: CD-ROM, hard disk, VHS, or super-VHS tape
- Editing goals: Precise editing, no editing
- Compression scheme: MPEG-1, Motion JPEG, Indeo, or Cinepak

The most versatile video boards use Motion JPEG compression, which allows you to save to an editable format and then recompress to a more compact scheme such as MPEG-1, or output to VHS or another tape format for analog playback. Less-expensive models, such as the Broadway Beginner, shown in Figure 22.4, lack M-JPEG editing.

Figure 22.4.
The Broadway Beginner uses one-step MPEG capture and compression to ease tough video capture tasks. (Photo courtesy of Data Translation)

Generally, capture boards fall into three categories:

- Under $500: Low-cost boards that use the system CPU to compress video to Indeo or Cinepak format.

- $800 to $1,400: Midrange boards with hardware for compressing to Motion JPEG, Indeo Video Interactive, or MPEG-1 formats.

- $2,000 and over: High-end boards with hardware for compressing to Motion JPEG or MPEG-1 formats. Also includes composite video inputs and outputs and accelerated effects generation.

The midrange boards provide the best combination of features and price. These products offer professional-looking results for less than $1,000. These products can help you whether you want to move your home videos to CD-ROM or edit hours of footage down to a few minutes and then record it back to VHS tape.

Compatibility Concerns

Before you buy, be certain that the board you purchase will work in your system. Some products are optimized for the Windows NT operating system and might lack drivers for Windows 95. Even if a capture board does have Windows 95 drivers, it might be optimized for NT. As a result, performance under Windows 95 might be disappointing.

Of course, you need to match the board with the add-in card bus in your system. Today, you'll have a hard time finding a video capture card for ISA or VL bus slots. Also be sure that the board you buy can fit inside the space available in your PC. Often, capture boards are full-length affairs, requiring more space than many compact systems provide.

Also make sure that the capture card you buy will work with your existing graphics hardware. Although most PCI-based capture cards will work with most graphics boards, some products still might want things their own way. This is particularly true of ISA-based capture boards, which often provide a dedicated graphics card connection (or even force you to throw out your graphics card) in order to work.

The Big Picture

If you want to purchase a capture board, you need to think big—not big bucks, big picture. To nab some quick snapshots from a sports broadcast or snap a few shots of your newborn, a $99 QuickCam or Snappy setup will do the job. Alternatively, you could invest in a graphics board that includes capture capability. Expect resolutions to be limited to 320×240 and compression to be handled by the host CPU.

If you want to convert hours of camcorder video to digital format—whether for edited output to tape or archived to CD-ROM—your investment gets more substantial. Here you'll need the talents of a true video capture board.

In order to get at least VHS-quality results, you'll need to spend about $800 to $1,200 on a Motion-JPEG capture card. Other alternatives exist as well. Data Translation's Broadway will capture your tapes straight to MPEG-1 format—perfect for moving your clips to CD-ROM while preserving video quality. Digital Video Arts' WakeBoard Multimedia Pro uses Intel's Indeo Video Interactive codec to provide a similar level of quality. Both provide interim formats that allow for frame-accurate editing.

Beyond this price, you enter the level of video production products. Better input filtering, enhanced special effects handling, and multichannel audio all set these products apart.

In all cases, you can expect to get some software in the deal. For true video capture boards, look for applications such as Adobe's Premiere 4.2 or Ulead Video Studio. If possible, get a card with the full version of the software—not a limited or special edition (often called SE) that leaves out features. Low-end graphics-capture card hybrids generally provide more consumer-oriented software aimed at capturing TV broadcasts or video, but editing options might be limited.

Diagnosing/Troubleshooting

Video capture is a complex task that involves many of the components of your PC. Problems that arise might reside in the video capture card itself, or they might come from the hard disk, sound card, operating system, capture software, or even the analog source device. One thing to keep in mind is that it often takes several passes to get things right. A healthy respect for trial and error will help you solve most glitches and obtain the best results.

Capture Setup

Getting ready to capture video is as important as—if not more important than—the actual act of capturing itself. Before you can begin pulling in a video stream, you need to define many parameters, from the name of the file to be created to the video's frame rate and format. Often, neglecting to pay attention to one of these details can yield subpar video or result in unexpected trouble.

Because the software used to capture video varies from product to product, I can't give you precise step-by-step instructions. However, I can tell you what you probably need to be aware of. From there, it should be a simple matter of making the proper settings in your capture software.

Preparing the System

Before you start capturing, you need to make sure that your system is ready for the task. Here are a few tips that can help boost the quality of your captured video:

- Check your specs: You'll need a fast Pentium CPU and a large 2GB or more hard disk to ensure reasonable capture. Although you can get by on 32MB of RAM and an EIDE hard disk, you're better off with 64MB of RAM and a fast SCSI hard disk.

- Defragment the hard disk: During capture, digitized video is laid down on the hard disk as it's captured, making the disk a potential bottleneck that can result in lost frames. Before you start, defragment the hard disk using Windows 95 Defrag or another utility. It's also a good idea to do a surface scan of the disk once in a while. These steps will allow video data to be laid down contiguously, speeding performance.

- Shut down software: Turn off any unnecessary background utilities or applications. These consume valuable system memory and CPU resources. Network software, in particular, chews up a lot of CPU time as it prompts your system to keep a constant eye out for traffic.

- Work with the latest: Make sure that the compression software you use is up to date. Current versions can provide more attractive results and demand less horsepower.

Lights, Camera, Action

Once your system is up to snuff, you can get ready to capture video. There's a good deal of setup involved, and neglecting any part of it will result in problems. Before you start capturing, make sure you have done the following:

- Watch those wires: Make sure your cables are properly set up. Make sure the red and yellow S-Video leads match up with the same-colored connectors on both the output device (camcorder, VCR, and so on) and the capture board. Also make sure that the white audio lead connects to the audio in port, whether on the capture card or a separate sound board.

- Set your source: Make sure you set your capture program to recognize the inbound analog signal. Most U.S. users will select NTSC. Likewise, you'll need to set the source device from among selections such as S-Video, Composite Video, and Component Video.

- Define your target: Before capturing, you need to tell the program how to save the inbound video. Set the compression type (Motion JPEG is typical for digital editing jobs) as well as the pixel resolution and color depth. You can also set the frame rate to as high as 60 fields per second. You'll also need to provide a filename and location for the video file.

Technical Note: When people talk about units of video, they speak of frames. *Frames* are the atomic unit of digital video—the individual snapshots that, when played in rapid succession, create the illusion of motion. Your TV displays video at 30 frames per second (fps), the same pace considered optimal for PC-based video. Movies actually run at 24fps. For PCs, 15fps is considered the acceptable minimum frame rate before playback becomes noticeably jerky.

Although 30fps is considered the optimal video frame rate, some capture boards actually go higher. The best boards provide the ability to capture 60 *fields* per second. This approach comes from broadcast video, which is almost always interlaced. Interlacing separates the even and odd scan lines, first displaying all the even lines and then all the odd lines. If you

continues

look closely at a TV screen, you'll notice a jagged effect along the edges of objects. This is an artifact of the video's being separated into fields.

Capture cards can either grab all the even lines, wait, and then fill in all the odd lines as they arrive, or they can capture the individual fields. The setup for capture cards normally lets you select one of these options.

Symptoms and Solutions

In case you're having trouble with your video capture, the following is a short list of things you can look into.

Distorted Video Picture

- Confirm that the input video source matches the incoming NTSC, PAL, or SECAM signal.
- Make sure that the source tape and playback device are in good working order.
- Try replacing the video cable.
- Make sure your capture driver supports Windows 95 and the version of DirectX installed on the PC. Windows 3.x drivers are generally incompatible with Windows 95, while DirectX 5 drivers can enhance capture quality.

Sound and Video Both Fail to Work

- Make sure that all cables are properly installed.
- Check the IRQ and DMA settings of your sound and video capture boards. A resource conflict will cause these peripherals to fail.

Video Fails to Display

If there is no video, try changing the video input source to the correct setting. If you aren't sure which is correct, try different settings among S-Video, Composite video, and Component video.

Sound Fails to Work

- Make sure that the capture program is set to record audio.
- If there is no sound with an S-Video configuration, make sure that a separate audio cable has been set up, because S-Video doesn't carry audio signals.

- Check the sound level on the analog source device.
- Check the sound level on your sound board. Also make sure that speakers are properly plugged in and turned on.

Upgrading for Video Capture

Unfortunately, installing a video capture board ranks right up there with installing a sound board as a surefire way to ruin a weekend. For this reason alone, you should think carefully about a video capture upgrade before you jump into it.

The following section will step you through installing two major video input-related upgrades—a videoconferencing system and a video capture board.

Upgrading to a Videoconferencing System

Adding videoconferencing to a PC is difficult because so many subsystems are involved. Assuming that you have an older modem, you might need to install a new modem and sound card. The following components might be involved:

- Video capture card
- 33.6 or 56Kbps modem with V.80 video handling capability, or ISDN adapter
- Monitor-top camera
- Microphone and speakers (integrated into a headset or separate)
- Full-duplex sound card
- Video-aware graphics accelerator

Warning: If you're attempting to upgrade a networked PC, think hard about what you're about to do. Videoconferencing upgrades are tough under normal circumstances, but they get brutal when you try to put these components on top of a networked system. If you're in an office environment, you should make sure that your IS staff does the upgrade. For home or small office networks, consider removing the network card and drivers, turning the PC into a stand-alone desktop. Once you've successfully installed the video capture board, you can try to reinstall the network hardware.

Upgrade Advice: Many kits include everything just listed except the sound and graphics cards. However, PCs purchased within the last year or two probably include the proper

continues

graphics and sound hardware. Check your system documentation to see if full-duplex audio and video-accelerated graphics are supported. You might even be able to avoid buying an upgrade kit if all you need is a single upgrade for, say, the video input and camera.

Because videoconferencing systems come in so many different configurations, installation routines will vary widely. As a rule, it's a good idea to proceed with caution whenever you install a complex multicard upgrade such as a videoconferencing package. Before you start, make a point to record all your current hardware settings—IRQs, DMAs, address ranges, and the like. Also record any free resources that might be available. That way, you'll have a ready inventory of available resources that you can apply to the new hardware.

Warning: To their credit, vendors try to ease upgrades by using software to automatically find free resources for the new hardware to use. However, these resources can fail and can even result in system crashes and aborted installation routines. Don't leave this to chance. Make sure you record your system's resource profile before you start so that you can take control if the need arises.

Video Capture Hardware

Depending on the package, a separate video capture board might be included in the box. Higher-end ISDN-based conferencing products, in particular, employ dedicated video capture hardware to receive analog signals from the camera and compress them into digital format for transmission.

Less-expensive systems, such as those that work over analog phone lines, often lack hardware-assisted compression and decompression. These products call on the system CPU to do the hard work of crunching in- and out-bound video data into manageable sizes. This scheme puts a lot of pressure on the CPU and limits video quality, but it can save $100 to $300. In either case, the video capture capabilities might be combined with communications hardware on a single card, saving valuable add-in slots.

For more on USB, see Chapter 24, "I/O Add-Ons."

PC97: The Universal Serial Bus connectors on PCs sold during the last year might eliminate the need for problematic video input card upgrades. Expect to see new USB cameras that send digital signals to your PC over a USB connection, which can then be sent directly over the phone line. USB's Plug and Play features and simple external connection promise to simplify complex videoconferencing upgrades and ease the crunch on scarce system resources. Just make sure that the USB camera you purchase features

precompression hardware so that the video stream is cut down to size before being sent out over the 12Mbps USB bus.

Communications Hardware

There are two classes of videoconferencing products: those that work over standard analog phone lines, and those that work over fast ISDN phone lines. Generally, ISDN-based products are appropriate for business applications, and standard phone line packages will work for consumers. The primary difference is video quality. The 128Kbps data rate of an ISDN connection is nearly four times that of the optimal 33.6Kbps connection possible over analog modems.

Note: ISDN has many advantages when it comes to videoconferencing. In addition to the 4X data rate advantage, the all-digital ISDN communication scheme avoids the vagaries involved in working with analog tones to transmit data. Line noise and drop-outs, which sap bandwidth and unceremoniously end connections on standard modem calls, are simply not a problem with ISDN. Call connection is also much quicker, since the digital link doesn't require the time-consuming handshake process needed by modems.

The drawback is that a very small percentage of homes and businesses have ISDN lines installed. Your ability to use ISDN videoconferencing will be limited to the small universe of fellow ISDN customers who have videoconferencing systems installed. In contrast, analog phone lines are universal.

For more information on ISDN and communications, see Chapter 23.

Today, most users will consider an analog setup, if only to enjoy the widespread compatibility that a modem-based package delivers. The modem in these packages should be at least a 33.6Kbps model. 28.8Kbps might be adequate, but every bit counts with videoconferencing. More importantly, the modem needs to be tweaked for video transfers using a standard called V.80. Modems provided in analog conference packages provide V.80 compliance.

Technical Note: You can't use any old 28.8Kbps modem for videoconferencing. In order for the modem to work with the H.324 video standard employed in analog videoconferencing packages, it must support an industry protocol known as V.80. This protocol determines how videoconferencing software runs on analog modems, providing a streamlined path for video and audio coming over the wire. Before buying a modem, make sure that V.80 support is built in so that you can take advantage of software-based videoconferencing packages in the future.

Warning: Don't expect a 56Kbps modem to improve things. These products only provide enhanced data rates going to your computer, for applications such as Web browsing and file downloads. You'll operate at 33.6Kbps when doing symmetric transfers such as videoconferencing. Also be aware that 56Kbps standards remain in flux. You might want to wait before jumping into this arena. Regardless, a 33.6Kbps modem will suffice for now.

As with the video hardware, the modem may be combined with video and audio handling onto a single card. This integration might help avoid space constraints, but it won't reduce system resource requirements. Whether on a single card or scattered among three separate cards, the video, comm, and audio hardware needs the same system resources in order to function.

Full-Duplex Sound

One area that gets overlooked is audio hardware. With all the excitement over being able to see other people during a video phone call, it's probably not surprising that speech gets short shrift. After all, we're already used to gabbing on the phone. But PCs aren't designed to be telephones. The sound hardware in your system might lack even the rudimentary features that make your $9 phone such a useful device.

You'll need the following features in your sound card or hardware in order to make videoconferencing effective:

- Full-duplex audio
- Noise cancellation
- Microphone and speakers (or, better yet, a headset)

Full-Duplex Audio

By far, the most important feature is full-duplex audio operation. *Full-duplex* means that your sound card can simultaneously accept both sound input and output. Consider a telephone call. When you talk on the phone, you can hear what the other person is saying even as you talk. Full-duplex sound boards allow the same thing.

The problem is that most older cards provide only half-duplex capability. If the card is accepting sound, it can't produce audio output. If the card is playing sound, it can't accept incoming audio. In the case of videoconferencing, this means that one person's speech gets cut off when someone else decides to speak.

A good example is CB radio communications. People can't both talk and listen over CB radio at the same time. They must stay off the microphone if they want to hear what the other person is saying. The effect is a very annoying—and, ultimately, unacceptable—break in conversation flow.

Noise Cancellation

Noise cancellation is critical to full-duplex operation. If you use desktop speakers, the sound from them will reach the microphone. The result is that your audio card ends up listening to the same sound input from both ends, making it impossible to use the microphone for speech.

Noise cancellation knocks out duplicate input by filtering the analog wave signals. Noise-canceling microphones also eliminate extraneous sounds that come from the periphery—such as office noises. So-called unidirectional microphones help focus on the speaker's input only.

Microphone and Speakers

For best videoconferencing results, you might consider using a headset microphone. The proximity of the microphone to your face will cut down on extraneous sounds being picked up, while the headset speakers reduce interference and desk clutter. A headset with a nice long cord also allows for better hands-free operation, since the microphone always moves with you.

Many kits also use lapel microphones that clip onto your shirt or collar. Like a headset, these microphones stay with you when you move in your chair or walk around. However, they require external speakers. One advantage is that a compact lapel mike won't mess up your hair.

Finally, desktop microphones keep you free of entangling wires. Just make sure that the unit provides unidirectional operation so that it won't pick up every sound in your home or office. Also make a point to keep it away from your desktop speakers.

Graphics Accelerator

A graphics card won't usually be part of a videoconferencing upgrade kit, but you might need to invest in a new one nevertheless. To get reasonable results from video playback, you'll need a graphics card that can take some of the processing burden off your CPU.

For more on graphics boards, see Chapter 19.

Fortunately, nearly every mainstream graphics board now includes a strong suite of video-handling features. Color space conversion lets your graphics board turn video data into a format recognized by your display, while pixel interpolation lets you zoom up tiny video windows without producing horrendous blockiness.

Not even a video-savvy graphics card can turn spotty modem-based video into VHS-quality fare, but it can help improve a bad situation. More importantly, it lets your system do a better job at other tasks, which is critical for sharing applications and data.

Video Capture Card Upgrade

So you want to turn your home or office PC into a desktop video studio. The good news is that $1,000 and a weekend's worth of work can actually make this happen. The bad news is that it could be a very, very long weekend.

An Ounce of Prevention

The lesson is clear: When you install a video capture board, proceed with caution. Start by taking note of all your PC's hardware resources. Note the exact IRQ, DMA, and address range resources consumed by components such as your graphics card, sound card, and modem. Also make note of which specific settings are free. Often, adapters will have preferred configurations—Creative's Sound Blaster sound boards, for instance, always want to grab IRQs 5 and 9—so knowing these preferences ahead of time can help avoid problems later.

Once that's done, back up your existing data. Back up both data and system files, because an installation can conceivably wreck key Windows 95 executable files. Make sure you also have a Windows 95 startup disc handy (including CD-ROM drivers!) so that you can start from scratch if necessary.

Finally, check out the video capture card vendor's Web site for possible driver or installation utility updates. Newer software might eliminate conflict problems with other hardware and even improve capture performance. You might also find online documentation that reveals common problems and solutions—information not available when the manual was put together several months before the release of the software.

Step-by-Step Installation

Installing a video capture card is similar to installing a sound card in that the hardware requires a number of specific IRQ, DMA, and base address resources. For this reason, I can't stress enough how important Plug and Play is to making a video upgrade work.

To install a new video capture card, follow these steps:

1. Shut down the PC, unplug the power cord, and remove the case.
2. Make sure you're properly grounded. Identify an appropriate PCI card for the installation—preferably one that has enough room for a full-length card.

> **Troubleshooting:** Older PCI systems might not have PCI bus mastering available in all slots. You might need to refer to system documentation to check which slots are bus-master-enabled. Without bus mastering, your capture card will be unable to achieve maximum performance.
>
> Likewise, some systems don't activate all the PCI slots. You might have to go into the system BIOS (accessed during the boot sequence) to actually turn on PCI bus slots. Again, your system documentation will provide the necessary information.

3. Use a Phillips-head screwdriver to remove the backplate that lines up with the slot you want to use.

4. Install the video capture card into the PCI slot. Make sure that it is firmly seated.

5. Power up the PC. Windows 95 will detect the new hardware.

6. Insert the video capture card's driver diskette into the A: drive.

7. Click the radio button labeled Driver from disk provided by hardware manufacturer, and then click OK.

8. Windows 95 will read the driver information from the disk and attempt to configure the card to match your system.

9. Shut down the PC, screw in the capture card's backplate, and reattach the case.

10. Reboot the system and install the card's application software, which probably can be found on CD-ROM.

Summary

Is video capture for you? It might be. Streaming video software for Web sites makes it possible to post your digitized home movies on the Internet. Video capture boards also provide a great way to boil down hours of agonizing video into an entertaining, edited final product. The cards let you distribute to other PCs, or you can play back out to VHS tape to send to others.

Whether you want it or not, video capture will join the PC platform. Video phone initiatives from Intel and others are pushing things forward, making ubiquitous videoconferencing a possibility in the next few years. Whether you want to try your directorial hand or want to place video calls to Grandma, you should keep an eye on this changing field.

Peter Norton

VI

Connectivity

23

Modems

Peter Norton®

The entire Internet revolution—you know, the one that's changing the face of communications and commerce—comes down to a single, inexpensive device: the modem. Three or four years ago, modems were just another option on desktop PCs. Today, they are nearly ubiquitous on nonnetworked PCs.

It's no surprise that modem technology has advanced along with all other aspects of the PC. These advances have improved the speed of transmission over phone lines and added useful capabilities while reducing costs enough to make modems standard issue on even entry-level systems. With PC users making ever greater use of the Internet, new modems can have a greater impact on your productivity and experience than any processor or RAM upgrade. In addition, nifty features such as simultaneous voice and data (SVD) and distinctive ring recognition that can route voice, fax, and data calls can help you make the most of a single phone line.

This chapter covers

- The workings of PC modem hardware, including analog modems, digital ISDN modems, and new xDSL and cable modems
- How to purchase a new modem that is right for your phone line and needs
- Dealing with and resolving modem problems
- Installing a new modem

Overview

As you probably already know, modems let PCs communicate with each other over telephone lines. The word *modem* is a contraction of the term *modulate-demodulate*, which effectively describes how the device turns binary bits into an unintelligible analog screeching and back again.

It's easy to overlook the hard work that modems undertake. Unlike most other PC components, modems straddle the difficult line between the digital universe inside PCs and the analog world we occupy. What's more, these devices must ply bits over a ragged telephone network that is fraught with limited bandwidth, noise, and interference.

Actually, analog modems are only the most common wide-area communications hardware for PCs. People who have digital phone lines—such as Integrated Services Digital Network (ISDN) or the emerging xDSL (digital subscriber line) service—can use all-digital interface devices that support superior performance. Because the vast majority of PCs connect to each other via standard phone lines, we will focus on analog modems.

For more information on ISDN and xDSL modems, see the section "ADSL: The New Grail."

Modem Characteristics

Although all modems do essentially the same thing—provide an interface to the analog phone network—they vary in performance and capabilities. Here are some of the varying capabilities:

- Data rate: The number of bits per second (bps) that a modem can send or receive.
- Protocol compliance: Compatibility with international standards to achieve specific data rates and other characteristics.
- Fax: Allows fax transmission and receipt using the PC.
- Error correction: Ensures that data arrives uncorrupted at the other end.
- Compression: Reduces the number of bits in a transmission.
- Voice mail services: Allows the model to act as an answering machine and to provide services such as call forwarding, fax-back, and multiple voice mailboxes.
- Distinctive ring: Allows the modem to recognize incoming calls as voice, fax, or data and to respond accordingly.
- Voice capability: Allows voice and data to be carried over the same line on the same call.

A lot of technical stuff goes into making modems work. Generally, you don't need to be up to speed on the very latest International Telecommunication Union (ITU) compliance and other issues, but this can help.

Modem Magic

How do modems communicate? Essentially, they use agreed-upon standard methods to express digital 1s and 0s as analog tones. However, unlike the digital domain, in which the lack of a charge indicates a 0 bit and the presence of a charge indicates a 1 bit, working with analog sound is more troublesome.

Turning Bits into Tones

In order to send and receive 1s and 0s over phone lines, modems must code and decode bits into waveform audio. To do this, modems employ a variety of modulation techniques. At the core of this approach is *frequency key shifting*, which uses standard analog frequencies (or tones) to denote a binary 1 or 0. Table 23.1 lists the frequencies that indicate a 1 or a 0 to a modem.

Table 23.1. Frequency key shifting standards.

Modem Side and Value	Frequency
Sending 0	1070Hz
Sending 1	1270Hz
Receiving 0	2025Hz
Receiving 1	2225Hz

Imagine two piano players suffering from laryngitis. They can't speak, but they can use their keyboards to respond to yes-or-no questions. Player 1 agrees to use the note A to signify no, while a C note signifies yes. Player 2, in order to avoid confusion with his partner's playing, uses an E to signify no and a high G to signify yes.

This approach runs out of gas fast. Modems take up to three cycles to lock onto a note change, limiting maximum data rates to just 300 bits per second—the rate achieved with the old Bell 103 standard.

To squeeze more bits into a transmission, new modems use a method called phase *key modulation*, in which transitions in waveform timing designate a 1 or a 0. By managing and accelerating frequency transitions, modems moved up to speeds of 9600bps.

Current schemes add volume to the mix, using changing amplitudes to designate additional bit transitions. The result is modems that can reach data rates of 28.8 and 33.6Kbps—more than 100 times faster than the original Bell 103 specification.

Setting Standards

In order for these ambitious modulation schemes to work, however, everybody needs to agree to work the same way. Modems must be able to assume specific frequencies, timings, and amplitudes in the analog signal. They must also be able to tell other modems in some standard way exactly what their capabilities are.

Setting the standards is the International Telecommunications Union (ITU). The ITU provides the forum for developing and ratifying modem communication standards, ensuring that a US Robotics modem you buy at CompUSA will be able to talk to the Hayes modem installed on your friend's PC.

Table 23.2 shows the series of ITU standards employed in the PC modem market.

Table 23.2. Modem standards.

ITU Standard	Data Rate
V.32	4800 and 9600bps
V.32bis	14.4Kbps
V.34	28.8Kbps
V.42bis	36.6Kbps
56Kbps*	56Kbps

*This ITU standard is still under development. 56Kbps operation occurs in only one direction.

56K Modems: Myth and Reality

The newest modems—so-called 56K models that can receive up to 56,000 bits per second—present a real buying dilemma for users. At the time this chapter was written, the ITU was still working on a ratified standard protocol for 56K operation—with one expected before the end of 1998. At the same time, North American companies hoped to adopt an interim standard. This is not the first time this has happened: Popular V.34 modems (28.8Kbps operation) were preceded by interim models using the V.fast protocol.

Right now, you'll find two proprietary schemes being used for 56K modems: The x2 standard from US Robotics (now 3Com), and the K56-Flex standard from Hayes, Lucent Technologies, and others (see Figure 23.1). Both do the same thing—provide fast 56Kbps downstream data access on certain phone connections—but not in a compatible manner. This means that a K56-Flex modem won't get 56Kbps operation dialing into an ISP using x2 modem technology.

Figure 23.1.
Diamond Multimedia's SupraExpress 56E provides K56-Flex-compliant 56Kbps capability in a convenient external design. (Photo courtesy of Diamond Multimedia)

For more on purchase issues with 56K modems, see the section "56K or 33.6Kbps?".

This new class of modem is optimized for the digital phone connections often employed by larger organizations, such as big companies, ISPs, and information services such as CompuServe and AOL. The secret is the fact that much of the phone network is already digital.

When you make an analog call, it travels over copper wires to the local phone-switching station. In most newer facilities, the call is converted to digital format and routed over the phone network to the switching station on the other end. Here, the call is converted back to analog form and sent over copper wires to the other phone. Similarly, signals coming from the far end to you are converted to digital format and back again.

But if your ISP connects to the phone system via a digital T1, T3, or even an ISDN connection, there is no need to convert analog impulses at all. Instead, everything travels as straight bits from the outbound connection all the way to your local switching station. It is only here, perhaps a few thousand yards from your home or office, that any analog signals get involved at all. The result is a much cleaner, sounder analog signal than one that has been converted twice.

Note: 56K modems might have to be renamed "53K modems." That's because current implementations violate FCC frequency limits, which are set to prevent unacceptable levels of crosstalk in the phone network. When operated within FCC-approved specifications, these modems are capable of 53Kbps downstream transfers. This matter was still under review at the time this chapter was written.

56K modems take advantage of the enhanced quality of these digitally originated connections. However, like any modem, the quality of your local line and switching station, as well as your distance from the station itself, will determine whether you get anything close to 56Kbps for data coming to you. What's more, outbound communication occurs at only 33.6Kbps maximum.

Compatibility: The good news is that most 56K modems provide compliance for existing ITU standards, including the V.42bis protocol used for 33.6Kbps operation. Your 56K modem should work like any standard 33.6Kbps product when calling into a system or ISP that doesn't employ the matching 56K technology.

Modem Reality

Advances in modem speeds have been nothing short of remarkable. In fact, engineers have repeatedly predicted the demise of modem speed increases. Modem data rates, they said, could go no faster than 14.4Kbps, and then 28.8Kbps, and finally 33.6Kbps. If you had told a modem engineer in 1990 that 56Kbps modems would be all the rage in 1997, he would have said you were crazy.

But it's not all that easy. The specified data rates often have little to do with reality. Line noise, modem design quality, and system resources all combine to drag actual performance below the line set by the standard. In fact, most 28.8Kbps modem calls occur at rates of 20 to 26Kbps. What's more, modems send and receive additional start and stop bits, as well as bits for error correction. These consume part of the bandwidth pie, further reducing the actual data being sent each second.

Driving the Dirt Road

Al Gore and others might like to go on about the Information Superhighway, but in reality, the public telephone network is a rutted dirt road. Aging telephone switching hardware introduces noise and crosstalk to the phone signal, while exposed phone lines stretch for miles in proximity to power lines that emit electric fields. Meanwhile, some second phone lines might be installed using a multiplexer box that tricks a single line into doing double duty, thus reducing performance.

The result is an infrastructure that is hostile to reliable data communications. Generally, those in metropolitan areas can expect the best level of service. Growing communities and new neighborhoods often enjoy new, all-digital telephone switches. Older neighborhoods and rural areas, however, might have to make due on aging analog equipment. Even the newest equipment, such as Diamond's 56Kbps-capable PC Card modem, shown in Figure 23.2, can't overcome poor line quality.

Figure 23.2.
The Diamond Supra PC Card can deliver 56Kbps capability to your notebook. But you'll be hard-pressed to predict line quality while on the road. (Photo courtesy of Diamond Multimedia)

Peter's Principle: Check the State of the Local Phone Network
Before You Set Up Shop

Modem communications and real estate sales operate under the same catch phrase:
Location, location, location. If you plan to set up shop and you rely heavily on modem-
based communications, make sure you investigate the state of the local phone network
first. If you have a short list of locations you're thinking about moving to, inquire with the
local telephone service provider about the state of the switching hardware that services the
areas. Try to find out when the infrastructure was installed and whether any upgrades are
planned.

You also might be able to get the phone company to conduct a loop qualification test. This
routine provides critical signal data that defines the quality of the line. It can also tell you
how far you are from a switching station—often a predictor of relative performance. You
need an active line to conduct this test, so you might have to ask someone in the area to
request the service for you.

Beyond analog communications, access to digital services such as ISDN, xDSL, and enhanced cable
service are all very much geographic issues. Again, new neighborhoods in metropolitan areas stand
the best chance of having access to these services. You'll need to contact the local phone and cable
companies to determine what services are available.

Tip: Don't be surprised if you can't get straight answers about digital services from the
phone company. You might have better luck talking to a local Internet service provider
(ISP). These folks often know the local communications landscape better than some call-
center rep and might even be able to steer you to the right people inside the phone company to answer your questions.

Compression and Correction

To work around the potholes and cracks in the phone network, modems use data compression and
error correction. The data compression process isn't hard to understand. Hardware in the modem
takes groups of bits and crunches them into a more efficient format.

The Compression Question

This process is similar to what happens with compression programs such as PK Zip or hard disk compression. Data is compressed on-the-fly by the modem before it is sent out. On the receiving end,
compressed data is expanded in the modem and sent to the system over the standard COM port.

Of course, both modems need to use the same compression scheme, or the squeezed bits will be unintelligible to the receiving hardware. That's where ITU standards come in. In addition to setting communications protocols, the international body defines compression formats. Backward compatibility ensures that the newest 33.6Kbps modem will recognize the compression of both new and older models.

Performance: Depending on the types of files being moved, compression might not have a significant impact. Many of the largest files are already compressed, meaning that modem-based compression is unable to find efficiencies in the data stream. Graphics files such as .GIF, .JPG, and .TIF are already compressed, as are files with .ZIP and .ARC extensions. Video files (.AVI, .MPG) are also cut down to size. Modem compression does help with text-based documents, including those ubiquitous HTML pages, and most uncompressed application files. If a modem maker says that compression provides 2X performance over the rated speed, be sure to take that figure with a grain of salt.

When two modems connect, they generally try to use the most efficient compression scheme supported by both. The ITU-established V.42bis protocol is preferred, because it offers better compression rates than MNP-5. If the modems fail to establish V.42bit compression, they will move to MNP-5.

The Correction Section

Far more important is error correction, which ensures that data gets to the receiving modem intact. Problems arise when noise in the phone line interferes with the signal, impairing the receiving modem's ability to detect the inbound signal. When this happens, the modem might guess wrong, putting 1s where there should be 0s, and vice versa. Without a scheme to detect and correct such mistakes, most modem transmissions would end up as gibberish.

Two kinds of error correction are built into modems today: forward error correction and data-level error correction. Forward error correction consists of redundant bits built into the data stream that can be used to rebuild lost or mangled data on-the-fly. This scheme reduces the bandwidth available for usable data but avoids time-consuming retransmission when minor errors occur. It is the first line of data defense for modems.

Data-level error correction uses a checksum scheme to compare chunks of data against expected results in a small header field. To do this, the sending modem breaks the data stream into standard-sized blocks, which are bookended by information about the data itself. In front of the block, a header provides information on where the data inside the block must go with respect to other blocks. This allows blocks of data to be sent out of order and reconstituted on the receiving end.

On the back end of the data block, the sending modem uses a standard algorithm to compute a series of error correction bits. Based on the data inside the block, these bits allow the receiving modem to distinguish errors in the transmission. The receiving modem uses the same algorithm to determine the appropriate error correction data. If the result matches that sent by the other end, the block is assumed to be whole. If the result doesn't match that of the other end, the receiving modem tells the other side to resend the corrupted block of data.

There have been several standard error correction schemes over the years, but only V.42 and MNP-4 remain important to modem users. Compliant modems can negotiate among themselves to come up with the optimal scheme for each transmission. Typically, two modems will first attempt to use V.42 and then move down to MNP-4.

Other Talents

Of course, modems do more than just screech bits at each other. For years, most modems have included fax send and receive capability, and many new models provide voice and data capability. Many are also telephony mavens, providing services such as voice mailboxes and messaging, distinctive ring capability, and the like.

PC-Based Faxing

Today, virtually all new modems provide fax capability. This allows your PC to send and receive fax transmissions, whether from another PC or from a standard fax machine. What's more, the advent of power Pentium-class systems and the multitasking talents of Windows 95 have made the PC a much more attractive fax platform than before, when such operations would slow system operation to a crawl.

It's no surprise that standards lie behind the fax capability. Most modems comply with the Class 1 specification, which places most of the fax processing burden on the system CPU. Windows 95's fax facilities are tailored to Class 1 operation. Class 2 products add some modem commands and intelligence to offload the work from the CPU to the modem itself, but the lack of support in Windows 95 makes it a less attractive option for most users.

In general, fax transmission may occur at data rates as high as 14.4Kbps. However, older fax machines and modems might not be able to support anything beyond 9600bps. Given that long-distance fax calls can add up to hefty phone bills, the higher fax data rate might make an upgrade worthwhile in and of itself.

> **Note:** If you have an Internet connection, you can use an Internet-based fax service to help trim the cost of long-distance faxing. A wide variety of free and pay services use different methods to handle your transmissions. Some turn simple e-mail messages into fax transmissions, and others, such as FaxStorm, take document files and transmit them as fax output. In addition to possibly cutting down long-distance charges, useful features such as fax broadcasting and transmission status updates can help people who send many faxes. You can find a wealth of information and useful links on Yahoo's Internet Fax page:
>
> `http://www.yahoo.com/Computers_and_Internet/Internet/Internet_Fax_Server/`

Voice and Data Handling

Many modems allow simultaneous voice and data communications over a single line. This feature is useful for everything from online technical support to online gaming (in which gamers can follow through on their burning need to mock their opponents). The voice-data capability was originally launched using two approaches:

- Radish VoiceView: The modem switches rapidly between voice and data operation, suspending data briefly while analog voice signals are carried through.
- DSVD (digital simultaneous voice and data): The modem parses out a section of the 28.8 or 33.6Kbps bandwidth to transmit digitized voice.

Today, DSVD is firmly entrenched as the standard technology for putting voice and data into a single call. This scheme is useful for allowing voice communications, but it does have a cost. Data throughput drops, because as much as 9.6Kbps of the available bandwidth gets handed over for voice operation. Still, if you plan to use your modem for online gaming or direct PC-to-PC collaboration, a DSVD modem might provide very useful capabilities.

Digital Domains: Modems for the New World

Analog modems top out at 33.6Kbps for symmetric data rates and about 56Kbps for downloads. These speeds are impressive given the challenges of the phone network, but they are woefully inadequate for the burgeoning demand presented by Web browsing, telecommuting, and other applications. To get better performance, some form of digital network needs to be put into place.

Technical Note: The telephone companies have a strong vested interest in changing the current data-carrying landscape. The phone system is what is called a *circuit-switched network:* When you initiate a call, you grab a line and keep it until you hang up the phone. This is fine, until a lot of people want to use the network at the same time—say, following an earthquake. At that time, the network simply runs out of circuits. The result is circuit-busy messages and even the lack of a dial tone altogether.

Enter the Internet. Phone companies install switching capacity according to well-researched historical usage patterns. For example, the phone company knows that the average phone call lasts about two or three minutes. Given that fact, they can assume that a reserved circuit will probably come free within minutes of being engaged. But the average data call (faxes aside) lasts 45 minutes or more. And often circuits are engaged for hours because users simply forget to log off. The result is the equivalent of a small natural disaster every evening as millions flock to their modems and tie up circuits to browse the Web.

The answer is the use of so-called *packet-switched systems,* which are similar to that of Ethernet networks, in which a fixed amount of bandwidth is shared among users. Although an overstressed packet-switched network will bog down, it won't deny service during periods of heavy usage. Asymmetric Digital Subscriber Line (ADSL) and cable-based Internet access both use a packet-switched scheme to split the bandwidth pie among consumers.

ISDN Modems

ISDN stands for *integrated service digital network,* and the telephone companies' efforts to roll out this service have been almost as clumsy as the name itself. For over 10 years, ISDN has been projected as the new face of phone service, providing an intriguing mix of voice services, digital controls, and high bandwidth to millions of subscribers. Today, ISDN is on the verge of becoming a telecommunications footnote, in part because ISDN suffers the same problem as standard phone lines—data calls tend to tie up available capacity and result in service outages.

An ISDN modem (see Figure 23.3) needs an ISDN line. This line actually consists of three channels: a 16Kbps D (data) channel that carries commands and control data, and a pair of 64Kbps B (bearer) channels that carry the data itself. That adds up to as much as 128Kbps of sustained bandwidth—about four to five times that of V.42bis modems and enough for business-grade video-conferencing. Web surfing gets a big boost as well.

Because ISDN is entirely digital, the term *modem* is a misnomer since no modulation or demodulation takes place. ISDN adapters provide an interface between your system and the digital ISDN network. The advantage is huge: Digital connections can be initiated much more quickly than their analog counterparts and are not plagued by performance-sapping line noise. Once you start an ISDN connection, you can rely on its staying put—unlike analog calls, which can drop off unexpectedly.

Figure 23.3.
3Com's Impact line of ISDN modems come in both external and internal varieties. You'll want to use the internal model to get the maximum 128Kbps ISDN data rates. (Photo courtesy of 3Com Corp.)

In order to get ISDN access, a modem must incorporate an NT-1, or network terminator component. The NT-1, which used to be handled as a separate box, lets you enable a connection to the telephone company's ISDN network, while an ISDN adapter hooks to your computer and serves as the interface between your PC and the NT-1. Today, most ISDN modems incorporate these functions, eliminating the need for separate modules.

Unfortunately, ISDN access can be limited. Outside of metropolitan areas, expect distances to be too great to support ISDN's line loop limit (some 18,000 feet, or just over 3 miles). Even if you're within a service area, ISDN can be maddeningly complex to set up. Remember, we're talking about phone companies here. You'll need to come to terms with esoterica such as service provider ID numbers (SPIDs), switching hardware, and NT-1 boxes before you can get going. Even then, things can go wrong.

ADSL: The New Grail

In the next few years, expect to see ADSL service emerge. This stands for *asymmetric digital subscriber line*, and it promises big bandwidth to end users over standard copper wire. Like 56K modem communications, ADSL is asymmetric, which means that downstream data comes faster than upstream. Data rates vary from 1.5 to 5Mbps downstream and from 64 to 640Kbps going up.

The biggest advantage of ADSL is that it works on the existing copper wire infrastructure already laid out by the telephone companies. This happens because the digital information is sent in the high-frequency area of the phone lines, where voice data signals aren't present. In essence, ADSL signals run along free lanes available in the phone lines. In fact, voice and ADSL transmissions can occupy phone lines at the same time. What ADSL does require are new switches to manage the digital signals, as well as a new class of adapters to hook the PC into the ADSL network.

Don't hold your breath. Unless you live in a few select trial areas where phone companies are sponsoring ADSL tests, this new service could be many, many years in coming. If the ISDN is any gauge, it might never get there at all. Still, the packet-switched scheme provides a terrific incentive for phone companies that are running low on dedicated circuits.

Cable Guy: Window of Opportunity

Another emerging option comes in the form of cable modems, which connect to the thick coaxial cable used to supply cable TV transmissions. Coax is a bandwidth hero, able to shove 6MBbps or more to the receiving PC. Unfortunately, because the cable network was laid with only TV broadcasts in mind, upstream facilities are limited in all but a small portion of installations. Without modification, there is no way to direct that bandwidth for applications such as Web browsing.

Cable companies are working on the problem. Newer networks routinely include upstream capability, and plans are in place to upgrade existing infrastructures. Cable access trials are underway in a variety of areas, with cable modems being used to interface the PC to the coaxial-based cable network. Like ADSL, cable modems provide asymmetric access, with 128Kbps or higher upstream service.

Satellite Systems

Today, the most widely available high-bandwidth Internet access option is via *direct satellite system* (DSS), such as DirecPC from Hughes Networks. (Check out the Web site at `www.DirecPC.com`.) A compact 18- to 21-inch dish, identical to those used for satellite TV services, receives downstream data from the Internet. With up to 400Kbps data rates, and access from even the most remote locations in the continental U.S., satellite service is the most widely available service.

There are several drawbacks. For one, you can't use the dish for fast upstream communications— you must use an analog modem and phone line to send data from your PC. In addition, obstructions such as buildings and trees make reception impossible. And although the satellite dishes are compact, mounting them on rooftops and building walls can be either hazardous or expensive. Finally, inclement weather, such as heavy downpours and snowfall, can reduce signal strength to the point that Internet connectivity is lost.

Buying Bandwidth: Shopping for Modems and Other Devices

So you want fast Internet access, do you? Today more connectivity options are open to PC users than ever before. Modems of varying speeds and talents can fire bits over standard phone lines and even turn your PC into an answering machine. Real bandwidth jockeys might consider one of the several digital infrastructures available, from ISDN to direct satellite systems. Table 23.3 will help you decide.

Table 23.3. Bandwidth options at a glance.

Type	Data Rate (Inbound/Outbound)	Cost of Installation	Monthly Cost	What It's Best For
33.6Kbps modem	33.6/33.6Kbps	$100	N/A	Casual Web browsing and e-mail, home and small office. This type of modem is ubiquitous.
56K modem	56/33.6Kbps	$189	N/A	Casual and heavy Web browsing and e-mail, home and small office, server access. The lack of a single 56K standard could make some products obsolete.
ISDN	128/128Kbps	$400	$36 to $100	Heavy Web browsing, small office, video-conferencing and data conferencing, Web publishing uploads. Limited availability.
Satellite	400/33.6Kbps	$500	$40	Heavy Web browsing and e-mail, small office, and server access. This is the best option for rural locations.
Cable modem	4Mbps/33.6Kbps	$800	$60	Heavy Web browsing and e-mail, home and small office, server access. This is still in trials.
ADSL modem	1.6Mbps/128Kbps	$800	$50 to $100	Heavy Web browsing and e-mail, home and small office, server access, Web publishing FTP uploads, videoconferencing, and data conferencing. This is still in trials.

The vast majority of users will remain with analog modems for years to come. Digital technologies are either too expensive, too complex, or too limited in their availability to make them worth buying. In the meantime, expect 56K modem technology to fill the gap while the phone companies, cable companies, and others lay down the infrastructure needed to make higher-bandwidth connections ubiquitous.

Peter's Principle: Digital Alternatives to the POTS Modem
Are Still Plagued by Problems

Remember, super-fast whizbang technology isn't worth much if no one on the other side of the connection has the same capabilities. Whether it's the vexing 56K standards problem or the stunning lack of ISDN service among ISPs, many of the more attractive-looking bandwidth options are plagued by questions. Until they get answered, those bandwidth alternatives might be offering a very quick road to nowhere. Just ask anyone who bought a Betamax VCR.

Buying a Modem

A new modem is a smart upgrade if your PC is more than a year old or so. If you access the Internet with anything slower than a 28.8Kbps modem, run—don't walk—to the nearest store for an upgrade. The same goes for anyone using a modem for e-mail, file downloads from a remote server, and other time-consuming pursuits.

The economics of modem upgrades are among the best in the PC marketplace. For one, modems are cheap. A 33.6Kbps modem from a top-flight manufacturer can cost $120 or less. Depending on your usage and the billing patterns of your ISP, you could recoup that entire amount within a year. If you make long-distance calls to transfer files to and from a remote server, the upgrade will probably pay for itself sooner than that.

Still, there are plenty of questions. We'll try to answer them one by one here.

56K or 33.6Kbps?

The 56K format wars might be raging, but that doesn't mean you can't place your bet. At the time this chapter was written, US Robotics' x2 standard enjoyed a strong market lead, with compatible modems appearing in PCs from market leaders such as Dell and Gateway. These vendors ship hundreds of thousands of PCs every month, which might be enough to push cautious ISPs and information services to support this scheme.

Still, expect K56-Flex to make a run of it. Between Lucent and Rockwell, you're talking the majority share of the modem controller chip market. K56-Flex modems should ship from everyone this side of US Robotics (now 3Com).

Of course, an ITU standard is pending, and it's anyone's guess whether modems sold prior to its ratification will provide compatibility. In other words, both choices could end up being wrong!

The good news is that all 56K products provide complete compatibility with existing V.42bis modems that operate at 33.6Kbps. For this reason alone, a 56K modem is worth considering if you use your PC for Web access. Before you decide, call your ISP and find out which 56K standard it intends to support.

Buying Tip: 3Com and other vendors are offering a free upgrade to the future ITU standard for their proprietary 56K modems. If you go 56K, you should definitely pursue one of these investment-saving upgrade deals. But be warned: Upgrade programs like this have a notorious history of being short on service. Long delays, lost records, and other hassles often occur because vendors underestimate the complexity and popularity of their upgrade programs.

If your ISP doesn't support 56K, or if you don't do much Web browsing, a 33.6Kbps modem might be had at a bargain. You can save $30 to $60 over the cost of newer 56K models and still get very fast performance. Also look for products that offer free or low-cost upgrades to 56K technology down the road.

Internal or External?

Personally, I prefer external modems. They cost about $20 more than internal ISA cards and add yet another cable to the rat's nest behind your PC, but the convenience of the external device is terrific. External modems can be easily moved and shared among systems (including notebooks), and they come in handy when things go wrong.

Peter's Principle: The Advantages of External
Versus Internal Modems

One reason I've come to value external modems is that they come in handy when things go wrong. Occasionally I run into situations in which the modem stops responding to commands and just sits there, screeching nonsensically into the phone. I can shut down communications apps, try killing the connection from software, and even issue hang-up

continues

command codes from the Windows Terminal applet. But the modem won't let go of the line. At this point, if you had an internal modem, you would need to reboot your PC to get your phone line back. An external modem, however, can be powered down from a toggle switch on the unit, freeing the line. After you turn it back on, you're ready to go.

An external modem also gives you visual clues when something is wrong, unlike an internal. If I'm in the middle of a lengthy download and data stops coming, it helps to be able to see the SD (send data) and RD (receive data) LEDs. If the RD light never comes on while the modem polls periodically, you know that the connection might be kaput. On the other hand, if the RD LED stays on but your software says no data is arriving, the PC itself, or the connection between the modem and the PC, becomes suspect. Although Windows 95 includes RD and SD lights on the Taskbar modem icon, these sometimes don't reflect all the activity on the modem itself.

So why do people buy internal modems? For one thing, they don't consume any desk space and don't require serial and power cables, which both add to the wire pollution at the back of the PC. Internal modems typically sell for $20 less than their external counterparts—an additional advantage.

Internal modems are worth considering, though. For one thing, far too many devices want to use the same serial port that your modem connects to. PDA connectors, sheet-fed scanners, and who-knows-how-many-other peripherals make their living off scarce serial port space. An internal modem frees that connector, eliminating the hassle of plugging in and unplugging devices.

In addition, an internal unit might be a must for older systems. That's because old PCs can't accept serial port data quickly enough to keep pace with 14.4Kbps and faster modems. The culprit is an obscure chip called the UART (universal asynchronous receiver-transmitter) that acts as a middle-man between the modem and the CPU. The old UART lacks a memory buffer to store incoming data, so it must constantly pester the CPU every time bits are received. Not only does this bog down the entire system, but the lack of buffer means that faster modems simply overrun the UART's ability to get data to the CPU. The result is lost data.

Internal modems provide their own UART—the 16550—which provides a 16-character buffer for inbound and outbound data (see Figure 23.4). If you use an external modem rated for 14.4Kbps or faster, however, your system needs to use a 16550 UART in order to keep pace. The deeper buffer in the 16550 UART allows the serial port to keep pace with the fastest analog modems, providing data rate services of up to 115Kbps.

Figure 23.4.
Diamond Multimedia's SupraExpress 56i internal modem packs its own fast UART chip, allowing older systems to deal with fast data downloads. (Photo courtesy of Diamond Multimedia)

Upgrade Advice: If your PC has a slow UART but you want to upgrade to an external modem, you still can. You'll just need to shell out a few more bucks for an I/O upgrade card that provides backplane connectors for serial and parallel port connectors. This card will include the 16550 UART, allowing mainstream modems to operate normally.

Other Choices

Once you've decided on modem speed and location, you can start looking in earnest. That said, many folks might consider paying extra for DSVD modems (assuming that there is someone on the other end with compliant hardware). Game players will get a kick out of the gratuitous verbal sparring (at the expense of a response), while office users can use the modem to combine audioconferencing and data conferencing.

You might also consider a so-called Win modem. These modems rely on the system CPU to handle the job of juggling bits instead of relying on an internal chipset. Win modems are inexpensive—they cost as little as $50 or $60. The name Win modem comes from the fact that these products work only under Windows (they won't work with DOS-based games) because special driver software is needed to shuttle the modem duties to the system CPU. What's more, Win modems tax the system CPU with extra work, which can be a problem if you multitask Web browsing with the latest cycle-sucking software. Still, for light online duty, a Windows modem might be a great bargain.

Beyond Modems

If you have an ISDN line, you face some similar decisions with ISDN modems. For example, you can pick up internal or external ISDN adapters. Again, that external adapter gives you easy access to controls and, more important, gives you a view of the informative status lights that tell you about B channel access, whether you are getting a digital dial tone, and other goodies.

However, if you use both B channels for maximum 128Kbps operation, an internal modem might be your best option. The serial port used for external devices poops out at 115Kbps, which means you'll be falling short of the top speed needed for videoconferencing and other cutting-edge applications. An internal device can offer the full bandwidth range.

Otherwise, look for products that combine the necessary components of ISDN connections—the NT-1 and ISDN adapter (see Figure 23.5). You'll also want to check with your phone company *before* buying to see which switch they use. Some ISDN modems might not be compatible with all switch manufacturers. Also look for automated setup routines to help with hooking to the phone network. These can sniff out the switch type and line SPIDs without intervention, saving you time and frustration.

Figure 23.5.
The 3ComImpactIQ provides slick, automated line detection and all the hardware you need to interface to the ISDN network. But you'll get faster access from an internal model. (Photo courtesy of 3Com Corp.)

Moving on Up: Upgrading a Modem

Once you've decided what kind of modem you want, upgrading should be fairly painless. Because modems operate over a serial port, they use the IRQ base I/O address of the serial port itself. That said, you will have to deal with the PC's COM port weirdness.

Understanding COM Ports

Your PC has four COM ports, numbered 1 through 4. These logical ports work with the two physical serial connectors found on the back of your PC. Because of the way COM port addresses work, you can only be certain that the lower two COM ports—numbers 1 and 2—will always be available for your modem.

Before you install a new modem, check Windows 95's Hardware Device Manager. This useful facility can give you detailed information on COM port status. To check for available COM ports, do the following:

1. Select Start | Settings | Control Panel.
2. Double-click the System icon. In the System Properties dialog box, choose the Device Manager tab.
3. Click the plus sign (+) next to the item Ports (COM & LPT).

> **Tip:** If a red X or yellow exclamation point appears next to either of the COM port items, a conflict of some sort is preventing normal operation of the indicated ports. For more information on how to troubleshoot COM ports, see the section "Troubleshooting COM Ports."

4. Double-click the COM port you want to examine. (On most PCs, you should see two COM port entries and one LPT port entry.)
5. In the Communications Port (COMx) Properties dialog box, choose the Resources tab to view the IRQ and address range settings for the COM port.
6. If both COM ports are without conflicts, you should be able to make use of either of them for your modem.

Installing Modem Hardware

If you spent the extra money for an external modem, you'll get some return on your investment when you install the hardware. External devices are easier to install, if only because you don't have to open the case to do so.

External Modem Installation

The following steps show you how to install your modem hardware. First you will need to find the appropriate serial port on the back of your system. Most PCs have two serial ports, which usually appear as a pair of nine-pin connectors, or as one nine-pin and one 25-pin connector on older machines. Depending on the cable provided with the external modem, you'll plug into either the nine-pin or the 25-pin serial connector. The other end plugs into the 25-pin connector on the modem itself.

Likewise, you will see two phone jacks (known as RJ-11 connectors) on the modem. One of these must be connected to the phone jack on the wall, and the other may be attached to a telephone. The second line acts as a passthrough, letting you use the phone line for both your phone and modem.

1. Attach the modem cable to the 25-pin connector on the back of the modem.

2. Attach the other end to the appropriate nine-pin or 25-pin serial port connector on the back of the PC.

3. Plug the phone cord into the wall jack and the other end into the RJ-11 jack on the modem. Make sure you plug this line into the connector on the modem that is intended to be hooked to the wall.

4. If you want to connect a telephone or fax machine to the modem, attach a phone cord from the device to the second RJ-11 jack.

5. Plug the power cord into an outlet and attach the round connector component into the modem's power input jack.

Internal Modem Installation

Installing the hardware for an internal modem is in many ways similar to doing so for external hardware. For example, cable setup is the same. Likewise, internal modems often provide two RJ-11 jacks like their external counterparts.

Otherwise, you need to follow the same steps as those for an internal card installation:

1. Shut off the PC, unplug the power cord, and remove the case.

2. Make sure you ground yourself by touching a metal portion of the PC chassis. Better yet, use a grounding mat and wrist strap.

3. Use a screwdriver to unscrew the backplane of a free ISA card slot. Pull out the backplane connector.

4. Seat the card into the ISA slot. You might need to rock the card slightly from back to front to ease it into the connector.

5. Plug in the serial cable and phone cords.

6. Power up the PC, and then follow the steps for setting up the new modem hardware under Windows 95.

7. Once you've determined that the modem is working properly, shut down the PC, secure the ISA board backplane with a screwdriver, and reattach the case.

Setting Up a New Modem

Installing a modem should go quickly. Generally, your biggest worries come from possible mouse conflicts, because many pointing devices use a serial port to hook to the PC. You can check your mouse settings from the Mouse icon in Control Panel. If you have a PS/2-style mouse, you should be in the clear.

Once you've installed the hardware and decided which COM port you want to use, do the following to set up the new device:

1. Start up the PC. If your system auto-detects the modem, follow Windows 95's Plug and Play routine (skip to step 4).

2. Go to Control Panel (select Start | Settings | Control Panel) and double-click the Modems icon.

3. Click the Add button. Click Next to proceed.

4. In the next dialog box, select the Don't select my modem check box. This will allow you to identify the modem yourself.

5. In the Manufacturers scroll-down list box, select the name of the vendor that made your modem. The Models list box should list product names specific to the company you selected.

6. In the Models scroll-down list box, select the specific model you're using, and click Next.

7. If the specific model isn't listed, insert the floppy disk that contains the modem's installation files into your A drive. Click the Have Disk button, and then double-click the .INF file that appears in the dialog box. Click Next.

8. In the next dialog box, select the COM port to use. You must click one of the choices in the box called Select the port to use with this modem.

9. Windows 95 will take a little while to install the driver software and update its records.

10. Click the Finish button to return to the Modem Properties page. You should see the newly installed modem listed in the text box.

Note: One welcome bit of news is that it is unlikely that you will find yourself messing with jumper switches during this routine. New modems do all their stuff in software, allowing you to change port settings without fishing around inside the case.

Dealing with Modem Trouble

As is the case with so many other PC components, you won't find yourself doing a lot of true repair jobs. Modems are solid-state devices that resemble sound and graphics boards in their make-up. When a chip or other component gets damaged on the modem card or inside the case, it is often most economical to have the unit replaced. In any case, it takes professional tools to fix major damage to modem components.

That said, a lot can go wrong. Modems must be installed around the PC's sometimes-elusive COM ports, and they can be dragged off-line by conflicting hardware such as mice. In addition, the interface to the public phone network opens all sorts of possible problems.

Troubleshooting COM Ports

Many modem troubles are caused by conflicts with mice, because both modems and mice want to use COM ports to connect to the PC. However, other devices can muscle in on your modem's territory, grabbing the IRQ or port address that your COM port has reserved.

> **Troubleshooting:** If you experience chronic or intermittent mouse problems that you can't figure out, you should check on your modem. You might be experiencing a COM port conflict, in which both the mouse and the modem want to use the same port. Because many users make use of the modem only occasionally, the perceived mouse problem might not crop up enough to warrant an aggressive look.

If you can't get your modem to respond, try changing its COM port setting. The second port might be free, allowing reliable operation. Do the following:

1. Double-click the Modems icon in Control Panel.
2. In the Modems Properties dialog box, select the device you want to adjust, and click the Properties button.
3. Click the Port drop-down control, and select a COM port setting other than the one that is active. If no other port is available, you might have to first add a new COM port by going to Control Panel, double-clicking Add New Hardware, and selecting Ports.
4. Click OK, and then click Close in the next dialog box in order for the changes to take effect.

Dealing with Dialing

Often, what seems like a modem problem is nothing more than a glitch in your modem's dialing properties. Windows 95 lets you assign permanent dialing routines to access outside lines, disable call waiting, and use a telephone billing card.

If the modem begins dialing but can't seem to connect with another line, do the following:

1. In Windows 95, from Control Panel, double-click the Modems icon.
2. Click the Dialing Properties button.
3. Check to make sure that the area code item matches the area code you're calling from.
4. In the How I dial from this location area, make sure that the settings for accessing an outside line, using a phone card, and disabling call waiting are set properly.
5. Also make sure that the phone is set to tone operation.

Troubleshooting: Under Windows 3.1 or 3.11 (Windows for Workgroups), modem installation and troubleshooting can be more difficult. It's important to keep track of IRQ assignments, COM port assignments, and I/O assignments, because the earlier versions of Windows won't do this for you. A common mistake is assigning the same value to the port address and the modem address, in the case of an internal modem. The COM port is the logical address that is assigned to a physical serial port connector, or it can apply to an internal device. The port address and modem address are not the same, so setting them to the same value will result in a resource conflict that produces unusual and confusing symptoms, such as having a modem that will go off-hook but not dial, or dial but not detect a carrier signal.

When you're troubleshooting modem difficulties under Windows 3.1 or 3.11, take care to write down the system settings as they are before you begin, and then document each change made until the system works and the modem responds correctly. Here are the most important parameters:

The COM port to be assigned to the modem

The IRQ to assign to the port and modem

The I/O address of the modem

The I/O address of the COM port

If problems occur with a non-Plug and Play modem under Windows 95, it is often more time-effective to replace the modem with one that is Plug and Play rather than manually wrestling with device conflicts and Plug and Play's attempts to intervene. That's what today's harried field technicians do. A new modem costs less than the time they would otherwise spend scratching their heads. On the other hand, who wants to trash a perfectly good modem that is only configured wrong?

Modems are often misidentified, especially by telecom software running under Windows 3.1 and 3.11. Also, sometimes hardware-specific default values are stored incorrectly. For this reason, your software might fail to identify the make and model of your modem.

continues

Software like that used to install America Online, for example, might misidentify your modem, even sometimes getting a very well-known model wrong, or it might not see your modem at all. If this happens and you're quite sure that the jumpers (if any), ports, and addresses are set correctly, try running Windows' dumb terminal program, found in the Accessories program group. If you can type AT (which means "Attention!" in modem-speak) and then press Enter and see the modem respond with OK, and then you can dial ATDT 12345 and press Enter and hear the modem dial, the fault can be placed on the telecom or application software that's attempting to identify your modem. Go back into that software and opt to manually specify the modem type instead of asking the software to do so. Select the most generic option on the list, usually "Hayes-compatible generic modem." If that selection doesn't work, try choosing a generic US Robotics modem of the correct maximum speed.

Summary

The arrival of the Internet has made the modem one of the most critical components of any PC. Yet many older systems came without a modem, or with one that operates at 14.4Kbps or slower data rates.

Fortunately, modems are affordable, costing as little as $100 for cutting-edge 56Kbps models. Meanwhile, Windows 95's improved communications facilities have helped take much of the sting out of modem setup and configuration. Given that a faster modem can enhance your Web browsing, cut your ISP bills, and save you time, it's clear that a modem upgrade is worth considering.

Meanwhile, the rapid growth of the Internet has prompted many developments in the digital realm. ISDN, ADSL, cable modems, and satellite systems are all competing to provide much greater bandwidth and reliability to your connections. Although all these options suffer from some drawback, such as limited access, high costs, or difficult setup, it is likely that the Internet connection of the future will not remain analog.

24

I/O
Add-Ons

Peter Norton®

Processors get faster, hard disks get bigger, and RAM gets less expensive. If all this seems woefully predictable, you can take heart in the vagaries of new, enhanced input/output technologies. Although improvements in the capabilities of SCSI and IDE bus technologies have been welcome, a spate of new buses are helping extend the capabilities of desktop and notebook PCs.

From wireless infrared communications to daisy-chained Universal Serial Bus, these new technologies make it easier than ever to move data among systems and peripherals. This chapter covers the following:

- The various types of enhanced I/O systems and devices and the means of adding their capabilities to existing PCs
- Advice and information to help you decide which I/O technologies are worth purchasing
- Upgrade instructions for various I/O peripherals
- Troubleshooting and repairing strategies for I/O products

I/O Upgrades: Let's Get Serial

Some of the most exciting upgrade opportunities for your PC might be components that enable advanced I/O capabilities. Behind these devices are a flurry of new standards and improved existing technologies. From enhanced printing to easy remote file access, these upgrades might be worth a look—particularly if you want to make use of new peripherals that take advantage of these I/O technologies.

The technologies involved are

- Universal Serial Bus (USB)
- IEEE 1394 FireWire
- PC Card (or PCMCIA) and CardBus
- IrDA-compliant infrared communications

PC97: If you want to make PC97 spec, you need these buses. Microsoft, Intel, and others are pushing hard to enhance the ease of use and installation of external devices, and these bus technologies are critical to that push. Plug and Play-aware designs in USB, FireWire, and PC Card/CardBus are make-or-break issues for PC makers trying to move their products into the consumer electronics mainstream.

Infrared communications, meanwhile, provide a critical wireless data on-ramp for devices. Remote controls, keyboards, and controllers running over a standard IR bus allow the creation of effective home-entertainment PCs. The ability to set up inexpensive ad hoc IR networks will be critical as more and more homes own multiple PCs.

One thing we're seeing is the adoption of streamlined serial bus architectures. Buses such as SCSI, enhanced IDE, and even PCI and ISA are all parallel bus technologies. In other words, they move groups of bits across many wires in lockstep. This approach works: PCI can push 132MBps by running 32 bits across at 33MHz. A proposal for a 64-bit PCI version running at 33 or 66MHz promises to extend that rate to about 264MB and 528MB in the future.

But parallel has problems, particularly when it comes to external buses. Getting lots of bits to cross wires in lockstep isn't easy, and timing issues get more and more difficult as speeds move up through 33MHz and beyond. This is particularly true of external bus architectures, in which electrical signals must travel long cables, braving external interference and crosstalk from other wires within the cable to deliver bits safely. Parallel schemes also get expensive, because the number of wires and pins needed for multiple data lanes adds cost to peripherals and systems.

Serial approaches, in contrast, use a single lane moving very quickly to meet or beat the performance of parallel buses. Again, the absence of complex timing interaction among multiple wires allows for much higher clock speed operation, even across a cable running several meters in length. Better yet, those speeds can be packaged into affordable, space-saving designs—making them potentially appropriate for desktop and mobile use.

Universal Serial Bus: First Among Equals

Of all the new I/O schemes being bandied about by engineers, this one stands the best chance of making an immediate impact on the platform. Several things account for USB's probable success, including low cost, powerful corporate backing, and a raging market need. In fact, many systems sold over the past six months already include USB connectors—although they're worthless until enabling driver software and compliant peripherals reach the market.

USB aims to take over the tasks now handled by your PC's overworked serial and parallel ports. Everything from printers and scanners to speakers, microphones, joysticks, and PDAs would hook into this standard port on the back of your PC. You already have enough ports, you say? Consider this: USB brings several critical talents to the PC that the serial and parallel port lack:

- 12Mbps throughput
- Plug and Play
- Hot swapping of circuit cards (allows swapping without restarting the PC)
- Daisy-chaining or the operation of more than one device on a single cable or bus
- Autotermination and detection

What It's For

More than the other new I/O technology, USB solves problems that are present right now. Both the parallel and serial ports are seriously overworked, forcing users to juggle peripherals that compete for scarce connector space. Things can get ugly fast. Anyone who has fished around among the tangle of cables at the back of a PC knows how difficult it can be to keep things straight.

USB can solve this problem by using a standard port to serve all sorts of peripherals. With a data rate of 12Mbps, USB is 10 times faster than the current serial bus and about 50 percent faster than the most advanced parallel port. That makes the bus appropriate for uses ranging from keyboards and mice to scanners, printers, and even telephones.

More important, USB is Plug and Play. With the proper device drivers and operating system support, devices plugged into the USB port are automatically detected and enabled by the system. Windows 95's virtual device drivers (known as VxDs) allow for dynamic loading and unloading of device capabilities. Unlike SCSI, in which each device must be manually identified via SCSI IDs, USB does all the work automatically.

Here are some of the peripherals that could employ USB for enhanced operation:

- Basic input (mouse, keyboard)
- Game controllers (joysticks, gamepads, head-mounted displays)
- Digital USB cameras for videoconferencing
- Digital audio speakers
- Scanning
- Printing

How It Works

USB frees up the connector logjam by allowing peripherals to hook to the USB bus through other peripherals (see Figure 24.1). Like SCSI, a peripheral such as a scanner or printer will generally have more than one USB port, allowing the device to hook to the system and to serve as a conduit for other devices downstream. Some devices, such as monitors, might feature *hubs*, which provide several ports.

Figure 24.1.
USB hubs can be found on monitors, scanners, or dedicated devices that serve as data centers for your USB peripherals.

Data moves up and down the four-wire USB cable. Devices can sit up to 50 feet from the host PC, and a maximum of 127 devices can run off the PC's USB controller. Higher-bandwidth devices such as scanners, printers, and sound hardware can run at up to 12Mbps, while less-demanding mice and joysticks run at a low-bandwidth mode of 1.5Mbps.

PC97: USB capability is part and parcel of the PC97 and PC98 specifications, and it's on Microsoft's menu for its Simply Interactive PC (SIPC) initiative. The reason is that USB eliminates the need for ornery parallel and serial ports and provides Plug and Play outside of the box. If you purchase a new system or motherboard, make sure that USB ports are provided. Often you'll see twin connectors placed low in the chassis, just off the motherboard plane.

Unlike the chaining SCSI specification, USB works using a star topology scheme, as shown in Figure 24.2. In this design, all devices operate downstream from a single USB controller—you can't install a second USB controller in a PC. Most desktop PCs have two USB ports coming from the central controller. Devices hanging off these ports might themselves serve up to three other devices. A maximum of 127 devices may be installed on the USB bus.

Figure 24.2.
USB allows a wide variety of peripherals to connect to each other, all answering back to a single host USB hub on the system. (Figure courtesy of the USB Organization)

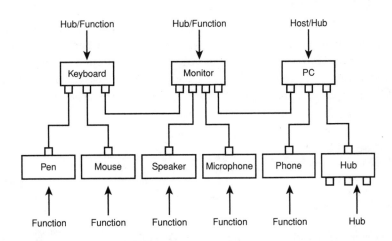

USB also allows low-power devices to run without an external power supply. Mice, keyboards, and joysticks are good examples of such devices. Scanners and printers will continue to need a separate power connection, whether working over USB or a parallel port.

IEEE 1394 FireWire: Convergence Cabling

USB is a sure bet to enhance the PC platform, but don't ignore the potential of the IEEE 1394 bus—more memorably known by its Apple-trademarked name, FireWire. This fast and furious serial bus takes aim at high-bandwidth peripherals such as video cameras and remote hard disks. Down the road, FireWire will be a viable successor to the IDE and SCSI buses. There is even speculation that FireWire could transform into a general-purpose system bus, supplanting PCI as the backbone of system communications (just don't hold your breath).

FireWire provides the following capabilities:

- Data throughput rates of 100, 200, and 400Mbps (with 800MB and greater data rates provided for in the new 1394.b specification)
- Plug and Play
- Hot swapping
- Daisy-chaining
- Autotermination and detection

As you can see, FireWire has many of the same attributes as USB, with one prominent exception— speed. Expect to pay for the added performance, because FireWire-enabled peripherals and adapters must use more sophisticated electronics and chipsets to manage the higher data rates.

What It's For

Where USB solves current problems, FireWire does more to open new opportunities. Video capture, for example, can take place over a general-purpose FireWire bus rather than a dedicated capture card. FireWire is already being used by consumer electronics companies such as Sony to connect new digital camcorders to PCs. Similarly, FireWire looks like a good bet to play a key role in PC convergence, connecting the PC to TVs, stereos, and other general-purpose devices (see Figure 24.3).

Figure 24.3.
FireWire covers some of the same ground as USB but weighs heavily on consumer electronics and multimedia. (Figure courtesy of Texas Instruments and the 1394 Trade Association)

Among the applications FireWire addresses are these:

- Digital camcorders and VCRs
- Videoconferencing
- Direct-to-home (DTH) satellite video and audio MPEG-2 data streams
- Musical synthesizers with MIDI and digital audio capabilities
- High-speed printers
- Hard disk drives
- Networking—in particular, home networks
- Cable TV and MMDS ("wireless cable") set-top boxes
- External DVD drives

How It Works

Like USB, FireWire is a self-terminating Plug and Play serial bus that can automatically detect devices as they are installed and removed. Again, dynamic device driver management is the key. 32-bit OSs such as Windows 95 and NT can load and unload device system software on-the-fly without requiring a reboot. In the case of FireWire, Microsoft expects to add support with the Windows 98 operating system, due in the first half of 1998.

FireWire is described as a noncyclic network that has finite branches. *Noncyclic* means that peripherals can't be set up to create loops, while a maximum of 16 devices may be strung together, daisy-chain fashion, between nodes (the *finite branch* part). The maximum distance between each device is 4.5 meters (although bridging hardware can extend this distance), allowing a daisy chain of 16 peripherals to extend up to 72 meters. FireWire can support up to 63 peripherals in this manner (see Figure 24.4).

Although FireWire supports up to 400Mbps operation, not all configurations take advantage of it. Most FireWire adapters, such as Adaptec's FireCard, provide 200Mbps operation. FireWire-compliant peripherals, meanwhile, are generally tuned for 100, 200, or 400Mbps operation.

Buying Tip: A 200Mbps FireWire peripheral will work on a 400Mbps FireWire adapter, but the reverse isn't true. If you plan on using FireWire for demanding, professional video-capture applications or the like, consider getting a FireWire adapter set for 400Mbps data rates. This will ensure that you have headroom for optimal performance. Also, if a 400Mbps device is daisy-chained between two 200Mbps devices, it can only run at the slower 200Mbps data rate.

It will be a while before you find any FireWire ports built into mainstream PCs. In addition to being an Apple-sponsored technology, FireWire's added cost makes it more difficult to incorporate into the PC platform. Expect Microsoft's support for FireWire in Windows 95 to lag well behind that of USB. In the meantime, add-in adapter cards and manufacturers' driver software allow upgraders to turn their PCs into FireWire-capable systems.

Figure 24.4.

Thin FireWire cables can carry video, audio, and data between connected peripherals over distances as great as 4.5 meters. (Photo courtesy of 1394 Trade Association)

Infrared Device Association: IrDA Beams Onto the Desktop

USB and FireWire are welcome technologies, to be sure. They're fast, they're convenient, and they bring Plug and Play technology to peripherals sorely in need of its benefits. What they won't do is alleviate the nasty tangle of wires and cables that plague virtually every desktop PC. These technologies cut down on the clutter by using a single cable standard, but the cables are there nonetheless.

Enter infrared communications. By managing the timing of invisible light pulses, infrared light can be used to pass bits back and forth between devices, without the use of connecting wires. This is the same concept used in TV remote controls. All that is needed are an IR emitter and receiver for each device and a standard way to interpret the light signals.

The Infrared Device Association (IrDA) got things moving by establishing a standard specification for IR communications. Although IrDA hardware is most frequently found on notebook PCs, a wide range of systems and peripherals can benefit from IR facilities.

What It's For

Obviously, IrDA is about communications. But more precisely, it is about convenient, cable-free connectivity, allowing PCs to access external devices or other systems without clumsy cables.

The following devices benefit from IR capability:

- Notebook PCs
- Handheld PCs, or Personal Digital Assistants (PDAs)
- Networked systems
- Ink jet printers and black-and-white laser printers
- Cordless mice and keyboards

Today, IR ports can be found on almost all notebooks and a good many handheld PCs. Many personal printers include IR ports as well. The benefit is obvious to anyone who has taken a notebook into a remote office and who needs to print documents. IrDA lets you simply beam your print job across the desk to a waiting printer. You don't need to hunt up a parallel cable or—worse yet—haul your own cable along to do print jobs on the road.

Even more promising is the ability to share files between notebook and desktop PCs. You can get your notebook on the network using a PC Card network interface card, but they tend to be pricey and prone to loss. Parallel or serial port communications over Windows 95's Direct Cable Connection facility or Traveling Software's LapLink are clumsy, requiring users to fish around behind the overcrowded backsides of PCs to hook up cables.

Unfortunately, desktop IR never took off. You won't find many PCs with IrDA ports on their front bezels. However, you can purchase IR ports that hook into a dedicated IR card. The small module hooks to the back of your PC using a cable (ironic, isn't it?), allowing it to be placed for maximum convenience. These ports can be used to talk to notebooks, printers, or other IrDA-compliant devices.

How It Works

The first IrDA peripherals ran at a relatively pokey 115.2Kbps. That's fast enough for simple file transfers and print jobs, but not enough for more-demanding uses. Reconciling the contents of a notebook and a desktop hard disk, for example, can involve hundreds of megabytes. Likewise, complex print jobs can be several megabytes in size.

The Fast IrDA specification, called FIR, addresses this problem by boosting maximum bandwidth to 4Mbps. Although this isn't as fast as the USB specification, it's more than enough for the vast majority of IR-based transactions. After all, you probably won't have to run real-time video over a wireless connection. More important, FIR peripherals can talk to older IrDA devices (see Figure 24.5).

Figure 24.5.
You'll need an external IR transceiver, like this ActiSys model, to share data between your desktop and IR-equipped notebooks. It can handle up to 4Mbps. (Photo courtesy of ActiSys)

IrDA has its drawbacks. For one thing, the infrared signal requires a direct line of sight, because any objects between the two ports will make data transfers impossible. Likewise, the IR ports need to be aligned to facilitate line-of-site communications, which can be a challenge, depending on where the ports are installed on some devices. You'll also need to dedicate your second serial port to the IR device, which really limits your options for other devices if you already have an external modem.

Mobile Marvels: PC Card and CardBus

In 1990, a group called Personal Computer and Memory Card International Association (PCMCIA) ratified a standard for credit card-sized peripherals that plug into tiny slots. Designed specifically for notebooks, this standard has helped create a market of tiny modems, LAN cards, and even multimedia peripherals. Today, any notebook you purchase will probably have one or more slots for the PCMCIA specification—known as PC Card.

The original PC Card specification has since been improved. Driving the move was the need for faster data rates and more direct access to system resources in order to support a wider range of peripherals. The enhanced bus, called CardBus, promises to deliver PCI-like bus performance over a modular, externally accessible bus architecture.

PC Card

There are actually several varieties of PC Card peripherals, demarcated by the height of the card. Right now, three official categories exist, and a fourth is under review. All three existing categories use the same 68-pin design. Table 24.1 outlines the categories and their intended markets.

Table 24.1. PC Card types.

PC Card Type	Card Height	Products
Type I	3.3mm	Flash memory
Type II	5mm	Modems, LAN adapters, audio/game cards, SCSI interface
Type III	10.5mm	Hard disks
Type IV	To be determined	To be determined

The current PC Card bus uses a 16-bit wide interface, running at 16MHz. The resulting throughput is roughly equivalent to that of an ISA bus card. This is more than enough speed for most communication and even mass-storage peripherals. Even fast 100Mbps LAN cards will run acceptably on the PC Card interface, although the faster CardBus scheme will allow greater performance in some applications.

Perhaps most important, PC Card was Plug and Play before Microsoft's Windows 95 turned it into a catch phrase. Thanks to a complex system of BIOS updates and PC Card drivers, these devices can be plugged in and taken out at will. Device drivers load and unload automatically, a process known as *hot-swapping*. You can complete a dial-up session with a PC Card modem, yank the card, install a LAN adapter, and be ready to log on to the network within a few seconds.

However, PC Card lacks direct memory access (DMA) and bus mastering, thus limiting performance for multimedia data transfers. The lack of DMA capability means that Sound Blaster-compatible PC Card products are impossible to build, because the standard demands a DMA address. PC Card also lacks power management features, which means that PC Card modems, for example, draw power even when they're not in use.

CardBus: The Second Coming

CardBus builds on the success of PC Card while addressing its most glaring problems. What's more, CardBus is intended to serve as a true, modular, general-purpose bus, just as PCI does for desktops. The difference is that you don't need to come face-to-face with intimidating circuit boards and silicon chips in order to install a device.

It's no surprise that performance gets a big boost. CardBus beefs up the data pathways to a hefty 32 bits running at a fast 33MHz. The result is a bus that is as fast and wide as PCI, matching its impressive 132MBps bursting data throughput. CardBus also moves to a 3.3-volt design that reduces power draw and heat dissipation.

CardBus peripherals are now starting to hit the market, but many notebooks continue to ship with the older (and cheaper) PC Card slots. Desktop PCs, meanwhile, can be outfitted with a PC Card reader, as shown in Figure 24.6. If you're buying a new notebook, definitely look for one with a CardBus slot. Over the next three years, CardBus peripherals will add tremendous value to existing notebooks. If you're stuck with an old PC Card bus, you won't be able to take advantage of these products.

Figure 24.6.
If you want to share PC Card peripherals with your desktop, you'll need to buy an adapter such as Card Dock to do so. (Photo courtesy of Adaptec Corp.)

Architecture: In addition, CardBus will probably adopt some implementation of a proprietary Toshiba technology called Zoomed Port Video (ZPV) or Zoom Video (ZV), depending on who's doing the marketing. Zoom Video specifically addresses video capture and playback on notebook PCs, allowing video data to be transferred directly to the graphics adapter frame buffer without going first to the host CPU or memory. At the same time, audio data is streamed directly to the digital-to-analog converter.

ZV allows for high-performance video capture on notebook PCs. By setting up direct data pathways to sound and graphics hardware, the system CPU can stay out of time-consuming transactions and focus on other tasks. ZV peripherals plugged into enhanced CardBus slots will be able to grab video streams, perform compression or decompression, and move the data to sound and graphics hardware on-the-fly.

Buying Bandwidth: A Guide to the New I/O

So you want to add I/O capability to your new or existing PC. What's the best option? It depends on what you need to do. Although USB, FireWire, and IrDA all boast intriguing capabilities, they all serve very different needs.

That said, even the best technology won't go far without support. Even if USB or FireWire sounds like something that can help you get more out of your PC, check to make sure that peripherals are available to work with it. Otherwise, you will end up buying the digital equivalent of an exercise machine—perfectly good technology that never gets used.

Compatibility: In most cases, none of your existing peripherals will be set up for USB or FireWire. This means that you should factor in the potential cost of upgrading these peripheral devices alongside the cost of adding a bus adapter. More important, you must make sure that USB-compatible products are available for the types of peripherals you're considering.

When Do Upgrades Make Sense?

Upgrading to a bus is like buying a house: It's not serving its purpose until you furnish it. In the case of USB and FireWire, actually furnishing your bus upgrade might be tougher than you think. New peripherals can take a long time to emerge, because vendors move cautiously before adding the cost of new connectors and drivers to their existing products.

USB is a case in point. USB ports have been appearing on desktop systems for nearly a year, and Microsoft has told anyone who will listen that native USB support will be woven into the Windows 98 operating system. Yet as of summer of 1997, very few USB-compliant peripherals had reached the market. The lesson is that you need to be patient. No multibillion-dollar industry changes overnight, and the potential risk for vendors moving to USB (or any other standard) too soon is enormous.

More important, you should time an upgrade with a peripheral purchase. For example, if you're thinking about buying a new scanner, you might want to look into available USB-compatible models. If you find something you like, this might be a good time to start the switch by purchasing a USB adapter card and a USB-compatible scanner to run off it (see Figure 24.7). Future peripheral purchases, whether joysticks or mice, could also take advantage of the new hardware.

Figure 24.7.
Older PCs can get access to USB peripherals by way of an inexpensive Adaptec card. The PCI-based CSA 6700 from CMD costs $59. (Photo courtesy of CMD)

Buying Tip: Keep your wits about you. A USB scanner might sound cool, but if it's the only external device you use (aside from a keyboard or mouse), USB probably isn't worth the added expense. You can save more than a few bucks by getting a low-cost parallel port scanner (such as Visioneer's PaperPort). Without other peripherals to contend with, you will never run across the port-shortage problems that plague many users.

The following sections discuss three general application areas:

- Mainstream home and office
- Video capture and connection to consumer electronics
- Mobile computing

Mainstream Home and Office

If you have a PC that you use for office-centric productivity applications and multimedia games and titles, USB will provide the most value. With its 12Mbps data rate, USB promises to become the workhorse external data bus of mainstream PCs. Best of all, USB is as close to a sure thing as you will find in the sometimes-slippery arena of PC standards.

Just take a look at the devices USB is tailored to service: scanner (see Figure 24.8), printers, mice, keyboards, digital cameras, PDAs, joysticks—even speakers. We're not talking about rocket science here. Although USB's Plug and Play and dynamic device loading are neat features, the bus itself basically shoulders the unglamorous work now performed by serial and parallel ports.

Figure 24.8.
The Logitech PageScan USB scanner is one of the first scanners to use the USB bus. One advantage: It doesn't require a separate power cord as other scanners do. (Photo courtesy of Logitech Corp.)

Here's my advice: If you're buying a new PC for a home office, make sure that USB is part of the picture. If possible, get started now by configuring your new PC with USB peripherals whenever possible.

Performance: Gamers in particular should check into USB for joysticks, gamepads, head-mounted displays, and other devices. For joysticks, the digital USB connection significantly improves the precision and efficiency of joystick performance over that of standard analog models. Your system must constantly poll analog joysticks for positional data, tying up the processor and affecting performance by as much as 10 or 15 percent. A digital USB joystick, on the other hand, could use a standard software interface—such as Microsoft DirectInput—to send data to the CPU without requiring constant hand-holding. The result is more-up-to-date joystick data gathered at a fraction of the cost in system resources.

Upgrade Advice: One great way to get started with USB is to purchase a monitor that has a USB hub built in to the bezel. These displays use a standard VGA connector to handle video signals, of course, but they also provide several USB ports conveniently embedded into the front panel to plug in compliant peripherals. This setup makes it easy to hook mice, keyboards, and joysticks into a single hub rather than daisy-chaining them awkwardly around your desktop.

Small and home offices might benefit from IR communications as well, particularly if notebooks are being used as either primary or travel PCs. IR makes great sense if you want to share a printer among two or three PCs but you don't want to set up a formal network. Each user can simply beam his or her print jobs directly to the printer.

Likewise, an office that has a mix of desktop and notebook PCs might benefit from the use of IR adapters on desktop systems. People who travel can quickly replicate files on their notebook PCs, eliminating the need to swap disks or use external Zip drives or other media.

Digital Consumer Electronics and Video

If USB is for the computer crowd, FireWire is the stuff of home theaters and video studios. Although the high-bandwidth FireWire bus won't get the mass market support that USB is wrapping up, the architecture serves its niche extremely well.

Who needs FireWire? If you do any video capture or editing, consider this technology. Vendors such as Sony, Matsushita, and Panasonic all sell FireWire-enabled digital video products, such as camcorders and VCRs. The bus allows for easy transfer of digital video to your PC, without the use of bulky and difficult video capture cards. Because most system vendors are unlikely to build FireWire connectors into their designs, you will probably need to add a FireWire adapter card to your system (see Figure 24.9).

Figure 24.9.
Adaptec's AHA-8945 card is a combination FireWire and SCSI PCI adapter. (Photo courtesy of Adaptec Corp.)

Likewise, FireWire might become the common currency between PCs and consumer electronics. Hitachi, for example, plans to introduce FireWire to its DVD players in 1998, which should allow them to be used both as DVD-ROM drives for the PC and as DVD players for the TV. Likewise, Sony and others expect to add FireWire connections to upcoming consumer audio components.

Another possible area is for home networks. PC makers such as Compaq and IBM see a future for home-based networks, where a single server PC might work in conjunction with other devices. FireWire plays a key role in many of these plans. The Plug and Play technology, high bandwidth, and prospects for adoption by both computer and consumer electronics companies position it as a superior bus for this application. Certainly it beats trying to foist cantankerous Ethernet network interface cards and cabling on the home market.

Mobile Computing

With powerful MMX-capable notebooks providing nearly all the power of cutting-edge desktops, the need for effective notebook buses is vital. Here, a combination of enhanced performance and wireless capability is in demand. Notebooks now need to be able to do everything that desktops do—including video capture and playback—as well as provide easy data-sharing capabilities.

For high-performance peripherals, the emerging CardBus architecture is the way to go. On notebooks that have CardBus slots built in, credit card-sized peripherals can provide data rates of up to 132MBps, matching the performance of the desktop PCI bus. Of course, you'll need to have a CardBus-capable notebook.

On the connectivity side, IrDA-compliant infrared communications make it easy to share data. This standard allows printers, scanners, PDAs, and notebook systems to share data without using bulky cables or wires.

Anyone who travels with a notebook computer appreciates the importance of a wireless bus. Each additional device and wire represent yet another valuable component to be lost or damaged. Additional components quickly become a huge nuisance as they join the unruly pile of batteries, power cords, external power supplies, PC Card modems, phone cords, and external floppy drives that are already stuffed into many PC carrying cases.

There's one problem. If you have a notebook PC that lacks IrDA, you won't be able to add it without actually buying a separate IR port. If you've purchased a notebook in the last two years, however, it should come equipped with an IrDA port.

Buying Tip: If you're thinking about buying a new notebook, look for an IrDA port before you make your purchase. Usually the port appears as a flat, smoke-colored, rectangular panel on the side or back of the notebook chassis. This panel must face the other IR port in order for communications to work. This is one reason why notebooks that have a rear-mounted port, or that have two separate ports, are preferable to those that have a single side-mounted IR port.

Upgrading to a New Bus

If your PC doesn't have one of these buses already built in, you'll need to upgrade. In general, the best way to do so is to install a multi-I/O card into an add-in card slot. The ports for the newly added bus will be available on the backplate of the card.

When Not to Upgrade

Before you rush out and buy hardware, take an inventory of your system. You might find that your PC is already outfitted with the connectors you need, and that an upgrade is really just a matter of handling drivers. You might also be able to get by with an external device, avoiding the hassle of installing an add-in card.

Older 486 PCs might lack the facilities to support some I/O upgrades. For example, an old 486 PC outfitted with only ISA bus slots won't have what it takes to support the fast-moving FireWire bus. It might also lack key Plug and Play BIOS facilities. Likewise, if all the fast PCI slots on your PC are taken, you'll have to find a way to free one up before you can install a FireWire upgrade card.

Also, keep your wits about you. A 400Mbps FireWire connector might sound really cool, but do you need that kind of bandwidth? If you're slinging mice and keyboards instead of high-quality video, you should stick with more mundane technologies like USB. Likewise, if your setup works well with existing parallel and serial ports, you can't go wrong by waiting. All this stuff will only get cheaper.

Making the Upgrade

So you've decided to upgrade to one of the new I/O technologies, and your system has what it takes to do the deed. Now it's time to roll up your sleeves and get to work. The following sections give you brief insights into installing each of the four buses.

USB: Upgrades for the Everyman

The most likely upgrade you face is to USB, since it's gaining the most support among peripheral product makers and is reasonably affordable. Although there were very few USB upgrade cards at the time this chapter was written, CMD Technology of Irvine, California was marketing an upgrade card for PCI-based systems. The following steps are based on their product:

1. Shut down the PC, unplug the power supply, and remove the case.

2. After grounding yourself, find a free PCI bus slot and remove the protective backplane cover (you'll need a flat-head or Torx screwdriver).

3. Install the USB controller card, being careful to press it firmly but carefully into the open slot.

4. Plug in the USB cable and hook it to a USB-compliant device, such as a mouse, keyboard, joystick, or monitor-top camera.

5. Start the PC. Windows 95 will detect the new hardware and will launch the Add New Hardware wizard.

6. Insert the driver disk that came with the USB add-in card. Click the Next button to start the installation routine.

7. When you're asked to detect hardware, click the No radio button, and then click Next.

8. In the Device Type scroll-down list box, select Unknown Device and click Next.

9. In the next dialog box, click the Have Disk button, and then double-click the appropriate .INF file on the file menu that appears.

10. Windows 95 will load the new driver and inform you when it is done.

11. Restart the PC. Your USB card will now be active. If everything works normally, close and seal the case.

FireWire: Now We're Talking Hot

For high-performance peripherals and convergence-oriented electronics, FireWire is the way to go. You'll need to be careful about your selection of products, though, because Microsoft isn't rushing to get FireWire drivers and support built into its operating system. Still, a reliable vendor should be able to provide a card that delivers on the attractive promise of FireWire.

In many ways, a FireWire add-in card upgrade is almost identical to that of a USB peripheral. Here are the steps to follow:

1. Shut down the PC, unplug the power supply, and remove the case.

2. After grounding yourself, find a free PCI bus slot and remove the protective backplane cover (you'll need a Phillips-head screwdriver).

3. Install the FireWire controller card, being careful to press it firmly but carefully into the open slot.

4. Plug in the FireWire cable and hook it to a FireWire-compliant device, such as a mouse, keyboard, joystick, or monitor-top camera.

5. Start the PC. Windows 95 will detect the new hardware and will launch the Add New Hardware wizard.

6. Insert the driver disk that came with the FireWire add-in card. Click the Next button to start the installation routine.

7. When you're asked to detect hardware, click the No radio button, and then click Next.

8. In the Device Type scroll-down list box, select Unknown Device and click Next.

9. In the next dialog box, click the Have Disk button, and then double-click the appropriate .INF file in the file menu that appears.

10. Windows 95 will load the new driver and inform you when it is done.

11. Restart the PC. Your FireWire card will now be active. If everything works normally, close and seal the case.

PC Card: Convenience Upgrades for Frequent Swappers

A PC Card adapter might not be an obvious upgrade choice for desktops unless you need to do things like swap hard disks (or store them off-site for security). A PC Card adapter is also a terrific way to share peripherals and data with notebooks.

Unlike the previous two installations, installing a PC Card adapter and reader means digging into drive bays. An adapter card interfaces with the system, while a PC Card reader gets mounted into one of the externally accessible drive bays, allowing you to add and remove cards conveniently.

Here's what you do:

1. Shut down the PC, unplug the power supply, and remove the case.

2. After grounding yourself, find a free PCI bus slot and remove the protective backplane cover (you'll need a Phillips-head screwdriver).

3. Install the PC Card controller card, being careful to press it firmly but carefully into the open slot.

4. Install the PC Card reader. Find an open externally accessible drive bay (preferably a $3^1/_2$-inch bay) and pry off the bezel cover that conceals it.

5. Fit the power and data cables into the appropriate sockets on the reader, being careful to match up the pin 1 orientation. Thread the wires through the front of the drive bay so that they hang loose onto the motherboard.

6. Slide in the PC Card reader module, lining it up with the mounting brackets.

7. Line up the mounting screw holes in the drive with the spaces in the drive brackets. Hold the drive in place and screw in the supplied screws.

8. Once the reader is in place, connect the data cable to the matching port on the adapter card. Again, be careful with connector alignments.

9. Now connect the power cable to the device.

10. Start the PC. Windows 95 will detect new hardware and will launch the Add New Hardware wizard.

11. Insert the driver disk that came with the PC Card or CardBus add-in card. Click the Next button to start the installation routine.

12. When you're asked to detect hardware, click the No radio button, and then click Next.

13. In the Device Type scroll-down list box, select Unknown Device and click Next.

14. In the next dialog box, click the Have Disk button, and then double-click the appropriate .INF file in the file menu that appears.

15. Windows 95 will load the new driver and inform you when it is done.

16. Restart the PC. Your PC Card reader will now be active.

Infrared: Blinded by the Light

An infrared adapter upgrade is the easiest of the group from a hardware standpoint, because it doesn't involve cracking open the case. IrDA-compliant IR ports run directly off the serial or parallel bus—although you can also find ISA-based adapter cards.

The bigger challenge is software. IrDA ports need to access those elusive COM resources, inviting potential conflicts with modems, mice, and other peripherals. Before you start, make sure you take a good hard look at your COM port resources. Figure out who's using what. Check the Modem icon in Windows 95's Device Manager to see what COM port it's using. Also make sure that your mouse isn't riding the other COM port. (It won't be if it's a PS/2-style unit.)

If you have a COM port to spare, you're ready to roll. Here's what you need to do:

1. Shut down the PC.

2. Plug in the IrDA-compliant transmitter/receiver device.

3. Start the PC. Windows 95 will detect new hardware and will launch the Add New Hardware wizard.

4. Insert the driver disk that came with the IR module. Click the Next button to start the installation routine.

5. When you're asked to detect hardware, click the No radio button, and then click Next.

6. In the Device Type scroll-down list box, select Unknown Device and click Next.

7. In the next dialog box, click the Have Disk button, and then double-click the appropriate .INF file in the file menu that appears.

8. Windows 95 will load the new driver and inform you when it is done.

9. Restart the PC. Your IR module will now be active.

Summary

Some of the coolest things in the evolution of the PC architecture are happening among buses. USB and FireWire represent the first mature external buses for PC users since the introduction of SCSI. And if things go well, they will boast greater ease of use and affordability than their predecessors. Now the wait is on to see how large a market exists for these peripherals and their drivers.

Meanwhile, IR and PC Card technologies significantly enhance notebook computing. They also might play a growing roll on desktop PCs as more and more users seek ways to juggle files among multiple computers. If you find yourself struggling with floppy disks or Windows 95's less-than-perfect Direct Cable Connection facility, an IR port or PC Card drive could be a terrific addition.

25

Networks

Peter Norton®

The explosive growth of the Internet has transformed the PC into a vital communications device. But anyone working in a corporate office probably saw the revolution coming five or 10 years ago, in the form of PC-based networks. E-mail, shared files, and network-based applications and services have long been critical tools for corporate PC users.

Today, networks are pervasive. Everyone from Fortune 100 businesses to the local coffee shop run connected PCs to share data and handle communication. And now networks are poised to enter the home. For instance, you might be contemplating hooking your work laptop to your home PC. With many home users buying their second and even third PC, a network makes it possible to get further use out of aging systems that would otherwise be put out to pasture.

In this chapter, you will learn to

- Understand how networks work, including the functioning of individual network components such as interface cards and cabling

- Make proper buying decisions for network hardware and software

- Recognize and troubleshoot common network problems

- Set up and maintain a Windows 95-based local area network, using Ethernet network interface cards and 10-BaseT wiring

Overview

The basic mission of any network is to move information from point A to point B quickly, efficiently, and inexpensively. Networks let you distribute information and services, whether between two computers sharing a printer or among the millions of computers that make up the world's largest network, the Internet.

The *local area network,* or LAN, is just one of many tools that lets a computer communicate with other devices. LANs let one computer share information and resources with other computers that have a need for this information (or resources). The goal of this chapter is to teach you about some of the more common networking technologies and show you how you can implement or augment them.

Networks, Networks Everywhere

The pieces of a local area network seem simple when viewed from a distance. If you look more closely, you'll see that each piece constitutes a complex system of its own. Perhaps most critical is that all the components of a network—whether network interface cards (NICs), cables, routers, or drivers—must work in conjunction with all the other networking components, often from a wide variety of vendors. With that in mind, we will start with the "big picture" and move in.

The following components make up a network:

- Server and client/workstation computers or peer-to-peer workstation computers
- Network interface cards (NICs)
- Network hubs and cabling
- The network operating system

Servers and Clients

Like love, war, and the tango, it takes at least two to make a network. In its simplest form, a network might be just two PCs, one being the server that shares its resources with other computers on the network. The resources can be anything from peripherals such as printers and modems to application software such as spreadsheets and databases. In many home networks, a peer-to-peer scheme is used, in which all PCs on the network act at the same level and share resources with each other.

The second computer in our novice network is the client, or workstation. This is the computer that needs to use the resources that the server or other peer computer makes available. In an office, clients are the systems sitting on each employee's desk. If you're browsing the Web, client machines are those being used to view data (while servers "serve it up"). Note that you will often hear the term *peer-to-peer network*. What this means is that all computers on the network fill the role of server and workstation. In essence, a peer-to-peer network is when no single computer maintains the dedicated server role. Basically, it is a peer of the rest of the computers on the network.

> **Note:** In actuality, any computer can be a server or a workstation. It's just that we tend to designate the role of a computer based on which role it fills most of the time.

Network Interface Cards

Networked PCs need to connect to each other somehow, which is where the network interface card, or NIC as it is known in the industry, comes in. The physical workhorse of your network connection, it translates information moving over the network into standard-sized "packets" of data. These packets are translated into electrical signals, which are passed onto the cable.

On the receiving side, a network card receives the electrical signal and then decodes and reassembles the individual packets for delivery to your computer. As part of its job, the NIC checks incoming packets to make sure all the packets were received correctly—a function called *error checking*.

NICs plug into the add-in card slots of PCs and are available for ISA, PCI, and EISA bus slots. Although in the past most clients used ISA-based NICs, the higher bandwidth, faster processing (bus mastering and so on), and Plug and Play convenience of the PCI bus have made PCI NICs a growing market. The act of upgrading your network speed will definitely benefit from the fast PCI bus connection. Companies such as 3Com, Intel, and Adaptec sell NICs.

Network Card Considerations

There are a multitude of NIC cards on the market today, manufactured by companies big and small. In my experience, one thing holds true: You get what you pay for. If you buy on a budget, you might have to put up with some tough compromises. For example, Windows 95 Plug and Play capabilities—an important consideration—might be lacking, or the drivers might lack full compatibility with your software and hardware. Unless you've had extensive experience with NIC cards, I suggest that you buy a NIC from a well-known manufacturer such as Intel, IBM, or 3Com.

> **Note:** A NIC can cost anywhere from $50 on the low end to $100 for the top of the line. You must weigh the monetary savings against the amount of time it takes to install and maintain a NIC. How much is your time worth?

Once your NIC is physically installed in the PC, you need to hook it to the network cable. If you're using an Ethernet network, you'll find yourself looking at two possible connectors on the back of your PC. The first will be a small circle that looks similar to the cable TV connector on your television; it services a coaxial or BNC connector. The other connection, which looks like a common phone jack—although it's a bit larger—is for twisted-pair wiring. You will use only one of these connectors, and you'll know which one after you've gotten through configuring the card (see Figure 25.1).

Figure 25.1.
Not all NICs are created equal. Here, one card provides both coaxial and RJ-45 network connections. (Photo courtesy of Adaptec, Inc.)

You also need to configure Windows 95 to use the NIC. If you're willing to shell out a little extra money, it would be worth your while to get a NIC that is Plug and Play. It can make building your network much less complicated.

Cabling

Not to understate the issue, but networks are really about plumbing. Exchange bits for drips and packet sniffers for adjustable wrenches, and suddenly you're a plumber. It's no surprise, then, that the physical media or cable used by networked PCs to communicate plays much the same role as a water pipe running from one area in a house to another.

Of course, your pipes need to fit and be appropriate for the job. The type of cable you will choose depends on the environment in which you build the network, as well as other mitigating factors such as cost and availability. The most common cable you will hear of is unshielded twisted pair, or UTP. There are others as well, such as coaxial and fiber optic.

Down to the Wire: A Critical Choice

Networked PCs must have some sort of connection, whether via physical cable, radio, or infrared transmission. But there are serious repercussions in choosing cabling. You must balance cost against efficiency and usability. If you buy cheap cable and your LAN grows, you might end up having to rewire the entire network—a potentially costly and disruptive process with larger networks.

For the purposes of this chapter, we will limit ourselves to a discussion of physical cables. Three common types of cable get used in most networks:

- Coaxial cable: Similar to the cable found in your cable TV hookup, network-based coaxial cabling comes in two varieties: thinnet and thicknet. The difference boils down to the distance these cables can support before signals degrade. Thicknet can carry a signal about 500 meters, and thinnet can run for 200 meters. However, thicknet is physically less flexible than thinnet, making it difficult to wire, and it is more expensive. Both types provide good resistance to interference, which reduces transmission problems. One problem with coax is that if one of your workstations goes down, all of them go down until the problem is resolved.

- Twisted pair: The most common network cable, twisted pair also comes in two flavors: shielded (STP) and unshielded (UTP). Most ethernet networks use unshielded category 5 twisted pair, which can run about 100 meters on a 10Mbps ethernet network. (Lengths for 100Mbps operation are shorter.)

- Fiber optic: Fiber optic deserves passing mention as an upcoming transport of network traffic. Limited to professional installations for networks requiring high speed and reliability, fiber optic cable often serves as backbone wiring for large LANs or other data networks.

It is much faster than 10Mbps ethernet, immune to electromagnetic interference, and can run longer distances without signal degradation. The problem is that this miracle wire is much more expensive than the other cabling and is more difficult to install. Of course, we can hope that one day all cabling will be fiber optic!

If you're building a small network in your home or in a small office, the best thing to do is grab some precut lengths of UTP (unshielded twisted pair) cable and set up your network that way. If you're designing a bigger LAN, I suggest that you get help. In all the corporate environments I have been in, outside contractors have always handled the cabling. This is because cabling an office is difficult and time-consuming and must be done right the first time. Having your LAN administrator or office manager test cables with a voltmeter is not a productive use of that person's time.

> **Note:** Not only is wiring an office expensive and time-consuming, but it's extremely disruptive as well. Employees often need to vacate their work spaces during the wiring process, and network service can be disrupted as well. For this reason, most corporate wiring jobs occur over the weekend—but even then, the complexity of the task can spill over into the work week. Your best bet is to spend a lot of time planning and preparing for problems.

The Network Operating System

The network operating system—or, more precisely, an operating system designed to control and operate a network—is needed to optimize the sharing of resources among machines across a distance. Novell NetWare (or, more recently, IntranetWare) and Microsoft Windows NT Server are just two examples of network operating systems. These are usually installed on server PCs, or they can be added to the existing operating system.

Client PCs, meanwhile, run standard desktop operating systems but require tweaks to talk to the server and its OS. Windows 95, for example, comes with drivers and protocols for the more mainstream networks such as NetWare and NT Server.

In addition to the network operating system, you will need to choose the protocol that the network will use. This is kind of like air traffic controllers all agreeing to speak English, whether the airport is in Osaka or Omaha. You might have heard terms such as TCP/IP, IPX, and NetBeui mentioned before. These are the three most common transport protocols used today. We will examine each of these protocols to help you decide which one is right for you.

NetBeui

NetBeui is an extremely fast network protocol. Unfortunately, it can be used only on small local area networks. This is because NetBeui lacks any real "addressing" overhead that other protocols carry. It is designed to operate on small-to-medium-sized LANs. You can liken this to a small cocktail party where all the people know everybody's names. You don't need name tags, so there are no awkward introductions or "addressing" that can slow a conversation.

This is a Microsoft-designed protocol and therefore is limited to Microsoft networking—which is ideal if you're going to connect three or four Windows workstations and you want an easy implementation. (NetBeui is included with the Windows 95 CD.)

IPX/SPX

IPX/SPX is a Novell network protocol that is designed specifically to work with Novell's NOS (NetWare). However, it will work with Windows NT and Windows 95. (Microsoft calls its version of IPX/SPX NWLink or NetWare Link.) Small, fast, and relatively efficient, IPX/SPX is only slightly slower than NetBeui. IPX/SPX is a *routable* protocol, which means that the "addressing" is more specific than with NetBeui.

The postal system works as an analogy here, since it is essentially a network in its simplest form. If I lived in a very small town that had its own post office, I could write a letter to another local person and address the envelope (or the packet in the case of a network) using the recipient's name and nothing else. The mail carrier, as well as everybody else in town, knows where each person lives and doesn't need a street address or zip code. The mail carrier will look at the recipient's name and put the letter in that person's box.

NetBeui is like that. You want to send a file to computer1. The file is broken into packets by the NIC and sent to the network. Since there is only one computer1 on the LAN and the LAN is limited in size, only one box will receive these packets.

With IPX/SPX, the system changes. The network expects more address information and also expects that not every computer is on the LAN or in the same "town." Therefore, IPX carries more addressing information in its packets. This allows the information to be routed, or sent to another LAN that is attached to your LAN with a router. (Think of a router as a post office that sorts by zip code and then sends the mail to the "local" post office.)

Using this example, think of the extra addressing information (in IPX/SPX) as the city, state, and zip code of a mailing address. Now, when you want to send mail (or a network packet) to a friend in another city (or another computer on another LAN attached to your local network by a router), the mail carrier reads the zip code and knows to forward it to the post office at that zip code. Then the second mail carrier will deliver the mail. That way, your carrier doesn't have to know everyone in the entire world in order to deliver mail.

Perhaps you're thinking, "That's great, but how does it affect me?" Well, the truth is, probably not much. If you're building a small network, the extra addressing information that the IPX has is just overhead slowing down your network.

TCP/IP

TCP/IP (transmission control protocol/Internet protocol) was developed to allow dissimilar machines to talk to one another. The Department of Defense wanted their computers to be able to communicate with other machines of different types, so they built this suite of protocols to deal with the problem. Since then, TCP/IP has grown into the protocol used by the Internet. It lets all sorts of computers share information across the world's largest network.

Like IPX, TCP/IP (IP for short) is a routable protocol. It is meant to be passed through the router on its way to its destination. You might have had some experience with TCP/IP if you have an Internet connection on your PC. The downside of TCP/IP is its addressing scheme. Each PC or node on your network must have a specific address assigned to it.

Building a Network

The following sections outline the construction of a very simple network. They describe an environment that has one machine acting as a server and two machines acting as workstations.

In order to build our network, we need the following parts:

- Three computers
- Three pieces of cabling (UTP CAT 5, with RJ-45 connectors)
- One hub
- Three NIC cards
- A protocol (NetBeui)

Note: A *hub* is a networking device to which multiple computers can connect (see Figure 25.2). It functions as a type of large intersection, where the hub acts as the traffic cop, directing network traffic to and from the correct port. It allows computers in a network to be arranged in a star rather than a continuous ring (see Figure 25.3). Small hubs are relatively cheap, costing about $100 for a five-port hub. This is a good investment when you're building a network.

Figure 25.2.

An inexpensive hub lets your networked PCs pass data back and forth freely.

Figure 25.3.

Star hubs versus ring hubs.

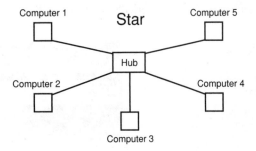

Building the Infrastructure

In order for our three computers to talk to each other, we need to put the cabling in place. First, place the hub somewhere central to all three computers. Connect one side of each cable to the first three ports available on the hub. The other end of each cable goes into the matching port on the back of your NIC, which we will now install on your PC. (Make sure you plug in your hub!)

Installing the NIC

Installing the physical NIC card is the same for each of the computers. You open the back of your PC and choose an available slot that fits the bus type of your card (PCI, ISA, and so on).

> **Note:** As I mentioned, using a NIC that is Plug and Play is an excellent way to avoid configuration conflicts.

It is important to ensure that the NIC card is seated properly. I have seen many NIC cards get fried because they weren't inserted correctly. Once you have your NIC card securely installed, close the computer and start Windows 95.

If your NIC is Plug and Play, Windows will recognize it and add it to your configuration. If your NIC is not Plug and Play, you need to follow these steps:

1. Select Start | Settings | Control Panel.
2. Double-click the Network icon. In the Configuration window that appears, click the Add button.
3. From the list of choices, shown in Figure 25.4, choose Adapter and click Add. (The network interface card is also referred to as the network adapter.)

Figure 25.4.
Tell Windows what type of network hardware you have installed.

4. Windows might build the driver database needed to present you with the list of choices for network cards. After a short wait, the list will appear.
5. Scroll through the list of choices and find your NIC manufacturer and model, as shown in Figure 25.5. It's important to know exactly which model you have. Choosing incorrectly can lead to hours of troubleshooting and frustration.

Figure 25.5.
Windows 95 gives you a handy list of applicable NICs to choose from. Unfortunately, vendor names can be a confusing jumble of numbers. Choose carefully, or you will face intractable installation problems.

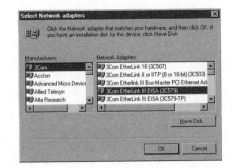

6. If your card doesn't appear in the list, check the box that your network card came in. It will probably have a 3$^1/_2$-inch disk or a CD that contains the necessary files to install your driver. Insert the disk or CD and click the Have Disk button. (You might be able to find the correct drivers on the Internet at the manufacturer's Web site.)

7. You will be asked for a path to the files. Type in the correct drive and click OK. Windows will search the specified drive and display the associated driver. Click OK to begin copying files.

8. After you have chosen your NIC and clicked OK, you will return to the screen at which you started. Your new NIC and a couple of lines referring to protocols and client software will have been added.

The default for Windows 95 to install is the adapter (which you already chose), Client for Microsoft Networks, Client for NetWare Networks, IPX/SPX, and NetBeui. Depending on how you want to configure your network, not all of these items are needed. The next section covers choosing a protocol.

Speaking the Right Language

As soon as the NIC card appears in your network list (in the Configuration tab window), you will see a number of other items listed as well. By default, Windows 95 installs IPX/SPX, NetBeui, Client for Microsoft Networks, and Client for NetWare Networks into your network configuration. Here is where you have a choice of which protocol or protocols you want to use. For our example, we will use Microsoft's NetBeui because it is fast, easy to install, and very common among small networks.

This means that we want to remove IPX/SPX form our list, as well as its accompanying Client for NetWare Networks. Do the following:

1. Highlight IPX/SPX (or another item if you aren't following the example).

2. Click the Remove button.

3. Click OK.

Options in the Network

Before you click OK (in the Network window) to install your network card, there are a few options you might want to check out.

Identification

Choose the Identification tab. This information can be configured only if you use the Client for Microsoft or Novell Networks.

The Computer name field lets you uniquely identify your computer, as shown in Figure 25.6. This name must be unique to allow efficient resource sharing. For example, imagine that two of your neighbors are named Bob Smith, and your spouse tells you to go over to Bob Smith's and borrow his weed whacker. You get the picture.

Figure 25.6.
What's in a name? A lot, if you're a network. You need to uniquely identify your systems and networks in order to ensure correct operation.

The Workgroup is the name you will give your small network. It might be something like BobNet or Network1. You want to have all the computers on your network join the same workgroup.

The Computer Description is just a small comment field that helps identify your computer when you see it in Network Neighborhood or another browser. This field is optional.

Technical Note: In general, there are two types of networks: peer-to-peer and server networks. A peer-to-peer network is generally a small network in which the individual PCs tend to be more powerful (although this isn't a requirement) and the access of shared resources is fairly small. This is ideal for a startup network. You'll make a smaller investment in money and time, and you won't need dedicated network specialists.

A server network has a computer or computers dedicated to the network that do nothing but service workstation requests. In addition, they tend to manage the logical network. This means that, among other services, they provide a central point for logging on to the network by maintaining a user database of sorts. This model is used for larger networks that have specific needs beyond basic file sharing.

Access Control

The last tab is called Access Control. In a workgroup environment, you will want to specify how a resource from your computer can be accessed (that is, who can read a file). You can specify either share-level access or user access. Share-level access lets you give outside parties full read/write or read-only access to a PC's drive, or it can disallow external access altogether. User access lets you provide access to specific users, setting up user names and passwords to gain access to resources.

The access control options can be changed at any time, so it isn't important to set them now. Leave them at share level; you will discover how this affects you later. Go back to the Configuration tab to get back to where you started.

File and Print Sharing

Note that in the middle of the Network Configuration window is a button labeled File and Print Sharing. This button is where you allow your resources (files and printers are resources) to be shared with others on the network. This is why you wanted a network in the first place. When you click this button, a small dialog box appears that gives you the option of sharing your files and printer on the network.

Check the boxes to share your resources with others on the network. (You don't have to check the second option ("printers") if you don't have a printer attached to your computer.)

Primary Logon

One other option, Primary Logon, decides how Windows 95 will start itself—whether it should look for the network first or log you into Windows first. If you're going to be working with a network, choose Client for X Network (whether Microsoft or NetWare).

You're Finished (Well, Not Yet)

When you click the OK button at the bottom of the Network window, several things will happen. Windows will attempt to begin loading the files and drivers necessary to control your NIC card. Depending on your computer, it might ask you for the Windows 95 CD-ROM. You should have this available. Once the appropriate files have been copied, Windows will want to restart the computer so that it can load the new NIC and the new protocol so that the computer can be networkable.

Before you click Yes, you might want to check a couple of things, perhaps to avoid the mistakes that plague even the best networking specialists:

- Is your network cable plugged into both the port in your NIC card and the wall jack (or hub)? (Check the back of the NIC and see if it has the connectivity lights. If it does, check that they are green.)

- Is your hub plugged in?

- Did you give your computer a unique name?

Any one of these things can lead to hair-pulling and teeth-gnashing, but these problems can be avoided if you double-check. Now click Yes. At this point, if all went well, your computer should be up and talking on the network. Now you can set up the other two computers.

Troubleshooting

In a perfect world, you wouldn't have to bother with this section. However, because computers want everything to be just so, sometimes things don't go as planned. So we will begin this section with some basic troubleshooting techniques for networking. The first step is to identify the problem. Problems can be broken into these categories:

- Resource conflict: Somewhere at the hardware level, two pieces of the computer's hardware are competing for resources.

- Connectivity: The NIC isn't receiving, sending, or translating data correctly.

- Configuration: Something about the configuration of your network or protocols is interrupting or preventing communication.

- Physical: There is some sort of physical (hardware) problem that can't be corrected through configuration.

Resource Conflicts

Pieces of hardware in your computer need specific memory allocations and interrupt requests (IRQs) in order to function. Generally, different types of cards will by default take certain I/O ports and IRQs. It isn't important to know the function of these settings, but it *is* important to know what the values of these settings are in case you need to change them. Again, Plug and Play will minimize or even eliminate a great deal of frustration.

IRQ

IRQ stands for Interrupt Request Line. When your network card (or any other card) wants to send a signal or an interrupt to the CPU, it must have its own distinct line on which to send. That way, the computer knows which card the interrupt is coming from. Network cards generally use IRQ 3 or 5. Check your NIC's documentation to discover the default value.

Table 25.1 is a general guideline to IRQ settings. Your system might very well be different.

Table 25.1. IRQ preferences.

IRQ Setting	Preferred Hardware
2	Cascade from IRQ9
3	Available (unless you have a second com port)
4	COM1, COM3
5	Available (unless LPT2 exists)
6	Floppy disk controller
7	LPT1
8	System clock
9	Video Graphics Adapter
10	Available
11	Available
12	Mouse (PS/2 systems)
13	Math coprocessor (if applicable)
14	Hard drive controller
15	Available

Troubleshooting: A classic network "gotcha" occurs with sound cards. Sound Blaster-compatible boards like to grab IRQ 5 by default, which happens to be one of the preferred IRQs for many network cards. If you're installing a network card on a machine with an installed sound board, be sure to check on the status of IRQ 5 first. You might even want to nudge the sound board to another IRQ (perhaps 7) to avoid problems. Just remember to also change any references to the sound board found in your AUTOEXEC.BAT file, or the change might not take hold.

I/O Port

Base input/output indicates through which path data flows between the card (NIC or otherwise) and the CPU. As with the IRQ, all cards must have a different I/O port through which to communicate. Network adapters generally use 300 to 30F or 310 to 31F.

If your NIC has caused a conflict in one of these two settings, it is fairly simple to discover the problem:

1. Go to the Start menu, select Settings, and go to Control Panel.

2. Double-click the System icon.

3. Choose the Device Manager tab.

4. If Windows 95 has a problem with your NIC, under the Network Adapters section your network adapter will have a yellow circle with an exclamation point next to it, as shown in Figure 25.7.

Figure 25.7.
Windows 95's Device Manager provides instant insight into the operation of network hardware.

5. Highlight the item that has the exclamation point, and click the Properties button.

6. The Device Manager will bring you to the properties screen of your NIC. It is here that we will try to discover the problem.

7. If under the Device Status you see Device failure, you know there is a problem. Click the Resources tab to find out more.

8. You might be given a choice to set the configuration manually, or you might see the screen shown in Figure 25.8. If you do see the button for setting the configuration manually, go ahead and click it.

9. Check out the conflicting device list. This will tell you if there is a problem, such as when both the IRQ and I/O port are in use. These values must be changed to ones that are not in use.

Figure 25.8.
Windows 95 keeps track of hardware settings, allowing you to quickly diagnose conflicts and make changes.

10. Highlight the resource type item in question (for example, Interrupt Request or Input/ Output Range) and click the Change Setting button. When a box appears, scroll through the available choices until the conflict information box says that no devices are conflicting.

11. Click OK and repeat step 10 for any others.

12. Click OK.

13. The system will want to reboot, so go ahead and shut down.

Connectivity

In its simplest terms, connectivity boils down to a clear-cut question: Is there a clean connection from the computer to the network? If your phone doesn't work, the first thing you check is the phone cord. The same applies to your PC network. Symptoms of connectivity problems include Windows not recognizing the card, and an inability to browse the network. Here is a list of items that you can check to see if you are connected:

- Ensure that the NIC card is seated properly. If the card is even a little misaligned, it won't initialize.
- Look at the back of the NIC. If it has lights on it, are they on? Are they green? Usually this indicates that the card is functioning correctly. Check the NIC documentation for more details.
- Check your cable connections. Is the cable plugged into the NIC securely? Is it plugged into the hub securely?
- Is the hub on? Try switching ports on the hub.

Case Study: I once had a coworker who had gone through all the configuring of his brand-new PC. He spent two hours trying to troubleshoot a problem to no avail. In the end, it was discovered that the hub was unplugged. This is an example of the importance of looking for the obvious first, because it's often the answer.

One important thing to remember about connectivity is electricity. Connectivity involves getting an electronic signal from one place to another intact. If there is a broken piece in the chain, the signal won't get transmitted, so check all your physical connections.

Configuration

Configuring your network settings can be tricky and confusing. You have to go back through each piece and recheck each entry. Here are some common problems and solutions:

- Did you enter the correct protocol? IPX won't talk on a network running NetBeui. It will look like it's running correctly, but the components won't be speaking the same language.
- Did you enable File and Print Sharing? This is important. Others on the network won't be able to see you unless you enable this setting.
- Check the identification for the computer. If the computer's name is the same as one already on the network, your PC won't be allowed to join the network.
- Did you install the correct NIC card software for your NIC? (Check the Network icon in Control Panel.) Manufacturers tend to name NICs with numbers that can cause two cards to look alike. However, Windows 95 won't raise a flag. Because the cards are so similar, Windows will assume that you know which one you're installing. Be sure to choose the right NIC when installing!

Physical

I saved physical for last because it tends to be the most expensive problem and the most uncommon one during installation. However, physical problems aren't out of the realm of possibility. You must realize that, outside of technical professionals, very few people can really tell when a piece of hardware has gone bad.

The surest means of checking is one of two ways:

1. Replace the item in question with one that works.
2. Put the item into a working environment and see if it functions.

I prefer the second method because of the certainty involved. If I suspect a NIC is bad, I will pull it out and place it in a system that works. If it doesn't work, I know it's broken. If it does work, I have considerably narrowed down the possibilities. Here are some problems that might be plaguing you:

- Bad NIC: Generally, when a NIC card goes south, the green activity lights won't activate. Also, Windows 95 won't be able to find your card. Your best bet is to swap the card out with another one and try again. Unless it is the exact same model of NIC card, you will have to reinstall the card.

- Bad cable: This is the easiest and cheapest problem to fix. If you suspect a cable is bad, swap it out with one that you know works. Look for fraying, or, if the connectors on the ends of the cable are clear, check to make sure that the wires inside aren't loose. Sometimes I swap out the cable just to be sure. Since the only thing you have to do to your computer is reboot, this is a no-hassle fix to try.

- Bad hub: This problem is the most infrequent, but it can happen. Check to make sure that all the lights are on. Also, try moving your cable around to different ports. If one PC works on the hub and another doesn't, you can be pretty sure that the problem is not with the hub.

- Bad slot: It's possible that the slot in which your card is in is bad. However, this is highly unlikely. Try switching slots and rebooting your PC. Windows doesn't care in which slot the card rests.

> **Troubleshooting:** On some early Pentium computers, it is necessary to "activate" a PCI slot. If your NIC card is PCI and isn't responding in any way, check your computer's documentation regarding the installation of PCI expansion cards. If you're a little more comfortable in a computer's BIOS, check the settings and ensure that your slot is active or not in use by something else.

Most troubleshooting involves using your head and following logic. Windows 95 has an excellent troubleshooter when it comes to network cards. Select Start | Help, and then search in the index for "troubleshooting network cards." This can point you in the right direction. Just be methodical in your approach, and check your documentation. Usually that is good enough to solve any problem.

Sharing Your Network

Here is something you might want to remember as your budding network takes form: If you want to share some files or even your entire hard drive, you must create a share "point" from which the rest of the network will access (assuming, of course, that you enabled File and Print Sharing back in the Network icon in Control Panel). To share a directory or drive, follow these steps:

1. Bring up My Computer or Explorer.

2. Highlight the item or drive you want to make available to others. (Only directories or drives can be shared, not individual files.)

3. Once the directory or drive is highlighted, right-click it to get the dialog box shown in Figure 25.9.

Figure 25.9.

The Sharing sheet of your drive's Properties dialog box lets you assign and control access to your data.

4. Choose the Sharing tab. You will be asked for information about how you want to share this resource.

5. Click the Shared As radio button. The Share Name field will become active.

6. Type a name that you want the rest of the network to see. This is how other computers in the network will identify this resource.

7. Choose the type of access you want to grant. You can choose Read-Only or Full or set it according to a password.

8. When you click OK, you will notice that the directory or drive you chose to share now has a small hand icon next to it. This indicates that the resource has been shared.

9. Double-click Network Neighborhood, and watch as the list of computers in your network appears. Then double-click your computer. (The computers are listed according to the names you gave them in the Computer Description field earlier.)

10. You will see the names you gave your resources (share points) earlier. Double-click a resource to view its contents.

11. Alternatively, you can map a drive letter to that resource. Click the Resource name (for example, CD-ROM), and then right-click. This will bring up the option to map a network drive. Choose to do so.

12. A dialog box will appear. Choose the drive letter you want to represent this resource. Then decide if you want to reconnect to this resource when you next log in. (I recommend doing so unless you're going to use this resource only once.)

13. Click OK. Now you have utilized your first network drive! (For fun, check My Computer to see the new drive listed there.)

Summary

Networking is becoming an essential tool in our everyday lives. Some people even think that the appliances in our homes will be networked. The alarm clock will contact the coffee maker 15 minutes before it is set to go off so that the coffee can get started. Don't laugh. The technology already exists—it's just a matter of time.

If you plan on building a small network, I can give you a few words of advice. Plan ahead! Once the people in your office or organization get a taste of it, the demand will be extreme. As far as troubleshooting goes, use your head and go with your instincts. They are usually right. Good luck!

VII

Input and
Output

Peter Norton™

26

Printers

Peter Norton®

When it comes to PC upgrades, it might seem out of place to talk about printers. After all, these devices aren't actually part of the PC. Instead, they are independent devices packed with enough silicon and electronics to make them a qualify as a computer in their own right.

But printers do, in fact, contribute a great deal to the overall value and effectiveness of any PC. For all the benefits of digital technology and ubiquitous Internet-based communications, sometimes you just gotta have it on paper. And a good printer can help you produce incredibly professional-looking output, whether it's a million-dollar sales presentation or a birthday card for your eight-year-old.

This chapter will help you understand what's involved in buying, using, and maintaining a printer. Here are some of the things you'll learn:

- How the various types of monochrome and color printers work, be they laser, ink jet, dye sublimation, or some other process
- What is involved in purchasing a new printer, with specific advice for home, office, and specialty buyers
- How to diagnose and resolve common printer problems
- Tips on routine maintenance of print engines and print media such as toner and ink
- How to upgrade your PC with a new printer
- What repair opportunities are available for printers that have problems, helping you avoid expensive servicing or even the replacement of the unit

Printers Are Improving

The great thing about PCs is that everything gets better, faster, and cheaper. Printers are no exception to the rule. In fact, they often seem to deliver the most telling examples of runaway advancement, as clever engineers and designers learn to squeeze more dots into ever-tighter spaces.

It all started back in 1984, when Hewlett-Packard released the HP LaserJet Series I. This 300dpi laser printer, and the HP LaserJet Series II that followed in 1986, helped usher in the desktop publishing revolution, transforming small offices into self-sufficient publishing operations. It also pushed noisy and slow daisy-wheel printers right off the mainstream market.

Today, over a dozen years later, PC-based printing is moving again—this time into color. Although it's not appropriate for everyone, inexpensive color ink jets provide an incredible range of talent, producing near-laser-quality text and rich, not-quite-photographic-quality color. Whether you work in a home office or a huge office or just have a PC for your home, the latest printers can help turn the bits and bytes inside your PC into attractive, compelling output (see Figure 26.1).

Figure 26.1.
Epson's affordable Stylus Color 400 is one of the dozens of low-cost color ink jets that have changed the face of desktop printing—particularly for the home user. (Photo courtesy of Epson America)

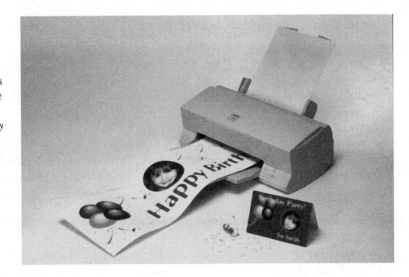

Desktop printers fall into three main categories, each of which employs a unique method for putting information on paper:

- Monochrome laser printers
- Monochrome and color ink jet printers
- Advanced color printers

Laser Printers

Laser printers use fine black toner—nearly identical to that used in copiers—to produce sharp text and graphics on the page. The toner is made from magnetic iron compounds, plastic, and pigment, which allow it to be shaped, applied, and melted onto the page. Laser printers get their name from the laser light that is used as part of the process.

Here's how it works: An optical photoconducting (OPC) drum is used to transfer toner to paper. First, the OPC drum is charged with static electricity, causing it to repel the toner. Then a very thin laser beam strafes across the OPC drum, strobing at a rate of 300 pulses per horizontal inch (in the case of a 300dpi print job). Each strobe of the laser represents a single microscopic printed dot. The laser strobe removes the static charge from the drum, allowing toner to adhere to the point where it impacts.

The OPC drum turns beneath the laser as the paper moves, advancing each printed line into position beneath the laser. The now-uncharged point attracts and holds a bit of toner, so a magnetic roller covered with toner is brought into the proximity of the OPC drum. Toner then transfers to the magnetic roller, where it is then exposed to a strong static charge called a *corona*, which is situated beneath the moving paper. The corona draws the toner off the turning OPC drum and onto the paper. An instant later, the plastic toner is melted onto the page by the heated Teflon fuser roller.

> **Architecture:** Some printers use an array of tiny LEDs (light emitting diodes) instead of a laser to dispel the charge from the OPC drum. Exactly $8\frac{1}{2}$ inches wide, this array flashes light onto appropriate points on the turning drum below to achieve the same effect delivered by lasers. LED mechanisms can also be less prone to breakdowns, because there is no moving laser gun. The drawback is that LED resolutions are limited to the number of lights that can be physically placed across the width of the page.

A printer's resolution is determined by how finely the printer's laser can describe charged areas on the drum. A 300dpi printer puts as many as 90,000 black toner dots on each printed square inch. A 600dpi printer lays down four times as many pixels in each inch. Print enhancement technologies further enhance the image by laying down gray half-toned dots.

Most laser printers employ their own pool of memory to store pages being processed. However, all these dots can demand a lot of space. Although a 300dpi print-out needs less than 1MB of memory to print, a 600dpi page requires nearly 4MB. This number goes up further still if enhancement technology is used, because each dot must now store more than simple black-and-white data.

The process is quite versatile: Laser printers present a wider range of print speeds and resolutions than any other printing technology. Small personal laser printers, for example, print four to eight pages per minute (ppm), and larger network models can push 30 to 40ppm or more. Likewise, resolutions stretch from 300dpi to 1200dpi or more. Often, higher resolutions have extreme memory requirements. A full $8\frac{1}{2}\times11$-inch page printed at 1200dpi can require more than 16MB of printer memory.

In general, laser printers are very easy to maintain and care for. They use modular toner cartridges that ease the replacement of consumables. Most cartridges integrate the print drum and toner, although some models use separate cartridges for each, allowing slightly less expensive operation by extending the life of the drum.

One drawback of lasers is their prodigious power consumption. These printers consume a tremendous amount of energy in order to produce charges for the drum and, to a lesser degree, to melt the toner onto the page. The previously mentioned corona is created by passing a 10,000-volt current through a wire near the paper. In fact, there are actually two coronas, called the *primary corona* and the *transfer corona*. Even when the printer is idle, power draw is significant. You might even notice that the lights dim when the laser printer in your home office begins to print a page. For obvious reasons, it is important that your laser printer be well-grounded. Not only can unanticipated capacitance kill you, it can also kill your printer.

> **Buying Tip:** Whatever you do, make sure you get an Energy Star-approved laser printer. These devices provide sleep modes that kick in after adjustable periods of inactivity, reducing power draw tremendously. That way, you can leave your printer on all day to occasionally print documents without pouring money down the electrical outlet.

Ink Jets: Squirting Pages

Ink jet printers have become the most popular option for home printing, thanks to very low prices, improved print quality, and the ability to cheaply produce color output. Some color Canon printers and HP DeskJets, for example, can be had for about $200. They offer 300dpi color printing, perhaps not too fast or very brilliant, but quick and brilliant enough for the cost.

They are also compact and consume little power. In the past, buyers had to choose between monochrome and color models, although both work on the same principle. Today, most personal ink jet printers are color, because this capability costs little more than straight monochrome while adding significant value.

Ink jets work by spitting tiny dots of colored ink onto the page. In this sense, they are similar to older impact printers, which repeatedly struck a ribbon of ink placed in front of the paper to form letters and graphics. The ink is stored in a reservoir, which often consists of replaceable cartridges that are swapped out when the ink is consumed. In the case of color ink jets, there are separate ink cartridges for red, green, blue, and black ink.

> **Buying Tip:** Some color ink jets—particularly older models—omit the black ink cartridge. To create black (say, for text), the printer shoots all three other colors to form a dark dot. The result, however, is usually closer to brown or gray than true black—a real problem for anyone who prints any amount of straight text. In addition, the use of three ink cartridges for each black dot increases the rate of ink consumption. If you buy a color ink jet, make sure you get a four-cartridge model.

The action happens at the nozzles, which place the ink on the page. Behind the nozzles, an interface circuit applies charges to a series of impulse drivers, corresponding to the appropriate color of ink. These drivers push a tiny drop of ink through the nozzle in one of two ways:

- A charge is applied to a pizoelectric driver (an electronic crystal often made of synthetic quartz), which causes it to expand. The controlled expansion pushes a known amount of ink through the nozzle and onto the page.

- A charge is used to heat a small amount of ink, producing a ball of vapor that pushes the ink onto the page.

In both cases, a print head positions the nozzles by moving across the paper as it is fed through the printer. Often, you can hear the operation of the print head moving back and forth as a print job is underway. Through the exact positioning of the print head, resolutions of 720dpi and higher are possible on the most sophisticated ink jet products.

Unlike laser printers, ink jets don't employ their own memory to store the entire image of the page to be printed. Instead, they accept data from your PC in real time, placing it on the page as the bits arrive. To do this, most ink jets employ a small buffer (from 128 to 512KB) to hold incoming data. The lack of dedicated memory is one reason why ink jets can cost hundreds of dollars less than laser printers.

Performance: The memoryless design of ink jets can save you a few bucks—but not without a cost. Ink jet printers put a greater load on your computer's CPU, in part because it must finesse the data flow to avoid sending too much or too little data at one time. Unlike laser printers, in which your PC can fire off and forget about print jobs that it hands off to the laser printer, the system stays engaged in ink jet print jobs until the very end.

Technical Note: Ink jet printers can get by without memory because documents don't have to move through the printer at a constant rate of speed. If your PC falls behind the ink jet's output, the printer merely waits for the data flow to catch up and starts laying down dots where it left off. Laser printers, in contrast, are committed to a set output speed when the print job begins. Because the paper is in precise physical contact with drums and rollers, stopping the mechanism will result in slippage, and the output will be distorted. For this reason, laser printers ensure that the page will run smoothly through its mechanisms by first assembling the entire print job in printer memory before starting to print.

Although ink jet resolutions have improved, they still lag behind their laser counterparts in print speed on longer documents. The reason for this is that once a page has been assembled in a laser printer's memory (some laser printers have more sophisticated motherboards than their host computers), the printer can then print as many copies as you want without any significant amount of further processing. Every page that a lower-end ink jet prints must be reassembled and sent to the printer by the CPU. Ink jets also can't produce black-and-white text that is as sharp as that of good laser printers.

Performance: You can usually tell what is ink jet output from the lower-contrast text. Letters might not appear truly black, even on ink jets that have a true black ink cartridge, and edges can look less than smooth. Still, top ink jets can produce text results that mirror lasers under casual observation. (Just don't let the ink get wet!)

In the past, ink jets were notoriously persnickety. Nozzles could gum up and jam, impairing output quality. Even today, you'll need to recalibrate your printer after replacing ink cartridges—a simple process in which you tell the printer which test pattern looks best. However, ink jets are very much affected by the paper stock they print on, because the absorptive properties of the stock determine how the dots look on the page.

Note: Recently, a new category of personal printers has emerged—true-color photo printers, designed to produce near-photo-quality snapshots from digital image files. As digital cameras become less expensive and more popular, photo printers provide a convenient and inexpensive way to view digital snapshots. Most of these products are small (see Figure 26.2), printing onto specially coated 5×7-inch paper that provides outstanding quality. They also use advanced color printing processes such as thermal dye transfer or dye sublimation. However, at least one printer, the Panasonic TruPhoto, actually produces images by heating chemically receptive paper stock. Instead of laying ink or wax onto paper, the paper itself changes to reveal the desired image. These parallel-port printers are compact and easy to install, but the coated paper makes them expensive to operate.

Figure 26.2.
Hewlett-Packard's PhotoSmart printer outputs photo-quality color snapshots using an inexpensive thermal dye transfer process. (Photo courtesy of Hewlett-Packard)

Advanced Color Printers

Most PC users have been working with ever-improving laser and ink jet printers, but a small portion of graphics professionals need more. Enter high-end color printers, which employ a number of different processes to produce precise color documents.

Although physical approaches vary, all these printers share two key qualities: They are very expensive (from $2,500 to $10,000 or more), and the cost of printing each page is much higher than it is for standard laser or ink jet printers. Both of these issues are enough to make advanced color printers a niche for people who need better fidelity, whether to proof documents before they go to press or to produce professional-quality color output for distribution.

There are three main areas of high-resolution color printers:

- Color laser
- Solid ink
- Thermal dye transfer
- Thermal wax transfer

Color Laser Printers

Costing $3,000 to $10,000, color lasers use the same toner and drum process employed by their monochrome cousins (see Figure 26.3). Instead of just black toner, four separate toner colors (cyan, magenta, yellow, and black) are employed. But unlike other color printers (including ink jets), color lasers can produce top results on regular copier paper—a potential huge savings in consumable costs over the life of the printer.

Output is very good. Monochrome text handling and speed are identical to standard lasers, making color lasers the only advanced color printer appropriate for monochrome output. Color quality has improved markedly over the last two years as well, and prices have come down to the point where many small departments or offices can afford to consider one for their pre-press work.

Solid Ink Printers

Costing about $3,000 to $4,000, solid ink printers can be thought of as thermal wax transfer printers. These models melt solid sticks of colored wax and spray the resulting liquid onto the page, much like an ink jet printer does. Some newer models actually apply the melted wax to a rotating drum, which then transfers the material to the page—similar to the operation of laser printers.

Because solid ink models can use plain copier paper for output, these printers reduce cost per page and are appropriate for mixed text and graphics output. However, resolutions are low enough that image quality might fall behind that of other models.

Figure 26.3.
Hewlett-Packard's Color LaserJet 5 provides attractive, versatile color and monochrome output. Falling prices have made color lasers a growing market segment. (Photo courtesy of Hewlett-Packard)

Thermal Dye Transfer Printers

The most expensive color printers at $7,000 to $15,000, thermal dye transfer models also produce the best overall quality. This is stuff for true professionals. Printing is agonizingly slow, and it must be done on custom polyester-coated paper that can push costs per page to an astounding $10.

The process works by rolling a dye-saturated ribbon across the page. The ribbon is heated to transfer the dye to the page, with separate passes for each color. Thermal dye models are one of the few printers to provide continuous tone printing, producing 16.7 million separate colors to eliminate dithering patterns.

Thermal Wax Transfer Printers

Costing $3,000 to $4,000, thermal wax transfer printers might be on their way out. These printers work much like their pricier dye transfer siblings, in that they heat a wax-coated ribbon as it rolls against the paper. The melted wax is laid on specially coated paper, which makes this sort of printer expensive to operate. They also produce dithering patterns, which detracts from their high contrast and excellent color production.

The Software Behind the Scenes: Languages and Drivers

Like any device, hardware is just a bunch of well-engineered parts until some software comes around to make it do something. Such is the case with printers, which require two things to operate—a device driver to access printer capabilities, and a page-description language to render pages into a format that is intelligible to the print controller.

Page-Description Languages

Until recently, Adobe's PostScript was the only printer language that let printers do neat things like produce adjustable-size fonts, white-on-black text, and rotated or scaled images. With its roots in the Apple Macintosh arena, PostScript has been the *lingua franca* of publishing, with almost all service bureaus using PostScript devices to produce physical output.

A more recent version of PostScript, PostScript Level 2, is optimized for color output. PostScript 2 provides complex color-handling and color-matching capabilities and is used almost universally among high-end color printers as their page-description language.

Over the past four years, Hewlett-Packard's PCL language (now at PCL 6) has matched PostScript's monochrome capabilities. Powered by the market juggernaut of its LaserJet line of printers, PCL has become the PC standard for print-based output, although PostScript continues to enjoy a niche among people who produce proofs for professional output. Today, many non-HP printers provide PCL emulation, allowing them to use the standard HP drivers supplied with Windows 95 to operate.

Drivers

Printer drivers act like any other hardware device driver. This segment of code acts as the emissary between your system and the printer hardware, telling it what it needs to do in a form it understands. Windows 95 provides a standard minidriver that addresses most of the base printer functions for all models, while an enhanced driver component provides access to custom features.

Custom drivers address features such as bidirectional communication, PC-based printer controls, resolution-specific operation, and the like. These drivers are critical to the optimal operation of your printer and can affect both features and quality of output.

Tip: Stay on top of driver updates. Vendors often update their driver software to provide enhanced features or better output quality and speed. New drivers might also fix inevitable bugs that crop up when the code interacts with system-level stuff such as the graphics device interface (GDI). Usually you can get the latest driver versions from your vendor's Web site. In fact, you should make a point of checking for updated drivers when you first install your printer, because the driver disks in the box might be up to six months (and several revisions) old.

Making Connections

Of course, your printer needs to get bits from the PC somehow. The most common transport is your PC's parallel port. For one thing, the parallel port is ubiquitous: Printer vendors don't need to worry about including an interface card or other hardware to ensure that PCs can send jobs to the printer. For another, it's the fastest ubiquitous external bus. Parallel ports run at speeds of 120KBps to 2MBps, depending on the type of parallel port involved.

Table 26.1 lists the three styles of parallel ports on PCs.

Table 26.1. The three types of parallel ports.

Parallel Port Type	Throughput	Description
Centronics	40 to 300KBps	Standard issue on PCs through the early '90s. Highest level of compatibility with all devices.
Enhanced Parallel Port (EPP)	2MBps	Better performance and allows bidirectional communication, but EPP mode might preclude the use of other peripherals.
Enhanced Capability Port (ECP)	2MBps	Provides multitasking tweaks to the EPP specification.

You'll need an EPP or ECP port in order to take full advantage of Plug and Play capability. The new specs convert four of the parallel port's data lines into a two-way data bus that allows for more complex configuration and control.

Compatibility: Before you get worked up over promises made by vendor advertisements, check your PC's hardware. If you lack an EPP or ECP configuration, your machine might not be able to make use of those features. If this is the case, you'll need to add an I/O card that includes the new features (see Chapter 24, "I/O Add-Ons").

A printer shared among users might employ an Ethernet network connection, often residing as a node on the network. Network connections can significantly improve the speed of print jobs with faster printers, because the throughput of the network—when not congested—might be 100 times that of a parallel port. Printers can often be upgraded with a network access card that fits into a slot in a printer's side panel.

Finally, some high-end printers feature a SCSI connection to connect to an individual PC (which might itself reside as a network print server). SCSI provides fast transfer and also allows the use of a local hard disk inside the printer to store frequently accessed graphics such as fonts, forms, and bitmaps. Although a printer hard disk adds expense, it can save hours of time by eliminating the need to pipe repetitive graphics and fonts over congested connections.

Purchasing a Printer

Since the LaserJet Series II, monochrome laser printers have become indispensable tools for offices large and small. And no wonder: They can produce sharp black-and-white documents that are nearly indistinguishable from professionally printed materials. Today, your options are much more varied. You can choose from among monochrome or color; laser, ink jet, or dye/wax transfer; personal or workgroup; and a variety of other options.

How do you decide what to buy? Ultimately, no printer can cover everything. That fast, inexpensive, razor-sharp text output of most lasers will let you down when you want to create a fun color invitation for a party. Likewise, ink jets can make you wait around while that 80-page document gets painted oh-so-slowly by overworked nozzles. And if high-end color printers don't bankrupt you, they will probably let you down when it comes to workaday monochrome documents.

So you need to decide what kind of printer will cover the most ground for you. Table 26.2 should help you focus on a specific printer class. Then you can move on to more specific breakdowns to determine the type of printer that suits you in each class.

Table 26.2. Choosing a class of printer.

Printer Type	Cost	What It's Best For
Monochrome laser	$300 to $3,000	Business documents, newsletters, fast printing of large documents, workgroup printing, fast personal printing
Color ink jet	$150 to $700	Home and small office, simple design work, personal home or office printing
Advanced color	$3,000 to $15,000	Prepress output for professional design, professional presentations

Laserpalooza: Monochrome Laser Printers

Laser printers helped launch the desktop publishing revolution, and their value is still evident today. You won't find a wider variety of printers within a class than with lasers. These versatile machines run the gamut from inexpensive, light-duty, personal printers to monstrous 40ppm workhorses that churn out the workload for an entire network.

Laser printers fall into the three broad categories listed in Table 26.3.

Table 26.3. Main laser printer categories.

Printer Type	Printing Speed	What It's Best For
Personal	4 to 8ppm	Small and home office, private office printer
Workgroup	8 to 16ppm	Small office, departmental printer
Network	16 to 40ppm	Medium and large departments

Regardless of the type of laser you select, you'll need to decide if you want to pay a little extra for a PostScript-capable printer or one that uses HP's PCL language. As explained earlier, the decision really boils down to compatibility with service bureaus and Macs.

Buying Tip: When you're buying a new laser printer, it's a good idea to look for models that use standard RAM SIMMs for their on-board memory. Many printers use proprietary memory cards, which vendors might sell at a stiff premium. By using a printer with SIMM-based memory, you will be able to shop around for the best price when you upgrade down the road.

Printers with Personality

If you're reading this book for advice on how to stock your home office or your personal space at work, you should consider a personal laser or LED printer (see Figure 26.4). These mighty mites provide an impressive blend of speed, affordability, high resolution, and reliable operation. With resolutions of up to 600dpi, you can produce professional-looking monochrome documents from your desktop.

In particular, personal lasers are great for office workers who need to output confidential documents. They can churn out up to eight pages per minute, and most models take a good deal of the printing burden off your PC, allowing you to get back to work quickly when you're printing large documents. However, personal models run at speeds one-half that of workgroup-capable printers and often lack paper-handling capabilities. For instance, the compact form can result in circuitous paper paths that make it inadvisable to use some personal lasers for printing adhesive labels and transparencies. Paper trays might be limited to just 100 pages, requiring frequent reloads, and output trays might be nonexistent, causing finished pages to spill onto the desk or floor.

Figure 26.4.
The EPL-N1200 from Epson is small, quick, and inexpensive. It features Energy Star operation but lacks the paper-handling capacities of larger workgroup models. (Photo courtesy of Epson America)

Peter's Principle: If You're Running Windows 95 or NT, Now's the Time to Consider a GDI Printer

There's a new take on an old wrinkle with personal laser printers. So-called *GDI printers*, or Windows printers, can cost significantly less than traditional printers that use HP's PCL or Adobe's PostScript language. These printers produce output based on the raw GDI graphics data sent from the PC. Because the printer doesn't interpret the incoming data, there is much less need for intelligent (read: expensive) controllers and on-board RAM. By the same token, these printers must make use of processing power and RAM on the PC itself, which can slow overall performance significantly.

GDI printers were actually introduced several years ago but failed to take hold because they suffered from slow performance and failed to work with DOS and OS/2 applications. Since then, Windows 95 and NT have reduced the importance of the OS question, while low-cost RAM has reduced the performance hit on host systems. The emergence of fast Pentium CPUs didn't hurt either.

Is a GDI printer for you? If you use and print from Windows-based applications exclusively, you're certainly a candidate. However, you should also make sure that you have enough processing power—a Pentium-166 is a good idea if you multitask applications—and plenty of RAM, on the order of 32MB. Note that 16MB RAM systems will run into trouble, because Windows 95 itself grabs 12MB, leaving little RAM for running applications and print jobs side by side. Also, you might want to avoid a GDI printer if you print a lot of long documents. These will hobble your PC during the length of the print job—and, for an 80-page manuscript, that can be a while.

Workgroup Printers

Workgroup printers run at speeds of 8 to 16ppm and provide the best mix of performance, resolution, and affordability. LexMark's Optra L, for example, can produce stunning 1200dpi output that is almost indistinguishable from professional linotype prints. Likewise, Hewlett-Packard's Si line of network printers can produce crisp 1200dpi pages 24 hours a day if asked to. In addition to parallel port connections, you can expect to see network and possibly SCSI connectors on these printers.

Workgroup printers are best for departments and offices that have 10 to 50 people, depending on how much printing goes on. Often these models are highly flexible. Memory might range from 2 to 40MB, and paper trays can be bulked up to handle 500 pages or more at a time. Some models also provide duplex printing add-ons that allow the printer to run pages through twice—once on each side—before depositing them in the output tray.

These models might also suit single users who either need to print at very high resolutions or who frequently output many longer documents. You'll pay for this privilege, however. Although workgroup models can be had for about $1,000, prices quickly move up as you add memory for high-resolution operation. A well-appointed workgroup laser can cost $1,600 to $1,800.

Network Lasers: The Big Time

Finally, a word about network laser printers (see Figure 26.5). These behemoths are best for big offices and departments that want to share a printer on an Ethernet or Token Ring network. With paper capacities in the thousands of sheets and the ability to push 30 pages or more per minute, network laser printers can quickly recoup their big $4,000 or higher price tags.

Although many network lasers offer 600dpi and higher operation, they usually run at a more pedestrian 300dpi. The lower resolution allows quicker, more efficient printing while still producing good results.

Home Color: Ink Jets

Ink jets are best for home and small office users who want versatility and low cost. Although the text quality won't match that of top lasers, it's good enough for everything short of business proposals. And the ability to add a splash of color to any document can be a real boon for both home and business users alike.

Figure 26.5.
Fully decked out with paper-handling options, Hewlett-Packard's LaserJet 5Si can meet the printing needs of a large department. (Photo courtesy of Hewlett-Packard)

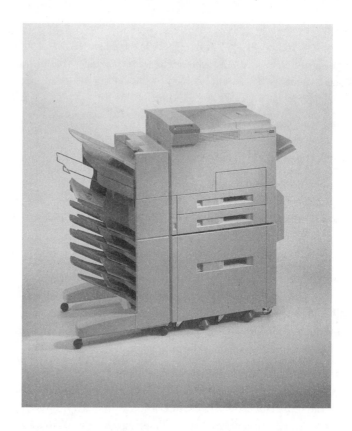

Expect to pay $150 to $400 for an ink jet, with the higher-priced models pushing resolutions up to 600dpi or even 720dpi. Although all these models work on standard paper, you'll get much better color output on special coated paper (often customized for the specific printer model). Coated paper will run you up to 10 cents per sheet, about seven to eight times the cost of standard stock.

Of course, speed is a problem. A quick ink jet hooked to a fast PC can spit out a single page nearly as fast as a personal laser can, because lasers usually don't start printing until the entire print job is spooled at the PC. However, subsequent pages take longer than those printed on laser printers. If you need to print lots of multipage text documents, consider a personal laser printer over an ink jet.

Artistic License: Dye Sublimation and Thermal Wax

If you're looking for professional color output to proof materials headed for press or to produce professional-quality output for distribution, the stakes get much higher. Still, $4,000 or less will get you a good color laser printer—about one-half to one-third the cost of such hardware just three years ago.

In this area, you need to decide what level of output you need. For drop-dead-gorgeous color, thermal dye transfer is your best choice. But the $10,000 and over price point might make you drop dead yourself. A solid ink printer might be the best choice for dedicated, high-quality color output. With a price of $3,000 to $4,000, it is certainly a competitive option.

For mixed use of color and monochrome, you have two choices: a color laser printer or a high-quality ink jet printer. The best ink jet printers can produce 720dpi resolution that, on specially coated paper, approaches the quality of other processes. However, they also give you the option of decent black-and-white output. Particularly useful are large-format ink jets, which can produce magazine-spread-sized print-outs.

Note: Epson now offers ink jets capable of 1440×720 resolution, including the wide-format Stylus Color 1520 (see Figure 26.6) and Stylus Color 3000 (see Figure 26.7). These printers bridge the gap between advanced color and standard ink jet processes.

Figure 26.6.
Epson's Stylus Color 1520 has 1440×720 resolution color output. (Photo courtesy of Epson America)

Diagnosing/Troubleshooting

Unlike many of the components inside a PC, printers are complex beasts with a lot of moving parts. The HP LaserJet Series II, for example, has over 2,000 parts. Problems can occur with the printer's gearing or head motor, for example. Toner and ink can get dirty or old, causing nozzle jams, uneven distribution, smearing, and other problems. And printer memory is just as likely to fail as a PC's main memory. Of course, you also have software to worry about.

Figure 26.7.
Epson's Stylus Color 3000 also has 1440×720 resolution color output. In addition, it has Adobe PostScript Level 2 and faster page output. (Photo courtesy of Epson America)

Clearly, we can't cover every problem for every type of printer. The best advice is to keep your eyes open. If you suspect a problem with print quality, try closely examining a variety of different types of print-outs. Do problems occur with color or monochrome jobs? Does the problem occur throughout the print-out, or only along the far edges? By looking closely at anomalous behavior, you can cut down the number of suspects.

The most common problem, if you can call it that, is running low on toner or ink. Usually you will see a message on the printer LCD indicating that the toner level is low, or a simple LED light might tell you that the medium is running out. Another symptom of low toner or ink levels is fading print quality as less of the medium is transfered to the page. To fix this problem, simply replace the cartridge or canisters as instructed in the printer's documentation.

Dirty Old Laser

Laser printers are particularly susceptible to dirt because toner is already dirt of a sort. Loaded with iron oxide, it is, naturally enough, abrasive. And the strong static charges involved in the printing process attract airborne dust. The result is that, over time, a machine will become quite grimy inside, and the dirt can eventually wear down and break internal parts.

The most common part destroyed by dirt is the Teflon upper roller in the heated fuser assembly. Parts inside that heated assembly attract partially melted toner, which forms into spikes and stalactites that are significant enough to dig through the microscopically thin Teflon coating on that upper roller. The next thing you know, every printed page has ugly vertical streaks.

It's much easier and less expensive to avoid a broken fuser than it is to replace one. You can use a clean, dry paint brush, a can of compressed air, and a few QTips to thoroughly clean the insides. Many printers also come with their own brushes for sweeping out toner particles and dust.

Warning: Never, ever use any liquid or liquid solvent to clean the insides of a laser printer.

With proper care and maintenance, your laser printer can serve you faithfully for years. Many 8ppm HP LaserJet Series II printers are still alive and printing, with page counts in excess of one million.

Tip: If you have a heavy-use office printer that you rely on, it's a good idea to have a knowledgeable printer or copier professional clean the machine once a year or so. Not only will this keep your office workhorse online, but it can also ensure that the fan (if there is one) continues to circulate air. A working fan is needed to make sure that ionized or "fried" air passes out of the printer before it begins to corrode plastic parts.

Easy Outs

Whether you've just installed a new printer or have an old warhorse, things can go wrong. If your printer refuses to print, don't panic. Because printers are external devices with their own power and internal settings, you should check a few simple items before you go fishing around for deeper issues in the printer or your operating system:

- Check the cable: Is it fitted tightly into both the PC and the printer? Also make sure that the cable is a proper 25-pin parallel cable, not a 25-pin serial cable (they look a lot alike!).

- Get online: Make sure that the printer panel indicates that the unit is online and ready to accept data.

- Check paper, toner, and ink: Make sure that there is paper in the input trays, because print jobs will fail otherwise. Also make sure that there isn't a paper jam holding up the works. Toner or ink cartridges need to be properly installed as well. Be sure that you have removed the plastic tab and the tape seal from the toner cartridge.

- Try a print test: There is often a test button on the front panel of the printer. If pressing this button produces a print-out, but the printer won't work otherwise, the problem doesn't reside within the printer itself.

Troubleshooting: There is an exception to the preceding point: If the I/O port hardware on the printer has failed, the print test will work despite the fact that something is amiss with the printer itself. Many laser printers have a small circuit board containing the Centronics connector and perhaps a UART. If one of the few chips on this board burns up, your printer is an orphan.

- Check the power: Don't laugh. Many personal printers and ink jets make almost no noise when they are on. Worse, some vendors have all but eliminated front panel lights and panels, making it hard to tell if the printer is actually on.

- Check your printer settings: Are you printing to the right device? From your application, select File | Print, and then choose the Name scroll box to view the available printers, as shown in Figure 26.8.

Figure 26.8.
Windows 95 will let you set up multiple printers. It also treats PC faxing and a few other electronic output applications as print jobs. Check the Print properties dialog box to make sure you're printing to the intended device.

- Be suspicious of printer pass-through devices: If you have multiple devices working off a single parallel port, you might be using a pass-through port to let both work without having to swap connectors. Unfortunately, pass-throughs don't always work. Try printing without the pass-through hardware in place.

Pop Goes the Port

One common problem is when your applications or operating system can no longer find the port leading to the printer. This can happen due to a classic hardware conflict, in which another device grabs the resources reserved for your parallel port.

A hardware or software installation might cause this problem. If several devices are sharing your LPT port, make sure that none of them redirected the address information for the device.

The parallel port leading to the printer is usually referred to as LPT 1. To check if you printer is properly installed, do the following:

1. Go to Control Panel (select Start | Settings | Control Panel) and double-click the Printers icon.

2. Select the installed printer, and then select File | Properties.

3. In the printer's Properties page, choose the Details tab, shown in Figure 26.9.

Figure 26.9.

Most local printers use the LPT1 parallel port. Make sure you have yours set up correctly.

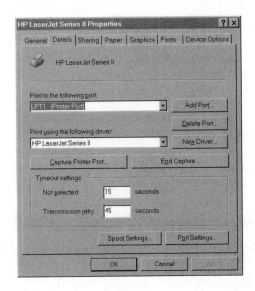

4. Check the Print to the following port drop-down list control. If it says LPT1: (Printer Port), your printer is probably properly installed. If it doesn't, select the LPT1 port from the list and click OK.

If the printer is properly installed on the LPT1 port, the problem might be with a port conflict. Use Windows 95's Device Manager to ferret out conflicts here:

1. Open Control Panel (select Start | Settings | Control Panel) and double-click the System icon.

2. In the System Properties sheet, choose the Device Manager tab.

3. Click the View devices by connection radio button.

4. Click the plus sign (+) next to the Ports (COM & LPT) item.

5. Look at the Printer Port (LPT) item that appears below it. If you see a red exclamation point or a yellow question mark next to the item, some sort of conflict is occurring. Double-click the item to access its properties sheet.

6. In the Printer Port (LPT1) Properties dialog box, choose the Resources tab and look at the information in the Resource settings box.

7. If a conflict exists, uncheck the Use automatic settings item and click the Change Setting button.

8. In the next dialog box, use the spinner control to change either the IRQ or base address setting to one that doesn't conflict with the other hardware on your system. Click OK in several dialog boxes until the changes take effect.

Language Barriers

Another frequent problem can be language mismatches between your PC and printer. If your PC is speaking PostScript but your printer understands only PCL, the result will be unintelligible pages of PostScript code.

Most new laser printers can automatically detect incoming PostScript and PCL data, switching to the proper mode on-the-fly. But if the printer has been set to specifically receive either stream, the auto-detect feature won't work. (This might have been done to speed up print jobs or because the auto-detect feature wasn't working properly.)

Installing a New Printer

So you bought a new laser or ink jet printer and you need to install it. Fortunately, printers are among the easiest devices to install. There are no pesky add-in cards to deal with and, as long as your LPT addresses are OK, no IRQ weirdness to deal with either.

First, get the physical stuff set up:

1. Place the printer on a flat, stable surface where it will be used.

Tip: A flat, stable surface is key to getting acceptable printing results. The calibration of ink jet nozzles and lasers can be affected by less-than-level surfaces. Over time, an unlevel setup will cause toner and ink to distribute unevenly in their cartridges, affecting the even distribution of media onto the paper.

2. Connect the 25-pin parallel port cable to the printer and the parallel port on the PC. The PC side parallel connector is often a pinch type, and the PC side uses pins.

3. Plug the printer's power cable into a grounded outlet.

Warning: Printers can draw a lot of power, so failing to ground them can pose a potential fire hazard. Make sure you plug into grounded, three-pronged outlets. You should also make sure that the electrical circuit you are running off of can handle enough amperage to support the printer and any other equipment on the circuit (including your PC and monitor).

4. Open the printer chassis and install the toner or ink cartridge as shown in your printer's documentation.

5. Power up the printer and wait until it has initiated.

6. Conduct a print test routine (usually from a test button found on the outside of the printer).

7. If the print test completes successfully, your printer is working properly. Proceed to install the software.

Now install the printer into Windows 95. All your Windows applications will take their cue from the settings you apply during the Windows 95 installation. If you set the new printer as your default, all these applications will print to the new device unless told otherwise.

1. Turn on the printer and the PC.

2. When Windows 95 starts up, double-click the Add New Hardware icon in Control Panel.

3. Click Next to start the installation. If you trust Plug and Play, you can let the OS try to recognize the printer. Otherwise, click the No radio button to control the installation yourself.

4. In the Hardware types scroll box, select the Printers item and click Next.

5. In the next dialog box, click the Local Printer radio button.

6. In the next dialog box, you can select the printer from the lists of Manufacturers and Models. However, doing this will use Windows 95's bundled drivers. A better option is to click the Have Disk button.

7. Place the printer's driver disk in the A: drive. Then click OK in the Install from Disk dialog box.

8. If the install routine doesn't begin, you can use the Browse button to search for the proper .INF file on the floppy disk.

9. Once the installation routine is complete, you can check your printer's settings from Control Panel in Windows 95. Double-click the Printers icon. If the new printer icon appears in the Printers window, the printer has been properly installed.

10. To make sure the new printer is set as the default, click the printer icon and then select the File menu. If the Set as Default menu item has a check next to it, your new printer is the active default printer.

Tip: You might be able to get better results from your existing hardware by using high-quality toner. The finer granularity of enhanced toner can provide more precise dot placement and better contrast.

Adding Memory to Your Existing Laser Printer

If you want to take full advantage of your current printer, you might need to add RAM. After all, a 600dpi print-out needs about 4MB, and even more if any gray-scale enhancements are involved.

You can usually easily install RAM in the back of a printer. Although access varies among different models, most printers have a liftable panel that exposes memory sockets and sometimes slots for Ethernet or other cards. Simply install the memory modules as instructed by the printer's manuals. The printer will automatically detect the larger memory pool at startup, allowing you to process larger print jobs more quickly.

Summary

Low-cost desktop printing was one of the great drivers of the PC revolution. Once people could produce professional-looking output using their PCs, the value of these machines grew immensely. Today, businesses large and small rely on the faithful operation of these devices. Just as the fax machine changed the way people do business, the printer helped transform the business document.

The wide array of printers provides terrific options for anyone who has a PC. Home users can find outstanding low-cost ink jet printers that can produce party invitations and family newsletters and even crank out great-looking digital photos. Small and swift laser printers serve home and small offices alike, while midrange and network printers provide output for busy departments. Finally, high-resolution color printers improve the ability of designers to quickly and effectively proof their work before sending it to press.

27

Keyboards

Peter Norton®

The most important peripheral connected to your computer isn't your graphics card, your printer, or even your monitor. The single most critical piece of hardware aside from the CPU is the keyboard. It's not high-tech, and when it works, it doesn't get noticed at all. But the PC's keyboard is absolutely critical to your productivity, comfort, and health.

You need look no further than the ever-expanding number of repetitive strain injury (RSI) cases plaguing corporate America. As people spend more and more time at their computers and work longer hours, the likelihood that a poor or malfunctioning keyboard can cause permanent injury grows.

This chapter will

- Help you understand how keyboards work and explain the differences among keyboards
- Introduce buying alternatives for keyboards
- Help you install and maintain a PC keyboard, and show you how to fix ergonomic dangers

Overview

There are many reasons to consider a keyboard upgrade, not the least of which is *ergonomics*. Ergonomic devices such as keyboards, office chairs, and desks are designed to minimize strain on the human body, which can lead to painful injury over time. Although numerous factors go into a friendly environment, your choice of keyboard is extremely important. In addition, you can find compact keyboards that save desk space, remote keyboards that use infrared or radio signals, and multimedia keyboards that integrate speakers, microphone, and audio controls. There are even keyboards with embedded scanners.

For all the variety—and a little weirdness—the devices we'll look at here perform similar tasks.

How Keyboards Work

Believe it or not, there's actually a spark of intelligence inside your keyboard. A small microchip called a *keyboard controller* plays interpreter, turning the presses of keys into recognizable input for the CPU.

It works like this: The keyboard keys are arranged above a sensor grid that detects key impacts. To do this, the keyboard controller constantly checks the state of each point on the grid, corresponding to each key on the keyboard. It does this by sending intersecting signals from the top and sides of the grid.

Of course, this polling happens very quickly. When the controller detects keyboard contact, it sends out a signal to the CPU (called an *interrupt*) that tells the system which key was pressed. By checking the keyboard thousands of times each second, the controller can "see" every keyboard event.

Physically, the keyboard is a rectangular circuit board encased in a plastic housing. The keyboard keys rest atop a base plate over the circuit board, which is itself protected by a plastic surface, or shield. The shield does two things. It prevents dirt, water, coffee, donut crumbs, and other assorted trouble from getting into the keyboard electronics and stopping up the works. It also provides a backstop for heavy-hitting typists who might otherwise damage the contact between the key and the circuit board.

There are two types of keyboards: mechanical and membrane. Mechanical keyboards, which mount the keypads on a post and spring, are used in almost all keyboards. They're cheap, reliable, and easy to maintain. Membrane keyboards are often used in industrial environments or areas where sparks must be prevented. In this case, a conductive membrane is used in place of a mechanical switch. When contact is made with the membrane, the keyboard controller detects it and passes a signal to the PC.

Most keyboards plug into one of two types of connectors: a DIN5 keyboard connector or a smaller MiniDIN6—often called a PS/2 connector—keyboard port. The two look similar—both are round plugs with oriented pin-outs—but the MiniDIN6 connector is much smaller.

Tip: You'll do better with a MiniDIN6 keyboard if you have the port for it. The compact connector is identical to that used on almost all notebooks, meaning that you can use your keyboard on a notebook system should the need ever arise. The larger DIN5 connector will require a separate adapter in order to work.

Different Types of Keyboards

If you're like most people, you think a keyboard is a keyboard. It's not. Keyboard makers have been busy cooking up models of every size, shape, and function. Ergonomics has driven much of the design innovation: Split keyboards, sloped keyboards, and keyboards with non-QWERTY layouts or radical one-hand designs have all been tried.

On the feature side, keyboard manufacturers have added everything from sheet-fed scanners and mouse pads to multimedia sound systems. The common thread is that every desktop PC comes with a keyboard, so the desk space is already being used. Why not make it work for you?

The following sections give a rundown of the types of keyboards you might select from.

Standard Keyboards

You know the, ahem, type: 101 keys aligned horizontally in five or six rows, with a classic QWERTY layout, and function keys arrayed along the top, the left side, or perhaps both (see Figure 27.1). You might also find an extra *macro key* or two tucked in a corner. These macro keys can assign complex actions to simple keystrokes, allowing you, for example, to fire up your Web browser with a single click, or shut down your PC in one step. Gateway's AnyKey keyboards have long included macro capabilities.

Figure 27.1.
The classic design of the NMB keyboard is familiar to anyone who has used a PC. (Photo courtesy of NMB Technologies)

Warning: Keyboard macros are nice, but they have their drawbacks. For one thing, the macro keys you assign might conflict with the key combinations assumed by applications—you won't know which operation will get executed until you actually press the keys. Worse, programmable keyboards can get horribly confused. Gateway's talented AnyKey keyboards carry a Tech Note sticker telling people how to cease macro operation should they inadvertently invoke a macro mode that knocks out the keyboard's functionality.

Otherwise, the picture is pretty basic. For any keyboard, you'll want to select based on comfort. For many people, this boils down to "clicky" versus "mushy." Another concern is the amount of key travel, which determines how far down the keys can be pressed—a critical concern for notebooks. You might also want to go with a keyboard that offers an expanded cursor key set (set up in a square with diagonal cursors, as opposed to the up-down/left-right upside-down T arrangement on most keyboards). If you do much data entry, a dedicated numerical on the right side is a must.

Split-Fingered Fastballs

The last couple of years have seen a flood of split-design keyboards intended to improve ergonomic typing. These products, such as Microsoft's Natural Keyboard and Cirque's Wave Keyboard 2, split the keyboard roughly down the center—between the G and H keys on a QWERTY layout—and slope the two sides down from the midpoint (see Figure 27.2). You'll also find adjustable split keyboards, which let you customize the angle and width of the split.

Figure 27.2.
Microsoft's Natural Keyboard features the same split-and-sloped design seen on many ergonomic keyboards. (Photo courtesy of Microsoft Corp.)

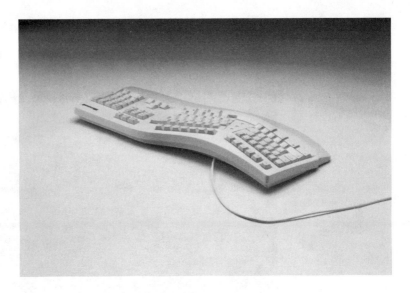

The idea is to eliminate the unnatural positioning of your wrists, elbows, and shoulders required by traditional keyboards. When you type on a traditional keyboard, your palms are set flat, with your hands close together on the home row—a situation called *pronation*. Pronation can bind tendons, cut circulation, and crimp nerve bundles. Irritation leads to chronic inflammation of soft tissue, which can soon lead to irresolvable RSI symptoms. This problem can show up in the wrists, hands, elbows, shoulders, and even upper and lower back.

The sloped keyboard does two things. It turns your palms inward—a more natural position that doesn't require any twisting or flexing—and it sets your hands further apart. When you place your hands closer to shoulder width, you are again assuming a more comfortable position.

Although these products might look very different from your usual keyboard, their physical operation is the same. You'll need to give yourself time to master the new orientation, however. In fact, some users might find that the unfamiliar layout can actually aggravate things, because they strain against the altered positioning. In addition, accomplished typists will find themselves initially poking at the unused space in the middle of the keyboard and generally fighting against the angled surface.

Multifunction Keyboards

Just as printer vendors have transmogrified some of their products into printers/scanners/fax machines, keyboard vendors offer multiple-personality products of their own. Not surprisingly, some of the components built into keyboards fail to match the performance of the best stand-alone peripherals. An integrated black-and-white sheet-fed scanner, for example, won't do for high-resolution color work, and keyboard speakers lack the power of their desktop siblings. You might also have to contend with extra wires attached to the keyboard, which can complicate your desk space. Among the variations you'll see are these:

- Multimedia keyboards: NMB Technologies' ConcertMaster Multimedia Keyboard, shown in Figure 27.3, adds stereo speakers, a built-in microphone, and even SRS surround sound capability to a standard keyboard. It also includes useful audio controls.

Figure 27.3.
*NMB Technologies'
bulky ConcertMaster
Multimedia Keyboard
is an attractive
alternative to
monitor-mounted
speakers, which can
cause interference
with the display.
(Photo courtesy of
NMB Technologies)*

- Scanner/keyboards: Visioneer sells a $250 keyboard with its popular PaperPort monochrome sheet-fed scanner attached to the back (see Figure 27.4).
- Keyboards that point: Any number of products integrate a trackball, trackpad, or even IBM TrackPoint devices into the design (see Figure 27.5). The advantage is that they save space consumed by mice and other roaming rodents.
- USB keyboards: USB-equipped keyboards can act as a peripheral hub for other USB devices, turning them into command central for your USB peripherals.

Wireless Keyboards

Wireless keyboards let you work more flexibly by untethering you from the PC (see Figure 27.6). These products typically include the keyboard and a separate receiving device that plugs into the standard PS/2 keyboard port on the back of your PC. A length of cord lets you place the receiver where you need it.

There are two types of wireless technologies: *infrared* (IR) and *radio frequency* (RF). IR has the distinct advantage of being inexpensive: You can find IR keyboards for less than $150. The drawback is that IR requires line-of-site placement of the keyboard and receiver. If you turn the wrong way or place the keyboard behind a stack of papers, the connection will be lost.

Figure 27.4.
NMB Technologies offers a keyboard that integrates a sheet-fed scanner. (Photo courtesy of NMB Technologies)

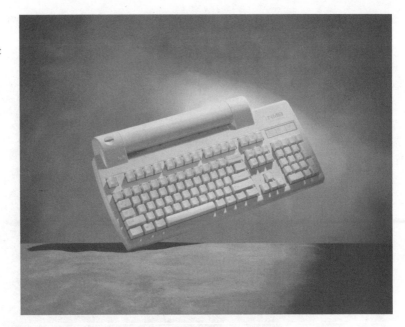

Figure 27.5.
The Cirque Wave Keyboard 2 features a built-in trackpad for pointing, eliminating the need for a separate mouse. (Photo courtesy of Cirque Corporation)

RF wireless keyboards, on the other hand, let you work from almost anywhere. With ranges of up to 50 feet, you can type in documents in the next room. (This isn't practical, but it's kind of cool.) Unfortunately, this capability will cost you. A good RF keyboard can cost $400 or more. In both cases, you have to worry about the incremental expense of batteries needed to power the small transmitter and keyboard controller.

A Lesson in Ergonomics

PC keyboards have been at the center of the ongoing controversy over RSI and other repetitive strain ailments. And no wonder. Keyboard-related health care costs are rising rapidly among corporations, forcing everyone from Fortune 500 corporations to home-based business owners to think about their working habits and environment.

Figure 27.6.
Wireless Computing's Wireless SurfBoard uses radio transmissions to provide excellent flexibility in a small form factor. But you'll have to invest in batteries to make it go. (Photo courtesy of Wireless Computing)

The problem is that you use the keyboard so much. If you spend most of your work day in front of a computer, the keyboard is your primary means of communication with the device. Sure, you click the mouse now and then—inviting an injury to your arm and shoulder, by the way—but the keyboard acts as the bridge between your analog self and the digital guts of the PC.

What's more, you probably use the keyboard more than ever. E-mail, Web browsing, and corporate networks have all eliminated the need to do things away from your desk. No more penning a letter and licking stamps—you just pound out an e-mail message and fire it off. And who goes to the library anymore to look up back issues of magazines? You just search a publisher's archives on the Web.

There's one problem: Way too many people think that a sloped or split keyboard will solve their problems. The theory behind the designs sounds good, but there is no conclusive data that shows that alternative keyboard designs actually help. And I've heard anecdotal stories of healthy workers who, upon switching to a split keyboard, promptly developed RSI symptoms.

Ultimately, ergonomics is about work habits. A split keyboard won't help if you're slouched over your desk or plagued by a chair that completely lacks lumbar support. Follow this checklist:

- Posture: Keep your back straight, shoulders back, and eyes looking at the monitor at a slight downward angle. Both legs and forearms should be parallel to the ground. A keyboard tray eliminates bending up at the elbows, while a foot rest or a good thick book (like this one!) ensures that your thighs won't press down against the chair and cut off circulation.

- Chair: You need a firm-backed chair that keeps you sitting upright, not tilted back or spilling forward. Lumbar support is key—you should be able to feel the chair press into the lower part of your back (not painfully, mind you). Armrests are a no-no: They force your shoulders up when you type, aggravating pronation and introducing neck strain.

- Monitor: The monitor should sit on the desk in order to ensure the proper viewing angle. If it's up on a computer case, you'll invite neck strain and headaches from looking up all the time. Here's a separate but related point: You'll want fast 80Hz and higher refresh rates to eliminate perceived flicker in the image.

Note: Small 14-inch monitors invite RSI injuries by requiring substantially more keyboard and mouse activity than do spacious 17-inch displays. The need to constantly click scroll bars and press cursor keys also slows productivity.

- Keyboard: A split-and-sloped design is worth trying. Remember that the keyboard should be low to keep your forearms parallel to the floor—otherwise, the alternative design won't help much. If your desk is too high, consider getting a slide-out keyboard tray, or try adjusting your chair height so that you are over the keyboard.

- Lifestyle: This is the last and most critical piece of the puzzle. No ergonomic setup will relieve symptoms unless you take frequent breaks from work—stretch, go get a cup of coffee, talk to people. Computer work is unique in that it tends to lock people into unhealthy positions. For example, studies have shown that people blink much less often than usual while working in front of a PC monitor. You should arrange to get up from your chair at least two or three times an hour, to ensure that you don't lock up.

Purchase Decisions

The keyboard is a very personal purchase, and one that can have a real impact on your productivity. In addition to personal preference, you'll need to consider issues such as your work space, ergonomic needs, and the possibility of springing for a multifunction keyboard.

First Impressions: Try Before You Buy

The funny thing about keyboards is that either you like one or you don't. Prices, specs, and slick advertising won't change that. For this reason, it's a good idea to actually use a keyboard before you buy it. Try out several keyboards at a local retail store if possible, or sample keyboards on different systems at the office.

Look for a level of firmness and feedback that is good for you. Heavy-handed typists might want the tactile click and pop of IBM-style keyboards, while less exuberant typists might opt for smoother travel. The following are points to consider. Remember to go with your preferences.

- Tactile feedback: Are the keys firm or mushy? Do they provide a confirming click or a silent rebound?

- Key tops: Pay attention to the tops of the keys: Are they indented to aid precision? Do they feel slick and slippery, or do they provide a little grab during impact?

- Sound: Do you want they keys to be silent or clicky? Does the keyboard rattle against the desk when you type?

- Construction: Heavy or light? Do the keyboard feet provide a stable platform, or does the unit shimmy and rattle during use? Is there unwanted flex or bend in the keyboard?

- Cord: Look for a long one. Too many keyboards skimp on a short cord that won't give you enough leeway to properly set up your desk space.

Features and Fun

If you're upgrading your existing keyboard, now might be a great time to add some neat capabilities to your PC—without eating an extra inch of desk space. If you have USB ports on your system, for example, you should really consider getting one of the new USB-capable keyboards, such as one from NMB Technologies. Not only are USB cables longer and less obtrusive than standard keyboard cables, but the new keyboard will include ports that let it act as a USB hub for future peripherals.

On the multifunction side, you should be cautious. Keyboard-based speakers won't match the quality and power of traditional desktop-based models—and you certainly won't get a subwoofer with them. Likewise, integrated scanners offer fewer capabilities than their stand-alone counterparts and might be restricted by your setup. After all, you won't be able to scan cardboard stock if your keyboard is set straight against the monitor—the paper will get jammed against the display bezel on its way out.

However, an integrated pointing device might be worth considering. Mice are a source of back and shoulder strain as well as desk clutter. The Cirque Wave Keyboard 2 keyboard puts a trackpad directly on the split-style keyboard, while IBM sells a keyboard that has a TrackPoint device positioned in the middle of the keys.

Keeping Keyboards Alive

More than any other component, keyboards are subject to abuse. Hard disks and CD-ROM drives are tucked away safe inside the PC's case, while your monitor sits back from the action. But the keyboard is front and center, sharing space with—and sometimes the contents of—coffee cups, Coke cans, and Chinese food containers.

Fortunately, keyboards are built to take the pounding. The plunger-and-switch mechanisms used by the keyboard keys are simple and hardy. In addition, most keyboards feature a plastic shield that keeps dirt, food, and liquids from striking the key contacts or underlying circuitry. This shield is constructed so that the plastic pops up beneath each key, providing a dam against foreign invaders.

Things do go wrong, though. The following sections contain a couple of tips.

Waterlogged Keyboards

Perhaps the most common problem comes from spilled liquids getting into the keyboard. Depending on what you spilled, you might have a good shot at recovering your hardware. If you spill something, do the following:

1. Unplug the keyboard immediately. Don't wait! You need to cut power to the device in order to avoid a possible short circuit that will fry the electronics.
2. Turn off your PC using the mouse.
3. Tip the keyboard upside down and drain out as much of the liquid as you can.
4. Use a blow dryer or fan to run air over the keyboard face. Make sure to set the blow dryer air to cool—you don't want to cook the keyboard, just dry it out.
5. Allow the keyboard to sit for 12 hours, preferably in a dry spot under direct sunlight.
6. Reattach the keyboard and boot up the PC. Keep your fingers crossed...

Other Liquid Assaults

The preceding approach will work well for water, but the situation is more grave if you spilled soda or coffee into the keyboard well. Once dried, these liquids will leave a residue of sugar and other sticky stuff that will coat contacts and electronics, stopping conduction and rendering the keys inoperable. You'll also have problems with stuck keys and plungers.

You can try to rinse out the gook by, ironically, plunging the keyboard into water immediately after the accident (unplug the keyboard first!). Be sure to work the water thoroughly so that the other substance is washed out of the well. Then follow the procedure just mentioned for drying the keyboard. You'll probably need to leave more time to dry—up to 24 hours.

Keep in mind that this is radical stuff for severe spills. If you spill a little liquid on the keyboard, you should simply mop it up with a rag or paper towel and see if the keyboard continues to work normally. Your keyboard should contain minor spills well, so dousing the unit will probably do more harm than good. If you do end up dunking the keyboard, don't get your hopes up. If the coffee or soda didn't kill the keyboard, the dousing probably will. Still, it's worth a shot, since you know that the keyboard will be doomed otherwise.

Cleaning the Keys

Keyboards are made to get dirty, and most are made to get cleaned as well. If lots of gunk is jamming your keys, or maybe you want to fish around for some loose change, you can clear matters by popping off the keys. Do the following:

1. Turn off your PC.

2. Select the key you want to remove. Using a small screwdriver, gently pry the key up, being careful not to damage the other keys.

3. On most keyboards, the key should click off its plunger, revealing the layer below.

4. To reattach the key, press it on top of the plunger and push down until it clicks into place.

5. If you remove multiple keys, be sure to return them to their proper spots!

Easy Money: Keyboard Upgrades

Installing a keyboard might be the easiest upgrade there is. In fact, the hardest part of the whole thing might be prying the keyboard out of the box. However, you need to check the port on your system first to make sure that you buy a keyboard that matches it. The smaller MiniDIN6 connector is now used on virtually all new systems and is often called a PS/2 keyboard port. Even if you end up with a mismatch, you can buy a simple converter at any computer store that lets you plug larger keyboard connectors into MiniDIN6 system ports, and vice versa.

Keyboards access dedicated system resources, which remove the uncertainty of resource conflicts found with sound boards, modems, and the like. Although USB-type keyboards change the rules a bit, the Plug and Play facilities of the USB bus should keep installation equally simple.

The only place where you can expect trouble is with multifunction keyboards that have scanners and sound systems. In these cases, you'll have separate wires leading to their respective ports. In the case of the scanner, you'll have to locate the resources for the included serial or parallel port scanner.

Summary

Ultimately, a quality keyboard can make a huge difference in your productivity, comfort, and work environment. If you bought a PC a couple of years ago with a chintzy, small-form-factor keyboard— you know, the cheapest the vendor could find—you would do well to consider an upgrade. Basic keyboards are cheap at around $100, while snazzy enhanced models can be had for $150 or less.

Ultimately, it's about your comfort. If you're OK with what you have, then by all means, stick with it. But if you feel you need to make a change, give yourself enough time to make an informed decision. If possible, try out a new keyboard before buying it—or at least test-drive a model by using a coworker's system for a couple of hours. Your body will thank you for the extra consideration.

28

Point and Shoot: Of Mice, Joysticks, and Other Controllers

Peter Norton®

If you buy a PC today, you absolutely, positively have to have a pointing device. On the vast majority of PCs, that means a mouse. These versatile little creatures let you point and click your way around the screen.

Like keyboards, mice are relatively simple devices that are easy to install. Still, not all pointing devices are equal. You'll find a variety of mouse designs and styles, as well as alternative pointing devices. And let's not leave out some of the most sophisticated controller devices—gaming peripherals such as joysticks, gamepads, steering wheels, and even foot pedals.

This chapter covers the serious business of pointing under Windows 95. You will learn

- How mice and other pointing devices work
- What to look for in a pointing device or game controller
- How to install pointing devices and deal with problems that can arise

Pointing Places

Many PC users will never buy a mouse or other pointing device. Nearly all PCs now come equipped with a mouse, which, if cared for properly, can last the life of the PC and beyond. That said, there are some pretty pathetic mice out there; some users might need to explore options beyond the traditional pointer.

There are several types of pointing devices for PCs, including

- Mice
- Trackballs, trackpads, and IBM TrackPoint devices
- Joysticks and gamepads
- Other gaming devices

Inside Mice

Along with the keyboard, the mouse is one of two primary input devices found on most PCs. The workings are simple enough: A rubbery little ball inside the mouse housing rolls against the surface of your desktop or mouse pad as you move the mouse. This ball is nudged up against a pair of perpendicular roller bars inside the mouse housing, so that when the ball moves, the roller bars move in lockstep. Move the mouse forward or back, and the vertical (or y) roller spins with the ball; move it left or right, and the horizontal (or x) roller does its thing.

How the Mouse Works

A motion digitizer reads the turning of the two bars, interpreting them as increments of travel (measured in hundredths of an inch). The controller then sends digitized signals telling your PC that the mouse has been pushed forward half an inch and left three-quarters of an inch. Keep in mind that the mouse sensor has no idea *where* the mouse cursor is on the screen—it simply reports relative positions over known periods of time.

Most mice can detect motion to as little as $1/400$ of an inch—more precision than most users will ever need. This level of precision is up almost four times since about five years ago, when a typical mouse provided precision to $1/100$ of an inch.

You'll also find two or more buttons on the top of most mice, as shown in Figure 28.1. Like the roller bars, these buttons have sensors that send a signal each time a button is pressed or released. Your PC's operating system and applications keep track of where the cursor is on-screen, interpreting movement and clicks based on the small bits of data sent by the reliable rodent.

Figure 28.1.
The new Microsoft IntelliMouse offers a few new features, but it's based on the same ball-and-roller mechanism found in almost all mice. (Photo courtesy of Microsoft Corp.)

Note: A few mice actually use an optical system in which positional information is determined by bouncing a beam of light off a reflective mouse pad. Although these mice don't have moving parts—and therefore don't succumb to dirt in the works—they do require the mouse pad to be clean and in good shape. Dents or nicks in the reflective pad can return spurious positional data, causing cursor fits.

Mice don't live on clicks alone. A small amount of electrical power must be available to the mouse in order for the sensors to work. In the past, this power requirement meant that mice needed a dedicated adapter card to operate. Today, low-voltage designs allow mice to operate over the serial port or dedicated mini-DIN6 connector, also called a PS/2 mouse port.

Like all hardware peripherals, mice talk to the system by way of a software driver. Windows 95 comes with a variety of standard mouse drivers, including those for Microsoft (surprise), Kensington, Logitech, and others. You can also go with the plain-vanilla PS/2 mouse driver, which lacks product-specific features. For most users, the vanilla driver will suffice (it's just pointing, after all). The generic driver also stands the best chance of avoiding compatibility conflicts.

Issues and Problems

Mice aren't perfect. They have moving parts, so they need maintenance, and because they spend all day shuffling around dusty and dirty desktops, their innards can get gummed up. You'll need to do routine maintenance every few months or so, depending on the state of your work area.

In addition, mice have a bad rap as an ergonomic troublemaker. Users tend to lean into their mice, causing shoulder, arm, and back pain over time. The act of moving the mouse around aggravates things, because your shoulder and elbow are moving and straining. These two drawbacks are enough to fuel a market for alternative general-purpose pointing products (now that's a lot of alliteration!).

Rodent Alternatives: Inside an Un-Mouse

Most desktops are equipped with mice, but not all of them. Tight work spaces, specific ergonomic needs, and sometimes just plain old preference make alternative pointing devices desirable. Among them are trackballs, trackpads, and eraserheads (such as IBM's TrackPoint). You'll also find some truly goofy and innovative stuff out there, such as Diamond Multimedia's gyroscope-driven GyroMouse.

We're Talking Trackballs

The most popular mouse alternative, trackballs are simply mice turned on their backs. They employ the same roller bar and button design found in mice, except that the roller ball is positioned on the top of the device for the user to move (see Figure 28.2). When you spin the ball forward with your thumb or finger, the trackball's y roller bar goes into action, signaling the motion detector to send updated positional data to the PC.

Figure 28.2.
The Logitech TrackMan Marble is one of the most popular trackball products. (Photo courtesy of Logitech)

Trackballs come in many shapes and sizes, ranging from tiny notebook-oriented dealies with a ball the size of a BB to colorful, honking desktop jobs designed for the kiddies to slap around (see Figure 28.3). In between, you'll find products such as Logitech's TrackMan Marble, which features a marble-sized ball and three buttons along the right-front edge (refer back to Figure 28.2).

Figure 28.3.
The Microsoft EZ Ball is tailored for kids, with an oversized roller ball and big, colorful buttons. (Photo courtesy of Microsoft Corp.)

Trackballs address the two major drawbacks of mice: their tendency to get gummed up with dirt, and the ergonomic problems associated with pushing the mouse all day long. Because the trackball roller never touches the surface of the desk, the only dirt that gets into the mechanism is from your thumb or airborne particles. Likewise, trackballs let you remain stationary while pointing—no more leaning into those mouse clicks—which can reduce cumulative strain.

Unfortunately, trackballs bring their own baggage. For one, the thumb is the least-dexterous finger, which means that many trackball designs make it difficult to precisely manage the cursor. What's more, simple operations such as clicking and dragging become difficult with a trackball, because you must apply pressure on a button with one finger while using another to roll the ball.

Mouse Innovations

3-D mice are beginning to emerge, and this should be no surprise. Applications ranging from first-person shooting games (can you say Quake?) to VRML browsing environments and low-cost 3-D authoring demand a whole new dimension in pointing. These products often depart from the slip-and-slide mouse design and are used in the air or manipulated on a base.

The Diamond GyroMouse, for example, is mounted on a base and recognizes pressure going from side to side, front to back, and up and down (see Figure 28.4). The result is that you can tell your application to move the cursor upward in a 3-D environment simply by pulling up on the mouse device.

Figure 28.4.
Diamond's GyroMouse provides six degrees of freedom and a whole new way to point. (Photo courtesy of Diamond Multimedia)

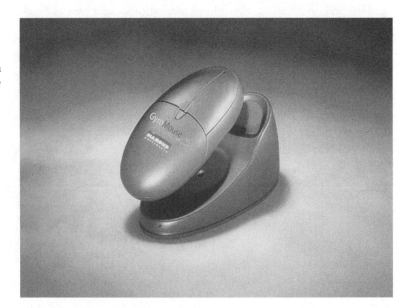

Road Pointers

For a while, trackballs were also a fixture on notebook PCs. Apple's PowerBooks really got the, um, ball rolling with its front-and-center trackball and handy wrist-rest design. But trackballs, like mice, are prone to sticking over time as particles get inside the housing. And unlike desktop trackballs, there is no convenient way to pop open the notebook pointing device and scrape out the insides.

IBM's TrackPoint

Enter IBM's innovative TrackPoint pointing device. This eraserhead-size nub sits in the middle of the keyboard and provides good pointing control without forcing your hands to leave the home row. The device is pressure-sensitive. Resistors at the base of the nub sense contact pressure, speeding or slowing the motion of the cursor to suit. Depending on which contact or contacts are pressed, the device sends positional information in the desired direction.

Because the TrackPoint doesn't roll, no furious spinning needs to occur. Better yet, dirt has no way to enter the device, so the TrackPoint won't gum up over time. However, the pointing experience is very different from mice and trackballs—enough so that many users find it difficult, and the presence of the device among the keyboard's keys can invite unintended key clicks.

You won't find eraserheads on many desktop systems. IBM sells a keyboard with a TrackPoint II pointer built in, but that's about it. But you might see TrackPoint-like devices on notebooks from IBM, Acer, Toshiba, and others.

Trackpads: The Emerging Notebook Standard

The newest notebook pointing device is the trackpad. First seen on Apple PowerBooks, this device appears as a simple black square embedded into the notebook's wrist rest. Their biggest advantage is that trackpads use the most natural of interfaces—your finger.

Trackpads use conductive material to sense where your finger is on the square. A steady, if small, current runs through the square. When you drag your finger across the square, it disrupts the signal. The trackpad's sensors can follow the direction and speed of the disruption by identifying which sensors have changed state.

The big advantage is that the trackpad has no moving parts. It is also sealed against dirt and grime. Still, the finger is a pretty blunt instrument. If you change the angle of your fingertip as you drag along, the on-screen cursor might jump left or right as different sensors get triggered.

Again, you won't find many of these on desktops, although companies such as Cirque sell keyboards with embedded trackpads. You can also buy a separate desktop trackpad module that plugs into the standard mouse port.

Who's Game?

Nowhere will you find more innovation, ambition, and engineering effort than in game controllers. Gamers are notoriously serious about their pointing devices. After all, a good controller can literally mean the difference between life and death.

Joy to the World

The joystick is the quintessential gaming peripheral. Appropriate for flight simulations and many other PC games, these devices work like the control stick in a fighter plane. The user pushes the stick left to right and forward to back to initiate motion, while two to 20 or more buttons provide weapons control and other features.

Joysticks work by placing four resistors in the base of the stick. When the stick is pushed forward, an electric charge is moved into the resistor. The further forward you push, the greater the rate of charge. Sensors check the resistance and report changes in the attitude of the stick. Driver software turns the signals into program-specific commands for down, up, left, right, and so on.

The problem with most joysticks today is that they need constant attention. Your CPU must continually poll the joystick port (usually the game port found on the sound card) to get the latest stick status. When your CPU is busy displaying rich 3-D scenes, the extra workload can drag frame rates and responsiveness down considerably.

The solution is a new generation of digital joysticks, including the Microsoft SideWinder Pro 3-D, Logitech Wingman Digital (see Figure 28.5), and CH Force FlightStick. These joysticks speak in your PC's native tongue—those ubiquitous 1s and 0s—to pipe positional information directly to the system. However, older systems might need an upgrade to provide digital joystick support, such as a USB connector.

Gamepads and Other Gear

Outside of joysticks, you'll find other sundry pointers. Gamepads are identical to the controllers you find with Nintendo or Sega game consoles (see Figure 28.6). These two-hand devices usually have a directional pointer on one side and a number of function buttons on the other. Functions can often be customized.

Figure 28.5.
Logitech's Wingman Extreme Digital maximizes your survival skills with enhanced precision and less CPU overhead than analog joysticks. (Photo courtesy of Logitech)

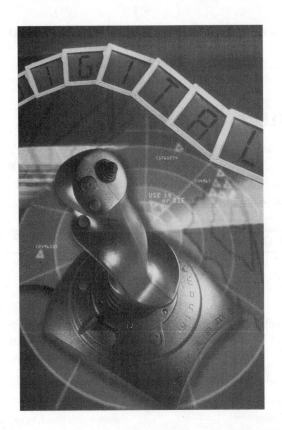

Figure 28.6.
Creative Labs' Blaster Gamepad gives you all the controls you need to jump, kick, run, and otherwise fight your way out of trouble. (Photo courtesy of Creative Labs)

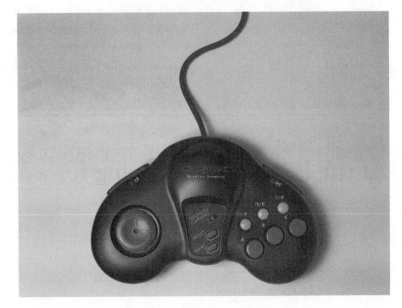

Other input devices include steering columns, such as the ThurstMaster Formula T2. This two-piece set includes a full steering wheel with shifter, which attaches to the desk and includes a small clamp to keep you from twisting it into the air. A foot pedal unit includes accelerator and brake pedals.

Pointer Purchases

Like keyboards, you'll want to buy mice and other devices with comfort in mind. For example, a small child wouldn't do well with the relatively large Microsoft Mouse 2.0, while lefties might want to avoid the right-sided buttons found on the TrackMan Marble. Likewise, a flight sim junkie wouldn't know what to do with a gamepad. Table 28.1 will help you figure out what to purchase.

Table 28.1. Choosing pointers.

Device	What It's Best For
Mouse	General-purpose home and business desktop computing, multimedia, and Internet applications
Trackball	Same as mouse, but optimal for space-limited environments and for users with mouse-related repetitive strain injuries (RSI); also notebooks
Trackpad	Space-limited and dirty/dusty environments, users with mouse-related RSI, notebooks
TrackPoint	Same as trackpad; easier keyboard access
Joystick	Gaming: Flight sims and other flying games; also suitable for some racing and water games, as well as first-person shooters such as Descent
Gamepad	Gaming: Best for side-scrollers (Mario), shooters (Quake), and fighting games (Mortal Kombat)
Steering wheel and foot pedals	Gaming: Driving/racing sims, some flight sims

At the Pet Store: Shopping for a Mouse

There are several types of mice to choose from. They include

- Standard serial port or PS/2 mice
- Wireless mice (infrared or radio frequency)
- Two- or three-button mice
- Enhanced functionality mice (such as the Microsoft IntelliMouse)

The variety is by no means as staggering as what you'll see with keyboards, but it is there nonetheless. For the vast majority of users, a trusty wired, serial, or PS/2 mouse will do the trick. These mice are proven, they don't require batteries, and they provide access to all the standard features in Windows 95 applications.

When it comes to ports, you might look into a USB mouse—if your system has the ports and drivers to support it. However, you'll be choosing from a limited selection of mice. Otherwise, a PS/2 mouse works best, plugging into the dedicated round mouse port (found next to the keyboard port) on the back of the PC. Best of all, it keeps your serial ports free for other devices, such as modems and PDAs.

In general, expect to pay $20 to $100 for a new mouse or trackball. Although most people can certainly get by with a basic mouse, you can choose from the advanced features that many products offer. Programmable button and keyboard combinations let you create nifty shortcuts to programs and OS features.

For mice, you might consider something like Microsoft's IntelliMouse, which puts a small daisy wheel between the left and right buttons (refer back to Figure 28.1). On IntelliMouse-aware applications, turning the wheel with your finger causes programs such as Web browsers to scroll up and down. When you press the wheel down, you can scroll up and down by moving the mouse back and forth.

Some mice feature three buttons. Although Windows 95 and most applications don't recognize the third button by default, your mouse's software can assign a universal function to it—for example, double-clicking or pasting from the Clipboard. Usually you can set these capabilities to suit your needs in software, as shown in Figure 28.7. (In Windows 95, go to Control Panel by selecting Start | Settings | Control Panel, and then double-click the Mouse icon.) In general, neither of these enhancements is enough to lure me away from a comfortable mouse design (although Microsoft has gotten it right with the Mouse 2.0 design used in the newer IntelliMouse product).

Figure 28.7.
Visual utilities make it easy to customize mouse settings.

Buying Game Gear

It's 1 a.m. You've been up half the night trying to get an urgent report in by the deadline. The spouse and kids have been asleep for hours, but you're too keyed up to go to bed just yet. Looks like a splendid opportunity to fly a loaded A-10 "Warthog" attack jet low into North Korean territory and give the business to some invading infantry.

Or it would be if you had the tools to fly the mission. Imagine trying to drive your morning commute with nothing but four cursor keys to control steering and speed. Or imagine that you're an airline pilot taking a stab at a cross-wind landing using only a keyboard. You can be sure that both will be very short rides.

Considering that top-notch PC games cost upward of $50, it makes sense to own a game controller that lets you get your money's worth. Still, price is a problem. You can buy a perfectly compatible four-button joystick for $30, but it might not last long. A joystick I was once given as a gift worked for about two and a half hours before I destroyed it while playing F14 Fleet Defender.

If you're buying a joystick, seriously consider a digital model. Microsoft's SideWinder and CH's Force Flightstick are two outstanding devices. The SideWinder, for instance, offers a neat yaw feature (you twist the stick) for rudder control or rotation. At $70, the SideWinder 3D Pro is among the better buys.

More intriguing are the Force Flightstick and SideWinder Force 3D (see Figure 28.8), both of which actually buffet and resist your hand as you play. These force feedback joysticks use small motors in the base to make you feel, as well as see, the effects of a high G turn. You have to fight the stick during a dive, or try to keep it level as turbulence or enemy fire buffets your plane. If you're serious about gaming, you simply must try one of these new joysticks. The drawback is that you need software that is written to take advantage of force feedback capability.

Figure 28.8.
The Microsoft SideWinder Force 3D lets you feel the buffet of heavy AA fire as you make your bombing runs. Best of all, it works off the standard MIDI/game port found on almost all sound cards. (Photo courtesy of Microsoft Corp.)

Nonflyers might consider a gamepad or similar device. These compact controllers let you conduct complex maneuvers in a wide variety of games. You'll want a device that provides comfortable spacing of buttons and controls and that feels sturdy enough to handle the relentless pounding that gameplay invites. Also consider buying controllers in pairs if you think you'll be playing against human competitors.

Installing and Caring for Pointers

In general, installing a new pointing device is quite easy. PS/2 mice and trackballs, for instance, use the dedicated IRQ 12 resource—meaning that every system, OS, and pointing device manufacturer knows exactly where to put its resources.

Serial mice are a bit trickier, because they must grab one of four (but really, two) available COM port addresses. The biggest danger with serial mice comes from modem conflicts. You need to double-check your modem settings if you plan to install a serial mouse.

Trapping a Better Mouse

Still, Windows 95 makes installing a mouse simple. To do this, go through the following steps. Note that this procedure assumes that you are installing a new mouse over an existing one.

1. Open the Windows 95 Control Panel (select Start | Settings | Control Panel).
2. Double-click the Mouse icon.
3. In the Mouse Properties dialog box, choose the General tab.
4. You will see your current mouse listed in the Name text box. Click the Change button.
5. Place the driver disk for your new mouse in drive A:
6. In the Select Device dialog box, click Have Disk.
7. Select the new device's appropriate .INF file. The device will be installed.
8. Shut down the PC and remove the old mouse from the serial or PS/2 port.
9. Plug the new mouse into the proper port and restart the PC. Your new mouse should be active.

The routine for installing new trackballs and other pointing devices is identical. In general, these devices behave very similarly and use similar system resources.

Setting Up a Joystick

Joystick installation is similar as well, because it uses the same Windows 95 install facility. Here, the thing to remember is that joysticks come with much customizable functionality. Your hot new joystick has many buttons that won't really do anything until you tell them what to do in the joystick's setup program (see Figure 28.9). (You can reach this dialog box by selecting Start | Settings | Control Panel and then double-clicking the Joystick or Game Controllers icons.)

Figure 28.9.

Logitech's Wingman Digital gives you plenty of feature choices for buttons. (Figure courtesy of Logitech Corp.)

Troubleshooting: Before you get too involved with installing that new joystick, check the Windows 95 Control Panel (select Start | Settings | Control Panel) and make sure that a Joystick icon is present. If it isn't, you might have a problem with the game port on your sound card, and the system won't be able to see your gaming device. Refer to your sound board's documentation to explore the problem further.

To install a new joystick, do the following:

1. Open the Windows 95 Control Panel (select Start | Settings | Control Panel).

2. Double-click the Add New Hardware icon.

3. In the dialog box that appears, click the Next button to start the process.

4. In the dialog box that appears, you will be prompted to have the system automatically check for new hardware. Select the No radio button and click Next.

5. In the Hardware Types scroll box, scroll down to the listing for Sound, Video, and Game Controllers and double-click it.

6. Insert the driver disk for your new mouse into drive A:. In the Select Device dialog box, click Have Disk.

7. Select the new device's appropriate .INF file. The device will be installed.

8. Shut down the PC.

9. Plug the new joystick or other device into the game port of your PC (most likely the sound board's combination MIDI/game port). Your new joystick or device should be active in Windows 95.

Note: Keep in mind that games played in DOS mode won't have access to Windows 95 drivers or capabilities. These games must provide direct support for your joystick in order for it to work. Failing that, your joystick should provide emulation for one or more popular models—similar to the way many sound boards make software think they are Sound Blaster cards. Even under Windows 95, you might find that you get the best results when using emulation mode. Check your device's documentation for details on setting and working with emulation.

Caring for Mice

Pointing and gaming devices do wear out. Button contacts get worn, springs give way, and roller mechanism can eventually jam or stick chronically. Crimped and pulled wire leads can also decapitate your mouse or joystick, cutting it off from the system altogether or resulting in maddeningly intermittent operation.

An Ounce of Prevention

Your best weapon is prevention. The following points will extend the life of your mouse:

- Clean out the interior of the mouse periodically to keep too much dirt and gunk from accumulating inside the mouse housing.

- Keep the mouse pad or desk area where the mouse resides clean and clear of dust and dirt.

- Avoid pulling the mouse wire taut or otherwise straining the leads to the device. Also try not to crimp or crush the wire.

- Go easy on the buttons—there's no need to smash them. Repeated heavy blows will only shorten the life of the springs.

- For joysticks, avoid slamming the stick to the wall. Heavy-handed use won't help you pull any extra Gs, but it will wear out or even snap the metal contacts at the base. Keep it up, and you'll be flying a keyboard.

Mouse Cleaning

One thing you will have to do periodically is clean out the insides of your mouse. The ball that pops out the bottom is designed to be tacky enough to grip the surface and provide friction to move the roller bars inside the mouse. Unfortunately, that same characteristic also ensures that dirt and particles on the desktop will stick to the ball and end up inside. Over time, the cumulative covering of grime will cause the cursor to stick annoyingly.

If you notice the mouse sticking, it's easy enough to clear up the problem. Do the following:

1. Shut down the PC. (You don't want to send all sorts of accidental mouse clicks to your waiting system!)

2. Turn the mouse on its back and look for the circular ball plate.

3. Press down on opposite ends of the plate with your thumb and forefinger. Twist the housing in the direction indicated.

4. Hold your hand over the mouse and turn it over. The housing and ball will spill into your palm.

5. Examine the rubbery ball. If you see any matter stuck to it, use your thumb or fingernail to scrape off unwanted particles.

6. Look inside the mouse housing. You will see the two perpendicular bars. Use your fingernail to scrape along each bar, removing any dirt.

7. Make sure to turn both roller bars and scrape along the entire length. Shake out the mouse to ensure that the dirt doesn't end up right back in the mouse.

8. Turn the mouse on its back, plop in the mouse ball, and place the ball plate back into the mouse. Twist the plate to tighten it into position.

9. Turn on your PC and start mousing around.

Summary

Windows 95 and the emergence of USB support will change the input marketplace. Over the next six to 12 months, expect more and more products to support the fledgling USB bus. Although USB should ease installations and cable clutter, it won't radically change the way you use these devices. Most important, comfort will remain the key decision point with any of these devices.

For serious gamers, the future is definitely digital. If you can, purchase a digital joystick with USB support. You'll enjoy better overall system performance, quicker and more precise response, and more advanced features and flexibility. Most important, you'll kill more bad guys.

29

Digital Cameras

Peter Norton®

Digital cameras might be one of the coolest things born of the PC revolution. These nifty gadgets let you snap photos that can be instantly downloaded to your PC. No going to the corner store to develop rolls of film, or scanning photos late at night. You just snap the picture and download it to your PC.

Digital cameras aren't new; in fact, they've been around for several years. What is new are lower prices and improved image quality, which finally makes these cameras a reasonable alternative to traditional silver-film photography. In fact, digital technology might soon replace your camcorder. (Sony sells a $2,000 digital camcorder.)

This chapter will help you understand the following:

- How digital cameras work
- Whether a digital camera purchase makes sense for you, and which is best for your needs
- How to operate a digital camera, including bus issues

The Photo Revolution

Ten years ago, computers were for geeks. Today, my mom sends me more e-mail than snail mail, and many television commercials include Web site addresses. With over 100 million Web pages out there, and near-photo quality ink jet printers costing less than $300, digital cameras play to a ready audience.

Most important, digital cameras are finally affordable. You can buy many models for under $250, and $1,000 will get you unprecedented image quality and features. Today's midrange cameras will snap 640×480 pixel resolution shots at true color (see Figure 29.1), and some push resolutions as high as 1024×768.

The attraction of these products is obvious. Digital cameras can readily move images to Web pages and color printers. Many people need to quickly move photos to the digital domain, and digital cameras are the fastest way to do so. In addition, a growing number of niche markets benefit from all-digital photography, including

- Real estate agents
- Insurance adjusters
- Newsletter publishers and online media organizations
- Law enforcement
- Home and small businesses

Figure 29.1.
The Epson PhotoPC 500 looks a lot like a standard 35mm camera and provides 640×480 pixel images. An optional LCD viewer allows in-camera viewing. (Photo courtesy of Epson America)

Peter's Principle: What Digital Cameras Can't Do

Digital photography is intriguing technology, but don't sell your Kodak stock just yet. Digital cameras still cost much more than their 35mm counterparts and fail to match the resolution of analog film. In fact, if you want the best possible digital output, you should use a high-resolution color scanner to capture images from 35mm slides or prints. Printing photo-quality pictures gets expensive as well. The cost of a good ink jet or photo printer, combined with expensive coated paper, can make digital output more expensive than traditional film processing.

That said, digital cameras excel at convenience and flexibility. These products eliminate troublesome scanning and can save you precious days or hours of processing time when you're in a hurry. The best cameras, which now push up to about 1000×800 pixels, even come close to matching analog output under casual scrutiny. The lesson here is that if you don't expect too much of these much-publicized products, you'll probably be more satisfied with them.

How Digital Cameras Work

Digital cameras are similar to scanners in that they employ thousands of tiny light sensors to turn reflected light into electrical impulses. The challenge is greater with digital cameras, however, because they must capture all the information in a single instant, whereas scanners can take 30 seconds or more to pass over a page.

Taking a Picture

When you take a digital photograph, the camera's lens snaps open just like with a normal camera. But instead of silver-halide-based film waiting in the back of the chassis to receive a dose of reflected light, a microchip with thousands of light-sensitive transistors is there. These transistors, known as *charge-coupled devices* (or CCDs), turn light into electrical pulses. The brighter the light, the greater the charge.

CCDs can discern levels of brightness, but they don't recognize color. Like all digital devices, these products create natural-looking colors by compositing three building-block colors and mixing them into each pixel. To do this, digital cameras must take three snapshots in order to complete a single color picture.

Digital cameras use three colored filters to deliver the proper light to the CCDs: one each for red, green, and blue. For each color pass, the camera stores 8 bits of color information per pixel, or 256 colors per pixel. Add up the bits per pixel for each of the three passes, and you end up with 24 bits of color information for each pixel. That equals 16.7 million colors—more than the human eye can discern.

The precision of the CCDs determines the top resolution, an important consideration in any digital camera purchase. That said, lens quality and image processing techniques can affect the end result significantly.

Managing Images

Once the lens and CCDs have done their work, the resulting color image is stored to memory in a compressed image format. A dedicated compression chip—often tailored to the standard JPEG compression scheme—squeezes the original bitmap image down by a factor of 10 to 100 times. The bits are then moved to the camera's memory buffer, a nonvolatile store of silicon memory.

Most cameras let the user set image quality to at least two settings—high and low quality. High-quality snapshots often come in at 640×480 pixels and go easy on the compression to maintain visual fidelity (see Figure 29.2). Cameras can store only a limited number of high-quality images—often about 20 to 30.

The low-quality setting usually employs a lower 320×240 resolution and more aggressive compression. It's no surprise that image quality suffers, with perceptible graininess and loss of detail. That said, you can often pack 100 snapshots into the installed memory of a digital camera when using the lower-resolution setting. Low-res images also download to your PC more quickly and use less hard disk space.

Today, most cameras use integrated silicon memory. However, Intel, Kodak, and others are pushing a specification for PC Card-based memory to be a digital camera standard. The main advantage is modularity. When your camera runs out of memory, you simply snap in another PC Card, the way you would snap in a new roll of film. To take additional pictures with an integrated memory camera, you must go to a PC, download the photos, and clear the memory—hardly an option when you're at the Grand Canyon, for example.

Figure 29.2.
This 640×480 resolution JPEG image was snapped by a $300 digital camera. Not bad, huh? (Photo courtesy of Epson America)

Moving Pictures

Your pictures aren't worth much if you can't get them into your PC. There are several ways to get images from the camera to the PC:

- Serial cable
- USB cable
- Flash memory cards

Today, most cameras use a standard serial port cable. The serial port connection means that virtually any desktop or notebook PC can communicate with the camera (provided that it has the right software, of course). However, the serial connection itself is slow and invites conflicts and clumsy cable swaps.

Expect newer cameras to begin offering USB bus capabilities. The faster 12Mbps throughput will be a welcome relief: Serial-based downloads can take much time. The daisy-chaining USB bus also means that you won't have to unplug a modem or other serial device to free up a port for the camera.

Another burgeoning option is the use of the standard-factor PC Card modules just mentioned. These Flash memory cards, shown in Figure 29.3, can store up to 10MB or more of data, and they let you swap cards if the memory gets full. This option is key when you're on the road and you don't have a PC around to download your full memory buffer to. They can also move images to your hard disk very quickly.

Figure 29.3.
Flash memory cards from Intel and others can put megabytes of swappable storage in your wallet. Flash memory is the best solution for taking pictures far from your PC. (Photo courtesy of Intel Corp.)

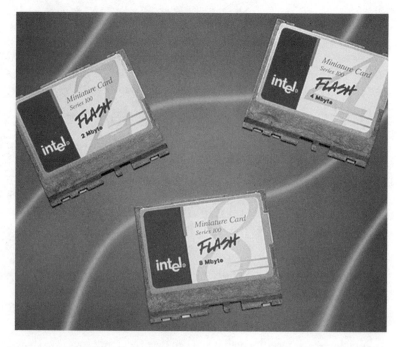

Both the USB and Flash memory implementation suffer a basic drawback—most PCs aren't equipped to deal with them. This means that you might face an I/O upgrade in order to make use of newer cameras. If you're unwilling to do this, a serial-based camera is your best bet.

Sundry Concerns

Although everyone is legitimately excited about digital cameras, there are many drawbacks. First, you won't get the level of quality you see with regular cameras, so you won't want to throw out your pocket 35mm camera anytime soon. Second, although digital cameras do away with film, they'll have you buying batteries by the palette.

What's more, digital camera owners face challenges with their image archives. Everyone is used to buying new photo albums to hold their growing collection of pictures—and the same holds true for digital snapshots. If you plan on taking a lot of photos, you'll need to find a place to archive them before they completely overrun your hard disk. The best solution is a CD-R drive that can write the files to a CD-ROM disc.

All that said, these cameras get a boost from the emergence of cheap, photo-quality ink jet printers. Printers such as the HP PhotoSmart and Epson Stylus Photo can produce true-color output at resolutions of 1,200 to 1,400 dots per inch (dpi). The result is instant print-outs that look nearly as good as their Fotomat counterparts.

Other Cameras

There's more to this market than digital Instamatic cameras. Sony has been selling a consumer-minded digital video camera for over a year, and others are expected. As low-cost video conferencing and Web video become mainstream, more and more PCs also sport small, monitor-top video cameras. The following sections tell you what to look for.

Direct to Video

Digital video cameras work much like their still-photo counterparts, except that they must function much more quickly (see Figure 29.4). As with digital cameras, CCDs capture light and convert it into analog electrical impulses, which are then converted into digital 1s and 0s. Color cameras often use three CCD chips to build a true-color composite in a single pass.

There's just one problem. Digital video cameras must take up to 30 snapshots each second, converting light into electricity into binary bits so that the individual images can be strung together into a coherent video. What's more, these cameras must also capture analog sound, sampling the waveforms and converting them to binary as well.

If this sounds like a lot to do, it is. For this reason, digital video cameras cost thousands—not hundreds—of dollars. In addition, these cameras use a digital tape-based medium or small hard disks rather than the solid-state memory found in digital cameras. The reason is that video files are too large to store economically in silicon.

Figure 29.4.
Sony's DCR-PC7 isn't cheap—it costs over $4,000—but it will stream digital video directly to your system over its FireWire connector. (Photo courtesy of Sony)

Looking Ahead: The future of digital photography might be found in the Hitachi MPEG Camera, shown in Figure 29.5. This compact, lightweight camera takes full-motion MPEG-1 compressed videos at 30 frames per second and uses a Flash memory card to move files to the PC. Compression happens in real time on the camera, keeping video files small. The MPEG Camera can also take still photos and record audio.

Digital video cameras also present challenges for moving data to PCs. Even USB's 12Mbps data rate is insufficient to conveniently move enormous video files. For this reason, many vendors look to the IEEE 1394 bus standard, known as FireWire, to provide fast downloads to the PC. FireWire can move data at rates of 200 to 800Mbps, and it also provides easy Plug and Play installation. However, few PCs feature FireWire ports (most now come with USB ports), adding to the expense of these peripherals.

Figure 29.5.
Hitachi's MPEG camera takes high-quality motion video, yet keeps file sizes compact with its on-board compression hardware. (Photo courtesy of Hitachi)

Monitor-Top Models

Perhaps the most prevalent type of camera is the inexpensive monitor-top models used for desktop video conferencing, Web-based video, and other PC-connected applications. Unlike stand-alone digital cameras and video cameras, these units don't use their own on-board memory to store and later upload images to the PC. Instead, they send data to the system in real time.

Most users will find these cameras as part of a larger bundle, whether included with a new PC or as part of a video conferencing upgrade kit such as Intel's ProShare. Controls are often limited—in fact, Connectix's QuickCam models have no controls at all.

Like digital video cameras, these units use a three-pass method to turn light detected by CCDs into true-color images. The data is then streamed to the PC through a cable of some sort, where it is displayed on the monitor or compressed and sent to the modem for transmission to a remote receiver. Unlike other cameras, these desktop cameras do not download data to your hard disk.

Many modern monitor-top cameras, such as the Connectix Color QuickCam, use—surprise—the serial bus. Expect that to change, however, as the faster, more convenient Plug and Play USB bus becomes entrenched on PCs. If you have a USB-capable PC, a USB camera is a very good idea, particularly since the higher data rate can yield better image quality and smoother video.

Purchase Decisions

When it comes to buying a digital camera, you have plenty of choices. Price remains a big issue. Generally, cameras with higher resolutions and attractive storage and image control features command a premium. That said, you can find excellent products for as little as $300.

Here are the main issues to watch for when buying:

- Color depth: Accept no less than 24-bit color.
- Resolution: 640×480 is a good minimum, but better cameras push resolutions up to about 800×600 pixels.
- On-camera storage: PC Card storage is the most flexible, but you should make sure that you have at least two of these cards so that you can swap out a full card for an empty one.
- Controls: Zooming, adjustable photo quality settings, and the ability to view and delete images from the camera are all useful.

Color Depth

The decision here is very simple: Accept nothing less than 24-bit color. Fortunately, most cameras today provide this level of color capability, making them a good match for printers and graphics display subsystems that are also tuned for 24-bit operation.

Resolution

Expect resolutions to continually improve. Two years ago, 320×240 was the resolution offered on affordable digital cameras. Today, most mainstream models provide 640×480 resolution—four times that of earlier models. You'll also find a few products pushing pixels further still, to resolutions of about 800×600 and even 1000×800.

Unless your needs are very specific, you'll want to buy a model that provides a resolution in the range of 640×480 pixels. These cameras produce attractive output that looks great when printed on new photo-quality ink jet printers. Of course, higher resolutions will eke out more detail.

Keep in mind that not all resolutions are created equal. Lens quality and image compression will both affect the end result. You should try to purchase all the resolution you can afford, but be sure to read the latest comparative reviews to get the skinny on which models do the best job. Keep in mind that this technology moves fast. What was a winning product six months ago will probably be in the middle of the pack today.

Short-Term Memory

Storage is a big deal. A camera with a small integrated memory store will have you running back to your PC every 10 shots or so so that you can make space for more pictures. And if you take that camera with you on a vacation, your PC probably won't be close at hand.

If possible, consider a camera that uses PC Card Flash memory (see Figure 29.6). These credit-card-sized modules plug into the back of your camera and hold 2 to 10MB of images. To transfer the data to your PC, you simply plug the card into a PC Card reader (often sold separately) and download the files.

Figure 29.6.
Flash memory is good stuff. Digital audio recorders, like this small Olympus model, can use the same Flash cards used in digital cameras. (Photo courtesy of Intel Corp.)

PC Card memory enjoys two major advantages over the built-in stuff found in most low-cost cameras. First, it's swappable. When you run out of storage space, you simply pull out the module and plug in a fresh one. You're then ready to snap another round of photos without having to go back to your PC, fire up the camera's desktop software, and move images to the hard disk. Of course, once you've downloaded your images, the card is free to accept another round of photos.

Second, PC Card memory can get images into your computer much faster than a serial cable can. Downloading a full set of photos over a serial cable can take 10 minutes or more—an agonizing process when you want to just grab a couple of images quickly.

Viewing Options

Another key feature is viewer options. All digital cameras include an inline viewer, which you must hold up to your eye in order to aim the camera. However, like camcorders, many digital cameras offer tiny color LCD view panels. Often available as an option (expect to pay $150 to $250 for this perk), the LCD lets you size up images without putting your face to the camera.

The big attraction of the LCD panel is viewing. The LCD lets you immediately view any photo stored in the camera's memory. Although the screens are tiny—about $1^1/_2$ inches on a side—their active-matrix design provides a crisp, bright display that can be viewed in sunlight.

Another advantage of the display is the fact that you can manage images without the PC. Cryptic but usable controls can often be found on the top or back of the camera. They let you delete the active image, making it easy to reclaim valuable storage space when you're on the road. The ability to proof images before downloading them can be helpful as well, prompting you to retake a picture that didn't work out, for example.

The Battery Issue

Digital cameras might seem like the soul of convenience—no floppy film strips to thread, no rushing to Walgreens to make the 11:30 a.m. deadline for next-day processing. What you *will* be doing is buying batteries and fretting about existing charge in the cells.

Digital cameras chew up batteries at a ferocious pace, particularly if you use an LCD attachment or take flash pictures. If possible, look for a unit that has a rechargeable battery pack rather than one that uses common but nonrechargeable AA or AAA batteries.

Tip: Save yourself some money by practicing good power management. Try to minimize the use of the LCD display when possible—it's a big consumer of power. Also, make sure that you purchase the optional AC adapter and power cord when you get the camera. Downloading images can take a while for many of these products, and doing this on a battery will shorten its life considerably.

Diagnosing/Troubleshooting

Digital cameras are highly integrated sealed-box peripherals. If something goes wrong with them, you won't be able to effect repairs without voiding the warranty and potentially damaging the product. As with so many computer components and peripherals, your best bet is to pursue a warranty repair or replacement of the camera through the manufacturer. Failing that, you can try to have the unit serviced.

The outlook for damaged cameras might be gloomy, but often things aren't as bad as they seem. A camera that fails to download images, for example, might simply be suffering from a loose connector or a dying battery. Here are a few simple things to look for:

- Check those batteries: Digital cameras consume batteries at an alarming pace. A fresh set of batteries can wear down fast if you've been using the LCD viewer or you've monkeyed with the power-down settings so that the camera fails to turn itself off when left unattended.

- Tighten connections: Cables can get bumped and stretched when you're downloading images. If you can seem to make the connection, ensure that the connectors are fitted tightly.

- Watch those modules: By the same token, you need to make sure that PC Card memory modules are fitted firmly in their sockets. Also, when you're juggling multiple memory cards, it's easy to accidentally swap in an empty card for one that has the photos you want. Make a point to mark your modules with an indelible ink pen so that you can keep track.

- Use fresh batteries: Be careful not to team fresh batteries with older ones. This mismatch can result in wacky behavior, including lost data and unexpected shutdowns. When you replace batteries, replace them all at the same time.

- Check the Twain drivers: If your PC can't see the camera, this might be a software problem. Make sure that the proper drivers (called Twain, an industry standard acronym that has no meaning) are installed (they're included with the camera) and that you're using the correct serial or other bus port.

Summary

Digital cameras are where the geek culture meets the mainstream. With Web sites turning into an accepted means of keeping ties among scattered family members, a good digital camera can help bring people closer together. Meanwhile, professionals can greatly enhance their productivity and speed to market by using all-digital photography.

And more is on the way. Intel is pushing for lower-cost cameras by shifting the burden of image compression and other operations to fast, MMX-enabled PCs. The FlashPix file format, developed by Kodak and promoted by Intel, employs variable-resolution output, making it easy to use one shot for high-resolution printing and low-resolution Web pages—without converting formats.

Just be warned: Digital photography is not for the meek. You still won't get the quality provided by 35mm film—that is still years away. You'll also want enough system horsepower and available storage to manage, manipulate, and store your growing library of digital snapshots. All that said, digital photography is one of the coolest—and most useful—things to come out of PCs since the spreadsheet.

30

Scanners

Peter Norton®

The past few years have seen an explosion of devices connected to the personal computer. PC speakers, monitor-top cameras, personal photo printers, and connected PDAs have all staked out a piece of turf on your desk. You can add scanners to that list. These useful peripherals can turn your boring old PC into a desktop photo studio, document imaging center, or working fax machine—all for as little as $200.

This chapter introduces you to scanner upgrades, ranging from inexpensive monochrome handheld devices to full-blown color flatbed models that are appropriate for professional artwork. In this chapter, you will learn

- How the different types of scanners work, including the interaction of the hardware and software
- What to consider when purchasing a new scanner, including what type of scanner is best for you
- How to install a new scanner and its software and make sure it's operating properly
- Tips and tricks for creating good scans
- How to resolve scanner problems ranging from software tweaks to mechanical problems

Overview

When it comes right down to it, a scanner upgrade might be one of the best ways to extend your PC's capabilities. After all, a faster CPU or a large hard disk won't give you the ability to grab objects in the real world and turn them into digital images and documents. But a low-cost desktop scanner can. And it will do so—in full color—for as little as $200.

Scanners are basically desktop analog-to-digital converters. They take analog visual things—documents, magazine pages, photos, business cards, and so on—and turn them into digitized bitmaps that your PC can understand. Bundled software lets you capture data and change settings that affect the visual quality of the captured images. In addition, optical character recognition (OCR) software is usually included to let you scan text and have the digitized information converted into usable text.

All scanners take the same basic approach to capturing visual information. A light source is aligned horizontally across the face of the scanner and is used to illuminate the target document. Reflected light passes through a lens, where it is detected by a row of charge-coupled devices (CCDs). The CCDs convert the reflected light into electrical impulses that vary in voltage according to the intensity of the reflected light. There is one CCD per pixel of resolution, so a 600dpi scanner would have 600 CCDs arrayed across the scanner's sensor head. Finally, one or more analog-to-digital converters turn the analog electrical signals into the 1s and 0s that your PC can understand.

Types of Scanners

You'll find a real variety of scanners on the market, ranging from precise, high-resolution scanners intended for professional artwork to small, quick-reading models designed to grab documents at a moment's notice. With the size, shape, and capabilities of scanners varying so widely, it's important to understand how they work and what you want before going in.

There are three types of scanners for the PC:

- Flatbed scanners
- Sheet-fed scanners
- Handheld scanners

Flatbed Scanners

The most popular and versatile type of scanner is the flatbed scanner (see Figure 30.1). As prices come down, the flatbed is the scanner of choice for more and more users. Flatbed scanners look like a rectangular box, usually 10 inches wide by about 12 or 13 inches long, which allows them to conveniently scan an $8^1/_2$×17-inch piece of paper.

Figure 30.1.
The UMAX Astra 1200S flatbed scanner provides top resolution and quiet operation. (Photo courtesy of UMAX)

Like a photocopier, flatbed products scan documents by running a sensor across the length of the document. The sensor itself lies underneath a glass scanning surface, while a top door closes over the scan table to control lighting, allowing for better results.

Flatbed scanners enjoy the highest level of accuracy because the document isn't moved during the scan. In addition, the sensor array travels along a finely-controlled path in a sealed environment, allowing for fine control that can enhance effective resolutions. However, you have to manually feed each page to the flatbed scanner unless you want to invest in a document feeder that can move paper in and out of the scan table automatically.

Sheet-Fed Scanners

Sheet-fed scanners (see Figure 30.2) are a popular alternative for crowded office desks and other places where the large footprint of flatbed scanners just won't do. Sheet-fed models use a motor to pull documents past a scanning head that is about $8^1/_2$ inches wide. The biggest advantage is that sheet-feds can capture an entire standard page in one pass, without consuming a lot of desk space.

Figure 30.2.
The Umax PageOffice 11C is compact, yet it provides color scanning capability. (Photo courtesy of UMAX)

Sheet-fed models have a few telling shortfalls. For one, they can handle only loose-leaf pages. You can't scan material from a book or magazine without first ripping out the page to be scanned. For another, these products can choke on thicker media, such as cardboard, and they can be tricky to use with small or odd-shaped paper, such as business cards. And because pages are pulled through the device past the scanning head, the scan isn't as accurate as that of a flatbed, where the medium is stationary.

Sheet-fed scanners range in price from about $100 to $250, and resolution ranges from 200 to 400dpi. In general, sheet-fed scanners are excellent for OCR work, as well as serving as input scanners for faxing. Some, such as Visioneer's popular PaperPort Vx, provide a software interface to launch fax, OCR, and image-editing software from within the scanner application.

Handheld Scanners

Handheld scanners (see Figure 30.3) are a diminishing breed in the scanner market. As its name implies, you use a handheld scanner by moving it over the item being scanned. It's no surprise that this type of scanner can be a bit imprecise—especially after that second cup of coffee—but it has the key advantage of being inexpensive and portable.

Figure 30.3.
Easy does it.
Logitech's ScanMan
Color can capture
300dpi color images,
but you'll need a
steady hand and
much patience for
larger documents.
(Photo courtesy of
Logitech)

Handheld scanners use a scan head that is 4 to 6 inches wide, allowing them to take in about half the width of a standard page at a time. To operate the unit, you must pull the scan head slowly and evenly across the document, maintaining a constant rate of speed to avoid overtaking the scanner's capacity to capture the data. A tracking roller records the distance and rate of travel, allowing the scanner to know exactly where each visual bit of information belongs.

Because the scan head is only half the width of a piece of paper, most units come with software that lets you stitch scan passes together into a single bitmap. The software attempts to anchor the two scans together to provide a close match, but the results are usually disappointing. If you need to capture entire $8^1/_2 \times 11$-inch documents, a handheld scanner probably won't be suitable.

Most handheld scanners are limited in resolution to about 400dpi, and many are monochrome models. Prices are attractive, though: You can find models for $150 and less. Logitech's aging ScanMan 256, for example, can be had for about $70. One area in which handheld scanners might be useful is with portable systems, because the scanner can be easily packed for travel and then operated in a cramped space.

Color Scanning: Three Times the Work and Worth It

Not more than a couple of years ago, it was hard to decide whether to go with color or black-and-white. A black-and-white scanner could be had at a reasonable price, but color-capable scanners still commanded a premium. Compact scanners, meanwhile, might lack color capability all together. Today, color pervades the entire range of scanner products, from low-cost handheld and sheet-fed models to powerful flatbed scanners.

The reason it took color a while to hit the mainstream is that capturing all the color data gets complex. For now, you need to understand how scanners see color. Like a dog, a scanner's CCDs see only in shades of gray—or, more accurately, in levels of voltages that can be assumed to be gray. To process color, scanners must take three separate snapshots, each tailored to a specific area of the color spectrum, and composite them to yield a color scan.

Here's how it works: By limiting the scanned light to one area of the spectrum, a typical flatbed scanner can capture 8 bits of color data for that color. By doing this for three building-block colors—usually red, green, and blue—the device can composite the information from the three scans to yield a range of 16.7 million distinct colors per pixel—more than the human eye can fathom.

Scanners can take color-specific snapshots in one of two ways: They employ a light filter to limit the reflected light to the desired wavelength, or they shine a specific color of light onto the document. In either case, by applying three different color "looks" to each line of the document, the scanner can put together an accurate picture of the colors it is seeing.

Technical Note: Here's where things get weird. The way your scanner deals with color depends on whether it uses color filters or different colors of scanning lights to read color information from documents. It all goes back to the area of *color modeling*—elaborate logical systems for specifying colors in digital equipment. Don't panic. Unless you want to delve into the arcane art of color matching to make sure your screen-based designs look just-so when printed professionally, you can still lead a full and rewarding life without mastering this stuff. Still, it's useful to know if you're printing scanned images to a color printer.

Here's how the process works: If your scanner employs a light filter, it is built around the RGB color scheme, which keys on red, green, and blue to build 16.7 million possible colors. To come up with colors such as maroon, yellow, and aqua, the PC mixes varying levels of red, green, and blue inside each visible pixel. By applying a certain number of bits (usually eight of them) to represent each color value in a pixel, you get the relative color depth available to the scanner.

The RGB color model is *additive*. In other words, RGB devices combine elements from building-block color to produce the desired color for each point. Both monitors and scanners that use color filters employ the RGB color model. The common bond is that color is perceived after it is passed through a filtering medium (such as color-specific phosphors or filters).

A different color-modeling scheme gets used by printers and by scanners that employ different scanning light colors instead of filters. In this case, color isn't achieved by filtering through a medium. Instead, color is produced by bouncing back the desired spectrum to the viewer. Called *subtractive mixing*, this approach works based on what light does *not* get passed through or absorbed by the target. What is left over gets bounced back to the eye— thus the phrase *subtractive mixing*. (Can you tell that this name was thought up by someone who spent *way* too much time in a lab?)

In the subtractive universe, the color model is called CMYK, or cyan, magenta, yellow, and black. (K is used for black to avoid confusion with blue). Cyan, magenta, and yellow are the primary colors in this scheme. Black gets thrown in to ensure that true black can be produced, because mixing cyan, magenta, and yellow really yields a brown or gray rather than true black. (With additive mixing, black is produced by the absence of light—you just turn off the pixel.)

Of course, moving to color means that you are, in effect, scanning your document three times. In this case, there are two approaches:

- Take three passes at the document: An option available only to flatbed scanners, this approach has the scan head scan the document three times—once each for red, green, and blue light. After this is done, the three images are merged using software to create the composited full-color image. Of course, even a slight variation in scanner movement will yield registration problems, possibly causing the individual red, blue, and green colors to become visible.

- Alternate the light or filters in a single pass: Every color handheld and sheet-fed scanner takes this approach. The scanner switches rapidly among the three color settings as it scans, yielding three color looks in a single pass. Although this is useful for limiting possible registration problems, the quick alternating of filters or lights poses a design challenge. Also, much more data is being grabbed in a single pass, so the scanner must capture and transfer information quickly enough to avoid data overruns.

Dots, Spots, and Spurious Specs

Of course, one of the first things any buyer looks for in a scanner is resolution. How many dots per square inch can the device detect? This seems like a straightforward question. Unfortunately, scanner marketers and engineers have teamed up to create really innovative ways to make this a tough question to answer.

Basically, there are three types of resolution in a scanner, all of which can come into play:

- Optical resolution
- Mechanical resolution
- Interpolated resolution

Let's walk through each.

Optical Resolution

This is the one that really matters. Optical resolution is directly associated with the number of CCDs (those small light-gathering sensors) mounted on the scan head. The quality of the scanner lens also comes into play.

If a scanner has 300 CCDs strung across each inch of the array, its optical resolution is 300dpi. If it has 600 or 1200 CCDs per inch, the optical resolution is 600 or 1200dpi, respectively (see Figure 30.4). Optical resolution defines the scanner's horizontal resolution—what it can see from side to side as it reads each line.

Figure 30.4.
The Epson Expression 636 can capture 600 dots per inch horizontally and 1200 dots per inch vertically. (Photo courtesy of Epson America)

Mechanical Resolution

Our first step down the slippery slope starts here. Mechanical resolution is determined by the number of steps per inch that the scanner's sensor array takes as it passes over the target. A 300dpi mechanical resolution means that the sensor array stops every $\frac{1}{300}$ of an inch to take a snapshot of the line, while a 600dpi unit stops every $\frac{1}{600}$ of an inch. Although mechanical resolution is a legitimate measure of fidelity, it works only along the vertical access. The optical resolution will always define the horizontal fidelity of the scan.

The limiting issue is the precision of the scanner's motor. Flatbed scanners, with their sealed sensor array and stable document platform, enjoy the biggest advantage here. These tabletop units can achieve mechanical resolutions of 1200dpi by providing minute control over the travel of the sensor array.

Although this is all based on good principles, problems arise in how this capability is reported to consumers. Often, vendors put the mechanical resolution ahead of the true optical resolution, calling their device a 1200×600dpi scanner. (The bigger number looks really impressive up front, no?) Worse, these products might be referred to only by their mechanical resolution when you're shopping at a store or talking to friends. So what you think is a 1200×1200dpi scanner is actually a 600×1200dpi scanner.

Interpolated Resolution

Finally, scanner makers talk about the top resolution that their products can provide. Using software to guess what lies between its CCDs, scanners can produce effective resolutions of up 2400dpi. Called *interpolation,* this process simply averages the known values of adjacent points and fills in the result between them.

Interpolation can be useful, particularly if you need to blow up a small image to a large size. If you captured a 300×300dpi image and increased it to 600×600dpi in a graphics program, the result would be a blocky graphic. By processing the picture using your scanner's interpolation software, you can get much better results, because the original dots aren't just replicated, but smoothed out.

In general, interpolation happens on your PC, not inside the scanner. For this reason, a quick system with lots of RAM can help speed up this kind of scanning. However, no amount of processing power can overcome the basic fallacy of interpolation. You simply can't reliably produce something that isn't there.

Think about it. Unexpected changes in color information between CCDs can yield unrealistic results. And when you double the resolution of an image, basically, half the dots *aren't really there.* If someone tries to sell you a scanner based on the interpolated resolution, look elsewhere.

Tip: Be aware that the interpolation algorithms within image-editing packages such as Adobe PhotoShop might be superior to those supplied with your scanner's software. If you have a new scanner and a favorite photo editor, you might run a little contest to see which really does a better job.

Software

Don't underestimate the importance of software. Virtually all scanners include a bundle of photo- and image-editing software, as well as utilities for managing and tweaking images. There are four main areas:

- Twain driver software
- Photo-editing applications
- Optical Character Recognition
- Utilities

Twain Software

Virtually all scanners come with so-called Twain software, an industry-standard interface designed to take the guesswork out of scanning. Established as a software driver, Twain lets any compliant application provide instant scanning capability. A Twain-compliant word processor, for example, could offer a Scan menu option that activates any installed Twain-compliant scanner.

Over the years, Twain has grown from a software driver layer (plumbing, if you will) into a useful interface for scanning hardware. Depending on which product you buy, you might find that any Twain-compliant application will have access to powerful scanning controls. In fact, your word processor or spreadsheet might have all the trappings of a photo-editing applet.

Photo-Editing Software

You might think you're buying hardware, but the software bundles that scanners provide can be attractive—particularly if you don't already own any image-editing software. Adobe PhotoShop or PhotoDeluxe, Ulead's PhotoImpact, and Kai's PowerGoo are just a sample of the powerful programs often included with scanners.

Also included might be image-management utilities that let you organize and search for graphics files. For example, you can assign key words to captured images—say, "beach" and "swim" with a scanned image of your family on the beach—so that you can use quick text searches to find images later.

Optical Character Recognition

One of the key components of many scanners bound for business duty is optical character recognition (OCR) software. This software processes the scanned bitmap image and converts the legible images of text into text that can be imported into a word processing program. The software allows for quick conversion of paper documents into digital format.

Here, even low-cost handheld and sheet-fed scanners provide adequate resolution for OCR work. What is more important is the quality of the OCR software—some *serious* math goes into character recognition. The raw horsepower of your system will make a big difference as well, because a slower 486 will grind to a halt trying to work through the complex recognition algorithms. A fast Pentium-class or better CPU is a good idea for frequent OCR work.

Bus Interface: Connecting to the PC

Today, most scanners hook to your PC in one of two ways: over the parallel port or over a SCSI connection. Although some serial port scanners are available, the port really lacks the bandwidth to keep up with the data flow from a scanner.

Parallel Port Scanners

Most handheld and sheet-fed scanners will join the clamor of peripherals vying for your parallel port. If you don't have too many parallel devices, this won't be a problem. Setup is almost always painless, and virtually all PCs have a parallel port. Most of these scanners include a parallel pass-through device that lets you keep your printer hooked up along with the scanner.

Compatibility: If you end up using a pass-through port with your scanner, keep a couple of things in mind to avoid trouble. First, don't try to print and scan at the same time. The pass-through device is there as a convenience to eliminate the troublesome plugging and unplugging of connectors—it can't juggle multiple jobs on the same port. Second, be aware that enhanced parallel port operation might not work over a pass-through device. If you experience printer trouble after installing a pass-through device, you should check your system CMOS utility and try setting the parallel port to standard Centronics operation.

SCSI Scanners

Until very recently, flatbed scanners and SCSI were a joint proposition—and no wonder. The SCSI bus has more than enough bandwidth for high-resolution scan jobs, provides standard external access, and has the flexibility to allow other devices to daisy-chain off the scanner. What's more, SCSI was a fixture on computers usually used by people who needed tabletop scanners—graphics professionals who had Macintosh computers or high-end workstations.

Unfortunately, for many PC users, SCSI has spelled trouble. Until the arrival of user-friendly 32-bit operating systems and useful SCSI tools such as Corel's EZ SCSI software, SCSI peripherals could be very difficult to install and manage. There was also the little problem of added expense: The cost of a SCSI card ($100 to $200) must often be considered as part of a scanner purchase.

Today, many SCSI headaches are starting to subside as drivers and operating systems improve. However, unless you have an existing SCSI interface on the outside of your PC, a SCSI-based scanner means that you will have to add an add-in card to your system.

USB Scanners

If you're in the market for a scanner, it might be a good idea to look for one that has USB capability. Provided that your PC includes USB connectors, this Plug and Play external bus can greatly ease hardware setups. Like SCSI, you can string USB peripherals to each other, making it easy to find enough connector ports and avoid evil cable tangles behind your PC. The bus also supports 12Mbps data rates, more than enough for scanning purposes.

If you don't have a USB connector, you might consider an upgrade as part of your scanner purchase. Although only a handful of USB-capable scanners are available now, expect more to arrive as Windows 98 and USB-equipped systems fill the market.

Buying a Scanner

How do you go about buying a new scanner? If you read the preceding section, you probably have a pretty good idea of what's out there. Now you just have to figure out what you want to do.

Table 30.1 provides a breakdown of common scanner usage scenarios and the hardware for the job. Keep in mind that these are minimum requirements—you might want to buy more scanner than you need right now, with the expectation that you'll make use of those features down the road.

Table 30.1. Scanners for every job.

Task	Mechanism	Minimum Requirements
Professional artwork	Flatbed	1200×1200dpi resolution, 36-bit color
Business and home artwork	Flatbed	600×600dpi resolution, 24-bit color
Business and home documents	Sheet-fed	300×300dpi resolution, monochrome
Portable	Handheld	300×300dpi resolution, monochrome

Professional Artwork

If you're buying a scanner to create accurate reproductions of photos for publication or distribution, image quality is your overriding concern. Your scanner must provide optical resolutions of 1200dpi to ensure fine detail under close scrutiny. Color depths should be 30 or 36 bits, which is high enough to smooth subtle color gradients and enhance dark images.

Scanners in this range can get pricey, mainly because of the added expense involved in scanning 30-bit and greater color depths. Expect to pay $3,000 or more for a scanner that has these capabilities. Here are things you should look for in a top-of-the-line scanner:

- Optical resolutions of 1200dpi
- Color depths ranging from 30 to 36 bits
- Fast SCSI or USB interface
- An optional slide scanner attachment for making scans of 35mm slides and transparencies (see Figure 30.5)
- Professional photo-editing software, such as Adobe PhotoShop

Figure 30.5.
The UMAX PowerLook 2000 includes a transparency adapter for scanning photographic slides. (Photo courtesy of UMAX)

General Business and Home Graphics

This fast-growing area of the market offers greater capabilities and lower prices than ever before. Here, scanners can be expected to be pulled into mixed duty, capturing high-quality color photographs one minute and scanning a five-page technical report bound for OCR processing the next.

Depending on the relative demands you put on image-capture quality, a flatbed model is probably best for this type of work. This is certainly the most versatile design, because it can scan pages directly from books, magazines, and boxes—scans that a sheet-fed model can't cope with. Prices are very competitive: Many top-notch flatbed scanners sell for $200 to $500 and offer more than enough resolution and color handling for heavy artwork.

If you're looking for lower prices and smaller footprints, a color sheet-fed scanner is a good idea. Generally, you'll give up a couple hundred dots of resolution (400dpi is a frequent sheet-fed spec), as well as the ability to read thick media. But scanners such as Visioneer's PaperPort Strobe offer unmatched automation (stick a piece of paper in the slot, and it starts scanning) and provide neat hooks to your day-to-day applications, turning your scanner into a real part of your PC's tool set. These scanners run $120 to $300.

Here's what you should look for in a scanner bound for home and business use:

- 300×300dpi optical resolution
- 24-bit color support
- SCSI, USB, or parallel port interface
- Good OCR software
- Photo-editing software, such as Adobe Photo Deluxe, that stresses usability over esoteric feature sets

Business and Home Document Scanning

Suppose you don't care about art or images but you need something to turn your bills and documents into electronic files. If you don't want to spend extra money for the ability to keep your records stored on your PC, a low-cost black-and-white sheet-fed model is your best bet. Resolutions really don't have to go beyond 300dpi, because that is enough to support effective OCR processing.

Note that if you're scanning many documents, you might need to buy a flatbed scanner that has an optional paper feeder attachment. Unfortunately, these can get expensive, so be sure to shop around for availability and cost of attachments for various scanners before deciding on one.

You can expect prices for these scanners to be at $150 and below. Here's what you should look for in a document scanner:

- 300×300dpi optical resolution
- 256 grayscale support
- USB or parallel port interface
- Good OCR software
- Small footprint and automation features

Portable Scanning

Portable scanning is a niche application, to be sure, but this is one of the few markets left for handheld scanners. And it's an intriguing one. Partnered with a notebook, a parallel port-based handheld scanner can capture business cards, legal documents, and other business-related fare—whether in a trade show booth or in a hotel meeting room.

Keep in mind that a scanner that travels is likely to suffer some abuse, so low-tech is really the way to go. A black-and-white handheld scanner can provide 300 or 400dpi optical resolution for $100 or less. Here's what to look for:

- 300×300 dpi optical resolution
- 256 grayscale support
- USB or parallel port interface
- Good OCR software

Working with Scanners

You've got your new scanner home, so now what? It's a good question. Like any external peripheral, a scanner needs to be connected to your system and given resources to be able to access what it needs in order to work. More important, actually making scans can be very tricky. This section will help you install and effectively use your scanner.

Installing a Scanner

Installing a scanner can be tricky, usually because you must deal with connectivity issues associated with the parallel port or SCSI bus. The following sections give you a heads-up on obstacles that you might encounter during installation.

Installing a Parallel Port Scanner

The good news is that you won't have to tear the case off your PC and fish around for free bus slots. The bad news is that, depending on your parallel port settings, you might have to fish around in your system CMOS and Windows 95 Device Manager to free up parallel port resources.

The easiest way to install a scanner is to closely follow the manufacturer's installation instructions. Scanners often provide a fully automated installation from a CD-ROM or floppy disk. However, if you choose to use Windows 95's Add New Hardware wizard, do the following:

1. Shut off the PC. Place the scanner on a flat, stable surface within a few feet of the PC.

2. Plug the 25-pin female end of the supplied parallel cable into your PC, and plug the pincher or end that mates with the scanner's port into the scanner.

3. Plug the scanner's power cord into an outlet. Make sure that all cables and cords are firmly seated.

4. Turn on the scanner (in some cases, the scanner comes on as soon as it's plugged in). You should hear the motor initiate. Turn on the PC.

5. Windows 95 will detect new hardware and launch the Add New Hardware wizard.

6. In the Hardware Type box, select Other (it has a yellow question mark icon).

7. Click Next. When prompted to detect the hardware, click the No radio button and then click Next.

8. From the Manufacturers list, scroll down to Unknown Device and select it.

9. In the Models box, select Unsupported Devices.

10. Place the scanner's driver diskette into drive A: of your PC.

11. Click Have Disk and double-click the .INF file for your scanner.

12. Windows 95 will update the drivers and then present a dialog box prompting you to select which port to connect the device to.

Parallel Problems

Parallel port devices are supposed to be easy to use. And although I complain vigorously about over-crowding on the parallel port, in general these devices are simpler to use than those using SCSI or proprietary bus cards. Still, the parallel port has its moments. And when it does, it's usually bad news, because your printer and perhaps a few other devices will all get dragged down with it.

Parallel port scanners often require you to turn off enhanced parallel capabilities. If you're having problems, check your system BIOS to see if the parallel port is set to Enhanced Parallel Port or Enhanced Capabilities Port. If it is, set it back to Bi-Directional Parallel Port, sometimes called PS/2 mode.

Many scanners feature a pass-through connector to allow you to hook both a printer and a scanner to the parallel port. Be sure not to try to use both peripherals at the same time, because the conflicting signals will cause your active jobs to fail.

Installing SCSI Scanners

Installing a SCSI scanner isn't too tough, provided that you already have a working SCSI daisy chain on your system. If you're familiar with the workings of SCSI, you'll be ready to deal with terminator plugs, SCSI ID settings, and even the vagaries of what-goes-where on a daisy chain to make everything work properly.

If you don't already have a SCSI adapter installed in your system, you can find out what you need to do in Chapter 11, "Control Freaks: IDE and SCSI Controllers." To install a new SCSI scanner onto an existing SCSI adapter, do the following:

1. Shut off the PC. Place the scanner on a flat, stable surface within a few feet of the PC.

2. Locate the peripheral you want the scanner to operate off of. Or, if the scanner is the only external SCSI device, plug the SCSI cable into the SCSI port on the back of the PC.

3. Set the scanner's ID number to a unique value between 1 and 7. The control for this setting can usually be found on the back of the scanner.

4. If the scanner is the last piece of SCSI hardware in the daisy chain, you must terminate the device. Plug the supplied terminator plug into the outbound port on the back of the scanner, or remove the terminator from what was previously the last device in the chain, and plug it into the scanner.

5. Turn on the scanner (in some cases, the scanner comes on as soon as it is plugged in). You should hear the motor initiate.

Tip: In general, it's a good idea to power up external SCSI devices, such as scanners, before you start the computer. This ensures that the devices are up and ready when the SCSI bus interrogates them.

6. Windows 95 will detect new hardware and launch the Add New Hardware wizard.

7. Click Next. When prompted to detect the hardware, click the No radio button and then click Next.

8. In the Hardware Type box, select Other (it has a yellow question mark icon).

9. From the Manufacturers list, scroll down to Unknown Device and select it.

10. In the Models box, select Unsupported Devices.

11. Place the scanner's driver diskette into drive A: of your PC.

12. Click Have Disk and double-click the .INF file for your scanner.

13. Windows 95 will update the drivers and then present a dialog box prompting you to select which port to connect the device to.

Getting Good Scans

If you think using a scanner is like making copies, think again. Scanning can be very complex, particularly if you're trying to optimize your scans for one or more print output devices. Resolutions, color depths, and gamma correction (color level) settings all need to be taken into account before you begin your scan.

A few things to keep in mind can help you get the best results and save you a lot of time.

Don't Overscan

A common mistake is scanning at the top resolution when in fact the graphic is bound for a 300dpi laser printer or, even worse, an on-screen Web graphic. If you capture a 600dpi image and print it on a 300dpi laser printer, you'll have wasted a lot of bits and time.

Table 30.2 lists the output resolutions of devices you might be scanning for.

Table 30.2. Output resolutions.

Device	Resolution
High-end laser	1200dpi
Midrange laser	600dpi
Low-end laser, ink jets	300 to 400dpi
PC display	72dpi

As you can see, a 600dpi scan won't do you much good on many printers. The situation is even worse on monitors, which can display only about 72 dots per inch. High-resolution scans for these devices only consume bits and time.

The exception is if you plan to enlarge the image after the scan. In this case, the extra resolution is critical to keeping the image quality acceptable. A 600dpi scan enlarged to twice its size will look about right for a 300dpi output device.

Work Outside the Box

Although most scanners come with their own utilities for sprucing up scans, you might be well advised to disregard them. In general, you'll get better results from a full-fledged photo-editing package such as Adobe PhotoShop than you will from bundled utilities.

Choose Your Media

Don't expect too much from magazine photographs and other printed matter. Newspapers, magazines, and books use halftone graphics to produce visual detail. The use of these mixed dots often creates a distracting moiré pattern in the scan—a perceptible flaw in the image. Where possible, you should use true photographs, because these won't produce a moiré effect.

Scanner Maintenance

Scanners can be troublesome devices. After all, anything on a PC that uses a SCSI interface will need some care and feeding to ensure cooperation. You'll also need to worry about the health of rollers used to move scanning heads or paper through the chassis. Still, depending on how often you use your scanner, your maintenance might amount to little more than occasionally cleaning the scanning table glass.

Summary

Professional-quality scanning became affordable only recently. 600dpi flatbed scanners can now be purchased for $250 and up, meaning that almost any desktop can afford to become a photography studio.

Of course, not everyone is interested in art. Sheet-fed models make excellent corporate sidekicks, turning printed matter into editable text, faxable documents, or shareable images. Although options such as automatic sheet feeders or slide adapters can run up the cost a bit, they add important features for people who need them.

Perhaps most important, the arrival of USB should launch a new generation of scanners. Gone will be the pricey and challenging SCSI bus for higher-end models. Once scanner makers update their designs, USB promises to greatly enhance the ease of use and affordability of flatbed scanners.

A

What to Do with a PC That's Beyond Recovery

Peter Norton®

There comes a time when even the most aggressive upgrade can't save a system. Whether overcome by the ravages of obsolescence or damaged beyond repair, every PC will eventually need to be retired.

What do you do with a PC that can no longer run the applications you need to use every day? Actually, there are a variety of options:

- Donate it to charity
- Cannibalize what parts you can for use in another system
- Place the system into limited, modified duty
- Recycle the PC components with a reclamation company

Donating a PC

Perhaps one of the best ways to dispose of an aging PC is to donate it to charity. Not only do you get the old hardware out of the house, but you also gain a nifty tax deduction. Many organizations are in need of PCs, ranging from schools and churches to nonprofit organizations.

In order for the PC to qualify as a tax-deductible donation, you need to make sure that you meet the following criteria:

- The PC is in reasonable working order
- You receive a dated and itemized receipt from the organization confirming the donation

If you're not sure where to take your PC, a number of charitable organizations specialize in handling PC donations. A further advantage is that these organizations know how to handle the specifics of PC donations, including assessing the market value of your PC.

The following are a just few of the charities that specialize in PC donations. These companies will accept your hardware and distribute it to organizations such as schools, churches, and nonprofit institutions:

- Computer Recycling Center
  (415) 428-3700
- Computer Recycling Project
  (415) 695-7703
- Detwiler Foundation
  (619) 456-9045
- East-West Education Development Foundation
  (617) 542-1234

- Educational Assistance Limited
  (708) 690-0010
- National Christina Foundation
  (800) 247-4784
- Non-Profit Computing
  (212) 759-2368
- The Lazarus Foundation
  (410) 740-0735
  (805) 563-1009

If you decide to donate a PC, be aware of the tax implications. Claiming excessive deductions on your return for computer donations can draw the attention of the IRS. You'll also need to keep receipts from your donations in case you face an audit.

Of course, you'll need to itemize your return in order to apply charitable deductions. If you file a 1040EZ return, or if you have less than $6,500 in possible deductions on your 1040 return, you probably won't be able to take a deduction. You should check your current tax situation or consult a tax professional to determine whether a charitable contribution makes sense.

Fine Young Cannibals

That old PC might be beyond help, but it can still help other systems. Several components inside it might be useful to your primary system:

- RAM
- Hard disk
- Modem
- Display

RAM

You won't always be able to use your old RAM in your new system. If your old PC uses 30-pin DRAM, it might be incompatible with newer 72-pin EDO DRAM used in modern Pentium and Pentium MMX PCs. You need to check the RAM SIMMs closely to ensure that the relative speed and type of RAM are compatible.

If the RAM is incompatible, you might be able to at least get some money back by selling the old memory. Check with local computer stores and memory retailers to find out how much your memory might be worth.

Hard Disk

The hard disk in your old PC might be tiny in comparison to the multigigabyte jobs you see in new PCs, but the disk itself might be in fine shape. If both systems use enhanced IDE drives, it's very easy to plug the drive from the older system into your newer PC. The drive could then be used to archive and back up important data from the faster primary disk, just in case something goes wrong.

Modem

Your new PC probably shipped with a 33.6 or 56KBps modem, but your older system might be equipped with an adequate 28.8KBps modem. If so, you can install the old modem into the new system and possibly use it to nearly double your Web-browsing bandwidth.

How? New software can bundle dual data phone calls, allowing two modems to aggregate their bandwidth into a single wide data pipe. Using this capability, you can add the 28.8KBps bandwidth to the 33.6 or 56KBps data capability already present on your PC. Of course, you'll need a second phone line to make this work. Windows 98 will add the capability as part of its dial-up services. You can also buy third-party packages that can turn your dual-modem phone calls into the equivalent of a single higher-bandwidth connection.

Display

Why would you want to use an old graphics card and 14-inch display on your new system? For one thing, Windows 98 will allow multiple displays and graphics cards to work together. The interface of a single application can be stretched across two monitors, or you can dedicate the 14-inch display to viewing one thing while the larger monitor displays another. This is useful if you need to compare the data displayed by two separate programs, for example, or if you want to use one monitor to browse the Web while the other displays a program.

Recycling Components

For true dinosaurs, there may simply be no prospect of giving away or reusing the system or components. In this case, the best option might be to discard the PC. But just throwing the old dog out might not be a great choice. PCs aren't exactly biodegradable—they're built of metal and plastic, and the monitors include hefty glass CRTs.

You might find a more environmentally friendly option by having the old components recycled. Some companies specialize in reclaiming the PCB boards, metal traces, and gold plating found on many PC components. Check with your local recycling company to see if it can make use of these parts, or contact one of the charitable organizations mentioned earlier.

Peter's Principle: The Leasing Alternative: Exchanging Your Old
Computer for a New One

One concept that is gaining ground in PC buying is the lease option. Businesses have long used lease agreements, which give them the option of keeping or giving back their PCs once the end of the lease term has been reached. Recently, Dell Computer inaugurated a consumer-oriented two-year lease program for its Dimension desktop and Latitude note-book PCs.

Leasing can help you stay on top of the latest technology and avoid accumulating old, useless PCs. At the end of the lease period, you can buy the computer outright for a small sum, making it yours for good, or you can return the system to the vendor and replace it with a new leased PC.

Leasing doesn't make sense for everybody. Over two years of payments, you'll probably pay a couple hundred dollars or so more than you would if you purchased the system outright (assuming that you don't carry the purchase on a revolving credit card debt). If you generally use a system for three, four, or five years or more, you're probably better off buying your PC. Still, if you find that you need up-to-date hardware for your applications, leasing might keep those aging PCs from stacking up in your home or office.

Summary

Even when a PC has grown too old and tired to be of use to you, it might be able to serve others. Donating your old PC is the most attractive option. It effectively disposes of your old PC, helps those who need a system, and even nets you a tax break. Of course, cannibalizing the parts for use in your existing system is a good option as well, because it can help extend the capabilities of the machine you use every day.

Glossary

Peter Norton®

10BaseT   The 10Mbps Ethernet LAN that uses a central hub in a star configuration. Uses Category 3 twisted pair wiring that is similar to phone wires.

100BaseT   The 100Mbps version of Ethernet LAN that uses higher-quality Category 5 twisted pair wiring. Requires 100Mbps-capable network cards and hubs.

80x86 or x86   A generic term referring to the Intel CPU architecture established with the 8086 processor used in the first IBM PC. The term *x86-compatible* refers to compatibility with the instruction set used in all Intel processors, including the new Pentium II CPUs.

accelerated graphics port   See AGP.

access time   The time it takes for a device to retrieve the first piece of requested information. A critical spec for storage media, including RAM and disk drives, access time is generally measured in milliseconds or nanoseconds, although tape drives can take several seconds to access data.

address bus   The electrical connections over which the CPU sends and receives information.

active-matrix   A type of LCD display that produces high brightness and contrast by directly applying an electrical charge to each pixel on the screen.

ActiveMovie   The successor to the Media Player applet, ActiveMovie provides the playback and control interface for video, audio, and animation. Developers can use ActiveMovie to create interactive effects-laden video and audio content.

ADSL   Asymmetric Digital Subscriber Line. A new digital phone service that promises downstream data rates of up to 6Mbps. ADSL requires changes to central telephone switches, as well as ADSL-specific modems. It is available in limited markets.

AGP   Accelerated Graphics Port. A new graphics bus that allows 3-D programs to use main system memory to store large amounts of texture data. Based on the PCI bus specification, AGP runs at 66MHz and adds pipelining and address queuing to optimize performance. Systems must be built with AGP support in order to accept AGP graphics cards.

American Standard Code for Information Interchange   See ASCII.

API   Application Programming Interface. A method of defining a standard set of function calls and other interface elements. It usually defines the interface between a high-level language and the lower-level elements used by a device driver or operating system. The ultimate goal is to provide some type of service to an application that requires access to the operating system or device feature set.

application programming interface   See API.

areal density   An expression of the number of bits that can be stored on a square inch of media. Typically used for hard disks, CD-ROM drives, and other spinning-disk media. The number of bits on each linear inch of track (bit density) is multiplied by the number of concentric tracks on each inch of the medium (track density).

ASCII   American Standard Code for Information Interchange. A standard method of equating the numeric representations available in a computer to human-readable form. For example, the number 32 represents a space. There are 128 characters (7 bits) in the standard ASCII code. The extended ASCII code uses 8 bits for 256 characters. Display adapters from the same machine type usually use the same upper 128 characters. Printers, however, might reserve these upper 128 characters for nonstandard characters. For example, many Epson printers use them for the italic representations of the lower 128 characters.

asymmetric digital subscriber line   See ADSL.

ATA   AT Attachment interface. The standard 40-pin connection and logical interface used in IDE devices. ATA-2 provides faster transfers and logical block addressing, which allows for large and fast hard disk drives.

ATAPI   AT Attachment Packet Interface. Defines a standard interface and behavior for peripherals connected to the IDE bus, including hard disks, CD-ROM drives, and tape drives.

AVI   Audio Video Interleave. The video file format developed by Microsoft that is often used in multimedia titles and software designed for Windows. AVI files combine audio and video into a single track to enhance synchronization of audio and images during playback.

bandwidth   A generic term that expresses the data or signal carrying capacity of a bus, cable, or other connection.

bank   The block of system memory that can be read by the CPU in a single clock cycle. The data width of a bank of memory must match that of the motherboard bus. For example, on a 64-bit Pentium motherboard, two 32-bit SIMMs compose a single bank.

bidirectional parallel port   Defines a printer's ability to transfer information both ways on a printer cable. Input usually contains data or printer control codes. Output usually contains printer status information or error codes.

BIOS   Basic Input/Output System. Code burned into read-only memory (ROM) or contained in Flash memory found on the motherboard. Provides communication between the computer and peripherals.

bps   Bits per second. The number of bits transmitted per second. Often used to express the speed of modems and other peripherals.

bus   A set of wires or traces that carries data and other electrical signals to one or more devices. ISA, PCI, and USB are all examples of PC buses.

bus master   A peripheral that can take control of the bus to transfer data without requiring the CPU's intervention.

cache   A generic term that describes a small pool of fast data storage used to augment a device's performance.

CardBus   An updated 32-bit PC Card specification that provides backward compatibility with existing PC Card peripherals. CardBus allows for 3.3-volt operation, better power management, and DMA capability for video capture and other multimedia applications.

CCD   Charge-Coupled Device. A sensor that responds to exposure to light by emitting an electrical impulse. Digital cameras and scanners interpret images from the relative electrical strength at each point on the CCD.

CD-R   Compact Disc-Recordable. Up to 640MB of data can reside on 5^1/$_4$-inch CD-R media, which can be read by standard CD-ROM drives. Desktop CD-R drives use laser light to mark changes into a chemical media layer on CD-R discs, which then behave like standard CD-ROM discs during playback. Once they're altered, CD-R media can't be changed, so multiple writes aren't possible.

CD-ROM   Compact Disc-Read Only Memory. Up to 640MB of data resides on 5^1/$_4$-inch CD-ROM discs, which consist of reflective media marked with pits and lands (nonpits). CD-ROM drives use a yellow laser to read pits and lands, which a microprocessor translates into digital 1s and 0s.

CD-RW   Compact Disc-Rewritable. Up to 640MB of data can reside on 5^1/$_4$-inch CD-RW media, which can be read by standard CD-ROM drives. Desktop CD-RW drives use laser light to mark changes into a phase-changing media layer on CD-RW discs, which then behave like standard CD-ROM discs during playback. The phase-changing CD-RW medium can be rewritten many times.

CDFS   Compact Disc File System. The portion of the file subsystem specifically designed to interact with compact disc drives. It also provides the user interface elements required to tune this part of the subsystem. The CDFS takes the place of an FSD for CD-ROM drives.

charge-coupled device   See CCD.

CISC   Complex Instruction Set Computing. Describes the type of instructions used by a processor. Intel x86-type CPUs feature a large set of instructions that are complex in nature.

client   The recipient of data, services, or resources from a file or other server. This term can refer to a workstation or an application. The server can be another PC or an application.

CMOS   Complementary Metal Oxide Semiconductor. Normally refers to a construction method for low-power battery-backed memory. When used in the context of a PC, this term usually refers to the memory used to store system configuration information and the real-time clock status. The configuration information normally includes the amount of system memory, the type and size of floppy drives, the hard drive parameters, and the video display type. Some vendors also include other configuration information as part of this chip.

coaxial cable   A type of wiring, identical to that used to connect cable TV boxes, that is sometimes used to connect network computers. Coaxial cable is notable for its high bandwidth and heavy shielding.

codec   Coder-decoder or compression-decompression. Refers to software used to compress and decompress audio, video, and other media files.

COM port   A logical resource that can be assigned to a PC serial port or other serial device.

compact disc file system   See CDFS.

complementary metal oxide semiconductor   See CMOS.

coprocessor   An additional processor in the PC that takes the load off the CPU by handling various tasks such as graphics operation, video playback, and communications.

CPU   Central Processing Unit. The brains of the PC, the CPU is the most complex and most powerful chip in the system, consisting of millions of transistors.

CRT   Cathode Ray Tube. The large glass vacuum tube mounted inside the PC monitor. An electron gun mounted inside the tube shoots a focused stream of electrons at a layer of phosphors on the inside of the glass, causing them to emit light.

daisy chain   A string of connected devices in which electrical signals move from the first device to the last. The SCSI bus is a daisy-chained bus.

DAT drive   Digital Audio Tape drive. A tape drive that uses a cassette to store data. The cassette and the drive use the same technology as the audio version of the DAT drive. However, the internal circuitry of the drive formats the tape for use with a computer system. The vendor must also design the interface circuitry with computer needs in mind. DAT tapes let you store large amounts of information in a relatively small amount of space. Typical drive capacities range from 1.2 to 8GB.

device driver   Device-specific code that allows the operating system and hardware to speak with each other.

digital audio tape drive   See DAT drive.

DIMM   Dual Inline Memory Module. The standard module format used by SDRAM system memory found in Pentium MMX and new Pentium II PCs.

direct memory access   See DMA.

DirectX   A suite of programming APIs and technologies that allows compelling multimedia content under Windows 95. DirectX includes the following components: DirectDraw (graphics and video), Direct3D (3-D graphics), DirectSound (audio), DirectInput (game controllers), and DirectPlay (network game play). Hardware devices must use DirectX-aware drivers in order to take advantage of the DirectX services built into the operating system.

disk defragmenter   An application used to reorder the data on a long-term storage device such as a hard or floppy disk drive. Reordering the data so that it appears in sequential order (file by file) reduces the time required to access and read it. Sequential order lets you read an entire file without moving the disk head at all in some cases and only a little in others. This reduction in access time normally improves overall system throughput and therefore enhances system efficiency.

DMA   Direct Memory Access. A memory-addressing technique in which the processor doesn't perform the actual data transfer. This method of memory access is faster than any other technique.

docking station   A hardware module that connects to a notebook and provides desktop-like capabilities such as networking and expandability.

DOS protected-mode interface   See DPMI.

dot pitch   Defines the width of pixel dots on a monitor. Measured in millimeters. The smaller the measurement, the greater the potential precision of the display.

DPMI   DOS Protected-Mode Interface. A method of accessing extended memory from a DOS application using the Windows extended memory manager.

DRAM   Dynamic Random Access Memory. The standard memory found in most PCs. DRAM must be constantly refreshed with electrical signals in order to maintain their data state.

dual-ported video RAM   See VRAM.

dual-scan passive-matrix display   A variation of passive-matrix display technology. The screen is divided into two horizontal sections, doubling the number of transistors available to send charges to pixels on the screen. See passive-matrix display.

DVD-R   Digital Versatile Disc-Recordable. The recordable version of DVD-ROM, DVD-R drives can write up to 3.6GB of data to DVD-R media. DVD-R discs can be written to only once.

DVD-RAM   Digital Versatile Disc-Random Access Memory. The rewritable version of DVD-ROM, DVD-RAM drives can write up to 2.4GB of data to DVD-RAM media. DVD-RAM discs can be rewritten.

DVD-ROM   Digital Versatile Disc-Read Only Memory. A new specification for $5^1/_4$-inch optical discs that can store up to 17GB of data. DVD-ROM discs provide higher capacities than CD-ROM discs by more closely spacing the pits and lands. DVD-ROM discs can store data on both sides of the disc and on two layers on each side.

Dvorak layout   An alternative method of laying out the keyboard so that stress is reduced and typing speed is increased. It's different from the more familiar "QWERTY" layout used by most keyboards and typewriters.

ECC memory   Error-Correcting Code memory. A type of system memory that employs additional bits to track and correct errors.

ECP   See enhanced capabilities port.

EMM   Expanded Memory Manager. A device driver such as EMM386.EXE that provides expanded memory services on an 80386 and above machine. (Special drivers work with 80286 and a few 8088/8086 machines.) An application accesses expanded memory using a page frame or other memory-mapping technique from within the conventional or upper memory area (0 to 124KB). The EMM usually emulates expanded memory using extended memory managed by an extended memory manager (XMM) such as HIMEM.SYS. An application must change the processor's mode to protected in order to use XMS. Some products, such as 386MAX.SYS and QEMM.SYS, provide both EMM and XMM services in one driver.

EMS   Expanded Memory Specification. Several versions of this specification are currently in use. The most popular version is 3.2, even though a newer 4.0 specification is available. This specification defines one method of extending the amount of memory that a processor can address from the conventional memory area. It uses an area outside of system memory to store information. An EMM provides a window view into this larger data area. The old 3.2 specification requires a 64KB window in the UMB. The newer 4.0 specification can create this window anywhere in conventional or UMB memory.

enhanced capabilities port   An extension of the bidirectional parallel port specification that increases performance.

enhanced IDE   Enhanced Integrated Drive Electronics. A standard low-cost interface for internal hard disk, CD-ROM, and other drives.

enhanced parallel port   An extension of the bidirectional parallel port specification that increases performance.

EPP   See enhanced parallel port.

expanded memory manager   See EMM.

expanded memory specification   See EMS.

FAT   File Allocation Table. The method of formatting a hard disk drive used by DOS and other operating systems. This technique is one of the oldest formatting methods available.

FAT32   File Allocation Table 32. An enhanced version of the FAT disk-formatting scheme, introduced in the OSR2 version of Windows 95 and, soon, Windows 98. FAT32 allows enhanced IDE hard disk capacities of just over 2GB in a single partition and reduces the amount of so-called "slack" associated with files, particularly smaller ones.

file allocation table   See FAT.

FireWire   See IEEE 1394.

FTP   File Transfer Protocol. A networking protocol commonly used for Internet downloads and uploads.

full-duplex   Describes a signal flow in two directions along a connection. Full-duplex sound cards allow speakerphone capability, in which both sides of the call can speak simultaneously, or in which a card can record and play back at the same time.

GB   See gigabyte.

GDI   Graphics Device Interface. One of the main Windows root components. It controls the way that graphic elements are presented on-screen. Every application must use the API provided by this component to draw or perform other graphics-related tasks.

general protection fault   See GPF.

gigabyte   An amount of data equal to 1,024 megabytes, or 1,073,741,824 bytes.

GPF   General Protection Fault. A processor or memory error that occurs when an application makes a request that the system can't honor. This type of error results in some type of severe action on the part of the operating system. Normally, the operating system terminates the offending application.

graphical user interface   See GUI.

graphics device interface   See GDI.

GUI   Graphical User Interface. A system of icons and graphic images that replaces the character-mode menu system used by many machines. The GUI can ride on top of another operating system (such as DOS or UNIX) or reside as part of the operating system itself (such as Windows or OS/2). Advantages of a GUI include ease of use and high-resolution graphics. Disadvantages include higher workstation hardware requirements and lower performance over a similar system using a character-mode interface.

half duplex   A connection in which signal flow can occur in only one direction at a time. Half-duplex sound cards are unable to allow efficient audio or videoconferencing because of their inability to allow both sides to speak at once.

hard disk   The PC's primary permanent data store. Hard disks consist of a coated medium that is magnetically charged to indicate 1 or 0 bits. The drive head floats over the spinning disk, reading and writing data.

heat sink   A metal or plastic device attached to a chip that helps dissipate heat away from the chip.

hertz   Indicates a signal frequency that cycles once per second.

IDE   Integrated Drive Electronics. Initially described the class of hard disks that had the controller circuitry built into the drive instead of on a separate card. Today IDE is often used to describe ATA-compliant devices.

IEEE 1394   Also known as FireWire. A high-speed Plug and Play external bus designed for applications such as video capture and consumer electronics connectivity.

Industry Standard Architecture   See ISA.

.INF file   A special form of device or application configuration file. It contains all the parameters that Windows requires to install or configure the device or application. For example, an application .INF file might contain the location of data files and the interdependencies of DLLs. Both application and device .INF files contain the registry and .INI file entries required to make Windows recognize the application or device.

ink jet printer   A printer that produces monochrome or color output by spraying ink onto the page.

interlacing   A way of scanning a CRT screen in which the electron gun paints every other line from top to bottom and then paints the remaining alternating lines. Older interlaced displays cause visible flicker, which can result in eyestrain.

interrupt request   See IRQ.

IPX   Internet Packet eXchange. The networking communication protocol for Novell's NetWare network operating system.

IrDA   Infrared Device Association. A specification, named after a standards-making body, that provides a standard way for devices to communicate using infrared light. The initial 152Kbps data rate was later improved to 4Mbps.

IRQ   Interrupt Request. The set of special address lines that connect a peripheral to the processor. Think of an IRQ as an office telephone that has multiple incoming lines. Every time a device calls, its entry lights up on the front of the phone. The processor selects the desired line and picks up the receiver to find out what the device wants. Everything works fine as long as there is one line for each device that needs to call the processor. If more than one device were to try to call in on the same line, the processor wouldn't know what was at the other end. This is the source of IRQ conflicts that you hear about. Older PC-class machines provided eight interrupt lines. The newer AT-class machines provide 16. However, only about 10 of those can be used, because several are used for internal purposes.

ISA   Industry Standard Architecture. The standard expansion bus on PCs since their inception. The current ISA bus runs at 8MHz and features a 16-bit connection. Common ISA peripherals include sound cards, internal modems, and LAN adapters.

ISDN   Integrated Services Digital Network. A digital phone service provided by telephone companies that can transport up to 128Kbps of data. PC-based ISDN communication requires an ISDN adapter, often called an ISDN modem.

jumper   Used to set hardware resources on motherboards and peripherals, a jumper is a plastic-covered contact that fits over dual pins protruding from a circuit board.

LAN   Local Area Network. A combination of hardware and software used to connect a group of PCs to each other and/or a mini or mainframe computer. Two main networking models are in use: peer-to-peer and client-server. The peer-to-peer model doesn't require a dedicated server. In addition, all the workstations in the group can share resources. The client-server model uses a central server for resource sharing, but some special methods are provided for using local resources in a limited fashion.

laser printer   A printer that works like a copier to cook toner onto the page. An image of the page is etched onto a rotating drum, so that toner adheres to the etched area.

LCD   Liquid Crystal Display. Flat-panel displays used in notebook PCs. Images are displayed by charging individual liquid crystals suspended between glass panels.

liquid crystal display   See LCD.

local area network   See LAN.

magneto-optical (MO) drive   High-capacity disk media and drives, often used to archive and exchange files. MO drives use a laser to heat the underlying magnetic medium to a state where it can be rewritten. The thermal threshold of MO disks makes them less susceptible to data loss than magnetic media such as hard disks.

MCA   Microchannel Architecture. A specialized bus introduced by IBM. It's faster than the old ISA bus and gives the operating system information about the peripheral devices connected to the bus. It also provides the means for devices to become self-configuring.

mean time between failure   Also called MTBF, this is a measure of the statistical probability that a device will fail within the indicated time. Usually expressed in hours.

microchannel architecture   See MCA.

MIDI   Musical Instrument Digital Interface. A standard scheme for expressing musical notes using a series of instructions. MIDI files are very compact, but they allow MIDI-aware sound cards to play back realistic-sounding musical scores.

miniport driver   A specialized Windows component that provides access to a resource, normally a peripheral device of some type. It's also used to access pseudo-devices and network resources.

modem   Short for modulate-demodulate. Modems let PCs send and receive data over standard phone lines by translating digital bits into analog sound.

motherboard   The PC's main board, upon which the CPU, chipset, system memory, and expansion slots are all mounted.

Motion Picture Experts Group   See MPEG.

MPEG   Motion Picture Experts Group. A standards group that provides file formats and other specifications in regard to full-motion video and other types of graphic displays. MPEG-2 is a high-quality video format used in DVD-ROM titles, and MPEG-1 provides low-bandwidth playback for use on CD-ROM titles.

multiple-boot configuration   A method of creating a configurable environment that was first introduced with DOS 5.0. The user simply selects the operating environment from a list of environments presented prior to the boot sequence. This technique provides an additional layer of flexibility and allows the user to optimize the operating environment to perform specific tasks.

multitasking   The ability of some processor and environment/system combinations to perform more than one task at a time. The applications appear to run simultaneously. For example, you can download messages from an online service, print from a word processor, and recalculate a spreadsheet all at the same time. Each application receives a slice of time before the processor moves to the next application. Because the time slices are fairly small, it appears to the user that these actions are occurring simultaneously.

near-disk storage   A generic term that describes large, fast, removable media that can be used to augment existing hard disk capacity. Magneto-optical drives and Jaz drives are examples of near-disk media. Also called near-line storage.

network interface card   See NIC.

NIC   Network Interface Card. The device responsible for allowing a workstation to communicate with the file server and other workstations. It provides the physical means of creating the connection. The card plugs into an expansion slot in the computer. A cable that attaches to the back of the card completes the communication path.

NTFS   Windows NT File System. The method of formatting a hard disk drive used by Windows NT. Although it provides significant speed advantages over other formatting techniques, only the Windows NT operating system and applications designed to work with that operating system can access a drive formatted using this technique.

NTSC   National Television Standards Committee. Used to describe the video format standard employed in television broadcasts.

parity   A type of random access memory (RAM) that incorporates additional bits to confirm that data wasn't corrupted.

passive-matrix display   Inexpensive LCD display. Individual pixels are lit when charges from the horizontal and vertical edge of the screen intersect. Passive-matrix displays lack brightness and contrast because pixels are not frequently refreshed.

PCI   Peripheral Component Interconnect. A high-speed general-purpose peripheral bus that runs at 33MHz and is 32 bits wide. Often used for graphics cards, network interface cards, and other high-speed devices.

peripheral component interconnect   See PCI.

Plug and Play   The combination of BIOS, operating system, and peripheral device components that provides a self-configuring environment. This self-configuring feature allows the operating system to avoid potential hardware conflicts by polling the peripheral devices, assessing their requirements, and determining and implementing optimal settings for each device.

POST   Power-On Self Test. The set of diagnostic and configuration routines that the BIOS runs during system initialization. For example, the memory counter you see during the boot sequence is part of this process.

power-on self test   See POST.

protected mode   The processor mode in which the processor can access all of extended memory. This mode also provides a better level of application error detection as part of the processing cycle.

QIC   Quarter-inch cartridge. A specification for tape backup cartridges.

RAM   Random Access Memory. The generic term for the volatile, silicon-based data storage used in PCs.

real mode   A Windows operating mode that supports the capabilities of the 8088/8086 processor. This essentially limits you to loading one application within the confines of conventional memory. Windows versions after 3.0 don't support this mode. You must use these versions with workstations containing an 80386 or higher processor.

remote access   The ability to use a remote resource as you would a local resource. In some cases, this also means downloading the remote resource to use as a local resource.

RISC   Reduced Instruction Set Computing. A type of processor instruction set that runs very quickly using a few simple instructions rather than a larger set of complex instructions.

SCSI   Small Computer System Interface. The fast internal and external bus standard frequently used for scanners, hard disk drives, and other high-bandwidth peripherals. Flavors of SCSI include Fast SCSI, Wide SCSI, and FastWide (UltraWide) SCSI, which tops out at 40MBps.

SCSI manager   Windows NT introduced something called the miniport driver. With Windows 95, you can use the Windows NT miniport binaries. However, before you can actually do this, Windows 95 must translate its commands to a format that the miniport driver understands. The SCSI manager performs this service for SCSI devices.

SDRAM   Synchronous Dynamic Random Access Memory. A new type of memory that improves performance by working in lockstep with the system clock.

server   An application or workstation that provides services, resources, or data to a client application or workstation. The client usually makes requests in the form of OLE, DDE, or other command formats.

small computer system interface   See SCSI.

SMP   Symmetric multiprocessing. PCs equipped with more than one CPU, with all CPUs able to take part in all tasks. SMP systems require an SMP-aware operating system, such as Windows NT Workstation or OS/2 SMP.

symmetric multiprocessing   See SMP.

system resource   Data, peripheral devices, or other system components used to create, delete, or manipulate documents and produce output.

TAPI   Telephony API. An interface used by applications to interface with various types of communication equipment. This currently includes both modems and fax devices.

task switching   The ability of an operating system to support more than one application or thread of execution at a time. The foreground application or task is the only one that executes. All other threads of execution are suspended in the background. Contrast this with multitasking, in which all threads—background and foreground—execute.

Telephony API   See TAPI.

texture maps   Images that are laid over 3-D objects to add the illusion of reality to rendered 3-D scenes.

UAE   Unrecoverable Application Error. A processor or memory error that occurs when an application makes a request that the system can't honor. The operating system normally doesn't detect this type of error. The result is that the system freezes or becomes unstable to the point of being unusable. Also see GPF.

ultra ATA   An enhancement to the enhanced IDE specification that allows for 33MBps data rates, twice that of earlier drives.

universal serial bus   See USB.

unrecoverable application error   See UAE.

USB   Universal Serial Bus. A medium-speed (12Mbps) Plug and Play external bus designed for devices such as mice, keyboards, scanners, and digital cameras.

VESA   Video Electronics Standards Association. A standards group responsible for creating display adapter and monitor specifications. This group has also worked on other standards, such as the VL bus used in some PCs.

VESA Local Bus   See VL-bus.

VFAT   Virtual File Allocation Table. An enhanced method of disk formatting based on the FAT system. It allows for additional functionality, such as long filenames.

Video Electronics Standards Association   See VESA.

virtual device driver   See VxD.

virtual file allocation table   See VFAT.

VL-bus   VESA Local Bus. A 32-bit 33MHz bus found in 486 systems. The first industry-standard, high-speed expansion bus, it was replaced by PCI in Pentium-based PCs.

VRAM   Dual-Ported Video RAM. A special form of memory that uses dual ports to allow simultaneous reads and writes.

VxD   Virtual Device Driver. A 32-bit driver DLL that allows dynamic loading and unloading and other low-level features under Windows 95.

wave audio   A digital representation of analog sound. Wave audio files can produce accurate recordings but take up a great deal of hard disk space.

WDM   A common device driver scheme for the Windows 95 and Windows NT operating systems that allows peripheral makers to write a single 32-bit driver for both OSs.

Win32 Driver Model   See WDM.

Windows NT   A 32-bit operating system tailored for network servers, corporate workstations, and high-end graphics. Windows NT provides greater reliability and stability than Windows 95.

Windows NT file system   See NTFS.

wizard   A specialized application that reduces the complexity of using or configuring your system. For example, the Printer Wizard makes it easier to install a new printer.

Index

MACMILLAN COMPUTER PUBLISHING USA

A VIACOM COMPANY

Technical ----┐
                 └--- ## Support:

If you need assistance with the information in this book or with a CD/Disk accompanying the book, please access the Knowledge Base on our Web site at **http://www.superlibrary.com/general/support**. Our most Frequently Asked Questions are answered there. If you do not find the answer to your questions on our Web site, you may contact Macmillan Technical Support **(317) 581-3833** or e-mail us at **support@mcp.com**.